Books by Hajo Holborn

A HISTORY OF MODERN GERMANY
The Reformation

(1959)

A HISTORY OF MODERN GERMANY
1648-1840

(1963)

A HISTORY OF MODERN GERMANY
1840-1945

(IN PREPARATION)

THE POLITICAL COLLAPSE OF EUROPE

(1951)

THESE ARE BORZOI BOOKS
PUBLISHED IN NEW YORK BY ALFRED A. KNOPF

A
HISTORY OF
MODERN GERMANY

1648-1840

A
HISTORY OF
MODERN GERMANY
1648-1840

BY

H A J O   H O L B O R N

Yale University

ALFRED A. KNOPF *NEW YORK: 1966*

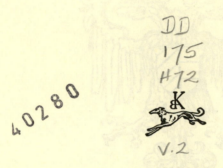

L. C. catalog card number: 59-5991

THIS IS A BORZOI BOOK,
PUBLISHED BY ALFRED A. KNOPF, INC.

PUBLISHED 1964
REPRINTED 1966

TO ANNEMARIE

Foreword

WHEN *A History of Modern Germany: The Reformation* was published in 1959, I expressed the hope that I would be able to cover the history of Germany from 1648 to 1945 in a single volume. This has proved to be impossible. It would have necessitated a compression of the history of the last century that would have blurred the understanding of the complex developments which enabled Germany twice during the last fifty years to challenge the traditional world order. Although Germany's drive for world power in many respects served only as a catalyst for the radical transformation of our world, her part in this historic process deserves a full treatment.

The history of Germany from 1648 to 1945 is therefore presented in two volumes. The present volume, deals with the institutions and events from the end of the Thirty Years War to the threshold of the German revolution of 1848–49. The political background and the origins of this revolution that ushered in the age of national unification will be described in the opening chapter of the next volume, *A History of Modern Germany: 1840–1945.*

I wish to record my appreciation of the unfailing assistance I have received from the members of the College Department of Alfred A. Knopf, Inc. I am deeply grateful to my wife for the part she has taken in every stage of the preparation of this book.

HAJO HOLBORN

New Haven, Connecticut
April 3, 1963

Contents

Maps

BY THEODORE R. MILLER

P A R T

I

The Age *of* Absolutism, 1648 – 1790

CHAPTER 1

The Empire After the Peace
of Westphalia

ᔕᔕ The German Constitutional Struggle

ALL THE CARNAGE AND DESTRUCTION of the Thirty Years' War had not changed the old dilemma of German history.[1] Ever since the breakdown of the might of the medieval emperors four centuries earlier, the particularist forces had been able to thwart the rebuilding of a central German authority. Twice the emperors had come close to imposing their will on the recalcitrant German territorial rulers. Charles V seemed to have won such a chance after the defeat of the Protestant princes in the battle of Mühlberg of 1547. Again, Ferdinand II saw practically all of Germany lie at his feet when, in 1627, his armies had reached the shores of the Baltic. But both times the fruits of victory had been elusive, and the German princes had been able to turn the tables on the emperor. In both cases the princes had relied on foreign support. As a matter of fact, the exertions of the German princes in the Thirty Years' War had meant little compared to the active intervention of Sweden and France.

The extension of the German constitutional struggle into an issue of European power politics was the inevitable result of the universal nature of the imperial dignity. For Charles V, the achievement of monarchical power in Germany was only a part of his much wider scheme for the revival of a universal empire. Ferdinand II, too, subordinated national aims to the planned restoration of a religious and dynastic universalism, which, as the Thirty Years' War proved, was forever unattainable. The common defense and promotion of orthodox

[1] For a discussion of the history of the German constitution prior to 1648, cf. the author's *A History of Modern Germany: The Reformation* (New York: Alfred A. Knopf; 1959), chapters 2, 3, and 9.

religion did not keep the papacy from withdrawing its support from the Habsburg emperors in the hours of triumph, nor did the Catholic princes show themselves loyal allies whenever the emperors approached a position of supremacy in the Empire.

✎ *Weakening of the Empire and of Religion*

THE RISE OF NATIONAL MONARCHIES in western and northern Europe had weakened the institutions on which both the universalism and the religious motivation of the medieval *respublica Christiana* rested. The Westphalian peace settlement treated the emperor simply as one among other major rulers of Europe. The participants completely disregarded the capacity of the papacy for contributing to the lasting stability of the new international order. Quite to the contrary, the signatories officially agreed that they would pay no attention to any possible objections of the pope, and the protest of Pope Innocent X (1644–55) actually went unheeded. The group of states which formed the new Europe regulated its order on the basis of mutual power relations. The statesmen believed that a political balance offered a greater guarantee for the preservation of peace than did religion. In the Peace of Westphalia, the signatories specifically assumed the common obligation to maintain the established international order, irrespective of religion.

While religion became a secondary influence in international affairs, it remained a fundamental force in the internal integration of all states. In this process, as Leopold von Ranke has pointed out, religion lost much of its universal character. With the official recognition of Protestantism, the individual was faced with a more conscious choice than in the past, when the single Christian faith was an unquestioned common tradition. But few people of this age met the challenge as individuals. For a long time to come, religion served as the visible representation of the communal spirit. The states, in Ranke's words, became "great ecclesiastico-political individualities." The various types of Protestantism molded the spirit of such nations as modern England, Sweden, Denmark, and the Netherlands. But Catholicism developed similar national differentiations, particularly through the distinctive attitudes which the various national governments took toward the Vatican and the internal Church administration. French, Spanish, and Polish Catholicism acquired very different colorings.

In Germany, religion, whether Catholic, Lutheran, or Calvinist, did not become an element in the growth of nationality but rather accentu-ated the character of the particular states. The latter appeared as the chief beneficiaries in both the political and spiritual field. The Peace of Westphalia had given the individual princes and cities practically full power over their subjects. Furthermore, it had sanctioned their right to conclude alliances with foreign states, with the significant, though in-effective, reservation that alliances should not be directed against the emperor and the Empire. In all legislation, taxation, levying of troops, conclusion of alliances and peace treaties, as well as in the declaration of war, the emperor needed the approval of the diet of the Empire. The Peace of Westphalia failed, however, to define the obligations of the more than three hundred territorial princes, represented in this diet, to their emperor.

The emperor retained certain undisputed rights of his own, the so-called "reserved rights," which stemmed mostly from his position as feudal overlord, such as the right of investment with inherited or vacant fiefs and the grant of nobility or privileges. The fees collected, though not entirely negligible, were quite insufficient to enable an emperor without other resources to conduct policies of his own. Yet for more than two hundred years the imperial crown had been in the possession of the Habsburg family, and in the hands of a powerful dynasty the "reserved rights" could be used for many political ends. Even after 1648, the Habsburgs, through their dynastic might, were the natural protectors of the small princes and lords of Germany. In the first place, the Catholic estates, especially the large group of prince-bishops and abbots, looked upon the emperor as the traditional de-fender of the Roman Catholic faith. Even on the election of the ecclesiastical princes, the emperors could attempt to exert a stronger influence after 1648. In addition, the free imperial cities and all the small princes sought to be safeguarded against their covetous big neighbors. Moreover, the larger German states, such as Bavaria and Saxony—or Brandenburg, which began to measure up to the other two only after 1648—often needed the emperor. They might, for example, wish him to confirm some hereditary claims to another German terri-tory or want him as an ally in some European enterprise. By offering posts in the Austrian army and civil service to scions of some fourteen hundred families of free imperial knights and to many of the younger sons of princely houses, the emperor won further friends and sup-porters in the Empire.

If held by the ruler of a great state, the imperial office, in spite of

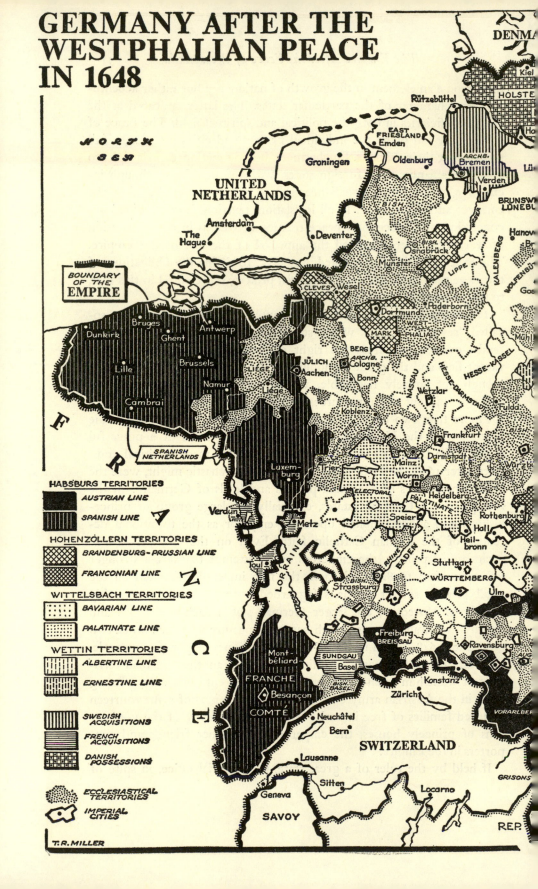

GERMANY AFTER THE WESTPHALIAN PEACE IN 1648

BOUNDARY
OF THE
EMPIRE

SPANISH
NETHERLANDS

UNITED
NETHERLANDS

NORTH
SEA

DENMARK

HABSBURG TERRITORIES
AUSTRIAN LINE
SPANISH LINE

HOHENZOLLERN TERRITORIES
BRANDENBURG-PRUSSIAN LINE
FRANCONIAN LINE

WITTELSBACH TERRITORIES
BAVARIAN LINE
PALATINATE LINE

WETTIN TERRITORIES
ALBERTINE LINE
ERNESTINE LINE

SWEDISH
ACQUISITIONS
FRENCH
ACQUISITIONS
DANISH
POSSESSIONS

ECCLESIASTICAL
TERRITORIES
IMPERIAL
CITIES

T. R. MILLER

SWITZERLAND

SAVOY

FRANCHE
COMTÉ

LORRAINE

Kiel
HOLSTE
Rützebüttel
EAST
FRIESLAND
Emden
Groningen
Oldenburg
ARCHB.
Bremen
Verden
BRUNSW.
LÜNEBU
Amsterdam
Deventer
The Hague
BISH.
Osnabrück
LIPPE
Münster
CLEVES Wesel
Dortmund
Paderborn
MARK
WEST-
PHALIA
BERG
ARCHB.
JÜLICH Cologne
Aachen
Bonn
Wetzlar
Koblenz
Frankfurt
Darmstadt
Mainz
Worms
Heidelberg
ELECTORAL
PALATINATE
Speier
Heilbronn
Stuttgart
WÜRTTEMBERG
Strassburg
Ulm
Freiburg
BREISGAU
Ravensburg
SUNDGAU
Basel
Konstanz
BISH.
BASEL
Zürich
Neuchâtel
Bern
Lausanne
Sitten
Geneva
Locarno
GRISONS
REP.
VORARLBER
NASSAU
HESSE-DARMSTADT
HESSE-KASSEL
Fulda
Rothenburg
Hall
BADEN
RHINE
Trier
Verdun
Metz
Toul
Mont-
béliard-
Besançon
Dunkirk
Bruges
Ghent
Antwerp
Brussels
Namur
Lille
Cambrai
LIÉGE
Liége
Luxem-
burg
Hano
Br
KALENBERG
WOLFENBÜ
Gos
Mühl
Würzb
AUG
MEUSE
MOSELLE
F R A N C E

its legal enfeeblement, was a source of considerable power. The interests of Austria were still tightly interwoven with those of crucial
German regions. Silesia was still Austrian, and thus the emperor controlled the major part of the Oder valley and was the guardian of
Germany's eastern frontiers. In the west, although Austria was forced
in the Peace of Westphalia to renounce her rights in Alsace, she
retained the strategic Breisgau, the district of the southern Black
Forest that was loosely connected with Tyrol by a string of other
south German possessions. This so-called Anterior Austria established
the closest contacts with the south German states, and in the defense
of her own lands against France during the next century, Austria
simultaneously shielded southern Germany.

It was not the rights that the German constitution gave to the
emperor but rather Austrian power that lent substance to the imperial
authority. Although the emperor possessed some monarchical attributes
as a German emperor, he could acquire influence within Germany only
by the careful exploitation of existing interests and conflicts of interests. This task could not be undertaken by a small prince, who was
likely to lose personal stature by the glamour of the imperial title. The
hapless Elector Charles Albert of Bavaria suffered such a fate when
France and Prussia engineered his election as Emperor Charles VII
(1742–45), the only time that a non-Habsburg prince was raised to the
imperial throne after 1438.

While the liberty (*Libertät*) of the territorial rulers of Germany
was codified in the Peace of Westphalia and thereby also guaranteed
by France and Sweden, the nature and extent of the obligations of the
estates to emperor and Empire were left to future discussions in a diet.
This diet was delayed till 1653, when it finally convened in Regensburg.
It was preceded by a meeting of the electors in Augsburg, where the
emperor's son was elected king as Ferdinand IV. The electors made
him accept a "capitulation of election" (*Wahlcapitulation*), into
which, as in all future capitulations, were written all the provisions of
the Westphalian peace protecting the rights of the estates. But Austrian
policy remained bent on winning maximum authority over the estates,
and the discord raging among the estates offered certain political opportunities. The electoral college, with the new Bavarian vote added,
contained a clear Catholic majority. The Bohemian vote was counted
only at the election of an emperor, but since it was in the possession of
the Habsburgs, this was an important element in safeguarding their
succession. The three Protestant electors, those of Saxony, Branden-

burg, and the Palatinate, would always find themselves in a minority in the diet and in its main organ, the so-called *Reichsdeputation*.

✍ *The* Deputation

THE DEPUTATION, created in 1555, had acquired a growing significance as an institution that prepared legislation for the diet. Although its labors did not replace the debates of the sessions of the diet, the small *Deputation* affected the legislative actions of the sprawling assembly. The *Deputation* was a diminutive diet composed of seven electors (the king of Bohemia was not included), and a curia of the princes and imperial cities. In contrast to the organization of the diet, in which the cities deliberated as a separate curia, the cities were here combined with the princes into a single curia. The Peace of Westphalia had provided that there would be an equal number of Protestants and Catholics in the "curia of princes" in the *Deputation*, and the Diet of Regensburg made the necessary arrangements. Since voting was in curias, however, this would have been of little practical consequence as long as the electoral college had a Catholic majority. It was the intervention of Frederick William of Brandenburg—the "Great Elector"—that forced the decision to give the three Protestant electors a fourth vote, to be held by each of them in turn.

In face of the Great Elector's leadership of the Protestant estates, the emperor was denied his wish to see the principle established that taxes approved by a majority of the diet were to be paid by all the estates. Frederick William argued that this would make the princes taxable subjects of the emperor and that more than a majority was necessary, especially since many voting estates had never contributed to the expenditures of the Empire. He asserted that the estates would not refuse to make "necessary" contributions in case of foreign aggression; but that any other contributions must be considered "voluntary," with the spending as well as the granting of such revenue controlled by the estates.

✍ *The "Youngest Recess"*

THE DIET OF REGENSBURG published, on May 17, 1654, its recess, known as the "youngest recess" (*Jüngster Reichsabschied*), containing a new statute for the organization and trial procedure of the Imperial Cameral Tribunal. Although this statute was a credit to the jurists who had drafted it, it failed to achieve its main purpose, namely, finding a way to help the court reduce its colossal backlog of unfinished business and expedite its work. The Tribunal, which moved from Speyer to Wetzlar in 1693, remained incapable of producing legal remedies with reasonable speed.

The "youngest recess" did not contain rules for the reorganization of the Imperial Aulic Council, as the Protestant princes had wished. The emperor issued such rules on his own authority and maintained the jurisdiction of this court in competition with the Imperial Cameral Tribunal. The Council had served as the chief political instrument of monarchical policy in Germany, and Ferdinand III wished to preserve it as such. But he did co-operate with the princes in another matter, one in which the princes, who were otherwise averse to having the Empire pass on their internal affairs, were glad to receive help from the Empire. Under the conditions of the dualistic state, it had been a problem whether the princes could grant taxes to the Empire without the approval of their territorial estates, though the diet had always affirmed that they had such a right. In Regensburg a new departure was taken. Article 180 of the recess stipulated that the "residents, subjects, and citizens" of the estates had the duty of providing their territorial lord with the funds necessary for the maintenance of existing fortresses and for the garrisons needed to man them. The authority of emperor and Empire was used here to make the princes independent of their own territorial estates, at least in matters of defense. Since only the prince himself could determine what was needed in the way of a garrison, the new imperial law permitted the formation of a standing army under the absolute command of the prince. It was not the Empire that started the rise of absolutist rule, but its paling prestige was employed to advance the cause of modern despotism in the territories.

∽ The "Eternal Diet"

WHEN THE NEXT DIET convened in Regensburg in 1663, it proved even less able to settle the fundamental problems of the constitution. The diet of 1663 became the "eternal" or "everlasting" diet, which came to an end only with the dissolution of the Holy Roman Empire in 1806. The attendance of princes at diets had been falling off for the last seventy years, and after 1664 the diet became a mere congress of diplomats which was permanently in session. No important legislation in political and constitutional matters was issued by the "eternal diet," with the exception of the law on the defense of the Empire of 1681. Among the economic laws the most useful was the order of craft guilds of 1731.

✑ Theories of Government

THE NATURE OF THE GERMAN CONSTITUTION was a topic of lively and heated controversy among contemporary jurists and statesmen. In the first year of the Thirty Years' War, a Lutheran professor, Theodor Reinkingk (1590–1664), published a treatise to demonstrate that the emperor, as the successor to the Roman Caesars and as feudal overlord, exercised monarchical power over Germany. It was this theory that obviously affected the policies of the Saxon government. In contrast, the Calvinists, as well as a large Lutheran school, tended to conceive of the Empire as a republican aristocracy. This was the theory of Althusius[2] and of Dominicus Arumaeus (1579–1637), a Dutch-born professor at the university of Jena, who was supported in these ideas by Friedrich Hortleder (1579–1640), his Calvinist colleague at this Thuringian university. The latter, a historian and the tutor of the Weimar princes, who had acquired great renown during the Thirty Years' War, was an impassioned republican. The republican doctrine reached its widest audience in a pamphlet by Bogislav Philip Chemnitz (1605–78), a Lutheran in Pomerania. In his dissertation *De Ratione Status in Imperio Romano-Germanico*, published under the name of Hippolithus de Lapide, Chemnitz presented the republican and aristocratic interpretation, turning it into a fiery attack against the usurped power of the Habsburgs and demanding the extirpation of "that family fatal to our Germany." Here was the voice of a Swedish partisan. Other learned men—among whom Johann Limnaeus (1592–1663), professor at Nürnberg's university of Altdorf and councilor of the margrave of Ansbach, was the most eminent writer—taught that the Empire was a mixed government. From the Peace of Westphalia they derived a confirmation of this view.

The theory of the Empire as a mixed government was probably still the best one, as long as one kept to the old Aristotelian forms of government. It was Samuel Pufendorf (1632–94), a young Heidelberg

[2] See the author's *A History of Modern Germany: The Reformation*, p. 260.

professor, who around 1664 issued under the assumed name of Severinus de Mozambano his *State of the German Empire*, which has been called the greatest pamphlet on German national affairs since Martin Luther's *To the German Nobility*. He pointed out forcefully that in the light of Aristotelian politics the Empire must appear as something of a monstrosity and that it could be understood only through a fresh analysis of its history and present conditions. Pufendorf's writings marked a new stage in German political thought, which will be discussed later.[3] With regard to the Empire and its constitution, which he described with earnest if slightly ironical realism, he stated that the Empire could not be classified simply as a monarchy, because the princes were not subjects of the emperor, although the emperor was their supreme feudal overlord, nor could it be called an aristocracy, as the emperor was not the servant of the princes. Essentially, the Empire had become a confederation of states with elements of a monarchical system.

In view of the divisions within the Empire—between emperor and princes, princes and cities, secular and ecclesiastical princes, and last but not least Catholic and Protestant estates—Pufendorf resigned himself to exhorting the states to unity. Suppression of special interests and mutually hostile federations might lead to a true confederation, which should form a permanent council. This council was to settle all common problems, and the emperor was to become merely president of the Empire. Pufendorf was not overly confident that this proposal would be accepted, because Austria would oppose such a development, while the conflicts between the estates and their alliances with foreign powers would militate against it. But the idea of associations of estates for common German ends, though not adequate to restore the Empire to statehood, was not entirely unrealistic as a means of organizing the smaller estates for the support of peace.

The ideas of Chemnitz, Limnaeus, and Pufendorf betray the new spirit of the generation that had lived through the Thirty Years' War or grown up under its shadow. To former generations the concept of the Empire had been embedded in metaphysical thought. To those who regarded it as the continuation of the Roman Empire, it was the fourth world monarchy, and even to those who avoided the scheme of the four successive monarchies, it was an integral part of universal history as planned by God. Now the idea of a *Holy* Empire was

[3] See page 146.

largely forgotten, and only in the ecclesiastical principalities did it continue to be expressed. The last support of the theory had been made questionable by a Frisian, Hermann Conring (1606–81), in Helmstedt. This founder of the critical study of German legal history showed that the "translation" of the Empire from the Romans to the Germans was an invention of priests. The Roman Empire had broken down much earlier. However, Roman law had infiltrated into Germany centuries later. It was therefore impossible to derive from Roman law an idea of the rights of the German emperor. Conring gave a clear, if not fully correct, picture of the development of Germanic law, demanding its reformulation and restatement in popular language by current rulers. Conring saw legal institutions closely related to human history and politics, and with all metaphysical concepts removed.

Yet all these professors of jurisprudence and politics were convinced that none of the estates of the Empire wished to secede, since they themselves patriotically hoped to see the "Empire," or "Germany," as Conring and Pufendorf preferred to call it, "united, strong, and prosperous." Pufendorf counted on the fact that none of the German princes, including the electors, would cut much of a figure if they ceased to be princes of the Empire and posed as European potentates. Certainly the ecclesiastical princes, and the small estates in particular, had no claim to rank except as members of the Empire. Pufendorf also trusted that the divergent interests of the great European powers would help to preserve the integrity of the Empire, as a gain made, at German expense, by one of these powers would arouse the jealousy of the others. He underrated foreign dangers, especially those brewing in the west, but he was right in judging that there were strong forces sustaining the existence of the dilapidated structure that the Empire had become. He was also right in quietly assuming that no secessionist groups would be found in Germany. The princes did come to use in reckless fashion their right to conclude alliances with foreign powers, but they were not motivated by separatist thought. Pufendorf might have added that for any member of the aristocratic society of German princes and estates, the Empire was the symbol of his liberties and superior rank. The Empire served not only as a loose physical framework but also as the ideological support of a national community that, for the time being, was entirely dominated by the princes and the nobility.

↶ The "Execution Diet"

THE PEACE OF WESTPHALIA was the work of the great European powers. By it they created a European balance founded largely on a balance of Catholic and Protestant forces within the Empire. But the Empire could not even hope to execute the treaty without foreign participation. We have seen what a problem the demobilization of the Swedish army in Germany and its withdrawal from the country had constituted at the conference table. But it is doubtful whether the restitutions and restorations stipulated by the Peace of Westphalia could have been realized, particularly in southern Germany, if the Swedish troops had not been in the country. The carrying out of these provisions, the payment of the indemnity to Sweden, and the simultaneous demobilization of all armies were made conditions of evacuation. This called for new, lengthy, and detailed negotiations, which the generals took in hand. From May, 1649 to July, 1650, an "Execution Diet" was held in Nürnberg. Prince Octavio Piccolomini, now Duke of Amalfi, represented the emperor. For the Swedes, the Count Palatine Charles Gustavus of Zweibrücken appeared. This young son of Gustavus Adolphus' sister Catharine had been appointed Swedish commander-in-chief in the summer of 1648. In 1654 he was to succeed Queen Christina on the Swedish throne as King Charles X Gustavus. Both of these men showed great talent in organizing the liquidation of the war.

Among their disagreeable assignments was the dispersal of troops. The Swedes had probably 100,000 men in Germany, among them 14,000 native Swedes and the rest chiefly German soldiers. On the imperialist side, even larger numbers had to be demobilized. In addition, there were exiled Bohemian Protestants, whom the treaty had not granted the right to return to Bohemia. Among both officers and men of the troops grumbling and even outright opposition to the peace could be heard. Most of them had lived on war for years, some of them growing rich. Many were homeless people who had never learned a civil occupation. A spirit of mutiny was rife, and the memory of the careers of such *condottieri* as Ernst von Mansfeld was beckoning in a situation still abounding in political friction. Whole units marched off to look for employment with the king of France, the republic of Venice, or even the czar of Muscovy. Serious rebellions broke out in a number of Swedish garrisons. Charles Gustavus, Elector Maximilian, and Piccolomini had to use iron fists to put down military revolts. Only a few of the discharged soldiers were absorbed into the rural population; large groups inflated the proletariat in the cities; a good many became brigands. Through the efforts of the generals, nonetheless, a problem that could have become a grave threat to the pacification of Germany was reduced to the point where local authorities could cope with it.

The "Final" Recess

WHEN DEMOBILIZATION WAS STILL UNDER WAY, the main political issues were settled with the "final recess concerning the execution of peace" of July 2, 1650. To many Germans, only this event marked the end of the war. But even afterward the clouds did not disperse. The Swedes made heavy demands before handing over East Pomerania to Brandenburg, delaying this action until 1654. They also attempted, when formally assuming the government of the bishoprics of Bremen and Verden, to compel the free imperial city of Bremen to accept Swedish domination. Furthermore, Elector Frederick William of Brandenburg, assuming the role of protector of the Protestants in Jülich and Berg, tried to conquer these territories by force. The attack against Count Palatine Philip William of Neuburg, ruler of Jülich and Berg, was badly prepared, and the Great Elector was saved from serious political embarrassment only by the mediation of the emperor. Still greater fear was caused by the unrest at the western frontier of Germany. Since neither Spain nor Lorraine was included in the Peace and their war with France went on uninterruptedly, Spain refused to evacuate the fortress of Frankenthal in the Palatinate. France, in turn, was unwilling to give up its strategic points on the middle Rhine. Charles of Lorraine, a cold-blooded marauder, liked to quarter his troops in the Rhenish lands, and as a result the population along the Upper and central Rhine continued to be exposed to the ravages of war. It is small wonder that the princes were eager to build police forces; the first associations or federations of princes for this purpose developed in the Rhineland and Lower Saxony.

Federation among the Estates

BUT CONTINUED HOSTILITIES on the Rhine gave reason for even profounder apprehensions. In the Peace of Westphalia, the emperor had undertaken to discontinue co-operation with Spain in her war with

France. But Ferdinand III had little intention of living up to this promise. His obvious support of the Spaniards in Lorraine, the Netherlands, and Italy would have given Mazarin justification for renewing the war against the emperor. The deep desire of the Germans for peace and their strong aversion to the Austro-Spanish collusion led to federations among the German estates, with comprehensive political programs. The most ambitious plan was presented by Count George Frederick Waldeck, the Great Elector's minister, in 1653–54. He aimed at a union of all the Protestant princes and estates. They were to look to France for support, exclude the Habsburgs from the imperial throne, and reform the Empire on a federative basis. It was a dangerous project and could have again divided Germany between the Catholic leagues and Protestant unions of the early years of the century. But this was probably not intended. Although in this proposed union, as in subsequent federations, the religious principle still formed an integrating bond within the two religious groups, the aims of such unions became more and more clearly constitutional and political.

✑ *Elector John Philip of Mainz*

IN THIS FIELD, the policies of Elector John Philip of Mainz had greater practical importance. This Count Schönborn was the first of a series of members of the Schönborn family who occupied sees in the century after 1648. He had become prince-bishop of Würzburg in 1642 and archbishop of Mainz in 1647. At the peace conference of Münster he had played a prominent role. Mainz, the foundation of St. Boniface, still breathed an air of high imperial traditions. John Philip was the archchancellor of the Empire, and this was not an empty title, though the functions of the office had dwindled. The archchancellor was the president of the electoral college and as such in charge of imperial elections. He was still the first officer in the Empire, announcing decisions of the emperor in matters of the Empire, and he was represented at the emperor's court by the vice-chancellor, who directed the Aulic Chancellery of the Empire (*Reichshofkanzlei*). It is true that the claim of the archchancellor to nominate the vice-chancellor had been virtually lost. Nevertheless, Archbishop John Philip was strongly conscious of the national responsibility of Mainz. Until his death in 1673, he was active in seeking to protect the Empire from another European war. In the early years after the Peace of Westphalia, he was aided in this by Count John Christian Boyneburg, his chief councilor, the man who later attracted young Leibniz to Mainz.

By bringing together smaller alliances already in existence, John Philip succeeded in forming the Rhenish Federation of December 1654. Its members were the three ecclesiastical electors, the prince-bishop of Münster, and the ruler of Jülich-Berg, but John Philip endeavored to secure additional members, particularly from among the Protestant princes. The approaching imperial election added momentum to his efforts. In July, 1654, Ferdinand IV, who had been elected king a year before, died, and his younger brother, Leopold Ignatius (born 1640), could not be elected because of his minority. After the death of Emperor Ferdinand III in 1657, there was a year's interregnum full of political scheming and bickering. Cardinal Mazarin used every weapon in the arsenal of French diplomacy to achieve the exclusion of the Habsburgs from the imperial succession and thereby isolate Spain. He would have liked to see Elector Ferdinand Maria of Bavaria crowned emperor, but the latter, who had succeeded his father Maximilian in 1651, did not trust his own gifts or his political power enough to accept this part in Mazarin's project.

John Philip was largely responsible for the election of Leopold, which took place in 1658, but only after Leopold had agreed to the "capitulation of election." John Philip drafted this document, whereby the emperor undertook to abstain from participation in the Franco-Spanish war, both in Italy and the Netherlands. This was a humiliating condition, which the Vienna government conceded most reluctantly, the more so since the possibility of Leopold's inheriting the Spanish crown was already in the offing. France was pressing to cut present and future ties between the two Habsburg countries, and presumably the German Empire had a similar interest. John Philip, having accomplished the election of a Habsburg ruler, was eager to make his peace policy effective by expanding the Rhenish Federation. In August, 1658, the original members of the Federation were joined in signing a defensive alliance for maintenance of the Peace of Westphalia by King Charles X Gustavus, as duke of Bremen and Verden, by three dukes of Brunswick, and by the landgrave of Hesse-Kassel. Among other things, members promised not to tolerate passage through their territories of imperial troops bound for the Netherlands. But the Federation was not strong enough to enforce its objectives in the event of a conflict with the emperor unless it had the support of a major power. France was invited to accede to this Federation of German imperial estates and did so as a signatory of the Peace of Westphalia. The Federation was to mobilize 10,000 men in case of war; of these, about a quarter were to be French troops.

An alliance between German princes and France was fraught with certain dangers, and John Philip did not intend to serve as a standard-bearer of the French in Germany. As a matter of fact, he would in all probability have turned against France if a Habsburg had not been elected emperor. The Great Elector also did not wish to advance the French cause in Germany when he joined the alliance in 1664. Actually, the war between Spain and France ended with the Peace of the Pyrenees of 1659, and with it one of the major reasons for the association of the German princes with France disappeared. In 1663–64 the Turks made a new attempt to extend their rule in Hungary. This threatened Austria directly and brought the Rhenish Federation, including the French, to the side of the emperor. Bavaria, Saxony, and Brandenburg acted independently and promptly in sending auxiliary troops to Austria, and in 1664 a corps of over 7,000 was sent by the Rhenish Federation. This corps was supplemented by a slightly larger French force under Count Coligny-Saligny. Officially, the French troops were under the command of Count Wolf Julius Hohenlohe, the military chief of the Rhenish Federation. Thus the Rhenish Federation, together with the French, helped defend the Danube. Their contingents made a real contribution to the victory of Montecuccoli, the imperial general, at St. Gotthard on the Raab.

In hoping to build, through an association of German princes in the heart of Europe, a mediating power that could keep Germany, and possibly even Europe, at peace, John Philip had overestimated the potential strength of the small German states. Among the statesmen around him there was an awareness not only of German national needs but also of the common life of Europe, a matter little thought of in this age of ruthless prosecution of individual political interests and growing indifference toward the religious division in Christendom. Here the reunion of Christian churches was considered as more than an academic dream. Leibniz was to devote himself to this reunion under the protection of the court at Mainz. But noble ideas could not make up for the weak political basis on which John Philip built his policies. In the 1660's the frightening strength of the monarchy of Louis XIV became apparent, and all expectations of establishing an intermediary or third position between France and Austria began to look utopian. The Rhenish Federation was not renewed in 1668, and a period of

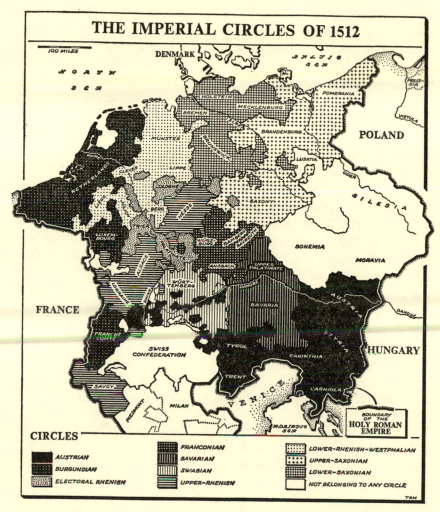

THE IMPERIAL CIRCLES OF 1512

divided policies followed. But co-operation was revived in 1670, when Louis XIV's full annexation of Lorraine aroused the greatest fears in all of Germany.

∽ *The Circles of the Empire*

In 1681 the diet of the Empire passed a law concerning the military organization (*Reichskriegsverfassung*) of the Empire. Defense was put in the hands of the ten Circles of the Empire.[4] Together they were to maintain in peacetime a force of 40,000 men, which was to be

---

[4] Cf. the author's *A History of Modern Germany: The Reformation*, pp. 43–5.

expanded in case of war. This system had its weaknesses. The emperor, whose lands composed the Austrian and Burgundian circles and were supposed to provide almost one third of the army, could not be subordinated to the general system, and the same was true of other "armed estates," as states that had developed their own standing armies were called. Brandenburg, which belonged to three different circles, was particularly evasive in doing its part. Accordingly, the new form of organization was followed chiefly by the circles composed of small estates, the two Rhenish, the Franconian, Swabian, and Westphalian circles. The troops created were not the best. Usually even their cadres were not up to full strength, and their arms and supplies left much to be desired. But these Empire soldiers made a great contribution to the defense of the Rhine frontier when they fought under Margrave Ludwig of Baden against the French, while the imperial army was fighting the Turks. The whole circle organization was badly shaken when the election of the Bavarian Charles VII as emperor, in 1742, set the members of the circles against one another. The army of the Empire became the subject of much ridicule when Frederick the Great sent it in headlong flight in a brief afternoon's battle at Rossbach in 1757. Still, in the war of the French Revolution the circle system of levying troops functioned.

✌ The Emergence of Independent Territorial States

ALL ATTEMPTS to give the Empire new life by grounding it on a free federation of its members had failed. All that was achieved was a modicum of co-operation among the small estates, particularly in the southwest of Germany. Except for this, all political life in Germany had its beginning and end entirely in the territorial states, which controlled the life of the individual in almost every respect and prepared a new stage of German historical development. Among these territorial states, some stood out more clearly than in the time before the Thirty Years' War. Apart from the Austrian territories under Habsburg rule, Bavaria and Saxony seemed to be the strongest territories during and after the war, but both were soon outdone by Brandenburg-Prussia. The Palatinate, in spite of the loss of the Upper Palatinate to Bavaria during the Thirty Years' War, seemed to regain its significance in the decades after 1648, but the cruel fate it suffered when it was devastated in 1689 brought a new decline.[5] Nor did Württemberg reach top rank

[5] See page 94.

among the German states in the next 150 years. But a new center of political power came into being in Lower Saxony.

Since the breakdown of the power of Henry the Lion in the twelfth century, the Guelf dynasty had owned only parts of the old tribal duchy of Saxony, and even these possessions were continuously broken up and divided among the members of the Guelf family. But in 1635–36 an agreement was reached among the various lines about the future distribution of their dominions. The elder branch received the duchy of Brunswick-Wolfenbüttel; one line of the younger branch got Lüneburg-Celle and Grubenhagen, another, Calenberg-Göttingen with Hanover. The close co-operation of George William of Celle and Ernest August of Hanover, two gifted brothers, made their territories a new political center in Germany, even before 1705, when George Louis, the son of Ernest August, inherited Celle at his uncle's death. In 1715 the former bishoprics of Bremen and Verden came into the possession of Hanover, whose ruler had the year before become king of England.

The secular states definitely possessed more power and political initiative than the ecclesiastical territories, which, however, still maintained their rank in the institutions of the Empire. The disparity between the great voting strength and the small capacity for political action which the ecclesiastical principalities displayed was probably another reason why it was unattractive for the secular princes to give the Empire greater attention. While the Holy Roman Empire, after 1648, lost its directing influence on German political activities, the territorial states integrated the German people ever more closely into their own system. The prevailing trend in the political development in all these states was diametrically opposed to that of the Empire. Practically everywhere the dualistic state was abolished, and the princes emerged as absolute rulers. The estates were either suspended or their rights curtailed. Exceptions to this general development were Mecklenburg, East Friesland, and after the transfer of the dynasty to England, Hanover. Württemberg also preserved its old institutions; they were, however, disregarded by its rulers all through the eighteenth century. Thus, the rise of absolutism in Germany was the chief political consequence of the Thirty Years' War.

CHAPTER 2

Economic and Social Conditions
After 1648

AT NO OTHER TIME in her history has Germany suffered such destruction as during the Thirty Years' War. The extent of damage defies exact description. Modern research has done away with the exaggerations that were common in nineteenth-century historiography, and has given a much more differentiated picture of the impact of the war according to regions and classes. Some regions, such as Salzburg and the Austrian territories with the exception of the land north of the Danube, were not exposed to the ravages of the war. Northwestern Germany was little affected by it and probably lost no more than the natural increment of births. The most severe losses were suffered by the Rhenish Palatinate, Württemberg, parts of Thuringia and Silesia, Mecklenburg, and parts of East Pomerania. In these areas the population dropped to one third of the prewar figure. But even in Brandenburg, northern Bohemia, Hesse, Trier, Franconia, Bavaria, and the Upper Rhine valley the average losses amounted to about half the population. Within the various territories the differences in the amount of damage suffered were great. Whereas, for example, the city of Göttingen was frightfully injured, Hanover came through relatively unharmed. In general, destruction was greatest along the roads that the armies had traveled and least in remote areas. In southern Germany most of the Black Forest served as a relatively safe refuge. On the whole, the countryside suffered more than the cities, as urban walls provided at least some protection.

ᴠ Population Changes

POPULATION LOSSES for the whole of Germany are estimated at one third of the city population and two fifths of the rural population. It should be added that further losses were suffered in the devastations of the wars of Louis XIV and of the Nordic War. The Palatinate and Mecklenburg again became victims of devastation, and Prussia, which had not felt the Thirty Years' War, suffered severely. As a result of the Thirty Years' War, Germany lost her position as the most populous country in Europe, her population of about 20 million having dropped to between 12 and 13 million. France, which had grown to about 24 million in 1660, was to take the lead among the European nations for a long time to come. But the restoration of Germany's old population level took only a century. The major reason for this impressive revival was an amazing fertility, sufficient to overcome even the high rate of child mortality of the period. The high German birth rate was in strong contrast to that of other European countries in the century after 1650; the population declined in France, Sweden, Denmark, Belgium, Switzerland, and northern Italy, while in England it increased only slightly—from 5.6 to 6 million.

But the high birth rate alone could not have restored the German population level so quickly. During the century after the war many immigrants came to Germany. Most came from Switzerland and settled in the Palatinate; subsequently, other Swiss settlers went to Brandenburg, where they established communities of their own. Substantial numbers of Walloons and Dutch also came to Germany, as well as some Scots and Scandinavians. The largest single group, the Huguenots, arrived from France after the renunciation of the Edict of Nantes in 1685. Through his Edict of Potsdam, the Great Elector invited them to come to Brandenburg, and 20,000 settled in the Hohenzollern territories, while others went to Ansbach-Bayreuth, Hesse-Kassel, the Palatinate, Brunswick-Lüneburg, Frankfurt, Emden, Bremen, Hamburg, and Lübeck. Württemberg, which was strictly Lutheran, refused the Huguenots admission, but at the turn of the century joined Brandenburg, the Hesses, Nassau, Baden-Durlach, and other Protestant communities in receiving hundreds of Waldensians who were driven out of Savoy.

The Protestant territories gained most from the foreign immigration. As will be seen later, they gained more than mere numbers. Their populations increased also as a result of migration within Germany, which went on for a considerable time after 1648. In addition to annihilating millions of people, the war had uprooted many thousands, perhaps hundreds of thousands. Soldiers did not always return to their places of origin, neither did the peasants who had fled to the cities. Actually, for years to come complaints were heard about peasants who had been given tax exemption and other assistance for a few years so that they could rebuild their farms, and who had left them before the end of the period to take up land under similar exempt conditions elsewhere. There must have been a rather large movement of people from war-protected regions to those that had been devastated—from northwestern to northeastern and central Germany and from Austria to southern Germany. In the latter case the migration of many thousands was prompted by the religious policies of the Habsburg government. Most of the Austrian Protestants went to the Franconian principalities of Ansbach-Bayreuth and to the Swabian and Franconian cities. Emigration from Bohemia reached high proportions after the war, when the Catholic Counter Reformation was pushed to its final conclusion. In Wallenstein's former principality Friedland, 7,500 inhabitants were left by the war, most of them Protestants. But when the new lord, Count Gallas, tolerated the Jesuits' efforts at Catholic conversion, all but 1,000 left. They crossed the frontier into Upper Lusatia, though they had to leave behind all their possessions. Seventy-five thousand Bohemian Protestants, among them many Czechs, are said to have come to Saxony and Lusatia as a consequence of the war. A belated expulsion on religious grounds took place in Salzburg under Archbishop Firmian in 1731. King Frederick William I invited the refugees from Salzburg to settle in East Prussia, and 20,000 answered his call.

৵ Agrarian Production

IT WAS AT THIS TIME that Frederick William I made his oft-quoted remark that "people are the greatest wealth of a country." This saying aptly epitomized one of the chief political concerns of all German princes who actively strove for the restoration and advancement of their territories. They were eager to find man power for the reconstruction of destroyed farmsteads and the recultivation of fields, which in many cases had lain unattended for years and become overgrown with weeds and brushwood. Cattle had been killed; farm implements were scarce and in disrepair. In the end the efforts to bring the land back to agrarian production were successful. Most villages were eventually brought to life again, though often by colonists from distant lands.

For a time land went begging. In certain regions, some peasants freed themselves of servitudes, while others became more dependent as a consequence of debts. But in most of Germany the legal position of the peasant was not changed. In southern and western Germany, peasant land here and there was temporarily added to the lands of the noblemen, and the obligation of peasant children to serve as maids, servants, and in other menial capacities for a period of years was extended to counteract the scarcity of labor. The nobility of these regions showed little inclination to turn to agrarian enterprise. It preferred to collect its rents and other dues, as it had done before the war. The incentive for taking up large-scale farming was not great in southern Germany because of the catastrophic fall of grain prices after the war, which in turn led to a serious decline in land values. Under these conditions the burden of debts became unbearable. The territories passed legislation providing moratoria, lower interest rates, and drastic curtailment of debts. The emperor went even further by stimulating legislation which, on the whole, favored the nobility and wrote off a substantial part of urban wealth. Moreover, it enabled the noble landowners to let land lie fallow till sufficient agrarian labor became available and the market for agrarian products began to recover.

In contrast to southern and western Germany, where the landholding rights of the peasants were relatively secure, they were less safe in the northwest, while the personal liberty of the Lower Saxons was rather greater than that of the south Germans. During the war much land had fallen into the hands of the nobility. With utmost energy, the dukes of Brunswick compelled the landowners to return the peasants' former holdings to them without any diminution. In view of the tax exemption of the nobility, the chief interest of the territorial princes lay in the preservation of a taxable class. In Lower Saxony the traditional social position of the peasants was not only restored but even strengthened by law.

In the Germany east of the Elbe—with the exception of Silesia, which belonged to the Habsburg territories—the Thirty Years' War brought to a conclusion a development that had earlier beginnings.[1] Here the noble landlords had not been satisfied to collect rents from their peasants but managed their estates themselves. The growth of *Gutsherrschaft* in contrast to *Grundherrschaft* made northeastern Germany a distinct part of the country. In the preceding centuries, princely power had been weak in Brandenburg, Pomerania, Prussia, Mecklenburg, and Holstein. In all these provinces the nobility had

[1] Cf. the author's *A History of Modern Germany: The Reformation*, pp. 64–5.

throughout the sixteenth century increased its own land at the expense of the peasants. But as its demesnes had expanded, the need for additional labor had become greater. Important political rights held by the *Junkers*, such as local police and justice, had allowed them to subvert the position of the peasants and exploit their labor for their own economic ends. The boom of agrarian prices in the period from 1550 to 1648 had sparked these efforts. The collapse of the market for agrarian products at the end of the war, together with the great loss of human life and destruction of property occasioned by the war, drove this policy in an even more radical direction.

The chief reason for the decline of agrarian prices was the decrease in the size of the urban population and its poverty. There was relative agrarian overproduction, and it was made more serious by the difficulties of export caused by foreign control of German rivers. It was not enough to hold labor on the land; labor had to be cheap. Ever-growing demands were made upon the work of the peasant, and social and political control over him by the *Junkers*, as the noblemen were called east of the Elbe, was ruthlessly extended. Thus peasants and their families were tied to the soil and practically became serfs (*leibeigen* or *erbuntertänig*). Since the *Junkers* had to give assistance in the rebuilding of peasant places, by imposing certain conditions they had an additional method of lowering the legal status of a large group of peasants. The situation of the peasant was better on the domains of the prince, particularly with regard to required labor services, and in some regions free peasants survived, but they were a small minority and everywhere they lost their voice in public affairs. The Thirty Years' War did not turn northeastern Germany into a *Junker* land, but it completed and solidified the position of social power which the *Junker* class had been acquiring.

✑ *Urban Commercial and Industrial Life*

AFTER THE MIDDLE of the sixteenth century the commercial and industrial life of German cities began to stagnate.[2] The loss of accumulated wealth during the Thirty Years' War ruined the foundations of the German standard of living, which had been high in spite of the adverse developments of the preceding century. The destruction of buildings and other assets, as well as the loss of human life, was smaller in the cities than in the countryside, but German capital resources

[2] Cf. the author's *A History of Modern Germany: The Reformation*, pp. 79–86.

were destroyed. In view of the new international trade situation, impoverished Germany had no chance of regaining the prosperity she had enjoyed in the early sixteenth century. Active participation in large-scale international trade became impossible for Germany after the creation of the modern national economies of the Netherlands, France, and England, which deprived her of access to the western European market. The rise of Sweden and subsequently of Russia diminished the commercial opportunities to the north and east also, especially since Dutch and English traders dominated Baltic commerce. Only in the course of the eighteenth century did German trade with the East assume large proportions, giving Germany a kind of middle position.

Broadly speaking, however, Germany became for the next 150 years a back yard of the emerging Atlantic world, a world whose maritime and colonial enterprises created the wealth on which the modern societies of Europe were founded. Germany had no part in these colonial enterprises. Even her connections with the Mediterranean world shrank. Austria's victories over the Turks did not give Germany or Austria a full chance for the exploitation of Near Eastern trade, since France and England were already too powerful in this field. If Germany had been united, she might have been in a better position to save or regain a place in world trade, but even then she would have required greater capital than the war had left her. Colonial enterprises called for large investments; such investments would also have been needed to stimulate industrial production capable of competing in international markets. Thus Germany was almost completely hemmed in and thrown back on the development of her internal economy. This economy could be made viable only on a much lower level than before the war, and only by relying more heavily on its agrarian resources than before. Under these circumstances the German cities could not be brought back to their former position of prominence.

Economic activity never came to a complete standstill in the majority of the large German cities. Safe conducts from military commanders had sometimes enabled merchants to lead their wagon trains through war zones. The southern German cities had somehow managed to maintain their trade relations with Venice and Lyons; but the staggering tributes imposed on them by friend and foe alike wrecked them financially, and the formation of some new fortunes by the war did not remotely make up for their tremendous losses. Some people had grown rich in the war. The generals, many officers, and merchants of military stores reaped great profits, and these were not altogether invested in land. Austrian refugees brought some capital to the upper German cities which was employed in urban commerce. All these funds, however, were small judged against the national needs. Even the German market offered only limited opportunities. How could the countryside in its desolation purchase urban products as long as its own chief produce, grain, could not fetch a decent price owing to the impoverishment of the city population?

Restoration of the crippled industry of the cities to the prewar level of production alone would have been extremely difficult, and mere restoration would not have been enough. Because of better methods of production developed abroad, Germany became flooded with foreign wares more appealing to the contemporary taste than domestic goods. German cloth could no longer compete successfully with textiles from the Netherlands and England. Wool or half-finished fabrics were now exported from Germany, later to be brought back as finished products. New French luxury goods, such as silk, gobelins, and damask, attracted the fancy of the rich, who were impressed by French manners and French style. Leibniz estimated, in 1670, that 10 per cent of the national income went to foreign nations, and this does not seem incredible. Mining had suffered most severely. The sources of precious metals were already drying up at the beginning of the seventeenth century, and many German mines were not reopened after the war. The revived silver production apparently went entirely into domestic coinage. Copper was still exported to some extent.

The German cities could not cope successfully with the new situation. Of the approximately fifty imperial cities, only a handful survived as major economic centers. A large number became small towns, with no influence beyond the crests of the hills that could be seen from their towers. Biberach, Rottweil, Isny, Kaufbeuren, Ueberlingen, Hall, and Gmünd in Swabia, or Windsheim and Rothenburg in Franconia, might serve as examples. Even more important cities, such as Worms and Speyer, were in full decay when the French burned them in 1689. By 1648 once-glorious Augsburg had lost more than half of its population, and it was only with difficulty that it maintained itself on the level of 20,000 inhabitants through the eighteenth century. It continued to trade with Austria and Venice and northern Italy but was no longer prominent beyond this region.

Nürnberg emerged from the war the strongest of all southern German cities. It had reached 40,000 inhabitants at the beginning of the seventeenth century and apparently regained that figure by the end of the century. Nürnberg profited from its possession of the largest territory of all the German imperial cities and from the fact that its financial activities—which culminated in 1621 in the founding of the Banco Publico—were supported by large industrial enterprises. During the war it had entertained a considerable production of, and trade in, arms, based on iron from Styria. After the war it re-established its world-famous toy production, and became active also in branches of the metal and textile industries. Nevertheless, although the Banco Publico lasted into the nineteenth century, Nürnberg did not achieve a far-reaching influence on the economic life of southern Germany as a whole. Moreover, it declined throughout the eighteenth century. After the middle of the century, the flow of emigration from the city increased considerably and by 1800 its population had fallen to between 25,000 and 30,000.

Frankfurt was the only southern imperial German city—with the exception of Strasbourg, which was soon to come under French domination—that both regained the position it had held in the second half of the sixteenth century and substantially retained it until the end of the Holy Roman Empire in 1806. It was an ideal center for the distribution of imports from Holland to all of southern Germany, and also, along the old route through Fulda, Eisenach, Erfurt, and Leipzig, to central Germany. Frankfurt's trade rested on its connections with the West, with regard to both commodities and finance. Its further growth in the eighteenth century was limited by the rise of Basel and the young city of Mannheim. These cities proved keen competitors of Frankfurt in the Upper Rhine valley, while its opportunities in central and eastern German trade were increasingly monopolized by Leipzig. Leipzig's fairs soon outshone those of Frankfurt. From the beginning of the seventeenth century, Leipzig supplanted Frankfurt as the leading center of the German book trade.

In northern Germany fewer free cities existed, and some of them were deprived of their freedom in the period after the Thirty Years' War. Both Münster and Erfurt had to forego all attempts to attain full independence. In 1661, the bishop of Münster subjugated this Westphalian city, and three years later Archbishop John Philip forced Erfurt to accept the rule of Mainz. In 1666 the Great Elector of Brandenburg compelled the city of Magdeburg to admit a Brandenburg garrison. Magdeburg was then a small town, which had not yet recovered from the disaster of 1630. The Brandenburg elector and the dukes of Brunswick were largely responsible for the defeat of

Swedish designs on Bremen, which, however, had an unchallengeable claim to the status of a free city; though it was small, this Calvinist community had courage and arms for its defense. However, the dukes of Brunswick used their new military power to subdue the Hanseatic city of Brunswick, which was surrounded by their own territories. In 1671, after a brief siege, Brunswick was incorporated into the duchy of Brunswick-Wolfenbüttel.

The coastal cities had not suffered damage during the war, and they had been able to maintain contacts with the outside world. Hamburg had for the most part kept aloof from the convulsions of war. As a matter of fact, the populations of both Hamburg and Bremen had increased through the arrival of refugees from war-torn regions. In 1650 Hamburg had about 40,000 inhabitants, more than any other German city except Vienna or Danzig. It grew rather steadily during the next 150 years; by 1800 it had a population of 100,000 and was bigger than any other German city except Vienna or Berlin. Since the early years of the sixteenth century Hamburg had been the central place for English goods on the Continent, but it also became the main distributing center for Dutch, and eventually French, goods in the wide market accessible from the lower Elbe. In view of Hamburg's importance as a distributing center, all the maritime powers were anxious to see it maintain its independence. Sweden's acquisition of the land on the left bank of the Elbe enabled Hamburg to play Sweden off against its northern neighbor Denmark, which pressed hard on Hamburg's freedom.

Hamburg's position, however, was not such as to make successful trading an easy matter. On the contrary, its situation in national and international politics was fraught with grave dangers, and its economic endowment was rather slim for the business enterprises into which the Hanseatic merchants ventured. Circumstances called for bold and prudent men, who were determined and adaptable. It may be assumed that the absorption of many foreigners—Flemings, Walloons, Portuguese, Jews, Huguenots—served as an important element in saving Hamburg from the fate of most German cities, which tended only to preserve their old institutions and habits. It was equally important for its success that the city kept its gates open to immigrants from Germany and was liberal in granting citizenship to newcomers, although non-Lutherans remained excluded from political office. Hamburg showed an unusual capacity for adopting new people into its communal life and public service. The number of people born outside of

Hamburg who rose to prominence in the city was considerable. This in general was the most democratic side of Hamburg's social development. The city displayed strong burgher pride. In contrast to the southern German cities, no nobleman could acquire citizenship or real estate in Hamburg. Theoretically, equality existed among all classes, although in practice this meant primarily recognition of the successful entrepreneur and did not eliminate a stern government by the ruling groups. In 1602 the city council admonished the citizens in good orthodox Lutheran fashion that "even if magistrates were godless, tyrannical, and avaricious, subjects ought not rebel and disobey but should accept it as the Lord's punishment which the subjects deserved for their sins." Still, the Hamburgers had sufficient political spirit to revolt against the formation of an exclusive patriciate. In the late seventeenth and early eighteenth centuries, popular unrest, which led even to co-operation between the internal factions and outside powers, brought about a revision of the city's constitution.

The new constitution of 1712, which lasted until 1862, was very complex, and it is doubtful whether it gave the average citizen actual participation in government. But it gave widespread representation, it provided the individual with a feeling of communal membership, and it preserved considerable social mobility, which was appropriate to the nature of an active commercial society. It was the basis of Hamburg's steady progress. The city overcame its original lack of financial capital, and the Bank of Hamburg, founded in 1619, was the only German banking institution of international rank in this period. Slowly industry developed and gave the commercial business diversified strength. All through the age, however, shipping remained predominantly in foreign hands. Of the 2,000 ships a year reported to have used the port of Hamburg in the second half of the eighteenth century, only 150 were owned by Hamburg merchants. Behind the bustle of economic enterprise the city gave much attention to cultural activities. Its economic policy was directed, after 1665, by a commercial deputation on which its foremost merchants served in an honorary capacity; similarly other citizens gave their time and energy to church, education, and the arts. Hamburg's cultural influence soon extended not only into Protestant Germany but also into Scandinavia. The close link between Danish and German civilization during the eighteenth century resulted largely from the influence of Hamburg.

Bremen followed the same pattern of development as Hamburg, though it remained less prominent, while Lübeck, the old leader of the

Hanseatic League, declined during this period. Danzig, which was outside the Empire but still enjoying corporate rights within Poland, reached its high point of expansion after the Thirty Years' War. Thereafter, it remained the greatest center of the Baltic grain trade, but hostile Prussian policy during the eighteenth century contributed to its decline. The population of Danzig—60,000 to 70,000 around 1650, dropped to less than 40,000 by 1793, when it became a Prussian city. Although Danzig's position was peculiar in many respects, it may be adduced as an example to show that only the independent German cities at the periphery of Germany and close to the international trade routes were able to retain the vitality necessary for autonomous development. In the interior of Germany the future belonged not to the free cities but to the "territorial cities"—the cities under the suzerainty of a territorial prince. In earlier periods the distinction between imperial and territorial cities had not been too clearly marked. In the old "dualistic" state the corporate rights of the towns that belonged to the territorial estates gave them a practical autonomy often hardly distinguishable from the status of imperial cities. A great change occurred after 1648. The rebuilding of the German economy could only be achieved on a basis that transcended the narrow limits of local government as represented by most of the old imperial cities, and for that matter, by territorial cities as well. The leadership in an active economic policy went to the territorial princes, who enforced their control by closing their territories against others, by breaking the corporate autonomy of the territorial cities and imposing their own direction upon these centers of economic activity. The rise of the new absolute state and its mercantilist policy stymied the life of practically all imperial cities but also overrode the traditional forms of town government and economic organization in the lands of the new state. Whatever the price may have been in terms of social and political values, a problem we will discuss later, important economic gains were doubtlessly achieved.

The first city to rise to national prominence under these new conditions was Leipzig. Its location in what was probably the most industrial region of Germany, as well as the privileges it acquired, with the help of the Saxon government, over the roads of central Germany and the Elbe valley, explain its remarkable growth in spite of its losses during the Thirty Years' War. It had 14,000 inhabitants before the war, 20,000 at the end of the century, and 32,000 in 1750. The economic activities of Leipzig centered around its great fairs and commercial relations, which were close with Frankfurt in the west, Hamburg and Bremen in the north, Breslau in the east, and Nürnberg in the south. But the large commodity market that Leipzig built up was supported by a considerable number of industries in the Saxon hinterland. Without its territorial basis and the protection of the Saxon government, which was needed in particular to keep open the channels of trade to more distant regions, Leipzig could not have gained its prominence. The rise of Berlin in the second half of the eighteenth century placed limits on the growth of Leipzig, and Prussia's acquisition of Silesia after 1740 made Leipzig's relations with Breslau more difficult. The latter, an important center of German trade with the East, had already under the Austrian government become a city more populous than Leipzig.

✑ Changing Social Organization of Production

AFTER 1650 urban development in Germany centered chiefly around the courts. Without the court, the government, and the nobility, a large and unusually wealthy class residing within its walls, Vienna could not have become the largest and richest city in all Germany during the eighteenth century. In the middle of the eighteenth century it had a population of 175,000. The geographical location of Vienna was definitely favorable to the development of commerce and the same could be said of other capitals. The seemingly artificial founding of Mannheim, started in 1609 and renewed with vigor after the devastation of the Palatinate in 1689, clearly took advantage of the propitious location at the confluence of the Neckar and Rhine rivers. Berlin, Dresden, Kassel, and Stuttgart also were favored by nature, but this was only a subsidiary element in the rise of these cities. All of them were dependent on a society grouped around a court and government that included servants, from secretaries to lackeys, as well as artisans catering to the habits of the wealthy. In 1783 two fifths of the 141,000 inhabitants of Berlin were soldiers, government officers, servants, or members of their families. In other capitals the army was not so predominant as in Berlin, but the circles around court and government had more lavish manners than the frugal Prussians, and commerce and industry served largely, and sometimes exclusively, the needs of court and aristocracy.

These governmental centers were in a way new developments, even where they had their roots deep in the past as, for example, in Mainz,

Würzburg, or Bamberg. As a rule they were built on the economies of territories larger than any the old imperial cities had acquired, and these economies were centrally directed by absolute governments that completely disregarded the traditional corporate rights and privileges of the towns. With the few exceptions already mentioned, the German towns, whether imperial or territorial, proved incapable of transforming their social institutions to meet the changed nature of economic life. The old town economy had aimed at providing for the upkeep of a local population. Of course, trade beyond the confines of the community had been sought as a source of income and wealth, and improvement of the quality of products had become a deliberate policy for strengthening the competitive position of urban industries. But the towns had not controlled the sources of raw materials, the extra-urban market, or the labor supply. Already in the later sixteenth century the guild organization of the towns had proved incapable of coping with the new conditions of industry and trade. The guilds were becoming agencies that limited production through holding down employment and immobilizing the market.

The effects of the Thirty Years' War brought this process to an end. The impoverishment of the population in town and country cut trade to a bare minimum. Apart from producing the essentials of life, in these circumstances cheap products, industry worked chiefly for the new armies, for the luxury demands of the courts, and for export. Standardized mass production of essential goods, particularly in the textile and metal trades, and the fabrication of high-quality products became the need of the age. The old guilds proved incapable of organizing the production of quantity goods, and as a rule, were able to restore the high-quality work by skilled German handicraftsmen only after a while. While the import of foreign luxuries was thereby slowly reduced, the export of high-quality goods from Germany remained for the next two centuries relatively insignificant. Practically everywhere, it became the policy of the old guilds, and of the town governments dominated by them, to restrict admission to the guilds and to press for exclusive rights in the only market they could hope to control, that of the town itself. There were a few attempts to expand production by going beyond the individual town and bringing the guilds of a whole region into a productive association. The cutlers of the Wupper valley around Solingen banded together, and in Swabia the cloth company of Calw brought together the clothiers and dyers of a whole region. But this company, which existed from 1650 to 1797, could not have functioned without the support of the Württemberg government, and almost inevitably the territorial governments assumed the direction of industry and commerce.

The shrinkage and immobility of the guilds naturally caused great tension between masters and journeymen, and this led to attempts by the Empire to establish new legal forms. Its legislation, which culminated in the guild recess of 1731, broke up the national associations of the journeymen, but at the same time abolished the judicial power of the guilds. The guilds were placed under the supervision of the governments and their functions confined exclusively to economic tasks. The practical execution of these rules, however, depended entirely on the determination of the individual governments. Little could be expected from those of the imperial cities, whereas the territorial princes used their power. So far as they cared for higher standards of guildlike production, they preferred to fight the monopoly of the old guilds by granting trade licenses to so-called "free masters," that is, masters outside the guilds. Frequently the "free masters" who received licenses were foreign immigrants who were being encouraged to practice a trade in which their native countrymen had achieved higher skills than the Germans.

Actually, however, the guilds henceforth ruled only a segment of industrial production. As early as the sixteenth century the organization of industry had passed increasingly into the hands of commercial entrepreneurs who used the cheap method of the "putting-out" or "domestic system" (*Verlagssystem*). Since the late seventeenth century this system had increasingly drawn wider groups of the population, including women and children, into its operations. Especially in the textile field—in spinning, weaving, knitting, and needlework—the poor toiled endlessly for little pay. Along with this decentralized form of production, the highly centralized form, the factory, made its appearance. Ready labor was often not easily available, in spite of the fact that Germany, like all other European countries in this period, abounded in idle people who existed as beggars and loafers. The large size of this group is hard to explain, even if one keeps in mind that it included all the physically unfit or incapacitated. But regular working habits are a result of long training, which in Germany became a task of the governments. The exploitation of forced labor—for example, providing a factory with the work of the inmates of orphanages or workhouses—was a common method of state support. Apart from giving support by supplying labor, governments assisted factories by granting them monopolistic privileges. State ownership and management was not the rule, though it occurred not infrequently, particularly in the arms industry and in mining.

With the development of manufacturing, industries spread through the countryside. The domestic system mobilized the countryside, while certain industries settled outside the cities because they needed the water power of rivers or fuel from the woods. With the decline of the towns the landowning nobility found an opportunity for entering mercantile activities on a larger scale. The expansion of brewing other than for home consumption, the development of trade in connection with sawmills, and the participation in grain trade are illustrations of the locally and regionally variegated struggle between urban and rural interests. Some governments, for example that of Brandenburg-Prussia, tended, for tax reasons, to frown upon an extension of industrial and commercial enterprise outside the towns.

∽ *The Structure of Society*

THE RUIN OF THE imperial cities, the loss of corporate rights and self-government by all towns, and the shift of the directing powers of economic policy from the towns to the territorial governments were events of the greatest magnitude in the social history of Germany. In the sixteenth century the German cities had attained a high level of economic productivity and had made great cultural and intellectual contributions. Their policies, especially in national matters, were open to some criticism, but public spirit was unquestionably alive in these cities and the sense of independence of the townspeople had enabled them, even amid the tragic misfortunes of the Thirty Years' War, to prove their loyalty to their religious convictions by many courageous deeds. After the war a timid and small generation grew up in the German towns, people who stooped to the forces in power and even in their cultural activities took their cue largely from the established authorities. It would be misleading, however, to speak of the burghers as a single group. The vast majority of the German towns were actually small hamlets. In many of them, particularly in the northeast, *Ackerbürger*—burghers living on farming—formed a substantial part of the population. Considering the burghers of the larger towns, Veit L. von Seckendorf in 1680 distinguished at least two classes—burghers of means and common burghers. The last dress regulation (*Kleiderverordnung*) issued by Frankfurt in 1731 names five classes: families eligible for public offices (*ratsfähig*); city officers, people of wealth, and doctors of law; guild masters and lesser merchants; artisans and storekeepers; and servants. The separation of the first and second groups probably occurred only in the big cities, particularly in the free cities. Otherwise the scale was representative of the division of urban society in Germany which has left an indelible mark on the history of the country. The social compartments became very rigid, and each group cultivated its own social honor and ideals.

The patriciate wished to be considered as an aristocracy and emulated the manners of the nobility. Since the nobility itself looked to the new civilization of the French court as its model, French habits and fashions gained admission to the town society through this upper-burgher class. Artisans and small merchants remained closest to German traditions and outlook. Far enough removed from the court and nobility but, as time went on, enjoying a modestly safe economic position, they were most anxious to improve their local, and this meant their German, world. Only a few were able to rise above their station to higher status through industry and commerce. But a good many could at least hope to see their sons rise through academic study to become civil servants or professional men. The academic way remained open as a method of social advancement, and students at the small German universities were obviously aware of this. The conduct and manners of these students were a vulgar copy of those of the German nobility. Dueling and drinking bouts were the cheap outlets of people who were impressed with the combative spirit of military officers and their contempt for the civilian classes.

But it remained quite dubious whether in later life these boys would be received into a higher class. The bureaucracy offered a certain chance. In the seventeenth century fewer councilors of common birth attained high rank in the state than in the sixteenth century, though some individuals succeeded and received the patent of nobility. The old nobility regarded these individuals disdainfully, but eventually they or their children were absorbed. The patriciate of the towns also adopted some of them. An academic diploma was, therefore, of value for maintaining a certain social mobility and nonfeudal selectivity. But on the whole society was strictly organized as a pyramid, and no equalization among the classes took place for more than a century. The commoner who stayed in the place in which he was born had to be satisfied with his narrow world and had to demonstrate obedience to the rules laid down by the authorities. Even privacy he enjoyed only if he was more than a servant or laborer. If he wished to participate in the political concerns of the community, he had to adjust his thoughts and manners to the style of the ruling class.

Accordingly, an independent political and social attitude on the part of the burghers, comparable to that of the Western European bourgeoisie, could not develop in Germany. The merchant and industrial producer depended on the assistance and favor of the government, as did also the ambitious university graduate whose career was tied up with the civil service. In Protestant Germany the church ministry was also linked up with the government. The Catholic Church preserved more of its corporate rights, but also more of its aristocratic character. Bishops' sees and chapters were still a monopoly of the nobility. The German universities had always relied greatly on the protection of the princes. The impoverishment of the universities through the war deprived them of all means for resisting the guardianship of the absolute state, which treated them as fully subordinate to its will. The professors made no effort to question this control. Like members of a guild, they preferred to defend their outward privileges. Extensive inbreeding was more prevalent at this time than in any other period of German academic history. Where men of spirit sought to expand their horizons, they could do so only in connection with a court or government. Conring and Pufendorf were typical professorial counselors of princes. Leibniz was never attracted by the universities and became dependent upon princes. Inevitably, even the eminent thinkers of the period were profoundly affected by the interests of the governments, while persons of weak character became fawning servants of the existing regimes.

When Milton, in 1656, spoke of the *"Germanorum virile et infestum servituti robur"* ("the manly strength of the Germans opposed to servitude"), this could be taken as descriptive of Germans only in an age past. The Germans of Milton's time were just becoming subjects of the social and political system created by the new absolutism and showed no signs of opposition to command. Avidly, they snapped up titles as a means of creeping a few inches closer to the thrones and of feeling superior to their fellow men. The nobility, for its part, carefully guarded its own social privileges and did not mingle with burghers. After 1650 special schools for sons of the nobility, the so-called knights' academies (*Ritterakademien*), were created all over Germany, particularly in the capitals, to teach social skills and manners to the young chevaliers. On leaving school they were sent on the grand tour through the Empire, France, and Italy, provided their families could afford the great expenses. The number of impoverished noble families was large. Scions not only of these families but also of families with wealth wished to gain a living or add to their fortunes by court, government, and military service. Although the old political power of the estates no longer existed, a memory of this power lingered on, persuading noblemen that appointments to such service were their proper due. The quasi-princely function of noblemen on their own estates and the community of feeling that existed between them and the princes, created by the fact that both followed the same aristocratic style of life, made the subordination of noblemen to princes a less bitter experience than that of the burghers to authoritarian command.

This fact explains, too, why the noblemen were always supporting the princes in attempts to abolish the freedom of towns and regulate their life. There was a deep gulf between the noblemen and burghers. Still, the caste system was not completely rigid. Education, scholarship, science, and technology remained the domain of burghers. Although noblemen did less for their own education than princes, not all of them lacked intellectual interests. When German thought began to gain fresh strength, its influence was felt also among the nobility; after the middle of the eighteenth century it went so far as to change their outlook.

✎ *General Economic Policies of the Absolutist State*

THE PRINCES EMERGED AS THE DOMINANT FIGURES of German life after the Thirty Years' War. Indeed, the fact that there were so many of them and that so many considered their princely dignity an excuse for profligate living impeded Germany's recovery. Yet there can be no question but that the poverty which followed the war and the efforts of the absolutist governments to overcome the devastation produced the transformation that made the German people into one of the most industrious and hard-working on earth. In Protestant Germany, Luther's conception that the individual Christian should obey God's will by fulfilling the demands of his occupation only now came to full fruition. Reducing the excessive number of Christian holidays was in itself a contribution to higher production. Even in Catholicism a new discipline of work was apparent. Its spiritual sources lay in the revival of religious asceticism, which was not confined to the monasteries.

Education for work was one of the main objectives of the general economic policies of the absolutist state in Germany. These policies all aimed at the stimulation of productivity. It is doubtful whether mercantilism is a good name for this period of German economic history. The merchant played a relatively minor role in German life, and an aristocratic society entertained many prejudices against him. Furthermore, he was chiefly an importer in Germany and therefore suspected by the governments as a man who carried good money away. The emphasis of German economic policies was on agrarian and industrial production rather than on commerce, and the endeavor to achieve a favorable balance of trade was dictated by the wish to keep the princely treasuries supplied with funds. Contemporary German writers spoke repeatedly of "cameralism"—*camera* meaning the princely treasury.

It is not known whether Germany as a whole had a favorable balance of trade, and it would be difficult to describe the situation even for individual German states with any preciseness. A policy of self-sufficiency obviously was impossible for the fragmentized German territorial states. Apart from trading, money transfers made as a result of hiring soldiers tended to equalize the differences in the standard of living between smaller and larger states. The national balance, however, was improved by large sums paid by foreign powers to the German princes as subsidies for their political and military services. During this whole period commerce in soldiers was of major significance, although it was no longer carried on by private entrepreneurs of the Wallenstein type, but by princes. It was the German form of the slave trade around which the colonial enterprise of Western European countries centered so largely during this age.

Repeated attempts were made by German rulers to acquire colonies, but they were in vain. Bavaria negotiated for a while with the Dutch, who seemed inclined to cede New Amsterdam, but the English occupation of this colony in 1664 destroyed all hopes for a New Munich in Manhattan. Prior to this time the Great Elector had urged the founding of an East India company, to be financed by the emperor, the king of Spain, Brandenburg, and other German princes, but the project, which sought to exclude the Dutch from control of the German market and envisaged the development of naval strength on the part of the Empire, was dropped, and instead the Great Elector strengthened trade relations with England. He resumed his active interest in maritime affairs during the war against Sweden, after 1675. He chartered Dutch ships for warfare, and after the war the Dutch commodore, Benjamin Raule, persuaded the Elector to send an expedition to the coast of Guinea. In 1682 an African Company was founded, with the Great Elector as the first shareholder. It established two military forts on the coast of Guinea by 1684. In the following year it acquired the right from Denmark to establish a settlement on St. Thomas Island in the West Indies in order to carry on the import of African slaves into the Western Hemisphere. The estates of East Friesland became partners of the African Company, and this made it possible to transfer the seat of the company from the Prussian Pillau on the Baltic to Emden. The elector of Cologne also invested some money, but the capital of the company remained small.

It is doubtful whether a large investment of capital would have made the venture more remunerative. The hostility of the Dutch toward the Brandenburgers who invaded their mercantile hunting grounds created continuous difficulties, which probably would have grown in proportion to further investment. The enterprise had no real protection, and it is questionable whether it would ever have produced profits. Frederick III, son of the Great Elector, kept the company active for reasons of political prestige. But his successor, King Frederick William I, declared colonial business a "chimera" and sold the African Company for a small sum to the Dutch West India Company.

In 1714, after his acquisition of the Spanish Netherlands, Emperor Charles VI founded the Ostende Company with a considerable capital investment. Business in Africa, India, and China developed auspiciously, but as early as 1727 he suspended the company for four years, and later dissolved it, because it aroused the enmity of the maritime powers and he wished to preserve the friendship of England. The only lasting German colonial enterprise, which, however, played no part in the growth of the German economy, was the emigration of dissenting Protestants from the Rhineland to the American colony of William Penn in 1683. A good many people from the war-ruined Palatinate followed them in the early eighteenth century. But these emigrants retained no economic or political ties with Germany.

CHAPTER 3

Absolutism in the German States: The Rise of Brandenburg

↪ The Political Situation in Europe after 1648

THE PEACE OF WESTPHALIA had broken the link between the two Habsburg powers, Spain and Austria, which had held France dangerously encircled for more than a century and a half. After another decade of war between France and an isolated Spain, the Peace of the Pyrenees of 1659 ended forever any serious threat to France from the south. The France of Louis XIV, therefore, found herself in a position of preponderance which allowed her to expand into the Netherlands and Germany. French power, which was to be materially buttressed by commercial and colonial dominance, was so great during the latter half of the seventeenth century as to give the French virtual leadership in the political affairs of Europe. French policy had a hold on Stuart England, and it had the co-operation of the Turks. In northern Europe it relied on Sweden, its wartime ally, and collected new allies among the princes of Germany. If we consider the great influence that French civilization wielded over the whole Continent, it is almost surprising that Louis XIV did not turn the whole of Europe into a universal monarchy in the second half of the century.

By the end of the seventeenth century the general military progress of France had been brought to a standstill. It was of decisive importance that Holland survived the attack by France and that William III of Orange, in the Glorious Revolution of 1688, removed French influence from England. In the battle of La Hogue, in 1692, the British navy established its superiority over the French fleet. It was equally important that in spite of suffering grievous losses the Empire held the Rhine line. During this same period Austria achieved full liberation from the Turks of southeastern Europe between the Carpathians and the Adriatic. It became impossible for France thereafter to unleash the Turks against the Empire at will, and the shift in the Franco-Austrian balance of power was considerable. Finally, the decline of Sweden, the rise of Brandenburg-Prussia, and the appearance of Russia on the European scene made the work of French diplomacy more complex than before.

This transformation of the European system of states deeply affected the political life of Germany. The danger that international conflicts might again be fought on German soil, as in the Thirty Years' War, was present for a long time. It did not lead to greater national unity but was overcome by the power of a few individual states. Brunswick-Hanover and Brandenburg-Prussia virtually removed Sweden from northern Germany, and the Hohenzollern state succeeded in gaining a base that kept Russian progress along the Baltic within limits. Austria, never without help from Germany, threw the Ottoman Empire back behind the Iron Gate and stemmed the French advance at the Meuse and Rhine. In making all these efforts, the German states reached a new stage of internal development which was quite the opposite of that of the Empire as a whole. Whereas in the Empire the estates, as we have seen, were victorious over the monarchical power of the emperor, everywhere in the territories the princes emerged as the absolute rulers of their own states, irrespective of whether they abolished, or shelved, or seemingly tolerated the co-operation of the estates. The theory that the prince had the *potestas legibus absoluta* was not always applicable in a strict sense, but even where estates remained in existence, the will of the prince was supreme. The preceding period of war had demonstrated the perils, for the conduct of foreign affairs, of a division of authority. It had also shown the risks that prince and country ran if they relied on privately managed mercenary armies. On the other hand, the usefulness of soldiers for the subjection of dissenters and political opponents, in disregard of traditional laws and customs, had become fearfully evident, as well as their ability to collect financial contributions.

✍ *The Development of Public Finance and Taxation*

IN MANY RESPECTS it had been a new discovery to find that it was physically possible to siphon off so much money from the population. Public finance, including taxation, had been in its infancy before the war. Now it became a deliberate, if still clumsy, art. A century earlier it had been a widely held opinion that the prince was to defray the expenses of government with his own income from domains—mining rights, monopolies, tolls, etc.—usually called the *camerale,* and that taxes were to be levied only for extraordinary purposes, such as defense. But already at that time the medieval *Bede,* a land tax, had become a permanent instead of a temporary levy, and other direct and indirect contributions had been added. The estates had tried with fair success to collect these taxes, called *contributionale,* themselves and also to supervise their use. Often they had gone beyond control of the *contributionale* and demanded supervision of the *camerale* as well. For the prince, by running up high debts on his personal domains, was usually able to compel the estates to buy him or his heirs free by new money grants. Yet the estates had not been able to acquire or retain such power of supervision for more than brief moments. Throughout the war taxes had gone up, and even at the end of the war it was impossible to return to the earlier level. Payment of debts, resettlement of the population, land improvement, and maintenance of troops—all these called for revenue, especially since, as a consequence of the sale and mortgaging of domains, low grain prices, and other adversities, the *camerale* produced little income. In these circumstances direct taxes had to be maintained. The princes now demanded them as a matter of right and also claimed discretion in the use of the tax income. This called for an improved system of tax collection and administration, preferably through officials appointed by the prince. The most radical reform was the transfer of all these functions to a new type of official, which had originally come into being in connection with modern mercenary armies. Commissaries had been dispatched to the troops to check on the proper execution of the contracts between princes and generals or to act as intermediaries between the army and the country in such matters as requisitioning and quartering troops. In these emissaries of the prince a skeleton organization for a centralized system of government under the prince came into existence.

The subsequent history of this organization showed certain complications. Even the war commissaries could be absorbed by the older institutions of the estates or at least be closely linked with them. The extent to which the prince could superimpose a centralized administrative structure of his own differed from state to state. There was great diversity among the territories as to the types of taxes chosen to satisfy the needs of the state budget. Beside direct taxation, indirect taxes on consumption or business transactions had occasionally been used. Even in the Middle Ages the German cities had rested their public finances on taxes on consumption and on duties, and in the Netherlands this urban system was carried over to a large territorial community whose economy aroused the admiration of all its neighbors. The "excise" became one of the foremost taxes for the development of the state-directed economy in the age of absolutism. In practice, excise taxes took very different forms in the different states, not only with regard to the categories of taxable commodities and transactions, but also with respect to the classes of people who had to pay them. In some states they were levied only in the towns, with the rural areas making their contributions in direct taxes; in others there were exemptions for individual social classes, such as the nobility or the clergy. Differences in the tax program and administration also existed in the various territories of a single ruler.

✎ *Absolutism in the Secular Principalities*

YET GREAT AS THE VARIETY of financial and political institutions and practical policies was, everywhere in Germany the princes emerged as absolute rulers. They were able to build a political economy that not only permitted them lavish personal display but also gave them full command over military and foreign policy. Except in Austria and Bohemia, the establishment of absolutism did not result from civil war. Rather, it was achieved quietly, though not always without struggle. So far as one major cause for the relatively easy victory of the princes can be singled out at all, it was not the weakened economic position of the estates as such, but rather the conflict of interests which developed among the estates and which was enormously intensified by the war. Princes could exploit the disunity between the nobility and the towns. Even where, as in Catholic countries, the clergy retained or regained a place among the estates, they were too closely tied to the government to co-operate consistently with either of the other two estates. In general, the towns were most disregarded in the three-cornered fight between princes and the two estates, while the noblemen won both recognition of their privileged position in the local sphere and preferment in the new military and civil service of the absolutist state. Through concessions and compromises, the princes won the battle to establish standing armies. Once a standing army—a *miles perpetuus* as it was called at the time—had been created with the assent of the estates, it became self-perpetuating; it gave the prince a weapon that could be used against the estates, especially since it could sometimes be financed by foreign subsidies.

✍ Absolutism in Bavaria and the Habsburg Lands

ABSOLUTIST GOVERNMENT APPEARED in Germany before all these military and economic forces had come fully into operation. In Bavaria the estates had already been deprived of all political power by 1618. The principle of religious uniformity served as the lever that accomplished this, and the assertions of the dukes that the nobility had contained many oppositional elements were hardly supported by facts. In this respect the development in Austria was quite different. In Austria large groups of the nobility and the towns formed powerful associations in order to defend their presumed political rights, or even to impose their will on the Habsburg rulers. The bloody conflicts that ensued had ended, with the battle of White Mountain, in complete victory for the royal or archducal cause in Bohemia and Austria. In the Habsburg lands no imperial cities had ever come into existence, and municipal life had always been closely supervised by the territorial rulers. The expulsion of a large part of the old nobility and the creation of a new nobility dependent on the favors of the dynasty broke the power of the estates. The Habsburgs could also count on the general support of the clergy, since their victory was achieved in the service of the Church.

The success of the Bavarian and Austrian rulers in depriving the estates of political power was so complete that they did not even bother to abolish the old political forms. No diets were called in Bavaria after 1667. The Upper Palatinate, acquired by Bavaria during the Thirty Years' War, was not only purged of all Protestants but also firmly integrated into the electorate. The existing role of the estates in financial administration was not abolished but allowed to operate along-side the elector's system. This divided system was in large part responsible for the poor management of Bavarian finances throughout the eighteenth century. The enormous expenditure of the Bavarian electors for political and private purposes would probably have been excessive for an agrarian state like Bavaria in any event, but in the absence of a rational administrative system it was not even possible to get a clear view of the relation between the country's income and expenditure.

In the Habsburg territories the diets of the estates continued to be called, and their administrative functions in the financial and military fields went on. The administrative offices of the crown existed side by side with the agencies of the estates. This dualism proved to be one of the chief obstacles to sound financial policies, and the difficulties were multiplied by the autonomy of the individual lands. Neither the exclusion of the estates from administration nor the integration of the various territories into a more closely unified monarchy was seriously undertaken before the days of Maria Theresa and Joseph II, after the Prussian system had proved its superiority. Before this time an appalling lack of co-ordination prevailed. Under Emperor Leopold I there were twenty central treasury offices, and the Austrian state debt increased at a growing pace. Integration was attempted chiefly by personal methods. The court of Vienna served as a means for creating loyalties that transcended the provinces. Imperial support of orders of Christian knights and similar methods stemming from a feudal past were freely used to create an imperial consciousness. Few important steps were taken in the organization of a modern political administration.

The separation of Austrian affairs from imperial German affairs reached a new stage in the seventeenth century. The Aulic Council of the Austrian archdukes had become the Imperial Aulic Council (*Reichshofrat*) and was the agency that performed the judicial functions of the emperor in Germany. Political administration was transferred from the Aulic Council to the Imperial Chancellery, but Austrian affairs were taken away from it when in 1620 a separate Aulic Chancellery was created for Austria. But in addition to the Austrian Chancellery there existed a Bohemian and a Hungarian Chancellery, and the full reconquest of Hungary at the end of the century added to the difficulties of centralization. The founding of a central council of imperial ministers in 1669, the so-called *Geheime Conferenz*, did not overcome the centrifugal tendencies in the government of the Habsburg territories.

The greatest new centralizing institution in the Habsburg realm was the standing army. It stemmed from Wallenstein's army. In 1650 Ferdinand III ordered the organization of nine regiments of infantry and ten of cavalry. This was a German army, at least in its rank and file. Only in the eighteenth century were Italian and Hungarian regiments brought into it. Yet from the beginning the officers' corps included, in addition to Austrians and Germans from the Empire, members of all European nations, a circumstance that inevitably weakened the army as a factor in the internal unification of the different Habsburg lands.

∽ Absolutism in Ecclesiastical Principalities

As IN BAVARIA AND AUSTRIA, absolutism in another group of territories, the ecclesiastical principalities, can be said to be a result of the religious wars. The ecclesiastical principalities would probably not have survived if they had not been needed to maintain the balance between Catholicism and Protestantism in Germany, and the restoration of the absolute power of the prince-bishops was largely a result of the relative victory of the Catholic German states. The absence of dynastic rights of succession and the elective rights of the chapters were of course an obstacle to absolutist practices. The complete domination of the nobility over the chapters in the past had made their noble members not only champions of the dualistic state but also of religious division. The restoration of episcopal authority in the Peace of Westphalia was, therefore, not confined to the religious field. Even after 1648 the nobility tried to limit the authority of the ecclesiastical rulers by "capitulations of election," but since, in their political demands, the nobility displayed an egotistical class interest, the other social groups rallied to the support of the prince-bishops and their unhampered exercise of power. Pope and emperor intervened in favor of the absolute power of ecclesiastical rulers. In 1695 Pope Innocent XII forbade all "capitulations of election" as well as all subsequent stipulations by the chapters, and Emperor Leopold I confirmed these rulings in 1698. After that time the ecclesiastical principalities closely followed the model of the secular principalities of the age. Certain bishoprics, primarily in the Rhineland and Westphalia, became directly allied with one or another of the secular states through their rulers. From 1583 to 1761 the archbishopric of Cologne was governed by a succession of Wittelsbach princes, and the bishoprics of Liége, Münster, Paderborn, and Hildesheim were, during most of this time, in the hands of Bavarian princes occupying the throne of Cologne. The bishoprics of Regensburg and Freising, adjacent to Bavaria, took their rulers largely from the Bavarian dynasty.

The Franconian bishoprics preferred to elect their bishops from the ranks of the nobility whose members formed the chapters. Among these bishops, members of the Schönborn family achieved the greatest distinction and, through their patronage of art, left behind immortal monuments. John Philip (1605–73), after military service against the Turks, became bishop of Würzburg in 1642, and five years later, archbishop of Mainz and bishop of Worms. His nephew, Lothar Franz (1655–1729), was elected to the see of Bamberg in 1693 and to the see of Mainz in 1695. Of Lothar Franz's seven nephews, four attained the episcopal dignity. John Philip Franz became bishop of Würzburg, and was succeeded by his brother Friedrich Karl. Damian Hugo became a cardinal of the Roman Church and bishop of Speyer; Franz Georg, elector-archbishop of Trier, bishop of Worms, and prince-provost of Ellwangen.

Although among the ecclesiastical princes there was occasionally a bellicose ruler, such as Bishop Christoph Bernhard of Münster, in general they directed their efforts toward the internal affairs of their dominions. In practice, this meant very different things. The emphasis could be on luxurious court life, or on a public-welfare policy, or on anything in between. No easy generalizations can be made about the ecclesiastical bishoprics, and the same must be said of the small Protestant principalities.

✍ Rehabilitation in the Small Protestant Principalities

THE WORK OF REHABILITATION and development in some of the Protestant principalities after the Thirty Years' War deserves highest praise. Apart from Margrave Christian of Ansbach, Elector Karl Ludwig of the Palatinate (1648–80) was probably the ruler most successful in restoring his devastated territories. After his return from exile in England, this eldest son of the Winter-King devoted himself with the greatest diligence to rebuilding the lands that the Peace of Westphalia had assigned to him. In a few years the Palatinate, of which Descartes wrote that its smallest part was worth more than the whole empire of the Tartars and Muscovites, began to prosper again. Its population was replenished by immigration; its fields, vineyards, and orchards were flourishing, its houses rebuilt. Heidelberg castle was made habitable again, and even its famous big wine barrel was repaired as a symbolic gesture. Karl Ludwig was an economical steward, more interested in the necessities than the luxuries of life. French immigrants introduced the exotic potato into Germany, but it did not become a staple food on German tables for many years.

Karl Ludwig's mercantilistic policies found their clearest expression in the refounding of the city of Mannheim in 1652. He planned the establishment of a great commercial center of the Dutch type at the confluence of the Rhine and Neckar. Decent people of all nations were invited to settle in the new town, which for an initial period was left free of taxes and customs. No guilds were introduced and full freedom was given to the three Christian churches. Karl Ludwig built in Mannheim a church dedicated to "St. Unity," in which alternately Catholic, Calvinist, and Lutheran worship was held. It was a monument to the enlightened ecumenical tendencies of the age, which, however, were rather rare in Germany. In the same year that Mannheim was founded, the University of Heidelberg was reopened with a faculty of eminent scholars. Samuel Pufendorf was professor of politics in Heidelberg from 1661 to 1668. In the university, too, the elector wanted the three Christian churches represented equally, but he went even beyond this aim when he tried to draw Spinoza to Heidelberg, promising him "the fullest freedom for philosophizing" if he respected the state religion.

Karl Ludwig was cautious in his external policies. He was convinced that the undisturbed development of the Palatinate depended on friendly relations with France, and he hoped that the marriage of his daughter Elizabeth Charlotte to the duke of Orléans would propitiate Louis XIV. He could not foresee that after his death and the death of his only son, Louis XIV would use the marriage as a pretext for French claims to the Palatinate. In the ensuing wars with France the Palatinate suffered a destruction more painful and thorough than that of half a century earlier. It recovered from the devastation only slowly, and the atmosphere of toleration was not restored under the new Catholic rulers of the Neuburg line. After these wars the Palatinate ceased to be one of the major German states.

Karl Ludwig was not fully representative of the contemporary generation of German Protestant princes, although the Great Elector of Brandenburg had ideas similar to his, ideas that were to come to the fore again in a subsequent age of absolutism. Closer to the thinking of the German Protestant princes of the later seventeenth century, though far above them in actual achievement, stood Duke Ernest the Pious of Saxony-Gotha (1601–75). He was an elder brother of Prince Bernhard of Weimar, who, after serving in the Swedish army up to the time of the battle of Nördlingen, settled down to govern his small Thuringian dominion in a spirit of strict, if mild, Lutheranism. Every aspect of the life of his subjects was brought under the care of the ducal government. Every inhabitant had to prove his knowledge of the catechism

and Bible. The state placed its full coercive power behind the rebuilding of church discipline. The sentiment expressed by Lutherans in
defense of the conclusion of the abortive Peace of Prague of 1635—
that the war deprived "our beloved youth of its most precious treasure
of education"—struck a dominant chord in the duke's character.
Luther's demand that everyone receive some schooling was for the first
time translated into a practical program in the school statute (*Schul-
ordnung*) of 1648. In its emphasis on an elementary school that would
teach not only the three *R*'s but also some general subjects, this statute
opened a new chapter in German educational history.

Duke Ernest also attended to the physical well-being of his territories. One of the projects that absorbed his energies was an attempt
to make the Werra river navigable, thus linking Gotha, through the
Weser, with Bremen and the North Sea. The enterprise suffered from
great technical handicaps and even greater political difficulties because
the duties levied by the various states along the Weser made most
exports unprofitable. However, Thuringian timber reached London
through this waterway after the Great Fire of 1666 and was used in rebuilding the city.

The political and economic ideas of Duke Ernest were clearly reflected in the books of Veit Ludwig von Seckendorf (1626–92), who
served for many years as his councilor. His *Princely State (Fürsten-
staat)*, first published in 1655, was reprinted many times in the following century, and his *Christian State*, which appeared in 1685, also went
through a number of editions. For a century Seckendorf's writings
were considered the classic texts of political ethics and practical statesmanship in Protestant Germany. In these writings princely absolutism
and the division of classes appeared as a God-willed order. But the
Christian prince was admonished not only to maintain justice and
security but also actively to support religion and education. He was
also counseled on the practical advance of economic welfare. This
interest in economic progress was a new note in political philosophy,
as was also Seckendorf's concept of the ruler, whom he regarded not
exclusively as the owner of a patrimony but as a man under obligation
to serve the general social and spiritual well-being of the community.
Still, this thought was little developed by the man whom his friends
admiringly called "the noblest among Christians and the most Christian among noblemen."

It would be a grave mistake to see in Seckendorf's idealistic writings
a true description of the actual condition of the Protestant states.

Leaving aside personal Christian morals, which did not fare well at many courts, the Christian patriarchal regime that Seckendorf described was already somewhat outmoded. Given a good prince, the ideal could probably most easily be realized in the petty states. On the other hand, it was least likely that the small princes would grow beyond "proprietary" concepts of government. Duke Ernest, for example, provided for the division of his tiny principality at his death among his seven sons. The bigger princes, who actively participated in the competition for power among states, were more likely, in spite of strong dynastic sentiment, to consider themselves as the agents of a dynamic historical process and to rise beyond the terms of private law.

∾ Early History of Brandenburg

IN FREDERICK WILLIAM OF BRANDENBURG (1620–88)—whom even his contemporaries called the "Great Elector"—this conflict can be seen clearly, although he was genuinely eager to live up to Christian ideals. It was Frederick William who almost overnight raised Brandenburg to the position of second in importance among the German states and to the rank of a respectable power on the chessboard of European politics. The Hohenzollern dynasty had been transplanted from the South into the Mark Brandenburg in 1415. It had been successful in establishing itself, during the fifteenth century, against strong internal opposition, but it had not played a very conspicuous part in the affairs of the Empire. In the great conflicts that tore the Empire asunder in the sixteenth century, Brandenburg followed a cautious and conservative policy. It adopted Lutheranism relatively late, and for a while in a half-hearted manner. Then it was usually found in the wake of the exceedingly timid policy of Saxony, though this course was often disturbed by jealousies between the two neighbors. Even rulers more eminent than those produced by the Berlin family of the Hohenzollern could not have made Brandenburg much more powerful. The sandy marshes between the Elbe and Oder were too poor in people and resources to serve as the base of an independent policy. The Hohenzollern gained by the secularization of the properties of the old Church, although they had to share their gains with the nobility, who defended their rights within the dualistic state most stubbornly. They also attended to the peaceful game of dynastic policy, that of concluding marriage alliances. But even if this was conducted with circumspection, it remained for obvious reasons somewhat of a gamble. It was after the turn of the century that John Sigismund inherited both the duchy of Prussia and that of Cleves, Berg, and Ravensburg. The latter Rhenish territories were actually only a part of the large Jülich-Cleves inheritance to which the Brandenburg elector laid claim, and he won even this part only on a provisional basis. As duke of Prussia, John Sigismund became a vassal of the king of Poland.

Through these acquisitions, however, Brandenburg moved into new political relations, which were bound to bring forth new policies. These also seemed foreshadowed by a change of religion, the acceptance of the Calvinist faith by John Sigismund and his son George William in 1613. But the illness that struck John Sigismund and the debility of the ailing George William, who took over the government in 1619, at the age of twenty-five, paralyzed all new efforts, and Brandenburg reached the nadir of its power during the Thirty Years' War. The Hohenzollern territories were without any unifying ties except the dynastic link, which was new and weak. Everywhere the estates had a strong influence, and they left the state defenseless. The policies of Brandenburg were irresolute and completely ineffective in protecting the state from the devastations and depradations of friend and foe alike. It was unfortunate that Sweden sought conquests in Germany primarily in the region of the Oder estuary, which, understandably, was a region much desired by Brandenburg as well. Through a marriage pact with the dukes of Pomerania, the electors of Brandenburg had acquired a strong title of succession to the duchy of Pomerania, but a powerful Sweden intervened at the very moment when they hoped to take possession of it. The conflict between Protestant Sweden and Brandenburg over Pomerania, which was to last about a century, was a major element in the vacillations of the foreign policy of Brandenburg which began when Gustavus Adolphus landed in Germany. Further difficulties arose from the location of East Prussia in the center of the struggle between Sweden and Poland and from the bonds of Prussia with the Polish crown.

In 1635 Brandenburg had joined the emperor, Saxony, and others in concluding the Peace of Prague,[1] and in 1637, after the death of the last duke of Pomerania, Brandenburg, under the all-powerful minister Adam von Schwartzenberg, attempted to organize strong military forces to dislodge the Swedes from Brandenburg and Pomerania. This was the first time Brandenburg had collected a considerable army, but it proved impotent against the much stronger Swedes, who were as-

[1] Cf. the author's *A History of Modern Germany: The Reformation*, pp. 352-4.

sisted financially by France. The situation of Brandenburg became quite desperate, and the court took refuge in Königsberg.

Brandenburg remained under the government of Schwartzenberg, who was also in command of the army. A Catholic, he was a partisan of the emperor's cause. He had taken the troops under oath to the emperor, though he himself appointed the officers. Schwartzenberg financed the army by levying contributions without the permission of the estates. His government was a military dictatorship in the Wallenstein fashion which superseded both powers of the dualistic state, estates as well as prince. When Frederick William, at twenty years of age, acceded to the throne, he was not even master of the government of his chief electoral dominion, while he had to pay homage to the king of Poland in order to be invested as duke of Prussia.

✑ *Frederick William of Brandenburg —*
The Great Elector

FREDERICK WILLIAM'S RECEPTIVE MIND had been impressed from an early age by an activist and politically minded Protestantism. His aunt, Queen Maria Eleonore, the widow of Gustavus Adolphus, told him about her great hero-husband. Through his mother, a sister of the Winter-King, he had contact with the Palatinate tradition. In 1634 he was sent to study in Leyden, where he acquired an excellent education and impressions which left indelible marks on his thinking. His interest in manufacture, commerce, land amelioration, and navigation was aroused by Dutch life. But the United Provinces excelled in the modern science of war as well as in the arts of peace. Gustavus Adolphus had learned his tactics from the Oranges, and the Dutch had also set new standards in army administration. Frederick Henry of Orange, whom Frederick William visited at his war camp, took a great liking to him. It was a greater world than that of the Brandenburg heath and the provincial Berlin court, and it awakened the imagination and also the ambition of the young Hohenzollern. His tutor had succeeded in inculcating in him, during his fiery and impressionable youth, strong religious and ethical beliefs, but Frederick William concluded that he who treads the paths of God could also achieve much through activity, courage, and prudence. He was able to listen to good counsel, though his temper sometimes flared up momentarily when his opinions were opposed.

The most urgent task that awaited him upon his accession to the

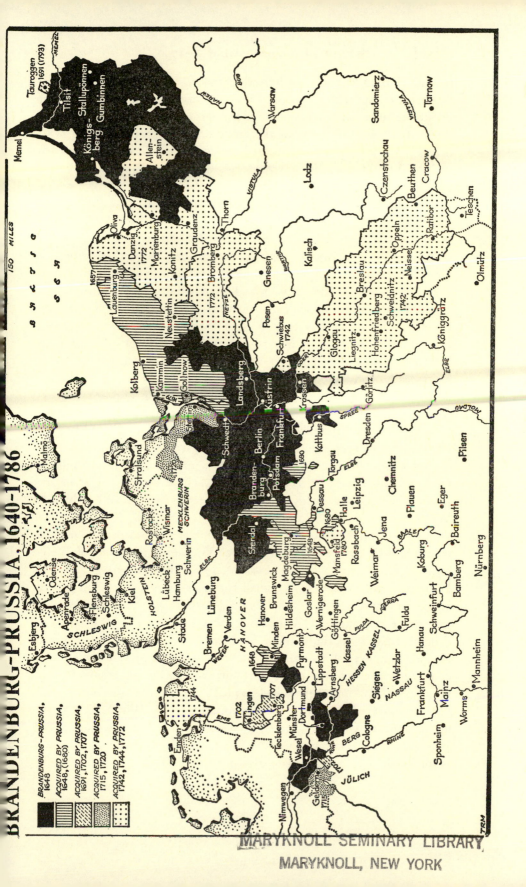

BRANDENBURG-PRUSSIA, 1640-1786

Legend:
- BRANDENBURG-PRUSSIA, 1648
- ACQUIRED BY PRUSSIA, 1648, (1680)
- ACQUIRED BY PRUSSIA, 1691, 1702, 1707
- ACQUIRED BY PRUSSIA, 1715, 1720
- ACQUIRED BY PRUSSIA, 1742, 1744, 1772

throne of Brandenburg was wresting the reins of government from Schwartzenberg without causing a major crisis. At home this meant greater reliance on the nobility; in foreign affairs, a slow revision of policy from an alliance with the emperor to an understanding with Sweden. Frederick William ordered the end of hostilities with Sweden and the disbanding of Schwartzenberg's forces, which were more of a terror to the people of Brandenburg than an annoyance to the Swedes. Schwartzenberg, who died shortly thereafter, was also deprived of his power as minister. Without an army, however, Frederick William was powerless in his negotiations with the Swedes. An armistice was signed which confined Swedish troops to certain places, but without troops it was not possible to hold them to the strict fulfillment of the agreement.

With the help of the Prussian and Brandenburg estates, the formation of a new army, sworn exclusively to the elector, was undertaken in 1644. This army was largely used for the protection of Cleves, however. For a while a marriage between Frederick William and Queen Christina of Sweden was under discussion; Gustavus Adolphus had already considered this possibility when he had seen and liked Frederick William as a boy. Christina, however, was opposed to marriage, and Frederick William once more gave expression to his preference for the Netherlands by winning the hand of Louisa Henrietta, the daughter of Frederick Henry of Orange. It was a marriage based on earnest common convictions, though as a means of political alliance the bond was not too effective after the eclipse of the power of the Oranges through the death of Frederick Henry in 1648 and of his son William II in 1650.

It is doubtful whether the European powers would have given the concessions that were made to Frederick William in the Peace of Westphalia to a less agile prince. He received only the eastern part of Pomerania, but in view of the small part that Brandenburg had played in the Thirty Years' War, the concession of Halberstadt and Minden and the expectancy of Magdeburg were great gifts. Serious new dangers arose with the coming of a new war between Sweden and Poland. The Swedish monarchy of that period, geared as it was to war, could feed its army only through conquests. In its new king, Charles X Gustavus of Zweibrücken, it had acquired a great warrior and captain. He overpowered Poland in 1655, before Frederick William had made up his mind whether to fight on the side of his Polish suzerain or, for a prize, on Sweden's side. In the Treaty of Königsberg of January 1656, Frederick William was forced to take Prussia as a fief from

Sweden. A popular national and religious revival in Poland enabled Frederick William to improve his position somewhat. In the Treaty of Marienburg of June 1656, he was promised some slices of the Polish booty in return for participation in the war against Poland. Then the newly formed Brandenburg army of over 8,000 men, about as strong as the troops of Charles X, together with the Swedes, advanced under the two princes into Poland to recapture the capital. In the grim battle of Warsaw, lasting from July 28 to 30, it won against a much larger Polish army, and Frederick William and Charles X rode into the city as victors.

The battle of Warsaw, in which the Brandenburg soldier proved himself equal to the Swede, marks the beginning of Prussian military history. But the victory of Warsaw turned out to be indecisive. In the fall of 1656 the Poles took Danzig and the valley of the lower Vistula, thereby cutting off the Swedes from their immediate naval bases and threatening Prussia. At this moment Russia turned against Sweden in order to conquer Livonia, and Emperor Ferdinand III moved to intervene on the side of Poland. Frederick William could now extract his price from Charles X Gustavus. In the Treaty of Labiau of November 1656, Sweden recognized Frederick William as sovereign ruler of Prussia. An inconclusive campaign against Poland followed, till Frederick William fell back into a state of military inactivity in Prussia, while Charles X Gustavus had to concentrate on Denmark, which rose against him. In a brilliant campaign the king drove the Danes out of Bremen, Holstein, Schleswig, and Jutland. A frozen sea allowed him, in January–February 1658, the unusual feat of marching his army to the Danish islands. In the Peace of Roskilde he forced Denmark to accept Swedish superiority.

Meanwhile, Frederick William found himself facing the Polish army alone, and he began to negotiate with Warsaw. In these negotiations the imperial master-diplomat, Marquis Francis Lisola, came to the assistance of Frederick William because he wanted to secure the latter's vote for the imperial election of Leopold, son of Ferdinand. King John Casimir of Poland hesitated to accept Frederick William's chief demand, Polish recognition of the elector's sovereignty in Prussia, but finally gave in, in accordance with the advice of his intimate councilors. In the Treaty of Wehlau of September 1657, Frederick William received this great concession and a few minor territorial gains. In return, he had to agree to military co-operation with Poland, and soon afterward, with the emperor against Sweden.

The Nordic War was opened by Charles X's attempt to take Copenhagen. He wanted to preclude the possibility that the Danes might again jeopardize his campaign on the Baltic mainland. But Copenhagen proved impregnable to quick capture, and as the siege dragged on, Charles X saw himself beset with grave dangers. Frederick William, leading a strong army composed of Brandenburg, imperial, and Polish troops, drove the Swedes out of Holstein, Schleswig, and Alsen. But the frost failed to build a bridge to the Danish islands, as it had done the year before for Charles X, so the Great Elector had to be satisfied with occupying Swedish Pomerania. With the exception of Stettin and Stralsund, he was in actual possession of this country by the end of 1659, and the moment seemed close at hand when the injustice of 1648, when Sweden had taken West Pomerania from him, would be undone.

At the height of his success, achieved by the bold exploitation of changing political constellations, Frederick William was stopped by French policy. With the end of the war between France and Spain in November 1659, France was able to exert her power all over Europe. Mazarin was not prepared to see Sweden reduced to a minor position in European or German politics and demanded general adherence to the Peace of Westphalia. This meant the cessation of Brandenburg's attempts to seize West Pomerania. Neither Poland nor the emperor felt any desire to stay in the war for the benefit of the elector of Brandenburg. Thus, after the death of Charles X Gustavus, in February 1660, the Treaty of Oliva denied Frederick William the acquisition of West Pomerania but confirmed his sovereignty in Prussia, as well as in some small territories ceded to him by Poland at an earlier date.

The Peace of Oliva of May 1660, was a disappointment to Frederick William, but actually the gains he had made in five years of war were of great historical significance. Brandenburg had shown herself a force in competition with European states. She was, to say the least, no longer the helpless victim of foreign power politics that she had been in the half-century before. Moreover, sovereignty in Prussia legally gave the ruler of Brandenburg the position of a European prince, in addition to his electoral dignity within the Empire. It enhanced his freedom of action in foreign policy and also strengthened his hand in domestic affairs. The Prussian estates had profited most from Polish suzerainty. Their rights and even their sheer local obstinacy had formerly found Polish support. Now they faced a ruler who had gained independence from outside assistance. Here in Prussia, as in the other Hohenzollern territories, the military exploits of the Great

Elector were most intimately connected with the establishment of absolute government at home.

∽ The Growth of Absolutism in Brandenburg-Prussia

FREDERICK WILLIAM HAD BEGUN his reign by restoring the influence of the estates, which had been suppressed by the dictatorial regime of Schwartzenberg. But he was convinced that the estates owed him the means for maintaining a standing army. Much wrangling took place over this issue, even in the early years when the army, except for a short period, was kept relatively small. The conflict became bitter when, in 1652–53, a Brandenburg diet was presented with definite requests for taxes. In its final recess of August 5, 1653, the Brandenburg estates granted the elector a sum of 530,000 thaler, to be paid in annual installments for the next six years, for the upkeep of his army. In return the elector recognized the political rights of the estates. He promised to call them in case of serious political decision-making and not to conclude alliances without their approval. He also bound himself not to change the method of taxation. More important than these concessions, however, which were soon to be flagrantly violated by the elector, was his recognition of the special privileges of the nobility. This amounted to full acceptance of the predominant position of the *Junker*, as it had developed in the last century and reached a new height during and after the Thirty Years' War.

The exclusive right of the *Junkers* to own land and their seignorial jurisdiction on their estates was reaffirmed. No enforceable limitations were placed upon the right to evict peasants and acquire their land. Even more far-reaching was the provision of the recess of 1653, whereby every peasant was assumed to be a serf (*leibeigen* or *erbunter-tänig*) unless he proved his freedom by title or through the good will of his lord. This provision was confined to the districts where serfdom had become customary, but since they were not named, the door was opened for an extension of serfdom to regions that had so far been less affected by its sinister growth. In addition to these guarantees of the social privileges of the *Junkers*, great economic advantages were heaped upon them. They were permitted to export their own products practically duty-free and to import their own basic provisions under the same conditions.

These were, indeed, concessions that made it seem that the dualistic state was to be eternalized. Only one important right was specifically reserved by the Great Elector. Although he promised to give preference to indigenous noblemen in making appointments to state offices, he refused to be bound by a law of indigenousness (*indigenatus*) and protected his power to appoint both foreigners and commoners. The governmental service was thereby declared the exclusive executive arm of the elector. The army also came to be directly under his control, and he used it to intimidate and overwhelm internal opposition. Already in the first years of the Nordic War the elector extracted sums from a population that was utterly exhausted and impoverished. The new power of the elector enabled him to secure continuation of the grant of 1653 without much difficulty. The Brandenburg estates had agreed in 1643 that the towns would pay 59 per cent of all taxes, while 41 per cent were to be collected by the tax-exempt *Junkers* from their peasants. In the towns payment of the contribution burdened the lower classes in particular, and the idea of replacing the direct contribution with an indirect excise tax had much support. But it met with the staunchest opposition from the *Junkers* because an excise tax would have destroyed their freedom from taxation.

The Great Elector did not succeed in making the *Junkers* accept the general change from the contribution to the excise tax. But the towns were allowed, beginning in 1667, to collect their tax quota through an excise system that was primarily a tax on consumption, although to some extent also on land and trade. Within fifteen years the excise was generally adopted and transformed from a municipal into a state tax; this meant that a surplus beyond the quota was to be retained by the government. The division of the tax system led to a strict separation of town and countryside. The traffic and movement of goods to and from the towns had to be closely supervised, and consequently governmental administration was bound to develop into two different branches. The new organization had an important impact on the institutions of the estates themselves. Co-operation of nobility and towns on the diet became impossible. Moreover, the excise tax was a permanent levy, which did not call for annual or regular review and discussion. The towns disappeared from the provincial diets (*Landtag*), and the only representative organs that remained truly alive were smaller local groups, rural county estates (*Kreistag*), in which only the local nobility was represented. Their meetings could never acquire political significance beyond the narrow local sphere.

Brandenburg was by tradition closely attached to the Hohenzollern dynasty, and this made it relatively easy for Frederick William to have the new regime accepted, although it was obvious that he would not have been successful without an army behind him. Even with it, he found it necessary to offer the nobility rather generous social concessions and economic bribes. In East Pomerania, which was officially joined to the Hohenzollern territories in 1653–54, the estates were accustomed to the contribution because of Swedish practices. No particular resistance was shown in the other territories acquired during this period, in Halberstadt and later in Magdeburg, though in Prussia and Cleves the absolutist changes evoked some active opposition.

The Prussian estates refused to recognize the sovereignty of the elector-duke as established by the Peace of Oliva because it had come about without their co-operation, and an angry conflict over tax grants ensued. The center of resistance was Königsberg, a city at least three times as big as Berlin and not very much smaller than Danzig, its closest commercial rival. The city, actually organized into three towns, would probably not have objected to the payment of taxes as such if it had not been aware that the creation of an electoral tax administration would mean the end of its freedoms. So far it had been able to preserve these by playing off the Polish king against his vassal, the duke-elector. The resistance of the city was broken by a show of military force, and by keeping the estates divided, absolutism was slowly introduced between 1660 and 1681. All types of petty and occasionally radical coercion were used against the estates, without strict regard for existing law. In the end, Prussian political conditions were similar to those in Brandenburg, except that in the latter urban development had always been weak, whereas the *Junker* influence in Prussia was strengthened through the economic losses that Königsberg suffered under the new system.

The development in Cleves-Mark followed a different course. The estates had enjoyed much independence throughout the century. Officially, the elector was only temporarily in possession of these territories. The Catholics looked to Jülich-Berg for support; the Protestants, to the Netherlands. The estates successfully defended their rights against the elector. They insisted on their privilege to meet annually even without his consent and to maintain diplomatic relations with foreign states. They compelled him to dismiss all officials who were not natives. Officials had to take an oath to uphold the laws as passed by the estates. The elector was not permitted to import troops or build fortresses in the country without the approval of the estates.

Cleves, on the Lower Rhine and adjacent to the United Provinces, and Mark, which contained a large segment of what has become in modern times the Ruhr district, were territories vastly different from those on the Elbe and Oder, or those east of the Vistula. Social divisions were much less pronounced in the west. There were free peasants or rent-paying peasants on practically hereditary leases. Few noblemen maintained large estates, and no seignorial jurisdiction existed. Noblemen contributed to the taxes on land, and, though not represented on the diet, peasants participated in the flourishing local self-government. The social structure received its main strength from the many towns. Though economically declining, some of them, for example Dortmund and Soest, had a great past as Hanseatic towns, and their civic pride was stimulated by the neighboring Dutch cities.

Here at the Lower Rhine, the Great Elector heard open threats that the country might deal with him the way the English people had dealt with their king. But by brute force he managed to draw considerable sums for armaments from Cleves-Mark during the war years of 1655–60, and after the end of the war his power had become sufficiently formidable to force a change of attitude upon the estates. They resigned the right of diplomatic intercourse with foreign powers and even with the emperor. They retained the *jus indigenatus*, but officials were no longer under oath to uphold the laws of the diet. The elector was permitted to maintain garrisons and fortresses, and there was no longer any doubt that the estates owed him taxes for defense. But the estates kept the right of assembly, though they had to make their intention to hold a meeting known to the government, and the diet would continue to pass not only on requests for revenue but also on the form of collection. While the diet did not refuse payment of taxes in the future, it defeated the introduction of the Brandenburg-Prussian system of taxation. In Cleves-Mark the old taxes continued, and with them the method of collection through the old institutions of self-government. As a consequence, self-government lived on in Cleves-Mark, though at the price of conformity with the demands of the Berlin government. Actually, Cleves-Mark was one of the few places in all Germany where corporative life survived the absolutist period.

The Great Elector attempted to introduce eastern German political methods into the western possessions of the Hohenzollern dynasty. In spite of his general admiration for the Netherlands, he apparently found it difficult to conceive of local government that was not in the hands of noblemen. He granted jurisdiction to some noblemen, and tax exemption to all, in spite of the customs of the land. With these moves he obviously tried to split the estates. But once the estates accommodated themselves to his wishes, Frederick William desisted from ruining them altogether, and his successors were to act likewise. Uniformity and centralization were imposed on the eastern and central German territories, whereas the peripheral western possessions were allowed great latitude.

✑ Development of the Agencies of Absolute Government

IT WAS CHIEFLY IN BRANDENBURG, Prussia, Pomerania, Halberstadt, and Magdeburg that the Berlin government developed a unified administration that tended to make the old, self-contained territories provinces of a greater state. The Great Elector was not only the founder of absolutist government, but also the creator of an incipient system of centralization. Technically, the so-called "governments" of all these territories remained. They combined political and judicial functions, which were carried on by native noblemen. But these governments were doomed because an entirely new administrative organization was springing up and taking over the political and economic tasks. The old governments were finally transformed into provincial courts of appeal (*Oberlandesgericht*). A similar development, toward confinement to judiciary functions, occurred with regard to the first princely organ devoted to solution of the problems transcending electoral Brandenburg. The privy council had been created in 1604, when the dynasty was about to launch a superlocal policy. It was somewhat more than a central council of the elector for Brandenburg affairs, because foreign matters were added to its special concerns. Under the Great Elector it became the true center of the new general policy and administration in all the Hohenzollern territories.

But the new centralized administration, which practically superseded the administrative agencies of the estates and eventually even eliminated the institution of the privy council, grew up around the new tax officers. In the towns so-called *commissarii locorum*—variously termed war and tax commissaries, and later, tax councilors—supervised and administered collection of the excise tax. Collection of the contribution in the country was in the hands of county commissaries (*Kreiskommissare*). Since both excise tax and contribution served exclusively military ends, the centralizing influence of the army was soon felt. Chief commissaries (*Oberkommissare*) were soon appointed for the provinces; above them was a war commissary-general (*Generalkriegs-*

kommissar). These two institutions rapidly blossomed into councils. In these agencies the new civil service of absolutist Brandenburg-Prussia originated. Aside from taxation, all general military administration—recruitment, quartering, and provisioning of troops—was directed by the commissaries. But the scope of their activities grew even larger. In order to increase the revenue, they proceeded actively to conduct economic policies. The tax councilors took over from the towns collection of the excise tax and began to regulate the economic life of the towns. This meant the virtual death of municipal self-government. In the countryside the war commissaries had originally played a supervisory role, while the contribution had been administered by the local estates of the counties under a "county director." But before the end of the seventeenth century the offices of director and war commissary were merged, with the result that also in rural regions the central government now had a reliable officer, though he was selected from the local nobility. In 1702 these officers received the elegant title of county councilors (*Landrat*).

The reorganization of the landed property of the elector, including his regal rights, such as salt production and mining, proved to be a slow process. It required a long renegotiation of lease contracts and, administratively, the building of local, provincial, and central offices analogous to the commissariats. They were called domain chambers and court chambers. The two major branches, the financial and domain administrations, formed the pillars on which the elector's state was built. During his reign state revenue trebled. In 1688 it reached nearly 3.4 million thalers. Whereas in the early years of his rule only about 40 per cent of the state revenue had come from taxation, at the end the *contributionale* and the *camerale* yielded about the same amounts. Taxes were most unevenly distributed among the territories and classes, and were a crushing burden on an impoverished population of about a million. The subjects of the Great Elector paid twice as much per head as those of the king of wealthy France. In contrast to France, taxes in Germany were not farmed out but levied by a corps of state officials. When the methods of collecting had become more rational and the economy had recovered from the war, the tax load, though heavy, was more bearable.

Half of the state revenue was used for the army, but even this proved inadequate and foreign subsidies were used to augment the funds available for military purposes, particularly in wartime. Frederick William took subsidies from the Netherlands, the Empire, France,

Spain, and Denmark. About one fifth of his expenditures for war and defense were derived from foreign sources. For this reason, foreign policy was greatly influenced by the need for financially strong allies. This explains some of the tergiversations of the elector's international policies as well as the fact that his allies were usually lukewarm in supporting his own political objectives in the councils of Europe. But he would not have found allies if he had not had resources of his own. As Frederick William put it, "Alliances, to be sure, are good; but a force of one's own, on which one can rely, is better. A ruler is treated with no consideration if he does not have troops and means of his own. It is these that have made me *considérable* since the time when I began to have them."

The army was the center of the new Brandenburg-Prussian state; even the new civil service was chiefly a means for the creation of military power. It was during the war of 1655–60 that the army was greatly expanded and placed under a single command. Field Marshal von Sparr united under his authority the hitherto separate contingents in the various electoral lands. Officially, General von Platen, the war commissary, was subordinate to him, but as a member of the privy council with direct access to the elector, Platen retained a great deal of independence. When Frederick William took command himself, Sparr acted as chief-of-staff, and a privy war chancery (*Geheime Kriegskanzlei*) was established in 1657 to take care of his military correspondence. After 1679 the general war commissariat became the most important agency of the state. It not only combined the functions of modern war and finance ministries but also became the chief agency for carrying through many of the mercantilistic ventures, such as population settlement and building of factories. The actual integration of the various lands into a single state was carried out most effectively by this central office of the co-ordinated military establishment. By 1656 the army already consisted of more than 2,000 men; in the years between 1660 and 1672 it grew to between 7,000 and 12,000, and in the subsequent war period, it grew at times to 45,000. At the time of Frederick William's death, in 1688, the army was estimated at 30,000 men.

A thorough internal reform of the army system went hand in hand with expansion in the number of troops. The army became a state enterprise, and everything in the administration that stemmed from the practices of private military entrepreneurs was eradicated. The key figures in the old system had been the colonels, who had undertaken to organize and maintain regiments by special contracts. The appointment of officers was considered their privilege, and their own sense of subordination to general officers was weak. Under the new system regiments were established and colonels appointed by order of the elector. But it proved difficult to accustom the colonels to a strict line of command, and even more difficult to wrest the commissioning of regimental officers from them. The process of creating a fully hierarchial officer corps was only completed under King Frederick William I.

Similarly, the social composition of the officer corps was somewhat less monolithic than it was to become under Frederick William I and Frederick II, but it was already assuming that character in the days of the Great Elector. Almost four fifths of the officers came from the nobility of the electoral territories. They were attracted not only by a natural relish for soldiering but also by the need to make a living, as large segments of the nobility were in dire straits. Under the Great Elector about 10 per cent of all officers were foreigners; of these, the majority were Germans from outside his territories. For a while the number of Huguenots was considerable, as the Huguenots were able military men. Of the Huguenots who came to Brandenburg, one sixth were soldiers, among them a good many noblemen who found appointment in the army. More than 10 per cent of the officer corps was made up of burghers. They were most strongly represented in the artillery and engineering corps, branches of the military service which at that time, and for many years to come, were not considered integral parts of the army. In the other branches burghers did not usually go beyond the junior ranks, but the Great Elector made certain exceptions. Field Marshal Derfflinger, the most brilliant officer of the young army, was a commoner. As in his civilian bureaucracy, Frederick William held firmly to the principle that birth of itself gave no assurance of excellence. In practice, the appointment of a few commoners to high command seemed to him sufficient to warn the nobility that they could not claim appointment in his service as a feudal right.

No change was made in the hiring of soldiers. As before, they were recruited by free enlistment. Attempts were occasionally made to use a peasants' militia in Prussia, the so-called "Vibrances," but the military results were not encouraging. A general arming of the population could have been accomplished only with the assistance of the estates, and this would have demanded the revival of a political system that had just been discarded. The army was to be the instrument for freeing the elector from the guardianship of the estates, enabling him to impose his absolute will. This meant that the ruler could exploit freely the resources of individual territories, weld them into a larger whole, and then use their accumulated strength in the struggle of European powers as well as for the advancement of internal welfare. The Great Elector believed that he had legitimate claims in Pomerania and also in parts of Silesia. His claims in Pomerania were especially close to his heart, because only by the removal of the Swedes from Stettin and West Pomerania could Brandenburg gain direct access to the sea, an objective desirable for reasons of strategy and internal welfare.

The Great Elector's foreign policy was not naked power politics. It stemmed from a strong conviction that his lawful claims were righteous and from considerations of internal welfare. Moreover, he was strongly motivated by religious ideas. The belief that European Protestantism would be endangered if the Protestant front of the Netherlands and Sweden was not further strengthened by a Protestant north German state was reflected in his actions over the years. This is not to say that he was not carried forward by the wish for power. Internal welfare inevitably resulted in greater strength in dealings with other states, and the religious idea gave justification to bold political enterprises. Much as he felt himself the champion of a religious cause, all his activities were dominated by the vision of a new state that had its existence and destiny in the secular order, although it was animated by ethical principles. In this new philosophy the medieval as well as the old Lutheran conceptions of state and church, history and individual duty, were transcended.

The vision of a new state was still largely personal. It was of relatively little significance that the elector taught his children to consider princely dignity not as a personal property but as a stewardship for the benefit of the people. He regarded his dominions not as an organic whole of which he, as prince, was helmsman but as a dynastic realm. The "proprietary" nature of his political thinking made him amenable to the persuasions of his entourage that he leave a testament providing for division of his territories. It might have led to Brandenburg's loss of important territories, but his life's work blocked the execution of his will. The trend toward a single integrated state which he had set in motion had grown too powerful to be resisted or deflected.

CHAPTER 4

Germany, the Wars of Louis XIV, and the Rise of the Austrian Empire, 1660-99

✍ The Problem of the Spanish Succession

THE OLD STRUGGLE between the Habsburgs and Bourbons was not settled by the Peace of Westphalia of 1648 or the Peace of the Pyrenees of 1659. The latter carried it to the point where possession of the Spanish crown became the coveted prize in competition between the emperor and the king of France. The Peace of the Pyrenees was based on the marriage of Louis XIV to Maria Theresa, eldest daughter of Philip IV of Spain, which took place in 1660. At the time of her marriage she had renounced all future claims to the Spanish throne. Her father had insisted on this, as he still thought in terms of the old tie that united the Spanish and Austrian branches of the Habsburg family. Emperor Leopold I married Margaret Theresa, the second daughter of Philip IV, in 1666, and in view of his marriage felt himself entitled to the Spanish succession. But Maria Theresa's renunciation had been surrounded, by French diplomacy, with conditional clauses that made even the legal issue extremely complex, and the actual succession of one of the contenders was, in any event, bound to depend upon more than legal arguments. It was not expected to be long before there would be a vacancy on the Spanish throne. A male heir had been born to Philip IV in 1661, but Charles (II) was a frail child and not expected to live long.

King Philip IV died in 1665. In 1661, after the death of Cardinal Mazarin, Louis XIV had personally assumed the reins of government in France. He devoted several years to reorganization of the military forces, and then steadily expanded them. France entered the War of

Devolution in 1667 with an army of 72,000 men and attacked the Netherlands with 120,000 men. In 1678 the French army numbered 279,000. For the first time in its history Europe saw armies larger than those of the ancient Roman emperors. The growing military might of Louis XIV was sustained by the great wealth of France, effectively mobilized for objectives of state. This wealth made possible not only a tremendous proliferation of arms but also many diplomatic triumphs. The royal government spent money with largesse, more liberally than the Dutch, to buy foreign alliances. The louis d'ors flowed freely into the coffers of princes and into the purses of collaborating ministers, mistresses, and courtiers. The weapons of persuasion and intimidation were wielded by generals and diplomats of highest ability. Small wonder that in many quarters there was a growing belief that France was destined to lead Europe.

∾ The War of Devolution

IN THE YEARS AFTER 1659 French diplomacy concentrated on protecting the internal consolidation that had been achieved. To demonstrate her solidarity with the Christian West, France even went so far as to send an auxiliary corps to the assistance of the emperor against the Turks in 1664. But the death of Philip IV induced Louis XIV to collect at least part of the Spanish inheritance. He was primarily interested in the Spanish Netherlands. Not only economic ambitions but also the strategic security of the French capital made expansion to the north desirable. The Peace of Westphalia had closed the Scheldt to commerce. In the hands of the French monarchy, however, Antwerp and the southern Netherlands could become the base of active colonial and mercantile enterprise. The power of the Dutch in this field was already being challenged by the English. War between the two so-called "maritime" nations was in progress. After futile negotiations with Madrid over cession of the Netherlands, and with The Hague over their partition, Louis XIV sent his army into the Netherlands in the spring of 1667. Among other places, Douai, Tournay, Charleroi, even well-fortified Lille were easily occupied. In the spring of 1668 France took also the Franche-Comté.

Louis XIV claimed that the Spanish Netherlands were his by right. The private law of Brabant recognized the daughters of a first marriage as privileged heirs before sons of a subsequent marriage. Under this so-called "law of devolution," Queen Maria Theresa's rights, so the French argued, superseded those of the child-king Charles II. The invasion of the Netherlands, in the War of Devolution, was diplomatically shielded by a series of agreements with Neuburg, Cologne, Münster, and Mainz. The French government had not simply relied upon the Rhenish Confederation. As a matter of fact, the ruthless action of Louis XIV caused great consternation among German princes, and the pamphlet *Le Bouclier d'état et de justice*, by Francis Lisola, was a clarion call to warn against Louis' plans for a universal monarchy. No individual prince making his peace with France could be sure he had gained lasting protection, nor could he enjoy the cold comfort of feeling he was the last to be swallowed by the Cyclops. But not even Lisola spurred the emperor into action. Under the influence of his leading ministers, Prince Weikhard Auersperg and Prince Wenzel Lobkowitz, Leopold I signed a secret treaty with France in January 1668, by which he recognized Louis's claim to the Spanish Netherlands and agreed to partition of the Spanish inheritance. France was to receive—in addition to Belgium—the Franche-Comté, Navarre, Naples, Sicily, and the African possessions, while Austria was to inherit Spain and the West Indies, Sardinia and the Balearic and Canary Islands, as well as Milan and its dependencies. It was a sign of the great discouragement prevailing at the court of Vienna that Leopold I could be maneuvered into a position that separated him from his Spanish relatives and also from advocacy of a strong German national policy.

The situation was, indeed, depressing. The Turks were far from subdued. The princes of the Empire were either openly flaunting their disregard of all national obligations, or were being successfully appeased by France. Even the Great Elector had found his best advantage in neutrality. But with the Franco-Austrian agreement of 1668 the emperor irreparably compromised his legal claims to the Spanish crown. The complete conquest of the Spanish Netherlands by France was prevented by non-German powers alone. The Netherlands and England settled their own conflicts in 1667 and, together with Sweden, formed a triple alliance that mediated between France and Spain. Since Louis XIV was not ready to fight a large coalition, and the terms offered were favorable, he accepted a peace that left him all his gains along the southern frontier of the Netherlands, among them Lille and Charleroi. It was a sign of the changing times that Protestant powers came to the rescue of Catholic Spain in bringing about this Peace of Aachen of May, 1668.

∽ Preparations for the Dutch War

IF THE TRIPLE ALLIANCE OF 1668 could have been held together and strengthened by the accession of the emperor and some of the German princes, it might have been possible to contain France in the future, but the alliance rested on shaky grounds. The weak Swedish regency was chiefly interested in subsidies. Charles II of England was contemplating a policy of re-Catholization of his country, which called for co-operation with the French king. In addition, commercial rivalry soon led to new incidents between England and the Netherlands. If the Netherlands had maintained a strong military posture, she might have attracted friends, but the flabby regime of the merchant patriciate, led by Jan De Witt, was unwilling to strengthen the army, partly out of fear of the party of the Oranges. Louis XIV was therefore able to prepare his next major action with complete calm. He decided to leave the Spanish Netherlands alone and direct his attack against the United Provinces. French diplomacy began to lay the groundwork for subjugation of the Netherlands.

In the secret Treaty of Dover of June, 1670, between France and England, Charles II undertook to enter the war against the Netherlands with a strong navy and token land forces. In return, France promised him generous subsidies, not only for the mobilization of his ships and men but also for the realization of his internal schemes. Sweden was won over by the ability of the French to outbid the Netherlands. She promised to attack any German prince who would assist the Netherlands. In the Empire France found active allies in Elector-Archbishop Maximilian Henry of Cologne and Liége and the bellicose Prince-Bishop Bernhard Christoph of Münster. The latter intended to go to war himself to expand his bishopric at Dutch expense. The elector of Cologne, a Bavarian prince, permitted the passage of French troops through his territories, handed over the fortress of Neuss as a main military base, and sent 18,000 men to join forces with the French army. Among other German princes who stayed neutral were the rulers of the Palatinate, Neuburg, Trier, and Württemberg. Elector Karl Ludwig of the Palatinate, in 1671, gave his daughter Elizabeth Charlotte ("Liselotte") in marriage to Philippe I, the duke of Orléans. If he thought that this alliance would remove the Palatinate from the repercussions of the European wars, he was soon to learn his mistake.

Grave concern was felt at the court of Archbishop John Philip of

Mainz. In 1668 John Philip had done his best not to have the Rhenish Confederation renewed. Plans for strengthening the constitution of the Empire were freely discussed in Mainz. But the archbishop was compelled by the general trend to move closer to France again. His own cathedral chapter had elected as his coadjutor Lothar Friedrich von Metternich, a man of French orientation. Thus John Philip had to promise to use all his influence to keep the Empire neutral. On the eve of the war he sent Leibniz to Paris to present to the French government the memorandum *Concilium Aegyptiacum* that the philosopher had drafted. This was an amazing attempt to channel French policy into entirely different directions by wise counsel alone. Leibniz reminded the French that he who occupied Egypt could control the trade of Asia and Europe and thereby become the leading state on earth. He also foresaw the possibilities that lay in building a canal connecting the Mediterranean with the Red Sea. While he recommended trade as the chief method by which France could build a great future, he wished to see her at peace with her European neighbors and a champion of Christian Europe against the Turks. As far as we know, Leibniz's ideas were not presented to members of the inner government. Paris was in the bustle of final preparations for war and not in the mood to listen to the young emissary of a German princeling.

Leibniz's project, which Napoleon is said to have studied with interest, raised issues that historians may wish to ponder. France's position in the modern world might have become more secure if she had endeavored to gain an unassailable place in the maritime world at a time when only the Dutch were in a position of real strength, with the English just beginning their expansion. Leibniz was certainly right if he expected such a policy to contribute to a more harmonious relationship among the European nations. But it was not to be expected that the French would discard their continental policies until they had fully freed themselves from fear of the Habsburgs, in whose encircling grip they had been held since the days of Emperor Maximilian I. As occurs with statesmen and others, the memory of past dangers had blinded them to the real situation. In both French and German history there are many examples of such human behavior. Louis XIV's headlong drive for European hegemony strengthened the divisive forces in Europe. By assuming the role of champion of the Catholic cause, he rekindled religious fanaticism, while his disregard of elementary rights stimulated national hatred.

Rather reluctantly, Leopold I, in November, 1671, signed a treaty of neutrality with France. Austria and France guaranteed the Peace of Westphalia and the Peace of Aachen, and the emperor promised not to intervene in the Franco-Dutch war, provided it did not affect the Empire and the Spanish monarchy. At this time the French had already occupied Lorraine—erratic Duke Charles IV of Lorraine had given them easy pretexts for this act of violence—and soon they swarmed into the electorate of Cologne. This time it was not the emperor but the elector of Brandenburg who chose an active anti-French course. Frederick William had remained neutral in the War of Devolution of 1667, and had even concluded an outright alliance with France. Apart from the fact that the treaty provided him with immediate subsidies, he felt that in case of a French conquest of Belgium his Rhenish possessions could be protected by the annexation of territories in the Meuse valley. But the subjugation of the northern Netherlands by France appeared to him as a threat not only to Cleves-Mark, but also to the commercial and political independence of the Continent and to the existence of Protestantism. He was heard to say; "Commerce lives and dies with the Dutch Republic," and "If Holland falls, the time will arrive when Louis XIV will throw German princes into the Bastille like his own *grand seigneurs*." After a long struggle against the advice of most of his political advisers, the elector decided to go to the assistance of the Netherlands. The Dutch treated this relative of the Oranges with petty condescension, but he overlooked all manifestations of ill will. In the spring of 1672 he concluded a treaty of alliance with the Netherlands by which he committed himself to help her in case of war with an army of 20,000, for which the Dutch were to pay half of the cost.

✑ *The Dutch War, 1672-78*

MEANWHILE HOSTILITIES HAD ALREADY BEGUN with English naval attacks on Dutch shipping, and in May, 1672, France, Cologne, and Münster opened war against the Netherlands. The main push was made from Cologne through Cleves down the Rhine toward Holland, while the bishop of Münster operated farther in the north. The campaign was stunningly successful and revealed the amazing unpreparedness of Jan De Witt's regime. He soon sued for peace, offering to cede large sections of the Netherlands. But French demands for even more territory, large contributions, and guarantees of Catholic rights set the spark to the popular revolution that led to the victory of the Orange party. Early in July, 1672, William, prince of Orange, became life-long stadholder, captain, and admiral-general of the Republic. Thus, indirectly, Louis XIV's most formidable enemy was launched on his historic career with French help. William III was not able to stage a military comeback, but the people were ready to wreck their own property to defeat the hated French. They cut the canal dikes, and the inundation kept the heart of the country from the invader. The spirit of fighting resistance appeared everywhere. In August 1672, the heroic defense of Groningen, the West Frisian capital, by garrison, citizens, and students defeated the heavy artillery of the bishop of Münster. This was the beginning of the end of the military enterprises of this warring bishop.

Taken aback by the display of French military power and the weakness of the Dutch, whose only ally he was, Frederick William of Brandenburg looked around for allies and found one in the emperor. In June, 1672, the emperor agreed to send an army of 16,000 men, who were to be joined by 12,000 Brandenburgers, to defend the frontiers of the Empire. This force was not strong enough to fight France. As a matter of fact, neither Leopold I nor Frederick William declared war on France; rather, they announced their campaign as directed against Cologne and Münster. The elector found himself in an embarrassing situation. The Austrians were not willing to conduct offensive operations, and Count Montecuccoli, the Austrian general, following instructions from Vienna, could not be persuaded by the Great Elector to cross the Rhine or co-operate with the Dutch army at the Lower Rhine. Understandably, the Dutch felt that Frederick William was not living up to his treaty with them, and they stopped paying subsidies. The elector quickly decided to make peace with France. On June 6, 1673, the Peace of Vossem was signed in Louis's headquarters near Louvain. Frederick William promised to desist from support of the Netherlands but reserved his rights and obligations as a prince of the Empire.

In the summer of 1673 Spain intervened in the war, and the emperor began to move against France. The recklessness with which the French troops were acting all along the Upper and Lower Rhine threatened to tear to shreds whatever political prestige Leopold still held in the Empire. In August 1673, the emperor, Spain, Lorraine, and the Netherlands concluded an alliance with the aim of rolling back French power to its boundaries of 1660. Then Denmark joined, as well as Elector

John George of Saxony, while the elector of Trier, whose territories were occupied by French troops, secretly promised his co-operation. For the first time a strong current of national sentiment was running through Germany. It was strengthened by the French action, taken during the summer, of incorporating the ten small Alsatian imperial cities into the French monarchy. The Peace of Westphalia had transferred to France only the loose overlordship that the emperor had exercised over the "decapolis." Over their resistance, the ten cities— among them Hagenau, Colmar, Schlettstadt, and Landau—were deprived of their local autonomy and absorbed into the absolute state of France. This act aroused the resentment of the estates of the Empire. In the spring of 1674 the Empire, too, declared war on France.

With great skill the old Montecuccoli had maneuvered the French army under Turenne out of southern Germany, gained the Rhine passage, and accomplished a junction with the Dutch army under William III. After a brief siege Bonn, the capital of the Cologne electorate, was captured on November 12, 1673. With their German base at the Lower Rhine lost, the French had to withdraw from the Netherlands. There was rejoicing in Vienna. Hope welled up that the moment had arrived to settle accounts with France, free the Netherlands, Lorraine, and Alsace, and bring the problem of the Spanish succession to a decision. Prince Lobkowitz was dismissed as minister and a new course of action inaugurated.

Political developments appeared to favor the anti-French allies. In the spring of 1674, under the pressure of Parliament, Charles II of England made peace with the Netherlands. The Dutch and Spanish navies had more than held their own against the English and French naval forces, and English commerce was suffering. Moreover, the estates of the Empire were now rallying around the emperor. The bishop of Münster made his peace with the Netherlands and concluded an alliance with the emperor, and Elector Maximilian Henry of Cologne followed his example. Then the new elector of Mainz, Lothar Frederick von Metternich, as well as the elector of Trier, Elector Karl Ludwig of the Palatinate, the dukes of Brunswick-Celle and Brunswick-Wolfenbüttel, and the administrator of Osnabrück all joined. Only the elector of Bavaria and Duke John Frederick of Hanover, a Catholic convert, kept aloof.

Frederick William of Brandenburg, whose French subsidies had not been forthcoming, was willing to join the anti-French allies, but the emperor pretended for a time not to be eager to accept him in the company. However, his good troops could not well be dispensed with, and he was admitted to the anti-French alliance in July 1674. Hostilities had been carried on since early spring. The French armies, brilliantly led by Turenne, Condé, and Luxembourg, were perhaps at their best in this war, as was the French navy, which, by the defeat of the Dutch and Spanish navies, gained complete mastery in the western Mediterranean. But the French carried on the war with a callous ruthlessness that was the result of both *hubris* and anxiety. Chief victim was the Palatinate. In order to make it impossible for the imperial troops to assemble there for an attack on Philippsburg, the main Rhine fortress, the French systematically devastated the surrounding country. In helpless anger Elector Karl Ludwig and the people of the Palatinate watched the destruction of all that they had labored to build over the last thirty years. They were fortunate in not knowing that the future held even greater misery for them.

The French concentrated their military efforts on the Spanish Netherlands, where they managed to maintain themselves. At the Battle of Senef, in August 1674, they inflicted such heavy losses on William III that in the future any idea of invading France from the north had to be abandoned. Meanwhile the French also protected their southern flank by occupying the weakly defended Franche-Comté and then awaited the German attack, which was to be launched from the Palatinate and Alsace, with relative confidence. The army of the Empire was superior to any Germany had produced in a long time. The large Brunswick contingent, in particular, displayed fine soldierly bearing. Once the Brandenburg army had joined forces with the troops of the emperor and the Empire, the Germans enjoyed numerical superiority. Frederick William assumed titular command of the German army, but by treaty the actual command was vested in a council of commanders, in which the fiery offensive spirit of the Great Elector was neutralized by the methodical caution of Bournonville, the imperial commander. A three-month campaign into Alsace was thwarted by the superior tactics and single-minded determination of Turenne. In early January, 1675, the German troops again had to take up winter quarters on the right bank of the Rhine. On his way, Frederick William received word that the Swedes had broken into Brandenburg. At once he felt that this would offer him an opportunity for conquering Pomerania. He negotiated with the emperor, the Netherlands, and Denmark for assistance. In May, 1675, he left Franconia with his army to go to Brandenburg. There he was to show what his imperious and bold nature could accomplish if unhampered by competing wills.

The year 1675 was one of relative success for German arms along the Rhine. For the last time Montecuccoli took command against Turenne, who died on the battlefield that summer. For a long while these two accomplished captains had played a war of maneuver, until the French had finally been pressed back over the Upper Rhine. But the reconquest of Alsace was not achieved. Only the right bank of the Rhine, with the exception of Philippsburg, was cleared of the French. The city and electorate of Trier were liberated, chiefly through the dashing valor of the Brunswick troops. In 1676, young Duke Charles V of Lorraine conquered Philippsburg, but his troops were not adequate to prevent the French from occupying Freiburg in the following year.

Meanwhile things had gone from bad to worse in the other western European theaters of war. Spain, beset with revolution in Sicily and threatened with financial collapse, had little left to contribute to the war in the Netherlands. Enthusiasm for the war had died in Spain once the French were no longer a menace to the country. The merchants wanted to go back to normal business. A costly reverse suffered by William III at Mont Cassel in April, 1677, caused strong opposition to his war policy among the Dutch. His marriage to the English heiress, Princess Mary, in November 1677, appeared to draw England over to the allies. Since 1676 a diplomatic conference had been in session at Nijmegen under English auspices, but Charles II was not willing to do more than mediate.

✑ *Peace of Nijmegen*

Louis XIV FOUND an opportunity to break up the coalition. He offered the Netherlands full evacuation of their country and a favorable trade treaty, and they accepted. In August 1678, France and the Republic signed the Peace of Nijmegen. A month later Spain gave in to French demands by ceding to France the Franche-Comté and sixteen fortified places in the Spanish Netherlands, among them Ypres, Saint-Omer, Cambrai, Valenciennes, and Maubeuge. Emperor and Empire were still at war with France, but the strongest armed estates of the Empire were fighting the Swedes in Bremen and Pomerania. It was doubtful whether the emperor could win a struggle that a large combination of powers had failed to bring to a successful conclusion.

In early February, 1679, the emperor concluded peace with France and Sweden on the basis of the Peace of Westphalia, except that France gave up Philippsburg, which had been won by German arms, in exchange for Freiburg, the capital of Anterior Austria, which had been conquered by the French. Lorraine was to be restored to its duke, but under such humiliating conditions that Charles V, who had married Leopold's sister, preferred to remain an imperial general. Brunswick and Münster followed the emperor in making peace.

Frederick William of Brandenburg found himself alone in facing France and Sweden. In the years before, he had gained great military triumphs, which suddenly became meaningless. In fast marches he had led his army from Franconia to northern Germany, while the Swedes had moved in more leisurely fashion, their units widely dispersed, toward the Elbe line. By an unexpected blow, a Brandenburg force took Rathenow on the Havel, placing itself in the center of the area of Swedish deployment. Taking his cavalry and placing some infantry on horse-drawn carriages, the elector swiftly rode on to meet one of the major Swedish corps. At Fehrbellin, in the swamps and marshes near Neu-Ruppin, he attacked them on July 28, 1675, with a force of 7,000 to their 12,000. The Brandenburgers fought with indomitable spirit against seasoned Swedish regiments, inflicting heavy losses and spreading consternation among them. It was a fierce battle, though by no means crowned with a great victory, since the Swedes managed to continue their retreat, retiring to Pomerania. However, the battle, the first won by the Brandenburg army alone, raised the prestige of Frederick William enormously.

Actually, the defeat of the Swedish plan to push beyond the Elbe and Weser was a great contribution to the war of the Empire on the Rhine. A Swedish army in northwestern Germany could have raised havoc with German dispositions against France. The elector proceeded vigorously to dislodge the Swedes forever from the southern littoral of the Baltic. Brunswick-Celle and Osnabrück, the bishop of Münster, the Netherlands, and Denmark turned against the Swedes. Bremen-Verden was easily overrun and Wismar taken by the Danes, while a combined Dutch and Danish fleet deprived Sweden of her naval command of the Baltic. This was one of the main prerequisites of a successful war in Pomerania, where the Swedes concentrated their defense. It took three years of grueling warfare before all of West Pomerania, including Stettin, Greifswald, and Stralsund—the city Wallenstein had once besieged in vain—the islands Usedom and Wollin in the Oder estuary, and the island of Rügen in the Baltic Sea, was in the hands of the allies. By November 1678, Frederick William was the ruler of all of Pomerania with the exception of Rügen, which fell to the Danish king.

ᔯ *Peace of Saint-Germain-en-Laye*

BY THIS TIME THE GREAT ELECTOR had already received word of the conclusion of peace between France, the Netherlands, and Spain; but more alarming tidings came from Prussia. As a last move, the Swedes had launched an attack from Livonia and flooded the province with numerous, if second-rate, troops. In the midst of a cold northern winter the Great Elector rushed to the rescue of his eastern province. The Swedes turned back without making a stand. In a frantic chase, with his foot soldiers on sleighs, Frederick William led his army over the frozen bays along the Prussian coast, cutting off all the easy roads of retreat. Of 16,000 men, only 3,000 hard-pressed stragglers reached the protecting walls of Riga. Magnificent military deeds were accomplished, but the Great Elector had forgotten that Pomerania could not be conquered from the Oder or Vistula but only from the Rhine. In Königsberg he learned of the peace between the emperor and France. His indignation was boundless. Not only was West Pomerania, including Stettin, lost, but the very existence of Brandenburg-Prussia was jeopardized. It was futile to hope that he might gain concessions regarding Stettin from Louis XIV. The Swedish government insisted upon the full restitution of Swedish Pomerania, and France, anxious to demonstrate her superiority, wanted to show that she would vindicate her allies. The electoral troops in Cleves were inadequate to stem the advance of the strong French army that reached Minden in May 1679. Frederick William signed the Peace of Saint-Germain-en-Laye on June 29, 1679. Except for some puny Swedish concessions, he had to restore West Pomerania, including Stettin, to Sweden. As compensation for war cost, he was to receive a consolation payment from the French king.

ᔯ *The "Close Alliance" of 1679*

THE GREAT ELECTOR'S ANGER was directed against Emperor Leopold. It was true that there existed in Vienna no inclination to assist in the aggrandizement of Brandenburg. In 1675, when the ducal dynasty of Liegnitz-Brieg had died out, the emperor had pocketed the Silesian principalities as fiefs returning to the Bohemian crown, in spite of a hereditary alliance between the Brandenburg and Silesian families. Pufendorf reported a remark made by the Austrian chancellor Hocher at the time of the discussion of a peace with France; namely, that it was undesirable to see "another king of the Vandals" rise on the Baltic. According to the alliance of 1674, the emperor was under no obligation to assist the elector in the expansion of his possessions, even though the expulsion of the Swedes from the Empire might have appeared as one of the natural duties of the German emperor. The Great Elector himself had insisted on the right of the individual allies to conclude a peace separately. He had considered it lawful to sign the Peace of Vossem in 1673, and had not cared about his ally Denmark when he had accepted the Peace of Saint-Germain-en-Laye. Actually, the Vienna government considered continuation of the war against France as futile, and was also conscious of the grave situation in the east. Revolts in Hungary were fomented by both France and Poland, where France had succeeded in bringing her candidate, John Sobieski, to the throne in 1674. It was fortunate that John III Sobieski was plunged at once into a war with the Turks in Podolia. Otherwise his policy might have become most nettling for both Leopold and the Great Elector during the Dutch War. The Vienna government was preoccupied not only with developments in Hungary and Poland, but also with its relations with the Ottoman Empire, with whom its treaty was soon to expire.

Leibniz spoke of Frederick William as "our Achilles" and disapproved of his rapprochement with France. How far the elector went in this, few contemporaries actually knew. On October 25, 1679, the "Close Alliance" (*Engere Allianz*) between Louis XIV and Frederick William was signed secretly. In return for a ten-year guarantee of all his territories, the Great Elector granted French troops free passage through his lands and reception in his fortresses. Furthermore, he promised to do his best to oppose the election of a member of the House of Austria as Roman king or Emperor, and to give his vote either to the French king or to the dauphin, or, if one of them could not obtain a majority, to a candidate approved by France. As a sign of his particular friendship Louis XIV declared his intention to pay the elector an annual sum of 100,000 livres for ten years. This pension enabled Frederick William to keep his armaments at a high level. His interest in receiving subsidies was of course the main reason for his going so far to the French side. He believed, furthermore, that through diplomatic co-operation German princes could exercise at least a moderating influence on Louis XIV, after they had given up opposing him in battle. The promise of his electoral vote, shocking though it may appear, was perhaps more of a symbolic gesture than a real commitment. The emperor was in the prime of life, and no election was close at hand. It was doubtful whether French diplomats put much stock in the election promise as such, although they had already obtained one from Elector Ferdinand Maria of Bavaria in 1670 and were to get still another, valid for four years, from Elector John George II of Saxony in November 1679.

✍ The "Reunions"

THE IMMEDIATE AIM OF FRENCH diplomacy was to encourage political division among the German princes in order to make recent French conquests secure. The treaties of Nijmegen marked the high point of Louis's power. The armies of the great coalition of 1674 had never been allowed to enter France, the alliance had finally broken up, and its members had yielded to French demands. It was true that the Dutch Republic had survived, but France had proved herself the strongest nation of Europe and was able to intervene in all the affairs of the Continent with a commanding voice. Not much was left of the seeming enthusiasm with which the German princes had closed ranks and thrown themselves into the war. To most Germans, Louis XIV appeared as an insatiable conqueror. However, Louis was too much of a courtier to try to become a true Charlemagne. Other contemporaries saw France as a fortress continually expanding the circle of its walls and forts. Defense, if carried to great length, inevitably takes on offensive forms, and is bound to appear as aggressive conduct in the eyes of those who are injured in the process. Moreover, in a ruler of Louis's arrogance and vaingloriousness, an expansionist urge often suppressed considerations of security.

Through the acquisition of the Flemish and Belgian fortresses, France was made safe in the north, while annexation of the Franche-Comté served as the southern anchor of her western frontiers. However, since no settlement had been reached with regard to Lorraine, it seemed desirable for France to gain an absolutely firm grip on Alsace. Absolute control of Alsace would at the same time increase the dependence of Switzerland on France, and Switzerland was still an important source of military strength for France. The Peace of Westphalia had failed to define clearly the character and scope of the concessions made to France on the Upper Rhine. The territories transferred to France were direct possessions of the emperor, and had actually already been given to Spain.[1] In this respect, the transfer of these territories became complete only through the Peace of the Pyrenees between France and Spain. Furthermore, in German constitutional law, it was perhaps possible to distinguish between the emperor's authority as a territorial prince and as feudal lord over the knights, counts, princes, and cities that were estates of the Empire, but in France the feudal law was more stringent, and did not interfere with the king's sovereignty. References to a bishopric in the treaties also gave rise to various interpretations. Did they refer to the secular territories of the bishop or the ecclesiastical diocese? The treaties were obscure also in many other respects. The estates of the Empire were aware of these ambiguities, but no one seriously wished to endanger the settlement of the Peace of Westphalia; all remonstrances were confined to one-sided declarations and protestations. France's position in the Upper Rhine was not clarified in the Treaty of Nijmegen either, although occupation of the Alsatian cities by the French had made the problem most acute.

After the Peace of Nijmegen the French pressed the enforcement of the full sovereignty of the French king over all the feudal entities with radical determination. To clothe the procedure in legal dress, three courts were established as "chambers of reunion" to decide which territories were, or had been, fiefs of the Alsatian lands and the Lorraine bishoprics, now in the possession of the French crown. This, of course, was contrary to all law, but it gave an excuse for the complete annexation of Alsace as well as for further expansion. This took place at the expense primarily of the Palatinate and archbishopric of Trier. It was at this time that France occupied a small part of what became known in modern times as the Saar district. Momentarily, she also advanced into Luxembourg. But the French dropped even the pretext of law when they massed troops around Strasbourg and forced the defenseless city to capitulate on September 30, 1681. The loss of the proud free city, which over many centuries had played a major role in its political and cultural history, was a terrific blow to Germany. The city was left its internal constitution. The year 1624 was recognized as the test year for the religious status of its citizens. The cathedral, however, was given to the Catholic Church, and the bishop of Strasbourg returned to the city.

[1] Cf. the author's *A History of Modern Germany: The Reformation,* pp. 362–3.

The "reunions" had caused deep indignation in Germany, and the act of violence which the capture of Strasbourg constituted aroused bitter hatred. The "reunions" spurred the diet of the Empire into action to complete the new military organization statute of 1681.[2] The initiative for a new European coalition came from William III of the Netherlands. The territory of Palantinate–Zweibrücken, which belong to Charles XI of Sweden, had been included among the French "reunions," and this led to a rift between Sweden and France. In these circumstances William III was able to form, in March, 1681, a Dutch-Swedish "association" to guarantee the peace treaties of 1648 and 1679. The emperor and Spain gave their adherence to this association half a year later. Plans for new unions within the Empire were discussed eagerly, and one at least was formed, the "Laxenburg alliance" between the emperor and the estates of the Franconian and Upper Rhine circles. It was joined shortly by Hanover, Saxony, and Bavaria. In Saxony the new elector, John George III (1680–91), was anti-French. He was also an army-minded ruler, and laid the foundation of the standing army in Saxony. In Bavaria young Max Emanuel (1679–1726) succeeded Elector Ferdinand Maria, a devoted friend of Louis XIV. He, too, was amenable to German patriotic sentiments and an ardent soldier. He was drawn to the court of Vienna also by the desire to win the hand of Maria Antonia, daughter of Emperor Leopold and Margaret Theresa, his Spanish wife. Archduchess Maria Antonia could be considered the legitimate heiress to the Spanish throne if Charles II died without issue, as was expected. Max Emanuel severed relations with France and signed a defensive alliance with the emperor against the Turks and France.

✍ *The Long Armistice; War with the Turks*

DEVELOPMENTS IN EUROPE AND GERMANY seemed to lead to a renewal of the war against France. That this war did not come about was largely the work of the Great Elector, who in the meantime had strengthened his relations with France. The rupture of Franco-Swedish amity had raised in his mind the hope of winning West Pomerania with French assistance. French diplomacy encouraged him in this, although France did not really wish to see a northern war and was set on eventually bringing Sweden back to her side. But France's encouraging words and growing payments were well placed in Berlin.

[2] See p. 19.

Frederick William turned into an ardent advocate of peace at the German courts and the diet of the Empire. His chief argument, that the chances of success in a new war against France were dubious, could not be easily refuted, particularly if he were not going to participate. Under the influence of the Turkish invasion, in the summer of 1683, the diet accepted the idea of a long armistice with France.

Leopold von Ranke has shown that it was not Louis XIV who induced the Turks to attack Austria. Franco-Turkish relations during these years were not free of friction, and Louis XIV did not wish to appear as the ally of the infidels in Europe—he even paused temporarily in his harassment of Germany. If the Turkish invasion nevertheless was blamed on him, it was because of the long history of collaboration between France and the Porte and France's attempts to take advantage of Austria's preoccupation with the Turkish war. The French government would no doubt have liked to see Austria remain in danger for a long time. If Vienna had fallen to the Turks, Louis XIV would probably have marched east as the protector of Christianity and established himself as the overlord of Europe, possibly claiming the imperial crown.

Since 1645 the Turks had again been on the offensive. Their efforts were directed at the exclusion of Venetian power from the eastern Mediterranean through the conquest of Crete, which had been under the Republic of St. Mark for four and a half centuries. This war lasted for twenty-four years and was fought with great tenacity and valor. German soldiers hired by Venice, particularly after the Thirty Years' War, played a conspicuous part in it. The Turks conquered Crete in 1669, and then turned their attention to the Black Sea. In 1672 the Poles were forced to cede the Ukraine and Podolia to the Ottoman Empire, and King John Sobieski was unable to regain them in a subsequent war. In this war, the Turks met the Russians for the first time and had to leave Kiev in their hands. Rebellion and chaos in Hungary encouraged the ruling vizier to advance through Hungary against Austria. The imperial army commanded by Charles of Lorraine was too small to meet the tremendous Turkish army, which rolled north through the Magyar plain under Kara Mustafa Kuprili. The Austrian court went to Passau. Vienna was left with 12,000 regular troops, while Charles retired to the north bank of the Danube. With an army of 100,000 men the Turkish crown-captain laid siege to the capital of the German emperor in the second half of July, 1683.

During the next two months Vienna fought a truly heroic defense under the leadership of its military commander, Count Rüdiger von Starhemberg, its mayor Andreas Liebenberg, and Bishop Kollonitsch. Resistance had entered a desperate stage by the time help arrived. In this war Austria was not without supporters. Christian sympathies were alive throughout Europe, even among the French nobility, but active help was given less freely. The devout Pope Innocent XI, however, gave the emperor both strong moral and financial aid. Papal intervention proved particularly valuable in Poland, where Austrian diplomacy scored a great success in persuading John Sobieski, who had come to the throne as the candidate of France, to join Austria in the war against the Turks. Help also came from Saxony, Bavaria, and from the Franconian and Upper Rhine circles. By September an army of 65,000 men had assembled on the Tulln field. Three quarters of it consisted of imperial and Empire troops. On September 12, 1683, it descended on a broad front from the Kahlenberg toward Vienna. A high crusading spirit animated the troops, and every contingent proved its worth. The imperial forces and the young Saxon army at the left wing along the Danube made the earliest gains, the Bavarian and other German units fought in the center against the elite regiments of the Janissaries, and the Polish army, well-supplied with cavalry, stood on the right wing, which provided the best terrain for deployment.

John Sobieski held the supreme command. His earlier military experience in Turkish campaigns and his bravery were of high value. The Polish participation in the battle at the Kahlenberg was the last historic contribution that Poland made to a common effort of the Western world. Charles of Lorraine deserves equal credit. This great general had drafted the plans for the attack and acted as chief field commander. His later pupil, the greatest of all Austrian military leaders, Prince Eugene of Savoy, then nineteen years of age, was a volunteer in the imperial army. Fierce fighting went on all day on Sunday, September 12. As night fell, the Turkish army fled from Vienna in disorder. Not only had the Turks been forced to a standstill in their pressure on the West as in 1529, but this time an opportunity for a far-reaching counteroffensive down the Danube had also been created.

King John Sobieski soon left with his troops for Podolia, and the troops from the south German circles went home. A first push of the imperial army into Hungary and an attempt to conquer Budapest failed. With the sultan arming feverishly, the emperor could not possibly fight a war against France to recover the "reunions." On August 15, 1684, a twenty-year armistice was concluded at Regensburg between the Empire and France; it left Louis XIV all "reunited" territories as well as Strasbourg. Thanks to the Turks, the Great Elector saw Leopold I take the line of policy vis-à-vis France which he himself had recommended and to which he was committed by his alliance with France.

Thus the war in Hungary was taken up again with vigor in March, 1684. Pope Innocent XI, Venice, and the emperor united in the Holy League for the common fight against the Ottoman Empire. Russia joined in later years, when John Sobieski broke into Moldavia and Walachia. Venice, half of her army composed of German soldiers from Brunswick, Hesse, Württemberg, and Saxony, attacked in Greece and conquered Morea. Next to Duke Francis Morosini, Count Otto William Königsmark had the greatest share in the successful direction of the campaign, which, in 1687, led even to the occupation of Athens. It may be mentioned in passing that it was not a German soldier who threw a bomb into the Parthenon, which was used by the Turks as a powder magazine.

An even greater outpouring of German manpower occurred in the main theater of war. Side by side with the Austrians fought the Bavarians and Saxons, soon to be joined by a strong Brandenburg contingent. Great military reputations were acquired by such German princes as the daredevil Elector Max Emanuel of Bavaria, feared by the Turks as the "blue King" because of the blue Bavarian colors, and the forceful and competent Margrave Ludwig of Baden, popularly known as "Turkish Louis." In 1686 Charles of Lorraine reconquered Budapest, and in the following year his victory at Mohács, near the battlefield of 1526, opened the roads to Transylvania and the lower Danube. Max Emanuel took Belgrade in 1688, and the imperial forces moved southward into Serbia. With the events on the Rhine, which compelled the German princes to recall their troops from the southeast theater, the war entered a quieter and less successful phase. Belgrade was lost to the Turks in 1690, but the Save-Danube frontier was held by the bloody battle of Slankamen in 1691. This was a victory for Margrave Ludwig of Baden, who soon left Hungary to take command on the Rhine. His successor, August the Strong of Saxony, did not prove to be a talented commander. When he was elected king of Poland in 1697, Prince Eugene of Savoy was entrusted with the command. A few months later the young prince annihilated the last large Turkish army in a brilliantly conducted battle at Zenta.

∽ The Habsburg Danubian Empire

THERE HAD BEEN TIMES WHEN the Austrians had dreamed of carrying the war as far as Constantinople. This might have been achieved if the Christian conquerors had been able to present themselves to the Balkan peoples as leaders in a movement of liberation rather than as men replacing their former lords. Actually, the support mobilized among the Balkan nations was limited. The diplomatic intervention of the maritime powers, which were worried about the loss of Levantine trade, caused in particular by Turko-Venetian naval warfare, brought the belligerents together for peace negotiations. Since the Spanish succession was now really imminent and Austria could not afford a long two-front war, the Vienna government made peace in 1699. In the Treaty of Karlowitz, the Turks gave up all of Hungary and Transylvania, with the exception of the Banat of Temesvar. It was an event of greatest historic significance, the actual foundation of the Danubian empire of the Habsburgs, which for more than two centuries constituted one of the main pillars of a European order. No longer was Austria "the garden fence of the Holy Roman Empire"—and for that matter, a fence that did not keep out intruders very well. A vast protective belt had been placed around the Austrian lands of the Habsburgs, and at the same time great resources were added to their empire.

After the fall of Budapest, the emperor was able to impose a constitution which made absolutism and centralism supreme in the Magyar realm. In the major part of Hungary, which had been under Turkish domination, the estates had sunk into oblivion, although on the local level some self-government survived. The magnates of Upper Hungary had to give up their resistance to the crown, which so often in the past had taken the form of open rebellion. When on December 9, 1687, Leopold's son Joseph was crowned in Pressburg, the Magyar estates had renounced their right of election so long as there was a male heir of the Austrian house. Two years later a beginning was made in establishing a standing army, but the building of large forces did not start before 1715. It was not until the time of Maria Theresa that the non-German troops became more numerous than the German regiments. In 1691 Transylvania was similarly absorbed into the Habsburg empire.

∾ *Realignment of European Powers after 1685*

THE VICTORIOUS PROGRESS of Austrian and German arms in Hungary, which enhanced the political and moral prestige of the emperor in Europe very considerably, was followed with grave misgivings in France. The successes of the emperor against the infidels spurred Louis XIV's ardor to contribute to the spread of true Christian religion and with this in view he introduced various measures in France. These steps were not taken to enhance the power of the Roman Church. On the contrary, while persecution of the approximately two million Huguenots was undertaken with growing violence, Gallican liberties were preached and practiced with complete contempt of all papal opposition. The outbreak of the brutal campaign for the suppression of Protestantism in France, which did not have the blessings of the pope, caused profound apprehension among the Protestant princes of Germany. A new era of religious wars seemed to be coming. In February, 1685, King Charles II of England died, and James II, a Catholic, became king. England, it was felt, was likely to follow French policy in Europe.

Anglo-French co-operation gave the renunciation of the Edict of Nantes by Louis XIV, in October of 1685, a particularly ominous character. New signs of French intervention in German affairs appeared in Louis XIV's brazen claims in the Palatinate. With the death of Elector Charles (1680–85) the Simmern branch of the Palatine dynasty had died out, and the Neuburg line succeeded. Philip William of Neuburg, the father of Empress Eleonore Magdalene, second wife of Leopold I, became, under the laws of the Empire, the new elector of the Palatinate. Though a Catholic, he confirmed the rights of his Protestant subjects. On behalf of his sister-in-law, Duchess Elizabeth Charlotte of Orléans, sister of the deceased Elector Charles, Louis XIV demanded from Philip not only Charles's private property but also a number of territories that were declared to be alodial possessions of the Simmern line. It was a ridiculous legal case, but recognition of the claims would have given France additional strongholds on the Rhine and the duke of Orléans membership in the diet of the Empire, as Count Palatine of Simmern and Lautern. For a while the French claims were sidetracked by haggling lawyers.

But the developments of the year 1685 led to important realignments of the powers in Europe. The Great Elector, impressed by the growing danger to Protestantism, revised his policies radically. It had already dawned on him that his expectation of finding in France an active supporter of his Pomeranian plans might be fallacious. On the other hand, Swedish control of the Stettin and the Oder estuary had become somewhat less oppressive by virtue of a canal that had been built between the Oder and the Spree, linking together the valleys of the two rivers and connecting Berlin with both. Still, it was not without an inner struggle that Frederick William turned to repair his relations with the Netherlands. He renewed the alliance with his nephew, William of Orange, for the unadmitted purpose of counteracting French expansion. The renunciation of the Edict of Nantes, in October of 1685, which destroyed all Reformed churches and exposed all Huguenots to the most cruel oppression and sufferings, outraged Frederick William. Although the Huguenots were forbidden under the heaviest penalties to emigrate, Frederick William issued, on November 8, the Edict of Potsdam, by which he offered all Frenchmen of Reformed-evangelical faith "a safe and free retreat" in his lands under the most favorable conditions of settlement. It was a courageous act, and it was considered possible in Berlin that Louis XIV might react to it violently. Although both sides pretended that the conflict should not affect their political relations, the French government could not be in doubt that its strongest German ally was veering rapidly from alliance with France. The Great Elector, indeed, was burying the political objectives that had led him to conclusion of the French alliance. He abandoned hope for the acquisition of West Pomerania in February, 1686, when he signed a secret defensive alliance with Charles XI of Sweden with a specific reference to the perilous situation of Protestantism.

ᴄᴐ *Political Reorientation of the German States*

MEANWHILE A RAPPROCHEMENT between Frederick William and the emperor was under way. Agreement concerning the military assistance Brandenburg was to send against the Turks was easily reached. In April, 1686, a strong Brandenburg contingent went to Hungary and participated with great credit in the siege and conquest of Budapest. However, negotiations for a general alliance proved more difficult. The Great Elector had resigned himself to the loss of West Pomerania. But it was too much for him to sacrifice Brandenburg's other major aspirations, in Silesia, as well. He was sincerely convinced of the righteousness of his claim to the principalities of Liegnitz, Brieg, and Wohlau, but the emperor was equally determined not to let any of the dependencies of the Bohemian crown pass out of his hands. Finally, Frederick William declared his willingness to give up his claims if the emperor would agree to make a token concession by transferring to him the district of Schwiebus, an area of a few square miles east of the Oder, separated from Silesia and surrounded by Brandenburg on three sides. But the imperial government was not prepared to buy the elector's rights even for so cheap a price. It declared such a transfer of sovereignty to be incompatible with the imperial dignity. In this critical situation the heir to the Brandenburg throne, who had always been hostile to the French alliance, offered to sign a secret declaration that he would return Schwiebus to the emperor after the death of his father. The intervention of the future Frederick III, of which the Great Elector never learned, was most irregular, to say the least, but it made possible the Austro-Brandenburg alliance.

The secret defensive alliance of March, 1686, between the emperor and the Great Elector, provided for mutual military co-operation and common resistance to all violations of the rights of Empire, under whatever pretext they might be perpetrated. Special mention was made of the conflict over the Palatinate. The elector also promised to support the imperial claims to the Spanish inheritance, to help in the defense of the Spanish Netherlands in case of a new attack, and to vote for the son of the emperor in a future election of a German king or emperor. In return, the emperor assumed the obligation to subsidize the Brandenburg army and turned over Schwiebus. The alliance was to remain binding for a period of twenty years. Actually, it established a relationship that was to last for more than forty. Although it did not always prove to be very firm, it exercised a most beneficial influence on the national history of Germany in this age.

With the Dutch, Swedish, and Austrian alliances, the Great Elector had defined the future political course of his state. In the last year of his life he became privy to the plans of William III to win the crown of England by direct intervention. During his last illness his mind was preoccupied with this project, which would have extended the anti-French coalition and removed the dangers that were threatening the existing Protestant states. On May 9, 1688, Frederick William died. Through his indomitable energy, he had played a part in the history of his time far greater than the political basis of his power could naturally sustain. But he had created a state that was to enable his successors to intervene in European politics with imposing strength.

While the policies of Louis XIV in the 1680's brought on the political reorientation of the northern states, they also had an effect on the southern German states. These came to feel strongly the need for military protection. In Franconia a movement began that led to the formation of a new association among the estates of the Empire with the purpose of mobilizing forces for the defense of the Rhine. Imperial diplomacy broadened this plan. In July, 1686, the emperor, Spain, Sweden, the Thuringian princes, and the Franconian and Bavarian circles concluded the Augsburg Alliance, which provided for the common mobilization of an army in case of attack by France. The elector of the Palatinate, the estates of the Upper Rhine circle, and the duke of Holstein joined a little later. The Augsburg Alliance alarmed the French, so much so that they named the subsequent war after it. In reality, the alliance did not have great practical significance, but it was a sign of the changing German mood. The spirit of resistance had become stronger in Germany.

A new conflict between the Empire and France developed over the succession to the see of Cologne. All through his reign, Elector Maximilian Henry of Cologne had remained closely allied with France. He was completely under the influence of the most unashamed partisan of France in Germany, William Egon von Fürstenberg, whom the emperor ordered abducted to Vienna during the Dutch war and whom he would have liked to dispose of as a traitor. Through French intercession he had become bishop of Strasbourg and had received a cardinal's hat. In January, 1688, French diplomacy engineered his election as coadjutor and successor to the ailing Maximilian Henry. The emperor objected officially, as did all the electors in surprising unanimity. The see of Cologne was traditionally considered a domain of the Bavarian dynasty, which a century earlier had saved the archbishopric from falling into Protestant hands. Prince Joseph Clement was the Bavarian candidate. He was only seventeen, though already titular prince-bishop of Freising and Regensburg.

⌒ The War of the League of Augsburg, 1688-97

WHEN, AFTER THE DEATH OF Maximilian Henry, in June of 1688, the Cologne chapter split in the election, Pope Innocent XI threw his authority behind the emperor and Bavaria and recognized Joseph Clement as archbishop. In Cologne the legal question was most complicated. In Liége, Münster, and Hildesheim—benefices that had been connected with Cologne—William Egon von Fürstenberg was not elected. Louis XIV was indignant at the pope's decision and prepared to back his satellite, who kept the Lower Rhine open for France. The conflict over Cologne in 1688 became part of the war the French king started in the same year, initiating another twenty-five-year era of almost uninterrupted war in Europe.

With jaundiced eye, the French government had followed events at the Danube. The coronation of Joseph, son of Emperor Leopold, as king of Hungary, in December, 1687, had shown that Austria was building a new empire. This time there was no question but that Austria received her gifts not from Venus but from Mars. Nor had her military *élan* stopped with the liberation of Hungary; she was pressing forward into the Balkan peninsula. It could be expected that Austria would at least win an advantageous peace from the Porte, unless events occurred that would induce the Turks to persist in warfare. If the war on the Danube came to an end, the emperor would be able to turn to the Rhine with full might and assert his and the Empire's rights with regard to Strasbourg and the French "reunions," which had been reserved under the Regensburg armistice of 1684. France, on the other hand, was isolated, unless England could be counted on as an ally. In addition to the Netherlands, Spain stood against her, the Polish alliance was lost, and the German princes were no longer tied, by chains of iron or gold, to the chariot of the Roi Soleil. On the contrary, they had banded together against France under the leadership of the emperor.

France was not well prepared for a big war, and the French economy was strained. But a long war was not foreseen. By a show of force, the French government felt it could compel the Germans to recognize the former French conquests and to respect the predominant position of France on the Continent. On September 24, 1688, Louis XIV issued a declaration against emperor and Empire, demanding the destruction of the fortifications of Philippsburg, a financial settlement of the claims of the duke of Orléans against the Palatinate, and confirmation of William Egon von Fürstenberg as archbishop of Cologne. He offered to return Philippsburg after the French army had done its work of dismantling, and even to restore Freiburg to the emperor, provided it remained disarmed. But all these modest demands and generous offers, which were cited as proof that the French king did not enter Germany as a belligerent, were conditional upon the change of the armistice of Regensburg into a definitive peace between France and the Empire by January, 1689. It was a thoroughly mendacious document. The confirmation of Cardinal Fürstenberg, for example, was beyond the authority of the emperor. In addition to being a political trap, this condition was a clumsy attempt to force the emperor into a common front with France against the pope. Louis XIV, in order to counter the support of Joseph Clement by the pope, had the obedient French Church declare the superiority of councils over the papacy. To make the emperor supplicate in Rome on behalf of the French candidate for the see and electorate of Cologne would have humiliated him, both as a ruler of Germany and as protector of the Church.

The invading French armies found little resistance on the left bank of the Rhine. Four electorates, the Palatinate, Trier, Mainz, and Cologne, were easily overrun. In the last one, Cardinal Fürstenberg opened to the French the gates of all fortresses except the city of Cologne itself. The archbishop of Trier maintained himself in Coblenz. Philippsburg, though weakly manned and ill-equipped, was ably and bravely defended for four weeks by Count Max von Starhemberg, brother of the defender of Vienna. French armies broke into Swabia and Franconia, extracting heavy contributions by violent and destructive methods. From the outset, the French were set on spreading terror. Louvois, the French minister of war and the evil genius of this war, wrote in October, "Do not think that you can achieve anything against the Germans with friendship or moderation; guns and fortresses will make them obey rather than anything else."

Yet Louis XIV and Louvois (1641–91) were gravely mistaken if they anticipated an easy victory. This time Leopold I accepted the challenge of the French and he enjoyed the active assistance of the German princes. His decision to do so was one of the most fateful he had to make during his long reign. He had been brought up to be an ecclesiastical dignitary and as emperor he had not become militaristic. He took an interest in books, in the theater, and especially in music. A composer of fair talent, he was the founder of Vienna's musical tradition. He did not relish the burdens of the imperial office, nor did he possess strong political gifts. But he was conscious of the Habsburg mission, which his piety turned into a religious obligation. He met changes of fortune with an enduring patience and proud determination. In the fall of 1688 he resisted the pressure of the German princes, and later of the maritime powers, to conclude a compromise peace with the Turks. Now Leopold boldly decided to fight on two fronts. On October 18, 1688, he issued a war manifesto against

Louis XIV, which shows the imprint of Leibniz's thinking, if indeed it was not written by him.

More than three months passed, however, before the Empire declared war on France. The great north German princes acted much faster. On the initiative of Frederick III, the new ruler of Brandenburg, John George III of Saxony, Ernest August of Hanover, and Charles of Hesse-Kassel formed with him the "Magdeburg Concert" of October 22, 1688. These princes sent an army of 22,000 men to the central Rhine, while the main Brandenburg army covered the Lower Rhine and sent strong units into the Netherlands. This deployment of the Brandenburg troops made it possible for William III to set out on his expedition to England, where he landed on November 15, 1688. With the help of Parliament, he soon put an end to the rule of James II and became himself King of England.

The southern army of the Magdeburg Concert assembled and advanced quickly. Frankfurt was shielded against French importunities and Franconia freed. In the middle of February the army approached Heidelberg from the east. The French troops were too weak to accept battle and had to retreat behind the Rhine. Louvois sent orders that in their retreat the French forces were to devastate and burn the Palatinate to the ground so that it could not serve as the base for an offensive by the enemy. From a strictly military point of view, this was an unnecessary step. As long as Mainz was in French hands, the Germans could not well cross the Rhine. The destruction of fortifications, the removal of stores, even the burning of places that resisted the imposition of contributions was considered permissible under the contemporary customs of war. But the systematic destruction by the French army of towns, villages, fields, and vineyards was outrageous, and there were signs that a good many French officers felt repelled by such cruelty. In Heidelberg the work of demolition was done hurriedly, and French officers closed their eyes when people fought the flames. Mannheim, however, was left an uninhabitable heap of ruins. Worms, Oppenheim, Frankenthal, and Speyer were burned. The graves of the medieval emperors in the crypt of the cathedral of Speyer were desecrated and destroyed, while all over the country towns and villages were left in ashes. Inevitably, soldiers driven to such brutal actions lost all sense of discipline and committed excesses of the worst type.

While clouds of black smoke hung over the Upper Rhine, the "glorious revolution" installed William III on the throne of England, and James II became a refugee at the French court. Negotiations were opened in February, 1689, between Austria and the Dutch and English governments. Emperor Leopold overcame his scruples and entered into co-operation with the man who had usurped the crown of a legitimate Catholic king. This step was facilitated by the obvious sympathies the pope harbored for the monarchy of William III, and by Leopold's hope of gaining the support of the maritime powers for the Habsburg succession in Spain. Thus the "great alliance" between Austria, the Netherlands, and England was concluded in May, 1689. William III was recognized by Austria as king of England in return for the promise of the maritime powers to support Austrian claims in the event of the death of Charles II of Spain and to support immediately the succession of Archduke Joseph to the German throne. William III wanted the emperor to break off hostilities with the Turks or make a definite commitment with regard to the number of troops he would use against France. But the emperor refused to be tied to specific obligations, and William III, still depending on Continental support, had to be satisfied with the hope that the exigencies of European politics would produce the strongest efforts against France by emperor and Empire. Savoy and Spain lined up against France in the fall of 1689 and summer of 1690, respectively.

The war in Germany in the summer of 1689 began most auspiciously for the anti-French allies. Duke Charles V of Lorraine led a strong army composed of imperial and Empire troops to the central Rhine and took Mainz after a siege of eight weeks. Then he assisted the Brandenburg army, strengthened by auxiliary Dutch forces, in the last phase of the conquest of Bonn, which in this age was a very strong fortress. The Lower and middle Rhine were thus liberated, but the situation on the Upper Rhine remained precarious for several years. With the death of Charles of Lorraine, in April, 1690, the allies lost not only a superb master of tactics, but also a superior will in the councils of war. The misery of discord among the princes and commanders of territorial contingents of the Empire army began all over again. The Rhine front also suffered from the demands of the Turkish war and from reverses in the allied theaters of war. New allied retreats from the Rhine to the Neckar line became necessary. Heidelberg was occupied by the French in May, 1693, and fire, this time not deliberately set by the French army command, destroyed the whole city with the exception of a few houses. The French blew up the castle and other fortifications. The new imperial commander, Margrave Ludwig of Baden, was unable to avoid the disaster that befell the historic capital of the Palatinate, but he succeeded in restoring a military balance in the last years of the war, although he had to fight chiefly with the limited forces of the Franconian and Swabian circles. It became a campaign of maneuver and position rather than of battle.

The war on the sea was originally not very successful. James II was able to go to Ireland, and only the battle of the Boyne of July 1, 1690, established William III's supremacy. In May, 1692, at Cap de la Hogue, the combined Anglo-Dutch navies annihilated the great French fleet that was supposed to cover the invasion of England. After this defeat France had to guard against possible English landings, and this tied down large French forces. An invasion of France by the allies would have required military progress in the Spanish Netherlands. But here they were not successful. On the day of the battle of the Boyne the Dutch army, under the command of Prince George Frederick of Waldeck, suffered a disastrous defeat at the hands of Marshal Luxembourg. The arrival of the Brandenburg army later in the month restored some strength to the allied forces, but their operations were confined to defense. In 1693 Marshal Luxembourg defeated William III in the battle of Neerwinden, but the victory was not decisive and the following years saw a military stalemate. The French were most successful in Spain, where they even achieved the occupation of Barcelona. In the Alps they fought Duke Victor Amadeus II, who was supported by imperial troops, to a standstill.

Even in her isolation France managed to defeat all attempts of the allies to break into the interior of the country. On most fronts she had military outposts well beyond French soil that remained unconquered, and although the French armies were incapable of assuming the strategic offensive, they remained formidable and able to inflict heavy blows on their enemies. The war taxed French resources to the utmost, however. Louis XIV had to use his full monarchical authority to exact the sums needed from a depleted economy and a tired and impoverished people. He sent out diplomatic peace feelers as early as 1693, but the price set by the allies was too high. The French government was not prepared to make a peace that would substantially cut the gains France had made since 1648. However, in the years after 1694 France learned that she would have to make concessions, but that they could be held within limits if made in such a way as to split the coalition. In the summer of 1696 Louis XIV declared his willingness to hand over two key positions, Casale and Pinerolo, to the duke of Savoy. The two fortresses had ensured France easy access to Italy, but now they bought the political collaboration of the Savoy dynasty. The duke was secretly promised the duchy of Milan out of the future Spanish inheritance. His daughter Adelaide, who was to become the mother of Louis XV, was engaged to the heir of the French throne. The separate peace between France and Savoy made warfare against France in Italy very difficult, and the emperor, trying to strengthen his forces in Hungary, proposed the neutralization of Italy. The transfer of the French army from Italy to the Netherlands, which became possible as a result of the subsequent neutrality agreement, increased the military problems of William III in the Netherlands. Diplomatic mediation by Sweden led to the opening of a general peace conference at Ryswick in May, 1697.

The French grant of a favorable trade agreement to the Netherlands and withdrawal of French support from James II and the Jacobites paved the way for a peace with the maritime powers. In order to complete the diplomatic isolation of the Empire and gain sympathy in Spain, Louis XIV offered Spain surprisingly easy peace terms. They amounted to the full evacuation of French troops from Spain and the return of practically all French "reunions" in the Spanish Netherlands as well as other territories taken during the war. French diplomacy could then take a rather firm line vis-à-vis the Empire. Here, too, France declared her willingness to restore the "reunions" and not to raise claims for territory in the Palatinate. The French gave up all places on the right bank of the Upper Rhine—Philippsburg, Kehl opposite Strasbourg, Freiburg and Breisach in the Breisgau. But Louis XIV absolutely refused to consider returning Alsace to the Empire, and although the restoration of Strasbourg was briefly discussed, he refused to return it also. Disappointment in Germany was great, particularly over the loss of Strasbourg, but since England, the Netherlands, and Spain had signed the Peace of Ryswick on September 20, the Empire followed their example on October 30, 1697.

ᔓ *Europe after the Peace of Ryswick*

CONSIDERING THAT ALMOST ALL OF EUROPE had fought against France, the peace settlement of Ryswick, which left France with very substantial strategic gains over and above her position in 1648 and 1659, was a great achievement of French arms and statecraft. But the Peace of Ryswick had forced France to give up some of her booty. It had set limits to her expansion and clearly shown the dangers of isolation.

Most important historically was the consolidation of the position of the other European powers in the course of war in the Palatinate. The establishment of the Protestant monarchy in England, which survived the early death of William III, in 1702, and led, through the reign of Queen Anne, to the Hanover succession of 1714, was the most far-reaching single development of the period. The battle of Cap de la Hogue, in wresting naval superiority from France, foreshadowed the ascendancy of England over France, which was largely won in the naval and amphibious struggles in the Mediterranean and America. With the acquisition of Hungary, Austria became one of the great European powers, more capable of stemming the French tide on the Continent than the former Austria had been. Imperial successes on the Danube and Tisza were bought at the price of old historic possessions of the German Empire. That Alsace and Strasbourg remained French was largely due to the need for Austrian and German troops for the war in Hungary. Without the whole imperial army, the German forces were not able to win decisive victories. The "armed estates" made great contributions, and even the efforts of the small estates of the southern German circles should not be underrated. It was the first war in a long time in which no German prince had fought on the French side.

But co-operation among the German princes during the war had proved uneasy. Most troublesome had been the ambitions of the dukes of Brunswick. After 1648 Brunswick had, like Brandenburg, risen to a position of political importance. It might indeed have reached an equal prominence with Brandenburg if the internal cleavages within the Guelf dynasty had been resolved earlier. Once Duke Ernest August had gained the virtual unification of the Brunswick lands,[3] he intended to crown his achievement by acquiring the electoral dignity. The expiration of the Protestant line in the Palatinate left only two Protestants among the eight electors of the Empire. This gave outward justification for the duke's demands, which were strenuously opposed by most German princes, who disliked the eminence claimed by the electors. Among the latter, sentiment was friendlier. Frederick III of Brandenburg, especially, was active in helping his Protestant neighbor and father-in-law. The decision, however, was in the hands of Emperor Leopold.

Leibniz's facile pen was at work to propitiate the opposition of the princely German chancelleries, but only massive political pressure, if

[3] See p. 21.

not blackmail, was to lead to the emperor's approval. Ernest August's efforts to build up in the Empire, a "third party," which would undertake to mediate between France and the allies, brought Leopold's consent. In March, 1692, the "electoral tractate," which created the electorate of Hanover, was signed in Vienna. In exchange for the electoral dignity the dukes of Brunswick promised their assistance in both the Turkish and French wars. Through a secret treaty, called the "eternal union," the emperor and the Brunswick-Hanover dynasty entered into a permanent alliance. It was agreed that the electoral vote would always be given to a member of the house of Austria, and that Hanover would lend military support to the emperor in the Spanish succession.

The creation of the Hanover electorate caused quite a stir at the German courts, as did also the sudden conversion to Catholicism of August II, "the Strong," the young elector of Saxony, who, in 1694, had succeeded his brother John George IV as ruler of Saxony. An uninhibited sensualist, he had lived for nothing but the pleasures of French and Italian courts. It was curious that this handsome worldling of artistic tastes and religious indifference should succeed to the line of simple Lutheran Saxon electors. He did not show military talent when he commanded the imperial army in Hungary in 1695–96. The following year, he turned to political gambling for high stakes. His conversion to Catholicism was the preparation for his candidacy to the throne of Poland. With Austria's support against the French aspirant, he gained substantial backing among the Polish magnates, and he was able to make himself king by marching his army into Poland. Austria had won a remarkable victory over Louis XIV just at the time of the Peace of Ryswick. In her subsequent struggle for the Spanish succession the exclusion of French influence from the east was of great consequence.

The Saxon acquisition of the Polish crown changed the relations between Vienna and Dresden. Saxony, the home of the Lutheran Reformation, though nearly always moderate in its opposition to the emperor, now became fully dependent on close collaboration with him. As it turned out, the Austrian orientation of Saxony was to last with little interruption till the end of the German Confederation in 1866. But contemporaries were disturbed most by the possibility that the conversion of the head of the *corpus evangelicorum* of the Empire might lead to complete control of the college of electors by the Roman Catholic Church, and even to forceful attempts at the reconversion of the Lutheran populace of Saxony. Although these fears did not prove justified in the end, they were not baseless, and they were further strengthened by a diplomatic trick France played on the Germans on the eve of the signing of the Peace of Ryswick.

At the instigation of John William, the Catholic elector of the Palatinate, the French demanded the insertion of a clause in the treaty stabilizing the state of religion in all the places handed back by France to Germany "as it is at the present moment." In open violation of the armistice of 1684, the French had propagated Catholicism in the German territories they occupied. The bigoted elector hoped to be able to achieve the conversion of his electorate on this basis. The refusal of the Protestant estates, with the exception of Württemberg, Frankfurt, and a few counts, to become signatories of the Peace of Ryswick did not change the outcome. The "Ryswick clause" produced endless controversies in the Empire. Moreover, it turned the Palatinate, under Karl Ludwig recently a model of toleration, into a center of acrimonious denominational conflict and oppression.

CHAPTER 5

Germany and the Restoration of the European Balance, 1700-21

THE PEACE OF RYSWICK of 1697, followed two years later by the Peace of Carlowitz, brought only a brief respite from war. Ill-boding clouds gathered over the Baltic. Poland, Denmark, and Russia prepared for the fight against Sweden, the contest that was to become the Nordic War. But the cabinets of Europe watched Spain with even greater concern. The problems of succession had not been settled at Ryswick. William III of England had committed himself to support the Austrian claims when, in 1689, he had needed Austria. In the strong position he had gained since then, he could approach the matter as an arbiter of the balance of Europe. Neither England nor the Netherlands wanted France to win the whole Spanish inheritance and thereby become the dominant power of Europe. Nor could either tolerate French acquisition of the Spanish colonies. Thus the principle of partition of the Spanish empire was adopted by the maritime powers, and it was not opposed by France and Austria under all circumstances.

A third claimant to the Spanish throne had appeared in the person of Elector Maximilian Emanuel of Bavaria, who had married the only child of Emperor Leopold and his Spanish wife, Margaret Theresa. In contrast to her elder sister Maria Theresa, Margaret Theresa had not renounced her hereditary rights, and Philip IV of Spain had intended that the Austrian line would succeed to the throne of Madrid in case Charles II should die without an heir. But the empress had died in 1673, and the only offspring of her marriage was Archduchess Maria Antonia, who had married the elector of Bavaria. Maximilian Emanuel, crowned with success in the Turkish war, had high ambitions, and he also had great appeal for the Spaniards, among whom the desire was great to see the Spanish monarchy held together rather than partitioned or annexed to Austria or France. In 1692 Max Emanuel had become regent of the Spanish Netherlands. When in the same year a son, Joseph Ferdinand, was born to him, the Wittelsbach succession in Spain gained fresh supporters not only in Spain but also among the other governments of Europe, which saw in the succession of a prince from a small German house the means of avoiding a Habsburg-Bourbon conflict.

✑ Treaties of Partition

IN 1698, ENGLAND, THE NETHERLANDS, AND FRANCE concluded the (first) treaty of partition. Joseph Ferdinand was recognized as the legitimate heir and was to receive Spain, the Spanish Netherlands, and the colonies. France was to gain possession of Naples and Sicily, while the emperor was to get Milan. The treaty aroused the weak spirit of the Spanish king, who now proclaimed Joseph Ferdinand the exclusive heir to the Spanish kingdom and all its possessions. Plans were made to bring the six-year-old boy to Madrid and to give him a Spanish education. However, he died early in 1699. In the spring of 1700 the maritime powers and France again agreed on a (second) treaty of partition. This time Spain, the Netherlands, and the colonies were earmarked for Archduke Charles, the second son of Leopold, while Naples, Sicily, Sardinia, and Milan were to go to France. This project was strenuously rejected in Vienna. French domination in Italy was completely unacceptable, and it was decided to forego claims to Spain rather than Italy. In Spain the second plan of partition was as much resented as the first, and over the deathbed of the enfeebled king, Charles II, the Spanish factions fought a war of poisonous intrigue. The party that saw in the succession of a younger French prince the best way to maintain the continued existence of the Spanish monarchy emerged with a testament of the dying king that left the throne to Philip of Anjou, second son of the dauphin. When Charles II died, on November 1, 1700, Louis XIV could not resist taking action. The treaty of partition was set aside and Philip proclaimed king of Spain. In January, 1701, Philip arrived in Madrid and was acclaimed by most Spaniards.

✑ War of the Spanish Succession: First Campaign

AUSTRIA REACTED QUICKLY, not only with declarations but also with actions. In May, 1701, Prince Eugene of Savoy, commanding Austrian troops, broke into northern Italy, where during the next sixteen months he conducted one of the most brilliant campaigns of his career. This first campaign of the War of the Spanish Succession finally came to a standstill, however, because Austria could not provide him with sufficient replacements and arms. The depleted condition of Austrian finances and the chaotic state of government administration had been the main objections raised at the time of Austria's decision to wage war. Emperor Leopold was sincerely convinced of his rights, and his two sons, King Joseph and Archduke Charles, together with Prince Eugene, had considered war an absolute necessity. But Austria needed allies and, even more, she needed money; this she could obtain only from the maritime powers, and in the form of loans or, as they were then called, "anticipations."

✄ *"Grand Alliance"*

WILLIAM III WAS CONVINCED that England should fight, and the leading Dutch statesman, Antonius Heinsius, urged a similar course for the Netherlands. If Spain with all her related realms and colonies were to fall to France, the whole naval and commercial position of the maritime nations would be placed in jeopardy. But the English Parliament was not easily persuaded to recognize its long-range interest. Louis XIV played into the hands of William III by committing a series of political blunders, of which the last and most serious was the proclamation of James Edward, son of James II, as king of England after the death of his father in 1701. In September, 1701, the so-called "Grand Alliance" was signed at The Hague by the emperor, England, and the Netherlands. The maritime powers were by no means willing to support the emperor's claim to the Spanish throne, but they found that he deserved "a just and reasonable satisfaction" of his claims, which was to be obtained in the Spanish Netherlands, Milan, Sicily, and other Spanish islands in the Mediterranean. With regard to Spain, the alliance contained only the provision that she should never be united with France into one empire. The maritime powers, for their part, reserved their own demands on Spain, which amounted to guarantees of freedom of trade and other colonial advantages. The "Grand Alliance" was the last great political achievement of William III. It had been preceded by the Act of Settlement of June, 1701, by which Parliament recognized the right of succession of Duchess Sophie of Hanover, the last surviving child of the Winter-King, in the event that

Princess Anne, the sister-in-law of William III, should die without issue.

Through this Act of Settlement, the elector of Hanover became an ally of the anti-French coalition. The strongest of the armed estates of the Empire, Brandenburg-Prussia, was already bound to it by special agreements with the emperor. Frederick III of Brandenburg had wanted to acquire the title of king after succeeding his father as ruler of Brandenburg-Prussia in 1688, but he did not feel strong enough to assume the title as a *fait accompli*. He wanted to have the emperor's approval, even though he proposed to build the kingship on the sovereign duchy of Prussia rather than on his electoral lands. Negotiations about this matter made little progress during the 1690's. Brandenburg played a conspicuous part in the Palatinate War, but the relations between Vienna and Berlin became ruffled over the Schwiebus affair. Schwiebus was returned to Austria in 1694. On this occasion the emperor recognized the hereditary alliance between the princes of East Friesland and the Hohenzollern dynasty, which half a century later brought this land under the Prussian crown.

After the Peace of Ryswick and the coronation of August II of Saxony as king of Poland, Frederick III pressed for approval of his project. The approaching death of Charles II of Spain dispelled all Leopold's misgivings. Two days before the death of the last Habsburg king of Spain, Brandenburg and Austria made a new treaty of alliance, which, except for minor concessions on the part of Brandenburg, was a renewal of the alliance of 1686; it also sealed the emperor's approval of Frederick's royal dignity. Frederick lost no time in assuming his new title. On January 18, 1701, he placed a new crown on his head and on that of his wife, Sophie Charlotte. The religious ceremonies were dispensed with except for the ritual of unction, which was performed by a Reformed bishop and a Lutheran bishop, especially named for this occasion.

Thus, Brandenburg, Saxony, and Hanover—the strongest north German states—were bound to the Grand Alliance, and almost all the other estates of the Empire followed the same political course, so that, with the usual delay, though with little opposition, the Empire declared war on France in 1702. The actual conduct of the war by the estates, however, left much to be desired. The "armed estates" preferred to hire out their troops to the highest bidder, as a rule England or the Netherlands. The emperor himself set a bad example by failing to supply the army of the Empire with adequate Austrian forces. In accordance with Austrian interests, he placed the main emphasis on the Italian theater of war. As a consequence, the imperial contingents of the army of the Empire were usually under strength or conspicuous by their absence. The army of the Empire had to rely on the small estates, of which only those of the Franconian and Swabian circles did their full part. It was a weak army that fought on the Upper Rhine, and Margrave Ludwig of Baden, now old, grumpy, and over-cautious in action, found it difficult to keep it together, let alone risk major battles. While German soldiers were in the majority in the English, Dutch, and imperial armies, which were employed mainly outside Germany, the southern German theater of war was short of arms and men. Small wonder that German interests were to receive no hearing in the final peace negotiations.

Only three estates of the Empire elected alliance with France. The first was Brunswick-Wolfenbüttel, ruled by Duke Anton Ulrich, who as head of the elder line of the Guelf dynasty was disgruntled over the sudden rise of the younger line, the house of Hanover. However, the considerable army that he had assembled was captured in a coup staged by his cousin in April, 1702, and Duke Anton was driven out of his country. More serious was the defection of the Wittelsbach dynasty. It began with the astounding pact between Joseph Clement, elector and archbishop of Cologne, and Louis XIV. This Bavarian prince, who had gained his dignity through the common efforts of emperor and Empire, handed over to the French all his military positions in Cologne and his other bishopric, Liége. His brother, Elector Max Emanuel of Bavaria, hesitated to take sides. As governor of the Spanish Netherlands he quickly recognized Philip of Anjou as Philip V of Spain and invited French troops into the Belgian fortresses, but at the same time he continued negotiations with all parties until September, 1702, when he took by surprise the free city of Ulm, the strategic key to the Upper Danube valley, thus causing an immediate threat to the defenses of emperor and Empire.

A strong hostile force now stood in the rear of the army of the Empire in Baden and the Palatinate. Margrave Ludwig had been able to take the offensive and had recaptured Landau, the gate to Alsace. But with this new development his forces were hardly adequate to cover the left-bank Palatinate, and they proved incapable of holding all Upper Rhine crossings against the determined French advance that was undertaken in 1703. After the successful siege of Kehl, a strong French army under Marshal Villars marched over the passes of the

Black Forest and united with the Bavarian army of Max Emanuel in May, 1703. Marshal Villars proposed to march down the Danube toward Linz and Vienna, while the French army in Italy under Duke Vendôme was to move against Tyrol from the south.

The situation in Italy had changed since the fall of 1702. Prince Eugene had maintained himself against growing French forces. But his own troops were exhausted and dwindling. A new battle was likely to reverse the fortunes of war. Neither reinforcements nor adequate provisions were forthcoming from Vienna. There was no money in the coffers of the Austrian government, but the military planners were proposing additional campaigns. In December 1702, Prince Eugene had hastened to Vienna, where with the support of the young archduke and King Joseph he struggled for months to make reason prevail. The bad tidings from Germany, as well as the spread of the new Hungarian revolution led by Francis II Rakoczy, caused Leopold I to change his ministers. In June, 1703, Prince Eugene became president of the Austrian war council (*Hofkriegsrat*), and the able Count Gundaker Starhemberg was appointed president of the financial administration (*Hofkammer*).

The young military genius from Savoy was now able to show his political sagacity as well as his skill in the conduct of war. He became the soul of the new Austria, which had become one of the foremost European powers. "Eugènio von Savoy," he often signed his name, and this signature reveals the three national strains in his personality. He came from a French line of the Italian dynasty of Savoy and grew up at Versailles. When Louis XIV passed him by in granting military commissions, Eugene went to Austria, the country that was fighting the battle of Christianity against the Turks. Since the glorious September Sunday of 1683 when as a simple volunteer he had descended toward Vienna from the Kahlenberg with the fighting armies, he had rapidly mastered the art of war in the school of Duke Charles V of Lorraine. He had endeared himself to his soldiers, who had carried his fame to the people. "Prince Eugene, the noble knight," was a folk song that rang through all of Germany. Actually, Eugene was not affected by German patriotism. The Empire of the German nation meant little to the man who wanted to be a loyal paladin of the house of Austria. But his belief in the European mission of the Habsburg empire was not conceived in an imperialistic sense. Rather, he saw in Austria the country that should help to hold Christian Europe together.

The year 1703 was a year of great danger for the allies. They assigned large forces to regain Cologne and Liége. Although these made good progress, they did not immediately bring about a strategic decision. The critical situation of Austria and Vienna was not overcome by the imperial government, though it was temporarily eased by Elector Max Emanuel, who would not agree to Marshal Villar's plan to march against Vienna. Max Emanuel saw in Tyrol the most desirable addition to Bavaria and the natural bridge to Italy, where he hoped to continue his empire-building.

In the ensuing fighting Vendôme was to occupy South Tyrol and be met at the Brenner Pass by the French-Bavarian army, but he began his operations late and ran into fierce opposition by the provincial militia. He got only as far as Trent by early September, when news of misfortunes befalling the Bavarian army induced him to retreat to Lombardy. Max Emanuel had taken North Tyrol easily and reached the Brenner Pass in July, when the militia, strengthened by native peasants and miners, had risen against him. A situation had occurred that was rare in this period of history, namely, popular feeling had burst forth with such vehemence as to lead to the defeat of a professional army. Popular animosity between Austrians and Bavarians had always been strong, and the Austrians were to bear the brunt of it during the next few years. Tyrol was ridden with dissatisfaction at the existing Austrian administration. The rising of the population against the Bavarian army in the name of loyalty to the ruling dynasty was curiously linked with opposition to the provincial Habsburg officials who, in addition to their old sins, were accused of lack of resistance to the invaders. In the mountainous land the fight of the people was very effective, and Max Emanuel had to beat a hasty retreat to Bavaria.

An attempt was made to encircle the French-Bavarian army in Bavaria through a simultaneous attack by the army of the Empire, which Margrave Ludwig led from the Rhine to Augsburg, and an imperial army, which under Count Styrum moved from Austria along the northern bank of the Danube, but it was frustrated by Max Emanuel. He defeated Count Styrum in the (first) battle of Höchstädt on September 20, 1703, before the latter could join forces with Margrave Ludwig. Then Max Emanuel was able to occupy the whole Danube line as far as Regensburg and Passau. The stage was set for a powerful offensive against Vienna. Louis XIV sent his main forces to Bavaria in 1704.

The situation of the allies was grave, nor was it greatly improved by the decision of Duke Victor Amadeus of Savoy to change sides. As the French strengthened their position in upper Italy, it dawned on him that he was becoming a mere underling of the French king. He renounced the French alliance, even though he knew he would not be able to count on allied help for a long time to come. On the other hand, the French army under Vendôme thereby was kept busy in Italy. In view of the supreme danger to Austria, Marlborough was persuaded to shift his Anglo-Dutch army from the Netherlands to Germany. John Churchill, Duke of Marlborough, was the real political heir of William III, but as a party head he was more dependent than the latter on parliamentary politics, and as a commoner, on the favor of the queen. This exuberant, highly educated, and ambitious statesman, who was at the same time a great military commander, thought in European terms. Neither in the Netherlands nor in England was the war in Germany popular. Belgium, Spain, and the colonies held the main interest. It was not an easy task for Marlborough to gain permission to take his Anglo-Dutch army into the heart of Germany. Such trusting co-operation as existed between Prince Eugene and Marlborough was rare in the history of combined warfare, which contains so much of disunity. The successes of the Grand Alliance were to a large extent due to the understanding between the two men. As Addison put it in the language of contemporary poetry:

> To souls like these in mutual friendship joined
> Heaven dares intrust the cause of human kind.

∽ Battle of Blenheim

IN A RAPID MARCH, keeping the French guessing about his ultimate objectives, Marlborough brought his army to southern Germany, where in the last week of June he started common action with Margrave Ludwig and Prince Eugene. The latter's attempt to keep a strong French army from crossing the Black Forest and joining the French-Bavarian army under Max Emanuel failed, but he himself was able to unite with Marlborough in time for the decisive battle of Blenheim on August 13, 1704 (called in Germany the [second] battle of Höchstädt). With a slight superiority on the French-Bavarian side, two armies, about 55,000 men, each fought at the Danube one of the most murderous battles of the new century. It was Marlborough's victory. Holding the chief command on that day, he recognized the tactical opportunity that made it possible to turn an initially discouraging battle into a full victory and led the final fight with the highest personal bravery. Prince Eugene, who commanded the right wing with his usual skill, gave Marlborough the best possible support. All troops—English, Dutch, Danish, and German—fought with great valor. The Hanover, Brunswick-Celle troops, and the Prussian corps under Prince Leopold of Anhalt-Dessau were singled out by the two commanders for special commendation. The victors suffered 12,000 casualties, while French and Bavarian losses were even greater; 13,000 men were taken prisoner, among them the French Marshal Tallard. This was the first great military defeat of Louis XIV, and it dealt a severe blow to the prestige of French arms.

The battle of Blenheim liberated all of Germany. The French retired behind the Rhine, and Elector Max Emanuel went to Brussels. On his way back to the Netherlands, Marlborough freed Trier and the Moselle valley. Bavaria came under Austrian administration, and the imperial commissars, in the ruthless fashion of the day, treated Bavaria like a conquered country and extracted heavy payments and deliveries. Peasants' revolts, which broke out in 1705, were suppressed with an iron fist. The Austrian occupation of Bavaria was looked upon with some misgivings among the German princes. It seemed like a prelude to annexation, and such a step could be regarded as the first in the revival of a centralistic policy by the emperor. Just then, in the dawn of the Austrian triumphs, Emperor Leopold died (May 5, 1705) and was succeeded by Joseph I (1705–11). The able and energetic young emperor had a high conception of the imperial dignity, which he intended to defend on a European plane and to reassert within the German Empire. He had already assisted in making Prince Eugene full director of military affairs. He remained devoted to him and also brought capable men to other posts.

With the approval of the electoral college, Elector Max Emanuel and his brother Joseph Clement were placed, in April 1706, under the high ban of the Empire and thereby deprived of their princely rank. It was the last time the declaration of the ban was executed with complete medieval ritual. But the annexation of Bavaria by Austria was not proclaimed. Only certain parts of the Bavarian state were severed from it. Austria took the "Inn quarters," Donauwörth was restored as an imperial city, other slices were given to neighboring bishoprics, and the Upper Palatinate was returned to the elector of the Palatinate. The future of Bavaria proper was left pending.

∽ *Treaty of Methuen*

ALL THE SUBSEQUENT MILITARY DECISIONS of the War of the Spanish Succession occurred outside Germany. Through the Treaty of Methuen of 1703 the English gained a strong foothold in Portugal. In 1704 they occupied Gibraltar permanently. With English assistance, Archduke Charles came to Spain and proclaimed himself King Charles III of Spain. But the Spaniards remained sullenly hostile to him, and though he twice entered Madrid briefly with Count Guido von Starhemberg's army, he could maintain himself only in Barcelona and Catalonia. Marlborough would have liked, in 1705, and again in 1706, to launch an offensive into interior France from the Upper Moselle, but Margrave Ludwig judged his forces ill-prepared for such a venture. The Netherlands urged the occupation of Belgium, and this the English commander achieved through his great victory over the French at Ramillies in May 1706. Most of the Spanish Netherlands was lost by the French and Max Emanuel, and fell to the Habsburgs. Charles III was now accepted as the new ruler.

The same year brought decisive events in Italy. With the help of substantial English loans, a strong imperial army was made ready. In a masterly maneuver, Prince Eugene led the army, to which large Hessian, Palatinate, Prussian, and Thuringian contingents had been added, from South Tyrol to Turin, the besieged capital of the duke of Savoy. Here, on September 7, 1706, within sight of the city, Prince Eugene defeated the main French army, which had followed him after failing to stop him in Lombardy. The victory brought about the evacuation of Italy by the French. Piedmont was restored to Duke Victor Amadeus and the Habsburg government established in Milan amid the applause of the populace. The English now insisted on the invasion of southern France, but Prince Eugene undertook this only reluctantly. French resistance in Provence was strong. The great naval base of Toulon, which constituted the real objective of England, proved unassailable from land and sea, and the whole project had to be abandoned. It was not without reason that the English suspected Emperor Joseph I of seeking primarily to bring all of Italy under his control. The best imperial troops were sent southward and, without meeting much opposition, occupied Naples in July, 1707. Pope Clement XI (1700–40) passionately opposed the revival of the imperial domination of Italy. In 1708 he mobilized troops, but he realized that he could only have provoked a new sack of Rome. Prussian regiments were quartered in the Church states, and Emperor Joseph refused to make concessions to the head of the Church. Thus Clement XI had to recognize the Habsburg supremacy in Italy.

Meanwhile things had gone rather badly along the Upper Rhine. In 1706 Margrave Ludwig with his weak Empire army was pushed back over the Rhine to the fortified defense lines at the slopes of the northern Black Forest. Ludwig retired from his command in the fall and died a few months later. He did not see the French breakthrough into Swabia in 1707, which threw the estates into a panic and made them readily pay all extortions. Fortunately, the French had to retreat to Alsace, but the Empire army had become unfit for any future offensive operations. Prince Eugene appeared, in 1708, with a strong army at the central Rhine. His plan was to invade Lorraine, while Marlborough advanced from Brabant. But Marlborough faced greatly superior forces and called for Eugene's help. Together they fought the battle of Oudenarde, in July, 1708, which not only made the Netherlands secure but also gave Lille, Louis XIV's most precious gain of the War of Devolution, into the hands of the allies.

The strong fortress seemed an ideal base for launching an offensive toward Paris. It had been increasingly difficult for the French government to find the funds and men with which to continue the war. But with desperate efforts Louis XIV succeeded in building a new army. At the same time he pressed for peace negotiations with new vigor. He had proposed negotiations since 1705, and at least in the Netherlands his suggestions had met with some response. In the spring of 1709 diplomatic conversations between the belligerents were held in The Hague. Louis XIV, deeply disheartened by the course of the war, went far in his offers. He was prepared to give up the whole Spanish inheritance, although he wanted Sicily and Naples left under his grandson; he was also ready to return Strasbourg and Alsace to Germany. But the allies were not satisfied. They demanded not only that Louis XIV urge Philip V to resign but also that he take part in driving Philip V out of Spain if the latter refused to give up the Spanish throne. In view of the attitude of the Spanish people, it was likely that Philip would refuse. Louis XIV could not accept such humiliating conditions.

The war was renewed. On September 11, 1709, at Malplaquet 100,000 allies fought 90,000 Frenchmen and forced them to retreat from the battlefield, though they retreated in good order. Marlborough and Prince Eugene had won only a Pyrrhic victory. The losses to their army were twice as large as those of the French, and the two leaders were still not in a position to carry the war into France. Again, in the spring and summer of 1710, the powers negotiated, this time at Gertruydenberg. Attitudes on both sides were little changed. Louis XIV offered to support an allied war against Philip V with subsidies but remained adamant in refusing military participation. Prince Eugene favored acceptance of a peace on these terms. But because of the influence of the Whigs, who found much advantage in the continuation of the war, the English rejected Louis's concessions as unsatisfactory. Thus the last opportunity for a return of Alsace to the Empire passed.

While diplomatic talks were still taking place, a great shift of power began in England. The Whig government was superseded by the Tories who had the active co-operation of Queen Anne; she finally dismissed Marlborough from all his offices. The Tories, representing the groups that contributed most to the cost of the war and profited least from it, were determined to conclude an early peace. After all, the Grand Alliance had not envisaged the grant of the whole Spanish inheritance to the Habsburg dynasty, but rather the creation of a balance of power on the Continent. The sudden death of Emperor Joseph I, in April, 1711, reinforced the need for a reappraisal of policy. Joseph I left only two daughters, and his brother Charles, at the time Charles III of Spain, became his successor. Was he to be given all the lands over which Charles V had ruled two centuries earlier? Charles III felt that this should be so, and when, very reluctantly, he departed from Barcelona, he left his beautiful and intelligent wife, Elizabeth Christina of Brunswick, the future mother of Empress Maria Theresa, as governor-general in Spain.

The new English government, however, conducted direct negotiations with France. In October, 1711, these led to an agreement on preliminary terms. The Spanish inheritance was to be divided. Philip V was to retain Spain and her colonies, but to renounce for himself and his descendants all claims to the French throne, while the French Bourbons were to give up their interests in the Spanish crown. Louis XIV accepted the English possession of Gibraltar and Minorca, the cession of Hudson Bay, Newfoundland, and Acadia in North America, and the dismantling of the fortifications of Dunkirk. These concessions established England's maritime position in the Mediterranean and the Atlantic, which was to be made lucrative by the grant of trading rights in both the New and Old Worlds. The disarmament of Dunkirk pacified the Channel frontier and enhanced the prospects of normal relations with France, which French recognition of the Hanover succession promised. England's allies protested the unilateral action of the British government, but the Netherlands soon dropped her opposition. She was anxious not to lose English support for her demand of a "barrier"—a line of Dutch-occupied fortresses along the Franco-Belgian frontier.

✍ *Peace Congress of Utrecht*

THE PEACE CONGRESS OF UTRECHT, which opened in January 1712, saw British and French diplomacy work together to isolate the emperor, now Charles VI, as the opponent of a settlement on the basis of a partition of the Spanish inheritance. The United Provinces were given the Spanish Netherlands, to be passed on to Charles VI after the emperor would agree to such limitations of his sovereignty as were required in setting up a Dutch "barrier" and the continued closing of the Scheldt to commerce. The British took special care to build up Duke Victor Amadeus of Piedmont-Savoy. Disregarding all Austrian titles, he was to succeed in Spain in the case of the death of the Spanish Bourbons. Meanwhile he was to receive the kingdom of Sicily. Prussia gained recognition as a kingdom by France and acquired Geldern (adjacent to Cleves) and the principality of Neufchâtel (between Switzerland and the Franche-Comté) out of the inheritance of William III of Orange.

The question of Bavaria was a major issue of controversy. Max Emanuel, like his brother Joseph Clement a refugee in France, aspired to a royal crown and wished to win chunks of the Spanish assets: the Netherlands, and possibly Sicily or Sardinia. In Vienna he offered to exchange Bavaria for the southern Netherlands, which he persuaded Philip V to cede to him. The Hague and London governments protested. They did not wish to get Belgium into the hands of a French satellite. Even the French did not like the project, since it would have strengthened the emperor's power in Germany. They wanted the full restoration of the elector in Bavaria. (He received, in addition, a promise on Sardinia, which the final treaty between the emperor and France did not repeat.) Austria succeeded, however, in having an article inserted in which the French king stated that he would not object if in the future the Bavarian elector exchanged his hereditary lands for others.

The decision not to annex Bavaria to Austria was of far-reaching consequences in German history, although the retrospective historian can define them only in a largely negative manner. The new Austrian empire which arose from the wars of the seventeenth century was no longer a predominantly German state. The acquisition of Transylvania, Hungary, Croatia, and a major part of Italy tended to make it a southern European state with a small German base. If Bavaria had been joined to Austria, the original German center of the monarchy would have been considerably strengthened, and even more important, Austria would have been closely tied to southern and western Germany. Through Bavaria, the outlying districts of Anterior Austria, particularly the Breisgau, would have been brought closer, and if in addition Alsace had come back to Germany, the emperor could have fulfilled his major national function—the defense of the exposed German boundaries—with greater hope of success. Assuming that Austria had retained such a position into the nineteenth century, a position which would have extended through southern Germany to the Upper Rhine, it is unlikely that Prussia could have driven her out of Germany.

Of course, these imaginary developments might not have taken place, even if Bavaria had become Austrian in 1714 or even sixty years later. The obstacles did not lie only in diplomatic circumstances. Like all German states, the Bavarian state was a dynastic one, but it was culturally and geographically a less artificial unit than even the original Germanic Austria, and with certain reservations this may be said of modern Bavaria as well. The absorption of Bavaria by Austria would not have been simple considering the popular antagonism between the two states, although it might still have been possible under the conditions of the eighteenth century. It is certain, however, that in the century and a half before Frederick II of Prussia the existence and preservation of a strong Bavaria was one of the major causes for a development which kept Austria at a certain distance from the rest of Germany.

For Emperor Charles VI, the Bavarian problem was less important than the Spanish inheritance as a whole, and he was even less inclined to make the recovery of Strasbourg and Alsace a prerequisite of peace. The Alsatian matter was left almost entirely to the German estates, which meant to the Swabian, Franconian, and the two Rhenish circles of the Empire. English policy in 1711–12 had still envisaged the restoration of Franco-German boundaries as defined in the Peace of Westphalia, but as England moved closer to France, and the French government, in order to strengthen the entente, proved rather accommodating in colonial questions, the German problems appeared of little significance. As Leopold von Ranke has expressed it, Newfoundland and St. Christopher were used to make up for Strasbourg. In vain did the German circles appeal to Queen Anne in a language that was often thereafter to be employed by disappointed Continental allies of England, to observe public and solemn assurances, "the sacred royal word," and "the sacred faith in the great seal of the kingdom so that it would not rest in the archive a sad memory." They pointed out proudly that they had fought the war without receiving subsidies. Unhappily, however, they had not been able to win any of the Alsatian places which they had hoped the peace would restore to Germany, and they could not well expect that the English government would care more about the Empire than the emperor. Thus the Ryswick settlement was reaffirmed.

∽ Peace of Utrecht

IN APRIL, 1713, THE PEACE OF UTRECHT was signed by England, France, the Netherlands, Savoy, and Prussia, but the emperor and the Empire refused to accede, largely on account of the provocative attitude which France assumed in her dealings with the emperor. Against the advice of Prince Eugene, the war of the emperor and the Empire against France continued. The emperor's chance of success might not have been so small if the large armed estates—particularly Prussia, Saxony, and Hanover—had joined in the campaign. But all of them were now involved in the northern crisis which Charles XII of Sweden had brought on. Moreover, the Dutch and English subsidies were no longer available. Prince Eugene led an army which, aside from good imperial forces, consisted only of auxiliaries, chiefly from southern Germany, and could merely attempt to shield Swabia and Franconia from a new French invasion. He was not able to keep the French from gaining successes on both banks of the Upper Rhine. They conquered Landau and subsequently Freiburg. It was fortunate also that Louis XIV had lost heart for the continuation of the war. The two commanders, Prince Eugene and Marshal Villars, were entrusted with the discussion of peace, which they held in the palace of the late Margrave Ludwig of Baden in Rastatt. On March 6, 1714, the Peace of Rastatt was signed by the emperor and Louis XIV. Prince Eugene achieved some minor improvements of the Utrecht settlement. On the other hand, Landau had to be left with France over and above the provisions of Utrecht and Ryswick. A special conference was held during the summer of 1714 to arrange peace between the Empire and France. Three months of negotiations produced, in September, 1714, the Treaty of Baden, which was identical with the Peace of Rastatt.

✑ *Nordic War*

EVEN AFTER THE PEACE TREATIES of Utrecht, Rastatt, and Baden, war was not entirely banned from Germany. Since 1700, the Baltic world had been aflame. Amazingly enough, unlike the War of the Spanish Succession, the Baltic conflicts had not merged into a world-wide struggle. A few times they had exercised an influence on the diplomacy of the larger war, but the impact of the northern hostilities had been felt most painfully in northeastern Germany. The Nordic War had its origin in the internal tensions of the Swedish empire. The earlier campaigns of 1675–79 had shown the serious weakness of Swedish imperial policies. A country so limited in its manpower and economic resources was actually incapable of maintaining an extended international position by its own strength. French funds and exactions from the occupied and invaded countries had carried Sweden through the half-century after 1630. Even then, Sweden had become increasingly dependent on the political assistance of France and had eaten deeper and deeper into her own internal reserves. The crown domains had largely fallen into the hands of the nobility. When King Charles XI (1660–97), attempted to restore them to royal control by drastic means, he was successful in most of his lands; in Livonia, however, the nobility revolted under Patkul, who continued his opposition from Poland even after being driven out of Livonia.

Sweden's deep social feuds, which Charles XI left to his fifteen-year-old successor Charles XII (1697–1718), were an encouragement to all those neighbors who had old scores to settle or novel ambitions to pursue. Denmark, Poland, and Russia joined in attacking the Swedish power. The Swedish possessions in Germany—Bremen, Verden, and West Pomerania—linked up Germany with the new conflict. Denmark, in addition to her foreign objectives, wanted to suppress the connivance between the younger line of the dukes of Holstein-Gottorp and Sweden. Poland and Saxony were dynastically united through August II. The Nordic War could not fail to affect Germany, and for the first time in history Russian power was brought to Germany by the alliance, made in 1699, between August II and Peter the Great.

When, in the spring of 1700, the war began with a rather unsuccessful offensive by King Augustus against Livonia, followed a few weeks later by a coercive move of the Danish king against the Gottorp duke, Charles XII was able to throw himself upon Denmark and force her to give up her alliance. The Livonian nobility became frightened and submitted to the Swedish king. Then Charles XII met a Russian attack on Estonia. With a small Swedish army he annihilated the vastly larger Russian army at Narva in November, 1700. The next years Charles XII devoted to the conquest of Poland. In the summer of 1702 he beat the Saxon-Polish army. In 1704, he had a Polish magnate, Stanislav Leszczyński, proclaimed king of Poland. In February, 1706, he defeated the last Saxon-Polish army decisively at Fraustadt and, violating imperial territory on his march, occupied Saxony and forced August II to accept the Peace of Altranstädt in September 1706. August the Strong abdicated in Poland and gave up the Russian alliance. Charles XII, who despised the licentious ruler and regarded him as a traitor to his faith, made the elector sign promises with regard to the rights of the Lutheran Church in Germany.

Inscrutable as to his further intentions, Charles stayed for a year in Saxony. Austria had every reason to feel uneasy. Denuded of troops and still troubled by the Rakoczy revolution in Hungary, Austria could have suffered untold damage from a Swedish attack. It was in the summer of 1701 that the French had successfully broken into Swabia. French diplomacy worked hard to bring about a renewal of the Franco-Swedish alliance, while the maritime powers did their utmost to smooth Swedish-Austrian relations. Charles XII turned down all French temptations. He was deeply resentful of the brutal extermination of the Huguenots by Louis XIV. On the other hand, he was pleased to act, as his great ancestor had done, as the protector of German Protestantism against the emperor. With Marlborough's prodding, the emperor promised to respect the rights which the Peace of Westphalia had granted the Protestants in Silesia. He even had to accept a mixed Swedish-Austrian commission to supervise the execution of this Swedish-Austrian convention of Altranstädt.

At the end of the year 1707, Charles XII left Saxony and marched east to fight Czar Peter. The years after Narva were the period in which Peter had laid the foundation for Russia's military power, which enabled the Czarist empire to intervene in the fate of Europe. The humiliation of Narva had evoked the whole strength of Peter's genius. A new Russian army was created, still largely staffed with foreign officers. In 1702–03 Peter the Great conquered Ingermanland, where he founded St. Petersburg, and in the following years he extended his conquests to Estonia, Livonia, and Courland. He would have made peace with Sweden if Charles XII had given him Ingermanland, but Charles felt confident that he could dispose of the new Russia altogether. The attempt to invade the center of Russia turned out to be his undoing. In 1708, he moved in the direction of Moscow, while his enemy evaded him. After a winter of hardships, Charles XII tried to win additional strength by uniting with the Cossack forces in the Ukraine. Here Peter annihilated his army in the battle of Poltava of July, 1709. Charles XII fled into Turkey, where, in the next years, he worked doggedly and vainly to establish a Turko-Swedish alliance against Russia. In 1711, the Turks opened war against Russia but were easily bought off with the cession of the recently acquired Azov. Peter the Great was not deflected from his Baltic objectives.

The catastrophe of Poltava was the signal for a renewal of the alliance among Saxony, Denmark, and Russia. August II renounced the Peace of Altranstädt and again made himself master of Poland, while Peter the Great extended his conquests of the Baltic coastlands. An attempt by the maritime powers to neutralize the German territories of Sweden failed. In the late summer of 1711, an army of Russian, Saxon, and Polish troops marched through Prussian territory to Mecklenburg to begin the siege of Wismar and Stralsund. Denmark was ready to try the occupation of the territory of Bremen. War seemed to engulf most of northern Germany.

Modern Prussian historians have found much fault with the policy of Frederick I of Prussia in the years after 1700. Johann Gustav Droysen has spoken of him as having conducted "war without a policy" in the West and "policies without war" in the East. It is true that Frederick's policy lacked great aims and was largely determined by his reliance on Western subsidies, which became more pronounced on account of the mismanagement of Prussia's own financial resources. But his policy was sound. His steady support of the Grand Alliance was a significant contribution to the successful conclusion of the War of the Spanish Succession, which freed Germany, including Prussia, from the dictatorial pressure of France. Leopold von Ranke correctly judged that only now an independent development of Brandenburg-

Prussia became possible. Apart from his royal dignity, Frederick I also gained important pieces of the Orange inheritance.

It is difficult to see what Frederick could have gained if he had recalled his army and entered the Nordic War. Whether he would have entered the war on the side of Charles XII or August II, neither of these rulers could have afforded to give him the land bridge connecting East Pomerania and East Prussia. An alliance against Sweden for the acquisition of Swedish Pomerania could at best be considered after Poltava. During all these years Prussian policy in the East was nervously scouting around. When Charles XII had conquered Poland, bringing the Prussian army back to Brandenburg seemed unavoidable. Marlborough came to Berlin twice, in 1704–05, to persuade Frederick to leave his troops with Prince Eugene. On the whole, Frederick felt that his state was still too weak to conduct a foreign policy all his own, and the risks involved in co-operation with Russia seemed unpredictable. Thus Prussia continued in her policy of neutrality in the north until the death of Frederick I, in February, 1713. His son, Frederick William I, was equally eager to keep the state out of the war. But the return of the battle-proved Prussian army after the Peace of Utrecht gave Prussia a much stronger position. While Charles XII was still in Turkey, Swedish circles had intimated that Stettin should be occupied by Prussia, and Peter the Great seemed willing to agree. Stettin, once won in strenuous fighting by the Great Elector only to be lost at the command of Louis XIV, was now offered to Prussia by both Sweden and Russia.

Owing to the resistance of the Swedish commander, Stettin had to be made to capitulate by Russian arms, but it was turned over to Frederick William I for safekeeping in exchange for Prussian payment of the war cost. The Prussian king, who was scrupulous about law, did not annex Stettin. His immediate aim was to keep all of Pomerania from becoming a battlefield or base of warfare. But he soon discovered that he might have to fight. Therefore, in the summer of 1714, he concluded a secret treaty with Peter—the first political treaty between Prussia and Russia—in which he declared his approval of the Russian annexation of Ingermanland, Karelia, and Estonia, in exchange for the Prussian acquisition of Stettin and the southern part of West Pomerania. Charles XII's return, at the end of 1714, and his attempt to reopen hostilities from West Pomerania, led to full Prussian participation in the war. Stralsund was besieged and Swedish resistance broken, though Charles XII escaped from the city. Thereafter Russia and Denmark continued hositilities against Sweden. In the course of these operations, large Russian forces were amassed in both Denmark and Mecklenburg. Russian expansion aroused misgivings in the West, particularly in England, which feared for her access to the Baltic. During the following years, Prussia's relations with the czar proved a source of discomfort for Frederick William I.

✎ *Settlement of the War*

IT WAS ENGLAND WHICH HAD the decisive voice in the Nordic settlement, as in the Peace of Utrecht. The union of Hanover and England under George I was reflected in England's support for Hanover's anti-Swedish and anti-Danish policies in northwestern Germany. In 1712, Hanover had occupied Verden and, in 1715, secured the former bishopric of Bremen in a treaty with Denmark. Access to the estuaries of the Weser and Elbe was a major interest of English commerce. The new connection between England and Hanover was beneficial for Hamburg, too. Henceforth the Elbe emporium was protected against serious interference from either Denmark or Sweden. But a general peace was delayed by controversies among the victors. Even the death of Charles XII, in 1718, which led to the collapse of royal absolutism in Sweden, did not bring an immediate end to the war. But in November, 1719, Hanover and Sweden came to terms. In return for the payment of one million thaler, Hanover kept Bremen and Verden. Prussia had to pay twice that amount, when, in February, 1720, Sweden ceded her Stettin and West Pomerania to the Peene River. In 1720, treaties with Sweden, essentially on the basis of the *status quo ante*, were concluded by Poland and Denmark. Finally, on September 10, 1721, peace was signed between Russia and Sweden at Nystadt in Finland. Russia received Ingermanland, Estonia, Livonia, and parts of Karelia.

✎ *New Order of Europe*

IN THE THREE-QUARTERS OF A CENTURY following the Peace of Westphalia a new political Europe had come into existence. The rise of England as the foremost world power was the greatest positive result; the collapse of the European influence of Spain and Sweden were the most obvious negative consequences. France was still the strongest nation on the Continent and the only one that could dare challenge

the maritime power of England. But France could no longer co-
operate with the Turks or Swedes and did not have enough strength
of her own to renew the struggle of Louis XIV for European supremacy. In the new Austrian empire, a state had arisen which, on
account of its composite character, was a more artificial creation than
the nationally homogeneous France but which served as a stabilizing
force of high order in Central Europe. The predominance of England
in the eighteenth century did not lead to attempts to control the Continent directly, as had been the case with Charles V, Philip II, and
Louis XIV. The insular nation was concerned with its overseas commerce and expansion. England, therefore, was content with manipu-
lating the political affairs of the Continent only so far as was necessary
to prevent the growth of a Continental power or coalition which
would be capable of depriving Britannia of her trident. In specific
terms, all through the century and beyond, this meant conflict with
France. Undoubtedly, Anglo-French antagonism often involved individual European states in controversies which were not germane to
their own life, but Europe could breathe more easily than in the centuries of Spanish and French preponderance.

An altogether novel event in European history was the appearance
of Russia almost at the precise moment when the Turks retreated from
the interior of Europe. The Turks had always been foreigners in
Europe. Except for the adoption of some elements of military art,
they did not take from the West ideas and institutions which might
have led to cultural exchange. Unable to reform its civilization by its
own strength, the Ottoman Empire stagnated and slowly decayed. In
contrast, the Russian "invasion" of Europe from its very beginning
was sparked by the desire to transform the Russian realities through
the acceptance and application of Western ideas. The westward turn
of Russian policy did not bring a reconciliation of Russian and Western
Christianity, which were separated by the difference in Church-state
relationship even more than by doctrines and ritual. What Peter the
Great imported from Europe were Western military and naval institutions, technology, manufacture, commerce, and last but not least,
rational forms of political administration. The technical equipment
which European absolutism and mercantilism had developed was transplanted to the soil of oriental despotism. A large number of Germans
took part in the westernization of Muscovy during the seventeenth and
eighteenth centuries. The marriage of Russian grand dukes and German princesses, as well as the entry of many Baltic-German noblemen

into Russian government service, increased this German influence.

Other Europeans were also admitted, and there seemed to be more hope than in Turkey that the country could become civilized along European patterns. In addition, every European power was eager to use the strength of the czardom for advancing its own objectives. Unfortunate Poland under August II allied herself with Russia against Sweden only to find herself thereafter facing a threatening Russia as eastern neighbor. The other eastern states—Prussia, Denmark, and Austria—did not hesitate to enter into alliances with Russia. Since the old European powers never managed to practice solidarity vis-à-vis the newcomer, Russia was able to edge forward into Europe. England was originally alarmed by the sudden westward thrust of Russia; but after her merchants had established commercial relations with Russia, apprehensions calmed down. After the death of Peter the Great, in 1725, and repeated internal crises, the Russian problem assumed smaller proportions. Frederick the Great could still consider it possible that the Russian empire might collapse someday as suddenly as it had arisen. This was an idle expectation, but for a generation or two Russia proved to be a great power which did not overstep the bounds considered proper in the community of European states.

German soldiers had fought in all the wars between 1660 and 1720, but the Empire played an insignificant part in the peace settlements. Not even the emperor had been able to make his will prevail in the councils of Europe. Alsace was definitely lost for Germany. On the other hand, the removal of Sweden from Bremen, Verden, and Stettin brought the mouths of the three main rivers again under full German control. That Sweden still retained the port of Wismar in Mecklenburg and the northern part of West Pomerania with the island of Rügen, was almost more of an anachronism than a serious imposition. On the whole, Germany gained by the relative stabilization of the European balance of power. All around Germany the sky showed fewer clouds. Even within the country, the party spirit had become less acrimonious, and in the Palantinate War and the War of the Spanish Succession, in spite of Bavaria and Cologne, the co-operation of the emperor and the estates had reached a level higher than any seen for a long time. The Austro-Prussian alliance, particularly, had proved its high value, not only in foreign battles but also in the internal life of Germany. If this collaboration between the emperor and the armed estates should break down in the future, there would result both internal war and a new intervention of the great powers.

CHAPTER 6

Religious, Intellectual, and Artistic Life in the Age of the Baroque

✍ Effects of the Thirty Years' War on German Civilization

THE SEVENTEENTH CENTURY was one of the greatest centuries in the cultural history of Spain, France, the Netherlands, and England. German civilization, on the other hand, offered a dismal appearance. It has often been said that the Thirty Years' War annihilated German civilization altogether, so that it had to be rebuilt from the bottom thereafter. But this is not true. All through the second half of the sixteenth century the cultural productivity of Germany had declined. Individual signs of new life came to the fore after the turn of the century and could be noticed even in the early years of the war. It is possible, though not demonstrable, that the war cut short an incipient cultural revival. In any event, though the half century 1630–80 showed few and sparsely dotted cultural landmarks, cultural life did not disappear. The mass of the people held on to the religious, moral, and intellectual substance of the past as best they could and tried to interpret their new experiences in the light of existing theory.

The common people, the average peasant and burgher, suffered the cruel hardships of the war with amazing stolidity and an unshakable faith in the metaphysical order of the world. The horrors which they experienced drove many to insanity and brought others down to the level of beasts. But to most of a generation which had been nurtured in the belief that this is an evil world, even great catastrophes assumed a logical character. Resignation to God's will was the prerequisite to salvation, and that meant entry into the life of true goodness. To be sure, the war did not produce high religious enthusiasm, but it demonstrated great loyalty to the existing churches in which Catholic priests and Lutheran ministers set shining examples. With the end of the war, the orthodox church leaders did not find it difficult to restore respect for the traditional religious concepts and morals, although the physical rebuilding of the church organization and the training of properly educated pastors took considerable time. But the century after 1648 saw the full restoration of the prewar forms of ecclesiastical life, at least in outward appearances.

If one probes deeper, new problems and trends can be discovered. The individual who had gone through the terrifying experiences of the war had developed an insatiable hunger for life and demanded greater opportunities for self-expression and self-satisfaction. Only princes and noblemen could give free vent to these desires, while for a long time to come the common man had to be satisfied with the vicarious pleasure derived from watching the glamorous life of the courts and the noblemen. In the highest classes of society, however, a great deal of skepticism about the truth of traditional religion had crept in as a result of the war which led to a secular opportunism in thought and action.

∽ State and Church

THE CHURCHES WERE NO LONGER in a position to curb the worldly life of the courts and the ruling classes. The state had assumed control over the churches and identified itself with them only insofar as it suited its own interests. This development began at the time when the Protestant reform movement had caused chaos among ecclesiastical institutions. Luther had called for the intervention of the state to save the essence of Protestant faith, while the Catholic Church had demanded the active help of the state in order to exterminate the heretics. The existence of the churches which emerged from the Thirty Years' War was largely the work of the states—states of enormously increased strength. These were no longer the feudal states with which the medieval papacy had clashed. Then the more highly rational organization of the Church had been vastly superior to the loose organization of medieval monarchy. Now the states, after suppressing the divisive forces within, exercised command over the moral energies of the peoples and were able to impose their will through their armies and bureaucracies. Moreover, the churches derived their newly won safety from the devotion of these Christian princes, who continued to strengthen the Christian symbolic character of the community. It was well-nigh unthinkable that the churches would desire to reassert their superiority over the state or would have any success if they did so. Religion found itself surrounded by new pressures.

The Peace of Westphalia had separated Protestants and Catholics as far as possible along territorial lines. As the religious system of Westphalia was consummated, it dug deep ditches and built high walls in the German cultural landscape. It is not surprising, for example, that the solid Protestant northeast came to differ sharply from Catholic Bavaria. But this differentiation also occurred between such closely related territories as Lower and Upper Silesia. Although for a complete description each individual Catholic and Protestant part of Germany would have to be treated separately, we must be content with showing the general characteristics of Catholic and Protestant Germany. Of all countries, Austria gained the highest degree of religious unity. She dispensed even with those concessions which the Westphalian Peace had made for certain Protestants in Catholic territories, until Charles XII made the Austrian government conform with them at least in the Silesian principalities.[1] Externally, the Catholic Counter Reformation was a complete success. Shortly after the war, visitors in Vienna were already impressed with the flourishing church life of the city. Worshippers were numerous. The old orders, such as the Benedictines, the Augustinian canons and the Premonstratensians, had been fully revived, often with the assistance of South Germans. New orders, such as the Piarists (*patres piarum scholarum*), undertook to develop the schools side by side with the Jesuits. However, the latter, at least during the whole reign of the devout Emperor Leopold I, remained the dominant order at the court, in the Church, and in the field of education.

✑ Catholicism in the Century after 1648

THE JESUITS WERE the chief ecclesiastical builders of the close marriage of Church and state. The government supervised the religion of its subjects and promoted the acceptance of new doctrines. Attendance at mass and fast-keeping were enforced; policemen were sent to St. Stephen's Cathedral to suppress "loud clatter"; every candidate for a degree had to swear his belief in the Immaculate Conception. Government officials set an example by leading processions and pilgrimages and church occasions were treated like state celebrations. Small wonder

[1] Cf. p. 117.

that heaven seemed a distant, majestic court. The popular, humane traits of Jesus or the Virgin were submerged in their positions as rulers of heaven.

This courtly religion was not given to either deep mystic or philosophical inwardness. No Pascal or Bossuet arose in Austria. The Jansenist movement, which had its origin largely in the Spanish-Austrian Netherlands, had an influence on Austria only at a very late stage, under Maria Theresa, and then through its theory of state-Church relations rather than through its central religious teachings. After such a long period of controversy and governmental guardianship, religious doctrines awakened only mild interest. The theology taught was the Spanish-Jesuit scholasticism, with its emphasis on logical technique rather than systematic knowledge. Only the Benedictine University of Salzburg cultivated a pure Thomism.

Religious life centered around the adoration of the supernatural that was present in the Church and accessible to the faithful who fulfilled the commandments of the Church. It called for dynamic, moralistic preachers. These were not lacking. The greatest among them was Ulrich Megerle, better known under his monastic name, Abraham a Sancta Clara (1644–1709). He came from the southern Black Forest to Vienna in 1662, and as Augustinian pulpit orator stirred up all of Vienna with an imaginative language and logic which overcame the buffooneries common in this age. The efficacy of the Christian sacraments, of Christian practices and consolations, was not a matter of much reflection but chiefly the subject of ever renewed admiration. The presentation of the glorious events of the Church year could not be dramatic and colorful enough to satisfy and lift up the senses. Here the Jesuit tendency toward the visual and sensual realization of divine history and the popular desire for actual religious participation were blended.

In this religion there was little room for deep conflict. Though the world was seen as the place of God's punishing justice, it tended to be understood as a world in which it was a delight to live. Thus even from the Christian point of view an optimistic philosophy of life developed which, in the latter half of the eighteenth century, merged with the secular optimism of the Enlightenment. Still another of the fundamental tenets of the Enlightenment had its psychological origin in this religion. In contrast to Protestant theologians, Jesuits stressed human freedom or at least the relative autonomy of human thought and action, a position close to that of philosophies which emphasized human reason and ethical freedom in contrast to divine omnipotence.

But this was a late development in Austrian or German Catholicism, which for almost a whole century after 1648 closed itself to novel intellectual influences. Originally, it faced new problems on an exclusively political level. The symbiosis of ecclesiastical and governmental values which characterized the half-century of the regime of Leopold I was challenged not by internal forces but by the deterioration of relations with the papacy. The Vatican's support of Louis XIV after Pope Innocent XI's death caused grave misgivings in Vienna. Under Emperor Joseph I, there was a recrudescence of the papal-imperial conflict reminiscent of the Middle Ages. Pope Clement XI reacted to the Austrian occupation of Italy with the papal ban and interdict, while in Vienna the establishment of a German patriarchate was considered. Under the staid and pious Emperor Charles VI, relations with Rome did not improve very much. When, in 1728, the pope extended the celebration of the sanctification of Pope Gregory VII to the whole Church, the Austrian government expressed its disgust, which was caused in particular by the pope's treatment of Henry IV's deposition. The imperial vice-chancellor Count Frederick Karl von Schönborn, who, a year later, became Bishop of Würzburg and Bamberg, spoke of these "poisonous" statements and principles that were "highly detrimental to the authority of the Emperor." The imperial attitude toward the Roman Church was practically undistinguishable from Gallicanism.

Still, the gate was not easily opened to the principles of Enlightenment. The councils of Joseph I and Charles VI showed great interest in the reconciliation of Protestant and Catholic faith. Prince Eugene was a warm admirer of Leibniz. But this concern was most closely connected with the projects for the renewal of the greatness of the imperial office and had no practical results in the ecclesiastical policies of the state. Religious uniformity was enforced in the Austrian lands even at a time when it had proved impossible to effect in other parts of the Habsburg Empire. In Hungary, the Evangelicals were definitely given religious freedom in 1691, and even an independent Greek Orthodox Church was tolerated. But as late as the 1730's Protestants were expelled from Upper Austria and Styria, although, unlike the Archbishop of Salzburg, Austrian mercantilists took care not to lose people: the Austrian Protestants were moved as colonists to Transylvania. Maria Theresa, no less than her father, was convinced of the necessity of orthodox uniformity, but events after the middle of the eighteenth century induced her to adopt new policies. In one respect, the assertion of the power of the state, these policies were the projection of older practices; but in content they reflected the victory of Enlightenment in the old Church.

The history of Austrian Catholicism in the century after 1648 may be considered broadly representative of the history of German Catholicism in general. The exclusive privileges which the Austrian Church enjoyed after the Peace of Westphalia did not lead to a separation of the Austrian Church from that of the Empire. On the contrary, the personal and religious ties between the Churches were extremely close. Germans from the Empire were constantly adopted by Austria and were advanced to positions of hierarchical and intellectual leadership. On the other hand, German bishops and theologians looked at the Austrian Church, more than in any other period, as the center of German Catholicism.

✌ Protestantism in the Century after 1648

GERMAN PROTESTANTISM and Catholicism of the age had one thing in common: the dominant position of the state in church affairs. On the whole the role of the state was even greater in Protestant than in Catholic states, and, at least in official Protestant theory, this was expressed with unreserved radicalism. After the Peace of Westphalia the authority of the individual prince was considered merely the effluence of his power as territorial prince. As a matter of fact, ecclesiastical responsibilities tended to be treated as merely a part of the general governmental functions. As late as the end of the Thirty Years' War princes and city councils still believed that the care for the spiritual welfare of their subjects was the chief duty of any Christian government. The restoration of church institutions was a major part of all state activities in the second half of the seventeenth century. Among the steps taken was the revival of the universities, which had had few students during the war and, in many cases, had practically ceased their educational work. But it was equally necessary to assist in the physical rebuilding of rectories and the living conditions of the clergy. It took the longest time to improve the lot of the large number of those ministers who depended for their sustenance on the *Junkers* as patrons of village churches. In general, the career of the average graduates of the theological faculties remained dependent on social conditions. Normally they had to wait for appointment as private tutors of the children of noble families or as teachers of the city schools, and many never got beyond subordinate teaching positions. Small wonder that they constituted a politically submissive group in society.

The interest of the governments, however, was not confined to the outward restoration of church institutions but was also directed towards the internal life of the churches. Visitations for looking into not only the state of the ministers but also the religious attitudes of the congregations were prevalent in Protestant territories. Knowledge of the catechism, attendance of church services and confessional, with the possible exception of the nobility, was practically everywhere enforced. But this enforcement of church obligations by the state governments stifled the growth of personal religion. It also interfered with the development of a trusting relationship between the individual layman and minister, since the latter appeared as a person of authority, practically just another governmental official, who could not easily be made a full intimate of the innermost concerns of individual church members.

❧ The Age of Orthodoxy

UNDER THESE CONDITIONS Lutheran orthodoxy revived. The second half of the seventeenth century may be more accurately called the age of orthodoxy than the century after 1555. The old conflict between Lutherans and Reformed Protestants continued with undiminished vigor throughout the Thirty Years' War. A voice like that of the Augsburg theologian, Rupertus Meldenius, was seldom heard. In 1626, he had described the misfortunes of the Evangelicals as caused by the ambitions of their theologians and recommended for their cure: "*In necessariis unitatem, in non-necessariis libertatem, in utrisque charitatem.*" (In necessary matters unity, in nonnecessary matters liberty, in both charity.) An exception was provided by George Calixt of Helmstädt (1586–1656) and his school. Calixt was a good Lutheran with a deep belief in the eternity of the Christian Church. He admonished his contemporaries that what had formed the basis of Christian faith in the first five centuries of Christian history ought to be considered adequate and basic for salvation, while all teachings going beyond the *consensus quinquesaecularis*, such as those concerned with the papal monarchy or the subject of predestination or the Lord's Supper, which were controversial among the Protestants, ought to be treated as human inventions. Although Calixt declared himself a faithful believer in practically the whole body of orthodox Lutheran doctrines and only demanded toleration for certain deviations, he was furiously attacked by the leaders of Lutheran orthodoxy. Abraham Calov (1612–86; since 1650 in Wittenberg) and Johann Hülsemann (1629–46 in Wittenberg, thereafter, until 1661, in Leipzig) carried Protestant polemics to their lowest level in these so-called "syncretistic" struggles.

The endeavors of Calixt for greater harmony had no visible results among theologians. Among Protestant laymen they seemed on balance rather to evoke a critical attitude toward the Protestant churches. A fair number of Calixtians ended as converts to the Roman Church. With dogged passion, however, the orthodox Lutheran theologians made the defense and diffusion of pure doctrine the supreme task of the universities. The "professor of controversies" became more important than the professor of biblical theology, and religion almost became identified with doctrine. In order to exclude subjective mysticism, the thesis of the divine inspiration of the Scripture was carried to extremes. Not only the general content but also the individual words were declared to have been formulated by the Holy Spirit, and the Bible was made the exclusive source of revelation as well as the only channel of communication with the divine. The theological interpretation of the Bible, was, of course, clearly established by Lutheran tradition, especially as it was embodied in the "formula of concord." But traditional teachings had to be explained and defended against modern opinion by philosophical arguments.

ᐧ Protestant Scholasticism

FROM THE BEGINNING OF THE seventeenth century Lutheran theology increasingly used the methods of scholasticism. Therefore, this period of Lutheran orthodoxy has often been called the age of Protestant scholasticism. But it should not be overlooked that then, as before, the scope of Lutheran theology was not as wide as that attained by medieval scholasticism. The latter, with the help of ancient philosophy, had built a universal system of knowledge in which the unity of reason and revelation was demonstrated, while at the same time the profundity of religion was fathomed through philosophical speculation and the full knowledge of a world related to the divine order of the universe.

Lutheran theology never intended to create a system of natural knowledge and bring it into a synthesis with religion. The first Lutheran theological text book, Melanchthon's *Loci* (Topics), set forth the chief points of Luther's faith on the basis of Luther's interpretation of St. Paul's *Letter to the Romans*. In subsequent editions, Melanchthon expanded the range of humanistic scholarship to be used for the further understanding and illustration of biblical wisdom. A large amount of practical and nontheological material found its way into the theological handbooks, but it was never intended to create an all-embracing philosophical system of knowledge.

For over a century and a half, the most widely studied handbook was the one by the Wittenberg professor Leonhard Hutterus (1563–1616), first published in 1610 (*Compendium locorum theologicorum*). It contains already much patristic and scholastic documentation and uses Aristotelian logic and dialectic for the refutation of Catholic and Calvinist doctrines. Hutterus' learned colleague in Jena, Johann Gerhard (1582–1637), went much further in this respect. He introduced Aristotle's *Metaphysics* into Protestant theology and thereby stimulated an intensive study not only of medieval but also of modern Jesuit scholasticism. Scholastic methods were employed for the strengthening of Lutheran convictions. Luther was eagerly read. On the eve of the Thirty Years' War Friedrich Hortleder (1579–1640)[2] began to write his extensive *History of the Schmalkaldic War*, while at the end of the century Veit Ludwig von Seckendorf's *History of Lutheranism* appeared. In 1661–64 the so-called Altenburg edition of Luther's works was published by Sagittarius. Most systematic treatments of theology thereafter contained a chapter entitled "On Luther's Vocation," showing the internal and external conditions of Luther's religious reform.

Lutheran orthodoxy of the seventeenth century was by no means inactive or thoughtless. It represented wide learning and earnest devotion. But it tended to be pedestrian and easily satisfied with the mere growth of its schoolbag. In general, the great majority of the orthodox divines conceived of the Church as little more than a teaching institution of limited scope. The teaching of the ministers was confined to the private life of the individual, and no new efforts were made to deal with the new political problems of the age. Johann Valentin Andreae's *Christianopolis* (1619), a Swabian version of Campanella's *City of Sun*, was a mere utopia and found its ultimate ideal in education. Secken-

[2] See p. 11.

dorf's *Christian State* (1685) was an edifying description of Christian patriarchism. The discussion of political philosophy and ethics became the domain of philosophers and jurists. Protestant theologians met political problems either by finding easy justifications for any action by an established government or by disregarding politics altogether. Not only was active participation of the Church in the molding of human society minimized but also certain traditional religious functions were neglected. The view of the Church as a community of Christian brethren who become brethren in the common experience of God's grace and express this common faith through social action, remained largely dormant in the age of orthodoxy.

The Protestant theologians of this period did not fail to stress the Lutheran conception of the sinful nature of man, who could not claim salvation by any merit of his own but only receive it as a gift from God. It was now emphasized that the justification of the individual must lead to good works not because of a presumed righteousness of man but on account of the urging of Christ with whom the faithful enters into a mystic union. Proper preparation for the act of justification by repentance was equally promoted. In Württemberg, Thuringia, and Mecklenburg these tendencies were most pronounced. Johann Valentin Andreae (1586–1654), as leading minister of Württemberg, developed a fruitful activity in the reform of the clergy and of congregational life. In Thuringia, besides the circle around Duke Ernest the Pious of Gotha, it was Johann Matthaeus Mayfart (1590–1642) who showed the way to a deeper personal appreciation of religion. But the most lively center of such reform throughout the seventeenth century was the University of Rostock. Its most influential representative was Theophil Grossgebauer (1627–61), who also brought a good many Puritan ideas to Germany.

Yet all endeavors to transform what was called a "fictitious faith" into a "faith of the heart" were not able fully to overcome some of the difficulties of Luther's religion, difficulties which were greatly enhanced by the domination of the Church by the state. It was not necessary to go so far as Liselotte, the Palatine princess who became the Duchess of Orléans. Quite innocently, she confessed that she could not assign much influence to the human will, otherwise one would have to feel sorry about one's own decisions in life. The temptation to accept Christian doctrine as a comforting message, while acting only intermittently in full accordance with it or even postponing the reconciliation with

God to the last moment, was very great and formed a continuous cause for complaint by the pastors. Without forgetting their responsibility for narrowing down religion so much to mere correct teaching, we must judge that the intensification of congregational life at that time would have called for the exercise of control over the daily conduct of the church membership through ecclesiastical bodies. The governments refused to surrender the authority over Christian discipline to the ministers, let alone to agencies composed of pastors and laymen. But inevitably the supervision of the inner life of the congregations by the state was bound to be legalistic, formalistic, and bare of Christian charity.

Perhaps a more friendly attitude could be found in the exertions of Protestant rulers to calm the theological feuds of their orthodox ministers, though the assertion of monarchical sovereignty in spiritual controversies was not an unmixed blessing. The Great Elector went farthest in this direction. Among all the German princes of his generation he was most deeply and genuinely concerned with the unity of the Protestant denominations as a prerequisite for the common survival of Protestantism in Europe. As a Calvinist ruler of such arch-Lutheran territories as Brandenburg, East Pomerania, and Prussia, he was eager to have the Reformed faith tolerated by the Lutherans. Since he himself did not espouse the more radical tenets of Calvinism, he felt it possible to find a common basis of peace in the Scripture and the Augsburg Confession, while declaring the subsequent special codifications of faith, including the formula of concord, matters for individual decision.

In 1662, an edict applied this policy to the examination and admission of ministerial candidates. Two years later a signed declaration was demanded from all ministers. They were to use moderation in the discussion of controversial subjects, not to identify their adversaries by name, and to lay aside the formula of concord. The dean of the St. Nicholas Church in Berlin, the famous and irenic Paul Gerhardt, refused to sign such a declaration, whereupon he was suspended and went to Saxony. Thereafter the Elector relaxed his attempts to impose uniformity. He had gained at least practical toleration of the Reformed Church, and the influx of the French Huguenots did not meet with opposition. Toward the end of the century, theological controversies began to assume a less shrill tone. Ever-larger groups lost interest in the dogmatic polemics of the theologians. This was true not only of the growing number of those who found ideals and purposes outside the Church, but also of those who tried to renew the Church by novel means.

✑ *The New Orthodoxy*

THE AUTHORITY OF THE STATE over the Church limited the opportunities for a vigorous development of religious life in Protestant Germany very severely. But orthodox theology, though erudite and active, was lacking in that ultimate intellectual determination which would have excluded disparate thoughts, and, on its own premises, it presented a system of thought that was not free of patent contradictions. George Calixt was the first theologian to adopt a new method of presenting a system of theology. While he had been unsuccessful in his irenic attempts at the reunion of churches, his new theological method was generally adopted by Protestant scholars. This so-called analytical method organized its material in the light of the supreme goal of religious life, the achievement of salvation. Consequently, the theological books of this school opened with the discussion of this aim. It was followed by an analysis of man as the subject of action and, finally, the treatment of the means of achieving salvation through Christ, the Scripture, and the sacraments. In contrast to the old method, which started with Scripture to proceed immediately to the doctrine of God and Trinity and finally ended with man, the analytical method wanted to captivate the personal interest of the individual from the outset. But the new form of presentation was more than a new literary style or pedagogic scheme.

This treatment of religion as a means of salvation departed from Luther's conceptions. To Luther, religion was absolute obedience to God's will or, in other words, the fulfillment of a supreme duty rather than the seeking of personal gain. Even the longing for salvation had seemed to him only a sublimated form of the pursuit of personal happiness. This had actually been one of the major causes of his revolt against the Catholic Church. In the doctrine of the justification of the individual and the origins of all moral life, Lutheran orthodoxy, too, endeavored to lay the utmost stress on the omnipotence of God. But in the general conception of religion the orthodox theologians defended the desire for ultimate happiness on the part of the individual, and it was only one step further to expect from God the granting of such happiness. At once the question arose why God, who was responsible for the well-being of mankind, admitted so much evil and suffering in the world. Orthodox theologians were inclined to answer that God tolerated rather than inflicted suffering. But this made God an observer instead of actor in human history.

The adoption of the analytical method by itself was proof that orthodox theology felt the need to satisfy the sentiments of more highly self-conscious individuals. It bore this out fully by making the pursuit of happiness a legitimate concern of religion and shifting the emphasis from sin to evil. Despite its apparent moral austerity, its aloofness from the political world, and hostility to modern philosophical thought, Lutheran orthodoxy did not actually place itself in absolute opposition to all secularism. It did not oppose the rise of the power of the modern state nor the growth of a more subjective approach to life, nor could it finally block the spread of a more optimistic interpretation of the world. The surface of its premodern teaching hid only incompletely the willingness to accept much of modern reality. In the course of the eighteenth century, Lutheran orthodoxy lost influence, but it never disappeared completely. In the early nineteenth century it extended its sway again, although it did not reach all classes of the people. This neo-orthodoxy was also distinguished by its absorption of other Christian ideals, which originally had arisen as a protest against orthodoxy but then merged with it in order to defend Christian transcendentalism against the philosophical rationalism and plain materialism which followed in the wake of the Enlightenment.

✒ Mysticism

MYSTICISM HAD CONTINUED to exist as an undercurrent in German Protestantism throughout the sixteenth century. Its main sources were Eckhart, Tauler, the *German Theology*, to which both the earlier classic texts of mysticism, such as Dionysius the Areopagite, and Jesuit mysticism were soon added. Johann Arndt's *True Christendom* carried this mystic thought to all classes. Arndt, who died in 1621 as chief minister of Brunswick-Celle, was a convinced orthodox theologian. Obviously he did not feel the contrast between his Lutheran tenets and the mystical approach which his general writings presented. This was different with Valentin Weigel (1533–88), who lived the life of an orthodox minister. In his writings, which were distributed only among a few intimates during his lifetime and were not printed before 1609, traditional mysticism was joined to a cosmological pantheism of neo-

Platonic origin. The latter had found its revival in the Italian Renaissance and reached Weigel chiefly through Paracelsus. God dwells in the universe and also in the human soul. He awakens faith and works purification from within. Christ's life on earth was taken as the model for every Christian in its humility and complete obedience to God. Luther's doctrines of justification, sacraments, and Scripture were totally rejected, and the existing churches—called mere "stone piles" by Weigel—were declared meaningless for the Christian, who needs no authority since he lives on an absolutely certain faith in the invisible church of the spirit. Weigel objected passionately to all force, to the control of the "stone-church" by the state, to war, and even to criminal law.

Such radicalism was rare in Germany, but both indifference toward the existing churches and the wish to reform them by the infusion of a personally experienced faith were widespread among the intellectually conscious groups of society. In the shoemaker-philosopher Jacob Boehme of Görlitz (1575–1624) this popular mysticism found its most original and powerful expression. He remained close to the Lutheran tradition insofar as the struggle between good and evil was to him the central problem, but this ethical dualism was transformed into a cosmological struggle which had its cause in the two aspects of God Himself. Luther, who had found in the contrast between God's wrath and love the greatest riddle of religion, would doubtless have opposed this metaphysical monism as blasphemous. But Jacob Boehme's mysticism constituted a link between Luther and certain schools of later German idealism, particularly Hegel, but even more Schelling and Baader.

Even Boehme retained an outwardly correct attitude toward the Church, though to him, too, it was a "stone-church," into which Christ's temple had to be carried. Profound disappointment with the official Church also was felt among the theologians. The longing for a restoration of nonlegalistic and nonauthoritarian beliefs was found generally in Europe, irrespective of whether it took more the form of a renewed awareness of the paradoxes of Christian religion or of an all-comprehending, harmonizing interpretation of universal life. Jansenism, Pascal, the mysticism of Molinos, Madame de Guyon, and Fénélon stood in the same front as Puritanism in England and the Netherlands and also the developing Pietism in Germany. Weigel and Boehme were read in England, but the influence of Puritanism on German Protestantism was far greater. It became effective chiefly through the Netherlands and the Reformed groups in Germany, in which Calvin's insistence on the sanctification of the orders of the world was not forgotten and congregational life remained active. Even in some of the orthodox theologians, especially in Grossgebauer, one can find Puritan ideas, but Grossgebauer remained an official churchman who was opposed to associations within the established Church.

↶ Pietism

THE FORMATION of special groups took place in Germany after Philip Spener (1635–1705) began his activities in Frankfurt in 1666. Here he first organized *collegia biblica* or *pietatis*, which meant special meetings for biblical readings, prayer, and the cultivation of individual piety. In this period, associations of individuals outside the existing authoritarian channels and the traditional class order sprang up in general German society as well. Free associations clearly had a wide appeal. *Collegia pietatis* spread rapidly over Protestant Germany, and very early laymen acted as the leaders of such groups. Spener, who in his *Pia Desideria* (1675) gave the new movement its first programmatic treatise, also stimulated a new enthusiasm for social work. Following the English model, a workhouse was founded in Frankfurt, and almost immediately was emulated in a number of cities, such as Nürnberg, Augsburg, Leipzig, Halle, and Berlin. These workhouses were soon overburdened with heterogeneous purposes. They were to serve impoverished and unemployed people as a base for a new start, but they were also used to compel the loafers and footloose elements, with which society abounded, to a routine of hard work. In addition, these houses were utilized for the development of new manufactures and further burdened with the housing and schooling of orphans.

But such subsequent developments, for which municipal niggardliness was largely to blame, could not detract from the new and earnest attempt to have the Church tackle social problems. A group of young Pietists became active in the University of Leipzig. Their foremost theologian was August Hermann Francke (1663–1727), with whom the jurist Christian Thomasius (1655–1728) co-operated. When, in 1686, Spener came to Dresden as chief court chaplain, Saxony seemed destined to become the center of German Pietism. But the Saxon government, interested mostly in avoiding controversy, took a stand against Pietism. August Hermann Francke was forced to leave Leipzig in 1690. Thomasius had left even earlier, though not for theological reasons. In 1696, Spener, too, left Saxony to spend his last years in Berlin.

The founding of a university at Halle by the Brandenburg government, in 1694, gave Thomasius and Francke a new academic home. The theological faculty was composed entirely of representatives of the new religious movement and soon outshone the smaller University of Giessen as the center of German Pietism. Thomasius, philosopher and jurist, turned away from Pietism, however, and the philosophical and law faculties of Halle were to become the first schools of German Enlightenment.

Nevertheless, through A. H. Francke, Halle became more than an academic center of Pietism. Rather, it became what one might call the "new Jerusalem" of the new piety. Francke began with the establishment of a school for the poor in 1695, and three years later founded the Halle orphanage, the first such institution devoted exclusively to the education of orphans. Later on, additional schools were joined to Francke's numerous foundations, which included an apothecary's shop and a big printing shop devoted to religious literature and the publication of Bibles for distribution in Germany and abroad. In addition to social activities (in the nineteenth century called "internal missions"), Francke tried to arouse an interest in foreign missions as well.

With the accession of King Frederick William I to the Prussian throne in 1713, Francke's activities enjoyed the active protection of the Prussian government. But Frederick II shifted governmental favors to the representatives of Enlightenment, and Pietism waned in the theological faculties. For almost an entire century, after 1740, the University of Halle was a school of Enlightenment in all its departments.

Francke also gave the clearest theological expression to the new religious aspirations. A systematic theology in the full sense could not be expected from a religious movement which was driven by warm hearts rather than subtle brains. Nor was this theology representative of all the individuals and groups of the early period of Pietism, though it became in time the most influential theoretical statement of the movement. Francke as well as Spener started from the central Lutheran question of justification and, in general, aimed at the conservation of Lutheran theology. The chief complaint about orthodox theology was its neglect of the personal experience of justification. Francke demanded actual experience of the terrors of conscience by the individual Christian. Out of a deep and crushing struggle of contrition the individual was to reach the brilliant moment of the assurance of God's grace, with which light and peace would settle in the soul. Only if justification is a true revival of the individual Christian can a transformation which creates moral renovation take place.

Even in this relatively conservative theological version strong radical trends were at once apparent. The reawakening and Christian revival was the result of the inner development of individual persons. The Church as institution became secondary if not irrelevant in religious life. Child baptism had no significance in the process of justification, and the Lord's Supper was not to be taken as the grant of the Church but as the symbol of the community of equally renovated souls. Nobody could be called a Christian minister because he was properly ordained and displayed formal doctrinal and moral rectitude as long as he had not undergone Christian revival.

The Pietists demanded a completely personalized religion which was gained by introspection and prayer. It found its source not in a body of rationalized doctrine but in the intensive reading of the Bible. Pietism carried biblicism to its ultimate conclusion. The more traditional approach to the Bible was to consider it as the means for the direct vision of the unique events of holy history in the past. As the receptacle of the divine spirit, the Bible had acted as God's message to man throughout the centuries down to the present moment. A careful distinction had to be drawn between letter and spirit, and the radicals could go a step further by asserting that orthodoxy, by its literal intrepretation, had been incapable of fathoming the secrets of Scripture, which had also been kept under lock by state control. In any event, the Bible was made the only tool of salvation, and its daily study by groups, the family, or individuals received tremendous stimulus. The Bible was the supreme authority and as such independent of the Church and its theology, which also introduced alien elements, such as philosophy and canon law, into the Christian faith. Through its efficacy in the conversion of the individual, the Bible proved its truth. Therefore, while Pietism was disdainful of theology, it was at the same time hostile toward the new rationalist philosophies. Where it did not directly attack such philosophies, it at least tried to insulate its own flock from their influence.

The opposition against the new secular thought which raised its head simultaneously with Pietism was also in line with the Christian ethics which Pietism derived from the Bible. The Pietists were convinced that Christian revival necessarily led to a break with worldly ways, and here they included the mores and customs approved by governments.

To Luther and the theologians of orthodoxy the state was an integral part of God's creation, though not its ultimate aim. The Pietists, who in their own days saw a more powerful state emerge than the one Luther had known, stressed the secular nature of the state and its unfitness to direct the religious and moral life of Christians. It was no longer enough to Christianize the state and public orders, since they were willed by God. True Christian morals could only be realized by and within groups of awakened Christians. One of the deepest of Luther's concerns was thereby brought to the fore again. Luther had not been willing to accept an ethics formulated by an ecclesiastico-political civilization and had postulated a Christian morality grounded in personal faith in the fatherhood of God. But whereas Luther had an unbounded confidence that the world would be reformed, Pietists did not believe that the secular order could be Christianized. Only the lives of individuals and of groups of individuals could be transformed. Nevertheless, most Pietists were satisfied to stay in the official Church as long as they were allowed to cultivate on the side their own religious practices and associations.

German Pietism was not entirely confined to this attitude, however. Where the pantheistic mysticism of the type of Weigel's and Boehme's, which was easily fused with pietistic religiosity, became the predominant force, the observation of strict separation from the general life of the Church markedly increased and here and there assumed sectlike forms. In Frankfurt, separatist elements, impressed by the example of William Penn, decided to emigrate to America. Since the law of the Empire forbade all new churches, the separatist Pietists could not hope to achieve the full realization of their ideals of a Christian community within Germany. The pietistic movement originally started with the upper burgher class and the nobility. In the seventeenth century many members of the imperial nobility in the neighborhood of Frankfurt were won and made their territories or estates homes for the new religion. In the nobility of Saxony and the Prussian provinces Pietism also found early converts and patrons. On the whole these social groups retained the leadership of the movement. Their political conservatism was not in favor of separatism and even made them look for governmental protection, which they found in Hesse-Darmstadt, Württemberg, Prussia, and Denmark. In the lower classes, among artisans and peasants, Pietism became more separatist, and sectarian enthusiasm and chiliasm frequently burst into the open. But after 1700, these latter groups were hardly heard of outside their immediate local sphere. Only in Württemberg did Pietism gain and retain a large popular basis, but under the guidance of the Swabian ministers it lost all tendencies to separate from the official Church.

On the other side, the most independent pietistic association had a rather strong and variegated social foundation. It was the work of Count Nicolaus Ludwig von Zinzendorf (1700–60), the descendant of an Upper Austrian Protestant family. Educated in Halle, he gave Pietism a different religious direction and a new form of organization. In order to create a home for Moravian Brethren who had escaped from Bohemia, he founded, in 1722, the Brethren's Community in Herrnhut, Saxony. Pietists and other German sectarians found a refuge here, too. Outwardly, the Community was within the Lutheran Church, but Zinzendorf was essentially indifferent to all confessional differences. He was willing to accept any Lutheran, Calvinist, and Protestant sectarian or even Catholic, as long as he worshipped Christ. With this statement he expressed the specific kernel of his own religion, which even abandoned the crisis of penance as a prerequisite of Christian revival and felt that through sensual and spiritual contemplation of Christ divine strength would fill the human soul. Luther's or Calvin's conceptions of original sin were suppressed. Man was not really evil, though he needed a guide and model to purify his heart.

One of the foremost objectives of the Herrnhut life was to produce and maintain the sentiment in which the presence and relationship of God was continually appreciated. Aside from private group meetings of laymen, the central cultic institution was the "singing hour," in which in Quaker fashion religious professions were heard and traditional or improvised hymns were sung. The harmony of the universe and of God and man, at all times of the day, found its expression in the music which was heard everywhere. The Brethren's Community was governed by elders, and when new communities came into existence, they formed a union bound together by a loose synodical organization. When, after 1740, Pietism lost its foothold in the state-controlled schools and universities, the Herrnhut institutions naturally became the mainstay of the movement to which the widely scattered pietistic groups and individuals looked for advice or where they sent their children to school. Among the leaders of future German idealism, Friedrich Schleiermacher and Jacob Friedrich Fries received their early education in schools maintained by the Brethren.

But this happened in the last quarter of the eighteenth century, when Pietism had lost its influence on the general life of the nation. Then it did no longer fight the Enlightenment in public, and the rise of the Enlightenment brought orthodoxy and Pietism closer together. Still, even in the second half of the century Pietism was a potent force in German life. There was practically no representative of classic German idealism who had not been impressed to a greater or lesser degree with pietistic religion, whether he had come in contact with the Herrnhut Community, the Württemberg congregation, or pietist individuals, so-called "beautiful souls," as in the case of Goethe. Commonly, the Pietists were spoken of as "the quiet people" (*die Stillen im Lande*), a label that, together with slight bewilderment, expressed the respect for their steady influence through personal example.

The Historic Significance of Pietism

THE RISE OF PIETISM in the last third of the seventeenth century was a sign of the pent-up desire for personal religion. The political and social conditions of Germany explain why the movement was so largely confined to certain social classes and never, like Puritanism or Methodism, aimed at a total reform of Church and state but rather concentrated on the regeneration of the private life of the individual. Among the motives which created Pietism, on the other hand, were hidden aspirations which went beyond the private existence of its members. This the Pietists showed not only by their social activities but also by their active interest in the improvement of general culture. As Pietism was a revolt against authoritarian and institutionalized faith, it was also a revolt against the blind acceptance of foreign models. Aiming everywhere at personal experience, Pietism took the individual German in all his narrow circumstances as the legitimate subject of the drama of life. Pietism was highly conscious of the popular or national scene, not in a political but in a cultural sense. And it approached German culture from a very definite angle. Essentially it cared only about the spiritual awakening of the individual. It was part of this process that the individual should become aware of the gulf between secular and religious pursuits. Actually, not even in a relative sense did Pietism assign to the life of the world a specific moral meaning. However, without the necessity to philosophize about secular life, it could be dealt with in a less dogmatic fashion than before, and the methods by which men could make it manageable could be more realistically explored. Pietistic schools, though never neglecting religious education, abandoned much of the humanistic and philosophical learning and emphasized realistic and practical subjects instead.

In spite of its own limited social basis, Pietism had a strong popular bent, and wherever it reached, it introduced a warm note into the relations of social classes which were usually distant and cold. In addition, pietistic culture was entirely devoted to the native life of Germany. But its most important contribution remained the development of a new type of individual character among Germans. Pietism did not produce a heroic man. This could not have been expected from a movement which did not recognize the issues of the world as worth the human struggle. Even in its inner religious life no great courage could be found. Pietistic religiosity was sentimental, aiming at peace and happiness, and its quietistic nature was easily satisfied with mere esthetic enjoyment of the divine. The moral impact of this religion was ambiguous. The consciousness of Christian revival often led to hypocrisy and Phariseeism, sometimes even to moral libertinage. The struggle for the experience of regeneration gave room to a great deal of self-deception and artificial vexation. But at the same time, Pietism created a remarkable power of self-observation and analysis. Since confessions of conversion were the chief means of winning new souls and enhancing the confidence of the members of the community, the capacity for expressing the experiences of the individual heart gained strength. For the Pietists all the events of their personal life were simultaneously divine actions. "God's finger" was easily, all too easily, seen in the course of human life. Yet intervention of the transcendental in human happenings gave to the actions and reactions of man's soul a central place in history. The beginnings of autobiographical understanding and critical interpretation of history as a psychological process were greatly advanced by Pietism.

Gottfried Arnold's (1666–1714) *Nonpartisan History of the Church and Heretics* (*Unparteiische Kirchen- und Ketzer-Historie*), 1699–1700, showed this trend most clearly. Arnold, who for a number of years was professor at the University of Giessen, was deeply moved by pantheistic mysticism, which made him skeptical about the Church and institutionalized religion. In his *History*, only the original Church of the Apostles was recognized as a Christian Church. Thereafter church history becomes the story of desertion from the Christian ideal. In the mass of disloyal name-Christians, only a few individuals stood out as true Christians, and they were found not only within the official churches but also within the heretical sects. The mystic-pietistic form of religion was made by Arnold the touchstone of pure Christianity without consideration of changing historical conditions. History of the Church was replaced by history of religion. Piety was considered both cause and achievement of history, and the institutional fabric, including orthodox doctrines, was judged completely meaningless. Arnold was still far removed from a modern, individualizing historical interpretation. His ideal of the pious individual was in all ages essentially the same. But he opened an entirely new view of history by moving the human soul into the center of all historical contemplation. The young Goethe was fascinated by Arnold, although from the outset he expanded his individualistic concept of religion.

Although Pietism took a hostile attitude toward all secular civilization, which included most aspects of the ecclesiastical life as well, it acted as a strong ferment in German cultural history. The most dramatic explosion of pietistic enmity toward the Enlightenment was the mean and false denunciation of Halle's most eminent philosopher, Christian Wolff. The same theological faculty which had found in Halle a refuge from the intolerance of Leipzig orthodoxy persuaded the dull-witted King Frederick William I that Wolff's philosophy would justify military desertion. The king exiled Wolff from Prussia, under pain of the gallows, on forty-eight hours' notice. Pietism also took a negative attitude toward art. Even music, if practiced as an art, was considered to be a devilish temptation. But beginning with the cultivation of the German language and culminating in the development of a culture of the heart, Pietism contributed to the growth of a new German civilization.

✑ *The New Concept of State*

PROTESTANT ORTHODOXY and Pietism, irrespective of the new trends expressed in them, were essentially attempts to interpret the world in terms of the old Christian tradition. Neither school of thought was any longer capable of comprehending the totality of life. Orthodoxy as well as Pietism refused to come to grips with the new political realities, and, we may add, the same was true of Catholicism. The Churches were incapable of bringing the modern absolute state under strict ethical norms. The moral conflict which thereby arose was covered up for contemporaries by the professed Christian attitude of the governments. But although one does not have to question the genuine character of the faith of many rulers, even devout princes used religion as a device for buttressing their power rather than as an absolute ideal to be humbly served.

Jean Bodin, through his theory of sovereignty, had taught that states were endowed with a central will which was supreme over the historical privileges and rights of special groups. But it had also been learned from Machiavelli and his Italian followers that pragmatic rather than moral rules determined the realization of control over the state and the preservation of the state among states. Each state had its own rational principle, its *raison d'état*, and its own interests which the statesman had to understand and pursue in his own policies. These political necessities, Machiavelli had written, took precedence even over moral laws. Religion and morality, and with them the foundation of law, were thereby challenged. Small wonder that all the Churches fought Machiavelli and Machiavellianism with great conviction. The Catholic Church placed the relevant literature on the index of prohibited books, while Protestant theologians never tired of inveighing against "the horrible beast *raison d'état*," as Grossgebauer called it. But the new naturalistic approach to politics could not be simply exorcised.

The death of Wallenstein was a disturbing example of the conflict between contemporary governmental practice and customary law. Careful legal discussions were held in Vienna before Ferdinand II consented to the killing of Wallenstein and his accomplices as guilty traitors. Only the threat to the very existence of the monarchy was found to give an excuse for proceeding against Wallenstein without a hearing, though not without legal argument. As the imperial councilor stated it, nobody was permitted for any reason to act against divine justice, but in an extreme emergency of the state it was permissible to use "extreme methods against extreme evils." The distinction between the absolutely binding natural and divine law and the positive law which the ruler might set aside under certain conditions if the welfare of the state demanded it, was drawn from the literature on the interests of rulers. This study of the *raison d'état*, which so far had chiefly been carried on in Italy and France, became quite widespread in Germany in the century after the Thirty Years' War, and here every effort was made to limit its moral implications. As late as 1739, Crown Prince Frederick of Prussia felt prompted to write his refutation of Machiavelli's *Prince*, following in the footsteps of the German anti-Machiavellians.

But it was of the greatest historical consequence that a difference be-

tween a sphere of action, however small, determined by its own im-
manent laws, and a world of religious and moral judgments was recognized by many writers and even more so by statesmen. Before the
conclusion of the Peace of Prague, in 1635, Emperor Ferdinand requested the advice of a conference of twenty-two theologians on
whether the treaty contained irreligious concessions which would make
it a sin for the Emperor to sign the treaty. The theologians were reminded, however, that it was not their business to pass on the question
of whether an extreme political necessity existed which made it ad-
visable to make certain concessions to the Protestants. This was a matter to be settled by the "politicos." Here was an early example of an
awareness of the existence of two realms of human action and reasoning, which grew throughout the century.

It was logical that the awareness of the naturalistic and pragmatic
side of political life led to historical study which was to demonstrate
the operation of the peculiar laws of politics. Samuel Pufendorf's[3] historical works were the most accomplished products of this new type
of history. Between 1677 and 1688, he composed for the Swedish court
his histories of Gustavus Adolphus and Charles Gustavus of Sweden.
Only months before his own death, the Great Elector brought Pufendorf to Berlin, where he wrote the history of the Great Elector and
started a history of Elector Frederick III, which remained a fragment
when Pufendorf died in 1694. The doctrines of *raison d'état* and the
interests of state formed the key to Pufendorf's monumental histories,
which, however, did not capture the complex motivations of the politics of his age, let alone define its individual character within the
stream of the general development of history.

∾ *The Study of Nature*

AS THE STUDY OF THE STATE revealed forces in history which followed
their own laws, the study of nature also produced new vistas. Germany
had not participated creatively in the studies of the science of nature
since the middle of the sixteenth century when Copernicus (1473–
1543) had still been stimulated by the Nürnberg school of Regiomon-
tanus, not only by what Italians had taught him about ancient and
modern science. Kepler (1571–1630) lived intellectually in a European
rather than German world. This is not to say that the Germans of the

3 See p. 12.

late sixteenth and seventeenth century lacked an avid curiosity about the problems of nature. They were not satisfied with what scholastic academicians, Catholic or Protestant, had to offer. The study of nature which the Italian Renaissance had created was cultivated in Germany even after humanistic leadership had disappeared. In many German cities, groups of burghers met regularly to discuss this type of speculation. The young Leibniz served briefly as secretary of such a group in Nürnberg, in 1667. In the mysticism of a Valentin Weigel and Jacob Boehme a reflection of this form of contemplation can be found. But the steps which led from Renaissance science to the beginnings of modern science that revolutionized man's thought and life as nothing else had done since the Greeks and early Christianity were taken outside of Germany.

Modern science did not rest on the quantitative expansion of knowledge but rather on a new form of it. The broadening of knowledge, as it occurred in the period of discovery as well as in the technology of the age of Leonardo da Vinci, was, no doubt, a great challenge to fresh thought, but by itself it would not have produced these new ideas. Medieval thinking had intended to reflect and describe the structure of being, which was conceived as an ordered cosmos. The study of nature was by no means excluded, but perception was confined to those finite and phenomenal objects which alone were within the ken of natural reason. With respect to both the reasoning subject and the objects of study, knowledge was limited. It is true that natural knowledge in medieval thought comprised more than the knowledge of physical and material objects. It included the social order as well as the fundamental truths of religion, but the "realm of nature" did not find its perfection except in the "realm of grace," and the *lumen naturale* could intellectually organize only part of the world and gain ultimate assurance and an apprehension of the absolute through revelation alone.

The scholastic world-view was replaced in Italian Renaissance philosophy by a new interpretation. Nature was declared not to have originated from a single act of God, and creation was conceived as a continuing process. God was assumed to be present in creation and his creatures to have part in the divine being unfolding in nature. The assertion of God's immanence in nature destroyed scholastic cosmology. The divine immanence could be philosophically construed in many different forms, and as pantheism it opened the doors to panpsychism as well as anthropomorphic speculation about the universe. Valentin Weigel's and Jacob Boehme's mysticism showed many traces of these ideas, which in vulgarized forms could even promote superstition and certainly substituted imagination for reason. But in critical minds this new religiosity, which so eagerly craved to discover God in nature, could lead in another direction. The participation of the individual in the divine could not merely mean that the individual was to be dissolved in infinity. Quite the contrary, the individual received a new dignity and through it justification of his own peculiar forces and character. This specific nature had to be understood as necessary and also as resting on innate principles amenable to clear definition. Mere imagination and sense impressions will not yield a valid description. Sensory observation must be confronted with mathematical description.

✎ *Johannes Kepler*

JOHANNES KEPLER TOOK this important step. Supported by the exact astronomic findings of the Danish astronomer Tycho Brahe, his predecessor as court astronomer in Prague, he worked out, in the most tedious and detailed studies, the laws which determined the course of planets and the velocity of their movement in relation to their distance from the sun. The hypotheses behind the studies of this Lutheran Swabian, who maintained his attachment to the Lutheran Church even at the imperial court, were all gained from his neo-Platonic pantheism. Mathematics was for him the means to understand God as creator. By the discovery of mathematical laws, the simple "harmonies" according to which God's wisdom has made the universe, are demonstrated, and a new trust in providence is aroused. On the other hand, if the earth and man are no longer in the center of the universe, man has won great new opportunities. Riding on a moving star through the sky enables him to learn the secrets of the universe. Kepler dismissed conflicts with the Bible by arguing that the Holy Spirit had to use popular language in order to be understood by common people. In science, rational proof was the only authority. In Kepler's scientific endeavor religion was the driving force, but both his methods and results already undermined his own religious symbolism.

Kepler's scientific research produced essentially factual findings. Galilei proceeded to a new stage. He realized that sensory observation was made more exact but was not transformed by mathematical measurement and did not afford an understanding of the necessity of the phenomena of nature. They could be understood only if their conditions were clarified, which required an analytical as well as synthetic method. Analysis had to lead to the distinction between the various elements in a natural process, which the senses reflected only in its general and indefinite totality. It is not enough, for example, to describe the path of a missile as parabola. In order to understand the parabolic movement of a heavy body, the individual movements, such as rise and fall, diminishing velocity, etc., had to be studied with a view to their conditioning factors. After an observed phenomenon had literally been taken apart, it could be reconstructed as a whole in terms of a true theory. The modern scientific approach was already present in Galilei's studies on dynamics, though his material results were less startling, partly because he did not completely overcome older ideas, and partly because experimental possibilities as well as mathematical concepts were still limited. It remained for Isaac Newton to lead the combination of analytical and synthetic methods to final victory. Kepler's laws of the movement of the planets were to Newton only the basis for an interpretation of natural events as the necessary results of conditions under which they came into existence. Once the complexity of a sequence of natural events was recognized, it was broken up into its constituent parts, which were analyzed singly to be brought together thereafter in the synthesis of a theory. Newton reduced Kepler's "laws" to the interaction of the law ruling the free fall of bodies and that of centrifugal movement. From mere contemplation and observation of nature he went to the understanding of nature through the formulation of theories which derived their claim for universal validity from mathematics.

The Rise of New Philosophies

THE SPREAD of the new scientific attitude did not have to wait for the perfection it received at the hands of Newton. Between the appearance of Galilei's works, in 1610–38, and the publication of the *Philosophiae naturalis principia mathematica* by Newton, in 1687, it gave rise to the new philosophies of Descartes (1596–1650), Hobbes (1588–1679), and Spinoza (1632–77), which found their German response and complement in Gottfried Wilhelm Leibniz (1646–1716). What all these philosophies had in common was the belief in the new scientific method which was far removed from a simple empiricism. Observation and experiment became significant only through the application of mathematical theory, which formed or transformed subjective sense impressions into objective knowledge. The scope of this knowledge was as infinite as the universe which it intended to explain, but its certainty lay in the combinative method which was universally applicable and understandable. Copernicus had removed man from the center of the world, but now man's knowledge of the universe was built exclusively upon his own reason. Traditional religion was not necessarily excluded thereby. While Descartes, who obviously took an indifferent attitude toward the Catholic Church, avoided religious conflicts, most seventeenth-century philosophers and scientists showed an even closer attachment to the established Churches. However, they tended to believe that the laws of nature would operate independently from God. Eighteenth-century deism was at least prepared in the philosophy of Descartes.

The great capacity assigned to man's reason raised at once the problem whether it could be trusted. The whole philosophical movement of European Enlightenment, therefore, was not only bent on completing the understanding of the universal mechanism of nature and on elucidating the relationship between mind and nature but also on making the validity of truth unassailable against all critical doubts. From Descartes, Leibniz, and Locke to Hume and Kant, theory of knowledge remained the central theme of all philosophizing. In Descartes and the first generation after him general epistemology was founded on a new metaphysics which derived from human doubt the necessity of God's existence and argued philosophically that the principles of human thought precede experience. Subsequent thinkers subjected human consciousness to a psychological study in order to make the process of thinking understood. In all circumstances it was mathematics which constituted the foundation of science and was essential in explaining a mechanistically conceived world. So exclusively mechanical was the world supposed to be that the Cartesian mode of thought was considered applicable to the social world as well. While Descartes himself paid little attention to social and political problems, Thomas Hobbes developed the first philosophical system which included politics as an integral part of its interpretation of the world.

↫ Hobbes and Grotius

HOBBES STOOD ON THE SHOULDERS not only of Descartes but also of the humanistic jurisprudence which had reached full maturity in

Hugo Grotius (1583–1645). The idea of natural law, which was born in man, had been passed on to the Christian Middle Ages by the Roman philosophers and jurists. Medieval ethical and political thought had subordinated natural law to divine law in various forms. Whether natural law was declared to be the law of the original state which man lost through the fall, or whether it was identified with the decalogue, it could be restored or perfected only through divine law. In Bodin, Althusius, and Grotius the Stoic conception of natural law experienced a renascence. A group of moral notions was assumed as common to all men and ages. The positive law was the result of human volition; consequently it was variable and arbitrary. The idea of justice appeared in those eternal principles that were grounded in the nature of man and things. These principles were gained by Grotius not by scientific logic but by practical reason. Supported by the wisdom of the ancients, the Bible, or religious arguments, the humanistic Calvinist appealed to common sense. The fundamental doctrines of Christian religion were not questioned by him. God has willed that the world should be ruled by natural law, which is identical with reason and has endowed man with social proclivity (*appetitus societatis*) and with the faculty of reason, which enables him to acquire knowledge of the laws of society and live in accordance with them. The law of creation and natural law are identical, and human reason grasps the idea of divine justice through the understanding of natural justice. For, as Hugo Grotius put it, "natural law is so immutable that not even God can change it . . . as little as He can turn what is evil by its inner nature into non-evil."

Thus Grotius prepared the field for the rational study of state and society. His study proceeded from a reduction of all positive laws to the fundamental natural law. Once this was achieved, new laws could be formulated through deduction. Herein lay the cause for the easy combination of Grotius' philosophy of law with Cartesian science which Thomas Hobbes achieved. The same method applied to the study of politics as to that of nature. Hobbes was able to accomplish this integration of politics into a universal philosophical system only by adopting a metaphysical materialism in place of Cartesian idealism, while Spinoza, who accepted Hobbes' thesis that the social order was to be treated by a method analogous to that applicable to nature, developed a pantheistic philosophy. Thus, already during the seventeenth century modern philosophy produced three of the basic forms of interpreting reality, all of them the result of a new faith in the power of reason to decipher the universe and live and act in accordance with these new insights.

Hugo Grotius was widely read in Germany, and Descartes' writings also quickly became known. Erhard Weigel (1625–99), with whom both Pufendorf and Leibniz studied at Jena, already tried to apply the Cartesian method to ethics and metaphysics. But it was Leibniz who gave currency to Enlightenment in Germany by absorbing the highest aims of the Western European movement and expressing them in his own creative thought. Leibniz's philosophy was the fourth of the great systems, those of Descartes, Hobbes, and Spinoza, which the seventeenth century produced.

✑ *Leibniz*

GOTTFRIED WILHELM LEIBNIZ, son of a Leipzig professor, was born two years before the end of the Thirty Years' War. An academic prodigy, he received his doctorate of law from the University of Altdorf at the age of twenty and could have lectured there. But the stale atmosphere of contemporary German universities held no attraction for him. He was happy to accept a position with the Mainz government, where he was connected with two eminent German statesmen of that period, Elector John Philip von Schönborn and John Christian von Boyneburg.[4] Under their eyes he launched his early political projects and his first attempts to bring about a reunion of the Christian churches. In 1672, he went to Paris, where he returned a few times during the next years. In Paris he made the acquaintance of many philosophers, among them Malebranche, Arnauld, Simon Foucher, and of scientists, such as Huygens and Mariotte. Twice Leibniz went to London, where he was elected a member of the Royal Society. In 1676, he met Spinoza in The Hague. The death of Elector John Philip made it unattractive to continue in Mainz, and reluctantly Leibniz accepted the invitation of Duke John Frederick of Hanover. In his small capital, which had nothing to offer outside the court, Leibniz spent the remaining forty years of his life, interrupted by occasional travel to Italy, Vienna, and various German capitals. In Hanover he was not expected to do the regular work of a governmental councilor but was supposed to write memoranda making policy suggestions and to prepare pamphlets defending claims or actions of the Hanover government. He took care of the library, and from time to time undertook lesser

4 See p. 17.

diplomatic missions. Unfortunately, Duke John Frederick died as early as 1679, and his two successors, Ernest August (1679–98) and George Louis (1698–1727; after 1714 King George of England), entertained only cool relations with Leibniz, in spite of his great services in the advancement of the ducal dynasty to the electorate and eventually to the English throne. Only Ernest August's wife, Sophie, daughter of the Winter-King, and her daughter, Sophie Charlotte, first Prussian Queen, were genuine admirers of the philosopher and gave him their friend-ship and intellectual companionship. If Sophie had lived a few months longer, she would have become Queen of England, with Leibniz one of her chief advisors. But George I and his ministers, though not una-ware of the renown which Leibniz's world fame gave to the court of Hanover, wished to keep him in his place, and he was not allowed to follow the court to London.

For a man as anxious as Leibniz to exchange ideas with his peers and, in addition, to make ideas reform the political world, Hanover was both too dull and small to constitute a satisfactory life setting. Leibniz's wide connections outside of Hanover were only a meager substitute for direct contact with the world. He exchanged letters with more than a thousand people during his lifetime. His renewed attempts to find a way for the reunion of the Christian churches, which this time led to a correspondence with Bossuet, and even a project for the reconciliation of Lutheran and Reformed Churches failed. He was more successful in his endeavor to see academies of sciences established. In Berlin, the Society of Sciences was founded with the help of Queen Sophie Charlotte, and Dresden followed suit. In Vienna, where he won the admiration of Prince Eugene, a similar project broke down, owing to the state of Austrian finances. Peter the Great met Leibniz in 1711, 1712, and 1716. He proved receptive to many of the ideas of the Ger-man philosopher, among them the blueprint of an academy. But the St. Petersburg Academy did not come into existence until after Leibniz's death.

Leibniz was one of the most universal minds the West has produced, and among Germans only Goethe can be compared to him. None of his contemporaries or successors could match the range of his seem-ingly unlimited learning, his profound curiosity, and the inexhaustible vitality of his intellect. Among the many fields of scholarship to which he devoted himself, history and politics found a place beside all the branches of natural science, and yet in no field did he appear as a dilettante. His historical studies, of which the most extensive work,

The Brunswick Annals of the Medieval Empire, was not published until a century after his death, show him ahead of the historians of his age with regard to method, but the real contribution he made to the growth of modern historical thought stemmed from the influence of his philosophy, rather than his historiography, upon the generation of Herder. It was in philosophy and mathematics that the full genius of Leibniz found expression. He has received much criticism on the ground that he dissipated his power by extending his studies to all fields of knowledge and, even more, by getting involved in practical affairs. It is true that these circumstances interfered with the systematic presentation of his philosophy. He published only a few of his writings during his lifetime. Most of his ideas he poured out in his correspondence and in innumerable drafts and essays. Even today, only part of his writings have been published.

But the diversity of Leibniz's interests and activities was inseparably connected with the mainsprings of his whole being. He wanted to embrace the world in its totality, because he believed in its goodness and meaningfulness. To make his faith generally acceptable was the essential aim of his life. In this respect he was a reformer, although at the same time he was a profoundly conservative man in the best sense of the word. He wanted progress—progress to new religion and thought, to a new society and state, but such progress was not to be bought by cutting the roots with the past. On the contrary, he wanted to project the legacy of history in undiminished form into the future. "It is strange," he said, "I approve of most I read." There was never a thinker who strove as ardently as Leibniz to reconcile the various historic schools of Western philosophy. They all formed in his opinion one *philosophia perennis*. With regard to the various denominations and sects he remarked that all of them were right in most of their affirmations, though not in their negations. Leibniz was possessed of an insatiable desire to make the spiritual aspirations of all ages part of his own inner experiences and hopes. The same hunger for life and spirit drove him into the extensive study of nature.

Leibniz's central philosophical effort was directed toward finding the key which would open the world. In the development of his own method he had before his eyes the method of Descartes and the science of Galilei. He also absorbed the systems of Hobbes and Spinoza. To all these philosophers reason was not an unlimited capacity. On the contrary, it was the philosopher's task to define the boundaries of human reason, which were found by Descartes and his Western European successors to coincide with those of mathematics. Leibniz expanded the mathematical and mechanistic "world picture" of these thinkers by the calculus, which he discovered independently from Newton, and by his studies on the continuation and preservation of energy. He even attempted to find a new language of signs and symbols more expressive of the peculiar types of truth in the various fields of knowledge and at the same time of the universality of all truth. In twentieth-century philosophy these studies have been revived. But the mere extension of mathematical method did not prove sufficient in Leibniz's thinking to embrace all valid truth, especially the cognition of the individual besides the general. Leibniz maintained the validity of the *vérités necessaires ou de raison* as the foundation and prototype of all knowledge, but under them there existed the realm of the *vérités de fait*. In other words, in addition to the logic of truth, there was a logic of probability, which organized the descriptive natural sciences and history according to certain rules.

It was this thought of Leibniz that created the conception of modern German science or *Wissenschaft*. Whereas in Western Europe "science" as the highest form of knowledge remained the study of nature exclusively and the studies of man were labeled liberal arts or humanities, any scholarly pursuit was called science or *Wissenschaft* in Germany, provided it proceeded on the basis of a method appropriate to the particular subject. The variety of methods only reflects the ultimate unity of the scientific mind. In contrast to the Royal Society in England, Leibniz's plans for "academies of sciences" envisaged not only the study of nature but of liberal arts as well.

∽ *Monadology*

The Leibnizian logic comprised all truths. Even Descartes had drawn a sharp distinction between philosophical and mathematical truth on the one side and theological truth on the other. Leibniz denied the difference between revelation and demonstrable philosophical truth. There was to him no subject matter which could not, or would not, eventually be understood through reason. In this respect Leibniz carried rationalism to greater length than had his philosophical predecessors. This required not only a new logic but also a new construction of the universe. The "necessary" truths as presented by mathematics or logic contain only the conditions determining organization of any possible world, but our world consists of facts which cannot be explained by these universal truths. A true understanding of the world cannot be reached by mechanistic or causal interpretations. It requires a different approach which considers value, meaning, and evolution. Leibniz achieved such a teleological interpretation by a new conception of "substance." Spinoza had assumed only one substance, which was beyond time and change. Leibniz thought of substance as a persistent thing, too, but he was a pluralist and not a monist. The universe consisted of a plurality, nay an infinite number of substances, which he called "monads." They were to him the real atoms of the universe, though they were completely different from material atoms. The monads had no extension, shape, or divisibility. Evolving in time, they were centers of action and consciousness. In both respects they varied greatly, and supreme power and reason were found only in the highest monad, God, who had created all of them. Each monad was unique and autarkic, which meant that it derived its energy from within itself. "Monads have no windows," they do not change their individual character through interaction among themselves or with the outer world. But monads have "mirrors," each reflecting the universe in a peculiar perspective and with greatly differing degrees of clarity. Their creator, however, has pre-established a harmony among them, which rests in their relations to him and to the general principles of his universe.

Frederick the Great once remarked about the *Monadology* of Leibniz that it was a "literary novel by a man of genius," and actually its concrete terms did not survive its author very long. But it represented the first attempt undertaken by a modern philosopher to formulate for the moral and intellectual world philosophical categories different from those describing physical nature, and this example had a great influence on posterity. Profound insights were everywhere woven into Leibniz's thought. He already knew about subconscious levels of human personality, though he was able to conceive of them only as layers of dimmed rationality. In general, his belief in the absolute supremacy of the universal laws of reason defeated much of his endeavor to justify the sovereignty of the individual soul. He wanted to save history and psychology as sciences, but in his system the development of the individual soul did not recognize the validity of individualized forms of truth but only of universal truth. The individual was born with notions of these necessary truths, and to clarify them into true ideas of reason was the goal of self-realization.

In Leibniz's system the problem of moral freedom constituted a difficulty, which he did not solve except to his own satisfaction. The monad was determined by its creator with regard to both its innate energy and its role in the world plan. Therefore each act of an individual was fixed. This Leibniz admitted, but he denied that it could be called necessary, since it was possible that God might have chosen a different person or action. But the fact that the individual person or event was not necessary in God's plan still left the individual without moral freedom. Metaphysical logic appeared suddenly substituted for ethics. If this could happen to a thinker of Leibniz's rank, it was due to his fervent faith that all determination of human action must derive from inner causes. Closely connected with the question of moral freedom was that of evil in a world created and guided by God. In his *Theodicy* (*Essais de Theodicée*), first published in 1710 and widely read in Europe throughout the century, even after Voltaire in *Candide* ridiculed its ideas, Leibniz argued that this world was the best of all possible worlds, because it contained the greatest sum of perfection. The infinite perfection of God could express itself only in a universe which was composed of all forms and levels of existence. Each individual was endowed by God with a perfection which gave him a unique value. He ought to realize this perfection, which cannot be highest perfection, since deficiency is the character of the finite. The divine perfection of the universe is to be found in the principles underlying its totality. Evil is only that degree of imperfection which attaches to the particular individual at his assigned place in a hierarchy of values which is founded on a teleologically necessary system. Man, being capable of knowing that the universe is moving toward perfection, ought to admire and love God and be prepared to accept his place in the total process. Contemplation, however, is not enough. The cosmos of the universe is dynamic action. The individual makes its contribution to the realization of God's plan by self-perfection and social action. Since other individuals have been given similar roles, loving them is practically identical with loving God. Those individuals who have learned to understand the universal ideas and assumed the ethical obligations which derive from them form the "divine society" and are the common builders of the transcendental city of God.

Thereby a religious goal was given to all human life and history, and no doubt Leibniz was sincerely religious. But religion was not separated from philosophy, and the idea of a highest being was the logical keystone of his system. It is doubtful, however, whether his attempts to fit a realm of grace into the natural causal nexus of the world were compatible with his philosophy. In this regard his own receptivity for spiritual forces of the past and present and his relativism as to perspective truth carried him to unsafe ground. Still, even his theological essays did not adopt the methods of the theological schools. Nowhere did he rely on proof from Scripture. The history of religions became the source of his definition of religion, and reason the criterion of its doctrines. In these circumstances the latter were of only secondary significance, and this made it possible for Leibniz to treat doctrines as a matter for compromise in his attempts at the union of Christian churches. This unity would have rested on natural religion rather than specific Christian tenets. His city of God was not really the communion of saints but the community of moral persons enlightened by reason. Leibniz was attracted by the catholicity of the Roman Church because he was conscious of the desirability of the harmonious unity of the West as a prerequisite for the full realization of its cultural values. But although it would have greatly improved his external position, he rejected the idea of conversion, since it would not have advanced the cause of Enlightenment which he wished to serve through his efforts for Christian agreement.

∽ A New Form of Religion

LEIBNIZ REPRESENTED A NEW FORM of religion. His Lutheran upbringing shone through many of his philosophical beliefs. In the construction of his monadology, with its refusal to admit the influence of monads on each other, Luther's insistence upon the absolute dependence of the individual soul on God assumed a new expression. Yet all similarities between Leibniz and Luther are of comparatively minor significance, in view of the radically different general outlook. Leibniz lived no longer in the faith that man was the real objective of God's creation. The earth was only a small part of the universe, and Leibniz thought that there could be other worlds in addition. Beyond this acceptance of the new scientific findings, Leibniz changed the central experience of Lutheran religion. The realization of man's utter moral depravity was the starting point of Luther's piety. For Leibniz, sinfulness was nothing but a relative debility. An angry God Leibniz could not see. Both as the architect of this world and the guarantor of the order of the universe, God appeared to Leibniz as an eternally friendly father. The world was not the unblessed place in which the individual Christian would act and suffer to save his soul. In spite of its finiteness, this world was for Leibniz a good world which could be further improved through man's activities. Luther would have called any of these statements colossal blasphemies and also would have condemned the whole character of this religiosity which identified soul and reason.

Spinoza's *amor dei intellectualis* could represent Leibniz's religious attitude as well. But the intellectual contemplation of God led to entirely different results in the two philosophies. In Spinoza's view the vision of the ineluctable order of nature brought all individual ambitions and passions to rest. Leibniz opposed this quiet mysticism. To him the universe was dynamic life progressing to ever higher forms. The knowledge of universal laws would silence passions but not individuation. On the contrary, since the realization of universal life was bound up with the growth of higher individual life, the individual derived from the understanding of the universe the incentive for action in the world and also the strength joyfully to live up to this moral imperative. The underlying sentiment was far removed not only from Spinoza but also from medieval German mysticism.

Leibniz's Political Thought

THE ACTIVIST NATURE OF LEIBNIZ's philosophy explains his ardent interest in both practical and theoretical politics. He accepted the doctrines of the school of natural law. The state was the result of a contract concluded among men for the establishment of social order. But the conclusion of such a contract was already determined by the innate associative character of man, and natural law was divine law. This metaphysical frame defined the political thought of Leibniz. The individual cannot be understood as an isolated being but, from the outset, is part of a teleological order, the realization of the state of reason or God. All concrete states find their justification in their role in this cosmic drama. The purpose of the state is a moral one, the progress toward the "republic of the spirit." For this reason absolutism finds its limits in the fundamental right of education. The right to develop into a reasonable being is inalienable, because it is founded on the laws of the universe. Leibniz did not base this right on the natural equality of individuals but on the common goal toward which all individuals tend in harmony.

This philosophy of history and politics discovered more than a superficially mechanical meaning in political institutions, but it also

lent itself easily to ascribing a deeper significance to political forms
and events which were lacking in ideal substance. Leibniz was a
passionate German patriot and anxiously endeavored to contribute to
the welfare and security of Germany. He was at his best in his efforts
to improve the cultural foundations of German political life. The man
who wrote the majority of his works in Latin and French was busy to
adapt the German language to the needs of universal education. His
projects for the founding of academies were equally directed toward
the accumulation and spread of knowledge within the nation and its
participation in universal culture. Here, too, Leibniz was looking for
the harmony between the individual and universal. But this view became more artificial when it was applied to the concrete political
conditions of Germany and when territorial states and Empire were
seen in a similar relationship. Reason was found where chance and a
lifeless tradition ruled supreme. The Empire held a strong fascination
for Leibniz. It was still a *holy* Empire, not in the former theocratic
sense, but as the highest potential embodiment of his religion of reason.
The obvious lack of subordination of the parts under the whole did
not discourage Leibniz. He felt that the Empire would regenerate if
its members joined in free alliances for the performance of common
tasks, such as defense, culture, and the building of a national economy.
The Empire should not claim universal dominion, but Leibniz was
sanguine enough to hope that in a balanced Europe, in which the individual nations would devote themselves to the cultivation of their
own life, the Emperor, owing to his eminent rank, would exercise
important functions as an arbiter in Christendom. With untiring zeal
Leibniz tried to persuade the princes of his age to act according to
what he considered reason in history. His fervor frequently induced
him to adjust his interpretation of the course of historical reason to
the circumstances which he wanted to see transformed. History and
politics appeared in a friendly and optimistic light, and the shrill dissonances between actual events and the postulated laws of reason
were muffled.

Leibniz has been called the father of German Enlightenment with
good right. As much as his philosophy—perhaps more in form than
in content—still contained elements of older thinking, he realized a
novel type of thought which was clearly separated from Lutheran
orthodoxy and Pietism as well as the tradition of German mysticism.
Without the model of Western European philosophy, particularly of
Descartes, the full work of Leibniz could not have come into existence.

On the other hand, its impact on Germany would not have been so profound if it had not contained ideas which appealed especially to the Germans of the early eighteenth century. As a matter of fact, its influence was so strong that Leibniz, who brought Western European thought to Germany and at the time of his death was more highly eulogized in France than in Germany, could be used by the next German generation as a shield against further Western infiltration. The turn toward empiricism and materialism which Western Enlightenment took in the course of the century, except for Frederick II of Prussia, found only a weak echo in Germany. What made the philosophy of Leibniz well liked in Germany was its combination of a reformatory spirit with an attitude which kept intact existing institutions, such as state and Church, and also intellectual patterns, such as the belief in a personal God and transcendental ethics.

To find a solution of the tension which existed between a religion based on eternal natural laws and a Christian faith in the unique historic and supranaturalistic events of human salvation, became a central problem, with which German theologians and philosophers wrestled throughout the century. Although many of the Christian dogmas were either totally abandoned or made relative in this process, the compatibility of natural religion and historical Christian religion was never questioned. In politics the early European Enlightenment generally favored absolutism, and it was natural that the Germans made no exception. If German political thought did not change in this respect, as it did in France, after the middle of the eighteenth century, Leibniz cannot be held responsible for this continuity, which reflected chiefly the continuity of social and political history. Leibniz helped, however, to set the mold of modern German political theory by his emphasis upon the freedom of education. But the protection of this freedom was made a duty of the government rather than a right of the individual. Leibniz, as we have seen, had endeavored to establish a firm identity between the function of the government and the spiritual aspirations of the individual. The synthesis which he assumed between rationalism and individualism was generally weakened by his German successors, but most decidedly so in political theory.

∽ Leibniz and the Eighteenth Century

LEIBNIZ CALLED PUFENDORF a "mere jurist" rather than a philosopher, but the latter's influence prevailed in academic political thought.

Pufendorf, Christian Thomasius (1655–1728), and Christian Wolff (1679–1754) followed Hobbes in the construction of the authority of the government, though with a few characteristic deviations. Hobbes founded the state on the contract which the mass of individuals had made with a ruler in order to end the war of all against their fellow-men which was the initial stage of human history. The right of natural law was thereafter superseded by the laws of the state. The German thinkers did not consider the first stage of history as such a chaotic and antisocial period of life. Sociability was one of the original qualities of man. Thomasius and Wolff preferred to think of a two-fold social contract, the first expressing the general will to found a community, and the second concluded between this community and a ruler. In this case the state was not of direct divine origin, and consequently certain unalterable and inalienable rights of the individual could be maintained against the state. In his compendious *Natural Law*, Wolff elaborated this theory, which had some influence on Blackstone, the author of the *Commentaries on the Law of England*, and through him possibly on the origins of the American Bill of Rights. But all eighteenth-century German political philosophers opposed the right of resistance to the government and refused to recognize popular institutions limiting the authority of sovereigns. As Kant put it later, there was only "the palladium of the pen" for the defense of natural rights. The government, though it should serve the welfare and happiness of the people, was actually free to act as it chose. Everything for the people, nothing by the people, was the practical maxim of this state, and no limits of state power existed except the respect for right which philosophy might plant in the heart of rulers. On the other hand, the state was a utilitarian institution, and outside of the obedience to its laws, the individual might live for the realization of his personal happiness.

Leibniz's attempt to find a harmony between a common culture and a common political organization was resumed in the German idealistic school on a new basis. The concept of the identity between *Volk*, people, and state has at least some roots in Leibniz. In this respect as in others, Leibniz was not only the father of German Enlightenment but also the progenitor of German idealism, particularly as represented by Herder, Hegel, and Schelling. It should be remembered, in this connection, that the writings of Leibniz were published only piecemeal over a long period of time. When, in 1765, his *Nouveaux essais sur l'entendement humain* appeared, the full scope of his thought could be grasped for the first time by a generation anxious to discover more than the mathematical and rationalistic side of philosophy.

ᴔ *Popular Enlightenment*

THE ENLIGHTENMENT was popularized in Germany by Thomasius (1655–1728) and Wolff (1679–1754). The jurist Thomasius was the first German professor who gave lectures in German. Developing character and an understanding of practical affairs were as much his aims as equipping men with a scholastic training. He conceived of jurisprudence as completely separated from theological ethics and deriving from a rationalistic interpretation of natural law. The *honnête homme* was his ideal, a man who lived according to the precepts of reason in frugal happiness, bent on the improvement of society. Thomasius's ideas lacked profundity, although he displayed both a great deal of common sense and civil courage. It is sad to report that none of the official churches ever undertook to abolish the crimes committed against the dignity of man in the execution of justice. Thomasius openly fought against the pagan superstition of witchcraft and the barbaric cruelties of torture. In certain respects at least the Enlightenment was more Christian than established Christian religion.

Thomasius exercised great influence on the future civil servants of the Prussian monarchy. The undogmatic but socially active Christianity of Francke and Thomasius's zeal for the reform of public administration gave the University of Halle an important place in German intellectual development and secured the support of King Frederick William I. Narrow-minded and unrefined as he was, he could see the advantages which accrued to his state from the spirit of Halle. He added to its faculty chairs of economics or "cameralism" as it was then called, in order to give the training of his bureaucrats still more practical substance. But it was difficult for him to understand the philosophical work of Wolff, who came to Halle in 1706. Wolff, his fame enhanced by his expulsion from Halle in 1723, was considered the great German philosopher of the century. Even Kant, who is responsible for the fact that Wolff's philosophy is nowadays forgotten, found his early philosophical orientation in Wolff. Quite apart from content, Wolff created the form of expression which made the German language suitable for original philosophizing. Thereby he fulfilled Leibniz's demand for the cultivation of a new German prose, as in most respects he was the heir of Leibniz, whose thought he systematized and presented in an academic manner. In Wolff's career the spread of the Enlightenment in Germany was clearly reflected. At the time when Frederick William I was persuaded by pietistic sycophants to drive Wolff out of Prussia, the professor was one of the pillars of Halle, but he was not yet widely known beyond his university. When Frederick II, immediately after his accession to the throne, in 1740, invited Wolff back, he returned from Marburg to Halle in triumph, but he never regained the attention of many students. By that time his ideas had become the common property of all academicians.

In spite of the deep cleavage which existed between the ideas of Pietism and the Enlightenment, both movements had some ideals in common. Both placed a new significance on the individual, whether it was the personal religious experience of the Pietists or the belief of the *philosophes* in the autonomy of reason. The two groups also were in contact with regard to their practical impulses. Both wanted a reform of social conditions and education. Both were interested in a native culture, even though the German Enlightenment took its models to a large extent from Western Europe. Thomasius had infuriated the orthodox professors of Leipzig not merely by announcing a course in German but also by specifying as its subject *The Rules of Practical Wisdom* of the Spanish moralist Balthasar Gracian, whose writings were much in vogue in France during these years. He boldly added the subtitle "In what way one should emulate the French in the conduct of life." But Thomasius and all German educators recognized that an improved style of life could be produced in Germany only through the cultivation of a German civilization, and not by the simple transplantation of French forms. The Enlightenment spread more rapidly than Pietism, since it entered with eagerness into an alliance with the political powers of the age and, through universities, high schools, and schools, affected Germany in all classes above the peasant level.

✑ *German Literature of the Seventeenth Century*

THE REFORM OF THE GERMAN LANGUAGE was a concern widely felt in Germany at the beginning of the seventeenth century. Luther's Bible translation and his own writings had not uprooted the German dialects. Particularly in North Germany, Luther's Bible was adjusted to local dialects, and sermons were preached in the local vernacular. Only between 1590 and 1650 did high German become the standard language in the pulpits and schools of North Germany, and Switzerland adopted high German as a literary language even later. For the future development of a German literature and the easy exchange of ideas on a national scale, this proved of importance, and mutual intercourse was further stimulated by the various societies, founded after the model of the humanistic academies of Italy, which included the use and improvement of German speech among their objectives. The "Fruit-bearing Society," the "Palm Order," or the "Pegnitz Shepherds" were associations in which aristocrats and commoners mingled and which even tried to disregard the denominational division in the heat of the Thirty Years' War.

Luther's language was a great instrument for the expression of religious sentiments but too rich in imagery and metaphor to serve as the instrument of exact learning. It was not in every respect suitable to the intercommunication of a highly stylized society. Latin and French words were abundant in the German of the seventeenth century. A general deterioration of all literary expression was the consequence. What Germany, in contrast to France and England, did not possess was a capital in which a differentiated society created standards of taste and forms adequate to express the full scale of human experiences. The active guardianship of language lay in the hands of small groups of intellectuals thinly spread over the Empire. As far as the nobility took part in cultural activities, it was widely attracted by modern French civilization. The scholars lived largely in the ban of a senescent Latin humanism. In these circumstances the struggle for the growth and revitalization of the German language lasted well into the late eighteenth century. It could be added that to the present time the standards of this language have not been very firm. Good German has remained a highly individualized art, while popular usage has been susceptible to obtuseness.

With few exceptions, the German literature of the seventeenth century has been forgotten. Actually the general religious and intellectual trends of this age were all reflected in this literature, which had its center in Protestant Germany, but hardly a single work broke through to a universality which characterizes a great monument of human expression and assures it an after-life. Martin Opitz, born the son of a Protestant minister in Silesia in 1597, published his book *On German Poetry* in 1624, and a year later his own *Poems*. For practically a century his theories and practical aims enjoyed canonic respect. Opitz wanted to create a German literature equal to that of the Netherlands and France, and for that purpose established a metric code and rules for the treatment of subjects which were derived from humanism. No doubt, German poetry could stand order both in form and substance. The insistence on the identity of word and verse accent was quite sound, and equally beneficial was his effort to steer German literature away from the plebeian and burlesque qualities in which it abounded. But both forms and objects of art were defined in a narrow and pedantic fashion. Poetry had a didactic task and was expected to bring wisdom and elevated feeling to the less learned people. All literary arts assumed a rationalistic and rhetorical character, and since they imitated foreign models, they spoke in stereotypes, substituting weak allegories for telling symbols. Artistic creation was not nourished by visionary power that springs from the genuineness of living experience.

Among the lyric poets, the warm and passionate Paul Fleming (1609–40) showed creative imagination, but real greatness came into the open only where deep religious faith dominated the lyric forms. The hymn book of the Rhenish Jesuit Friedrich von Spee, posthumously published in 1649, introduced the mysticism of the soul's love of Christ into the religious literature of Germany. In Protestant Pietism, particularly in the more than two thousand religious poems of Count Nicolaus von Zinzendorf of Herrnhut, this mysticism found further, often tortuous, expression. A pantheistic mysticism found its poetic voice in Johannes Scheffler (1624–77). He began as a Protestant physician and, through Jacob Boehme, was led to the medieval mystics, converted in 1653, and became a zealous Catholic priest. He published his *Cherubinic Wanderer* in 1657 under the pseudonym Angelus Silesius. His writings included religious hymns also.

The greatest religious poet was Paul Gerhardt (1607–76). The numerous religious songs of this loyal orthodox Lutheran minister, who stood his ground even against the Great Elector, made him the most creative song-writer of Protestantism after Luther. While Luther's hymns, such as *A mighty fortress is our God*, were intended as expressions of the faith and hope of a congregation, Gerhardt's hymns were the professions of faith of the individual believer in the objective truths of Christian religion before the congregation. In Gerhardt the consciousness of the assurance contained in the Christian message and membership was counteracted by a highly individualized piety. He accompanied the events of the ecclesiastical year in his poems, and they also depicted the divine presence in the world, particularly the peace and beauty of nature. The new poetic rules of Opitz and a purified simple language became the vehicle of a personal religiosity of unaffected depth. Under the influence of Pietism the Church lost significance, and the relation of the individual soul and God became the center of imaginary thinking again. Gottfried Arnold[5] and Gerhard Tersteegen (1697–1769) were the most eminent representatives of this later religious poetry, which was not only more mystical but also more subjective in character.

The seventeenth century by no means conceived of art as an expression of subjective sentiment. Art still had chiefly a social function. Its intent was to throw into bold relief the forces and virtues which would enhance the life of the community. At the lowest level, this could mean mere entertainment or the supply of fanciful material to satisfy curiosity. The novel in its manifold forms, heroic, court, travel, satiric, and moralistic narration, attempted to still this hunger. But only where a talent rooted in the richness of native popular life could transcend the imitation of foreign models were lasting works born. The *Adventurous Simplicissimus* of H. J. C. von Grimmelshausen (1625–76), published in 1668, followed the pattern of the Spanish picaresque novel but breathed the reality of German life not only in its subject, the development of the poor peasant boy Simplicius in the midst of the disasters of the Thirty Years' War, but also in its woodcut-like treatment. The Hessian author, who in his later years made his home in Alsace, had been a soldier in the War, of which he preserved for posterity a naturalistic picture. But both in literary composition and the deeper interpretation of human motives, the work was rough and uneven.

The "social" art above all others has always been the drama. General conditions were most unfavorable to the growth of a German dramatic art. Not only the lack of a capital but also the separation of the social classes deprived any potential dramatist of a public which was reasonably united in its ideals of life and esthetic taste. In France, where the civil wars had imperiled the cultivation of literature and theater, Richelieu's patronage of the Académie and the Comédie had been an important contribution to the flowering of arts in the seventeenth century. But the French rulers and the French nobility were truly representative of the cultural aspirations of the nation, whereas none of the German princes or aristocrats lived in such a natural relationship. Landgrave Maurice of Hesse, who built the first standing theater, a wooden shed, in 1605, and Duke Henry Julius of Brunswick were

[5] See p. 143.

princes who took an interest in a German dramatic art. But even if they had found successors in these pursuits, chances of a reform of the German stage were small. The Jesuits still carried on the tradition of the medieval church play; schools, Catholic as well as Protestant, had their humanistic plays, and the popular wandering theaters catered to low taste. The cheap comedy also was an outgrowth of the ecclesiastical culture of the Middle Ages and the carnival play.

To unify these heterogeneous forms into a single theatrical art proved impossible in the Germany of that age. The courts turned to foreign theater, be it French or, as in Vienna, Italian. The German theater was confined to the schools or the cheap, almost circus-like theaters, all living on a greater or lesser emulation of the Western European drama. The Italian comedy helped to revive the German popular play; the harlequin became the *Hanswurst*. In Vienna this branch of thespian art was especially popular, and in 1706 the actor Joseph Anton Stranitzky founded the first permanent German stage for this genre. A larger repertoire was presented by the migratory dramatic companies from England, which toured Germany from the end of the sixteenth to the early eighteenth century. Only after 1650 do they seem to have played in German. In this fashion, Shakespeare and Marlowe came to Germany, though in a frightfully mutilated form.

The greatest dramatic talent of seventeenth-century Germany was the Silesian Andreas Gryphius (1616–64). An earnest and somber figure, he acquired a broad philosophical education in Holland, and he also learned much from the Dutch drama. In all types of dramatic art, Gryphius actively tried to produce works of better form and higher meaning, but he could not help approaching an insensitive public with loud effects and exaggerated sentiments, which his less gifted successors of the so-called Silesian school carried to even greater length. A different kind of drama was created by Christian Weise (1642–1708), the school-principal of Zittau in Saxony. He made the transition to a natural style and rationalistic philosophy. But he could stage his plays only in his school. In the early decades of the eighteenth century, few plays were published in print.

The hold which Opitz maintained long after his death was superseded by that of Johann Christoph Gottsched (1700–66). Particularly between 1730 and 1740, he made Leipzig the center of German literature. Under his influence, the university, at which he taught from 1725 on, became a seat of the German Enlightenment like Halle. Through his literary periodicals he banned all bombast from German literature. French classicism was made supreme. With the help of Friederike Caroline Neuber, the most eminent actress of the period, he drove *Hanswurst* from the theatrical stage into the Punch and Judy play. Translations from the French and his own stage plays set a new elegant style. It was the transformation from the age of the long periwig to that of the pigtail. But together with the verve and *grandezza* of the Baroque, the free play of poetic imagination was discredited.

☙ *Musical Life*

THE LANGUISHING STATE OF THE GERMAN THEATER and of literature in general in the century between 1650 and 1750 was partly caused by the attraction of modern opera. This last great creation of the Italian Renaissance was ideally fitted to express the whole range of sentiments, passions, and poses in which the courtly society wished to live. It also provided the opportunity for lavish display which was the obsession of all high personages. After the middle of the seventeenth century the Italian opera found a permanent home in Vienna, Munich, and Dresden, and other courts followed. In Berlin the first Italian opera was performed in 1700, but Frederick the Great dedicated the opera house in Berlin to "Apollo and the Muses" as late as 1742. German princes spent enormous sums on Italian singers and ballet dancers as well as stage decorations. Composers, conductors, and vocalists were predominantly Italian. Among the instrumentalists, German musicians were rather frequent, and ultimately some Germans mastered the Italian style completely. In his lifetime the court conductor of Dresden, Johann Adolf Hasse (1699–1783) was considered the greatest German-Italian composer. Even the Italians spoke of him as *il gran Sassone*.

The Italian opera was of great consequence for the German musicians who absorbed a rich world of forms from it. But the opera had little influence on the German people. The attempts to create a German opera failed. In Hamburg a permanent theater was opened with the performance of a German opera in 1678. But its founders had overrated the possibilities of contemporary German language and poetry. Eminent musicians, such as Keiser, Mattheson, and Telemann, endeavored to develop the Hamburg theater. The young Händel performed his first two operas here in 1703–05. Still, whereas in the France of Louis XIV the Florentine Lully could create a French opera out of the spirit of Corneille and Racine, a comparable test in Germany was unpromising in the absence of a German drama. The world of ancient gods and heroes meant little to Hamburg burghers. Biblical subjects belonged to the Church. In order to keep a large enough audience, one had to reach out after a while for low comedy again. In 1738, the Hamburg opera was closed. A similar enterprise undertaken in Leipzig lasted only from 1693 to 1729.

The Church was still the natural place for the growth of musical art in Germany. It was understandable that German Catholicism for the time being was satisfied with cultivating the traditional and modern Italian music. The longing for the adaptation of Italian forms to different spiritual conceptions was more likely to come to the fore in German Protestantism. Slowly this trend gathered strength and artistic capacity. The merger of the lyric tonality of Italian music with the spirit of German Protestantism was first achieved by Heinrich Schütz (1585–1672). He came from a rather well-to-do Saxon burgher family, received his musical education under Gabrielli, and remained in contact with Italian composers, such as Monteverdi, throughout his life. From 1615 to his death, he was the director of music in Dresden. This brave man saved the existence of the musical institutions of the Saxon capital through the devastations of the Thirty Years' War and successfully strove to realize his own artistic ideals. In the last years of the War, the *Seven Words at the Cross* appeared, and in 1666 he saw the publication of his three great *Passions*, works which prepared the way for the oratorios of Bach and Händel. The years at the close of the century also produced great organists like Buxtehude (1637–1707) and Pachelbel (1653–1706).

✑ *Johann Sebastian Bach*

IN THE EARLY PERIOD of Lutheranism, the choral had served as an expression of congregational creed. But the Lutheran faith not only intended to engender the confidence which derived from a common belief in the Christian message but also wished to have the message understood as the confirmation of the individual's struggle for salvation. The religious hymns of Paul Gerhardt and others already tended to stress individual feeling, but the new musical forms as used by the cantata opened up entirely novel possibilities. Choral and choir lent themselves well to the presentation of congregational trust, while the recitative and aria became the means for expressing the interaction of the objective contents of religion and individual feeling. From here it was only another step to undertake the presentation of the contents themselves, as Bach did through the evangelist and the Jesus in his *Passions*, together with the reflections and moods which the fundamental Christian ideas awaken in the sensitive heart of an active believer. This oratorio became another form of Protestant service, including sermon and the administration of sacraments. Though grown on Protestant soil, the religious music of Bach transcends the walls of individual Christian churches. Shakespeare, using and expanding the forms of the Italian Renaissance, created in the midst of the national life of England a poetic world which was as English as it was universal. Bach, through the use of Italian musical forms, achieved something similar in many respects. Within the Lutheran society of Germany he made visible the deepest substance of Christian religion.

Johann Sebastian Bach (1685–1750) was the descendant of many generations of musicians in Thuringia and Saxony. The craft-guild tradition of his family lived on in him. He was a strong man and by no means aloof from the life of the community. Nor was his music confined to the church. He was productive in all fields of secular music as well. But it was not the circumstances of his final position as city-appointed cantor of the Thomas Church in Leipzig, which included much more than the direction of church music, that made him express his highest ideas in religious music. His piety was genuine, and although he resented the hostility toward art shown by the Pietists and looked for support from the orthodox ministers, his music showed the influence of subjectivist religion. Yet he belonged to a much earlier age than the one in which he actually lived. It seems amazing that he arrived in Leipzig in 1723 almost simultaneously with Gottsched and that Frederick the Great could welcome him as a visitor in Potsdam, in 1747.

✍ *G. F. Händel*

GEORG FRIEDRICH HÄNDEL (1685–1759) was born in the same year as Bach. The son of a physician in Halle, he came from a somewhat more intellectual and individualistic atmosphere. The choice to devote himself to music was his own, and throughout his life he hated dependence on others and wanted to be the creator not only of his own works but also of his own career and position. After an early musical education in Germany, which in particular set him on the way to becoming one of the greatest organ players, and after a few years at the Hamburg opera, he went to Italy, where he conversed with the Italian composers, the Scarlattis and Corelli, and soon was celebrated by the public as a great composer of Italian opera. In 1710, he was appointed conductor at the court of Hanover, but was almost immediately on his way to England. The move of the Hanover court to London, in 1714, made England his permanent home. He was luckier than Leibniz, who would have liked to exchange the great political and social scene of London for the narrow locale of Hanover. Händel and Leibniz were kindred spirits, each uniting a profound reflecting mind with the urge for practical action and the piety of individual sentiment with a confident faith in the world.

From 1720 to 1741 Händel struggled against tremendous odds to give the Italian opera a definite place in England. Italian forms were little modified by him, but his operas showed a deeper, less conventional expressiveness both in melody and harmony, and thereby greater dramatic powers. It was a curious fact that the German composer introduced the English vernacular to the Italian musical drama. His attempt to plant the Italian opera firmly on English soil failed, in spite of temporary triumphs. Elevated popular sentiment in England was still directly rooted in Christian religiosity, and the most vigorous musical practice was carried on by the fine English choirs. The financial collapse of his operative enterprises drove Händel to the full development of the oratorio, the musical form in which his genius reached its richest expression and, at the same time, closest consonance with the English life of the age. The denial of the stage and also the move from the church to the concert hall determined Händel's art of the oratorio. Even the characterization which stage-setting, costume, and acting had permitted in the opera had to be achieved in the oratorio by musical means alone. Händel's music assumed a new dimension, freely expressing outside the church the substance of Protestant religion. Biblical history, as the record of God's relations with his elected people, was depicted in his *Messiah* and *Judas Maccabaeus*. They were musical theodicies and ethics for heroically minded Christians. Herein they corresponded to the national temper of England, which had entered on a glorious period of her history full of outward successes but also of internal crises, such as the Stuart insurrection and the battle of Culloden, in 1746. This explains the veneration felt for the old Händel by much larger circles of the English people than his operas had ever reached. Not only a new form of music had been born but also a new public had been created. The concert hall, the center of modern musical culture, had come into existence.

No artist before Händel had been taken to heart by a whole nation during his lifetime. Fittingly, Händel was buried in Westminster Abbey. These events were a prelude to the modern adoration of the artistic genius, as Händel showed signs of the consciousness of the modern artist's freedom and mission. In Germany, Händel could not have expressed himself fully. Here his music did not become very well known until a century after his birth. Even Bach was known outside of Leipzig during the eighteenth century only for his chamber and organ music. The oratorios of Bach and Händel were included in a living musical tradition by the romantic school of the early nineteenth century. The connections between the classic Vienna composers and Bach and Händel were rather tenuous.

✍ Baroque Art

THE DISCONTINUITY OF THE MUSICAL TRADITION demonstrates that Germany was not only politically but also culturally departmentalized. The development of the visual arts mirrored the same picture. Whereas literature and music were the prominent forms of artistic achievement in Protestant Germany, the visual arts were the creative expression of German Catholicism. Neighbors of the Latin countries, in the case of Austria the actual government of large Italian provinces, and linked naturally with the Church of Rome, the Catholic states kept in contact with the art of Italy and subsequently France as well. The Catholic Reformation had created the Baroque style, or at least the Jesuit order had made it dominant and exported it on a world-wide basis. In Munich and Salzburg, the Italian Baroque was represented as early as the last years of the sixteenth century. The Thirty Years' War did not stop artistic work everywhere, but tended to end opposition to the Italian style which had existed in some parts of Germany. The international acceptance which the Baroque style had acquired by 1650 made it appealing even to Protestant patrons. There were, however, relatively few patrons of art in Protestant Germany. The Protestant churches had inherited enough church buildings, and the nobility was not very wealthy. In Austria, the end of the Thirty Years' War, and even more the liberation from the Turks, started an enormous building activity. The Emperors were not the chief sponsors of this architecture. The new wealthy nobility, eager to settle down to a life of splendor and worried about the inflation in Austria, invested in a grandiose manner in architectural projects, as did the monastic orders, which again enjoyed secure rents. The Jesuits did little building at this time and were far outdone by the old orders, the Benedictines and the Augustinian canons, and Premonstratensians. Ecclesiastical princes played a prominent part in addition to the secular rulers in the Empire. None of them did more than decorate their old cathedral churches in the new style. Insofar as they constructed churches, they were votive or pilgrimage churches. Rather, to exult in their sovereignty, they built themselves new palaces of extravagant dimensions.

Baroque is an ill-defined style. In a formalistic sense, Baroque art could be called a variation of Renaissance art. As a matter of fact, none of the individual structural or decorative patterns was original; all of them can be traced back to classic models. It was the way in which these forms were employed which made the difference, and this distinction rested on a change of human attitude toward life and art. In general, Baroque art tried to find a place for the metaphysical side of life besides the natural one, for the inward experience of the soul as distinct from the contemplation of objective beauty. The Baroque artist did not reject nature. In certain respects he employed color and sense impression in a more lavish manner than the Renaissance artist had done. Nor did he deny reason or even mathematics. For that it is only necessary to look at a Baroque garden. But the Baroque artist believed that proportionate forms did not express total reality, particularly not the supranational forces. Within this broad frame, a great variety of artistic solutions was possible, and the history of art in the various countries bore this out. Classicism remained present in Baroque art everywhere, even in the Spain of El Greco. In France, the classicist element was particularly strong, and Cartesianism made it still more so. Baroque feeling was weak in the visual arts of England, and in Dutch architecture the rational element also prevailed. Into the last years of the seventeenth century, Germany remained under the influence of Italian architects. Thereafter two generations of great German architects assumed the leadership and developed Austrian, Bavarian, Franconian, and Rhenish Baroque architecture. With its emphasis on dynamic emotionalism and its flowing forms, this architecture was one of the great contributions to European Baroque art.

In the decades after the Thirty Years' War and even after the victories over the Turks, Italian architects were the chief designers of all building projects in the Habsburg territories. Undoubtedly they accommodated themselves to the landscape and general conditions of Austria; on the other hand the Austrian artisans whom they employed participated in the execution of their plans with understanding. But it was a novel event when German artists began to replace the Italian builders. The first to acquire a prominent and even dominant position was Johann Bernhard Fischer von Erlach (1656–1723). Fischer received his decisive formative impressions in Rome, where he was still able to meet Bernini and saw the last works of Borromini. Fischer was a man of wide knowledge and had a reflective mind. Architecture, like music, belonged to the subjects in which an Austrian nobleman was to be educated. Fischer was selected as teacher of the heir to the throne, King Joseph (Joseph I), for whom he drew, among other projects, grandiose plans for an Austrian "Versailles," the palace of Schönbrunn. However, after the early death of the Emperor, these projects were executed only under Maria Theresa and in a more modest fashion. A good many other of Fischer's building projects did not come to fruition until after his death. The structures erected by him in Salzburg, Vienna, and Prague were too numerous to be enumerated here. Within Baroque art, Fischer represented a classicist taste. His younger peer among the Viennese architects, Lucas Hildebrand (1668–1745), followed a warmer and somewhat more popular style. Like so many of the architects of that time, he began as an army engineer and was made court engineer in 1701. He became the favorite of the greatest art connoisseur of the period, Prince Eugene, for whom he devised the Belvedere. Fischer and Hildebrand gave Vienna its Baroque face, which expressed the sentiment of Austria at the moment when it became the capital of the new Habsburg empire. But the new architecture was not confined to Vienna, Salzburg, and Prague. It flowered all over Austria. In the world of Jacob Prandauer (1655–1727), especially the magnificent abbeys of Melk and St. Florian, Baroque art assumed its most specifically Austrian character.

Austrian Baroque architecture, however, was only part of a wider German movement which sprang up simultaneously in Bohemia and Silesia and particularly in Bavaria, as well as in Swabia, Franconia, and along the Rhine. Everywhere it was represented by artists of extraordinary talent, such as Johann Michael Fischer (1691–1766), the Asam brothers (Cosmas Damian, 1686–1742, and Egid Quirin, 1692–ca. 1750) in Bavaria; Johann Dientzenhofer (died 1726) and Balthasar Neumann (1687–1753) in Franconia; and Maximilian Welsch (1671–1743) in the Rhineland. Italians remained active in Germany, and

German Baroque art never broke its connections with Italy, although after the War of Spanish Succession, first in the Wittelsbach courts of Munich and Cologne, French influence became important. But even this French influence was absorbed in the specifically German form of Baroque. It was characteristic, for example, that the so-called rococo pattern, used by French artists under Louis XIV exclusively as a decorative element, in the hands of the Germans became an element of architectural style.

Church and palace building were the chief tasks of art. One may be allowed to say that in the buildings of the orders the two fused into a single undertaking. The Austrian abbeys of Melk, St. Florian, Göttweig, Admont, the Bavarian Ettal, the Swabian Weingarten and Ottobeuren, and the Silesian Grünau were all monastic buildings centered around a church. They were Baroque castles of Christ. Outside of the monastic world, church and residence separated, and where a whole new city was planned, as in Karlsruhe or Darmstadt, it was oriented toward the princely palace rather than a church. Belatedly Emperor Charles VI attempted to create for himself an "Escorial." In Klosterneuburg construction of a great palace was started around the medieval church. Its finished central part was capped by the imperial crown, while its wings were to be covered by all other Habsburg crowns. The whole complex of buildings was to symbolize the universality of imperial dignity morally supported by universal religious faith. But Maria Theresa did not complete her father's project. Instead, she built Schönbrunn with its gardens. But even the prince-bishops of the Empire built themselves secular palaces, such as the grandiose *Residenzen* of Würzburg, Bonn (bishopric Cologne), Bruchsal (bishopric Speyer), and Pommersfelden (bishopric Bamberg). Nothing distinguished them from the contemporary palaces of secular princes, such as Schleisheim and Nymphenburg in Bavaria, Ludwigsburg in Württemberg, Rastatt in Baden, or Weikersheim in Hohenlohe.

The same artistic style dominated both churches and palaces, but the nature of the artistic task was different. The churches were intended to direct the faithful toward transcendental truth and joy. Their interior, composed as a single entity using sculpture and painting as supporting means of architecture, was designed to lift the believer from this earth toward heaven. The chief attention is drawn toward the main altar and the central cupola above it, through which light is flooding. If one raises one's sight, the cupola does not seem an enclosure of the room but, on the contrary, a direct panorama of heaven. If the eye falls back into the interior of the church, it discovers the angels and saints, freed of all weight and suspended in ideal space worshiping the divine or inviting mortal men to exaltation. Never before in the Christian ages had art seen the transcendental mystery in the full-blooded reality of human life, never before had it used sensual attractions to stir men to devotion to the same extent.

In contrast, the palace aimed at the display of human power. Already the park showed man's control over nature, but the building itself represented a world beyond the ordinary. These, indeed, were palaces fit for heroes to live in. Mingling with the classic gods, they could feel like Olympians themselves. Here the transfiguration of reality was a hymn to the greatness of man. It is perhaps natural that the two poles of art, the Christian heaven and Olympus, were moved closer together once religious sentiment grew weaker, as happened in the later eighteenth century.

Baroque architecture was the art of Catholic Germany. For a moment it seemed as if northern Germany would join the movement. Frederick I, who liked display, wanted to emulate the style of the South in order to glorify his new royal dignity. In Andreas Schlüter (1664–1714) he found an original talent. The royal palace of Berlin and that of Charlottenburg as well as the Armory were built while Schlüter was court architect. But building came to a practical standstill in Prussia under Frederick William I, except for the construction of some churches, and here Dutch classicism prevailed. What happened in Prussia was typical of all of Protestant North Germany. The few examples of German Baroque art in the North were singular cases. Only where Catholicism extended to the North, as at the court of August the Strong of Saxony, did Baroque art find a home. With the architects Matthäus Daniel Pöppelmann (1662–1736) and Georg Bähr (1666–1738) he transformed Dresden into a Baroque city, and its art collection and Italian opera turned the Saxon capital into what was properly called "the Florence on the Elbe."

↶ The End of the Baroque

THE MIDDLE OF THE EIGHTEENTH CENTURY brought the creative period of German Baroque architecture to its conclusion. To be sure, many Baroque buildings were still built down to the end of the century. Among them were some based on plans of the earlier masters, such as the palace of Schönbrunn or Balthasar Neumann's most beautiful

Church of the Fourteen Saints (*Vierzehnheiligen*), which was begun in 1743 and consecrated in 1792. In the Berlin and Potsdam of Frederick the Great there was a fresh spurt of Baroque architecture which was attractive but not really original. Frederick had a personal concern for literature and music, but architecture to him was rather one of the duties of his royal office. Lucas Hildebrand had died in 1745, Balthasar Neumann in 1753. In 1755, J. J. Winckelmann's first treatise, *Thoughts on the Emulation of Greek Works,* appeared. In it a scholar, not an artist, declared the whole Baroque art to be a false art and presented an entirely new ideal of beauty. By the end of the century the new ideal had captivated the thinking of Germany. But no new art was born from it. Winckelmann's ideas on art enriched the literary and philosophical movement of the late eighteenth century without stimulating the growth of a new representative visual art. More fortunate was the development of music after 1750, the year of J. S. Bach's death. The compositions of his two most gifted sons, Philip Emanuel (1714–88) and Christian (1735–82) left the ways of their father and developed forms which impressed Haydn and Mozart. While Baroque music drew to its end, musical creativity continued on the highest level and appealed to the whole nation. This Baroque architecture had not achieved, nor was the literary and philosophical movement after 1750 to reach such a position within national life.

CHAPTER 7

Austria and Prussia Under Charles VI and Frederick William I

FROM THE LONG PERIOD of wars which came to an end with the peace treaties of Utrecht and Rastatt, Austria emerged the largest European state. But the imposing array of kingdoms, duchies, and principalities which Charles VI called his own after the death of his brother Joseph I in 1711 did not constitute an empire which could make its weight felt with united strength. Territories such as Naples, Sardinia, or the Netherlands could neither be defended by Austria without strong allies nor, in an age of ruthless naval and commercial competition, be developed very well, without maritime strength. Even the defense of the central Danube countries depended to a large degree upon alliances, because the structure of government was incapable of producing the funds needed for an independent position in Europe.

↫ The Balance of Power

SOME INTELLECTUALS, at least, saw in the balance of power, the basis of the Peace of Utrecht, an opportunity to maintain peace with much less military power than had been required in the previous fifty years. The Abbé de St. Pierre, in his treatise *On Perpetual Peace between the Christian Princes*, published in 1713–14, proposed a general security pact and a settlement of conflicts by the majority decision of a congress of states, to be enforced, if necessary, by collective sanctions. Though such a system might have made it possible to reduce armaments, there is little evidence that the project of the Abbé made any impression on the chancelleries of Europe. Still it is noteworthy that such a project was conceived at this juncture of history. The plan was rash in assuming that the cosmopolitan outlook prevailing among so many of Europe's intellectual elite could be easily made the basis of

European statesmanship. It underrated the difficulties of constructing a society of states at a moment when a few of them were pre-eminent and proud of their superiority over the rest. On the other hand, the Peace of Utrecht had created a more solid foundation for the relations among the big states, and insofar as they agreed and acted in accord, they could have enforced peace.

∽ The Quadruple Alliance

CLEAR PROOF OF THIS is the original defeat of Spanish schemes to regain a foothold in Italy. Elizabeth Farnese, the wife of Philip V of Spain, announced claims of succession in Parma and Piacenza. Spain used Austria's involvement in a Turkish war to occupy Austrian Sardinia in 1717 and Savoyard Sicily in 1718. England, France, Holland, and finally Charles VI, concluded the Quadruple Alliance. A short war, in 1719, in which the Austrians conquered Sicily, while the French and English took some Spanish coastal towns, forced Philip V to dismiss Cardinal Alberoni, his cunning foreign minister, and make peace. Only now the War of Spanish Succession found its formal conclusion. Philip recognized the cession of the Netherlands to Austria, and Emperor Charles VI, who, as Charles III of Spain, had gone to Barcelona in 1703, recognized the succession of Philip V to the Spanish throne. Moreover, the hereditary rights of Infanta Don Carlos, the elder son of Philip V and Elizabeth Farnese, in Parma, Piacenza, and Toscana were acknowledged. The Emperor received Sicily, and Duke Vittorio Amedeo of Savoy received Sardinia. The concert of the four great powers had restored the balance of Europe with relatively little effort.

Yet, as was quickly shown, this concert was not firmly established. England, because of her own interests unwilling to enforce the peace settlement in every respect, wanted moreover to hold the balance rather than throw her weight on either side. In any event, she felt free to withdraw from the fray whenever her interests seemed satisfied, and these interests were increasingly defined in terms of commerce. Her imperiousness, fickleness, and egotistic materialism made her an unpopular ally. The revival of English-French commercial conflict dominated most of the eighteenth century. The exploitation of Spanish trade with Latin America, a right England gained at Utrecht, made the Spaniards squirm. The exclusion of the Austrian Netherlands from the Atlantic trade and the opposition to the growth of Austria's Mediterranean commerce embittered the Viennese government.

The other members of the Quadruple Alliance either were ineffectual or would not subordinate narrower and selfish interests to the cause of ensuring lasting peace. Fortunately, Dutch interests were compatible with those of England. But its international influence shrinking fast, the Dutch Republic, outside of its own orbit, was a negligible guarantor of the European order. For a short period after the Peace of Utrecht and the death of Louis XIV, France was too exhausted to conduct an active foreign policy. Under the regency of Philip Orléans she joined forces with England to maintain the balance. But the desire to complete the work of Richelieu and Mazarin in gaining unassailable continental frontiers made France a doubtful supporter of the Utrecht settlement. In particular, one great gap in France's eastern boundaries still existed in Lorraine.

Even Austria was not satisfied. What Austria needed most was a period of internal consolidation, similar to that of Prussia under Frederick William I. In order to gain time for domestic reorganization, strict adherence to the system of Utrecht would have been required. Actually, Charles VI, who still hoped that Spain could be brought back to Habsburg rule, did not believe in the Utrecht settlement. After Charles had accepted Philip's kingship in 1720, the dream assumed a different form. The Vienna treaty of 1725 between Austria and Spain made vague promises about a future marriage between the elder son of Queen Elizabeth of Spain and Maria Theresa. A pointedly anti-French and anti-English alliance was built upon these promises. The immediate reaction was an Anglo-French counteralliance, joined by Prussia in the Herrenhausen Convention of September 3, 1725. The very idea of a possible revival of the universalist Catholic policy of the Habsburgs frightened Frederick William I. In October, 1726, however, the Austrian statesmen succeeded in bringing the soldier-king back into the imperial camp. Frederick William had reached the conclusion that he was risking much without gaining anything through his alliance with the Western powers, especially since Peter the Great's successor, Catherine I of Russia, concluded a defensive alliance with Austria. On December 23, 1728, the Austro-Prussian treaty developed into a full-blown alliance through the Treaty of Berlin. Both governments pledged their mutual support in European, specifically Empire, affairs.

Thus for a while Austria, at least diplomatically, was the leader of a Continental bloc of states. But Austria's military weakness was not overlooked in the councils of Vienna, and it was not pleasant to contemplate what profits strong allies such as Russia or Prussia might derive from it in the event of war. The whole alignment, moreover, was insincere. Emperor Charles VI was undecided and eventually unwilling to have his daughter marry Don Carlos. Without assurance in this matter, Queen Elizabeth saw no point in continuing an alliance which exposed Spain to great dangers from England. Through the Treaty of Sevilla, of November 9, 1729, Spain joined the political and commercial system of England, France, and the Dutch Republic and, in return, was promised support for the advancement of her designs on central Italy. Finally, the emperor recognized that the policy of the last decade had to be liquidated. By now, however, this could only be done at a fairly high price. All plans to develop large-scale maritime trade and navigation for the Netherlands and Naples and Sicily had to be sacrificed and Spain had to be admitted into Italy. The (second) Treaty of Vienna, of March, 1731, which embodied these concessions, was signed after many months of great tension in Europe. It was the beginning of a period in which Charles VI concentrated on gaining general acceptance of the future succession of Maria Theresa to the throne of Austria without relating the state to other powers, such as Spain or, as Prince Eugene recommended, Bavaria.

✺ *The Austrian Succession*

THE PROBLEM OF AUSTRIAN SUCCESSION occupied Charles VI almost from the beginning of his reign. In 1703, when he had left for Spain, Emperor Leopold had written a "mutual succession pact," which was to settle the rights to the throne between the Austrian and Spanish lines. Reference was made to the succession of female descendants. The daughters of the elder Joseph were to precede those of Charles. Joseph I died, in 1711, leaving two daughters, and Charles VI felt free to change the mutual pact of succession in all the Habsburg lands in favor of his own male and female offspring. On April 19, 1713, when the new family law, called the Pragmatic Sanction, was announced in a secret session of the council of state, there was little reason to consider the matter as of first importance. But when the first-born infant died, in 1716, and two princesses were born, in 1717–18, apprehension was felt that no male heir would appear. After the birth of a third daughter, in 1724, it was much harder to suppress this fear.

After 1718, the imperial government publicly announced the Pragmatic Sanction and requested the consent of the estates of the various Habsburg countries. By 1732, all the estates had consented, but with the proviso that the act was not to lessen the existing rights and privileges of the component units of the Habsburg empire. Although the proviso was a declaration against a centralistic system of government, the unanimous consent still was an impressive demonstration of loyalty. The ruling groups of the many territories considered the unity and indivisibility of the Habsburg empire desirable and were to prove it in the years of crisis after 1740. After the approval of the estates had been given, the Austrian government sought the approval of the foreign powers. In 1731 England-Hanover and the Dutch Republic added their recognition of the Pragmatic Sanction to that of Russia, Spain, and Prussia. These letters of assent proved of doubtful value, although without some of them, particularly England's, the empire might not have survived. In 1732 the Empire formally expressed its consent. But at the same time the prestige of Habsburg power was gravely impaired by international developments which occurred after the death of August II the Strong of Saxony, King of Poland.

✧ *War of the Polish Succession*

FRANCE WISHED THE ELECTION of Stanislaus Leszczyński, who had been the favorite of Charles XII against August II, and had meanwhile become the father-in-law of Louis XV. He was elected, in September 1733, against Frederick August II of Saxony, the candidate of Russia and Austria. Both these powers moved troops toward the frontiers of Poland, but Russia had acted speedily when the election went to Leszczyński, and had the means to keep Poland crippled even from within. At this moment, France declared war on Austria. Spain and Sardinia joined France in order to extend their rule in Italy.

It was not Poland that caused France to go to war. Cardinal Fleury's objective was the acquisition of Lorraine before Francis Stephen, the heir of the senescent duke, ascended the throne. Francis Stephen, who lived at the Viennese court, was generally rumored to have been selected as the bridegroom of Charles VI's young daughter, Maria Theresa. The breach in the eastern defenses of France was to be closed for good.

In the summer of 1733, the French occupied Lorraine and in the fall, captured Kehl. In the spring of 1734, they began the siege of Philipsburg. Neither England nor the Dutch Republic was prepared to help Austria. Prussia was the only state to offer immediate assistance, an army of 50,000 men. But Austria, not unjustly, was wary of Prussia's designs on the Rhineland, and declined the offer, though insisting that Prussia could send 10,000 men as a contingent of the army of the Empire. In other words, the emperor was not willing to deal with Prussia as a European ally but only as an estate of the Empire. The Empire was prevailed upon to declare war on France in January 1734, but the customary weakness of the defense organization of the Empire showed itself again when Bavaria, Cologne, and the Palatinate protested the action. In the Empire the general impression prevailed that the war was not essentially concerned with German affairs but rather with Polish matters.

Prince Eugene proved his unflagging loyalty to the house of Habsburg by accepting the command of the greatly inferior forces which the emperor and Empire marshalled on the Rhine. But the victor of many historic battles, aged and ill, was unable to turn the fortunes of war. Philipsburg fell, and only defensive operations were possible, even after a Russian corps joined Prince Eugene's army at Heidelberg, in August, 1735. The outcome of the fighting against the French, Spaniards, and Sardinians in Italy, where the main forces of Austria were sent, was quite disastrous. Lombardy was practically lost in 1734. A Spanish army and fleet conquered Naples and Sicily. Still, Cardinal Fleury did not intend to carry the war to the length of a general European conflagration. Direct negotiations between Paris and Vienna led to a settlement. Lorraine was to be given to Stanislaus Leszczyński, from whom it was to go to France. Austria ceded Naples and Sicily to Spain. In return, she received Parma and Piacenza and also, indirectly, Tuscany, where Francis Stephen of Lorraine was to be installed as Grand Duke.

Soon after the restoration of peace, on April 21, 1736, Prince Eugene died at the age of seventy-three. In him the Austrian empire which had risen since 1683 was even better represented than in its Habsburg rulers, whom he had served with absolute devotion. He had always felt himself to be a vassal of the Austrian court rather than of the Roman Emperor. German national feelings were alien to him, though he was fully aware of the importance of the Empire for Austria. The monosyllabic prince was an understanding friend of scholars and artists. He had no taste for the nobility's superficial pleasures, and he possessed none of their vices. The ideal of the Christian knight was once more realized in this great soldier-humanist.

Though the loss of southern Italy probably was a blessing in disguise for Austria, the loss of prestige caused by the display of military and political weakness was serious. It was in these years that the Prussian crown prince took the measure of the strength of the Austrian Empire. Austria's—Prince Eugene's—last victories had been gained almost twenty years earlier. In 1714, the Turks opened a war against Venice and reconquered Morea. Realizing that further Turkish successes in the Adriatic would endanger her position in Hungary, Austria took up arms. At Peterwardein, Prince Eugene gained one of his most brilliant victories (August, 1716), and crowned the campaign by the conquest of Belgrade in 1717. In these years, another German general, Matthias von der Schulenburg, a Protestant *Junker* from an *Altmark* family, defeated Turkish attempts to build a position in the Adriatic. The Peace of Passarowitz (1718) gave Austria possession of the last parts of Hungary, of North Serbia with Belgrade, and sections of Wallachia and Bosnia. Austria also received important trading rights in the Turkish Empire.

But all these territorial gains, with the exception of the banat of Temesvar, were lost in the war which Austria, in concert with Russia, waged against the Turks in 1736–39. Russia, Austria's ally since 1726, demanded Austrian assistance in her own efforts to win access to the Black Sea. It seemed unwise to reject Russia's demand, especially since the Austrian government hoped to make conquests which would compensate for the recent losses in Italy. The war, however, was a series of military defeats. The organization of the army as well as the ability of its field commanders had fallen very low. The Peace of Belgrade (September, 1739) which fixed the lower Danube and Save as the southern frontier of the Habsburg empire, was not as calamitous as the manifestation of disorder and debility just at the time when the reign of Charles VI drew to its end.

❧ *Austria under Charles VI*

THE MELANCHOLY HISTORY of Austria's foreign relations under Charles VI cannot be understood without considering the lack of progress in the internal consolidation of governmental powers. The first steps in the direction of the establishment of an absolute regime had been taken in Austria much earlier than in Germany, especially Brandenburg-Prussia. But the relative success of the imposition of monarchical power over the estates, together with the truly gigantic tasks which the combination of such heterogeneous territories presented, brought the movement to an early standstill. The dualistic division between estates and monarch survived in all Habsburg lands. Everywhere estates granted the "contribution," which was a land tax, actually borne by the peasants, and they also delivered soldiers for the army. Through committees, the estates administered a good many military and financial matters, and although their members had to have the confidence of the crown, they remained representatives of the local estates. Besides this administration of the estates, a monarchical administration existed. The latter was responsible not only for the "camerale," i.e., domains, mines, and duties, but also for the taxation of the clergy, cities, and Jews and a great variety of indirect taxes levied on consumer goods and luxuries. Repeated attempts were made to group all of these indirect taxes around a universal excise tax. Only in Bohemia and Silesia was an excise tax collected, but it was just one among other levies.

Although the estates' political opposition to the crown had ceased by the time of Leopold I, the function of the estates in the general administration helped to preserve local interests and made it difficult to develop an effective central governmental organization. The Habsburg empire consisted of three major orbits: the German or Austrian "hereditary lands," the lands of the Bohemian crown, and Hungary with its "separate parts." In addition, the empire included the Italian possessions and the Netherlands. At the beginning of Charles VI's reign, three main governmental offices existed, the Austrian, Bohemian, and Hungarian court chancelleries. To these he added a "Netherlandic" and a "Spanish council," the latter designed to direct the government of the Italian possessions inherited from Spain. It was lavishly staffed with Spanish noblemen and adventurers, who had taken sides with the emperor during his Spanish expedition of 1703–11, and who constantly urged him to renew an Austro-Spanish connection. The loss of Naples eventually confined the Spanish council to more limited tasks. For the narrower field of German history, the Spanish and Netherlandic councils may be disregarded.

Understandably, it was impossible even to try to integrate the Italian and Belgian possessions into a single Habsburg empire, but the contiguous parts, especially the Austrian hereditary lands and Bohemian dominions, could have been brought into a closer political relationship. This would have required a simultaneous streamlining on the lower levels of administration. Silesia and Moravia had institutions of their own, which it was the function of the Bohemian chancellery to coordinate as best it could, whereas the Austrian lands consisted of six duchies. As a result of the division of the Habsburg territories after the death of Ferdinand I, in 1564, certain agencies had come into existence for groups of these Austrian lands, and not all of these agencies were abolished after the restoration of dynastic unity, in 1619 and 1665. Three territorial groups survived: Low Austria, containing Lower and Upper Austria, Interior Austria, comprising Styria, Carinthia, and Carniola, and Anterior Austria with Tyrol and the possessions in southern Germany. Considering the simultaneous existence of offices of the estates and of the crown, it was not surprising that the Austrian or Bohemian court chancelleries had their hands full.

At the time of Charles VI only two agencies existed which exercised functions for the whole empire. Characteristically, they were those supervising finances and defense, the court chamber (*Hofkammer*), and the court war council (*Hofkriegsrat*). In 1713, the court chamber was reorganized along functional instead of territorial lines, although this had to be modified twenty years later. In 1715, this reform was followed by the establishment of a state bank, which was to act as a general pay office, a depository bank, and administrator of the public debt. This so-called *Universalbankalität* to some extent became a competitor of the court chamber. The court war council exercised the supreme functions of command and army organization.

On the highest level, the "privy conference" constituted the chief advisory organ under the emperor. Attempts to make the Austrian court chancellery the central agency of political control succumbed to the resistance of the other chancelleries, including the court chancellery of the Empire. Still, the Austrian court chancellor, who, in addition to foreign affairs, took care of the over-all interests of the imperial family, albeit no prime minister, was always one of the leading political figures of the emperor's government. Together with the presidents of the court chamber and the war council, he was an influential member of a group of about a dozen men chosen from among the heads of the various top agencies. Its membership was never clearly defined, nor did it develop into a body which combined policy-making and executive functions with a division into departments, the main characteristics of a modern cabinet of state. In the days of Charles VI the Austrian chancellor Count Ludwig Philip Sinzendorf, Prince Eugene, and Count Gundaker Starhemberg were probably altogether the most influential members of the privy conference, though often their advice was only partially followed or entirely disregarded. In particular, Prince Eugene's proposal to form the monarchy into a *totum*, an integrated whole, produced few results.

The archaic organization of the Austrian government defeated many mercantilistic enterprises, or at least was responsible for the poor profits they yielded to the public treasury. A theoretical basis for Austrian mercantilism had already been laid in the age of Leopold I by three Germans, two of them converts from Protestantism. Many such converts were found among the Austrian intellectuals and even among the imperial councilors. Johann Joachim Becher, son of a Protestant minister in Speyer, alchemist, physician, and economist, was the most talented and original of the three. His brother-in-law, Johan Philip von Hörnigk, gave the economic ideas of this group their most impressive literary statement in his *Oesterreich über alles, wenn es nur will* (Austria above everything if it wills it), published in the year after the liberation of Vienna and for a full century the most widely read tract on Austrian economy. Wilhelm von Schröder represented the Austrian mercantilist school in a more academic form. All these men pleaded for the development of Austria's economic resources in order to make the empire strong. They demanded the stimulation of industrial production and the exchange of goods among all parts of the empire. A modest economic expansion occurred under Leopold I, but officials able to direct such work were lacking. Capital was scarce and not too well managed by the new manufacturers, many of whom were noblemen who had good connections with the government but little knowledge of production. The long period of war after 1680 made real progress impossible.

The government of Charles VI made a fresh start. A great deal was accomplished in many directions, even though on a small scale. Some local trade barriers were abolished, but not the high walls between the various lands. The local interests represented by the estates opposed unification of commercial policy and often blocked the way even to better communications. The building of the road over the Semmering pass (*Via Carolina*), linking Trieste with the Vienna basin, was the greatest achievement in this regard. With high enthusiasm, Charles VI turned toward the development of colonial trade. The unhappy history of the Ostende Company has already been mentioned. It fell victim to the political counteraction of England and Holland. In the Mediterranean, the political machinations of England and France were embarrassing. But the economic weakness of Austria was, in itself, a handicap to prosperous foreign trade. The Peace of Passarowitz (1718) gave Austria great commercial opportunities in the Turkish empire. But some imports from Turkey actually hurt Hungary, which might have exported similar goods to Austria. Moreover, Austria did not have many commodities for export, particularly of a quality to meet French and British competition. Thus the results of the oriental trade were disappointing. Still, a first step in the development of maritime commerce was made with the growth of the port of Trieste. It was a thorn in the flesh of Venice. If the city of the lagoons raised no open objections, this was a sign of the decline of the Adriatic's former ruler.

Many complaints were heard in Austria about the hostile attitude of the maritime powers toward Austrian commerce. But the Austrian mercantilist writers correctly maintained that the future rested on the development of internal resources and the domestic market rather than on foreign trade. Brandenburg-Prussia learned this lesson quickly and, with considerably smaller resources, built a viable economy strong enough to serve as the foundation of a growing military and political power. The Austrian economy remained too weak to sustain Austria's strength. Her indebtedness, high as early as the eve of the Thirty Years' War, doubled (from 30 to 61 million gulden) in the century between 1612 and 1711, and by 1747 climbed to 106 million. The highly competent Gundaker von Starhemberg, who became the director of Austrian finance in 1703, introduced many improvements, particularly by consolidating a substantial part of the public debt through the Vienna City Bank, but he had to bend all his efforts to camouflage what amounted to near-bankruptcy. While wars, of course, devoured most of the money, the expenditures of the court were also enormous. New credits and loans had to be sought for the payment of debts, which multiplied rapidly because they could only partly be serviced from revenues. When Maria Theresa ascended the throne, the Austrian exchequer contained only a few thousand gulden, despite a dangerous curtailment of military expenditure.

↭ The Rise of Brandenburg-Prussia

In the meantime, Brandenburg-Prussia had gained a new position. The government of the first Prussian king, which came close to imperiling the achievements of the Great Elector, certainly deserves no praise but it did not cause lasting damage to the rise of the Prussian state. Frederick I's love of wasteful pomp has rightly been criticized. His grandson, Frederick the Great, judged the acquisition of the royal title a costly gesture of vanity, unjustified so long as Prussia had not grown stronger. Yet in an age so devoted to the mere ritual of political rank, the sacrifices made for this purpose could not be considered altogether useless. Frederick's was neither an original nor an independent foreign policy. Considering the man, originality could not be expected. And by dissipating money, he increased his dependence on foreign powers. But by accepting subsidies, he managed to maintain, and even expand, the army which his father had created. Perhaps it was not harmful that in his internal regime he took a more conciliatory attitude toward the nobility than had the Great Elector. The latter's forceful policy had essentially established the supremacy of the monarchy over the estates. That under Frederick I the *Junkers* were helped in adjusting themselves to the new political situation was not a loss for the further growth of monarchical absolutism in Prussia.

For the first time in its history, Brandenburg attempted on its own initiative to participate in the best that the artistic and intellectual life of the age had to offer. In his support of artists and scholars, Frederick I was motivated to a large extent by his desire to embellish his kingdom. His wife, Sophie Charlotte, the understanding friend of Leibniz, took a deeper personal interest in these matters. Still, creations such as Leibniz's Academy of Sciences or the architecture of Schlüter had no immediate impact and remained a passing fancy, though later they influenced the young Frederick II. Founding the University of Halle was Frederick I's most important achievement in this area.

✑ *Frederick William I*

BUT EVEN IF WE AVOID HARSH CRITICISM of Frederick I, it is clear that under the rule of men like him Prussia would not have risen to more than medium importance. It would have remained a state comparable to Bavaria and Saxony. One can ask whether such a Prussia might have become a more comfortable state to live in and for others to live with, or whether a state of this type, with its scattered territories, could have survived in subsequent European crises. There are no answers in history to such queries, but it is clear that it was Frederick William I and Frederick II who lifted Prussia to greater heights.

The key to the growth of Prussian power lay in the management of the country's meager resources, and herein Frederick William I proved a master. His reign, from 1713–40, covers almost the same years as the reign of Charles VI. Behind Austria's glorious facade all political problems remained unsolved. Prussia showed a rather dismal outward appearance but gained granite-like strength.

Frederick William I was a boorish man, lacking not only in cultural graces but also in sensitivity for the human feelings of his fellow men. His irascible temper and violent manners made him a formidable tyrant over his family, entourage, and state. Being somehow unsure of himself, he passionately adhered to self-made homespun rules of religion and morals, so far as his choleric nature allowed. He wanted to transform in his own image countries and people whom God had chosen him to govern. Throughout his life, he drove himself hard. Except for an overindulgence in eating, beer drinking, and rough hunting, he knew no pleasures. He abolished all the pomp of his father's court and established himself and his family in an almost burgher-like fashion in a few rooms of the castle. The ground floor was turned into government offices, the basement into the state treasury. The pleasure garden in front of the palace was made into a military drill ground. Thus the chief activities of the Prussian state were under the king's eyes, for he did not trust anybody fully, with the possible exception of the theological professors in Halle. All others needed watching against a reassertion of the old Adam and a lessening of their sense of duty.

In contrast to his forebears, Frederick William I leaned toward Lutheranism. Though the Calvinist concept of predestination made him uneasy, the legalistic side of Calvinist puritanism, on the other hand, had one of its staunchest representatives in the king. Theology, however, was not his interest. For this reason he liked the less dogmatic and more practical Pietistic school.

What remained of religion for Frederick William did not go far beyond the acceptance of certain tenets of doctrine and the fulfillment of moral commandments. These were at the same time the principles which a good ruler had to enforce. A serious conflict between the duties of a Christian and a citizen could not arise as long as the individual subject obeyed the laws and did what his properly appointed ruler told him was his duty. Frederick William felt himself to be the executive manager of God in the affairs of the peoples entrusted to his care, or, since this proximity to the divine made him blush, he often placed an abstract king between himself and God. Said he: "I am the finance minister and field marshal of the King of Prussia." But from all his subjects he demanded absolute obedience. "Everyone has to serve the master with body and life, with his possessions and goods, honor and conscience, and must give everything but salvation; this belongs to God, but everything else must be mine."

In many respects, this uncouth and somewhat preposterous man resembled more the Lutheran princes of the sixteenth century than his crowned cousins of the eighteenth. His emphasis on simple, native customs and virtues linked him to an older generation, though his contempt of all French and other pretentious influences indirectly helped the coming of a new age. If we look at his political practices, the novelty of his regime is even more clearly revealed. The old functions of government, cultivation of pure religious doctrine and justice, were still maintained, but defense and economic production were added and actually formed the hard core of Frederick William's governmental activities. Over all of them he assumed a despotic control. Frederick I had not governed by himself. Eberhard von Danckelmann had been his leading minister. After the fall of this loyal official, in 1697, the result of court cabals, various favorites competed for leadership. Frederick William took the reins of government himself. Council meetings with ministers were no longer held. Except for the annual budget meeting, the ministers reported mostly in writing to the king, who decided matters in his study and gave his orders by rescripts or merely by marginal comments. (This system of personal government from the royal study or cabinet was called in Germany *Kabinetts-regierung*, which reflects the contrast to the development in England, where a different "cabinet system" became the vehicle of parliamentary government.)

Frederick William's autocratic government required an able administrator at the helm of the state. This he was as few other men. His shrewdness, practical sense, memory of detail and over-all policy, combined with his impetuosity and dynamic energy, made him the "greatest domestic king" in Prussian history. Like the Great Elector, he was convinced that the size of an army determined the rank of a state and that it was not enough to have an army if the state could not maintain it through its own resources. The abolition of the luxurious court of Frederick I was immediately followed by an order to augment the army by seven new regiments. It grew from around 40,000 men, in 1713, to 80,000 men, in 1740. Frederick William left his successor an annual revenue of seven million thaler. After 1713, all expenditure of the Prussian state was covered by revenue, and credits were practically never used. Frederick William left a stored-up treasure of eight million thaler. For the Prussia of 2 to 2.5 million inhabitants, of whom two to four per cent were soldiers, this achievement was colossal. A combination of measures, of which economies in all fields were only part, produced this result.

∽ Administration of Finances

OF THE TWO BRANCHES of state income, Frederick William found the *camerale* disorganized as a consequence of policies which had been adopted under his father. In order to acquire large funds for the needs of the court, Luben von Wulffen, domain administrator, proposed to parcel out a substantial segment of the domain properties through hereditary leases rather than the short-term leases previously granted. The project could have had very beneficial effects on the social structure of eastern Germany. A class of independent landholders would have come into being besides the nobility and the peasant serfs. The reform also would have freed the peasants on the domains and made them owners of inheritable farms. Luben was probably right when he expected from such change a considerable improvement of agriculture and therefore greater state revenue in the future, apart from the purchase-price paid when the lease was acquired. But his plans were not conceived in the spirit of social and political reform. They were designed to serve urgent fiscal needs. This contributed from the outset to the poor execution of the whole undertaking. Prices were fixed too high or incompetent people chosen. The state bureaucracy of that time was not capable of managing such a complex operation, and the new agencies established for this purpose met with growing opposition from the old domain offices.

In 1713, Frederick William issued an edict which declared all territories of the Hohenzollern state an indivisible whole and simultaneously all domain lands and forests an equally unsalable trust. The edict, testimony to Frederick William's proprietary conception of the state, has often been compared to the Pragmatic Sanction of the same year, but succession to the throne was no longer a problem in Prussia. The rules laid down with regard to the domains meant the return to conservative management. The edict also signified a conservative attitude toward existing class conditions. In the same year, the old court chamber, renamed "general finance directory," assumed the full direction of the *camerale* in the whole kingdom. All provincial "domain chambers" were subordinated to the central office. The financial results were highly satisfactory. Between 1713 and 1740, revenue climbed from 1.3 to 3.3 million thaler.

For the *contributionale*, a second financial administration emerged. War commissars had originally been created for a variety of functions. Some supervised the administration of the army; this included muster-

ing and paying troops. Others dealt with relations between the army
and the civilian population, seeing to it that the army received deliveries both in money and kind from the country. In arranging billets
and provisions, they were supposed to consider the necessity of the
army as well as the welfare of the country. The war commissar attached to the army became superfluous, since the colonels and captains
ceased to be contractors and assumed the position of salaried officers
of the king. The local commissars lost some of their original tasks
when the country began to consider the maintenance of the army as a
normal burden.

The characteristic difference between the Prussian countryside and
the towns affected the development of the roles played by these local
war commissars. In the rural counties the nobility had formed representative bodies, county estates, after the introduction of the modern
war contributions. They elected a director, soon called county councilor (*Landrat*), to represent their local interests with the army
through the local war commissar. But the war commissar disappeared
from the scene before 1700, and his functions were taken over by the
county councilor. He was still elected by the estates, but appointed by
the king. Since he received only a small salary, it was inevitable that
only a *Junker* of the district could be selected. Frederick William often
disregarded the electoral right of the estates, but Frederick II accepted
it completely. The scope of the task assigned to the county councilor
became very broad. He was the local executive officer of the king in
all matters of general administration.

In the towns, the evolution of the war commissar's role took a very
different course. The excise tax depended on the growth of economic
enterprise, and the petrifaction of municipal self-government and economic organization gave no assurance of high yields. The local commissars—or tax councilors, as they were called after a while—soon began handling not only the collection and administration of the excise
tax but also the policies which could lead to a higher income, such as
the regulation of prices and wages. The tax councilors became the
actual rulers of the towns. The small towns were usually placed in
groups of six to eight under an individual commissar.

Thus, in 1720, Prussia had two administrations of revenue. The
domain administration under the domain chambers and the general
finance directory attended to the time-honored tasks of agrarian husbandry. The commissariat agencies, in contrast, were driven by a desire
to expand the economy. They were the true organs of mercantilism.

Whereas in the rural counties no further extension of their power was possible once the contributional tax had been accepted, the weakness of the towns and the system of the excise tax opened a wide field for direct state intervention. But it was inevitable that the domain agencies would clash with the commissariat offices who wished to concentrate crafts and industries in the towns and to keep food and raw materials, such as wool, cheap. The commissariats advocated the prohibition of the export of domestic agrarian produce. The domain chambers, on the other hand, sympathized with the agriculturists in their desire for free movement of goods and economic enterprise.

Frederick William I settled this conflict by bold, drastic action. In 1722, he merged the domain and commissariat offices on both the central and provincial level. The unification of the general war commissariat and the general finance directory in Berlin produced the central office with the formidable name *General-Ober-Finanz-Kriegs-und-Domänen-Direktorium*, commonly known as the General Directory. In the provinces, the war-and-domain chambers came into being, and the county and tax councilors were subordinated to them. The whole interior administration was thus brought into a single centralized system. Certain older traditions were, however, continued in the new organization. The collegial and territorial principles of organization could be counted among them. The General Directory had four departments with one minister and a number of councilors for each. The departments were responsible for groups of provinces, though they did not settle policies individually and independently. All decisions were made by the council of ministers. A beginning was made, however, with the distribution of work along functional lines, since each of the territorial departments was simultaneously in charge of certain general matters, such as frontier questions, military economy, postal affairs, or currency. (Immediately after he ascended the throne, Frederick II began to establish additional departments, those of commerce and trade [1740], military administration [1746], excise and duties [1766], mining [1768], and forests [1771].)

Only two central political offices existed besides the General Directory, the foreign office, which received its final organization in 1728, and a department of justice and ecclesiastical affairs. Unity among the three departments was created exclusively by the king. A council of state comprising all ministers existed, but was of no political importance. In fact, the king also remained in direct contact with the provincial chambers and his *fiscals,* who acted as superiors and spies and kept him informed about the operations of the governmental machine. A machine it was indeed. Frederick William saw to it that his poorly paid officials, *royal domestiques* as they were called in this age, gave every ounce of their strength to his service. Strict execution of orders and utmost economy with public funds were prerequisites of acceptable performance. Failure to live up to the expectations of the king might not only land the official in a low job but even in the Spandau prison, if the king's ire was aroused.

Frederick William was the father of Prussian bureaucracy. For the eighteenth century this was a new and unusual achievement. In this age it was still customary to consider posts in public service largely as benefices or even sinecures. The distinction between public and private interests was not clearly drawn, not even on the side of governments, as the sale of offices and commissions, which remained common in many countries, indicated. Outside of Prussia, *travailler pour le roi de Prusse* became the ironic description of hard work with little pay and leisure, but to the corps of Prussian officials it seemed as an honor. Honesty and loyalty, virtues which Frederick William wanted to implant, fast became widespread. On the other hand, the civil service was not a good school for independent statesmen. Not even the highest officials had any knowledge of the ultimate policies, which were reserved to the king, and the automatic obedience expected from them stifled personal initiative. In its dealings with the public the bureaucracy displayed the imprint of the harsh, imperious language spoken by the king. It was worst on the lower levels, on which many old soldiers, former regimental quartermasters, scribes, and other noncoms were employed. The Prussian bureaucracy, though respected and feared for its efficiency, never acquired a reputation for courtesy and good manners. Subservient themselves to an ebullient supreme authority, the Prussian officials liked to show their own rank and power over those entrusted to their care.

With this bureaucracy, Frederick William perfected the system of Prussian finance and taxation. The "contributional" taxes fell entirely on the peasants. It is assumed that about forty per cent of the peasant's income was taken by the state. The nobility was exempted from the land tax, except in East Prussia, where such a tax had existed since the days of the Teutonic Order, and later in Silesia, where this Austrian tax was continued. Against much opposition, a small tax was introduced by Frederick William when he abolished the feudal services of the nobility. The theoretical obligation of the noblemen to do military service on horseback, the so-called *Lehnspferde* (literally: feudal horses), had become useless for modern warfare. In return for lifting his feudal duty and turning the feudal estates into alodia, i.e., lands not subject to services and in full personal ownership, a tax was levied.

The excise tax in the towns became not only the means for siphoning off the maximum of money for the treasury but also the tool for the domestic and foreign economic policies of the state. Originally, flour, meat, beer, wine, liquor, and monopolized commodities, such as salt and tobacco, were the chief sources of the excise tax, but the list grew steadily. Of consumers' goods, eggs, butter, cheese, fruits and, as one might expect, imported colonial products, coffee, chocolate, tea, and sugar were taxed. Many raw materials and some industrial products came under the excise tax, for example, timber, flax, hemp, cotton, leather, tallow, dyes, and all silk goods. Small wonder that revenue rose. But the burden on consumers was great and rested most heavily on the poor classes. The administration of the system was rather expensive, though much less so than the French system of tax-farming. An external customs line did not exist. The boundaries of the Prussian territories were too much broken up. Goods had to be examined from town to town and duties paid at the point of destination. The growing differences between the tariffs for foreign and domestic goods were the measure of state intervention in trade. Exports were at times forbidden, thus, for example, those of grain when prices were rising. When prices were falling, imports were limited. Also imports of manufactured products were prohibited before the industry to be protected could turn out decent substitute goods.

✍ The Prussian Army

THE FUNDS COLLECTED by King Frederick William were spent chiefly on the army. Eighty per cent of all revenue was assigned to it, in contrast to about sixty per cent in France, fifty per cent in Austria, and a little over thirty per cent in Bavaria. Austria and Bavaria had to use a quarter of their budget for service on debts. While Bavaria is supposed to have spent twenty per cent on the expenditure of the court alone, Austria under Maria Theresa spent around six per cent, Frederick William and Frederick the Great only two per cent on their courts. In Prussia the king was still able to devote close to twenty per cent of the annual revenue to the objectives of general administration and development. But the army was the chief consumer in the monarchy, and the civilian society benefited from at least part of the army expenditure. Frederick William said that when the army marched, income from the excise tax fell by one third. The soldiers were quartered in the towns. Some barracks were already being built, but in general the soldiers were billeted in burgher houses and had to buy their own provisions and even parts of their uniform. Their pay was inadequate, so that in their free hours they worked for low wages and profits, as did their womenfolk. Towns liked the income from a garrison.

Still more important was the influence of the army on the development of manufacture and industry. Powder factories and iron mines as well as the textile industry found a steady market. In fact, Prussian industries were not yet ready to satisfy demand. Frederick William I paid particular attention to the building of cloth factories to supply the army and home market. Subsequently, larger quantities of Prussian cloth were exported to Russia. But the export of manufactured goods from Prussia remained rather insignificant throughout the century. Agricultural products, such as grain, flax, leather, and timber, figured most prominently, even when Prussian exports grew at the end of the century. The demands of the army, together with a careful agrarian policy, stimulated the increased agricultural production which made these exports possible.

Welfare of the individual was not the aim of the policies of Frederick William I, any more than it was to be that of Frederick II's. Their dominant objective was the aggrandizement of the power of the state, to which every class and every individual was to contribute to the utmost. It was, of course, clear to these rulers that this required a minimum of welfare, and they wished to improve the lot of their subjects so long as this did not interfere with the growth of Prussia's military might. The army was the beginning and end of all policy.

The armies of the Great Elector and Frederick I had rested on free hiring. Like many other princes of that time, the Great Elector had tried to use additional popular militias, but they had always proved disappointing. No doubt, they could only be turned into more respectable military forces with longer training and better arms. But the arming of the local peasants was not an appealing thought to the nobility, and longer periods of service would have deprived them of labor on their estates. Thus at the beginning of Frederick William I's reign all ideas of enlarging the army through organized militias were abandoned. Yet the experiments with militias proved that the old idea of the duty of all men to fight for their country in an emergency had not completely disappeared. Already in the days of Frederick I, local authorities had occasionally been requested to deliver recruits against fixed government payments. Normally, recruitment was carried on in Prussia and in foreign countries, which meant chiefly in other German states, and in neither case did Prussian recruitment agents hesitate to employ fraudulent and violent methods. Worse things happened than those related in Voltaire's *Candide*. Man-hunting raids were staged into the neighboring Hanover and Mecklenburg, and Prussian press gangs also operated within Prussia. The East Prussian Gottsched, a tall young man, fled from Königsberg to Leipzig, because the recruitment officers showed an unwholesome interest in him. Frederick William I disallowed the recruitment of Prussian subjects with regular residence, in 1721. But this was only a transitional step in a process of recruitment which, in 1733, was formalized by royal edicts.

The monarchy was divided into so-called "cantons," districts of 5,000 hearths for infantry regiments or 1,500 for cavalry regiments. Only from its own canton, usually in the neighborhood of its garrison, was a regiment thereafter permitted to draw recruits. In the cantons the young lads were "enrolled," i.e., registered, and the regiments could call up a certain number every year. This canton system did not mean the introduction of universal military service. Whole social groups were exempted, namely all burghers, educated people, and also the workers in specialized manufactures. The obligation fell almost exclusively on the peasants and journeymen in the crafts. In addition, certain total regional exemptions were granted, which were further extended under Frederick II. The recruitment among the footloose at home and the hiring and impressment of foreigners was continued with great energy. In 1740, the army had two foreigners to one Prussian. Under the impact of the wars of Frederick II, the ratio was probably half and half, and during the later years of the Seven Years' War the number of foreigners dropped temporarily to one third. But both Frederick William I and Frederick II believed that Prussia, with her small population, could not afford to take too many people away from their occupations. Reasons of economic policy determined the compromise in recruitment and exemptions. For the same reason, the soldiers from the cantons, though, like the rest, belonging to the army for twenty years, were given leaves to return to their villages and estates after two years of training. Only during the spring months were the regiments in full strength. The *Junkers* did not lose much of their labor.

The Prussian army consisted of two categories of soldiers, the native peasants and craftsmen and the foreign hirelings. The second group contained the more unruly elements and the ones most likely to desert in war or peace. Barbarous discipline and military justice were applied to keep this hapless medley together. Frederick the Great never tired of explaining that the soldiers should be more afraid of their own officers than of the enemy. For such treatment the serf peasants brought some preparation with them. They were used to foul words and received beatings from their feudal landlords, whose sons and cousins they met as officers in the army. In an indirect way, some advantages accrued to them from their soldiering. They came under the jurisdiction of the king, and even permission to marry was given by the army rather than their feudal lord. On its side, the royal government had good reason to look into the state of the peasants. Frederick William, in order to have soldiers, fought any attempt of the *Junkers* to appropriate peasant lands.

The same king who abolished the feudal military duties of the noblemen by making the knights' estates free family property, achieved the practical continuation of military vassals' services by the *Junkers*. The officers were not yet fully separated from the rank and file. But the new discipline distinguished them sharply. The last vestiges of the craft-guild system, which had been an important principle of military organization at the time when the German *Landsknechte* had come into being, were suppressed. The army reflected the age of hierarchical social order. Frederick William I was convinced that an efficient officer corps could be composed only of noblemen. He weeded out not only the adventurers and questionable characters but also practically all officers of burgher origin. Except for the artillery, which was not a fully integrated part of the army, only a handful of burghers remained in the Prussian army. Instead, the officer corps was systematically staffed with noblemen.

The Prussian nobility was predominantly a poor class, and many families had nothing left but their social prejudices. Soldiering was fairly common among them, and a good many *Junkers* were found already in the army of the Great Elector. But many had gone to Poland or Denmark or, from the Rhenish lands, to Holland. Frederick William I barred service in foreign armies and insisted that the sons of noblemen be prepared for officers' careers. In order to make it possible for the sons of noble families to acquire a suitable education, the king founded a "cadet house" in Berlin. He did not hesitate to send out gendarmes to the rural estates to collect the boys. This policy was entirely successful. By 1724, there was hardly a family in Pomerania which was not somehow represented in the army. Absolute obedience to the king was made acceptable by the respect these people enjoyed within the army and without. They were the comrades-in-arms of the king. Every day, from 1725 on, Frederick William wore their uniform, thereby setting the style for all his successors on the Hohenzollern throne. Although the officers were sworn to absolute obedience, even the draconic regulations of Frederick William recognized that they were freed from this duty in case of an attack on their honor.

It is very doubtful even under eighteenth-century conditions whether noblemen made the best officers. The finest officer of the Great Elector, Field Marshal Derfflinger, was a burgher by origin. The sense of honor and *vertue*, which Frederick II could discover only in noblemen, was not as class-bound as that. But there can be no question that the homogeneity of ideals and manners which the Prussian officer corps possessed, as a result of its social exclusiveness, strengthend the cohesion of the army very considerably—and of the monarchy as well. The new caste, rooted in social privilege and the exercise of the profession declared to be the highest in the realm, became the chief defender of the existing political order. In France, the division between the officers of high and small nobility and the bourgeoisie proved one of the major reasons for the overthrow of the monarchy. The Prussian officer corps as created by Frederick William I was made of a uniform timber. It was so closely joined to the social and political aims of Prussian absolutism that it could not be split. Both Frederick William I and his son loved soldiers, but they knew what they were doing when they placed the most monolithic groups ahead of their civil servants. In the court ceremonial which the soldier-king introduced, generals took precedence over royal ministers, although the high positions in the civil service were also reserved to noblemen. But in some measure burghers were accepted and assimilated in higher posts. The civil servants of upper rank were not yet exclusively or chiefly university graduates, but appointments, including those of nobles, were already by examination. However, the so-called "ink-splashers" were aware of their lesser prestige as compared to the sword-bearers. In a state which, in Frederick's words, grew only "iron and soldiers" the bureaucracy was ancillary to the army.

With his usual grim determination, Frederick William I devoted himself to the training of his troops. They received good arms. The introduction of an iron instead of wooden ramrod and of the bayonet, which replaced all pikes, increased the fire power and tactical mobility of the infantry. In strange contrast to his normal parsimony, the king was willing to pay fantastic sums for tall soldiers. The penchant for giants, though not entirely without excuse in the conditions of contemporaneous warfare, was a mania with the royal drill sergeant. Linear tactics could only be prepared by drill, and the tireless efforts of the king and his chief military adviser, Prince Leopold of Anhalt-Dessau, created an infantry which in discipline, precision, and relative speed of tactical movement had no equal during the century. The Prussian cavalry did not reach the same level of perfection under Frederick William and had to be reorganized by Frederick the Great.

✒ *Despotism and Nobility*

FREDERICK WILLIAM WAS the founder of the military monarchy which his son made a European power. He could build on the achievements of the Great Elector, primarily on the exclusion of the estates from the government, which the latter had accomplished. Frederick William was always conscious of the political conflict between crown and nobility, which distinguished him from his father and also from his son, Frederick II, who did not have to feel serious concern over this problem any longer. Frederick William was still in a fighting mood about the political position of the *Junkers*. "I shall establish my sovereignty like a rock of bronze," was a remark he threw in their face when they opposed him. Yet annoying as the opposition of the nobility against many of his measures was, the king never had to go through such serious crises as the Great Elector had to suffer. Frederick William was able to exclude participation of the nobility in the actual conduct of government and thereby also to subordinate the old territories and provinces to an integrated single monarchy. But there were limits even to Frederick William's despotism, which on the surface seemed absolute.

Actually, in 1653 and later, the Great Elector had already made the concession of recognizing the social and political power of the nobility on their estates. Frederick William did not dare challenge this freedom of the *Junkers*. Hugo Preuss, one of the founders of the Weimar Constitution, has correctly stated that the Prussian monarchy stood on one long and one short leg. Whereas the Prussian government reached down to the last individual and his every action in the towns, its authority in the countryside ended with the *Landrat*, who, however, was a member of the landed gentry. On their estates, the Prussian squires ruled as absolutely as the king in Berlin and Potsdam. Within the monarchy, the *Junkers* had to accept the orders of the king, who gave them all the honors and positions of rank in the state. They were the only gentlemen, irrespective of property or education, and the king, in his own personal conduct, pretended to be one of them. The class lines of society were drawn as sharply as possible. The function of the burghers was to produce the money for the maintenance and expansion of the state beyond the traditional income from agriculture. In exchange for this, the townspeople received some privilege, but little honor, by exemption from military service. And below the townspeople were the mass of the population, the peasants, burdened, as Luben von Wulffen put it, with "Egyptian services," consisting of their endless toil for their landlord and state and military service.

∾ Foreign Policy

FREDERICK WILLIAM I WAS an unusual domestic administrator. As founder of a martial kingdom one would have expected him to take an active part in international affairs. But he did not think of himself as a military commander, and he felt quite unsure in diplomacy. Except for his brief intervention in the Nordic War, which was more or less imposed on him by circumstances at the beginning of his reign, he kept peace. While his participation in the Nordic War brought him the gain of Stettin and parts of West Pomerania, all subsequent negotiations, though backed by his powerful army, yielded nothing. Frederick William was poor at the game of high politics as it was played by the cunning statesmen of his time. He was too frank, but also basically peaceful. In this respect, too, he had much in common with the Lutheran princes of an earlier age. But he was also aware that empires like France or Austria might lose armies and still survive, whereas the king of Prussia, if deprived of his army, would be reduced forever to political insignificance.

From his father, Frederick William had inherited a policy of cooperation with the emperor. He himself felt no sentimental attachment to emperor and Empire, but it seemed natural to him that there should be a German emperor, provided he would respect the rights of the German princes, especially those of the strongest prince in the north of Germany. If the government of Charles VI had treated Frederick William I as the foremost northern pillar of the Empire, the latter would have been satisfied, and possibly even his successor might have hesitated to raise the sword against Austria. But the emperor would have had to pay a high price in order to keep Prussia's friendship, and it would have involved Austria in difficulties with other north German princes. Attention had to be paid to Saxony, not only in connection with the Empire but also with regard to the crucial Polish problem. The other neighbor of Brandenburg-Prussia, the elector of Hanover and king of England, demanded even higher consideration. Still, it remains true that Austria did not see the growing strength of Brandenburg-Prussia, and even pressed her imperial authority at the diet of the Empire against the Protestant elector in a thoughtless fashion, thus contributing to the surly resentment in Berlin.

The Prussian king based his entire foreign policy on legal and hereditary claims. As was customary in this age, the dynasty had a well-assorted shelf of titles. For Frederick William I, the claims on Jülich and Berg were the most attractive ones. In the early seventeenth century the territories of Jülich, Cleves, Berg, Mark, and Ravensberg had been divided between the Hohenzollern and a branch of the Wittelsbach family, the Palatinate-Neuburg line.[1] From 1685, this line also ruled the Rhenish Palatinate. But Elector Carl Philip (1716–42) had no male issue, and after his death the Palatinate was to go to another branch of the house, that of Palatinate-Sulzbach. The question could be raised whether Jülich-Berg should also go to these future rulers in Mannheim. Frederick William contended that Jülich-Berg ought to become his, and the emperor could make claims as the son of a Palatinate-Neuburg princess. It was a most complex legal issue, which could be settled only by a court, but it lent itself to much political maneuvering. The emperor, for example, might decide not to raise his claims, or the Palatinate-Sulzbach heir might resign his rights. Who, furthermore, was to take temporary possession of the territories while the matter was lengthily argued by the lawyers before the *Reichshofrat* after the actual death of Elector Carl Philip?

Frederick William I weakened his case considerably by declaring that he would be content with receiving Berg and the small Raven-

[1] See the author's *A History of Modern Germany: The Reformation*, p. 301.

stein, but all his negotiations failed to bring him real assurance of succession. In the Treaty of Berlin, of 1728, in which the king recognized the Pragmatic Sanction, the emperor had promised his moral
support for the eventual Prussian acquisition of Berg without, however, committing himself with regard to legal interpretation. Frederick
William soon recognized that he could not bend the emperor to his
wishes, but he did not withdraw his support in European politics from
Austria. These were the years in which relations between the Western
powers and Austria reached a high degree of tension, and serious
friction developed between Prussia and Hanover, which was only
superficially settled. At this time the English government decided to
complete the diplomatic isolation of Austria by winning over Prussia.
It proposed the conclusion of a double marriage tie between the court
of St. James and Berlin. Wilhelmina, daughter of Frederick William I
and Queen Sophie Dorothea, a sister of George II, was to marry the
prince of Wales. Simultaneously, Princess Amalie of England was to
become the wife of the Prussian crown prince. He was to reside in
the Hanover capital with his wife, whom the English government proposed to make governor of Hanover.

Crown Prince Frederick

THE PROJECT CAUSED A TURMOIL of feelings at the court of Prussia. It
had the blessings of the queen, who liked these matches and, in addition, enjoyed plotting. The young prince and princess suddenly saw
the dawn of the day which would allow them to leave their surroundings, which had become stifling through the oppression of a
tyrannical father. The king himself was brooding over the political
implications of such marriages, but from the outset was worried lest
the importation of a princess from the sinfully elegant London court
would further ruin his Fritz. He agreed to the marriage of his daughter,
but the English insisted on a double wedding. Negotiations were suspended, when an event occurred which ended the project. The crown
prince decided to go to England. Supplied with money from there, he
prepared his flight while he was accompanying his father on a visit to
Heidelberg. A frightened page told the king, who lost all self-control.

Frederick, who was eighteen, had, from early years, shown an independent mind and great aversion to the outlook and manners of his
father's court. His tutor, a Reformed Frenchman, was a man of broad
education and liberal religious views. Frederick took to books and

philosophical arguments with a natural delight, and French philosophy satisfied him more than the religion of his father. Music and reading seemed to him better nourishment than military drill and hunting. But he had to cover up his inclinations and opinions before his father, and the relations between them grew unnatural and even hostile. The king became alarmed at this resistance in his own family, especially since he craved the love of his son. When he discovered the contraction of debts and even an early interest in the opposite sex, angry scenes took place. The discovery of the planned escape to England aroused Frederick William's full fury. He treated Frederick as a deserting officer, had him imprisoned, and did everything to break his will and self-respect. The most abominable penalty which he inflicted was Frederick's forced attendance at the execution of his friend and accomplice in the intended flight.

In the midst of all these acts of insanity, Frederick showed great stoic qualities. He feigned repentance over the past and adapted his opinions to those of his father, whose ire finally relaxed. Frederick was then compelled to learn the business of provincial administration at the war-and-domain chamber in Küstrin. After he had made the greatest concession to his pitiless father and married a nondescript Brunswick princess, he was given a regiment and small household of his own away from Berlin, in Rheinsberg. Here he spent the years before his accession to the throne using his leisure hours for his beloved literary, musical, and artistic interests and also pondering what use he would make of Prussian power once his hour had come. But he kept these ideas strictly to himself. The struggle with his father had taught him not to trust others with his innermost thoughts. It had destroyed the last remnants of religion, except for a deistic faith, and given him a cold view of human nature in general. On the other hand, his experiences had not destroyed his belief in himself. As he began to understand the operations of the monarchy in both the civilian and military field, Frederick discovered what a mighty instrument it might become in the hands of a ruler of spirit and courage. This gave him respect for the task, while making him a most critical observer of the clumsy foreign policy of Frederick William I.

The projected Prussian-English alliance was called off. In 1731, Princess Wilhelmina was forced to marry an insignificant German prince, the Margrave of Bayreuth. The crisis in the Hohenzollern family enabled Austrian diplomacy to keep Prussia firmly on the side of the emperor during the next years. But Frederick William felt snubbed when during the War of the Polish Succession Charles VI refused to accept him as a European ally and allowed him only to contribute a contingent to the army of the Empire. When, during the Turkish War of 1736–39, the emperor asked for Prussian troops and a loan, the king declined to give armed help but offered 1.2 million thalers as a free gift, provided the emperor would give him the guarantee of Berg. Austria was unresponsive, because she wished to maintain her friendship with the Palatinate. France was also backing the Wittelsbach family, who had been so amenable to French wishes, while the maritime powers did not want Prussia to expand. Austria, France, England, and the Netherlands agreed that in the case of the death of the last Palatinate-Neuburg ruler all his territories should be occupied by the line of Palatinate-Sulzbach under reservation of the Prussian claim. This meant that Prussia would have to start legal proceedings before the *Reichshofrat,* and this litigation offered no prospect of success. In February 1739, the ministers of the four powers presented identical notes in Berlin requesting Prussian acceptance of the four-power agreement. Frederick William fumed over what he considered Austria's betrayal. He refused the demand and began negotiating an alliance with France. In January 1739, Cardinal Fleury had concluded a treaty with Austria confirming the four-power compromise. But he thought it advantageous to increase the split between Austria and Prussia and bring the latter closer to France. Therefore he concluded another secret treaty with Prussia, in April 1739, in which he guaranteed Prussia a part of the Jülich-Berg inheritance. Such were the practices of cabinet diplomacy which Frederick William was unable to grasp. Prussia and Austria had come to a parting of ways, and in Frederick a man stood ready who had no inhibitions to use Machiavellian methods and was scornful of the Holy Roman Empire. On May 31, 1740, Frederick William I died, and Frederick took over the Prussian government. On October 26, the last male Habsburg emperor died. A new era dawned on Germany.

CHAPTER 8

The Austro-Prussian Dualism and the Reign of Maria Theresa

FREDERICK II'S ACCESSION to the Prussian throne raised hopes that his father's militaristic and puritanical regime would be replaced by a luxuriant and benevolent reign. But such expectations were quickly disappointed. To be sure, changes occurred. Christian Wolff was reinstated with great honor in Halle, Maupertuis was invited to Berlin, direct contact was established with Voltaire, and plans were drawn for the erection of an opera house in the capital. The Prussian monarchy paid homage "to Apollo and the Muses," as Frederick's inscription on the opera building read. Interference with the doctrines and customs of the various churches was not allowed. "In Prussia everybody can seek salvation in his own fashion," the young ruler declared. Censorship was eased. Quietly, the administration of justice was modified. Torture was practically abolished and the most cruel penalties discarded. But at the same time, Frederick made it quite clear that nothing of the Prussian state's fundamental organization would be altered, and while he kept his father's ministers in office, he continued the autocratic direction of the government. He dissolved the Potsdam guard of giants, but the addition of seven new regiments to the army indicated in which direction the wind was blowing.

✍ War of the Austrian Succession

CHARLES VI'S UNEXPECTED DEATH gave Frederick the opportunity to lead Prussia on the road of military conquest. On December 16, 1740 the first Prussian troops moved into Silesia, which they occupied quickly without meeting serious opposition. The small Austrian garrisons withdrew to three fortresses. Frederick had invited his officers "to a rendezvous with glory." His desire to win fame for himself by making his monarchy respected as a power among the great nations of Europe

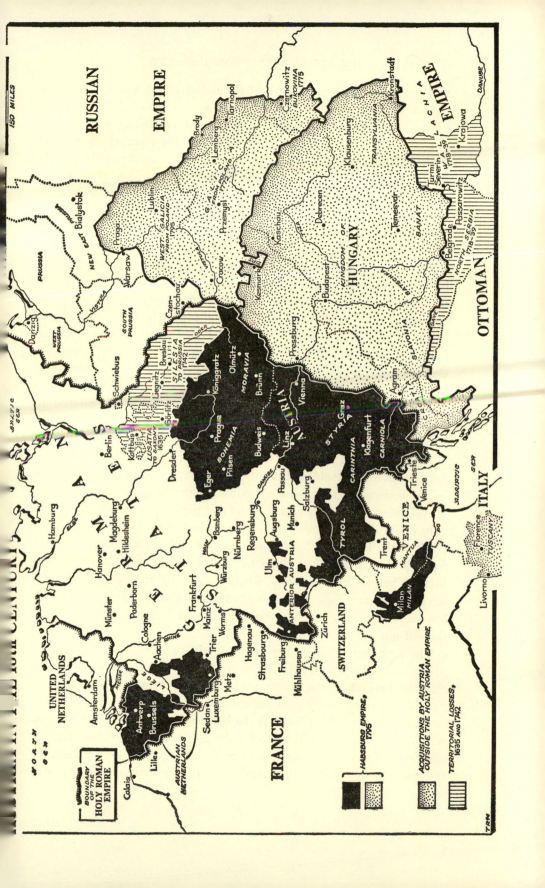

was the strongest single motive of his audacity. He was aware of the risks in "crossing the Rubicon," but he also believed that he had correctly calculated the future actions and reactions of the major powers and that the risks were worth taking. He counted on eventual support from one of the two groups of European states. In this he proved right, although in 1740 the French and British governments actually were not inclined to take advantage of the question of Austrian succession for a new test of strength. Frederick's initiative was the immediate cause for the War of the Austrian Succession.

There is no need to examine the legal claims to Silesia made by Prussian propaganda. Frederick himself cared little about them, though he was perhaps not entirely unaffected by the anti-Austrian resentment that had long been nourished over this affair in Berlin. The claims applied to only small parts of Silesia—the principalities of Liegnitz, Brieg, and Wohlau in Lower Silesia and Jägerndorf in Upper Silesia. Even with regard to these territories, they were trumped-up claims. As claims for all of Silesia, or even Lower Silesia, they were downright brazen. Frederick appealed to arms, not to a court of justice. After the occupation of Silesia had been accomplished, Frederick offered to assist the heiress of the Habsburg throne defend her possessions and to cast his vote for her husband at the imperial election. Though many in Vienna favored accepting Frederick's proposition, Maria Theresa's outraged sense of right and good political sense induced her to reject it. She recognized that Austria's power in the Empire and in Europe would suffer an irrecoverable loss and that giving in to blackmail would only invite demands from all sides. She had risen to the throne as a result of the Pragmatic Sanction. It seemed to her dangerous to depart from this law, which then might be flouted even within her dominions. Maria Theresa did not know whether war might not force greater territorial concessions from her than those that Frederick expected, but she felt certain that Austria would cease being a great power if she did not defend her rights.

The first battle fought between Austria and Prussia took place at Mollwitz on April 10, 1741. Thanks to Field Marshal Schwerin, rather than to Frederick, the battle turned into a Prussian victory. The Austrian cavalry had overwhelmed the Prussian battle lines in the beginning, and the king had left the battlefield convinced that the day was lost, when Schwerin restored the balance through the infantry and finally forced the Austrians to retreat. Few knew how precarious this victory was. A total reorganization of the Prussian cavalry was required. Frederick also realized that it was not simple to pluck laurels, and he knew all the time that his financial and military resources did not allow him to conduct a long war. Yet the news of the Prussian victory became the signal for France's entering the war against Austria. Marshal Belle-Isle, supported by the conviction in army and court that Austria was France's traditional enemy, forced the hand of the eighty-seven-year-old Cardinal Fleury. The goal of French policy was the transfer of the imperial crown from the Habsburgs to the Bavarian dynasty, which was to receive Bohemia, Tyrol, and Anterior Austria. Prussia was to get Lower Silesia, and Saxony Upper Silesia, Moravia, and Lower Austria. The formation of a single prominent power in the German Empire was to be forestalled.

✑ Franco-Prussian Alliance

ON JUNE 5, 1741, a Franco-Prussian treaty was concluded in Breslau. In exchange for the promise of Lower Silesia, Frederick agreed to vote for Elector Charles Albert of Bavaria as emperor. A few months later, Saxony joined the new grouping. Spain had already declared her intention to attack Austria's Italian possessions. The English government, burdened by a maritime war with Spain, was not ready to intervene in Austria's behalf. In June 1741, England promised limited help, but this was no more than a gesture, and King George II, who would have liked to fight on Austria's side, had to purchase Hanover's neutrality by promising his electoral vote to Charles Albert.

The Bavarian ruler, husband of one of Emperor Joseph I's daughters, had protested the accession of Maria Theresa as early as 1740. But only French support could make him a serious pretender. The phlegmatic son of the colorful and dashing Max Emanuel was an amiable man. Nobody disliked him; he did not hate anyone. But he lacked determination and serious application to political business. Even Maria Theresa took pity on him when he was in adversity.

At first Charles Albert was riding the wave of the anti-Habsburg alliance. In September 1741, a Franco-Bavarian army occupied Upper Austria. Everybody expected a direct march on Vienna, which was actually within the army's grasp, but the French insisted on moving north against Prague. They had not come to Germany to preserve the Austrian monarchy under a new ruler, but to create a divided Austria and Germany. In November, Bavarians, Frenchmen, and Saxons conquered Prague, and Charles Albert declared himself king of Bohemia.

On January 24, 1742, he was unanimously elected emperor. But on the day of his coronation in Frankfurt, Austrian troops entered Munich, and before long Austria occupied all of Bavaria. The new Emperor Charles VII, the first Roman emperor in three hundred years who was not a member of the house of Habsburg, was deprived of his own electoral lands. Popular feeling in southwestern Germany, where people were bound by old sentimental ties to the Austrian family, was hostile to him, in spite of his *bonhomie*. He was entirely dependent on the arms and political intentions of his allies.

Two events in particular had caused the reversal of the military situation. During the summer of 1741, Maria Theresa had gone to Pressburg (Bratislava) and crowned herself with the crown of St. Stephen. Long negotiations over the future government of Hungary were held with the Hungarian estates, who looked with suspicion at the daughter of Charles VI, because he had steadily whittled away the liberties and privileges of the Hungarian aristocracy. This course had to be reversed. As a matter of fact, Maria Theresa had to give the Hungarian estates guarantees of autonomy, which laid the ground for the future Austro-Hungarian dual monarchy. It was not the last time that Prussian pressure advanced the Magyar cause in the Habsburg empire. From 1740–41 to 1866–67, this interaction functioned continuously. Maria Theresa not only pacified the sulking noblemen but even aroused them to positive co-operation and sacrifice. Her natural charm and high courage evoked real eagerness to come to the defense of the queen. The organization of Hungarian regiments, which henceforth were to form a substantial element in the Habsburg armies, was begun immediately. Nevertheless, the months in Pressburg were exasperating for the young queen. Her enemies' advance into Austria and Bohemia continued unchecked, and her ministers urged her to make concessions to all of them.

But difficulties developed within the anti-Austrian alliance. Frederick was faced with a curious dilemma. The physical occupation of Silesia gave him no assurance for the future. If the alliance led by France was to gain all its objectives, French domination of the Empire would make Prussian conquest rather hollow. If, on the other hand, the queen of Hungary was to emerge victorious, she was not likely to condone the Prussian theft of Silesia. A strong, though not overpowering, Austria seemed to be in the Prussian interest. Here, too, a theme of future history was sounded for the first time. Even the Prussian king who first raised the sword against the old imperial power realized that somehow Prussia needed the independent existence of Austria in Europe and could not afford to contribute to her disappearance from the council of the big states. Until the end of the two monarchies, in 1918, antagonism was never carried to extremes, even in times of hostility, and there were to be long periods of co-operation as well.

Uncertainty about the best means of making the annexation of Silesia secure led Frederick to conclude the Convention of Klein-Schnellendorf with the Austrian commander, Count Neipperg, on October 9, 1741. In exchange for Neisse, the strongest fortress of Upper Silesia, and Maria Theresa's general promise to negotiate a treaty that would include the cession of Lower Silesia, Frederick allowed Neipperg to lead his army unmolested into Bohemia. The convention was a clear breach of his alliance with France and gave Frederick the reputation of moral recklessness. The allies' rapid progress in Bohemia induced him to repudiate the treaty quickly. He used the correct excuse that the Austrians had broken the secrecy that had been made a condition of the treaty.

The convention did not enable the Austrians to stave off the allied capture of Prague, but Neipperg's army was able to occupy southern Bohemia and Moravia and thereby cover the flank of the army that assembled at the central Danube, strengthened by the new Hungarian troops under the learned Field Marshal Count Khevenhüller. Among his forces were hussars and pandours, uncultured sons of the Hungarian steppe, the Croatian mountains, and the Turkish frontier, who injected an untamed barbarism into the fighting when the army moved into Bavaria. Charles VII's misfortunes brought Frederick back into the war. He led an army augmented by Saxon and French troops from Upper Silesia through Moravia against Vienna. But the campaign, undertaken in the unfavorable early months of 1742, failed. The strategic offensive could not be carried to such lengths under the conditions of eighteenth-century warfare. Armies depending on supplies from magazines could not advance far into enemy territory. With the loss of the many sick and deserters, and with his military prestige dimmed, Frederick retreated to Silesia.

Again negotiations between Prussia and Austria were opened. For two years, English diplomacy had admonished Maria Theresa to buy off Frederick in order to master her other enemies. The Convention of Klein-Schnellendorf had been the result of English mediation, and so were the discussions of 1742. But Maria Theresa was not persuaded to grant him peace, until Frederick's victory at Chotusitz, in May, 1742, had shown his ability as a commander of an army in which infantry, cavalry, and artillery demonstrated the highest efficiency and esprit de corps. The English mediator was generous at Maria Theresa's expense. In the preliminary Peace of Breslau (June 12, 1742) and the final Peace of Berlin (July 28, 1742), Frederick received all of Silesia except Jägerndorf and Troppau. The peace came at the right moment for Frederick, because his finances were drying up fast, but for the second time he was exposed to the accusation of being an unfaithful ally. It still remained doubtful whether Maria Theresa would respect his conquest if she defeated the hostile coalition.

Before the year 1742 was over, Bohemia was under Austrian control. Most of Bavaria had to be temporarily evacuated by Charles, but it was fully reconquered in the following year. In England, meanwhile, Lord Carteret had gained sufficient support for a policy of direct intervention in Continental affairs. He sought to chase the French out of the Rhineland and to restore the balance between Austria and France. An army was formed of British, Hanoverian, and Hessian troops, and this "Pragmatic Army" under George II, won a victory over the French at Dettingen on the Main, on June 27, 1743, that before long forced the French army to retire to Alsace. An Austrian army invaded Alsace, and the moment seemed at hand when Austria could recapture Alsace and the duchy of Lorraine. In these months, Maria Theresa contemplated annexing Bavaria. She felt that an Austria thus compensated and at the same time capable of restoring the Empire's old boundaries in the west could forget the loss of Silesia. Sardinia-Piedmont was brought into the war against the Spanish Bourbons in Italy. In the north, Saxony was won as an ally to strengthen the shield against any new Prussian intervention, for Frederick was rightly distrusted.

This development marked the beginning of more than a century of enmity between Saxony and Brandenburg-Prussia. In the century after the Reformation, Brandenburg had willingly followed the political leadership that the protagonist of northern Protestantism had exercised. But since the days of the Great Elector, Brandenburg had increasingly asserted its independence. Brandenburg-Prussia was clearly the state that attracted the Protestant sympathies that the Saxon dynasty had lost through its conversion to Catholicism. The acquisition of the Polish crown had not solidified Saxon power, whereas Prussian strength had steadily grown. The events of 1740–42 clearly demonstrated the military superiority of the northern neighbor, who, with the conquest of Silesia, placed himself between Saxony and Poland. Small wonder that Saxony had strong misgivings over Prussia's rise and was driven to the side of Austria and Hanover-Britain, and Elector Frederick August II was the Russian candidate on the Polish throne; important lines ran from Dresden and Warsaw to St. Petersburg.[1]

Frederick felt that the progress of Austrian arms and diplomacy was great enough to jeopardize his continued possession of Silesia. He decided to attack Austria before France gave up the war. In June 1744, he concluded an alliance with Louis XV. France found her war aims in Belgium, but the common conduct of the war was to lead to the conquest of Bohemia for Charles VII. The Prussian army was supposed to advance from Bohemia against Vienna; the French army was to operate along the Danube. Frederick had increased his army to 140,000 men and, through peacetime maneuvers, then still a novelty, trained it in the lessons learned during the last war years. He was confident that with such an army he could adopt a bold offensive strategy. Actually, the march to Prague, which he started in August, 1744, came off with clock-like precision. By disguising his expedition as one undertaken for the emperor, he forced his passage through Saxony. But the announcement of the intended restoration of Charles VII did not make the Prussian heretics more attractive to the population, which refused co-operation, particularly in provisioning troops. Prague was taken in mid-September, but far from becoming a base of operations against Vienna, it turned out to be an untenable position.

If the Austrian army on the Rhine, commanded by Maria Theresa's brother-in-law, Prince Charles of Lorraine, had a chance to conquer Alsace and Lorraine, Frederick's breach of the Berlin Peace of 1742 killed any such opportunity. In forced marches, Prince Charles's army moved to Bohemia. The French failed to follow and frittered away the rest of the year in secondary military ventures. Frederick's position in Bohemia became serious. The Saxons declared themselves openly against him, and 20,000 of them joined with the Austrian army, which, by a mere war of maneuver against Frederick's lines of communication, forced him to retreat to Silesia. The king tried in vain to come to a decision by battle, in which the technical training of his forces might have tipped the balance. As it was, his troops were worn out and demoralized. That greatest weakness of the army system of the *ancien régime*, desertion of the impressed soldier, proved catastrophic. Frederick lost 17,000 deserters before he got to Silesia in December. In

[1] See p. 183.

addition, heavy losses of matériel were suffered. The army's confidence in Frederick's leadership was badly shaken, even among officers.

These were not all his misfortunes. The death of the unlucky Emperor Charles VII, on January 20, 1745, ended the war between Austria and Bavaria. The young Bavarian Elector Max Joseph, supported by his Habsburg mother, was anxious to make peace with Vienna. A treaty was formally signed at Füssen in April, 1745. It became difficult for France to fight Austria in Germany, and French military efforts were centered on the Netherlands. Austria could direct her main power against Frederick.

The political and military crisis of 1744–45 matured Frederick. The boastfulness he had often displayed in his early years disappeared thereafter. But the resilience of his steely personality, which came into the open at this moment, he was to prove in many future hours of danger. He succeeded in restoring the order and morale of the army and spurred his civil servants to supreme effort. With superb generalship, Frederick defeated the Austro-Saxon army as soon as it crossed the mountains into Silesia. The battle of Hohenfriedberg, won in the morning of June 5, 1745, annihilated about one fourth of Prince Charles's forces. But Frederick did not dare move deeply into Bohemia again, and the political consequences of his victory were not great. Maria Theresa could have her husband, Francis Stephen, elected emperor over the protest of Prussia and the Palatinate. The jubilation of the people of Frankfurt over the election was great, and Maria Theresa was easily forgiven for not attending the coronation in the cathedral. To her, the diadem of a German empress appeared to be insignificant beside the royal crowns of Hungary and Bohemia, which were her own. People called her "the empress" just the same, and they seemed to be well satisfied that the Austrian dynasty had acquired again the highest German dignity.

Against tremendous odds resulting from Prince Charles' tactical cunning, Frederick won another victory over the Austrians at Soor, on September 30, 1745. But his dangers were mounting. Austrians and Saxons agreed to join forces for a campaign against Berlin, and Russia was also preparing military intervention against Prussia. Before Austrians and Saxons could accomplish their union, a Prussian army, under the old Prince Leopold of Anhalt, beat the Saxon army decisively. Frederick occupied Dresden. The remnants of the Saxon troops, together with Prince Charles's army, withdrew behind the Bohemian mountains. The dark shadow of Russian intervention was dispersed.

Maria Theresa, whose troops had suffered serious reverses in the Netherlands and Italy, would have liked to make peace with France in order to concentrate on the fight against Frederick. French diplomacy, however, not only insisted on the cession of Belgian places but also refused to discuss cutting Prussian gains in Silesia. Without consulting his French allies, Frederick offered to renew the Peace of Berlin. Nor did he demand any land from Saxony, though he extracted heavy payments from the Saxon government. Maria Theresa resigned herself to what seemed to have become inevitable. She authorized her minister in Dresden to sign the peace of December 25, 1745.

∽ Treaty of Aachen

FOR PRUSSIA AND THE EMPIRE this meant the end of war. Austria still had to bring the fighting in Italy and the Netherlands to a conclusion. The reconquest of Milan was accomplished in 1746, but the war against France went far beyond Austria's military capacity. Not even in combination with England and the Dutch Republic could Austria stop Marshal de Saxe's victorious progress. The decision lay in the maritime and commercial struggle between England and the Bourbon powers. As before at Utrecht, England was able to define the ultimate peace terms of the Treaty of Aachen (October 18, 1748). Maria Theresa's succession was generally recognized, as was her husband's imperial dignity. But Frederick received a European guarantee for Silesia. Parts of the Lombardy went to Piedmont-Sardinia; Parma, Piacenza, and Guastalla went to France; the Netherlands were restored to Austria. In Vienna, the English pressure for all these Austrian concessions aroused some pique, in which resentment against the big creditor nation was also noticeable. Yet despite all losses, of which Silesia was the greatest, the existence of the Austrian empire in Europe was saved, although Austria's position within Germany had changed. Nevertheless, Maria Theresa still could hope in her heart that Silesia was not lost forever, no more than the conflict between France and Britain was laid to rest by the Peace of Aachen.

∽ Maria Theresa

CONSIDERING THE ODDS against her, Maria Theresa had done extremely well by her valor, and high tribute must be paid to this extraordinary German princess. With two German parents and four German grandparents, she really was a German princess. It often has been said that though she inherited her Guelf mother's lively temper and spirit, she was a true Habsburg in her unshakable belief in her dignity. She had not been properly trained for the role of ruler of a far-flung empire, which was practically bankrupt and without an army to defend it against malevolent neighbors. Her father's senescent ministers offered her contradictory advice. A less courageous woman might have despaired or at least have turned over the government to her husband whom she loved. Her marriage, one of the happiest among crowned heads, did not affect her good judgment. She realized that Francis Stephen, a friendly, pleasant, comfortable family head with no particular interests except in occasional business ventures, was ill-suited for politics. The young, gay matron of twenty-three, who had already given birth to three princesses and was to become the mother of a prince, the future Joseph II, a few months later, decided from the outset to keep the reins of government firmly in her own hands. In Johann Christoph Bartenstein, who was the son of a Protestant Strasbourg professor and who had already risen high in her father's council, she found a minister who introduced her to state affairs and executed her orders, although they often were contrary to his counsel.

Maria Theresa put all the men around her to shame with her courage, which was built on natural pride in her dynastic inheritance and an unfailing belief in moral principles. Her womanly character showed not only in her unwillingness to have her moral judgment confused by men's prudent talk about expediency, but also in her ability to kindle enthusiasm for her monarchy through mere appearance and manners rather than argument and command. It was a political accomplishment of the highest order when she won over the Magyar estates to active support of her foreign policy in 1741, and the scenes of Pressburg were repeated in Prague and Frankfurt. Her good heart made her a poor hater. At times she even felt sympathy for the sufferings of the Prussian army, but she always detested "that evil man" in Potsdam. She did not overlook Frederick's abilities, but it was one of the sorrows of her later life that her son Joseph was so overly impressed with the model which Frederick had set. In the early years of her reign, she complained that her pregnancies did not allow her to mount a horse and lead her troops in the field.

Maria Theresa did not develop rational principles of government nor did she care much about systematic thought. Her strong convictions were maintained by a natural and simple faith, free from bigotry and superstition, though not from all intolerance. Her piety enhanced her strong maternal feelings toward her subjects. She gave birth to sixteen children, to whom she was a devoted mother, but she also defined her ideal duty as queen as that of the "first and universal mother" of the empire. She learned from practical experiences, and she learned quickly. Soon it became clear to her that whereas a change of ministers would not help much, a thorough change of the system of government was imperative. As soon as the wars of her first years ended, Maria Theresa turned her attention and energies to reforming her empire's institutions, and after the Seven Years' War she concentrated even more fully on reorganizing the state.

✌ Reorganization and Reform

FIRST, THE ARMY HAD to be strengthened. This required excluding the estates from influencing the administration of finances. Maria Theresa had promised to respect Hungary's special government, and she did not attempt to change the system of government in the Netherlands and Italy. Her reforms were confined to the "German hereditary lands," that is, Austria and Bohemia. In Count Friedrich Wilhelm von Haugwitz, governor of Austrian Silesia, she found a man who had studied the Prussian system closely and proved able to transfer its constructive ideas to Austria in a well-modified form. Count Wenzel A. E. von Kaunitz-Rietberg, after 1753 the unchallenged director of Austrian foreign policy, was her other great advisor on governmental reorganization.

After 1748, the estates of the individual lands were compelled to make greatly increased money grants for periods of ten years, and the collection of taxes was taken over by government officials. Opposition was vocal; the estates no longer were in a position to act. The Vienna government, showing an iron hand under a velvet glove, overcame the protestations of the estates within a few years.

The estates might now have disappeared altogether, as in France or Prussia, but this was not the case, since, in contrast to Prussia, increased taxes had to be voted. But the power to make political decisions was taken from the estates and, even more, their administrative functions. The newly created governmental agencies began redefining the antiquated system of tax assessments. Better distribution and higher yield were ultimately achieved. In this process one can discover the beginnings of the modern income tax, although considerable class distinctions remained. But a dent was made in the tax exemptions of the first and second estate (this did not happen in Prussia). Maria Theresa occasionally remarked upon the "God-willed equality" (*gottgefällige Gleichheit*) of all classes, and nobility and clergy were made to pay regular taxes.

For the execution of these new policies, the government created the so-called "representations and chambers" on the provincial level and under them district offices (*Kreisämter*). These agencies were quite different from their Prussian counterparts. A marked division of town and country did not exist in Austria. In Prussia the *Landrat* of the rural county was still largely a representative of the local estates; only the tax-councilor in the towns was exclusively a state official. The Austrian district officer had authority over both town and countryside. Further, separate taxes for town and country did not exist in Austria. The "contributional" as well as the excise tax applied to both.

The new organs of the Austrian state could reach down to every local level. This system proved effective, particularly in measures intended to protect the peasants. Military considerations underlay this concern for the peasants' welfare. Since responsibility for recruitment and general military administration was delegated to the state's local and provincial offices, the preservation of manpower became a natural policy. The Austrian recruitment system, which received its final form in the so-called "soul conscription" (*Seelen-Conskription*) of 1763, was practically identical with the Prussian "canton" system.[2]

The reorganization of local and provincial government was accompanied by a drastic reform of the central agencies. The Court War Council with the subordinate war commissariat remained practically unchanged. At its side was the State Chancellery for Foreign Affairs, founded in 1742. In 1753, when the long tenure of Kaunitz at the *Ballhausplatz* began, it was named House, Court, and State Chancellery (*Geheime Haus-, Hof-, und Staatskanzlei*). A significant characteristic of the internal government was the almost complete separation of the judicial and executive branches of government. The Supreme Office of Justice (*Oberste Justizstelle*) was established just at the time when Montesquieu advocated the division of powers in his *Esprit des lois* (1748). The direct influence of Montesquieu cannot be proved, however. Under the central office, provincial courts were established; they assumed jurisdiction formerly in the hands of the estates and of the state's administrative agencies.

[2] See p. 199.

Haugwitz, probably with the Prussian General Directory in mind, planned to keep the domestic and financial administration together in a single office. He merged the Austrian and Bohemian Court Chancelleries and added to their authority the financial administration of Austria and Bohemia, formerly carried on by the Court Chamber. The latter retained only the Hungarian finances. Under Kaunitz's influence, however, this *directorium in publicis et cameralibus*, of 1749, lost the financial administration to the Court Chamber again in 1761 and, thereafter, was named the United Bohemian-Austrian Court Chancellery. After the first Polish partition, the Galician administration came under the Chancellery as well. The Court Chamber functioned as the central financial agency for the monarchy. A general treasury and accounting office was associated with it, and the debt service was placed under its supervision. This change of 1761 led to a revamping of the provincial offices as well. The "representations and chambers" were turned into offices, mostly called *Gubernia*, each with a political, financial, and juridical department.

In 1746, a very modern institution was created, the Universal Directory of Commerce. Haugwitz took his cue from Frederick's department V of the General Directory.[3] From 1753 on, the commercial directory was linked up with the *directorium*, and its provincial offices with the representations and chambers or, subsequently, *Gubernia*. In 1761, the Universal Directory of Commerce, as Council of Commerce, became an independent central agency. Thus, supported by a foundation of a co-ordinated local and provincial administration, there were six highest offices of state—defense, foreign affairs, justice, interior, finance, and commerce—that stood directly under the monarch. In 1760, Maria Theresa created the council of state, which, in addition to the state chancellor, was to consist of three members of the high nobility and three knights. The state council, which had no executive or legislative authority, was the supreme watchdog committee and braintrust of the crown for internal administration and legislation. It was not a council of the chiefs of the highest departments but a committee of "wise men," who advised the empress. The Austrian council of state shows the contrast between Maria Theresa's system of government and Frederick the Great's. Carefully as the sovereign rights of the empress were guarded, hers was not an autocratic regime in the sense that she acted as her own minister. In many respects, one may call the Austrian system a bureaucratic

[3] See p. 195.

absolutism, of the sort introduced in Prussia only after 1807. But it was Maria Theresa's creation, and she devoted her life to it until, saddened by her husband's death in 1765, and exhausted by continuous controversies with her son, she finally allowed her efforts to slacken. Joseph II, who was elected Roman king in 1763, and became co-regent upon the death of his father, from the beginning took part in the state council's deliberations, and this institution proved its value for the monarchy even in those trying days. Frederick the Great, who admired Maria Theresa and called her "a great man," judged quite correctly, in his *Political Testament*, that she governed *"par elle même."*

On paper, the Austrian system of government looked more egalitarian than that of the Prussian kings. But the bureaucratic regime still had to struggle with estates, and its centralism had to overcome the strong consciousness of individuality among the territories. Maria Theresa had created positions from which diligent officials might have completed the task. But such officials did not exist in numbers large enough to make the regime fully effective. There was no choice but to appoint many noblemen who had served as executives of the territorial estates. No doubt some of them were competent, and many got used to receiving orders from Vienna. But in many, old habits or oppositional moods persisted. Few burghers were available for higher positions, and even the lower offices had to be filled with people of slight intelligence and reliability. Maria Theresa was aware of the bureaucracy's inadequacy and knew, too, that an improvement could not be expected except through the cultivation of a new public spirit and through better education.

∾ *Religion and Education under Maria Theresa*

MARIA THERESA WAS A DEVOUT Roman Catholic, and she was convinced that religious unity was a necessary element of a healthy public life. But compulsion of conscience was against her own feelings. Therefore, she had Protestants transferred from Austria to Transylvania, where the German colonists had been granted free exercise of their Protestant religion. The empress took exception to many of the exaggerated manifestations of piety that characterized Austrian religious life. Public flagellantism was forbidden as was the extravagant frequency of processions. The large number of Christian holidays was cut down, the number of monastic orders limited, and the taking of monastic vows made more difficult. Jansenist influence became strong in Austria, particularly after the acquisition of the Netherlands. If it was the chief original aim of Jansenism to reassert the primacy of religious faith over an easy synthesis of religion and reason, this did not affect Austrian thinking as much as the insistence on a practical conduct in accordance with Biblical rules. Still more important was Jansenism's advocation of maximum freedom of the national Churches from Rome, after it had been officially condemned by the Vatican. The foremost formulation of the arguments against papal absolutism in Germany was the treatise of the auxiliary bishop of Trier, Nicolaus von Hontheim, written under the name Febronius, *On the State of the Church and the Legitimate Power of the Roman Pontiff* (1763).

Austrian practice had always emphasized the rights of the state with regard to the Church. Strengthened by the fresh theoretical justification which it received from Jansenism, it was stirred into new action. The control of the Church by Rome or other non-Austrian authorities was narrowly circumscribed, but even more far-reaching was the virtual removal of ecclesiastical control from education. Originally Maria Theresa was most concerned with the universities, which were to train the leaders and officials of her state policy. A Dutchman of earnest Catholic faith, Gerhard von Swieten, court physician, became chief advisor in her efforts to turn the universities into state institutions. Swieten began with the reform of the medical faculty of Vienna University in 1749, the other faculties following shortly thereafter. The dominant position that the Jesuits had held for almost two centuries was thereby broken. Their ideal of education had aimed at training men able to understand and defend the faith. The new school thought that it had the same ultimate objective but considered the Jesuits' scholasticism and papalism incapable of achieving these results. The reformers wanted to introduce students to the full scientific knowledge that had been accumulated during the century.

Reason and practical common sense were given much wider room than before and given it confidently, since the truth of religion seemed so clearly rooted in the sentiments and actions of the heart. This synthesis of faith and reason appeared to many conscientious churchmen as the best answer to the religious indifferentism and immoralism that spread from Paris. Christian Wolff's philosophy served this Catholic thinking well. Vienna received its first professor of natural law. Actually, the old tradition of natural law in the Catholic Church was a better preparation for the modern legal ideas than Protestant theology had offered. Catholic Enlightenment, though it tended to draw both churches closer together, had a character of its own. It soon extended its influence from Vienna and the Benedictine University of Salzburg into the Catholic parts of Germany.

Maria Theresa's reforms of education were largely motivated by practical considerations. She wanted civil servants and people equipped to deal with economic problems and practical tasks. The law faculty in Vienna was strengthened through professors who, besides their teaching, were active in governmental affairs, particularly the attempts to create unified and reformed law codes for the monarchy. In economics or as it was still called "cameral science," Joseph von Sonnenfels (1733–1817) began his career in the university. This man of humble origin—his father, son of a Berlin rabbi, had immigrated into Bohemia and become a Catholic—was the most influential teacher of generations of Austrian bureaucrats. The school reform was originally begun by individual improvements, such as the introduction of a new curriculum at the Theresianum, the Vienna version of the German "Knights' Academy." But the pope's dissolution of the Jesuit order in 1773 made a thorough reform necessary and also made it possible to bring the schools almost completely under state control. In Maria Theresa's words, the schools were a "politicum," which, however, did not, in her opinion, necessitate excluding the clergy from school-teaching. As a matter of fact, the school reform could not have been carried through without the active co-operation of the clergy and some orders, such as the Piarists. The secondary schools began to emphasize such subjects as mathematics, history, geography, and German. Side by side with the *Gymnasia*, the still predominantly humanistic schools for future scholars, the so-called "realistic" schools (*Realschulen*) or "burgher schools" that concentrated their curriculum around the nonclassical subjects were developed.

For the organization of a universal school system one of the period's most eminent pedagogues, Johann Ignaz Felbiger, provost in the Silesian Sagan, was brought to Vienna. In 1744, he presented his plan, which was implemented by the founding of normal schools in all provincial capitals, and subsequently of village schools. These results were not won overnight. Most teachers were not able to teach more than the very elements of the three R's, school attendance was irregular, and the establishment of schools in many sections of the monarchy was lagging. Still, an important beginning was made, which the next generations were able to bring to full fruition. It is surprising, however, that all these new activities in education were not accompanied by some growth of literary productivity. The recognition of the German language in school and government may have contributed to the decline of the interest in the French theater, which had to be closed in 1772. When the Court Theater (*Burgtheater*) was turned over to a German company in 1776, it met with little popular applause. The Viennese preferred their light comedy, offered by the cheap theaters in the precincts before the city gates.

∾ Music in the Age of Maria Theresa

IT WAS UNDER THE REIGN of Maria Theresa and Joseph II that Austrian music completed its emancipation from Italian guardianship. Christoph Gluck (1714–87), son of a forester from the Bohemian-Franconian frontier, was a court conductor in Vienna from 1754–73, and he returned to live there again after leading his operas to triumph in Paris during the years of 1773–79. In contradistinction to the Italian opera with its emphasis on the vocal soloist, Gluck subordinated music to the drama. Unlike Richard Wagner, he did not aim at creating a naturalistic musical drama. Gluck chose classically simple subjects in which great heroic emotions could be expressed. One theme in particular dominated all his great operas—*Orpheus, Alceste, Iphigenia of Aulis, Iphigenia of Tauris*—the victory of love over death. Although Gluck restored significance to the drama as such, it served him chiefly to make the musical presentation a more highly organic whole than either the Italian operas or Händel's oratorios could be. Gluck had to go to Paris in order to gain recognition for his art. At that time Paris had come almost as much under the domineering influence of the Italian opera as Vienna, but the dramatic opera of Lully and Rameau was not forgotten in France.

∾ Joseph Haydn

JOSEPH HAYDN NEVER MADE any direct contribution to the development of the opera. Born in 1732, the child of poor artisans in a village of Lower Austria, he had to undergo many hardships until he rose from a choirboy to conductor of the rich Prince Nicolaus Esterházy's orchestra. This Hungarian magnate held court in Eisenstadt in the Burgenland and spent the winter with his retinue, including the orchestra, in the imperial capital. For almost thirty years (1761–90)

Haydn was in the Esterházys' service and had to deliver the music for all occasions as well as to fit this music to the artistic means at his disposal. These restricting conditions imposed upon the composer made it difficult for him to give full expression to his ideas. Yet with steady determination Haydn succeeded in fulfilling his artistic mission. He was first of all an instrumentalist, though vocal music helped to form the style of his compositions. But it was less artistic operatic singing than the folksong that influenced him. Maybe his love of melody went back to his infancy, when he heard his parents sing accompanied by a harp.

Haydn became the master of the new homophonic music, and he brought its classic sonata form to perfection. He exploited to the full the potentialities that the clavier offered, and by integrating the individual instruments of the string quartet and the symphony orchestra into a single sound-body he created a new musical "organ" fitted to express the vastly enriched tonality that the new melodic music required. Such an achievement could not have been the mere find of a naïve genius, as Haydn is usually misunderstood by the modern layman. Much conscious thought must have gone into the consummation of the musical revolution that he accomplished. But it is true that Haydn conceived of his musicianship still largely as artisanship rather than as the means of individual self-expression. The post-Rousseauan concept of art as a confession of personality did not appear in Germany before Goethe and Beethoven.

Haydn liked to take a cue for his compositions from the actual life around him, as the "hunt" or the "military" symphonies may illustrate. But whatever reality he set out to depict became at once transposed into the ideal world and had to submit to artistic laws. The gaiety of so much of Haydn's music was not the expression of a jovial composer but the intended reflection of the Olympic world of art. Haydn, however, was already affected by the age of sentimentality. Still, his sentiments were simple and ultimately were anchored in his piety. Haydn's religion was that of the German Enlightenment, the grateful worship of God as the creator of a world full of beauty and happiness, as expressed in his great oratorio, *The Creation*, which he wrote in 1798 after his return from England. He brought back with him the text of an adapted Miltonian poem. In these years Haydn also reached his peak as a composer of instrumental music with his "London" symphonies.

Although approaching sixty Haydn was able to learn from Mozart in a more than superficial way. His music gained a new depth by accepting the sweet melodic *cantabile* in addition to others of Mozart's tonal expressions, particularly a greater musical dynamics. While staying in England in 1790–92 and in 1795–98, Haydn became acquainted with the richly endowed musical life of Britain and with the flourishing cultivation of Händel. The acclaim that the English public showered on Haydn gave him world-wide renown and induced his Austrian patrons to grant him that comfortable independence that made his last years both happy and productive.

When Haydn died in 1809 during the French siege of Vienna, Ludwig van Beethoven (1770–1827) had already produced six of his nine symphonies. The Sixth, called the *Pastorale*, by its very name seemed closest to Haydn's art. But great as the debt of the young Rhinelander was to his Austrian predecessors, he belonged to a different age altogether. Rousseau, the French Revolution, and the new German poetry lie between Beethoven and Haydn, as they do also between Beethoven and Mozart.

✎ *Wolfgang Amadeus Mozart*

WOLFGANG AMADEUS MOZART (1756–91) came from an Augsburg artisan family. His father Leopold had turned to music and become a musician in the service of the prince-archbishop of Salzburg. Leopold gave his son, who turned out to be a child-prodigy both as virtuoso and composer, an extraordinary musical education and had him perform extensively in Italy, Germany, and France. While this work as a youth may have weakened his health, it gave him early in life a complete knowledge of Europe's whole musical culture.

For a number of years Mozart was employed, finally as organist, by the archbishop of Salzburg. But the despotic manners of the archbishop, who wanted to show his power by keeping the young man in his place, caused deep resentment in Mozart, and in 1781 he went to the Austrian capital in order to gain recognition of his talents. Mozart was anything but a social revolutionary, but he always refused to be treated as a servant. In the world of the courts and noblemen this was not the best method for winning favors. Artists, in order to be reasonably secure, still needed some sort of office like those occupied by Bach or Haydn. Beethoven in his later years was to become the first composer able to live largely on royalties from the publication of his compositions. In spite of many admirers Mozart failed to find patrons who would have freed him from worries about his material circumstances. None of the triumphs that he gained as a composer in Vienna or in Prague was sufficiently lasting to establish his musical supremacy and dislodge the conventional Italian music which still dominated. While he anxiously struggled with these adversities, a premature death took him away.

Mozart's artistic production was immense and ranged into all the fields of music. In instrumental music he developed Haydn's forms to new levels of musical expression. Gluck's influence on Mozart was not equally strong, although the dramatic side of Gluck's art made a contribution to Mozart's operas. Yet Mozart's imagination was not confined to the heroic life. He wrote only one opera in the high pathetic style, *Idomeneo* (1780), in which his talents somehow appear confined. There followed *The Abduction from the Seraglio* (1782), *The Marriage of Figaro* (1786), *Don Giovanni* (1787), *Così fan tutte* (1789), and *The Magic Flute* (1791); only the first and the last of these works had German texts. Different as the operas were in style and perfection, they demonstrated Mozart's capacity for embracing the whole breadth of human life by having characters from all social stations and from among all human types. Even figures seemingly belonging to a higher order of existence, such as the *governatore* in *Don Giovanni* or the Queen of the Night and Sarastro in *The Magic Flute*, act as feeling human beings.

Mozart possessed the highest sensitivity toward all phenomena of life and obviously desired to make the widest range of inner human experience his own. At the same time, he was endowed with an unsurpassed musical inventiveness that enabled him to translate any situation into a tonal or melodic form. But what made him the greatest dramatist of the eighteenth century, a figure of Shakespearean stature, was the incomparable architectonic gift that was an essential part of his creative genius and gave him the power to organize the vast variety of human experiences on all levels of life into dramatic events. In *Figaro* and *Don Giovanni* each figure is presented throughout in musical terms that never leave the fundamental character in doubt, while their various moods are revealed in the variety of melodic themes. In the multivocal arias each personality is made further explicit by being brought in contact or placed in contrast with others. Here Mozart made the fullest use of an advantage that the opera has over the stage-play, insofar as the opera can have a number of people express varying or even conflicting sentiments simultaneously. Bound together by melody and harmony, the great vocal sextets or octets impress on the listener at the same instance both the unity and variety of human life. Quite novel, too, was the use to which Mozart put the orchestra, employing it not merely for the accompaniment of the singers but as an instrument for bringing to life the underlying sentiment of the operatic scene as a whole.

Thus, Mozart's great operas, in their synthesis of musical expression of the various emotional levels of human life, display a structure that seems analogous to the widening horizontal and vertical circles of baroque churches. It was characteristic that early French critics complained about "too much music" in Mozart's works, and it is at least true that every part of his operas was so completely conceived as music that the music far transcended the meaning of the texts. The exclusively musical conception of Mozart's work also did not change when he adopted more classical lines in his last opera, *The Magic Flute*.

The musical representation of the world, not the confession of the artist's own personal struggle with this world, as later in Beethoven and his successors, was the supreme aim of Mozart's art. The harmonious beauty of Mozart's music sometimes seems to veil his awareness of the tragic element of life. As a matter of fact, many of his contemporaries in this age of the rococo took exception to what they called Mozart's melancholic moods. The Catholicism of the Enlightenment that he imbibed from his early youth might have led an artist in quest of beauty into a straight secularism. Mozart was little concerned with dogma and doctrine as such, but his attitude toward life was deeply molded by the fundamental emotions that the Church, through the meaningful ancient rites of its services rather than by the preachings of its clerics, had awakened in his heart. Mozart was acutely conscious that life is surrounded by death and recognized in the co-existence of life and death the will of a supreme creator. At the same time Mozart felt confident that man could grow toward higher virtue and love. This belief, that made him a Mason, was not in conflict with his basic religious sentiment. Rather, it was the free expression of his longing for moral perfection. *The Magic Flute*, embodying these feelings in their most elevated form, and the unfinished *Requiem Mass*, both composed in the year of his death, were complementary statements of the faith that gave depth to his work. Both in Mozart's work and person we can feel the stirrings of a coming modern world, but he was at the same time the last towering genius of Baroque art in Europe.

⌒ Austrian Weaknesses

THE STATE BUILT BY Maria Theresa was strong in eighteenth-century terms. Its weakness was still largely a matter of slow economic development. Some progress was made, particularly after 1763, and there was a spread of greater prosperity, in which the burghers shared. But even within the Austro-Bohemian complex, full economic integration could not be achieved by the administration. Tyrol, for example, had to be treated as a separate unit. Another handicap was the loss of Silesia, the realm's chief manufacturing province. Capital was scarce, and the expansion of transportation and factories kept within narrow bounds. Most serious was the state of public finance. The revenue from the contribution rose from 20 to 54 million gulden in 1773, the land tax from 14 to 19 million gulden during the same year. But the revenue never kept pace with the enormous expenditure for armaments and wars. At the end of the Seven Years' War, the Austrian government began issuing paper money, the so-called *Bankozettel*, a method that accelerated the accumulation of debts. In 1781, the bank debt amounted to 20 million gulden.

An even greater and more fundamental weakness was still hidden from the eyes of eighteenth- and early nineteenth-century men. The state's national diversity was still considered a technical rather than a constitutional debility. Leaving the Netherlands and Italian possessions alone, even the Danubian group of Habsburg lands was predominantly composed of non-German territories. Only Austria proper was a German country. With Silesia gone to Prussia, the lands of the Bohemian crown became predominantly Slavic. In the monarchy's so-called trans-Leithanian sections—that is the lands in the lower Danube basin—Croatians, Slovenes, and Rumanians, apart from Magyars, formed the major nationalities. With the acquisition of Galicia and Bucovina, two new nationalities, Poles and Ruthenians or Ukrainians, were added. They were on the eastern slopes of the Carpathian mountains, which made it extremely difficult to tie them closely to the center of the Habsburg empire.

For the unification of this southeastern European world, the dynastic idea was not by itself adequate unless it was embodied in an able ruling class. Maria Theresa knew this, and she did everything in her power to capture the personal adherence of the noblemen in her lands. But this was more of a palliative than a remedy for potential regional opposition. She trained a corps of officers and civil servants given to an all-embracing idea of superregional and supernational empire. For that purpose she had to rely on Germans, because their loyalty to the house of Habsburg was greatest and because relatively more education and talent were available among them. Modern nationalist thinking was alien to the empress, although the colonization of Germans along the military frontier against Turkey and in Transylvania was partly intended to inject a German element into the non-German population. By the end of the century, the Austrian bureaucracy had become a very effective arm of the government and undoubtedly, in this age, contributed greatly to the development of those peoples who later rose against it. The Austrian regime in Italy, for example, was better liked than that of the Spanish Bourbons. But a bureaucratic absolutism will always find it difficult to change and absorb new ideas and men from among those whom it rules.

Czech historians have judged that the subordination of the estates in the years after 1745 frustrated a development that might have led to a healthy federalism in the Habsburg empire a century later. But the decay of the diets had gone much too far to justify the assumption that in time they would have changed into democratic representative bodies. Everywhere the diets had become bulwarks of small social groups unable to show a way into the future. The modern history of Hungary, where the diet was preserved, does not prove that the problem of nationalities would have been more easily solved if the diets had retained their full political power.

✍ Seeds of War

WHILE ALL THESE PROBLEMS were still beyond the horizon, even for the most farsighted men of the age, a closer observer could not fail to notice that the concentration of Austrian statesmanship upon the unification of the Danube countries was indicative of a new attitude toward Germany. The Empire had played a secondary role in Austrian policy for a long time, but the preoccupation with the integration of the Habsburg dominions was bound to lead to a further diminution of Austrian commitment to the interests of the German Empire. This does not mean that Austrian diplomacy was not at all times active to line up as much support among the German princes as possible, but in a conflict of German and Austrian interests the latter usually prevailed. It was the full measure of Frederick's victory that he forced the old imperial power into a political course that was only slightly better than his own disregard of the Holy Empire's institutions. The hope of regaining Silesia, which Maria Theresa nourished in her heart, was born by the desire to restore this jewel to her own, the Bohemian, crown rather than the wish to rebuild in Germany the imperial prestige, which, unquestionably, had further suffered by Frederick's violence. In balancing these conflicting motives, Maria Theresa's offended moral sentiments were a most important factor. She was averse to war in general and thought of war of conquest as a crime, but defending a legitimate right and undoing an act of robbery was a different matter.

✑ *Count Kaunitz*

MARIA THERESA'S UNHEROIC and business-like husband recommended that she should maintain her alliances with the maritime powers and Russia. This would keep at bay "that Prussian," who was the only possible peacebreaker. At the same time, he warned her not to make Frederick angry through bitter words. But the empress trusted the advice of Count Kaunitz (1711–94), whom she appointed state chancellor in 1753. This strong-willed diplomat came from an old Bohemian family and from a Westphalian-Frisian mother. For forty years, beyond the death of Maria Theresa, he directed Austrian foreign policy almost single-handedly. In internal policy, too, his influence was greater than that of any other minister, although the empress tried to keep him out of Church politics. Even here, however—as has been learned only recently—he knew how to steer her into an attitude which did not fully correspond to her own thinking. Kaunitz was a pupil of French deism and the Encyclopedists, and a mechanistic rationalism also helped him to understand the interests and trends of the states of Europe. Every conception and move of his diplomacy was the product of rational calculation, and through logical reasoning he made himself effective with the partners of his negotiations. But if "the coachman of Europe"—as he called himself occasionally—thought that his "political algebra" gave him a perfect knowledge of his road, he deceived himself. Nevertheless, this priggish man possessed great political vision and extraordinary shrewdness in the execution of his schemes. Personal passions did not affect his policies.

Kaunitz agreed with the empress that the reconquest of Silesia had to be made the central theme of Austrian foreign policy. He saw that the alliance with England would be of no avail for that aim. England had not shown real zeal in defending the Pragmatic Sanction and, while expecting Austria to fight in the Netherlands in an Anglo-French war, would never be inclined to assist in a war for Silesia. Kaunitz proposed to seek an alliance with France by making concessions in the Netherlands and Italy. It seemed an overbold project, implying as it did that France could be persuaded to sacrifice her northern ally, who had taken Sweden's and Poland's place in the diplomatic arsenal of France and, incidentally, also to write off Turkey. Kaunitz would not have made any progress if the relations between England and France had not taken an unexpected turn. For the first time, events in America completely overshadowed and determined the political grouping of powers on the Continent.

The French attempt to link up their position in Canada with Louisiana by a chain of forts in the Alleghenies had aroused the ire of the English settlers along the Atlantic coast, who saw themselves cut off from future western expansion into the interior of the American Continent. The sparks that flew from incidents in the wilderness had set off a smoldering fire, which for almost two years went on as an undeclared war between France and England, until the English government officially opened war in May, 1756. Both powers would have liked to avoid war in Europe, but even neutralization of the Continent required diplomatic measures. France had an alliance with Prussia, and Sweden, Denmark, and the Ottoman Empire leaned on France. England relied on her close relations with the Dutch Republic and Austria. In case of war with France, this entente was to defend the Netherlands and thereby also prohibit a French attack against Hanover, though the latter might still fall prey to Prussian ambitions unless Austria would engage Prussia. Austria was assigned a big task by England. Kaunitz refused to assume the defense of the Netherlands, calling it a hopeless venture. He declared his willingness to undertake the protection of Hanover on condition that England would support Austria and Russia in their designs on Prussia.

ᴄ Russian Policy

RUSSIA HELD A VERY SPECIAL position within the system of European politics. The western expansionism that Peter the Great had implanted into his state continued under his three weak successors. As early as under Peter the Great's regime, two major directions had been chosen, which could be pursued simultaneously or consecutively. Access to

the Black Sea and an extension of Russian influence into northern
Central Europe were the two poles around which Russian policy
fluctuated in this period. Heavy pressure was already brought on
Poland from within and without. But the wish to acquire the *dominium
maris Baltici* was bound to create conflict not only with Sweden but
possibly also with Prussia. During the Nordic War, Prussia was still
able to profit from the war between Peter the Great and Charles XII
by the annexation of Stettin and the Oder estuary. The Russia of 1755
was no longer afraid of Sweden, but she resented the liaison between
Prussia and Sweden and had her eyes on eastern Prussia. Her anti-
Turkish plans brought Russia to the side of Austria, so much so that
during the War of the Polish Succession Russian troops appeared on
the Rhine as Austrian allies. Therefore it seemed that Russia could be
safely counted on as an enemy of the Franco-Prussian combination,
the more so since her material needs made her depend on England. The
English took most of the Russian exports, among them vital naval
stores, and provided the country with colonial goods in exchange. But
beyond mere commercial relations, England was the only possible
source for the subsidies required if a big Russian army was to move
westward.

When Austria balked at the defense of the Netherlands, the duke of
Newcastle turned to Russia and, in September, 1755, concluded a
subsidy agreement under which Russia was to maintain 55,000 men at
the border of Livonia. The duke thought of them as a warning to
Prussia to abstain from any threat against Hanover. In spite of its
moderate scope, the Russians saw in the treaty rather an encouragement
of their westward expansion, about which they were in lively negotiations with Austria. When Frederick of Prussia learned about the
Anglo-Russian subsidy treaty, he became greatly alarmed. Although
his remark after the Peace of Dresden, that from now on he would
not even attack a cat, was not to be taken too literally, he was no longer
the youthful daredevil who had plunged into war in 1740. He was
aware of the strength of the powers which he had once challenged too
boldly, and the activation of Russia made this hostile group most
formidable. Frederick felt certain, however, that the enmity between
France and Austria was immutable and that he could gain additional
consideration from the French government only if he did not place
himself unconditionally at its disposal. Anxious to cut British subsidies
to Russia, he offered himself as a guarantor of the neutrality of
Hanover. On January 6, 1756, the Convention of Westminster was

signed, which obliged England and Prussia to act together in keeping foreign—and this included French—troops out of Hanover. Frederick now believed that the Russian army could not march, that Austria would not move against him, and that military hostilities on the Continent would be confined to warfare in the Netherlands between France on one side and the maritime powers and Austria on the other.

✎ The Diplomatic Revolution

BUT FREDERICK HAD committed the gravest political error of his life. In Versailles, the Westminster Convention, which had been negotiated in dark secrecy, was considered an act of treachery, and the Franco-Prussian alliance was allowed to lapse. The moment of Kaunitz's triumph had arrived. On May 1, 1756, a first Treaty of Versailles was signed between Austria and France, which was still defensive in nature. But while Austria merely promised neutrality in the Anglo-French war, France, strangely enough, committed herself to come to Austria's assistance if the latter was attacked. Whereas Louis XV was driven into the nets of Kaunitz by his resentment against Frederick's part in the Westminster Convention, the Russian Empress Elizabeth grew indignant over the action of the British cabinet. Neither then nor later did it come to an open breach between Russia and England, but Elizabeth persisted in her war plans. She proposed to march against Prussia in the summer of 1756; Kaunitz persuaded her, and at this moment Maria Theresa also, only with difficulty to wait till spring, 1757. Kaunitz wished to solidify the French alliance and give it an offensive character chiefly by making France pay subsidies, without which Russia was unable to conduct an effective war. Austrian diplomacy had made considerable headway when Frederick struck. On August 29, 1756, he invaded Saxony after Maria Theresa had turned down his ultimate demand for assurances that Austria would not open war against him.

Frederick's aggression brought the Austro-French alliance into operation. This alliance provided for only very limited French assistance and not at all for French gains. On May 1, 1757, a new treaty was signed at Versailles. France undertook to participate in the war with an army of more than 100,000 men and pay subsidies to the amount of 12 million livres. Equally important was French approval of the total destruction of Prussia. Silesia was to go back to Austria, Magdeburg to Saxony, and Stettin to Sweden. Once Austria had won Silesia, France was to receive

Ypres and some other small places in Belgium. The Spanish Bourbon prince, Philip of Parma, was to be transferred to Brussels and the Austrian Netherlands to fall to France after his death. The treaty was a colossal blunder on the part of Louis XV's government. No French interest could justify the investment of such large amounts of money and manpower in Austria's German war. If it failed, France would get nothing. If, on the other hand, the alliance defeated Frederick, Louis XV would have helped to undo the work of French statesmanship since the days of Richelieu by re-establishing Austrian hegemony over Germany. But the most serious aspect of this French policy was the fact that it deprived France of substantial means for the effective conduct of the war against England. Pitt's remark that he conquered America in Germany was correct. The French alliance enabled Kaunitz to bring Russia into the war without committing himself to the future annexation of eastern Prussia by Russia. It is, however, difficult to see how he could have dislodged Russia from Königsberg if the war had been victorious. Kaunitz assumed a great responsibility in pulling Russia deeper into Europe.

The outbreak of the Seven Years' War, in 1756, found Austria in a situation very different from that of the year 1740. Austria was the center of an imposing group of major powers and could employ all her forces against Prussia. Maria Theresa's reforms gave her a strong army of high military quality. It was ably led by its commanders, among whom Count Leopold Daun and Baron Ernst von Laudon were most eminent. Because of them, Frederick the Great lost almost as many battles as he won. But in the end he proved invincible.

CHAPTER 9

The Seven Years' War and the Monarchy of Frederick the Great

✍ Frederick's Personal Qualities

WHEN, IN 1746, Frederick returned to Berlin from the second Silesian War, people acclaimed him "the Great" for the first time, and soon Europe joined in this accolade. However, many of his contemporaries called him "Frederick the Unique," which expressed admiration mixed with a certain bewilderment at his complex personality. His many-sided and paradoxical nature was perplexing. This complexity explains the conflicting interpretations of his personality, though some of them must be adjudged mere political legends. Frederick was a highly sensitive, originally even perhaps sentimental, human being. There was much in him that drew him to an esthetic and contemplative life. At the same time, he was driven to action that would impress people around him. This quality proved to be his strongest trait. The eminent German historian Friedrich Meinecke has rightly stated that the future ruler in Frederick was developed earlier than the philosopher. Though it is true that Frederick wished to work for objectives that would stand up in the light of philosophical reflection, his boldness as a statesman often carried him over the hurdles that philosophy placed in his way. Philosophy to him was a means for gaining fresh strength and seeing himself and his activity as part of a more comprehensive order of natural and historical events.

One of the earliest reasons for the conflict between Frederick and his father had been his belief in the Calvinist doctrine of predestination, and even as an enlightened philosopher in his later life he remained a strict determinist. This determinism reflected the force in his nature that enabled him to continue his father's work and suppress in himself much of his adolescent self-conceit and idle playfulness. The young king was not without vanity, which Bismarck considered one of his chief characteristics, and, as the events of 1740 demonstrated, had strong gambling instincts. But from the beginning he was determined to identify himself entirely with his royal position's objective tasks. He chose an ascetic life. The pleasant summer palace "Sans Souci," which he had built for himself between 1745 and 1747 in the neighborhood of Potsdam, was quite small and never saw any luxurious court life. Once Frederick became king, he set up a separate household for his unloved queen, whom he very seldom saw thereafter. Women did not play any role in his life, with the possible exception of his sister, Wilhelmina of Bayreuth.

As crown prince, Frederick imbibed Christian Wolff's philosophy. In his later years, he tended to prefer Locke. But the main influences that formed his thought came from France, to such an extent that Frederick became a virtual foreigner in Germany's intellectual development. Bayle, Voltaire, and d'Alembert were foremost among the authors who attracted him to the contemporary philosophy of France. With them he rejected all metaphysics, although he retained a general faith in God or a supreme providence, whose traces could be found in the general laws ruling nature and the universe. Human reason, however, was considered capable of raising man to the level of full humaneness (*humanité* or *Humanität*) and of making him master of his life. If principles of reason were applied to social life and the chaos that resulted from the unregulated passions and prejudices of the past removed, happiness could rule the world. Inevitably, the fragmentary nature of the individual was felt in this philosophy, as were the limitations of human cognition. Life was short, and though the philosophers knew about primary laws, they were unsure about the secondary causes of events. But, by irony and wit, an enlightened mind could rise even above these baffling questions. This philosophy's secular character made its believers immune against being deflected from the pursuit of their own happiness and that of their fellow men. In philosophy, science, history, and art a philosophical mind was able to depict the beauty and truth of the universe which the individual might enjoy.

The growth of the French language and literature gave Voltaire and his contemporaries the faculties to express these new ideas succinctly and brilliantly. What they lacked in depth, they gained in breadth and in their intimate relation to the practical life of the individual and society. They captivated the exuberant thinking of the young Frederick completely. Here was the rebirth of the glory of the Augustan age, a world of clarity and perfection as well as a challenge to the present generation's moral will. Frederick himself became a French *philosophe*, pouring out his thoughts in a stream of writings on philosophy, politics, and history and in a flow of poetry. None of his writings, with the exception of his two historical books, *Histoire de mon temps* and *Histoire de la guerre de sept ans*, could be considered an important contribution to scholarship or art, and the same holds true of the music he composed. They were, however, testimony to his active personal response to everything he learned and to his deep love for things of the spirit. He succeeded in drawing Voltaire to Berlin and Potsdam for three years, from 1750 to 1753. Although Voltaire's personal intrigues against Maupertuis led to a sharp rupture of relations, the king and Voltaire renewed their correspondence in later years. Every French writer who might fall out with the French government was sure of a refuge in Prussia, and the Prussian presses would even publish philosophical treatises with which Frederick disagreed. In 1744, the Academy was reorganized as the *Académie des Sciences et Belles Lettres*, and Maupertuis was persuaded to accept its presidency. Many other French scholars and writers of higher and lesser rank became members of this institution, whose publications were in French. The Berlin Academy became an outpost of France's scholastic civilization, according to the wishes of its founder, who surrounded himself in Sans Souci with a group of educated men, among them many Frenchmen, Italians, Scotsmen, and Germans, with whom he liked to spend his few leisure hours in lively conversation ranging from the loftiest subjects of philosophy and the arts to gay banter.

On the negative side, Frederick shared with his French philosophers the rejection of all historic forms of Christian religion. In his *Political Testament* (1768), he called it "an old metaphysical fairy tale, full of miraculous legends, paradoxes, and nonsense." He warned his successor not to allow "saintly charlatans" to gain influence. Another time, he defined theologians as "animals without reason." In the conflict "between Geneva and Rome" he declared himself to be neutral; Wittenberg he did not care to mention. Frederick was not certain whether religion would ultimately disappear. In general he recommended not giving offense to the religious feelings of the masses. "The state does not have to care what metaphysical image is in a human brain." Under Frederick's government churches were treated with cool toleration, which sprang from this indifference.

It is unnecessary to add that Frederick was not moved by any of the traditional religious justifications of kingship, nor, on the other hand, by a mere dynastic conception of monarchy. He accepted the contract theory, according to which the prince was originally elected by the people for the protection of their security and prosperity. Such a contract had laid in his hands absolute power, which, however, had to be used wisely for the benefit of the people or, as one may paraphrase it, nothing was to be done by the people, but everything for the people. As Frederick formulated it, probably in analogy to terms used by Bayle and Fénélon, the prince was only the "first servant of the state." Actually, this often-quoted expression was not entirely novel as a definition of the prince's duties. One could arrive at similar statements from a strictly Christian concept of monarchy. In Frederick's mouth it meant a denunciation of the "proprietary" state, and at the same time was closely connected with his belief that wisdom was to be found in the philosophical laws and moral ideals the Enlightenment preached. Here a dilemma arose that was to constitute an almost continuous theme of Frederick's meditations. Philosophy taught him that the ultimate aim of a policy directed by reason ought to be the advancement of human welfare. Right laws would create human happiness. But power alone could afford security in a world so largely dominated by ambition for power. Therefore even domestic government had to assume as its major task the production of military power for defense. The impact of international conditions upon interior politics was bound to limit the progress of welfare.

∽ Welfare and Power

FREDERICK WRESTLED with the conflict between welfare and power all his life. In his conscience it presented itself as a problem of the conflict of individual and political ethics. In the years before his accession to the throne, he had believed himself able to refute Machiavelli's teachings that a prince could only act in accordance with the interests of his power, and that this *raison d'état* overrides all considerations of law and ethics. In his treatise of 1740, best known under the title of *Anti-Machiavel* given to it by Voltaire, he attempted to demonstrate the applicability of the moral law to all, or at least almost all, circumstances of politics. But his own actions in 1740 and thereafter were not controlled by this moral philosophy nor even completely by the interest of the state. They were motivated largely by a passion for glory. After the first two Silesian wars, Frederick subordinated personal ambition to the demands of a rational policy, but utilitarian rather than moral grounds prevailed in his political thinking. The relative limitation of his policy's acquisitive aims came from the realization of the weakness of his own state within the European system of states. On the other hand, this weakness was an additional reason for disregarding law. Prussia could not afford to leave the initiative to others, or, as Frederick expressed it, in certain circumstances she had to "dupe" others before being duped herself. His decision to march into Saxony in 1756 was the most important act of such a defensive *raison d'état*. Frederick did not begin the Seven Years' War in order to conquer a new province. But had he succeeded in defeating his enemies decisively, there can be no doubt that he would have added Saxony to his own dominions.

At that stage, Frederick declared self-interest to be the ultimate moving force of politics. In self-seeking ambition he saw the only bond in the association of nations. Otherwise states would prefer to live in isolation. Thus, full contrast was reached to any ideal of a European community, which had been one of the constitutive forces of the European order and its consciousness of law through the Middle Ages. This ideal had lived on among both Catholics and Protestants through the sixteenth and seventeenth centuries. It was paradoxical that the Age of Enlightenment, with its strong cosmopolitan feeling among the educated people, should have banned any deeper European loyalties from politics. But the very rationalism that helped create the new cosmopolitan faith in humanity turned the states into separate machines of power to be run according to technical rules. Mercantilism strengthened this political insulation and cut the ties between the nations. It is true, however, that the rulers could carry out their policies without hatred and look at each other somewhat like competing businessmen in a free economy. In the eighteenth century, it was possible to civilize even war itself and begin to define its codes. It also was unnecessary to work up a feverish national sentiment. In war, patriotism was aroused, and agnostic monarchs unblushingly spread religious slogans, which had not lost their appeal with the common people. But in times of peace, despotic governments did not consider ardent patriotism a healthy attitude. Patriotism should be cultivated in peacetime only as a "mild passion," Frederick's minister Hertzberg declared.

The Prussia of Frederick II developed the principles of eighteenth-century power politics to their highest logical perfection. But it was the monarch alone who knew and practiced the game of power in accordance with its rational rules. If in following *raison d'état* the prince had to violate treaties or disregard ethical norms that were binding on private citizens, he could be morally excused, provided he acted in the interest of the state. Frederick had to admit that statesmen often enough did not execute a policy in harmony with the interests of their states. The Franco-Austrian alliance of 1756 was a shocking example of such an irrational policy. It made him more skeptical than before about the nature of man and the adequacy of the doctrine of state interests for the explanation of history. But at the same time, self-denying service for the state assumed an even higher value. The idea of the state for Frederick was something highly abstract and cold as marble. It could be suspected that "state" was nothing but a hypo-statization of the absolute king, much the same as Frederick William I's pretension that he served the "king of Prussia." However, this is not entirely true. To be sure, the state was not the people, of whom Frederick was quite unable to think as an organically growing community, but it was no longer exclusively identical with the dynasty or king. The state was a task of suprapersonal character to be performed by all classes. The king never forgot the duty to humanize the government to the highest degree compatible with outward security. In practice, this did not permit many reforms, because wars were costly, and to the end of his life Frederick believed that Prussia could not measure up to the great powers, England, France, Russia, and Austria, and had to make up for her external weakness by special efforts. In the conflict of power and humanitarianism, the latter had to take the back seat, but Frederick never lost sight of his humanitarian responsibilities. In his later years he was even more conscious of these responsibilities than in his youth.

∽ The Seven Years' War

FREDERICK'S CONCERN WITH foreign affairs was always uppermost in his mind. In 1756, it led him into the action by which he hoped to break up his enemies' alliance before it was capable of attacking him. This aim was not reached, and a struggle opened which required superhuman courage, resourcefulness, and endurance. Dresden was captured, and Frederick also captured the encircled Saxon army after beating off a supporting Austrian army at Lobositz (October 1756). Saxony was occupied, and all during the war the rich country was exploited to fill the Prussian king's coffers. But Frederick displayed shortsightedness in judging popular sentiment when he enrolled the whole Saxon army of 20,000 men without their officers in the Prussian army. Whole units deserted in subsequent campaigns. With Saxony as a base, Frederick hoped through a powerful offensive to confound the Austrians before they had deployed their armies completely, and to gain possession of Bohemia. The invasion of the country from Saxony and Silesia was accomplished, and the Austrian army under Marshal Browne and Charles of Lorraine was pushed back. On May 6, 1757, in one of the most murderous battles, the Austrians were forced from their fortified positions before Prague and shut off in the Bohemian capital. The moral effect of the Prussian victory was great, though it had been bought at a very high price, and though the Prussians were ill prepared for a long siege of a strongly defended fortress. Moreover, another Austrian army, under Daun, was still in the field. With part of his forces, Frederick marched against Daun, and, at Kolin, on June 18, suffered the first defeat of his life. It was the end of the Bohemian campaign. The siege of Prague had to be lifted, the king went back to Saxony, and the Austrians moved into Silesia.

The great strategic aims that the king had set for himself proved beyond his reach. Even after Kolin, he had a respectable numerical strength left. But an army of mercenaries, which had to be provisioned by a chain of magazines, could not operate on such advanced lines nor effectively occupy a large province. If battles could have completely annihilated the enemy's main forces, the wars of the eighteenth century would have assumed a different character, and Frederick the Great, more than any of his contemporaries, would have been the man to conduct wars of great strategic offensives. But this would have required a different type of army and, in addition, superiority in numbers. Napoleon had both and was able to revolutionize warfare by aiming at the single, decisive battle which in one day would settle the fate of empires. Frederick did not even enjoy larger numbers. On the contrary, most of the time his army was inferior in size to the individual armies that he took on in battle, and vastly inferior to the aggregate of armies that the members of the hostile alliance could muster against him. As these armies took the field, he was thrown on the strategic defensive. The latter had to be conducted by way of tactical offensives designed to make the union of allied armies impossible. Even the king's greatest victories, between 1756 and 1763, were strategically indecisive. The only hope Frederick had was that the sequence of battles would have a cumulative effect on his enemies' resources or upon the ties of alliance.

It was not easy to maintain even this much hope after the defeat of Kolin and the failure of the Bohemian campaign. The summer of 1757 brought additional bad news. A Russian army under Apraxin broke into East Prussia and defeated a Prussian corps. The loss of Prussia seemed imminent, and it could not be foreseen that Apraxin would withdraw upon receiving a false report of the czarina's death. Even more alarming were the events in Germany. The English had failed to re-enforce their army in Hanover, against which the French moved 100,000 men in the summer of 1757. The English army, composed of 45,000 Hanoverians, Brunswickians, and Hessians, was under the command of the duke of Cumberland, a son of George II. Beaten at Hastenbeck on the Weser, it retired to Stade on the lower Elbe, and the duke was persuaded to conclude the Convention of Kloster Zeven with the French commander, the Duc de Richelieu, on September 8. It provided for the dispersal of the Hanover army and left the country to French control, consequently as a possible base for action against Prussia. Another French army under Prince Soubise was detailed to co-operate with the forces mobilized by the emperor against the violator of the German peace. From Thuringia, the armies were supposed to carry out actions against Magdeburg and Leipzig.

Frederick marched against this allied group and, with 20,000 Prussians, routed the 50,000 French and Germans at Rossbach, on November 5, 1757. Hurrying to Silesia, he found his troops there in a grim situation. The chief fortress protecting Lower Silesia, Schweidnitz, had fallen into Austrian hands, and after a victory over the Prussian army the Austrians were able to make their entry into Breslau. Frederick restored the morale of his defeated Silesian troops and, with 35,000 men, attacked an Austrian army twice as strong at the village of Leuthen, west of Breslau, on December 5, 1757. His old stratagem, the oblique battle order, by which he held back one of his wings and threw himself with great force upon a single wing of the enemy, was executed to perfection. Napoleon remarked that this single battle would have sufficed to make Frederick immortal. Silesia had to be evacuated by the Austrians. Daun returned to Bohemia with only 30,000 men.

Frederick's victories made a tremendous impression on Europe. Not only the Empire's ill-trained troops but also French elite regiments had been beaten in a few afternoon hours, and the small Prussian army had proved superior against a mighty coalition. The battle of Rossbach awakened much admiration, in places even jubilation, in Germany. The alliance with France was most unpopular in the Empire, and obviously the military prowess of the Prussians was well liked. The *litterateurs* in Paris also applauded loudly. Inept French generals had been jeered often enough in France, but now the praise for the foreign victor was an expression of the contempt in which the brainless French rulers were held.

The greatest enthusiasm was displayed in London. On the night of Frederick's birthday, the city was illuminated. Methodists and other devout people hailed Frederick as a new Protestant hero. William Pitt, in his earlier career a staunch opponent of Continental entanglements, discovered the usefulness of Continental diversions. He advised the king to withhold ratification of the Convention of Kloster Zeven and to strengthen the Hanover army for new fighting. Prince Ferdinand of Brunswick, a Prussian officer and brother-in-law of Frederick, assumed command and proved himself a masterful strategist. He managed to tie down the large French army which France continued to send into Germany every year. This diversion aided England in her colonial wars. Frederick, for his part, was relieved from French threats against his western flank. He would have liked to see an English naval squadron in the Baltic Sea as a demonstration against Russia and Sweden. England was unwilling to enter into Baltic conflicts, but though Frederick's war contributed only indirectly to England's war against France, Pitt was willing to support it with the largest English subsidy ever paid to a Continental ally. On April 11, 1758, England and Prussia signed an agreement in which they pledged themselves not to make a separate peace. Prussia was to receive four million thaler (£570,000) in annual subsidies and remained free to choose her own military objectives.

∽ Prussian Reverses

THE POPULARITY WHICH Frederick had gained in Germany after Rossbach made it possible for him to replenish his forces through recruitment in Germany. Once more, in early 1758, he wanted to launch a campaign of great strategic possibilities. Again, as in 1742, Moravia was selected as the theater of operations. But the offensive bogged down at the fortress of Olmütz. Laudon endangered Frederick's communications with Silesia, and in July, 1758, Frederick had to retreat from Moravia. He bitterly complained that he had lost his superiority, and this proved perfectly true. From now on, he conducted only sorties against the foe who at any given moment was most threatening. In the summer of 1758, the Russians presented the greatest peril. A Russian army under Count Fermor had crossed into East Prussia in the first days of 1758. On the same January 24 when the Londoners had placed lights in their windows, the magistrates of Königsberg had to pay homage to the empress of Russia. There was no chance of freeing East Prussia from the Russians. It remained occupied to the end of the war. But the Russian advance to the *Neumark*, that is, the part of Brandenburg east of the Oder, had to be thwarted if there was not to be a juncture of Russians and Austrians. On August 25, 1758, Frederick met the Russians at Zorndorf close to Küstrin and found them more formidable enemies than he had anticipated. The bloody battle forced the Russian army to retreat behind the Vistula for the rest of the year. Quickly Frederick turned southward to protect Saxony and Silesia against Field Marshal Daun. Much as Daun was given to Fabian tactics, he did not fail to take advantage of Frederick's mistakes. On October 14, he surprised him at Hochkirch. The Prussians lost almost one fourth of their army. But despite this serious blow, Frederick managed to defend both Silesia and Saxony for the rest of the year.

The year 1759 dawned upon a greatly worried and haggard king. Replacement of the losses suffered by the army became difficult, and his best generals had been killed in battle. Even in discipline, the Prussian army was no longer what it had been in the early years of the war. Daun's strategy of maneuver did not achieve the union of his army with the Russians, who, under the command of Count Soltykov, had advanced again to the eastern bank of the Oder. But a strong Austrian corps under Laudon managed to join the Russians in the neighborhood of Frankfurt. Frederick was forced to fight to avoid losing Berlin and Brandenburg. On August 12, 1759, with 53,000 men he attacked the Russian-Austrian army of close to 70,000 at Kunersdorf. This time the oblique battle order was of no avail, and the king suffered the gravest defeat of his life. Practically half of his army was lost. Frederick wished for an enemy's bullet to kill him and actually almost fell into the hands of the Cossacks. To his minister in Berlin he wrote: "I believe everything is lost; I shall not survive the collapse of my fatherland." In those days he was afraid of his own soldiers, though he continued to trust his officers.

Consternation and despair gave way to new determination, and Frederick's enemies failed to throw the net over him. Daun wanted to conquer Silesia and Saxony for his queen, and Soltykov, whose losses at Kunersdorf had been serious, refused to march alone against the Prussian capital. This decision of his enemies, which gave him a new lease on life, Frederick called "the miracle of the house of Brandenburg." Soon he turned toward Saxony, where the army of the Empire had taken Dresden on September 4. But the capitulation of a Prussian corps of 15,000 men at Maxen made the recapture of the Elbe city impossible. The year ended in gloom, and the next year brought no decisive shift. What kept Frederick's situation from further deterioration was the inability of the Austrian and Russian military commanders to agree on combined operations. Maria Theresa reluctantly agreed to an Austro-Russian treaty, of April 1, 1760, which promised the Russians the possession of (East) Prussia after the war, provided Austria regained Silesia. But the hope that this political concession would smooth understanding on the military conduct of the war did not come true. Frederick increased his enemies' difficulties by his victory over Laudon at Liegnitz on August 15, 1760. As a sort of secondary operation, a thrust against Berlin was undertaken by detached Russian and Austrian corps in early October. Except for vandalism in the royal palaces of Charlottenburg and Schönhausen as well as the extraction of war tribute from the city, the Russian and Austrian troops did not behave badly during their week in Berlin. Word that Frederick was approaching made them leave the city by October 13. Again the king turned to Saxony to dislodge Daun from the strong position he had gained at the central Elbe. On November 3, 1760, at Torgau, Frederick beat the Austrians once more in a costly battle.

During the following year Frederick's situation grew more constricted. His army was poor. Two thirds of even the regular regiments consisted of foreigners. Officers were scarce, and fourteen- and fifteen-year-old cadets had to be appointed. Large numbers of less desirable people were organized in irregular "free battalions." Frederick conducted the campaign of 1761 by maneuvering tactics. The two chief fortresses of Silesia and Pomerania, Schweidnitz and Kolberg, were conquered by the enemy. For the first time, the Russians were able to take winter quarters in Pomerania and the Austrians in Silesia. With the occupation of these provinces, additional revenue was lost. Frederick knew that the Habsburg empire's financial difficulties were mounting and that, as a consequence, Austria had to curtail the strength of army effectives. This, however, was little comfort, since he felt that his enemies had ample power to snuff out his own light. His mind was made up not to survive the defeat of his monarchy. Secretly he advised one of his ministers that in case of his own defeat and demise, London, if necessary even Versailles, Vienna, or Petersburg, should be approached in an attempt to save as many territories as possible for his nephew and heir. There was still a ray of hope left in a possible war by Turkey and the Tartars of the Crimea against Austria and Russia.

For a few years, Frederick had been trying to persuade Sultan Mustafa III to take up arms. During the winter of 1761–62, the Prussian agent in Constantinople made the sanguine report that great preparations were being carried on, and a representative of the Tartar khan actually appeared in Frederick's headquarters. The king decided to wait till the middle of February.

Relief came through another event, the death of Empress Elizabeth on January 5, 1762, and the succession of her nephew, the duke of Holstein-Gottorp, as Peter III. A boundless admirer of Frederick, this drunken German prince, who succeeded in making more bitter enemies in a single day than other fools in a lifetime, was more interested in the restoration of his duchy, now in Danish hands, than in the government of Russia. But he changed Frederick's fortunes. Peter III renounced all Russian conquests in Prussia and advised his allies to make peace. The war between Russia and Prussia was officially ended by a treaty of May 5, 1762. Sweden, which since 1757 had conducted an ineffectual, if annoying, war against Prussia, followed suit. Peter III even urged a Russian alliance on Frederick. He proposed to send 20,000 Russians to Frederick's support if the latter would back the czar's claims for Holstein. The alliance was signed in June. It was a most unusual step for the king, because the Danish possession of Holstein had been guaranteed by France and England, and obviously England was not going to tolerate Russian occupation of this strategic corner.

The Anglo-Prussian alliance of 1758 had been broken off in the spring of 1762. After a slow beginning, England's war against France had gone from victory to victory. In North America, the West Indies, and India the French had completely lost control, the French navy had been swept from the high seas, and French foreign trade had been depleted. Yet the greatness of these successes, achieved under William Pitt's leadership, not only aroused the wish for peace with France but also made the war on the European continent appear rather insignificant. The most direct contribution to the war against France had been made by Prince Ferdinand of Brunswick and his army, which was composed of Hanover, Brunswick, and Hesse troops augmented by English regiments. Considering the strong forces that the French were continually hurling at him, the prince had done extremely well throughout these years. In June, 1758, he had driven the French over the Rhine and defeated them at Krefeld. But his army was not strong enough to hold the French on the western bank of the Rhine. His victory at Minden, on August 1, 1759, kept the French out of Hanover, most of Westphalia, and Hesse. Hesse was lost in 1760, but a French offensive against Hanover and Brunswick was thwarted in July, 1761. During the following summer, Prince Ferdinand was able to advance into Hesse again.

Even this war around Hanover, which was fought with English money and partly with English soldiers, became less important as the French suffered defeat overseas. An England that turned her attention to the empire lost interest in Hanover and, inevitably, even more in Frederick's war with Austria and Russia. The loss of popularity which the Prussian cause suffered in England was quite understandable. It was this change of attitude which enabled the placemen of George III, who came to the throne in October, 1760, to undercut the position of William Pitt. The "Great Commoner" left the government in October, 1761, and Lord Bute became the most influential member of the English government, which used the peace issue most recklessly to entrench itself in power and prepare the way for a return of personal government by the king. Spain's foolhardy entrance into the war, on the side of France, in January, 1762, which actually offered England a golden opportunity to solidify her colonial supremacy, made the incompetent Lord Bute doubly eager to liquidate English responsibilities with regard to the wars on the European continent. His suggestion to Frederick to come to terms with Austria met with the king's stern refusal. A direct British feeler in Vienna as well as the supposed anti-Prussian maneuvers of Bute in St. Petersburg left Frederick little choice but to accept the Russian alliance.

By the end of June, 1762, the imbecile czar had been murdered, and his wife Catherine, a princess of Anhalt-Zerbst, was empress of Russia. She renounced at once the alliance with Prussia and called the Russian troops back from Silesia. But she saw no point in participating in the Austro-Prussian war on either side and admonished both parties to make peace. The presence of a Russian army had given Frederick a chance to recover Schweidnitz and with it most of Silesia. His brother, Prince Henry, who was a master of eighteenth-century warfare of maneuver and had given his unloved brother most valuable services, particularly at the critical moments of the war, fought his first battle on October 29, 1762, at Freiberg in Saxony. It resulted in defeat for an Empire army strengthened by Austrian troops. Prussian light regiments began ranging into Franconia and Thuringia, holding up free cities and prince-bishops for war tributes. Frederick offered them neutrality agreements, and Bavaria, Württemberg, the Palatinate, and Cologne accepted these agreements without paying attention to Austria.

Meanwhile the Spanish war against England had led to nothing but disasters for the Spaniards. But Bute still wanted peace and even was willing to pay a good price for it. The preliminaries of a peace, which were signed between France and England at Fontainebleau on November 3, 1762, gave England tremendous gains, among which the French withdrawal from North America was the most important. The concessions made by Bute to the duke of Choiseul were, however, most astounding, especially the return of the British conquests in the West Indies which was to prove a serious handicap to English warfare in the War of American Independence. But equally amazing was the complete neglect of any consultation with Prussia during the negotiations and the gratuitous gesture of open disregard which the treaty contained. Cleves, Mörs, and Geldern on the lower Rhine were still occupied by French troops. Whereas the treaty carefully enumerated the territories of German allies which France was to restore to their sovereigns, the Rhenish possessions were only to be evacuated. In other words, France could turn them over to Austria and use them as a pawn in her negotiations with Prussia. It was a stupid act, not only because it outraged Frederick and drove him into the arms of Russia, but also because it gave England the reputation of always making peace at the expense of her European allies. At the Peace of Aachen, of 1748, Austria had been the victim; this time Prussia was to be deprived. The total isolation in which England found herself during the American revolutionary war went back to these events.

∽ Treaty of Hubertusburg

MARIA THERESA HAD the good sense to avoid a conflict over Cleves, which was quickly occupied by Prussian troops. While England and France ended their war through the Peace of Paris (January, 1763), and Russia was urging the German contestants to come to terms, direct Austro-Prussian negotiations had already begun. They took place in the dismal setting of a hunting lodge of August the Strong, which had been devastated by a marauding Prussian free battalion in 1761. Kaunitz had not given up hope that Austria might keep Glatz, which was still occupied by Daun, but Frederick was adamant in insisting on the *status quo ante* and in refusing any indemnity to unlucky Saxony, which had paid a major part of the Prussian war cost. At least he gladly promised his vote for the election of Joseph as Roman king. The treaty was signed at Hubertusburg on February 15, 1763. Prussia retained all her gains from the first two Silesian wars after fighting one of the most powerful European coalitions to a standstill. In this respect, she could be called the victor. But on the other hand, it was shown that Prussia could not further expand without the consent of the Continental powers. For Germany as a whole, Hubertusburg introduced a thirty-year period of peace. At last, the dream of enlightened thinkers for the exclusion of war from interstate relations seemed to move closer to fulfillment.

✐ An Uncertain Peace

YET THE INTERNATIONAL situation was not stable. Anglo-French antagonism continued, and Austro-Prussian relations remained full of jealousy and suspicion. The expansionism of Catherine's Russia pressed upon both Prussia and Austria. The alliance of Austria and France, the great work of Prince Kaunitz, which had led to the *renversement des alliances* in 1755–56, proved a solid element in European politics down to the French Revolution. Its advantages for Austria were considerable. Her Italian, German, and Belgian possessions were safe. From the French point of view, as even Kaunitz had to admit occasionally, the usefulness of the alliance was open to some doubt. But France was weakened and she cut her objectives after 1763. The marriage between Maria Theresa's daughter Marie Antoinette and the dauphin (Louis XVI), in 1770, was a symbol of the co-operation between Vienna and Paris. England stood aside from the Continent and soon saw herself embroiled in the American war. England's involvement in colonial struggles was the great opportunity for Russia's rise, and Catherine, the "Semiramis of the North," made the best of her opportunities.

After 1763, Russia became the chief concern of Frederick's diplomacy. He did not forget the grievous blows that Russia had inflicted upon him, and he well knew that he would have been lost without the freak of fortune that brought Peter III to the Russian throne. In his opinion, Russia was unassailable. The only method to hit at Russia would be to march an army along the Baltic shores against St. Petersburg, provisioned and protected by a fleet, which required an alliance with England. But Frederick argued that such an operation would be hazardous because of the many fortresses that had to be conquered on the way, and ultimately unavailing, since the Russians could simply withdraw into the interior. On the other hand, East Prussia could not be defended by Prussia in a single-handed war with Russia. Frederick felt sure that Russia would become the most dangerous power for Europe once it had settled its uncultivated lands, though, as so many statesmen have done in the subsequent two centuries, at times he comforted himself with the thought that Russia might split into two Russias. In 1768, Frederick could cry: "How insane and blind is Europe that she contributes to the rise of a people which some day may become her own doom." However, he failed to do some heart-searching of his own, although he pointed out that Catherine's present power was largely the result of the Austro-Prussian discord, which led to a race between the two German powers for Russia's favors.

∽ *Russo-Prussian Alliance*

THE WISH FOR A RUSSIAN alliance dominated Frederick's policy after 1763. Catherine had every reason not to tie her hands in one direction, because she wanted an understanding with both Prussia and Austria for the support of Russian policy in Poland. The death of August III, in December 1763, afforded the occasion for the creation of closer relations between Russia and Prussia. Since Austria was not prepared to support Catherine's candidate, Stanislaus Poniatowski, unreservedly, and France, Austria's ally, was even less so inclined, the empress accepted the alliance with Frederick. Thereby Russia recognized the Prussian acquisition of Silesia, against which it had fought a war in the past. But Frederick had to commit himself to far-reaching services, which included not only full co-operation in the election but also a guarantee of the unworkable Polish constitution with its *liberum veto* and common intervention in favor of the dissidents in Poland. By opposing a reform of the constitution and using religion as a pretext for intervention, the powers condemned the hapless Polish state to further internal chaos and foreign control. Frederick entertained no doubt that his policy was bound to lead to the ultimate demise of Poland. At this moment, he was not eager to speed up the process, which was to replace a weak neighbor with an immensely powerful one, but he wanted to get the Russian alliance. The two governments pledged themselves to assist each other with 12,000 men in case either was attacked, and under certain conditions with all their might.

The election of Stanislaus Poniatowski was achieved, and Austria and France let it pass. The enforcement of Polish Greek Orthodox rights by Russia led to internal unrest, which, in 1768, induced Catherine to send troops into southern Poland. A violation of Turkish territory gave Turkey a reason for declaring war on Russia. The Russians gained their first military advantages late in 1769, when they broke into Moldavia. In the following year they beat the Tartars and Turks in Bessarabia. A Russian navy sailed from the Baltic to the Aegean Sea, in order to stir up the Greeks against Ottoman rule, and annihilated the Turkish fleet in the bay of Tschesme on July 5, 1770. The Turkish government called for Austrian and Prussian mediation. The Russian demand to retain Moldavia and Wallachia met with the absolute refusal of Austria, which felt threatened with being cut off from her connection with Constantinople. As far as Austria was concerned, the stand she now took for the first time was on the whole to characterize her policy on the Near Eastern question until World War I. England was still favoring Russian progress. Without her benevolence, the Russian naval expedition into the Mediterranean could not have taken place, and the Russian fleet was largely commanded by Englishmen. England saw in Russia's southward expansion a useful counterpoise to French influence in Turkey and the Mediterranean.

✍ First Polish Partition

WAR BETWEEN AUSTRIA AND RUSSIA was imminent. It would have compelled Frederick to march against Austria again, this time for Russian rather than Prussian interests. At this moment, Frederick proposed to settle the conflict between the three eastern powers at the expense of Poland. Even as crown prince, in 1731, he had written that the acquisition of West Prussia, that is, the country on the lower Vistula, known after 1918 as the Polish Corridor, should be an aim of Prussian policy, but for more than thirty years thereafter he had thought of building a bridge between Pomerania and eastern Brandenburg on one side and East Prussia on the other by forcing small concessions on dilapidating Poland. His brother Henry was the man who sensed that the constellation of 1770 allowed a bigger grab. The Austrians unwittingly contributed to the idea of annexation by occupying, in 1769, a few parcels of Polish territory on the Hungarian slope of the Carpathian mountains, which supposedly had belonged to the Hungarian crown. In view of an apparent rapprochement brought about by meetings between Frederick and Joseph of Austria, Catherine deviated from her original political objective, that of ultimate Russian control of all of Poland. In February, 1772, Prussia and Russia reached an agreement on the despoliation of Poland, to which Austria acceded in August, 1772. Maria Theresa resisted the entreaties of her son and Kaunitz with deep moral emotion. It seemed to her unjustifiable that "if two people use their superiority to suppress an innocent, a third should emulate this and commit the same injustice under the mere excuse of expediency for the present and as a precaution for the future." She felt that she had gained Europe's admiration and even her enemies' respect by her strict adherence to law, truth, and moderation. Austrian participation in what became the first Polish partition was to the empress "a blot on her whole reign." A century later, Leopold Ranke found in the controversy between Maria Theresa and Joseph a landmark between two historic periods. What Frederick and Catherine practiced, was soon to be applied on a larger scale by Napoleon and his successors.

The treaty of 1772, which was ratified by the Polish diet under foreign duress, gave Russia the Polish part of Livonia and large areas of Lithuania and White Russia. Austria took Galicia and Lodomiria. Prussia annexed the smallest, if most valuable, lands. She received the bishopric of Ermland, an enclave within East Prussia, the districts along the Vistula, which later on formed West Prussia, and a district of Great Poland along the Netze river. Danzig and Thorn, however, remained excluded from Prussian rule. Prussia did not possess historic titles to these countries, though prior to 1466, West Prussia and Ermland had belonged to the Teutonic Order for more than a century. Under the regime of the Order many Germans had been brought to West Prussia, but in 1772 they were a minority, except in a number of towns. Particularly, so-called Pomerelia, the country west of the Vistula adjacent to Pomerania, was a land of Polish settlement up to the Baltic shore, as were the Netze district and the southernmost area on the eastern bank of the Vistula, the land of Kulm. For the time being, national consciousness was not very widespread in Poland. It was confined very largely to the nobility and clergy. An important Polish middle class did not exist, and the peasants, held in a serfdom that could be called slavery, lived in an abject state of poverty and ignorance. Poverty extended also to the greater part of the nobility, which often enough lived on little more than its social pride. It was said that Polish noblemen, in order not to be mistaken for peasants, would rather go barefoot than wear straw shoes.

Prussia's desire to link up East Prussia with Pomerania and Brandenburg was understandable, and actually she might have succeeded in winning the loyalty of the inhabitants of these new regions. The Prus-

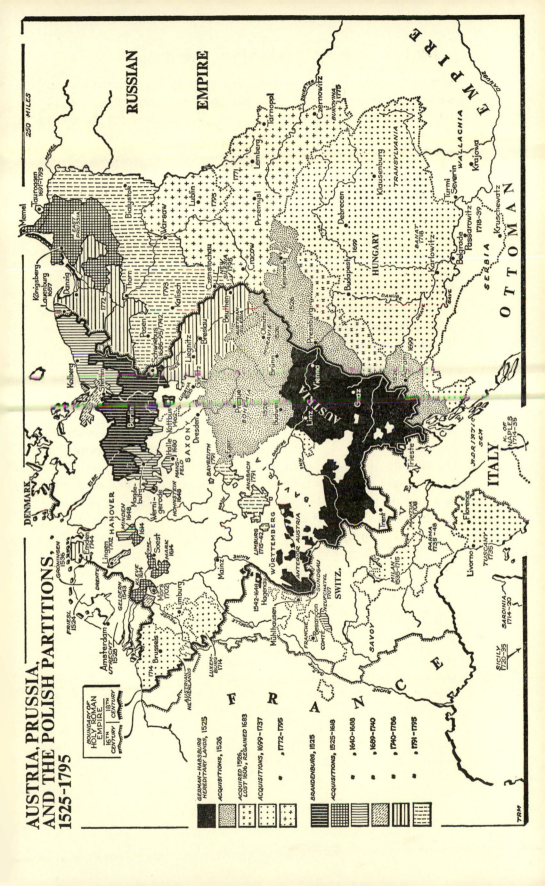

sian government was able at once drastically to improve the peasants' social position, and, a little later, the province's economic state. The large German element could immediately be mobilized for the task of development. But the use of Germans, particularly in areas formerly solidly Polish, had its political drawbacks, because from the outset the Poles played only a secondary role in the region's public life. This fact was further emphasized when many German settlers, artisans, and, most of all, bureaucrats were brought in. There was no intention of de-nationalizing the Poles. Frederick liked to employ administrators who knew Polish, and at times he talked with affection about his "Irokese." But only the Ermland was fully integrated into the Prussian state later on, and it was simply absorbed and Germanized by surrounding East Prussia. West Prussia became a country of mixed allegiances as soon as Polish national feeling became more intense under the influence of the death-struggle of the Polish state and that of the French Revolution. These happenings belonged to a new period, which was only partly foreshadowed by the events of 1772.

It is true that these events were not intended as the first step in a complete partition of Poland. Severe as Poland's losses were in 1772, the country was still a viable state which could have lived on if reformed internally. Actually, forces of regeneration came to the fore in surpris-ing strength during the next two decades. But everything depended on the attitude of the European powers. Austria and Prussia, one should have thought, had every good reason for keeping the Polish state going as a cushion between themselves and Russia. An awareness of this in-terest was not absent, yet a strong temptation to follow the road toward further partition lay especially in the nature of the Prussian acquisition. Danzig and Thorn had remained outside the new Prussian province. The former dominated the whole commerce of the Vistula, particularly the most important corn trade. It was altogether the biggest port on the southern littoral of the Baltic. The gains of 1772 gave Prussia a relent-lessly exploited stranglehold on the traffic and trade of the Vistula. Still, Danzig dangled as a precious fruit before Prussian eyes. Catherine had withheld it from Frederick, because she feared that Danzig would be-come the base for the development of a Prussian navy. It was clear that Russian resistance to Prussian annexation of the old Hanseatic city would subside only to the extent to which Russia would devour addi-tional parts of Poland. Thus the violence of 1772 became the prelude to the ultimate partition of Poland, in 1793 and 1795. Through these events, a dependence of the new Prussian monarchy on the new Russian empire was created, a relationship that went far beyond the normal interdependence of European nations. It has remained a determining factor in modern German history for the next century.

✑ Austrian Designs on Bavaria

THE RUSSIAN ALLIANCE was the mainstay of Frederick's foreign policy during the 1770's. In 1776, it was prolonged until 1788. Russia ended her war with Turkey and did not retain Moldavia and Wallachia in the Treaty of Kuchuk Kainarji of 1774. In 1776, the American Revolution began occupying all of England's energies and also deflected France's eyes to the Atlantic. It was in this situation that Joseph II, who, upon the death of his father in 1765, had become emperor and co-regent of Maria Theresa, and who was left much freedom in the direction of foreign affairs by his mother, launched his attempt to annex the major parts of Bavaria. In the last days of 1777, Elector Maximilian Joseph, son of Emperor Charles VII, died. He was the last of the "Wilhelmian" Wittelsbach princes, that is of the Wittelsbach line which traced its ancestry to Wilhelm of Wittelsbach, who had received Bavaria in the fourteenth century, while his brother Rudolph had been installed in the Palatinate. The Palatinate Wittelsbachs, for their part, had broken up in a number of branches. In 1742, Carl Theodore of Sulzbach (1724–99) had inherited from an older Rudolphian branch the Rhenish Palatinate and in addition Jülich and Berg; now he inherited the Wilhelmian possessions as well. But Carl Theodore liked Mannheim and his Rhenish lands better than chilly and uncouth Bavaria, and having no legitimate offspring, he did not care about the rights of his successor, Duke Palatine Charles of Zweibrücken. He was easily persuaded by Emperor Joseph II to sign a treaty, in which he recognized Austrian hereditary claims to those Bavarian territories which Duke Wilhelm of Wittelsbach had called his own in 1353, and which had been given in fief to Duke Albert of Austria by Emperor Sigismund in 1426. The legal basis for the case was flimsy and could not stand up under examination. In the middle of January, 1778, Austrian troops moved into Bavaria.

In the annexation of Bavaria, Joseph II saw a golden opportunity for strengthening the German center of Austria and also the imperial influence in the Empire. Naturally, the success of the *coup* would have made up for the loss of Silesia. For this very reason, Frederick, who still considered the balance between Prussia and Austria highly precarious, was fiercely opposed to tolerating Joseph's action. With his support,

Duke Charles of Zweibrücken brought his protest to the diet of the Empire, where the prevailing sentiment was unfavorable to the high-handed deeds of the emperor. Saxony, Austria's old ally, was particularly aroused against Joseph, but at the same time was the only German state willing to fight by arms with Prussia against Austria. Nor was foreign assistance forthcoming, as Frederick had expected on account of his Russian alliance. Catherine did not go beyond diplomatic steps in Vienna. On the other hand, the France of Louis XVI and Marie Antoinette, as Frederick II put it, proved less Austrian than that of Louis XV and Madame de Pompadour. In view of the American embroilment, Vergennes declared French neutrality, since the *casus foederis* was not given.

In July, 1778, the Prussian armies broke into Bohemia. But Frederick's military plans were frustrated. The Austrians conducted a clever war of defensive maneuvers and entrenchments. The Prussian troops suffered in the autumn cold, nor were they cheered by the potatoes they picked in the fields, which gave the whole campaign the name "Potato War." By the middle of October, the Prussian armies, under the king and his brother Henry, were back in Silesia and Saxony. But during this "insipid" campaign, as Frederick called it, diplomacy had not stopped working. This was due to Maria Theresa, who had had serious misgivings about her son's foreign policy. After the outbreak of hostilities, she addressed herself directly to Frederick in an appeal to find a settlement. However, these direct negotiations did not lead to any agreement. Austria invoked French mediation, which the French government accepted on condition of Russia's participation. Frederick's willingness to grant Austria a territorial concession made the Peace of Teschen (May, 1779) possible. The Bavarian territories went to Carl Theodore, and the hereditary rights of the Zweibrücken line were made secure. Austria received the *Inn Viertel,* a strip of land on the right bank of the Inn river, between the archbishoprics of Salzburg and Passau. France and Russia became guarantors of the Treaty of Teschen, and since the Treaty of Westphalia was inserted fully into the Teschen Treaty, Russia now became a guarantor of the whole constitutional order of Germany.

Frederick was afraid that after a while Joseph II would repeat his efforts to expand Austrian influence in the Empire, and in this apprehension he was not mistaken. But first Joseph II scored a success that could not be opposed by war. From the late sixteenth century on, the Bavarian Wittelsbach family had placed its younger princes on the thrones of the neighboring as well as Rhenish bishoprics.[1] There was a time when the Wittelsbach family held eight sees. The electorate of Cologne was in the hands of Bavarian princes continuously from 1583 to 1761. Thereafter, no Wittelsbach princes were left. In 1780, the appointment of Archduke Maximilian, the youngest son of the empress, as coadjutor of Cologne and Münster gave Austria a strong position on the Lower Rhine. In subsequent years, Austrian diplomacy endeavored to win for Maximilian the see of Hildesheim in addition.

This extension of Habsburg power to some of the prince-bishoprics was observed with displeasure in Prussia, but it was found disquieting even among Catholic estates of the Empire. For centuries the Habsburg emperors had buttressed their influence in the Empire by close co-operation with the prince-bishops. But the enthronement of Archduke Maximilian, together with the policies which Joseph II conducted with regard to the Church in Austria, raised the suspicion that the emperor's ultimate aim was the secularization of the Church. The southeastern German marches had once been Christianized from Passau and Salzburg, and the Austrian bishops had been suffragans of these two metropolitan sees. Moreover, both archbishops were still holding princely powers in some enclaves in Upper Austria and Carinthia. Joseph II, determined to subordinate the Austrian Church fully to the government, abolished the enclaves and placed the ecclesiastical communications between the metropolitans and the Austrian clergy under the strict control of the government. In 1784, he even came into the open with a project of absorbing the archbishopric of Salzburg and provostship of Berchtesgaden. But before this stage was reached, which coincided with a new attempt of Joseph II to acquire Bavaria, the domineering attitude of Austria in the councils of the Empire had caused unrest among both ecclesiastical and secular princes. Over some ridiculous question of protocol, the imperial minister at the diet in Regensburg brought the work of the "princes' bench" to a complete standstill. Consequently, the princes could not have effective recourse to the diet. To many it seemed a deliberate step toward the establishment of a "despotic" imperial regime. The commotion among the petty princes induced some of them to discuss plans for the formation of an association among themselves, and it was characteristic of the situation that Catholic and Protestant princes mingled in these talks. But even as a group they were powerless so long as none of the "armed estates," especially Prussia, would champion their cause.

[1] See p. 48.

Joseph II would not have risked a resumption of his Bavarian project if he had not trusted that he had blocked Prussian opposition by means of his European policy. In 1780, Joseph II and Catherine met in Mogilev, and the Russian empress found the emperor in sympathy with her anti-Turkish plans. Frederick, on the other hand, had annoyed her with his wishes for drawing Turkey into the Russo-Prussian alliance in order to make it more effective against Austria. In 1781, the two imperial rulers reached an understanding, which bore its first fruit in 1784 with the Russian annexation of the Crimea. Austria brought exceedingly strong pressure on the Sublime Porte to achieve this result, which was accepted by England and France. Prussia remained outside all these negotiations, and actually remained diplomatically isolated so long as Austria's alliances with France and Russia held together. Frederick began looking for allies and found them only among the German princes. The diplomatic offensive that Joseph II opened to win Bavaria finally induced Frederick to take up the idea of an association of German princes.

Joseph II proposed an exchange of Bavaria for the Austrian Netherlands. Elector Carl Theodore had found life in Munich disagreeable. Almost from the first day, he was unpopular with Bavarians, whose pride he had hurt by his willingness to give up the country in 1779. The offer of a Belgian crown and greater revenues than those from debt-ridden Bavaria made the elector amenable to Austrian coaxing. The "pantocratrice," as Frederick mockingly called Catherine, promised to support Joseph's enterprise, while the French government offered its support only on condition that an understanding with Prussia could be reached. France had reason to become worried about her ally. Austria's association with Russia in the destruction of the Turkish empire was not to France's liking. In addition, Joseph II got himself into a conflict with the Dutch Republic when he tried to rid the Austrian Netherlands of the limitations that the Westphalian Treaty had placed on navigation on the Scheldt. France favored the Dutch, who insisted on the preservation of the existing treaty obligations. But the French also remembered that France had no interest in letting Austria move so far west into the Empire and, in general, to strengthen her hold over the German princes. Emperor Joseph II had to drop the whole project.

∽ *The Association of Imperial Princes*

YET FREDERICK, THOUGH momentarily relieved, was still fearful that the plan might be once more revived upon the death of Elector Carl

Theodore. Concern over the course Austria might take led to the formation of a "Constitutional Association of Imperial Princes." On July 23, 1785, representatives of Prussia, Hanover, and Saxony signed the treaty in which the three electors pledged themselves to uphold the constitution and institutions of the Empire. Rights and possessions of all imperial estates, secular and ecclesiastical, were to be maintained. A "most secret" article bound the three electors to oppose the exchange or annexation of territories with arms. The accession of the "archchancellor" of the Empire, the Elector of Mainz, gave the Association half the votes of the electoral college. The assent of the foremost Catholic German prince, though he refused to accept the secret article, gave the league a neutral character in religious questions. Fourteen other princes joined the Association. Among them was Goethe's prince and friend, Duke Carl August of Weimar, who had been a most active promoter of the Association, as well as the princes of Zweibrücken, Baden, Ansbach, Anhalt, Mecklenburg and also the (Lutheran) bishop of Osnabrück, a son of George II of Hanover-England.

Frederick's creation of the Association, as to some extent his policy during the War of the Bavarian Succession before, aroused a great deal of patriotic sentiment in Germany. But the "pride of Empire" that it engendered was entirely dominated by the wish to make history stand still. Insofar as reforms were considered, one thought at best of an activation of the diet, but merely in the way the diet had functioned in the sixteenth century. It must be added at once that nothing whatsoever came of these reform ideas. The main wish was the old hankering for *Libertät* rather than for closer cohesion of the Empire as a whole. Least of all was Frederick motivated by national feeling, and not for a moment did he intend to use Prussian strength for a regeneration of the Holy Roman Empire. He never had the slightest attachment to that "antiquated and odd" formation, which was neither holy nor Roman. In 1750, he abolished the prayer for the emperor in the churches under his monarchy as an "ancient and ill-contrived custom." To him the Empire was a republic of princes whose existence and rights were maintained by the balance of power between Prussia and Austria. He believed that the number of imperial estates would decrease, because of the expiration of individual dynasties, and that in a more distant future the republic would finally dissolve and be superseded by new political groupings. In his *Political Testament* of 1768, he confessed that he could not foresee in what forms this might happen, but it is evident that the possibility of a reformed German national state was completely absent from his mind. The Association of German Imperial Princes of 1785 was used by Frederick merely as a means of restoring the balance of power. The involvement in the Russian war against Turkey and his internal difficulties kept Joseph II from continuing an active policy with regard to the Empire.

The founding of the Association was the last major action of Frederick in the foreign field. As a result of the king's warfare and diplomacy, Prussia had grown almost twice as large in the forty-six years of his reign. Nobody knew better than Frederick in his old age that Prussia still was not a great power. Except for the Rhenish-Westphalian possessions and East Friesland, the state had gained a better defensive stature than in 1740, but its boundaries were still overextended and highly vulnerable. An even clearer test of Prussia's weakness was the obvious fact that a full defeat in a major war would have wiped out its existence as an independent state, whereas England, France, Austria, and Russia would have remained considerable powers even though they had suffered grave losses. Frederick himself counted only these four as great powers, among which Prussia could maintain herself only by quite extraordinary efforts. Prussia's power rested on her army to a greater extent than that of any other nation. In a relatively small state with modest resources, the maintenance of the army dominated the whole life of the state.

Frederick went into the first Silesian War with 100,000 men, into the second with 140,000. He opened the Seven Years' War with an army of 154,000 and between 1763 and 1786 raised the army to close to 200,000. At the time of his death it was the strongest army in Europe. A comparison with the growth of population shows that on the average the army comprised 4 per cent of the population. In 1740, Prussia had a population of 2.5 million, the population of Silesia was estimated at 1.2 million and that of West Prussia at 0.5–0.6 million. Altogether, the population of the Prussian state, taking into account the natural increase in births and the settlement of 300,000 colonists, grew to 5.4 million by 1786.

✍ Frederick's Domestic Policies

FREDERICK WAS MORE a man of action than of organization. On the whole, he kept the government structure as his father had left it. The additions and changes he made were not altogether improvements. The creation of functional departments besides the old regional ones in the General Directory, which began in 1740 with the department of commerce,[2] produced some friction in the central administration. But the overlapping organization could hardly be avoided at a time not yet ripe for a fully centralized administration. Most dubious, however, was the establishment of separate treasuries, especially the chest at the exclusive disposal of the king (*Dispositionskasse*), into which the great expansion of revenue was flowing. Frederick instituted the system after the Seven Years' War, when he wished to have greater flexibility in employing funds than a rigid budget would have allowed him. The multiplicity of state chests made it finally impossible for anyone except the king to know the general state of public finance. Had Frederick not been an unusually shrewd and conscientious financial administrator, this would have created the most serious dangers.

Great complications of the existing administrative organization developed as a consequence of the introduction of the so-called *Regie* in 1766. Frederick believed that the yield of the excise tax could be raised considerably by using the refined methods the French had perfected. The excise and customs administration was set up as a separate administration on the local, provincial, and central levels, and about two hundred French professionals were appointed for its direction. The French techniques brought good financial results, but it may be questionable whether they were worth the resentment that the *Regie* and the subsequently instituted tobacco and coffee monopolies caused. The establishment of the French *Regie* was a clear declaration of lack of confidence in the ability of the Prussian bureaucracy, and the public tended to ascribe the guilt for the heavy and exacting taxation to the foreigners whom the king had imported.

The institutional changes that Frederick made in the Prussian administrative system necessitated an even greater centralization of all supervision and decision in the hands of the autocratic monarch. Frederick's regime was the utmost realization of the *Kabinettsregierung*, that is, government from the king's study, on the basis of reports, usually in writing, of government agencies and ministers. But the king's decisions were based also on opinions which he formed by regular inspections on the spot and through conversations with local people of various classes. Regular travels brought him to all of the provinces, where he inspected both his troops and civil administration. He also encouraged the presentation of complaints, which gave the lower classes the impression that the king was on their side against the bureaucracy.

[2] See p. 195.

On the other hand, the relative omniscience and omnipresence of the king drew him into the settlement of details which might more usefully have been left to the local official. His autocratic manner did not encourage initiative among his subordinates.

The Great Elector and Frederick William had built the structure of the new despotic state over and above the old dualistic state. Though they tore down many of the old institutions, they bent some of them as well as they could to their own purposes, while leaving others intact. Among the latter was not only the old class division as such but also the very special social privileges of the nobility. Frederick William might have gone still further in demolishing the exemptions of the *Junkers* if he had lived longer. He felt the tension between the new royal power and the old feudal traditions acutely. For Frederick this was a thing of the past, especially since, much more distinctly than his father, he felt himself an aristocrat, and his modern education rather confirmed this attitude. In Frederick's opinion, the interest of the state justified the privileged caste character of the Prussian nobility. It provided the state with its military officers and high civilian officials, and for this reason it deserved to be protected in its social and political rights. Frederick was most careful to preserve and even fortify the *Junkers*' existing position. He never contemplated extending taxation of the nobility to all Prussian provinces, a practice which had been customary in East Prussia and Silesia. He was most anxious to keep the *Junkers* owners of their landed estates. The best way seemed to him the creation of entailed estates, but meanwhile he disapproved the purchase of land by burghers and took steps to enhance the credit of the landowning nobility.

What endeared the *Junkers* to him, though he was not blind to some of their foibles, was their sense of honor, which he could not discover in most burghers, who had "low minds" and made for poor and useless officers. The fairly large numbers of nonnoble officers whom the king used in the last years of the Seven Years' War were dismissed after the war or transferred to the second-rate fortress troops. On the other hand, he realized that there were not enough Prussian *Junkers* for a greatly enlarged army and advised his successor to draw foreign noblemen into the Prussian army. Among the burghers, he found it worthwhile to give the sons of managers of royal domains commissions in fortress battalions, to knight them after ten years of satisfactory performance, and to allow them to serve with regular regiments thereafter. No doubt, Frederick's pragmatic justification of noble privileges was greatly tempered by his personal social prejudices.

In Frederick's view the burghers had the duty of producing the wherewithal for the army. Although there were among them some people of extraordinary intellectual gifts and even some people of noble honor and virtue, whom Frederick proposed to treat with special recognition, the burghers formed the class that by its industry contributed most to the maintenance of the government. For this reason they received their special privileges, which consisted chiefly in the exemption from military service and special assistance to new economic enterprises. Below the class of noblemen and burghers, lived the vast majority of the population, the peasants. To maintain and increase this class was of vital interest to the state. The livelihood and a substantial part of the income of the state depended on them, but even more important were their military services. In order to preserve the peasant population, at least one limitation had to be imposed on the *Junkers'* freedom. They were not allowed to add the acreage of peasants to their land, and the government saw to it that every peasant's place that fell vacant was filled again. Otherwise the state did very little for the peasants on the estates of the noblemen. Frederick wanted to limit the forced labor services of peasants to three to four days, but did not dare impose such a rule on the *Junkers*. Not even with regard to the peasants on the royal domains was he fully successful in this respect. The domain peasants at least received their land as hereditary holdings.

While these policies were entirely conservative, one could find a slightly different tone in Frederick's colonization of the state. This is one of the finest pages of his government's record. Over 57,000 families were settled during his reign. It is assumed that at the time of his death every fifth Prussian belonged to a family of colonists. One of the greatest achievements was the drainage and amelioration of the large marshes of the Oder valley in the years 1747–53, a work that was repeated in the Netze district after 1772. In these new lands, his peaceful conquests, Frederick settled free peasants, and the feudal structure of eastern Germany was avoided.

Frederick's economic policy remained mercantilistic throughout. What distinguished his policy from his father's was the greater emphasis on the development of manufacturing and commerce, although agriculture, still by far the most important part of the economy, was not neglected. Every effort was made to attract foreign capitalists, manufacturers, and skilled workers to Prussia. Berlin, Potsdam, and Brandenburg, which were singled out by the king as centers of manufacturing, were for this reason entirely exempted from the canton system. Special attention was given to transportation. The Oder river in its entirety was in Prussian hands after the acquisition of Silesia, and it was made safe for navigation by the building of dikes and the dredging of the estuary, at the entrance of which the port of Swinemünde was founded. Whereas the Great Elector was satisfied with linking up the central Oder with the Elbe and Hamburg through an Oder-Spree canal, Frederick wished to deflect some of the Elbe traffic to the Oder and Stettin. The Finow canal between the Havel and the Oder north of Berlin, built after 1746, served at the same time as a convenient connection between the Prussian capital and the Baltic.

Among the manufactures, the textile industries were the most important. The woolen cloth manufacture, relying on domestic wool production, was economically the most profitable industry, but the linen industries of Silesia and Westphalia were also of great significance. Frederick endeavored to develop the Prussian silk industry. But the stimulation of manufacturing was extended to practically every field that promised profit or at least the exclusion of the need for imports. In the years after the Seven Years' War, Frederick played temporarily with the idea of a completely centralized economy, steered and planned by the government, in whose hands capital and credit was to be fully concentrated. Little remained of this project for a complete state socialism or state capitalism. A royal bank was founded, as were a number of foreign trade companies and certain state factories. Besides some arsenals, the best-known of these factories was the Berlin royal porcelain factory. But the activities of the state as a rule did not take the form of ownership. In addition to exercising the close supervision over productive labor, the government promoted industries by grants of initial capital and credit, very often as a free gift. A frequently used method was the gift of buildings. Through the exclusion of competitive production, either by limiting the numbers of producers or the grant of exclusive market rights, governmental protection was quite common.

In these conditions, the growth of an entrepreneurial group was slow and devious. Frederick complained about the lack of enterprising spirit among the Prussian merchants. Most of them were satisfied to act as traders on a commission basis. The dependence on state capital and credit, as well as on state protection and guidance, did not permit the development of independent entrepreneurs either in the commercial or industrial field. A great number of eighteenth-century industries in Prussia were closely connected with agriculture. The *Junker* estates produced grain, wool, and flax for the market. At least in Silesia, linen manufacture was closely connected with the landed estates. Other industries, such as mills, sawmills, distilleries, and brick factories, were found on many estates. In the last years of Frederick's reign, the development of mining was given particular care. It was the work of Baron von Heinitz, a native of Saxony, whom Frederick brought to Prussia in 1777, and to whom he left more freedom than to any of his ministers. Under him, Count Reden devoted himself with great success to the opening of the large mineral resources of Upper Silesia, while the young Baron Stein was active in Westphalia. But here again the part played by the nobility was remarkable. In 1785, one year before the first coke-heated steel furnace was started in Germany, only 2 out of 243 mining enterprises in Upper Silesia were owned by merchants, while 20 were owned by the king, and the rest by the nobility.

At the end of Frederick's reign, Prussia had become the fourth largest industrial state, after England, France, and Holland, but actually she was so far behind the three others that the statement is not very meaningful. Foreign trade was small, too, though no longer insignificant. In 1781–82, imports and exports amounted to 26 to 27 million thaler, with a favorable balance of about 3 million. As industrial production was steadily rising, so was foreign trade. Yet the full benefit of Frederick's economic policies was reaped by the country only after his death. Some extraordinary circumstances contributed to this, for example, the lesser production of France during the years of the French Revolution and new opportunities for grain export. But by then Prussia had become capable of taking advantage of such conditions. In the five years after 1769, 200 to 300 Prussian ships annually passed through the Danish Sound; in 1798: 1,621; in 1804: 2,012. All this proved that Frederick's mercantilistic policies had laid foundations for a growing economic life, though a good many of their special measures and individual creations had to be discarded.

The whole system was violently criticized in Prussia and abroad as early as the 1780's. Excluding the criticism that stemmed from an absolute hostility to mercantilism—for how could small Prussia have turned liberal in a mercantilistic world?—it was obvious that internal trade barriers and customs, as well as the excessive concern with immediate tax revenue, albeit less pronounced than under Frederick William I, acted as brakes on the economic development. Frederick took deep satisfaction when he looked at the results of the *rétablissement* of his devastated provinces after 1763 and noticed the progress in the Prussian peoples' well-being. Nevertheless, his chief goal was the

power of the state. The growth of the population and economy was to
feed the expanding army and war treasury. Frederick had managed
to conduct twelve years of war without running up more than a negligible public debt. In 1740, the state revenues had been 7 million
thaler, and 10 million had been in the war chest left by Frederick's
father. In 1786, Prussia collected 23 million in revenues and maintained
a war chest of 54 million. It was as amazing as some of his most brilliant
military victories that Frederick proved able to finance the Seven
Years' War, although at times income from taxes dwindled to almost
nothing owing to the occupation of most provinces by the enemy. To
the actual war cost of around 100 million thaler English subsidies contributed 16 million. The major part of the funds was extracted from
occupied Saxony and Mecklenburg. Out of these unhappy states, 50
million and 8 million were exacted, respectively. Meanwhile, internal
payments were cut to a minimum. The Prussian state officials were paid
in promissory notes to be cashed after the war. Internal loans could not
produce much, and Frederick was finally driven to coin bad money and
pass it off not only on his own subjects but also on Poland and on
neighboring German states. It was a rather desperate means of war
financing, but it gave Frederick sufficient cash just at a time when he
resisted the importunities of Lord Bute for political concessions to
Austria. Although the consequences of these malpractices in coinage
were not easily overcome after peace had been made, Frederick had
money left in 1763 to begin at once the restoration of Prussia. It was
understandable that on the basis of his experiences Frederick considered
the accumulation of a war chest imperative, although he was not unaware of the deflationary impact that the hoarding and sterilization of
money was bound to have on the economy. However, it is true that
the chances for capital investment were limited so long as rigid mercantilistic laws prevailed.

✍ *"Old Fritz"*

THE POWER OF THE STATE was the lodestar of all of Frederick's policies
and autocratic management the method for the realization of his aims.
This autocracy extended to every corner of the government and was
exercised in a most personal manner. The king, who seemingly moved
simply and easily among all classes of the people, actually was a world
apart from them. The sensitive man had maintained his own courage
and determination under the enormous strain of the Seven Years' War,

which also demanded great physical endurance. The tragic emotions of his beloved Racine, the Stoic philosophers, and Lucretius comforted him in hours of defeat as well as victory. But he grew more skeptical and contemptuous with regard to man. In his testament, he expressed the wish to be buried on the garden terrace of Sans Souci close to the graves of his little French greyhounds, which he liked to spoil. His relationship with the French Enlightenment became more distant in his later years. The materialism of a Helvétius or a Holbach was to him the recrudescence of a particularly ugly metaphysics, and the signs of democratic thought that appeared among the young French writers annoyed him.

"Old Fritz," as the Prussians named him, was a lonely person among his people. He did not wish to make personal friends among his officers and officials. Rather, he wanted them to obey and do their assigned duty meticulously and with dispatch. Frederick was distrustful not only of their intelligence and industry but also of their integrity. In general, he believed that the members of this *maudite race* were moved chiefly by their desire for personal advantage and that a system of penalties interspersed with occasional premiums was the best way of keeping them on their toes. Frederick no longer knocked out the teeth of his officials nor beat them up, as his father had done. But his acid vituperations were equally wounding, and he was as quick as his father in sending officials to the Spandau prison. No doubt, there were cases of corruption. The days of feudal spoils were still in living memory, and officials served for starvation wages. But it is questionable whether abuses were really widespread. There is plenty of evidence that the number of officials and officers who took their duties with a deep sense of moral responsibility was great, and this sense of responsibility was much more than outward conformity with higher orders. Religion, whether of the orthodox-pietistic or enlightened variety, was a potent force in Germany, and Frederick knew little about such sources of loyalty.

Planting fear and trembling into the hearts of all subordinates produced automatons galore but not men of strong character and self-reliance. This was true even with the king's officer corps, which enjoyed more royal respect and attention than any other group in the state. But Frederick failed to replace Field Marshals Schwerin, Winterfeldt, and Keith, who met death in battle in the early years of the Seven Years' War, by officers of his own training. In Seydlitz and Ziethen, the Prussian army possessed cavalry generals of the highest talent and bravura. What was missing, however, was a group of generals fit for high command. There was nothing Frederick's generals feared more than being selected as leaders of detached armies. As a matter of fact, none of them ever did well in such a position, and, at least in some cases, this was due to Frederick's interference. Only one general was a born captain of war like Frederick; that was his younger brother Prince Henry (1726–1802), who resembled the king in education and thought as well as in the desire for recognition. This highly gifted, unhappy prince, who was obsessed by a consuming jealousy of his elder brother, was in a position to gain more independence, or at least distance, from Frederick than men of lesser birth.

Frederick was not unmindful of the necessity for training officers who were experienced in higher tactics. In the years after 1763, he attached a group of young staff officers to the quartermaster-general's staff and he himself taught them tactics. One of these officers, Baron von Steuben, was to become one of the chief organizers of the American army. But this training was discontinued after a few years. The king also attempted to raise the very low general educational level of the officer corps. Courses were introduced for junior officers. A small number of gifted cadets were brought together in an elite school, the "academy of nobles," in Berlin. But at best these efforts could have borne fruit only after a long period of time. Moreover, technical education was not the real answer to the weaknesses of the Prussian army, which were caused by the mechanical enforcement of rules and the suppression of the initiative of the individual. Frederick was greatly dissatisfied with the showing of the Prussian army during the war of 1778–79, but his dissatisfaction only served to make him an even tougher taskmaster in the subsequent years.

✑ *Frederick's Social Conservatism*

FREDERICK DID NOT CONSIDER it a structural infirmity of the monarchy that it demanded a king able to rule by himself as he had done. In view of Frederick's judgment of his prospective successor's character it is perhaps hard to understand why he tried to impress upon him the imperative need for royal autocracy and to warn him even against a chief minister or council of ministers. There was no intimation that the shortcomings of the heir to the throne might call for adjustments in government. He also was fully unaware of the changeability of social forces. They were to him timeless, and although he did not deny that they could get out of hand, he felt certain that a good government could hold them in their natural place. It was surprising that he did not see the conflict between the old feudal order and the new conception of equal service to the state, while as an enlightened *philosophe* he believed in the possibility of doing away with old prejudices and institutions. But a more conscious attack on the social order would have jeopardized the immediate use of the state's ready resources in the foreign field. Frederick's preoccupation with power politics dictated his social conservatism, which stands in contrast to his intellectual and religious radicalism.

Much of the steel frame which Frederick constructed for the Prussian state remained standing in the nineteenth and even twentieth centuries. This was partly the result of the incomplete character of all subsequent social reforms. But it was also due to the fact that Frederick's regime created certain institutions that were only loosely connected with the military objectives of the Prussian state and acted as channels through which the warmer air of humane ideals could eventually flow into the cold atmosphere of the northern Sparta.

In the administration of justice and education, Frederick reached most clearly beyond power politics. In describing the *ancien régime* in Prussia, Friedrich Meinecke has referred to the saying of an ancient Sassanide king: "There is no kingdom without soldiers, no soldier without money, no money without population, no population without justice." This is an apt description, and it is true that Frederick's reforms of justice and education intended to improve the economy on which the military state was built. But the scope of his reforms was broad enough to carry them beyond their original objectives. Frederick devoted himself to an improvement of the administration of justice in the years between 1746 and 1756. In Samuel von Cocceji (1679–1755), whom Frederick William I had appointed Minister of Justice in his last years, Frederick found the man who combined a belief in natural law with practical knowledge of state administration. Cocceji made short shrift of thousands of law cases, which had been piling up in all the provinces, and created a unified and centralized state court system on the local, provincial, and central levels. The judges became salaried state officials, and judges' personal fees were abolished. The procedure, for which the rules were laid down in the *Codex Fredericianus Marchicus* of 1748, was greatly simplified and expedited. The whole judiciary, which so far had retained much of the guild character, was made a branch of state government by Cocceji. At the same time, he gave it greater dignity by providing personal security and solid legal training. In the course of the reorganization of the courts, many incompetent judges were removed. Judgeships no longer could be purchased but required the passing of an examination and years of preparatory service with the courts.

Cocceji argued that the king, though supreme judge, should not interfere with the course of justice by personal rulings or decisions. Frederick agreed to this principle, for "in the courts the laws must speak and the sovereign must remain silent." But the king remained supervisor of the judges, whom he reprimanded or dismissed at his discretion. The independence of judges was by no means guaranteed. Another limitation of the courts' power resulted from the continuation of broad judicial authority in the war and domain chambers. They retained jurisdiction in all matters concerning the state's police, domain, and tax administration. On the other hand, the ecclesiastical consistories ceased to have judiciary functions, which formerly had been rather extensive in family law.

◡ *The Prussian* Code

COCCEJI DID NOT ACCOMPLISH the unification and modernization of the laws themselves. A new generation of jurists grew up, trained in the school of Thomasius and Wolff. From the Roman and German legal tradition, alive in the greatly diversified laws of the various provinces, these jurists tried to single out the norms which could express the practice of both an enlightened state and of natural law. After 1779, the work was taken up under Minister J. H. von Carmer (1721–1801). His closest associate Karl Gottlieb Suarez (1746–98) was the chief author of the Prussian Law Code (*Preussisches Landrecht*). Suarez, a student of Christian Wolff, attempted in this book of statutes to define and carry forward the moral principles that the monarchy of Frederick had developed. The *Code* was intended to give every citizen a clear conception of the state's purpose, and for that reason was not confined to private civil and criminal law but treated constitutional questions as well. The authors of the *Code* hoped to implant a public spirit that would make the enforcement of laws by the government an easy task. The sovereignty of the monarch was formulated in all its absolutist consequences. For the first time, the *Code* clearly defined as a right what so far had been only the practice of the Prussian rulers, namely to levy taxes without popular consent. But on the other hand, even the rights of the king were defined as duties as well. It was the king's obligation to act for the welfare of the people and respect those moral purposes that the human individual had a duty to realize in his life. "The general rights of man are founded on the natural freedom to seek and advance his own welfare without interfering with the rights of others." These rights were to be protected by reasonable laws administered by judges who were secure against the disturbing intervention of arbitrary government.

Carmer and his collaborators were believers in Montesquieu's division of powers and wanted to establish the judiciary as an intermediary power between the executive and the people. But they were not allowed to write this theory into the *Code*, which was not promulgated under Frederick but only under his successor. In vain did Suarez argue that a paragraph protecting the citizen against the arbitrary decisions of the crown merely meant the spelling out of the existing difference between the Prussian monarchy and oriental despotism. Frederick William II did not wish to see his absolute royal sovereignty committed in this manner, and the paragraph was dropped before the *Code* became law in 1794. Even the statement "mutual promises and contracts must be holy to the state and its citizens alike" had to go. Still the general tenor of the *Code* pointed in the direction of contractual rights. Alexis de Tocqueville later on described the *Prussian Code* as a constitution as well as a code of civil and criminal law. This is going too far. But it is true that the *Code* marked the beginning of a tendency for authoritarian government to limit its absolute powers by the rule of law or, in German terminology, that the *Obrigkeitsstaat* was supplemented by the *Rechtsstaat*. Then and later, it was easily forgotten in Germany that this rule of law depended on the absolute will of the sovereign and had no guarantee of stability without representative institutions or, in other words, without a popular constitution.

But neither was absolutism ready to abdicate, and the distinctions between classes were not abandoned. The *Code* defined the rights of the citizens according to the three social "estates"—peasants, burghers, and noblemen. It is characteristic that the peasants were now called an estate, and that in the opinion of the lawgivers an estate was constituted not only by "birth" but also by "main occupation."

The peasants had the right to remain on their land, while the nobility, still called the "first estate," enjoyed protection of its landholdings and had the first right to state positions. The latter, however, presupposed that the *Junker* had acquired the necessary skills for the job and was selected by the king from among a group of candidates. Thus the social distinctions were preserved in a scale of political and social rights that corresponded to the functions that the individual class performed for the community. General rights were recognized only in religion and, to a lesser extent, education. "Every inhabitant of the state must be granted complete freedom of religion and conscience," was the conclusion the *Code* drew from almost two centuries of denominational conflict.

The state did not relinquish its authority to decide what religions should be admitted, but the criteria applied were no longer theological but entirely practical ones. Obedience to the laws, loyalty to the state, and the inculcation of morally good attitudes toward fellow-citizens were expected from all religious groups. But Frederick followed a liberal practice even here. The Moravian Brethren gained exemption from military service in exchange for the payment of a tax. Antitrinitarians were allowed to have church buildings, and Hussites were admitted into Prussia. Frederick even invited Tartars to settle in West Prussia and promised to build mosques for them if they came. Still, the supervision of the churches remained strict. In particular, the churches were prevented from engaging in controversies with each other. The assertion of exclusive sovereignty, which tolerated no independent church government at its side, was naturally simple in the case of the Protestant churches, since the king retained the episcopal authority. This authority was exercised, through the control of church appointments, in molding the teachings of the Protestant churches. Differences between Reformed and Lutheran doctrine were played down, and the representatives of the Enlightenment given preference.

Protestantism continued to be the favored religion. Catholics were not chosen for higher state positions. Frederick showed great fairness in his dealings with the Prussian Catholics, most of whom were in Silesia. But he did not tolerate papal interference with the exercise of his royal control over the Catholic church in Prussia. This exclusion of papal authority might have led to conflicts between Prussia and the papal see had the Vatican not been pressed even harder by Spain, France, and Austria.

Closely connected with the policy toward religion were censorship questions. The state manifested its interest in the spread and expansion of knowledge by the maintenance of the academy and universities. With the division of labor prevailing in Frederick's state, however, the members of academy and universities were the only people who were free from censorship. Private persons had only limited rights of public communication. The *Code* contained severe penalties against the critical discussion of many subjects, particularly criticism of political conditions, derogatory statements about the laws, and the diffusion of ideas likely to endanger order. Beyond such penalties, censorship did its work. It could be fairly liberal, because the state authority was safely anchored and because German writers showed no revolutionary spirit.

In these circumstances of the age, the criminal law was also relatively liberal. Through the abolition of torture and many of the ugly penalties of life and limb, a great step was taken beyond the *Carolina* of the sixteenth century,[3] which was still the predominant code of criminal penalties. The protection of the community's security, peace, and welfare was the supreme principle that defined crimes. Not so much vengeance for committed crimes as deterrence from future crimes was sought. The absolute state could be lenient compared to practices of the past, since it could hope to be more effective in the prevention of crime. Through its officialdom, it felt itself to have the capacity to control the everyday life of the people and thus keep them on the right path. The bureaucracy had its eyes not only on all aspects of economic life but also on all private movements. They believed themselves able to direct everything through reputedly wise ordinances for the welfare of both the state and individual. But while the omnipresence and omniscience of the government was stifling, government was no longer justified in theological terms as punishment for human sin, but rather as an institution for the realization of the moral qualities of man. Government claimed to be the leader in the moral progress possible in this world and asserted an identity of objectives, if not of functions, between itself and its subjects. All this was still conceived in a crudely mechanistic spirit and largely concealed by practices which did not jibe with lofty ideal aims. But these ideas formed powerful incentives for the future reform of governmental practices and, more than this, for an attempt at finding true unity between people and government.

✑ Education

THE DEVELOPMENT OF EDUCATION added another element to this process. Frederick did not consider education an integral part of state policy, but his personal interest in it was lively, especially after 1763. The

[3] Cf. the author's *A History of Modern Germany: The Reformation*, p. 159.

notion that education would make absolute government more difficult seemed to him ridiculous. Education for him had a largely practical aim. It was to make people better fit for the performance of their work and was not designed to carry them beyond their station in life. To Frederick it was undesirable to give a peasant a schooling that might make him wish to become a secretary in a town. It was enough to teach him "a little reading and writing" and the moral commandments of Christian religion, which Frederick thought could be summed up in the single sentence: "Do not anything to others that you do not want to have done to yourself."

Not too much was accomplished in elementary education during Frederick's lifetime. A good many schools were established in villages and towns, but adequate teachers were lacking. Tailors and other artisans, finally even disabled sergeants, were widely used. Conditions were better in Catholic districts because of the Catholic orders. But at least the schools were drawn into the scope of state activities. Methods of inspection were devised, and schools for the training of teachers supported. In Karl Abraham von Zedlitz (1731–93), who was responsible for all cultural affairs in Prussia after 1770, education received a director of high talent and enlightened convictions. But utilitarian motives and a strong emphasis on socially divided education characterized Zedlitz's administration, and full contact with the new German literature was not established.

Frederick saw no need for rooting the life of the state deeply in a common civilization. Education was to provide the individual with a set of moral rules and equip him with the practical knowledge necessary in his occupation. Only a small group of the most eminent men was to be free to devote itself to the critical enjoyment of philosophy, literature, and art. A real understanding that civilization is largely a search for new ideals was alien to him. Without denying the expansion of knowledge over the ages, he conceived of truth and the ideals of beauty as essentially identical throughout the ages. The culture of the Augustan age was submerged by medieval superstition and stupidity, but had revived with the able men who lived under Louis XIV. French civilization was for Frederick the resurrection of the eternal beauty and truth of the ancients. He was greatly displeased to see new ideas presented by the post-Voltairean writers of France. He most emphatically rejected that "obsessed cynic" Rousseau, although he did not deny him a refuge in the Prussian Neufchâtel in 1762. But his rigid cultural concepts deprived him of any access to the ideas of the French thinker who had an infinitely greater influence on the thought and art of Germany than Voltaire. Even if Frederick had followed the growth of German literature in his later life, he would have pronounced the same negative judgment as the one expressed in his article *On German Literature*, of 1780. Klopstock, Lessing, or Wieland were not mentioned by the king. Goethe's *Goetz* he called an "abominable imitation" of Shakespeare's "bizarre aberrations." Although he held out some hope for the future, he found German literature without an educated language and sense of taste.

Frederick clung to the type of French thought that corresponded to his own aristocratic style. For his state, a utilitarian moral culture appeared to be the healthiest form of education. As a cement for the cohesion of the political community, cultural ideals were not considered of great importance. The authority of the government was firmly anchored. As Kant put it, a monarch "who enlightened himself has no fear of shadows and, in addition, has a well-disciplined and numerous army as guarantor of public peace, can say what a republic could not dare: 'Argue as much as you please and about anything you please, but obey.'" With the significant exception of politics itself, this definition was correct. The existing freedom at least stimulated intellectual growth, which, as Kant also predicted, was bound eventually to build a public spirit.

When Frederick died, on August 17, 1786, he left a state that he had raised to European stature by his military genius and by a government that mobilized every ounce of strength for the increase of Prussia's armed might. Frederick was fully aware of Prussia's precarious position among the European powers owing to her weak physical and material resources, but he had no idea of the tremendous forces which were hidden in the unawakened political energies of the peoples themselves. Frederick warned that an indolent ruler on the Prussian throne could ruin the state within thirty years. Actually it took only twenty years until Frederick the Great's monarchy crashed to the ground for reasons much more complex than he had foreseen. It is not surprising that Frederick's successors never mastered his method of government. They must be called his inferiors chiefly because they failed to remodel the state in accordance with the needs of a new historic age. Only after the disaster of Jena did a new generation of statesmen breathe a new spirit into the Prussian monarchy, though even nineteenth-century Prussia was built on the foundations which Frederick had laid.

CHAPTER 10

Germany on the Eve of the French Revolution

OVERSHADOWED BY AUSTRIA AND PRUSSIA, the rest of Germany played a minor political role in the second half of the eighteenth century. The troops of Hanover, Brunswick, and Hesse under Prince Ferdinand of Brunswick contributed greatly to the defeat of the Franco-Austrian alliance during the Seven Years' War. But the defeat of the Empire's army at Rossbach, in 1757, had made the southern German estates the laughing stock of Germany. However, in the small states of Germany great intellectual changes were going on and new political developments were beginning.

✑ The Impact of Prussia on Germany

THE RISE OF FREDERICK'S PRUSSIA could not fail to make an impression on Germany at large. Actually, few people thought very much of the peripheral northeastern state of Germany, which took its name from a territory outside the Empire. Prussians were not well liked either. They were noted for their self-consciousness, rather than nobility, elegance, or fine education. Yet Frederick's personality attracted all eyes as no German ruler had done in modern days. His heroic courage, military feats, devotion to the government of his people, philosophical mind, and wit furnished the material with which he could be transformed into a legendary figure at an early moment. To many a German nobleman and burgher he gave assurance that historic greatness had not passed with ancient Rome and might even flower in the small world of Germany. People were far from turning their sympathies to Prussia, but Frederick captivated their imagination. Thus Goethe wrote in his autobiography with reference to the sentiment in Frankfurt during the Seven Years' War: "We were no partisans of Prussia, but partisans of Fritz." Wieland expressed what probably was the feeling of the average burgher "King Frederick is a great man, but may a gracious God protect us from the good fortune to live under his cane or scepter."

The impact of Frederick's personality and deeds was most immediately felt among the German princes. His influence might be confined to the acceptance of certain administrative and military institutions, as in the Austria of Maria Theresa, or, as with Joseph II, might take the form of personal emulation of the style of kingship that Frederick had set. The emperor led enlightened despotism to its last consequences.

Alexis de Tocqueville has shown that the *ancien régime* prepared the ground for the French Revolution and in most every respect initiated the policies characteristic of the modern state. The creation of a centralized state, in which local and social privileges were uprooted in favor of an all-embracing secular government, had gone very far in France. Local and regional peculiarities were not fully abolished, nor were social inequalities. The French monarchy subordinated the nobility and clergy, but chose to identify itself socially with the old upper estates. It was the undoing of Louis XVI that he did not support the attempts of Turgot or Necker to shift the social and political basis of royal government. The absolute governments of Maria Theresa and Frederick represented, historically, the same stage of development as the France of Louis XV. It was Joseph II who tried to carry absolutism one stage further in centralization, in the leveling of class differences, and in the secularization of government. He was the most revolutionary reformer of all the eighteenth-century kings.

∽ *Joseph II*

Joseph, Maria Theresa's beloved "Phoenix," became German Emperor in 1765. His mother kept the reins of government, though Joseph's influence as co-regent was much greater than that of his father. The struggle between mother and son over principles of government and religion was pathetic, the more so since both were persons of deep and genuine convictions. But Maria Theresa failed to instill something of her own warm humaneness into her son's heart, which burnt to serve mankind but was so sure of its righteousness. Joseph did not know any personal pleasure except bureaucratic work and the display of superior wisdom. The comfortable elegance of Maria Theresa's court vanished when the puritanical Joseph II took over the government in 1780. His brothers and sisters moved away from the capital. They disliked the bleak atmosphere and commanding nature of the crowned head of the family. Joseph drove his ministers hard and treated most of them badly, since he distrusted them. Prince Kaunitz remained in his favor. Otherwise, fear that his edicts, numbered 6,000 in ten years, might not be properly followed by the population or executed by his officials led to the development of an elaborate police system. The various police departments in the provinces were subordinated to the chiefs of the provincial administration, but they also sent secret reports to the central government. In 1793, the Court Office of Police (*Polizeihofstelle*) came into being. It was to gain much notoriety in the Metternich era.

∽ Absolutism

ABSOLUTISM EXTENDED to every corner of the Habsburg possessions, which Joseph started to mold into a single unified empire. A single central office for Austrian internal administration was created. The Court Chancellery was merged with the Court Chamber. Interior and financial administration was fused into a single agency, as in the Prussian General Directory and as proposed by Count Haugwitz in the 1740's.[1] The United Court Chancellery was divided into thirteen departments, each headed by a court councilor. On this occasion the last essential functions that the Vienna Court Chamber exercised in the government of Hungary were transferred to the central government of Hungary in Pressburg (Bratislava), which thereafter also ruled Transylvania. The warnings of ministers that this might lead to a full separation of Hungary from the rest of the monarchy were disregarded by Joseph II in the conviction that the uniformity of political principles and administrative organization would block any secession of Hungary. Joseph had refused to be specially crowned Hungarian King and had the crown of St. Stephen brought to Vienna. Soon he was to abolish all self-government in Hungary, as he was to do in Lombardy and the Netherlands.

The organization of the United Court Chancellery in central departments could have produced a modern ministerial council as chief organ of government. *Kabinettsregierung*, that is the autocratic management of all the affairs of the state by the monarch himself, never reached the same degree as in Prussia. For this type of personal regime the Habsburg empire was too big, and the position of ministers, such as Kaunitz, and of the state council was too strong to allow even

[1] See page 221.

Joseph II, who had a temperamental bent toward *Kabinettsregierung,* to adopt this system. But the formation of a council of ministers who were at the same time heads of executive departments was not to the taste of the Emperor, who wanted to be free to intervene everywhere, thereby causing a great deal of confusion. Thus for over half a century Austria remained without a council of ministers like those introduced in practically all the European states within the next twenty years. The lack of such a council became a serious weakness once the hand of a strong emperor was missing. For Metternich, the loose structure of the supreme offices of the monarchy became the most annoying practical encumbrance of his long chancellorship. On the provincial level a new order was introduced. It will be remembered that not only diets of estates existed here, but also committees of the estates which attended to administrative tasks in financial, military, and other matters. These committees or "colleges," as they were called, were abolished. The whole administration, as was already the case in the local sphere, came into the hands of the state bureaucracy. In Austria the twelve provincial governments, which conformed to the historic territorial units, were superseded by six land governments, new *Gubernia,* a method of minimizing the significance of the old provincial estates.

Side by side with the general administration, the judiciary was organized in a parallel fashion. On the local level distinctions were not entirely extirpated. In the rural sections of the county the noblemen retained judicial functions, while in the towns there were local magistrates. But the judges had to be confirmed by the court of appeals and were supervised by the local district officer. Beyond the local courts, appeal could be taken first to the court of appeals in the lands and finally to the Supreme Office of Justice (*Oberste Justizstelle*). The separation of political administration and justice was more complete in Austria than in Prussia. Similarly, the civil and criminal law codes of 1786 and 1787 went much further in the liberalization of law than the Prussian law code of 1794, largely because Joseph II was considerably less willing to recognize social privileges. The criminal code embodied the ideas of Cesare Bonesano Beccaria, the Italian champion of a reformed penology. It was the first law code that abolished torture altogether and also removed the death penalty.

✍ Culture

THIS EXAMPLE ILLUSTRATES the fact that Joseph II took many of his ideas from non-German sources. As a matter of fact, intellectually he was almost as much a pupil of the French Enlightenment as Frederick, although he was even more scornful of the immorality and luxuriousness of the French ruling classes. In contrast to Frederick, Joseph did not turn into a skeptic under the influence of French philosophy. He retained an earnest faith in religion and the Church, even though his faith was barren of any understanding of the superrational. This religious note brought Joseph closer than Frederick to the prevailing sentiment in Germany. But his relationship to the burgeoning literary and artistic movement in Germany was most superficial. He read widely in his younger years, but as emperor he found a budget report or a political memorandum more exciting than a page of noble French or German prose. Projects for bringing Lessing, Klopstock, and Herder to Vienna never reached a decisive stage, since Joseph did not really consider them important. Concerning the commendations Joseph received in Germany for not making personal contact with Voltaire and other French writers, Goethe remarked: "This was not even to the credit of this prince, because it would not have been harmful to him and his enterprises if, with his great intelligence and magnificent convictions, he had possessed more sparkle and a higher esteem of the spirit."

Joseph did not intend to destroy non-German cultural institutions when, in 1784, he issued his edict regarding a single state language. Nor did he plan to impose German civilization on the various nationalities in the Habsburg empire. He wanted to spread civilization as such, largely of a utilitarian type, through the centralized monarchy. The German language was merely the vehicle for establishing political rather than cultural unity. His edict prescribed a knowledge of German for everybody who wanted to enter public service, and the schools in Bohemia, Hungary, and Galicia were provided with German teachers. In Bohemia and Moravia the language edict caused little trouble. Here it capped a development of more than a century. The nobility and high clergy used German. The Czech language had become the language of the "kitchen and nursery," in other words, an unrecorded tongue. This began to change after 1770, when the extension of schools propagated by Maria Theresa started to thaw Czech illiteracy. Still, only in conjunction with social and religious issues was the status of German as official language to become a political problem in the future.

In Hungary, where it appeared at the same time as the assault on the Magyar constitution, the edict met with fierce opposition, exclusively political in nature. Magyar was at best the language of half of the inhabitants of the lands beyond the Leitha, while the official language was Latin. The fight against German served almost entirely as a symbol of resistance against the centralism of Vienna. It should be added that the large colonization of Germans, particularly from Swabia, commenced by Maria Theresa and pushed forward by Joseph II with great success, inevitably appeared as an attempt to introduce a strong force loyal to the emperor in Hungary. Actually the chief motive was to increase population and thereby benefit mercantilism. Some Italians and Frenchmen from Lorraine were settled in southern Hungary as well. But Joseph II knew that in his centralistic policies he would find his main support among the Germans. Also his foreign policy was conducted with a view to strengthening the German element in the monarchy.

∾ *Religion*

His COLD-BLOODED RADICALISM also made the enlightened emperor the only sovereign over the Church. What Kaunitz had achieved under Maria Theresa with respect to the control and management of the Church in Lombardy, was now applied to all the Habsburg lands.[2] The remaining ties with the archbishoprics of Salzburg and Passau were cut. Even more drastic was the prohibition of all connections with Rome. The monastic orders were placed under the supervision of the indigenous bishops, and on this occasion all those monasteries that were exclusively devoted to contemplation rather than education or the nursing of the sick were dissolved. Four hundred convents were closed in the German lands of the monarchy and about eight hundred in the empire. This action was carried through with undue speed, and the corruption of officials and tradesmen was responsible for the loss of much property and the ruin of great cultural values. Still, the measure aroused only mild objections from the people. On the other hand, Joseph II organized a wider distribution of pastoral care. No village was to be farther off from a church than an hour's walking distance. Hundreds of new parishes were founded in the next few years.

Yet it was a new type of priest that Joseph wanted. In conformity with the basic doctrines of the Church, the priests were to preach moral conduct, including principally a zeal for the general welfare as

[2] See page 223.

interpreted by the state. In order to secure official champions of the enlightened state, Joseph II did not hesitate to take the education of priests away from the Church. "General seminaries" under the exclusive direction of the government were created in order to turn out devoted servants of the state.

Even this was not enough for the emperor. One of his most revolutionary actions, the introduction of civil marriage, including the possibility of divorce, may have stemmed from his conception of state and government rather than an intention to interfere with religious thinking. But regulating the frequency and forms of worship and tampering with old, hallowed popular customs was an open and deliberate intrusion into the inner life of the Church. His injunction against coffins at interments caused a storm of protests and had to be revoked very quickly. Nevertheless, he was convinced that his interventions in the government and cult of the Church were only purifying, and thereby elevating, the Church. Joseph II also refused to have his Edict of Toleration understood as an act intended to encroach on the position of the Church.

The Edict of Toleration, of October 13, 1781, ended the "Ferdinandean period" of Austrian history, during which the monarchy was completely identified with the Roman Catholic Church. In this period, the monarchy had first restored the old faith, then maintained its absolute dominance over the people. Joseph's edict gave all non-Catholics full rights as citizens and also the right of the private exercise of religion. Their meeting halls were not allowed to have spires, bells, or entrances on main streets. Catholic priests continued to keep the public registers. Full religious equality did not come to Austria until 1861. From the point of view of the enlightened despot, the existence of a single Church was naturally very desirable, particularly after it had been turned largely into an instrument of the state. But belief in the free trade of ideas and the interests of mercantilism recommended a different course. Joseph's Edict of Toleration was a compromise. But Joseph was mistaken if he hoped that Protestants might be more easily won over to the Catholic religion, which in his opinion had been brought back to the undogmatic simplicity of early Christianity. The number of conversions to Protestantism reached 70,000 in the first year after the edict.

For the first time in German history, the edict attacked the problem of the Jews in a rather sweeping manner. So far, the legal position of Jews, like that of all other groups, had rested on special privileges and not on general legislation. The very idea of equality, of course, had no reality so long as the society consisted of a plurality of groups with different legal status. Prior to the late eighteenth century, equality of Jews could only have meant equality with either the nobility or the peasants or burghers. But the question would still have remained in what class of burghers they should have been fitted. On the other hand, the Jews wanted to be a group of their own in order to cultivate their religion and live according to the law of their fathers. The special position of the Jews in the medieval and early modern world is not surprising, nor is the fact of their pariah role in a society dominated by a single orthodox faith. The centuries that saw the worst persecution of Christians who deviated from orthodoxy could not be expected to forgive the Jews their religion. Only a generation that began to see the different religions as emanations of a universal natural religion could become more tolerant in this respect.

✒ The Status of the Jews

IT IS WITHIN this framework that the history of the Jews must be seen. Had they not at all times fulfilled an important function in society, they would not have survived the Christian Middle Ages. Briefly stated, it can be said that the Jews attended to those tasks that medieval society was unable to perform, on account of the rigidity of its social structure and social philosophy. An economy of predominantly local and agrarian character, inclined to consider any living not derived from the tilling of soil or artisanship as dubious if not outright nefarious, was necessarily short of commercial middlemen and providers of credit. All during the Middle Ages, Jews managed a substantial part of the long-distance trade, particularly of luxury goods and of all money and loan operations. The canonic prohibition of usury had no parallel in Hebrew religious laws, and consequently Jewish social ethics presented no impediment to capitalistic attitudes. Dire necessity compelled the Jews to live outside the occupations and craft guilds, which were set up as Christian corporations. Moreover, the acquisition of landed property was forbidden, and schools, universities, and all public offices were closed to them. On the other hand, kings, princes, and bishops needed their services. The privileges and exemptions that the Jews received constituted a bare minimum of protection. Often they were swept aside when Christian religious feeling ran high or Jewish economic practices were rightly or wrongly suspected of damaging the livelihood of the Gentiles. The violent persecutions of the Jews in the fifteenth and early sixteenth centuries, which led to the emigration of many Jews to Poland, indicated the insecurity of the Jews in Germany.

In spite of these catastrophes, Jewish groups continued in many places. Some cities, such as Nürnberg and Augsburg, did not tolerate any Jews within their walls. Ulm harbored a single Jew. Frankfurt had the largest Jewish congregation of around 500 households. Because of the almost complete absence of outbreaks of anti-Semitic mob violence, the Jewish community in Frankfurt gained not only considerable prosperity but also cultural distinction. With the admission of Jews, Hamburg became another civic center of Jewish life. Although the Reformation did not change the status of Jews in any respect, the general conditions of the seventeenth and eighteenth centuries provided opportunities for improvement. The new territorial economies needed a wider distribution of goods over the country than the old local centers could provide. However, the ideal of maximum autarchy had cut normal connections by which the hunger of the rich for the luxury goods of foreign countries could be satisfied. The new absolute states of the era with their still far from perfect civil services needed men who could solve intricate economic tasks. In all these situations the Jews were of greatest assistance. Their ability to establish easy contacts over a whole country and even with distant lands enabled them, for example, to purchase and deliver quickly the provisions and supplies demanded for the mobilization of armies and their maintenance in the field. After 1648 Germany had to rely almost entirely on the importation of metals, and consequently Jewish connections with the sources of supply were of great value. Coinage and currency operations became main activities of Jewish bankers.

The decline of the guilds and the growth of the factory and "put-out" system opened the doors to Jewish participation in production. Jewish capital was welcomed. The rise of a number of Jewish families in Berlin, among them the Mendelssohns, Veits, and Friedländers, to wealth and eminence in the days of Frederick II was largely the result of the silk factories the king directed them to develop. But Frederick also employed Jewish bankers for his money manipulations. He disliked the Jews, and in his two *Political Testaments* he recommended to his successor not to tolerate their increase in numbers and to keep them away from big trade. However he obviously felt that individual exceptions should be made. In Austria, the Jews were expelled from Vienna in 1670. But it was soon discovered that the richest among them were needed for the financial administration of the state, and they received special permission to return to the Austrian capital. Samuel Oppenheimer, who died in 1703, became a mighty figure in Austrian financial history as merchant of army supplies and credit-giver of the period of Leopold I. Subsequently a number of "court Jews" continued these profitable enterprises.

In most German courts of the period it was usual to have one or more Jewish "factors"—financial and commercial agents—to service the personal wishes of the sovereign. These were either special personal matters, such as the purchase of luxury items, jewels, gobelins, or silk dresses, or they might amount to high state actions, such as currency devaluations, the provisioning of an army, or the investment of princely funds. The most famous, or notorious, of the eighteenth-century factors was *Jud Süss*—Joseph Süss Oppenheimer—who served Duke Carl Alexander of Württemberg from 1732 to 1737. Württemberg still had a dualistic constitution, and the estates saw an attempt to undermine their rights in Süss's activities for stabilizing the finances of the duke. Carl Alexander's successor sacrificed Süss to the ire of the people, and after an ugly travesty of a trial he ended on the gallows.

While a few individual Jews with special privileges acquired considerable fortunes and were able to afford a standard of life comparable to that of the nobility or rich burghers, the vast majority was confined to small country towns as tradesmen. They were exposed to innumerable indignities, but as far as can be seen they gained in security and prosperity during the eighteenth century. In its last quarter about 25 per cent of the merchants at the Leipzig fairs were Jewish, and comments were heard about the unusual variety of wares they displayed. Maria Theresa had still declared the "Jewish nation" to be "the worst pest for the state." Joseph II not only extended toleration to their religion but very considerably broadened their social rights as to choice of domicile and occupation.

Joseph II's reforms of Church and religion, accompanied by an active school policy, aroused great alarm in Rome, already hard pressed by France and Spain. Pope Pius VI took the unusual step of going to Vienna, where he was welcomed by the people and courteously received by the emperor. But neither Joseph II nor Kaunitz could be deflected from their course. Although these reforms caused much controversy among the populace, they among others were not altered after Joseph II's death. Actually, what has often exclusively been called "Josephinism" lasted until 1853. But there was another side to Josephinism which had a great influence on the future, though some of its measures were annulled after Joseph's death.

∽ *The Peasantry*

AT THE CENTER of all Joseph II's social and economic reforms was the endeavor to improve the lot of the most numerous class in the monarchy. Beginning with the edict of November 1, 1781, he concentrated on the advance of the peasants. The first law dealt with the personal servitude of peasants. Serfdom (*Leibeigenschaft*) in the strict sense of the word did not exist in any of the Austrian lands, but *Erbuntertänigkeit* ("hereditary subjection") existed. This meant that serfdom, though hereditary, was connected with the soil and not the person of the serf. He performed work, or as it was called in Czech *robot*, because he held land, and not because he was the property of his lord. However the peasant could not leave the land at will, and the lord determined the vocation of the peasant and regulated his marriage. These last obligations of *Leibeigenschaft* were abrogated by the edict of November 1, 1781. In this respect the peasant ceased being a mere subject of his landlord and became a subject of the state, which watched over the execution of the law through its district offices. Still, the peasant was not yet freed of work for his lord, or of tributes, nor did he become the proprietor of his own land. But the peasant became a renter, and subsequent legislation defined both the rents and tributes he had to pay as about 30 per cent of his income. The state was to take 12⅔ per cent as contributional tax, while the landlord was to receive 17⅓ per cent for all servitudes, labor, rentals in money or grain, and fees. Here again the state offices were to act as supervisors.

The general direction of Joseph's reforms was clearly indicated by what happened on the public domains. Here Joseph II vigorously continued what Maria Theresa had already begun. Obligatory labor was altogether abolished, and the acquisition of land by peasants was greatly facilitated. Thus the noble landowners saw in Joseph's legislation a thoroughly revolutionary act. They were immediately deprived of labor and income. So far the lord of the manor had been the owner of the land, tax collector, recruitment officer, chief of police, and judge. The burden of proof of any rights that a peasant might claim was on the peasant, and he had little chance to argue his case before an outside authority. With the intrusion of the state offices into the relationship between lord and peasant and with the introduction of new laws, the proof of the peasant's obligations was largely shifted to the landlords. Nevertheless, the new legislation was seriously limited in that it applied only to a minority of the peasants. A distinction was drawn between the "rustical" and "dominical" peasants. The latter occupied land used by the lord himself but partly rented to peasants, the former were traditionally hereditary tenants. The laws of Joseph II alleviated only the position of the "rustical" peasants and among them only those who paid an annual tax of two gulden or more. The exclusion of all "dominical" and a large segment of the "rustical" peasants was bound to create unrest and give the landlords an easy argument against the whole legislation. Thus of all the agrarian reforms of Joseph II only the abolition of *Erbuntertänigkeit* was retained after his death, while the social and economic emancipation of the peasants in Austria was not achieved before the revolution of 1848–49.

At the time of this revolution Austrian liberals decorated the statue of Joseph II. This seems surprising if one considers the extreme autocracy of the ruler who was convinced that once natural reason had been introduced, government would be loved by men. He had no idea that people seldom identify their happiness with the ideal welfare of the whole community, which is difficult to define. Still, Joseph II was a pacemaker of liberalism. The conception of a state built on an egalitarian society animated by a secular philosophy anticipated basic ideals of the French Revolution and of nineteenth-century liberalism. It was quite natural that the liberalism of southwestern Germany was definitely colored by Josephinism, since it had one of its most important centers in the Breisgau in southern Baden, part of the old Anterior Austria. Particularly among the peasants, Joseph II remained a hero. It must be assumed that to some extent the emperor's reforming activities were responsible for the lack of internal disturbances and reform. With the consequent stability the Habsburg monarchy could withstand the impact of the French Revolution and the staggering exertions of the Napoleonic wars. Moreover, it can be said that Joseph II would have had a very good chance of realizing his full program if he had confined himself to the Austrian hereditary lands. The resistance of Hungary and of the Netherlands reacted on Austria in such a way as to persuade his younger brother and successor, Leopold II, to revoke substantial parts of Joseph's work.

Leopold II (1790–92), who as grand duke of Tuscany had been one of the most successful of enlightened despots, was actually in agreement with Joseph's general aims. What distinguished him from his brother, apart from his great personal sagacity, was his belief in constitutional forms. Leopold reintroduced the provincial estates as they had still existed under Maria Theresa and also the constitutions of Hungary and the Netherlands. However the importance of these concessions, at least in Austria, should not be overrated. Real power had not rested with the estates for a long time, and already under Maria Theresa Austria's administration was carried on in a centralistic if motherly spirit. The change from Joseph II to Leopold II and thereafter to Francis II was not as profound as it might appear from the outside.

Another, though unintended, result of Joseph II's government lasted into the subsequent period. The concentration on the *universum*, as Joseph II called the Habsburg empire, produced in the army and bureaucracy, and beyond them particularly in the German territories, a preoccupation with specifically Austrian problems. This preoccupation could not fail to interfere with Austrian interest in the German Empire. It is paradoxical that this should have happened under Joseph II, who was far more conscious of being German than Frederick II of Prussia. Joseph II had promoted German civilization in his dominions more deliberately than his predecessors on the throne. He cared about Germany, and had he not continually been defeated by Frederick in his German policies, the Empire would probably have assumed an important place in his reign. As it was, the imperial dignity seemed to Joseph II just another historical institution that had become meaningless and useless to him. Thus the building of the Habsburgs' universal state consumed all his energies. The force of circumstances drove him toward a loosening of the ties between Austria and the rest of Germany. The final creation of an imperial crown for Austria, in 1804, would have been impossible without the relative unification of Austria in the age of Maria Theresa and Joseph II. However it was not caused by the integration of the Austrian territories but by the destruction of the Holy Roman Empire under the blows of the new power that emerged from the revolution in France.

The French Revolution influenced the collapse of Joseph's policies. The revolution of the Belgians, led by their bishops, could hardly have gathered such irresistible force if the convention of the estates general in France had not revived confidence in representative ideas everywhere. The internal struggle in France was damaging in itself to Austrian interests in Europe. The alliance with France became a weak reed, and Austria had to rely exclusively on Russia. Joseph II was bound to come to Russia's assistance when a Russo-Turkish war broke out in 1787. The military co-operation between Austria and Russia left much to be desired. Joseph had expected gains from the war, but instead found himself saddled with an extremely costly and hazardous campaign. Since the main burden of war rested on Hungary, much fuel was added to the flames of Magyar opposition against the "hatted," that is not formally crowned, king. The machinations of Prussian diplomacy appeared everywhere. Prussia supported Magyar and Belgian resistance as well as Galician revolts. Together with England, Turkey, Poland, and the Association of German Princes, Prussia hemmed in an Austria stuck in the quagmire of an oriental war. Joseph II recognized the grave peril and admitted defeat by restoring the old order in Hungary before he succumbed to his last illness. By adopting more elastic political tactics at home and abroad, his successor, Leopold II, succeeded in stabilizing the Austrian monarchy. Stability from this source, also, enabled the monarchy to carry the burden of the continental fight against the French Revolution and Napoleon during the next quarter of a century.

᧞ *Other German States*

BETWEEN AUSTRIA AND PRUSSIA stood the remaining, major, part of Germany. The existence of the two big powers made a reform of its confederate organization impossible. But reform of the individual state governments and administrations was not necessarily excluded. The general picture was as spotty as the political map of the Holy Roman Empire, and it may be overbold to attempt any generalizations. But from most descriptions the impression prevails that in the period between 1750 and 1790, and especially after 1770, the general situation of the middle classes became slightly more comfortable than before, both economically and politically. Reforms were carried out in a number of large and small states. Although the number of dull-witted, profligate, or vicious potentates was large, there were some outstanding personalities. The bureaucrats, if often corrupt and most of the time pedantic, showed greater competence and better education than in the early days of absolutism.

Two states, Saxony and Bavaria, had lost the leading role in Germany they had possessed in former centuries. Saxony never ceased to be in the vanguard of German cultural activities, and its commercial and industrial activities always remained considerable. But politically it was forever outclassed by Brandenburg-Prussia. Saxony had suffered greatly from the regime of Count Heinrich Brühl, the ruling minister from 1738–63 under Frederick August II (1733–63). He mismanaged Saxony's finances and directed her unhappy foreign policy. The Seven Years' War and the Prussian occupation had taken the remaining mobile resources of the electorate. With Frederick August III (1763–1827; from 1806 on King Frederick August) a ruler came to the throne who tended to emulate his sixteenth- and seventeenth-century forebears rather than his father and grandfather. He gave up their Polish aspirations and established close political relations with Prussia, leading Saxony into the Association of German Princes. Again Saxony received an economical and effective administration. The administration of mines was unequaled in Germany. Much was done to stimulate industry and commerce, though Saxony was enclosed by Prussia and Austria and thereby blocked in a free development of its trade. But prosperity returned to Saxony, and with it a modest elegance of life not commonly found in Germany. The sensual luxury of the first two Augusts, which had never affected more than the court and part of the nobility, did not revive. But the beauty of Dresden's architecture continued to spread its charm among a civilized population. The art collections, which, among other treasures, contained Raffael's Sistina from 1753 on, gave J. J. Winckelmann his first conception of classical art. They were to become a center of worship to the generation of classical art lovers then growing up. Frederick August III was not a man of high ideas, and the Enlightenment frightened him. But by now the Enlightenment was well entrenched even within the Lutheran Church of Saxony, and the Catholic elector was not inclined to interfere with the Church. He wanted to be a practical and paternal ruler.

Bavaria was in poor condition in the second half of the eighteenth century. Under Maximilian I it had been the strongest German state, but had declined rather quickly after the turn of the century. The wars for the Spanish and Austrian inheritance had swallowed enormous sums. Foreign soldiers roaming and occupying the country had taken a frightful toll. The zeal that Bavaria had shown in the defense of the Catholic faith at the same time resulted in a deep aversion against any foreign influences. No systematic reform of her public institutions was undertaken. The organization of her financial administration was antiquated. From 1671 to 1751, taxes were farmed out, and the people were exposed to arbitrary oppression. The situation did not improve when corrupt state officials took the place of the tax farmers.

It was unavoidable that an almost entirely agrarian country could not bear the burden of great schemes of foreign policy or huge expenditures for the grandiose opulence of the court. The *camerale* was relatively small, the income of the *contributionale* limited, partly due to the unusually large exempted Church properties. Debts were growing by leaps and bounds throughout the century. In 1760, more than one fourth of the state revenue had to be used to service the debt, and more than one fifth was spent on the court. Soon special taxes had to be raised and forced loans had to be imposed on landowners and the Church. Finally the "decimation," the seizure of a tenth part of all ecclesiastical income, was employed. The specter of the secularization of Church goods appeared in the very state that could rightly pride itself on having contributed more to the preservation of the old Church than any other state in Germany.

Bavaria's religious and intellectual culture was generally criticized, most sharply perhaps in the Austria of Joseph II. Nowhere in the eighteenth century was popular religion so deeply permeated with superstitions and pagan abuses as in Bavaria. Max Joseph III (1745–77), a mild and friendly man, was not inactive in the improvement of schools; in addition, he founded an academy of sciences in Munich. Still, progress against obscurantism was slow and came to a standstill under his reluctant successor, Carl Theodore of the Palatinate.

For thirty-five years Carl Theodore (born 1724; from 1742 on Elector of the Palatinate; 1777–99 also of Bavaria) had ruled the territories of the Palatinate and Jülich-Berg, when Frederick II's intervention against the scheming of Joseph II compelled him to move from Mannheim to Munich. In the Palatinate and the Rhineland Carl Theodore had been rather popular. However the Protestants of the Palatinate complained with good reason about the violation of their rights and thousands of them emigrated to America. Carl Theodore liked to live in great style. Even his *amours* were on a lavish scale, and in order to provide for his mistresses and illegitimate children many corrupt practices in the administration were forgiven. Carl Theodore was a gay and trusting man. The "first cavalier of the Holy Roman Empire" he was often called. He loved the arts, showed good taste in his buildings, and maintained a distinguished opera. The elector proved to be particularly interested in the cultivation of German literary art. In 1779, he founded the first court theater for German art (*Nationaltheater*), where the birth of the German classic stage was to begin under the direction of A. W. Iffland (1759–1814). In 1782, Schiller's *Robbers* was presented here for the first time. The galleries and art collections of Mannheim were exceptionally fine. In a few decades the Palatinate's new capital became something of a south German Dresden. This was the more important, since so much young talent began to make itself felt.

Carl Theodore's regime in Munich was a barren and disagreeable period in Bavarian history. He was viewed with deep suspicion as the prince who had wished to bring Bavaria into Austrian hands. It was correctly assumed that this plan had not been definitely buried. The hostility and intrigue that surrounded him in Munich made Carl Theodore an intolerant ruler. For a short time he made an effort to bring fresh ideas in agriculture and technology to Bavaria. In this endeavor an adventurous American, Benjamin Thompson, Count Rumford, served him. Carl Theodore also laid out Munich's famous "English Garden." But in order to keep his hold on the country, Carl Theodore soon relied entirely on his confessor, an ex-Jesuit Father Ignaz Frank, who opened a furious fight against all influences of the Enlightenment. While Bavaria suffered from tyrannical government in this respect, it suffered from too little government in all other fields. Public indebtedness continued on the increase, economic life stagnated, the streets of Munich were crowded with beggars, and highway robbery was quite common.

In the neighboring Württemberg, Duke Carl Eugene reigned from 1737 to 1793. He was educated at the Prussian court, and Frederick wrote for him a "mirror of princes," instructions on the duties of princes toward their subjects. Except for his useless love for soldiers, the Swabian prince brought no ascetic lessons from Berlin to Stuttgart. He conducted himself like an oriental sultan both in his private and public activities. Money was spent insanely on palaces, mistresses, court festivities, and hunting. To make up for some of the cost, the duke sold soldiers to the colonial powers for war overseas or auctioned off posts in the state service. But these were small gains compared to the waste of funds. When the estates objected, Carl Eugene disregarded the constitution altogether, and the estates appealed to the Empire. Prussia, England, and Denmark offered good advice in Stuttgart, but to no avail. The duke had the eminent lawyer of the estates, the brave J. J. Moser, imprisoned for five years. Later, his subjects and crowned European cousins were surprised to see the duke in a state of remorse. On his fiftieth birthday, in 1777, he had a declaration of repentance read from all pulpits, together with a promise of reform. Because of the catastrophic condition of Württemberg finances, he had to make peace with the estates. This step was the result of the persuasion of his last mistress, Francisca von Hohenheim. The prudent lady became his second wife and managed to stop Carl Eugene's private and political excesses, although he remained a ruler whose fierce temper and erratic manners were hard for his subjects to bear.

Duke Eugene was not the worst example of a mad German despot. The worst was probably Carl of Zweibrücken, whose protests against Carl Theodore's intended cession of Bavaria to Austria had been exploited by Frederick II. Fortunately, Bavaria was spared the yoke of Carl of Zweibrücken as he died before Carl Theodore, and Carl's younger brother inherited Bavaria in 1799. In the old Franconian Hohenzollern principalities of Ansbach and Bayreuth, a nephew of Frederick II, Carl Alexander, was margrave after 1757 and 1769. He spent his dominion's funds first on a French actress and then on a noble English lady, Lady Craven. He, too, tried to recoup his losses by selling troops to the colonial powers. In one of these transactions Neithardt von Gneisenau, then a lieutenant, reached America. When the Ansbach battalion reached New England in 1782, the war was practically over, and Napoleon's future conqueror did not see action in America. Lady Craven persuaded Carl Alexander to sell his principalities to the presumptive heir, the Prussian King Frederick William II, and to follow her to England in 1791.

Landgrave Frederick II of Hesse-Kassel was the greatest merchant in soldiers, and Hessian troops acquired an unenviable reputation in America. As individuals they do not seem to have aroused equal hostility, for many of them settled there after the war. Under Landgrave Frederick II, Kassel became an elegant city, where art and education were not neglected, despite the immoral court life. The landgrave, who was converted to the Roman Catholic Church, left his subjects' religion unmolested. But even apart from the shameful trade in soldiers, Hesse-Kassel was an ill-administered country. In the neighboring Hesse-Darmstadt Ludwig IX and Ludwig X ruled with more earnestness. Although the latter became a devotee of French literature under the influence of Frederick II of Prussia, he established friendly personal relations with Goethe and Schiller.

Created shortly before its dynasty ascended the English throne, the electorate of Hanover had its own peculiar conditions. The first two Georges still took a lively interest in the affairs of their German possessions. However George III liked to think of himself as an Englishman, and actual participation of the English kings in the government of Hanover sank to a low point except in foreign policy. George III

never visited Hanover after his accession to the throne and made no
strong personal demands on the electorate. No Hanoverian troops
were employed in the American war. In the absence of the elector-
king, the government of Hanover fell largely into the hands of the
high nobility. Its members occupied the seats of the governing body,
the privy council, and communicated with the king through a residing
minister in London. However, the actual administration was conducted by councilors from burgher families, who by themselves formed
something of a territorial political patriciate.

This oligarchy had many shortcomings. But since Hanover had
sound agrarian laws which protected the peasants, and since the nobility was not very numerous, its influence was not seriously damaging
to the country. It is true that the regime failed to tackle important
tasks. Politically, Hanover remained divided into six lands with that
many separate estates. Economically, a large part of the country—
estimated at two fifths—remained uncultivated. Conditions in a thinly
populated territory of less than 1.5 million people would have called
for an active policy of settlement. On the other hand, although Hanover was not endowed by nature with any riches, it was well off.
Except for Prussia, it was the only German state that did not have to
toil for the maintenance of a luxurious court. This advantage balanced
the military expenditure incurred during the wars between 1742 and
1762. The victories of Ferdinand of Brunswick over the French in
the Seven Years' War sharpened sentiment against France. The participation of substantial British forces strengthened the attachment to
England, with which the internal political practices of Hanover were
lightheartedly compared. In addition to the social prejudices of the
ruling class, the nearness of Prussia contributed to this blurred picture.
In contrast to Prussian despotism, the oligarchic regime under an
absentee king—the so-called "vicecracy"—was rather liberal. However social and local privileges prevailed in Hanover to a much greater
extent than in contemporary England. The link between Hanover and
England was also important in intensifying direct cultural relations
between Germany and England. Well into the first half of the eighteenth century, Germany had received a great deal of its information
about English ideas and affairs through France. What the Hanover
regime was capable of doing at its best was shown by the founding of
the modern University of Göttingen in 1737. The work of Adolf von
Münchhausen, it became, under his curatorship, the freest and most
flourishing German university after 1750. It was characteristic of the

political sentiment prevailing in the Hanover government that the excellence of the university rested to a large extent on its cultivation of the study of the Empire's laws. The preservation of the territorial states' liberties was a strongly felt concern in the state of the Guelfs.

In Hanover the influence of the nobility remained within limitations set by the traditions of the older princely power and by the freedom of the strong peasant population. However the institutions of the older dualistic state in Mecklenburg, or rather the two Mecklenburgs (Mecklenburg-Schwerin and Mecklenburg-Strelitz), had undergone a development comparable to that in Poland. The power of the dukes had become a mere shadow. At the time of the Nordic War, Duke Leopold had attempted to emulate Charles XII of Sweden and impose absolute authority. In this attempt he had not hesitated to call Russian troops to his support. His coup failed, and in 1755 the dynasty had to accept a "hereditary compromise" (*Erbvergleich*). With only small amendments, this compromise served as the fundamental law of Mecklenburg until 1918. These laws were divided into those applying to domains of the dynasty and those applying to the estates. The estates were composed of 700 noblemen and less than 50 mayors and magistrates of the few Mecklenburg cities. Outside of their own domains, which comprised about two fifths of the country, the dukes had little authority. On their estates the Mecklenburg *Junkers* pursued their selfish interests in the most ruthless fashion. The transition to cattle raising led to ever larger "enclosures" and evictions of peasants from the land. In contrast to England, it was cows, not sheep, that "ate men." The Mecklenburg cities, of which Wismar was in Swedish possession until 1803, were unable to absorb additional population. Under a petrified guild system even the port city of Rostock was languishing. Baron Stein spoke grimly of the houses of Mecklenburg noblemen as "the lairs of beasts of prey," around which all life would cease.

∽ Other German Princes

AMONG THE SMALL PRINCES many most offensive characters could be found, though also a goodly number of extraordinary figures. Best known in Germany and Europe were Duke William Ferdinand of Brunswick and Margrave Carl Frederick of Baden. The former was praised by the younger Mirabeau as a ruler of sounder principles than those of Frederick II. Like his uncle Ferdinand he had served in the Prussian army and had the reputation of being one of the ablest generals of his time. For a while the revolutionary government in Paris thought of winning him as commander of the French armies. Instead, he was to lead the German army on its ill-fated march into France in 1792 and to command the Prussian army at Jena in 1806. The duke was fully acquainted with French literature and philosophy but took a genuine interest in the modern intellectual movement in Germany. He visited Voltaire at Lake Geneva, toured Rome under the guidance of Winckelmann, and, in his young years, brought Lessing to Wolfenbüttel, the capital of Brunswick. When he acceded to the throne in 1780, he launched constructive reforms in all fields by stabilizing the budget, improving roads, and placing Joachim Heinrich Campe, one of the German Enlightenment's leading pedagogues, in charge of education. The duke practiced toleration toward the Jews and granted freedom to the press.

In Protestant Baden-Durlach, Carl Frederick came to the throne in 1738. In 1771, he inherited also the Catholic Baden-Baden. By the time of his death, in 1811, Baden had become the third largest state in southern Germany. This was largely caused by the upheavals that occurred in the Napoleonic period. But without the good government that Carl Frederick and his highly gifted minister Wilhelm von Edelsheim gave the small country, nineteenth-century Baden could not have come into existence. The margrave conducted his government in a paternal, though mild and enlightened, fashion. The government, a Baden statute declared, had to teach its subjects "even against their will how to manage their own affairs". Such guardianship was considered by Carl Frederick the "natural" order of things. He was a humane person and always eager to learn about new ideas in practical matters. He corresponded with the elder Mirabeau and Quesnay and became the first ruler who applied physiocratic theories to the economy of his land. In 1783, serfdom was abolished, though the obligations resting on land were not as yet lifted. Carl Frederick worked with energy on the improvement of education, while he was cautious in dealing with religious matters. He avoided the hurry and exaggeration of Josephinism. Later on, when the Austrian Breisgau fell to Baden, this was to prove advantageous. Small as the margravate was, it was important at the time of the French Revolution that this land, crucially located opposite Alsace, lived in happy contentment.

Carl Frederick attempted to draw Klopstock to Karlsruhe and discussed with Herder plans for a "German Patriotic Institute," an academy for the cultivation of a common German culture. But it was a young prince who made his little principality the living center of the young literary movement. The Duchy of Weimar, consisting of two separate patches on the colorful map of Germany, had been under the regency of the widowed Duchess Anna Amalia, a Brunswick princess, niece of Frederick II. She introduced the Enlightenment into this state of the descendants of Luther's princes. The most important step of her regime was the choice of Wieland as tutor of her son, Carl August, in 1771. This date is often called the opening date of the Weimar age of German literature. When, four years later, the eighteen-year-old duke became ruler, he persuaded the young author of *Werther* to join him in the small Thuringian capital. The next years were years of untrammeled revelry in human friendship, poetry, and nature, in which the old court etiquette was contemptuously thrown aside. But affairs of state were not neglected, and both the young duke and the poet as minister proved able administrators not only in matters of education but also in the tasks of economy and finance. In 1776, Herder was made head of the Church in the duchy, and ten years later Schiller became professor at Jena University.

∽ *Ecclesiastical Principalities*

A LARGE PART of Germany still lived under the crozier, and conditions in these ecclesiastical principalities were no less variegated than those in the secular dominions. One would look in vain for religious personalities or even learned men among the prince-bishops and prince abbots. All were scions of ruling dynasties or of the high aristocracy. They considered themselves political leaders who lived and acted in the style of the contemporary secular court society. Their sense of responsibility and their capacity for the administration of their territories varied greatly. Under its last Wittelsbach elector Clement (1723–61), Cologne had lived under a regime that followed the pattern of the court of Versailles under Louis XV, for the elector was a loyal henchman of France in foreign affairs. Max Frederick von Königseck, who succeeded Clement as archbishop in 1761, cleansed the court of frivolity but made little progress in the reform of government. The youngest son of Maria Theresa, Maximilian Francis, elected coadjutor in 1780 and elector-archbishop in 1784, did much to improve the electorate's economy and administration. In many of his policies he was under the influence of his brother Joseph II. By changing the academy in Bonn into a university and making study at this new university obligatory for the members of the clergy, he planned to make the electorate independent of the University of Cologne, which fought Febronianism.

In Trier, Clement Wenzeslaus, a brother of the elector of Saxony, ruled after 1768. He entered the ecclesiastical career late, after serving as an officer in the Austrian army. A man of high moral principles, he was not very effective as a governor. He had a great attachment to French things, one of the reasons why the French royalists found a hospitable refuge in his capital Coblenz after the French Revolution.

The see of Mainz still enjoyed the highest prestige as Germany's ecclesiastical center. But no outstanding man had become archbishop of Mainz and archchancellor of the Empire after Count Johann Philip von Schönborn. From the middle of the century on, strong attempts had been made to make Mainz a center of French Enlightenment. However this caused resentment among the lower clergy, which had ample support from the populace. The last of the electors, Frederick Carl von Erthal, was elevated to the throne as a defender of conservatism. He began his reign by removing all signs of mundane philosophy but soon became a champion of Enlightenment in its radical materialistic form. Voltaire and Helvétius were worshiped at the see of St. Boniface. The government was little affected by all these pretensions, which were a mere cover for the elector's sensual and luxurious secularism.

The last of the archbishops in Salzburg, Hieronymus Count Colloredo, was a strict believer in Josephinism, and the Enlightenment was also represented in Würzburg and Bamberg. Franz Ludwig von Erthal, prince-bishop of Würzburg, had the reputation of being one of the most benevolent and progressive German rulers. In other ecclesiastical dominions, such as Münster and Fulda, able ministers came to the fore. Still, the general picture of the ecclesiastical principalities in the last decades of the Holy Roman Empire was a curiously mixed one. For general national history, it was fortunate that these principalities opened themselves more freely than in the past to all the movements of thought and politics that characterized Germany at this time. But this is only saying that the ecclesiastical principalities had lost any specific task of their own. Even at their best, they could not achieve the continuity of government that some dynastic states began to acquire, especially those that were developing a corps of permanent officials. On the other hand, where government appeared immoral, it looked even more offensive if practiced by ecclesiastical rulers rather than by secular princes. The ecclesiastical principalities had come into being in an age of conflict between the universalist claims of Church and Empire. Now they served neither. It is true that in the eighteenth century they could still be considered the chief supporters of the institutions of the Holy Roman Empire, and their disappearance in 1803 was actually followed immediately by the demise of the Empire. But they acted entirely as guarantors of the Empire's inanimate state and were averse to reforming the Empire by the strengthening of the emperor's power. Mainz even joined Frederick II's Association of German Princes in order to thwart Joseph II. The prince-bishops were too weak and too little concerned with the common good of Germany to lead a federal reform movement in the Empire. As in the case of other territorial rulers, their policies were dictated exclusively by personal ambitions. This led the Rhenish prince-bishops into continuous co-operation with France.

It might have been expected that these ecclesiastical states would have come to the support of the papacy when it was so hard pressed by the policies of France, Spain, Naples, and Portugal, the same powers that had imposed the dissolution of the Jesuit order on the papacy. Finally Joseph II launched his own Church policies, which found some theoretical basis in the teachings of the auxiliary bishop Nicolaus von Hontheim, best known under his pen-name Febronius.[3] In his doctrines Hontheim brought together ideas that tended to elicit very different responses. In his book of 1763 he showed that the Catholic Church was not identical with the Roman Church. The primacy of the pope had been a historical development away from the early Church, which had been built on the apostolic office of all the bishops. The pope was only the first among equals and could not rightly claim any authority except that conferred upon him by general councils. Febronianism was radical episcopalism and as such likely to give the state considerable leeway. But in addition Hontheim was deeply influenced by Hugo Grotius's natural law theories on the power of the state. No doubt, Hontheim was more of an episcopalist, the representative of a German "Gallicanism," than a state absolutist, though his state absolutism caused the stronger practical reaction. This was to be expected in the case of secular rulers, but it proved also true with the German archbishops.

Carl Theodore of Bavaria was eager to extend the power of his government over the Bavarian bishops, but he was not strong enough to proceed by simple fiat in the manner of Joseph II. Instead, he pre-

[3] See p. 223.

vailed on the pope to appoint a nuncio with special powers in Munich. The establishment of this nunciatura came on top of a series of minor interventions by the pope and spurred the four German metropolitans of Mainz, Cologne, Trier, and Salzburg to protest. They viewed this intervention as a step toward the exclusion of their jurisdiction over their suffragans. In the Ems Punctation of 1786, they published a scathing challenge of the authority of Rome to intervene in the internal affairs of the German Church and demanded the full restoration of its original constitution. This was a political action entirely and had little to do with religious or philosophical convictions, even though it might use the language of Enlightenment. Gallicanism or the Church policies of Louis XIV had not been greatly different in an orthodox garb. The four German archbishops fought for their political position, but they misjudged their own power and determination.

Joseph II refused to do their bidding. He wanted a real state Church and not a bishops' Church. The German bishops saw in the move of the archbishops merely an attempt to exercise greater control over the suffragans. Not even the prince-bishops, such as those of Würzburg or Speyer, found any advantage in heightening the archbishops' role. Thus the Ems Punctation, once more sounding the war cries of the conciliar movement of the fifteenth century, did not lead anywhere. With the exception of Archbishop Hieronymus of Salzburg, who openly adhered to the doctrines of Febronius, every archbishop elector made his peace with Rome. The revolutionary events in Belgium and France were a warning to the Rhenish princes not to precipitate conflicts within the Church or in the Empire.

The French Revolution was to overthrow not only the ecclesiastical states but the whole ramshackle structure of the Holy Roman Empire. It was to do even more. From a quarter century of European revolution and war, not a single major state, with the possible exception of Austria, was to emerge unchanged in its basic nature. The pressure that triumphant France exercised upon all of Germany, and the foreign domination under which large parts of the country lived for a good many years, suddenly confronted the German people with entirely new problems. It is true that the German states accepted many French ideas for their solution and that this was not entirely without precedent in the age of absolutism. But equally important was the fact that the new social and intellectual forces which had been forming outside the old feudal society in Germany could gain recognition in the rebuilding of a new German political structure.

PART
II

Reform
and Restoration,
1790—1840

CHAPTER 11

German Idealism and Neohumanism

GERMAN INTELLECTUAL AND LITERARY LIFE gathered strength in the second half of the eighteenth century even though it had little support and little recognition from Germany's political rulers. After 1770, and even more after 1780, it burst forth in a stream of creative achievements that made this age of German civilization one of the greatest periods of Western history. In this spiritual revolution Western man gained a new dimension of consciousness of human existence. Even after 1780, the movement which started from small and modest sources was carried forward only by select groups. It gained a strong position in the general system of education in Germany after 1815, when it also began to be studied abroad. In the 1830's, the last great leaders of German idealism and neohumanism passed away, and new forces came to the fore.

∾ Social Structure

DURING THE EIGHTEENTH CENTURY, growing economic activities, combined with a relative security of life and property, created a more variegated society in a good many towns and cities. But it was almost exclusively the German burgher class that underwent important changes.

A very wealthy class did not arise in Germany. At the end of the eighteenth century, Hamburg, which had only a few dozen millionaire merchants—not many compared with Holland—towered far above the rest of Germany. Fortunes of 100,000 marks made a man rich in the eyes of his fellow-burghers in Berlin, Breslau, Leipzig, and Frankfurt—not to mention less important places. The majority of the rich or well-to-do were hardly to be found among the old families. There was, of course, no old patriciate in the new urban foundations of absolutism, such as Mannheim. In addition, mercantilism had given special privileges to many manufacturers and freed them from obligations to the guilds. It did not matter greatly that this excluded them from communal offices, for the city government in all the territorial cities was a mere facade, behind which state officials directed the affairs of the city.

In addition to this group of newcomers, all state and court "servants" were outside the traditional city organization. This category included not only the soldiers but also all civilian officials and the ministers. They took an oath not to the city but to their respective sovereign lords. Under governments which controlled every aspect of life, the officialdom was large and on the increase. Insofar as the members of the bureaucracy had gone through the universities, they mixed most easily with the other academic graduates in the towns—ministers and the learned professions, at this time chiefly composed of lawyers and, where high schools existed, teachers. The number of physicians also was slowly increasing.

With the growth of new groups of city-dwellers, social stratification became more elastic than in the past. Nevertheless, social mobility was still very limited. The rise of an individual from a low class to a high group was very exceptional, but a family could achieve it within two or more generations. Practically all the leaders of the German intellectual movement descended from families who over generations had been artisans, till their father, or sometimes grandfather, changed to a higher position, usually by way of academic study. A master's son might manage to get into a high school and university and ultimately become a pastor or teacher. His son might climb to a university professorship or even a post in the higher ranks of the bureaucracy. If he was very successful, he might become a privy councilor or state minister and receive a patent of nobility.

These new groups, unlike the sixteenth-century burghers, who had been integral members of a self-governing community, were burghers because they happened to live in cities or towns, and they were distinguished from the nobility and the peasants by lesser or greater rights. The traditional criterion of a social estate, birth, was subordinated to occupational skill and education. The new burghers cannot be considered as a class in the strict sense. In most cases, they, along with a large number of merchants and manufacturers, were directly or indirectly dependent on the state, and they were divided into various subgroups with different social codes.

But all groups accepted the nobleman as the type possessing the highest social graces and modeled their own style of life as much as possible according to the manners of the nobility. Goethe, in his novel *Wilhelm Meister,* the most profound statement of the educational program of German Idealism, characteristically considered it natural that the young burgher son received his education from a nobleman and actors. Two major weaknesses of the aspiring burgher are herein indicated. The stage taught him to co-ordinate his body, practically forgotten in schoolrooms and offices, with his inner being and to make appearance and gesture express some meaning. The nobleman, on his part, set the example of a fuller development and freer use of his total personal faculties and of greater confidence and courage. In 1782, a year after he had been knighted, Goethe remarked: "In Germany only the nobleman has the chance of a certain universal, if I may say so, personal, culture. A burgher can acquire merits and train his mind under great stress. His personality, however, gets lost in whatever way he may act."

Thus the German burgher had to crawl from under the shadow of the German nobleman, and he never fully succeeded in doing so, not even in the nineteenth century. But his early admiration was mixed with criticism, which became louder as time went on. The burgher was chafing under the privileges of the nobility and the arbitrariness of the freakish tyrant-princes. Still, the cities did not constitute any considerable power in an overwhelmingly agrarian Germany. Widely dispersed over the Empire, the burghers were confronted with different governments on which the middle classes depended through jobs in state and Church or through direct business contracts. Burghers found hope for relief in the expectation that more princes of enlightened character would appear and appoint able councilors. The burghers themselves endeavored to make a contribution by the promotion of education.

Reform through Education

LEIBNIZ HAD LIFTED his sights still higher than this, as did, in a lesser fashion, Pufendorf and Thomasius. Leibniz wished to see the Berlin Academy become a center of practical reform, to act as a sort of state advisory council in matters of education, economic development, and general culture. Frederick II monopolized all these practical tasks for himself and confined the Academy to philosophical and scholarly discussion. His own interest lay entirely in the Academy's new philosophical division, so much so that he did not discover that the Swiss mathematician Leonhard Euler (1707–83), a member of the Academy from 1741 to 1766, was the only scientist of real genius in the whole group. The predominance of Frenchmen, most of them of minor distinction, actually minimized the influence in Germany of Frederick's Academy. Germans preferred to read the great leaders of the French Enlightenment.

The attempt of the German thinkers to offer themselves as allies to the absolute rulers and co-operate with them on a level of relative equality, was rebuffed not only in Berlin but also elsewhere in Germany. Insofar as they wanted to move closer to politics, they could do so only through the civil service, but then they had to toe the line and were usually kept in lower posts.

It was only natural that German intellectuals turned from politics to the cultivation of their private lives and to the exploration of the world of the spirit. Here was freedom, in contrast to the mechanical order of the state. Here, too, was equality, of which enlightened rulers often talked but blatantly denied in practice. In these intellectual and artistic pursuits burghers were joined before long by a goodly number of noblemen who desired more individualized experiences than the circumscribed world of the courts, the army, and aristocratic mansions offered. Contacts of more than superficial nature also existed between burghers and noblemen in the bureaucracy and in the universities, although class differences were carried right into the classrooms, where the young noblemen had their own row of chairs. The latter also did not submit to the indignity of final examinations, but needed at least attendance at a university if they wished to enter the civil service. The masonic lodges—the first of which in Germany was founded in Hamburg in 1733—made an important contribution to bringing people of various social statuses together.

Yet the German intellectual and literary movement grew up essentially among the higher middle classes, primarily among the so-called "academic" groups. This characteristically and still common German usage includes in these academic groups not only the academicians but also everybody who ever pursued an academic study. The extent to which the university performed a function of social selection may be seen in the fact that the letters *Dr.* were officially considered part of the name, a kind of substitute for the *von*, the symbol of nobility.

In the late eighteenth century, many more sons of burghers went to the universities than could be easily placed in professional jobs. There was a glut of lawyers, though the plight of the young theologians was worse. It had been customary for theologians to go into high-school teaching for a number of years, since the office of minister seemed to call for seasoned men. Even at this time the teachers at the high schools were mostly graduates of the theological faculties, because the philosophical faculties still served predominantly as preparation for study in the theological, legal, and medical faculties. But the overcrowding in Church and school forced the divinity graduates into often miserable jobs as tutors of children in *Junker* and burgher families. Frequently these graduates were treated no better than butlers and valets.

Nevertheless, families were eager to have their children educated. And a growing number were no longer satisfied to accept the minister's word, or even religion itself as the exclusive subject of spiritual interest, but desired to arrive at their own opinions and learn about man and the world. Reading spread far beyond the learned circles. Whereas, in the second half of the seventeenth century, around half of all books issued in Germany were still in Latin, only one fourth were in 1754, one fifth in 1759, one eighth in 1781, one tenth in 1787, and one twentieth in 1799. Book production increased steadily both in numbers of titles and size of editions. At the end of the century, Leipzig had eighteen presses, each employing seventy to eighty people. The city, called by Goethe "a little Paris that educates her people," had more than fifty bookstores. Women took an ever greater part in literature, a first step toward an emancipation which at the same time enlarged their role in their children's education. The reading matter was of great variety, and the amount of flimsy stuff was certainly not negligible. A great appetite existed for travel books, both scholarly reports and books in novel form. Defoe's *Robinson Crusoe* (1719) was so popular that it was imitated in numerous German *Robinsonaden* for the next half century. Besides seeking knowledge of the distant world, exploration turned to man's own life and its expressions. English writers such as Richardson, Fielding, Goldsmith, and Sterne helped in the discovery of the poetic elements in all situations of human life, including that of the burgher, in whom the seventeenth century had seen at best a subject for comedy. Stories or plays depicting the stylized emotions of princes and noble heroes became rare. The first bourgeois tragedy was Lessing's *Miss Sara Sampson* of 1755, the first bourgeois novel Thümmel's *Wilhelmine* of 1764.

The growth of a reading public was stimulated by journals and magazines. The *Tatler*, *Spectator*, and *Guardian* found German counterparts that endeavored to popularize scholarship, present the products of literary schools, or merely entertain. Their existence showed that literary discussion had reached the burgher's home.

But serious literary interest was not yet cultivated by very large groups in the individual cities. The theater still depended on companies of actors moving from place to place, and although the art of acting showed great improvement, even the best companies frequently had to offer a low fare in order to attract a public. The effort to establish in Hamburg a permanent stage supported by private patrons and directed by Lessing, in 1767–69, failed, just as Händel's labors for a Hamburg opera had failed sixty years earlier. Also, no doubt, there were not enough German playwrights at that time. Only the state could provide the means for theatrical establishments. The example set by Joseph II in Vienna in 1776 and by Carl Theodore in Mannheim in 1779 was followed in Berlin, when, after the death of Frederick II, the new king turned over the French theater to German acting. In 1791, Duke Carl August founded the court theater in Weimar, which Goethe guided until 1817. Although the opera also remained in the hands of the courts, the cultivation of music was carried on more independently. Originally, as we have seen, it had its main center in the Church, but now it gained its firm place in the burgher's home. Musical demand spurred technological progress in the development from the cembalo or clavichord to the modern piano. The burghers had sufficient enthusiasm for modern secular music to contribute to the building of orchestras and glee clubs. The most eminent orchestra in Germany goes back to the initiative of Leipzig burghers. Its concerts were given in the building of a craft guild, Clothiers' Hall (*Gewandhaus*), and hence its name, the Leipzig *Gewandhaus-Orchester*. The glee club in its classic form originated with a Berlin association which became the *Singakademie*.

⌁ The Triumph of Enlightenment

IN THIS SOCIAL SETTING, the German burgher's new culture grew up with its own forms of sociability, centered around humanitarian and esthetic ideals. At the middle of the eighteenth century, the Enlightenment was triumphant, but orthodoxy and Pietism, though on the defensive, retained some influence on German life. Much as German Enlightenment depended in its origins and subsequent history on Western Europe, it displayed a more religious and philosophical bent than that of Western Europe. The belief in a personal God of supreme wisdom and benevolence, the creator of a perfect world, who had planted in the immortal human soul the power to rise—through moral virtue—to the highest objectives of the universe, was not questioned by any serious German thinker. Philosophical materialism, which became one of the important schools of thought in France, found no place in Germany. There was also much reluctance to follow the development toward an epistemological skepticism and empiricism that took place in England from Locke to Hume. In the early nineteenth century, Western Europe, without a break, proceeded in this course of empiricism, while Germany parted company with it in the idealistic systems of Kant, Fichte, Hegel, and Schelling.

✧ Enlightenment and Christian Theology

GERMAN ENLIGHTENMENT was not a passing episode or an artificial emulation of foreign models. Rather, it was a necessary preparatory stage for German Idealism, which contained many of the fundamental impulses of Enlightenment. Moreover, it survived the period of German Idealism as a popular force, and by 1840 became powerful again. To be sure, German Enlightenment had changed by that time, not only through the influence of French liberalism but also through modern scholarship, which had developed in the wake of German Idealism. Intellectual and spiritual movements of any given period will interact, and a nation's intellectual history can be compared to some extent to geological history, in which the different ages deposit one layer upon another. The history of ideas cannot be conceived as a sequence of stages in which one system of thought replaces another. A civilization can accumulate a variety of schools of ideas. Orthodoxy, Pietism, Enlightenment, and Idealism have existed side by side, though on different social levels, for the past two centuries of German history.

The German Enlightenment of the eighteenth century dealt a fatal blow to Christian theology, although its early representatives were unaware of this. If the benevolence and wisdom of God could be recognized in the immutable natural laws that determined the universe, God's belated and unique divine historic intervention in the world appeared incredible. The traditional Christian conception had assumed an active God with will and personality; the new philosophies accepted a remote God, whose action expressed itself in the original creation and in the laws with which He had endowed it. The fact that God should have desired to reveal His intentions beyond this general act was by itself a stumbling block. There was the additional difficulty that such a message should have reached people only in a forlorn corner of the world.

Reason was declared to be capable of grasping the divine intentions fully and clearly. Revelation, which for more than a millenium and a half of Christian theology had been held superior to reason, was now dethroned by autonomous reason. Christian Wolff described revelation as supplementary to reason; insofar as its contents transcended reason, they could not be in conflict with it. This was one of the numerous weak compromises made by many Germans of this generation who were anxious not to lose entirely the faith of their childhood. Every effort was made by theologians to explain everything in Holy Scripture, including miracles, in a rational manner. This was bound to lead to the boldest as well as most platitudinous interpretations.

✍ *Biblical Criticism*

AT THE SAME TIME, this tendency stimulated a critical study of the Bible as the source of Protestant faith. Johann Salomo Semler (1725–91) of Halle was the most eminent scholar. His many books, of which the *Treatise on the Free Analysis of the Canon* deserves special mention, made him the first great German scholar of biblical criticism. A Pietist who throughout his life retained a sincere and warm belief in Christ, he employed rationalism to destroy the very foundation of the Lutheran faith in the validity of the Scripture as the source of our knowledge about original Christianity. In his opinion, the bulk of the Bible set forth the teachings of natural religion, while a smaller part contained differing opinions. The latter, however, were uncanonic, since they had to be cleansed of the ideas and motives deriving from the specific historical circumstances of their origin. Christian religion was older than the New Testament, whose writings had served very specific temporal purposes. Semler hesitated to demand the complete disregard of the canon in the Church, but he drew a distinction between the statutory religion of the Church and free private religion. With regard to the latter, the removal of the canon's authority allowed him to postulate a religious individualism in the tradition of Gottfried Arnold.

Pietism was the fire that drove Semler to burn away all authority in order to reduce Christian religion to its pure core, the religion of the heart. A lonely figure, Hermann Samuel Reimarus of Hamburg (1694–1768) was already at work employing the weapons of rationalism against Christianity as such. Shortly before his death, he completed his *Apologia for Reasonable Worshippers of God*, which he did not wish to see published for the time being, in view of the prevailing religious sentiment. Lessing, who did not agree with Reimarus but wanted to stir up a discussion on the premises and principles of theology, published fragments of the book in 1774–77. Reimarus denied revelation altogether and declared reason the creative power of religion. In one respect Reimarus was less individualistic than Semler, in that he believed in the existence of absolute ideas of reason. Reimarus's attack on Christianity met with general rejection in Germany.

✎ Revision of Church Theology

THE CRITIQUE OF THE CANON was accompanied by a total revision of Church history. Johann Lorenz Mosheim (1693–1755), the first chancellor of Göttingen University, treated ecclesiastical history without any reference to the idea of a *corpus mysticum*. He called the Church "a society subordinated to the legitimate government and its laws and institutions of primarily moral and spiritual intent." Ludwig T. Spittler (1752–1810) made Church history completely part of general history. For about twenty years professor of history in Göttingen, this Swabian was the most eminent German student of Voltaire's historiography and essentially a secular historian. To him the Church was nothing but an institution for the enlightenment of the people. Both the enlightened statesmen of his own age and the great religious reformers were judged by Spittler to be the true promoters of historical progress. Gottlieb J. Planck (1751–1833) continued Spittler's work in Göttingen and also carried rationalistic criticism over into the history of Protestant doctrines, for which orthodoxy claimed the same authority as for the biblical canon. In Planck's treatment the doctrines appeared as "accidental opinions, arbitrary assertions, momentary impressions, aberrations of reason, and worse things."

Natural reason had become a more reliable source of all truth than divine revelation. Inevitably, the rules of piety and ethics were taken from philosophy rather than religion. Melanchthon, in contrast to Luther, had already declared the desire for salvation, the supreme happiness, an acceptable motive of religion. Lutheran orthodoxy had placed even greater emphasis on this eudaemonistic trend. The Enlightenment extended the pursuit of happiness to the whole human life. Leibniz had taught that the endeavor for further perfection and happiness was true morality. It was man's duty to aim high, but the highest happiness was seen only in the achievement of harmony with oneself or in the accommodation of egoistic and altruistic attitudes. In the utilitarianism of an eudaemonistic ethics the new secularism found its clearest expression. But the effort to realize virtue was taken very seriously by the German burgher. With the possible exception of some latitude in sexual matters, which was mild compared to the libertinage of the nobility, the German burgher was conscientious and charitable in his general conduct and frugal in his pleasures.

These generations were conscious of their own worthiness and unwilling to cultivate a spirit of penance. Kneeling disappeared altogether from Lutheran churches in this period, and with this symbol the practice of confession and penance. The Lutheran doctrine of justification was totally abandoned. It seemed objectionable that God should absolve sinners or judge good men sinners. Justice ought to be meted out according to law, and confidence was great that the human wish after goodness would be counted as fulfillment. After all, God had planted in man only the yearning for the good, without giving him the sure capacity for grasping it, while man, on his part, had to defend God for his toleration of evil in this world. The collapse of the trust in revelation and in Christian dogmas led theologians into an apologetic attitude which defended little of the substance of customary Christianity. Small wonder that educated men began to neglect their connections with a Church that had nothing to offer beyond what could be got from philosophy and science. It was also soon to be discovered that more mysteries might be hidden in art than in religion.

✍ *A Rationalistic Literature*

PROFUNDITY WAS NOT a characteristic of German literature in the earlier part of the century. German literature was animated by the religion and philosophy of the Enlightenment. In all its forms it espoused these new ideals. The didactic purpose of poems, plays, and novels was generally taken for granted. The perfection of the world and the beauty of nature formed the subjects of literature, together with man's moral capacity and the happiness he was able to enjoy close to nature. However, the greatest expression of these sentiments did not appear in literature but in Joseph Haydn's *Creation* and *The*

Seasons. A similar world could also be conjured up in a dream, as was done in idyllic poetry, or it could be contrasted with the existing society, which led to satire, although satire stayed away from politics in Germany. Man was the true center of art as a whole, as he was of philosophy. A better understanding of man, it was felt, could be reached if he was firmly placed in the realistic world of natural causality. The imaginative dimension of the world of Dante, Cervantes, or Shakespeare was reduced to mere mythology or allegory when used to interpret nature.

Thus wide provinces of reality were opened by the writers of the period. Their ideal aim was the demonstration of man's common nature and of the human capacity for moral progress. In this enthusiastic hope originated the *Hymn to Joy* of the young Friedrich Schiller, which to Beethoven expressed the noblest creed of mankind when he embodied it in his *Ninth Symphony*. But the rationalistic philosophies of the Enlightenment imposed definite limitations on the understanding of human nature. The heroes of plays and novels acted out of moral conviction, unaffected by passion. Their conflicts were the result of the clash with external forces, the opposition of a still corrupted world, in the form of cruel tyranny or the intolerance of the Church. The tragic which comes from life itself and is inherent in the very nature of man was hidden to the rationalists. The figures they created remained somewhat bloodless and artificial.

✆ *Esthetic Criticism*

THE GROWTH of artistic achievement had to overcome not only the limits of prevalent conceptions of man but also the narrowness of the theory of art. Esthetic criticism had been revived in the Renaissance and had flowered greatly from the time of Descartes on. For a long time Germany was a beneficiary rather than a full partner in this discussion. Its common thesis was that in some form art imparted rational knowledge or moral lessons. The closeness into which philosophy and art were thereby brought made some allowance for the creativity of the artist, thereby raising him beyond the status of a technical craftsman, but it posed serious problems as well. If there was a special logic of imagination as distinct from general logic, it could only be a lower form of knowledge. As such it was described by one of the foremost philosophers of the Leibniz school, Alexander Baumgarten, who, prior to Lessing, made the most important contribution to esthetic theory.

He gave philosophy of art, or as he called it for the first time *Esthetics* (1750), a definite place in academic philosophy. On the other hand, art was often understood as an allegoric presentation of morals. Regardless of whether art was seen to have a logical or moral meaning, the language of sensuous imagination was subordinated to theoretical knowledge.

These theories explain why theoretical minds could hope not only to assist or guide literary production but also to censor and police it, as J. C. Gottsched did. For at least a decade[1] he exercised dictatorial authority in the world of German arts and letters. In accordance with Aristotle, art was still declared to be the emulation of nature or of natural beauty. The decision of what this would mean in practice, however, inevitably depended on the taste formed by historic societies. Gottsched's endeavor to impose narrowly conceived French classicism upon the Germans was bound to dampen the spirit throbbing in the world of German cities. What this spirit was able to achieve as to good style and poetic form, Friedrich von Hagedorn (1708–54) proved in his lyric and epic poems as well as in his fables. Fully at home in both French and English culture, and living comfortably in prosperous Hamburg, Hagedorn expressed the Enlightenment's philosophy of life in such natural and faultless German as had not been heard for centuries.

✍ Swiss Influence

WHEN HAGEDORN'S MAIN WORKS appeared, Gottsched's star was waning. It was the lively and bitter feud with the Swiss school that ruined the belief in his infallibility. Swiss-German cultural relations grew close in the eighteenth century. Basel, Zürich, and Bern were civic communities that impressed the German burghers. With denominational differences between Reformed and Lutheran Protestants losing significance, the exchange of ideas intensified. Swiss feeling revolted at an early moment against the cultural ideals of the France of Louis XIV and Louis XV. The Swiss criticism of French classicism had a strong political undertone. Through the conquest of Alsace, France had become too formidable a neighbor of the Swiss Federation. The Swiss reacted by stressing their own history and character. In the intellectual defense of their political institutions against French

[1] See p. 168.

absolutism, recourse was taken to English constitutionalism, and in the literary field to Shakespeare and Milton.

The Swiss fully accepted the general esthetic theories of the age, though they wanted to change the contents of art. They did not wish to see religious subjects or history and uncultivated nature—they called it "the miraculous"—excluded from the realm of art. From this angle the two Zurich professors Johann J. Bodmer (1698–1783) and Johann J. Breitinger (1701–76) directed their attacks against Gottsched, and after 1740 the German literary movements began using imagination with greater freedom.

In Leipzig, Christian F. Gellert (1717–69) exercised the greatest influence. Even Frederick II found him bearable. Gellert tried himself in many fields. His poetic fables and religious poems, the latter perhaps the classic presentation of the religiosity of German Enlightenment, showed his unpretentious talent at its best. Another literary group assembled in Halle about the middle of the century, including J. P. Uz and J. N. Goetz, who published a German translation of Anacreon in 1746. To the same circle belonged J. W. L. Gleim (1719–1803) and Ewald von Kleist (1715–59). All of them started out in the Anacreontic style, singing of life, spring, roses, and wine. Much of this poetry has survived in German students' songs. Shallow as this Epicurean attitude was, it was often wittily and pleasantly executed, and both Gleim and Kleist went to more serious objects in later life. Ewald von Kleist was a Prussian officer, while all the others made a career in the service of Church and state. Through these men, poetic activities spread to the Prussian capital for the first time. Halle and Berlin were strongly influenced by Swiss esthetic theory.

Switzerland had not only its Bodmer and Breitinger but also in Albrecht von Haller of Bern (1708–77) a lyric and epic talent of distinction. His chief works appeared between 1725 and 1736 and gave vent to the strong sentiments of the Swiss school, the admiration of nature and a natural life joined with a lively patriotism. Haller had a Leibnizian outlook; travel and study in Germany, Holland, and England gave him a universal education. He was one of the eighteenth century's most eminent scientists. With Haller as its first professor of physiology from 1736–53, when nostalgia drove him home to patrician Bern, the new University of Göttingen won its first scientist of European renown.

Haller inspired a higher style among German poets, which was realized in the full sense by Friedrich Klopstock (1724–1803). Reared in the orthodox faith and in the classics, Klopstock left school determined to become the great epic bard whose ideal had been set up by Bodmer, the translator of Milton. In 1748, Klopstock published the first three cantos of his *Messias*, which twenty-five years later he completed with the twentieth canto. It was not a work of the rank of *Paradise Lost*, and outside of religiously conservative Switzerland its subject matter did not attract great interest from the literary public. Klopstock's *Messias* as well as his *Odes* won admiration for the intensity of passionate feeling which his whole poetry breathed and expressed in creative language and form. He succeeded in adapting German to Greek meters, particularly the Homeric hexameter, and he invented German rhythmic verse without rhyme. Klopstock's plastic imagination was inadequate. He was more of a musical spirit. The extraordinary impression that he made on his contemporaries lay in his capacity for setting the individual in relation to the infinite through the exaltation of individual sentiments untrammeled by reason. He liberated German lyric poetry from small prettiness and made it fit for dealing with great ideas. Though in his poetic work a full individuality, free of conformity with general conventions and rules, stood before the public, Klopstock did not have the gift of growing intellectually. He never moved from his original, somewhat archaic, position. He rejected the whole philosophical and literary movement of Goethe, Schiller, and Kant. He also resented the French and anti-Christian philosophy of Frederick II and generally castigated the autocracy and militarism of monarchs. Klopstock welcomed the French Revolution enthusiastically and called upon the German people to rise against their princes. The poet who found a protector in the Danish king and lived in Copenhagen for almost twenty years felt himself the liberator of the German language and turned to Germanic subjects in his later years. Together with Gluck, he hoped to see his *Arminius* turned into a musical drama, but the composer's death frustrated the project. The revival of the Teutonic age as musical drama had to wait for Richard Wagner's *Nibelungen*.

Christoph Martin Wieland (1733–1813) provides a full contrast to the Christian and Germanic Klopstock. Son of a Swabian minister, he lived in Weimar after 1771. Wieland was most indebted to the French literature of Diderot and Voltaire. Enlightened, secular, and elegantly sensual, he never lost himself in mere sentiment. Shrewd and wise through irony, he was endowed with an unusual sense for and mastery

of forms, and a delight in greatness. Wieland's capacity for enjoying
genius made him appreciate Klopstock as well as Goethe, Schiller,
and even the romantics. For the young literary movement in Germany
his understanding of Shakespeare was of greatest consequence. His own
prose and verse, as well as his critical writings display a pulsating and
supple style which was equal to any task he chose. Wieland demonstrated how far German literature had gone in the discovery of the
world, and to what extent even the sensuous world had become an
integral part of German culture. But Wieland's world was too roman-
tically playful and his art too much of a mere response to impressions
to serve as the vessel for the novel intellectual and artistic ideals of the
young. It was Lessing who added bones and marrow to the growing
literary movement in Germany.

✧ *Gotthold Ephraim Lessing*

GOTTHOLD EPHRAIM LESSING (1729–81) came from a Saxon minister's
family. He was the most courageous and effective of German writers
since Ulrich von Hutten. Among German burghers, such a thoroughly
manly character had not been seen before, nor was it often to appear
thereafter. Lessing embodied the ideals of the Enlightenment in full
measure. His lucid and searching mind insisted that human reason
should determine all actions. Man should leave the fear of the supernatural behind him and build a life and world of his own on moral
principles. In Lessing's philosophy nothing quite original can be found.
Rather, his originality lay in the force with which he revitalized the
ideas of the Enlightenment by following their genesis and clarifying
their original intent. This was particularly shown in his esthetic theory,
at which he arrived through a clairvoyant reinterpretation of Aristotle.
Lessing freed art and literature of most superimposed rules alien to
their nature, and thereby gave both the work of the artist and the
enjoyment of art a spiritual justification. Morals were stripped of their
eudaemonistic motives. The good was to be done for its own sake.
With earnest passion Lessing fought not only dogmatic orthodoxy but
also the intellectual shams of the "neologist," that is, rationalistic,
theologians. He conceived of God as actively expressing His infinite
essence in the universe. The individuals are contained in the Deity as
individual thoughts are in reason, and they participate in the divine
process by the development of their potentialities in an active life.
Progress was understood by Lessing as proceeding through various

stages. Returning to life, the migrating souls grow toward the ultimate goal, the absolute moral law, which God has revealed for educational reasons in the Old Testament, and more so in the New Testament. In the end, however, even these revelations will become superfluous, because each soul will find unity with the absolute by the compulsion of its own knowledge.

Lessing's philosophy depended on Leibniz, particularly in its emphasis on the universal development and on the individual. At the same time, it absorbed substantial elements of Spinoza's thought. Though Lessing did not think of himself as a poetic talent of the first order, he wanted to give the Germans a critical understanding of art, and managed to do much more. He laid the foundations of the modern German stage, not only through his constructive criticism, but also through his own plays, of which *Minna von Barnhelm* (1767) and *Nathan the Wise* (1779) are the finest. The former, a comedy, showed the enormous advance that German literature had achieved in the grasp of reality and the realistic visualization of individual persons. *Nathan the Wise* created the drama of ideas, which was to become so important during the next literary period. It was the artistic epitome of the Enlightenment. Lessing's strong plea for religious toleration was not simply the result of religious indifference. Christianity, Judaism, and Mohammedanism are all individuations of the single religion that was in the beginning. They are united both by their common origin and common objective, the perfection of humanity.

Lessing was the first eminent German writer who made literature his profession. He left his academic studies in Halle and, breaking with his parents, went to Berlin in 1748 to make a living with his pen. Later he acted in Leipzig and Hamburg as an adviser and playwright for theater companies. His life remained insecure and unrewarding. Finally he had to accept salaried positions, first in Breslau, then, in 1770, as librarian in Brunswick-Wolfenbüttel. In these hard-pressed circumstances, aggravated by bitter misfortunes in his own family and the invectives of his theological persecutors, the prophet of the "religion of humanity" kept his head high and his mind clear and active.

During his years in Berlin, Lessing gathered a group around him which after his departure exercised an influence greater than that of the philosophers of the Royal Academy. Outstanding among them was Moses Mendelssohn (1729–86), the man to whom Lessing created a monument in his *Nathan the Wise*. From a penniless Jewish youth, Mendelssohn worked his way up to the ownership of a silk firm. His few leisure hours were given to the study of philosophy and to writing. Mendelssohn built a bridge between modern thought and the cultural life of his isolated co-religionists. Remaining a devout member of the Jewish congregation, he participated fully and productively in the Enlightenment movement. Apart from Mendelssohn, Friedrich Nicolai (1733–1811) popularized the cause of the Enlightenment in his popular philosophical tracts and novels, until at the turn of the century the great in Weimar held up his prosaic rationalism to ridicule.

This Berlin school remained considerably behind Lessing in freshness of thought and failed completely to absorb the various new ideas which came to the fore very rapidly after 1770. Lessing himself, though a classic representative of Enlightenment, pushed forward to the limits of its thought. Lessing was still seeking a single rational truth, and even where he saw this truth as the result of an unfolding process, he tied this development to a general law of successive stages. He rejected the historical proof of Christianity as irrelevant to the formation of a philosophy of life because of the relativity of history. What was truth to the people of the first century was not necessarily true for other ages. But Lessing assigned to the individual a creative capacity, which was only uneasily harmonized with the uniform truth of reason. The term "genius" that he applied to the great artists of history merely implied knowledge of the right art rather than full spontaneity. Once the conception of the "genius" was broadened, it was inevitable to conclude that a single truth could not embrace all phenomena of the various stages of history. But it could also happen that through further analysis the individual elements of Western civilization separated. For all thinkers Christianity and classic antiquity had been complementary ideal forces, and Lessing did not depart from this tradition. But the men were already at work who were to break up the synthesis of antiquity and Christian religion and offer a new view of the creative power of man. Johann Winckelmann and Jean Jacques Rousseau were to make their influence felt.

✑ Winckelmann

JOHANN JOACHIM WINCKELMANN (1717–68) was born a poor shoemaker's son in the stagnant provincial town of Stendal in the Old Mark. He suffered great want in his youth, but later on was to suffer even more deeply from hunger for beauty. He was lucky enough eventually to find a noble patron, and in the art collections of Dresden he was able to develop his new vision of classic art. His burning desire to go to Rome was fulfilled, although at the price of his conversion to the Roman Catholic Church. From 1755 on, he lived in Rome enjoying the favors and friendship of Cardinal Alessandro Albani, a great art collector. Winckelmann's conceptions of art, which, at least in embryonic form, were already contained in a small book that he published in 1755 before he went to Rome, received their final elaboration in his *History of the Art of Antiquity* of 1764, probably the first German book read widely even outside of Germany.

In his original search for a new artistic taste, Winckelmann was affected by dissatisfaction with the new public spirit in Germany. Political freedom to him was the proper soil for art. His critique of Baroque art came from an inner opposition to the despotism of the age, which he identified largely as French influence, as the Swiss had done. From Bernini and Michelangelo, whom he condemned, he went back to Raffael, the classic master, and from him he reached out for ancient Hellas. In Greek art he found the normative ideal of beauty. Needless to say, it was not Winckelmann who was responsible for the demise of the Baroque. The latter was dying in the climate of rationalism, and enlightened despotism had already shown a growing taste for classic ideals. Winckelmann's thinking was deeply embedded in the general intellectual atmosphere of Europe. Shaftesbury taught him to find his way back to Plato, Montesquieu opened approaches to historical interpretation, and the French archeologist Count Caylus had given at least a hint about a certain connection between art and national character. But Winckelmann gave the classicist ideal both concreteness and a new justification. So far art had been understood by the critics through an attempted analysis of the creative act of the artist. Winckelmann placed the work of art itself on a pedestal and insisted that art should be seen not as a pleasant impression or charming decoration, but as the expression of a higher existence. The greatest art was to be not just beautiful but sublime. This Winckelmann found realized in Greek art, especially in Greek sculpture of the fifth century. Sculpture, with is reduction to simple lines and forms was to him the truest art. The sculpture of the Periclean age he considered the supreme fulfillment because it was natural, though not in the sense of naturalism. The Greek artists had emulated nature by revealing its ideal forms. Thereby they had uncovered the reality of the eternal, which, though invisible, was present in the work. Whereas the idea of the true or the good was elusive, the idea of beauty became real in the work of art.

This Platonic conception led Winckelmann to characterize Greek art as displaying "noble simplicity and serene calm," and to demand the imitation of the ancients as the only way to greatness.

Art thereby became a sacred matter, and its works were described by Winckelmann in the language of sentiment. Beauty was comprehended through impressions, not through rational argument. The sensuous and spiritual faculties of man together opened access to the work of art. This "inner sense," as Winckelmann called it, was a desire which, unlike other human cravings, was not aimed at possession but at experiencing the appearance of the absolute in the sensual. Closely analyzed, this desire is not stilled but only transformed into a deeper longing for the invisible world of absolute forms. The nostalgic sentiment that characterized Winckelmann's thinking was also reflected in the very fact that he found his ideal in the past. Although he recommended its emulation to his contemporaries, he was simultaneously convinced that this past was irretrievable.

Winckelmann was the father of a new history of art. So far the history of art had been the history of artists in the Vasari style. In his *History of the Art of Antiquity*, Winckelmann conceived of Greek art as the expression of a nation and saw the relations between the development of art and the change in general conditions. The historiography of Voltaire and Montesquieu with its "spirit" or "genius" of nations and ages prepared the ground for Winckelmann's history. In explaining the reasons for the excellence of the Greeks, he used the rationalistic terms of Western European Enlightenment rather freely. Nevertheless, he opened a new gate to the world of history, through which many others, and in particular Herder, were to follow.

Winckelmann's theories deviated strongly from the general course of German thinking. Art was no longer considered a lower form of knowledge or ethics but became autonomous, therefore calling for its own method of intuition rather than rational comprehension. Ideal beauty could not be constructed, but had grown in a unique historical climate. It was illogical that at the same time Winckelmann established this historic ideal as the absolute model of art. While in this respect he remained a child of the century that sought the absolute norm, this incongruity also betrayed the intensity of his feeling. The enjoyment of Greek art was his religion, compared to which Christianity was insignificant. Goethe had already commented on Winckelmann's pagan mind, on his "worship of the gods as ancestors," and "the admiration of them as if they were works of art." Antiquity and Christianity were divorced, and Winckelmann adopted an esthetic humanism. He was far from proclaiming a naturalistic or materialistic philosophy; on the contrary, it was a humanism built on spirit and resting on a Platonic monism. This new humanism became one of the great forces in modern German civilization through Goethe, Schiller, and Wilhelm von Humboldt. Friedrich August Wolf (1759–1824) became the founder of the new scholarship of the classics, which placed the Greeks as the more creative nation above the Romans and attempted to revive ancient *humanitas.*

✍ *Jean Jacques Rousseau*

BEFORE WINCKELMANN'S TEACHINGS could make their full impact felt, another influence was avidly absorbed in Germany. In the years 1761–62 Jean Jacques Rousseau's (1712–88) *Social Contract, Nouvelle Héloïse,* and *Émile* appeared, and he reached the height of his fame. The impression made by Rousseau on the young generation was great. His personality gave encouragement to all individualistic stirrings, and his writings helped to bring forth a poetry and literature that took as their subject the inner experiences of the author himself. Rousseau's impassioned protests against modern civilization and the crippling effect of a mechanistic rationalism upon man found a keen hearing in Germany. His ideas of a live nature as well as of the power of the human will and feeling, in which he saw the curative forces of humanity, had the warmest echo. Like his philosophical opponents in France, Rousseau was looking for general solutions. He was unable to illustrate or prove through historical argument his chief thesis that historical civilization had ruined man. His religion remained deistic. "Natural religion" was the normative truth. While all religions contained elements of relative truth, Christian religion and Protestantism approached natural religion most closely. But religious truth was not gained by reflection but rather a *sentiment intérieur,* which grows in the simplicity of an unspoiled heart.

In order to restore the capacities of natural man, Rousseau presented programs of the reform of society and education. It was characteristic that Rousseau's political creed contributed greatly to the revolutionary development in France, whereas the fundamental ideas on which his educational philosophy rested did not find a ready response there. These ideas became more persuasive only after 1815, when they began to infiltrate back in the guise of German idealism. In Germany it was

Rousseau's educational program that kindled a flame, whereas his political ideas, though exercising a certain influence on Kant and Fichte, failed to set a fire.

✑ *Herder*

JOHANN GOTTFRIED HERDER (1744–1803) early experienced the impact of Winckelmann's and Rousseau's ideas. An East Prussian by birth, he studied in Königsberg under Kant, who in these years presented the philosophy of the German Enlightenment in a form comparable to that of Lessing. But Herder was more deeply affected by the sibyllic wisdom of another Königsberg writer, J. G. Hamann, who, starting from a pietistic belief, had developed a radical antirationalistic position. As a young teacher and minister in Riga, Herder gained impressions of the Slav world and of the primitive culture of the Letts and Lithuanians. After two years of travel, during which the memorable meetings with Goethe in Strasbourg took place, and after a few years as ecclesiastic councilor in Bückeburg, the little capital of Lippe, Herder came to Weimar as head of the Lutheran Church. One of the richest and most fertile minds, he spread a wealth of fresh and original ideas. These were eagerly absorbed not only by his German contemporaries but also by subsequent generations of European, particularly Slav, intellectuals. Herder's ideas have been much misunderstood. They underwent great change and never were systematically summarized. His capacity for large-scale composition was weak, as was his ability to define terms sharply. Kant remarked that Herder lacked "logical precision of terms," although he possessed "a perfect sagacity in finding and using analogies." Herder's was an esthetic and poetic mind, which worked through the ear rather than the eye.

The trend toward a new concept of man, which had gathered momentum from Shaftesbury to Rousseau and Winckelmann, found its consummation in Herder. The very forces in man that most thinkers of the European Enlightenment had decried as unruly passions, ignorance, and superstition, were proclaimed to be an integral part of personality. Out of the totality of the human person sprang the "inner sentiment" which was the womb of all his ideas and actions. Truth was not the product of reason but of the whole creative power of the individual, and it was expressed in language, myth, religion, and poetry rather than reflection. Consequently, there is not a single truth or norm, but only the multiplicity of historical forms. No single region, age, or nation possesses the whole content of humanity, which runs through history in thousands of forms and in continuous change. Nor, in Herder's view, can a higher or lesser value be attached to early or late stages of civilization. As childhood is not a mere means toward manhood but has its own needs and ideals, primitive civilizations have their own worth. In their language and poetry, they express a more genuine truthfulness than the philosophies of ripe cultures, in which the harmonious totality of human beings has become subverted by artificial reflection.

It is not difficult to discover in these observations the contrast between the *homme naturel* and *homme artificiel* of Rousseau. But Herder approached the problem from a different angle. He was thinking exclusively in terms of culture. For Herder the absolute state, being a soulless machine, was an object of bitter hatred. He despised the monarchy of Frederick II, in which he was born, as a Pyrrhic realm and felt sure that his "subjugated fatherland" would be happy only if its parts were brought together in a fraternal confederation. Herder welcomed the French Revolution, because it brought absolutism in France to an end. But he criticized the regime of the Jacobins, those "daring, proud, and presumptuous men, who feel themselves chosen to organize everything and impress their image on everybody. It is fortunate that these demons appear infrequently; a few of them can spread misfortune for generations." The state, particularly the state built on cold power, seemed to Herder an institution that alienated man from his natural humane tasks. Herder was particularly critical of Frederick's monarchy, because it opposed German civilization. However, he could be friendly toward Peter the Great and Catherine as acting in conformity with nationality. His preference was an old-fashioned paternalistic state. Rousseau's ideal of equality left him unaffected.

Herder's thinking circled around the cultural activities of humanity, on *Volk* rather than *Staat*. The creativity of humanity realizes itself in human virtues, mores, and arts, and differs in different peoples and ages, with each expressing its innate natural qualities. Nations aim at their happiness, but even happiness assumes variegated meanings. "Every nation has in itself its center of happiness, as every sphere has its center of gravity." While Leibniz had spoken of the monads as "living mirrors of the universe," Herder took the nations as living mirrors, each reflecting humanity at its particular angle of refraction. Early folk-poetry is art as much as civilized literature, Homer as great as Sophocles. Herder admitted that individuality could not be catholic in its tastes and aspirations, but he judged such "nationalism"—a word he coined—a useful incentive for the vigorous growth of historic civilizations.

No direct way led from Herder's cultural nation to the modern political nation. Herder's nations, or *Völker*, were striving for *humanitas*, not for political organization. He did not endow them with the right of national self-determination. But Herder's nationalism could create a consciousness of cultural community of national scope, which was to gain high political significance in the future. If his political—or should we rather say antipolitical—ideas had not entered into relations with other thoughts, they would have led to a traditionalist and anticentralistic attitude. But where his quietistic nationalism was brought together with Kant's or Fichte's autonomy of the human will or with the ideas of the French Revolution, his philosophy acquired an explosive political force. This had already been shown in German national feeling during the Napoleonic period. It assumed larger proportions in the liberation movement of the Slav nations during the nineteenth century.

As a philosopher, Herder failed to produce a systematic view of history. On the whole, he represented a more or less qualified pantheism, although as a theologian he wished to retain some semblance of theism. Originally, he constructed universal history as guided by providence, but later he tried to imbed history in nature in vitalistic terms, though not in a materialistic or naturalistic fashion. Yet all his philosophical constructions still came down to the assumption of humanity as the genetic force producing true *humanitas* in its genuine historical realization. Religion to him was essentially an elevated form of humanity. The Bible was declared to be a human book "written by men for men." The Old Testament was a treasure of Hebrew folk-poetry. Theological exegesis with a view to Christian dogmas seemed to Herder an absurdity. This transformed even Christian revelation into a product of the *Volksgeist*. Herder was unable to establish a law of historical development. He was what he had originally wished to become, "the historian of the human soul." Culture sprang from the totality of feeling of young nations. This totality was in jeopardy through the artificial elements of subsequent cultural developments. But true genius could regenerate civilization. A genius such as Shakespeare rejuvenates language and poetry and with it the natural creative power of man.

◢ Goethe

WHEN HERDER BEGAN TO EXPOUND HIS THEORIES on the role of the genius, he had already come into contact with Goethe and together with him ushered in "the period of genius," or of "Storm and Stress" (*Sturm und Drang*) in German literary history. In 1773, Goethe published his *Goetz von Berlichingen*, a play in the Shakespearean manner, which disregarded all the classical forms of contemporary drama, including that of Lessing. Its subject was equally anomalous: it was the world of the German Middle Ages depicted as the age of genuine *humanitas*, of full-blooded life and heroic action. The *Goetz* was written as a protest against the artificial conventions and philistine dullness of the existing order. A year later, *The Sorrows of Werther* appeared, a novel in which a lonely soul of utmost sensitivity is disintegrating in its conflict with reality. *Werther* aroused a storm of feeling not only in Germany but also in Europe.

Werther surpassed Rousseau's *Nouvelle Héloïse* by Goethe's superior imaginative power, the like of which none of his closest literary friends and emulators possessed. Their revolt against the traditional order, however, was radical and went beyond literature to the critique of social and political conditions. In 1790 Goethe remarked: "It hardly occurred to anybody in my youth to envy the privileged class or grudge them their privileges. But knights, robbers, an honest Third Estate, and an infamous nobility—such have been the ingredients of our novels and plays during the last ten years." But the revolutionary drive launched by these young writers did not get anywhere. It may have created a certain predisposition toward social reforms; beyond that it only contributed to the reform of private social forms. This was quite important with regard to marriage and family, while of more symbolic significance in the case of dress. Goethe and his duke abandoned the rococo costume and were seen in the "Werther costume," which was less effeminate and more suitable for roaming the countryside.

H. L. Wagner, M. R. Lenz, and F. M. Klinger, whose play *Sturm und Drang* gave the whole movement its name, were soon forgotten as writers. Others, such as the champion of immoralism, Wilhelm Heinse (1749–1803), or the poets of the Goettingen circle *Hain* ("The Grove"), contributed little that survived these years. When the literary uproar seemed to have quieted down, a young Swabian, Friedrich Schiller (1759–1805), presented his *Robbers* in 1781, *Fiesco* in 1783, and *Love and Intrigue* in 1784, all of them passionate indictments of tyranny. These plays displayed a high talent for stage effect, and even though they were not free of clichés and literary exaggerations, they breathed a genuine and pure enthusiasm.

Goethe, in the meantime, had gone new ways after 1775, when he came to Weimar. His first decade in Weimar was the time in which he conceived his greatest visions, and works such as *Faust* and *Wilhelm Meister* were to accompany him through the rest of his life. His activities as minister of state gave Goethe concrete tasks and an insight into the life of the community. His love of Charlotte von Stein became the source of a happiness which rested on the feeling of personal growth. In these years Goethe's lyric poetry seemed to flow out of him without any effort, while at the same time he absorbed ever-expanding realms of the spirit. Next to Leibniz, he was the most universal mind of all historic Germans. When his personal duties and commitments in Weimar proved an obstacle to his search for development, he went to Italy in 1785. Under a southern sky, in the world of antiquity, he found assurance about his own personal existence. He returned from Italy in 1787 a classicist. As he thereby set limits to the freedom of esthetic style, he simultaneously began to fit his life into a definite pattern. His marriage, the resumption of some official duties, henceforth confined to the administration of education, the theater and the arts, as well as his complete devotion to his own productive work, characterized a life which moved on a steady and unbroken course. For the first time in 1790, he published a set of *Collected Works*. In addition to his great lyric poems, these *Works* included the new classic plays, *Iphigenia of Tauris* and *Tasso*, the *Faust* fragment, and the first part of *Wilhelm Meister*. Only now could the German public see Goethe's full stature and the new philosophy he expressed.

Although Goethe was the greatest German lyric poet, he is not an equal of Homer, Dante, or Shakespeare, in spite of the world-wide acceptance of *Faust*. But the unity of his personality and artistic achievement gave Goethe a unique position at the threshold of our own age. It was the inner life of the artist himself that became the subject of art. In his old age Goethe remarked that all his works were fragments of one single confession. He called his autobiography *Poetry and Truth*, not because he felt that he had mixed fiction with facts, but in order to indicate that he had raised the figures and events of his personal memory to symbolic validity. Rousseau had shown the path in this direction, but his ability to mirror the world outside was limited whereas Goethe's capacity for reflecting the world objectively was supreme. The miracle of his genius was the interplay of his artistic imagination with the passionate search for the perfection of his personality. Poetry was his way of bringing reality into clear focus and making it his own. But at the same time artistic objectivity was the means for harmonizing the deep feelings which all the phenomena of human spirit and life aroused in him. The continuous dialogue over great objects which went on in Goethe's heart and mind made such works as *Faust* possible.

Goethe was not a philosopher who thought in abstract, logical terms. Rather, he contented himself with finding wisdom in symbolic signs. To him, nature was a living universe. The infinite power by which it is animated produces the multiplicity of forms and the levels of life which rise from rocks and plants to the human being. Goethe's was a pantheism that accepted the world as a good world. This did not mean that everything in this world was to be judged good. The divine power which enlivened the world was pushing toward ever higher forms, and only where spirit and nature coincided was the fullness of life achieved. Thus the imagination of the artist continues the creative work of nature by perceiving the typical forms of nature and bringing them into consciousness. The universe was the emanation of primordial typical forms (*Urphänomene*). Newton's geometrical and mechanistic universe, a conception to which the future belonged, was disliked by Goethe. He disapproved of microscopes, because they presupposed that the observation of parts would lead to an understanding of the whole of nature, while, as in art, the parts could only be interpreted after the meaning of the whole had been found. But Goethe's own scientific studies, such as his morphology of plants or theory of colors, proved fruitful in physiology and biology.

Nature and individuality were the two poles of Goethe's thinking, in which Christian religion had no real place. He himself said that, though not anti-Christian or un-Christian, he was "decidedly a non-Christian." He had a deep respect for Christianity in its original period, but he saw it as a historical culmination, never as a source of absolute wisdom. Man was endowed by nature to grow and mature by his own effort. "If God had wanted me to be a worm, he would have created me a worm." With quite unusual acerbity he remarked that Kant had soiled his philosopher's toga by imputing a "radical evil" to man. Human self-perfection was achieved through the individual, not through society or the state. Goethe's grasp of the history of culture and art was extraordinary, and occasionally he showed deep insight into political history. But the latter was for him the least interesting part of nature, since chance played a deplorably big part, and the smell of death hung over it. The state depended for its health on the individual, who was expected to work actively for preservation of the natural social order. Prudent rulers and diligent citizens were called for. Goethe was a good representative of the spirit of enlightened absolutism of the antimilitary and benevolent variety. Still, his heart beat faster when he discovered great political figures, such as Frederick, and he became a great admirer of Napoleon.

Goethe, as he himself knew very well, was a product of the German burgher class in its eighteenth-century circumstances. As such he was driven into the inner and private life as the scene of all major human conflicts. The great political struggles among nations, as well as the whole world of social conflicts and sufferings, remained outside the purview of his poetic or philosophical work. The provinces of nature and spirit that he mastered were of such magnitude as few people ever commanded, and he molded them into a cosmos of beauty and wisdom. This he achieved after his return from Italy by confining himself to a predominantly contemplative existence. The volcano that burned in him was held back, and the tragic dissonances of human existence that threatened to overwhelm him in his youth were moderated. This *Entsagung,* or self-denial, was the personal sacrifice made to his work.

ᡃ Friedrich Schiller

AFTER A YOUTH MADE OPPRESSIVE by narrow surroundings and unbearable by the tyranny of Duke Carl Eugene of Württemberg, Friedrich Schiller found his first expression in the *Sturm und Drang.* The young Swabian, who in his *Robbers* turned Rousseau's call to nature into an idealization of gangsters taking to the woods in order to fight a degrading civilization, showed a strong political and revolutionary temper. In the years after 1784, he went through a transformation which led him, like Goethe, to a sublimation of his personality. As a writer, Schiller went beyond radical subjectivism to a restraining idealism and classic forms. Strength of character and will power carried him over chaotic years beset by poverty and profound worries until he was able to settle down and found a home in Jena, and afterward in Weimar. But the years of his highest productivity, between 1789 and 1805, stood under the shadow of growing illness, against which he maintained his unequaled purity of feeling and bold devotion to high ideals.

While Goethe was the poet who wished to expand his personality by developing the core of his own being and who found in nature the element of his existence, Schiller reached out in the sphere of human moral action. He had grown up in the tradition of the philosophy of Leibniz and Wolff and subsequently had absorbed the ideas of the Shaftesbury school. But out of these ideas he early formed a pantheistic interpretation of the universe which reveled in its beauty and the divine nature of man. More than anybody except Rousseau, Schiller was convinced of the solidarity of mankind and its destiny toward progress, perfection, and happiness. Rousseau's revolt against stifling conventions also found a fervent believer in Schiller. Civilization must be grounded in nature and achieve its ultimate goal in a free state of reason. Kant accepted the same scheme. But Schiller went beyond both Rousseau and Kant in his concrete ideal of *humanitas*, in which sensuality and reason were brought into synthesis. To art he assigned the function of raising man beyond mere knowledge, to the level of the beautiful and harmonious personality, for which the Greeks in the past and Goethe in the present served as models. Only after this new humanity had come into being was it possible to build the free state of reason. For this humanity was not yet prepared, as the course of the French Revolution proved to Schiller.

While Schiller thus gave up a revolution of the state, he clung to the educational and public task of the artist. Ethereal as many of Schiller's thoughts may appear, they never were mere esthetics. Sensuality, which craves possession of the object of its desires and thus forever ties man to a material world, enters into unity with spirit in art. The work of art, though enjoyed through feeling, does not elicit the wish for possession but, owing to its ideal character, elicits a consciousness of the transcendence of life. The experience of artistic form is the intermediary stage between the sensual and rational man. As Schiller put it: "Through the morning gate of beauty we enter into the realm of truth." But for Schiller it was the duty of the artist to use the key of art for opening the moral world and revealing the conflict between matter and spirit, freedom and destiny, as well as the tragedy they cast over the lives of the individuals. Man, however, gives the world form and meaning by his creative mind and thus achieves freedom. Even in defeat the idealist cannot lose his greatness, which does not lie in his physical or material existence.

From history Schiller took the subjects that were adequate to his heroic character. His tragedies *Don Carlos*, of 1787, then the sequence of the years 1799–1804, *Wallenstein, Mary Stuart, Maid of Orléans, Bride of Messina*, and *Wilhelm Tell*, attempted to present human nature and fate in great and ideal dimensions. The plays were constructed intellectually, and the didactic aim, to educate a future generation of free men, was not always successfully veiled, but Schiller had a supreme sense for the possibilities of the stage and dramatic action. Beyond that, he had at his command a language of plastic expression and musical rhythm that gave his plays a poetic beauty of rare quality. Schiller was the true creator of the modern German theater. Since he felt that the study of philosophical thought had liberated him from doubt and fear, he wished to speak of the philosophical position he was gaining in the course of these years. He overcame the danger of sermonizing not only through the magic of his language but also by showing the lofty sentiments which accompany sublime ideas. If Goethe prayed: "Give us a pure heart and great thoughts," this prayer was movingly fulfilled in Schiller, and if the latter maintained that art led the way to truth and reason, his philosophical odes and poems did just this.

In 1794, Goethe and Schiller met in Jena, and a close friendship developed, which lasted to Schiller's early death in 1805. It was a relationship that rested on mutual admiration and common literary and philosophical interests, as well as on the consciousness of their complementary characters. The direction of the Weimar theater by Goethe and Schiller's editorship of critical literary organs in the neighboring Jena provided the two men with the channels through which they addressed the educated public of Germany. In this decade they exercised a consular rule over the learned republic. Schiller's presence in Jena until 1799, when he moved to Weimar, and Goethe's administration of Jena University made the little academic town a center of attraction. Laying the foundation for his own humanism, Wilhelm von Humboldt lived here for some years in close contact with Schiller and Goethe. Through K. L. Reinhold (1758–1823) the university became the first school outside of Königsberg to represent the critical philosophy of Kant. Fichte came to Jena in 1794, Schelling in 1798, and Hegel in 1801. No place outside of classic Greece can boast of having been home to so many great philosophers in a single decade. That this should happen in the university of the duchy of Weimar was symptomatic of the close connection that existed between

the rise of the new German literature and philosophy. The two movements were only two branches of a single stream that produced the
transition toward a new German culture.

∽ *Immanuel Kant*

IMMANUEL KANT (1724–1804), on whose work the future German
philosophy depended, was born the son of a poor master-craftsman in
Königsberg. Throughout his life, he rarely ventured beyond the city-
line and never crossed the boundaries of East Prussia. In 1755, he became a lecturer at the university and patiently waited for a professorship in Königsberg, but Frederick II passed him by in filling a vacancy.
Kant became well known as an able writer on philosophical subjects
and formulated a theory of the origins of the universe which, as the
theory of Kant-Laplace, has played an important role in modern
science. Only in 1770 did Kant receive a professorship. He then was a
true representative of the German Enlightenment, probably next to
Lessing its best interpreter, and a most effective academic teacher who
was also befriended by the intellectually inclined members of the
Prussian nobility.

From scientific problems, Kant turned in his publications to esthetic
and moral questions, a change that reflects the impression that Rousseau made on him. But starting in the late 1760's a period of silence followed, during which he was completely absorbed in cutting loose
from existing philosophical traditions. He was almost a sexagenarian
when, in 1781, he published his *Critique of Pure Reason*, followed in
1788 by *Critique of Practical Reason*, and, in 1790, by *Critique of
Judgment*. In the remaining years of his life he issued other smaller
works, among them *Religion in the Limits of Pure Reason* (1793)
and *On Eternal Peace* (1795). The pleasant style of Kant's early "pre-
critical" writings is rarely found in his later works, which marked a
new period of Western philosophy.

Kant stood in the tradition of modern philosophy which Descartes
had begun. Like the great French thinker, Kant, in his intent to prove
the validity of knowledge as manifested in modern science, started
from the consciousness of the individual. Descartes, and equally Leibniz, had to overcome the difficulty of bridging the absolute gulf that
existed between human consciousness and the world of appearance,
and they had done so by the assumption of certain metaphysical
notions. Locke and Hume had criticized this metaphysical practice.

The British philosophers had expounded a strictly "scientific" empirical approach to reality and argued that no concept of reason could claim to be universal and necessary. General ideas did not go beyond the particular and were formulated by custom, not reason. British empiricism abolished not only metaphysics, but also the belief in the rule of reason over reality.

Locke had not gained many followers in Germany, where the Leibniz-Wolff school held almost absolute sway. This school, however, would not have held its own permanently, particularly after David Hume gave English empiricism a new and powerful expression. It was Hume's skepticism with regard to the capacity of reason to organize reality, rather than empiricism, which Kant opposed. Kant's philosophical "criticism" set limits to reason, but only in order to make the throne of reason secure against skepticism. He denied the whole metaphysical tradition as it had come down from Aristotle and the Stoa to Descartes, Spinoza, and Leibniz and confined all knowledge to experience, while remaining a staunch defender of rationalism. The *Critique of Pure Reason* demonstrated that British empiricists had not provided the means by which the human mind organized the objects of experience. Kant showed that the human mind arranged the manifold impressions and sensations through universal patterns, the forms of "intuition" (space and time) and of "understanding" (the categories), such as causality, reality, unity, and the like into a coherent experience. These concepts precede all actual experience, they are *a priori*, and as a matter of fact, only this *a priori* mode of human knowledge makes an ordered experience possible. Reality, as a necessary and universal order, originates with the subject through acts of intuition and understanding, which constitute the very structure of the human mind. They are not arbitrary acts of the individual but universal and necessary acts of objective judgments. The forms of intuition relate the variegated sensations and impressions in a spatiotemporal system, and the categories of understanding organize the objects of experience as reality, unity, cause and effect, and so on. All these acts of intellectual synthesis are ultimately unified in the "transcendental apperception," the consciousness, of the thinking subject, of the continuity of his experience and of his active thinking role in all his experiences.

The *a priori* concepts are operative only in the realm of sensations and impressions, which in turn become knowable within these concepts. But the "things in themselves," which we must suppose to exist outside these conceptual forms and to cause our sense impressions, cannot be known. Here then the limits of all theoretical knowledge were reached and thereby all metaphysics banned. In this respect Moses Mendelssohn could call Kant "the great demolisher" (*der alles zermalmende Kant*). Critical and methodological knowledge—or *Wissenschaft*—was confined to the science of nature.

Kant's epistemology was essentially a philosophical justification of Newtonian science. He found it in a radical departure from the traditional conception of science. Science to him was not the copying or depicting of nature but a synthesis of perceptions according to the universal norms of the human mind. It is philosophy's task to bring these norms into clear consciousness by removing dogmatic prejudices from science and restoring its creative spontaneity.

In this Kantian scheme theoretical reason remained excluded from an objective knowledge of the thing-in-itself, a skepticism much criticized by subsequent German philosophers, such as Schelling and Hegel. But Kant believed that theoretical reason was only one of the activities of the human mind. Thinking, willing, and feeling are the functions of the human mind, and in the study of the two latter Kant saw the way to enter into the region beyond the perceptible world. The *Critique of Practical Reason* analyzed the practical application of reason, or the moral will. Not the relationship between perceptions and theoretical judgments but that between will and ends is the subject of philosophical ethics. Here again a solution could not be expected from the contents of an empirical will but only from an *a priori* synthesis, which must assume the form of a moral law or imperative. Desires directed toward empirical objects are dependent on them and, therefore, not actions of a pure will. In practical life, naturally, an individual has to will certain means in order to achieve certain ends. From here, however, only counsels of prudence can be derived, or "hypothetical imperatives." True moral action cannot be built on any personal wish, even on such high wishes as those for happiness or perfection. If nature had intended to make happiness the destiny of man, it would have endowed him with an unfailing instinct rather than with a conscience constantly in conflict with man's desires. A rational moral will can never be defined philosophically by something that is outside the realm of reason. Nothing is good but a good will. Consequently, the moral law, or a "categorical imperative," must be the result of the autonomy or self-determination of practical reason. The human will must freely accept the duty expressed in maxims which could serve as principles of a general legislation for men of practical reason. Kant arrives at this formulation of the categorical imperative: "Never act in such a way that you could not will that your maxim should be a universal law."

A general moral law was thus established, which did not make any allowance for the individual, from whose consciousness it originally sprang. It was democratic in the sense that it demanded strict conformity from each individual. The dignity of man rests upon his capacity to respect a law without looking at his personal advantage. In this light man is a moral end to himself, and Kant demanded: "Act in such a way as never to use humanity, whether in your own person or in any other person, as a mere means, but always at the same time as an end." Morality is possible only as a result of freedom, and although theoretical reason cannot produce proof of the reality of freedom, it cannot refute it either. Since, however, freedom must be real if morality is to exist, the reality of the thing-in-itself is demonstrated by practical reason. But the certainty thus achieved is quite different from theoretical knowledge. Conscience and the belief in the ability to follow its advice make it necessary to accept the corollaries which make moral action possible. The conception of freedom is not an object of knowledge but a postulate, an act of faith, yet of a faith which is *a priori*, and therefore necessary and universal.

Practical reason was thus made independent from pure reason, and this brought the sensible world and the moral world into sharp conflict. As a member of the former, man was bound by the necessity that ruled nature, while as a member of the latter, the noumenal or intelligible world, man had freedom. Because moral consciousness opened the way to a sphere transcending the actual world, Kant saw in it the only way to justify religion. His own philosophical ethics showed its origin in the old Lutheran ethics, which his pietistic mother and early teachers had planted deeply into his heart. His criticism of the shallow utilitarian ethics of the eighteenth century bore a genuinely Lutheran stamp. In his philosophy of religion, particularly in his assumption of a "radical evil" in man, similar Lutheran traits became noticeable. But Kant did not think of himself as a real Christian. Theological ethics he rejected altogether. The natural religion of the *philosophes* became in his hands a rational religion of morality, and although he kept God, soul, and immortality as ideas, his rationalism completed the dissolution of the Christian dogma. The visible Church needs a statutory faith, which is, however, not absolute and certainly ought to be freed from "the stupidity of superstition and the madness of fanaticism." But the visible

Church was only an external representation of the Church invisible, which in turn remained a mere rational symbol as the spiritual community of moral men working toward the realization of the moral law in the history of humanity.

The state was the realm in which the relationship between moral freedom and natural necessity had to be worked out. Kant's political thought was fully developed only in the years immediately before the French Revolution and the years thereafter. Even before the Revolution, Kant had looked for the extension of moral freedom to the political world. In the Revolution, which he called an unforgettable act in human history, he saw a great moral act transforming the world of necessity. Throughout the 1790's he remained an admirer of the French Revolution, in spite of the "misery and atrocities" that followed in its wake. His early thinking about the state had not substantially differed from the customary theories about enlightened absolutism. Since the faculties of reason will be fully developed in the species, not in the individual, a "civil society" is needed which enforces the general will against refractory individual wills. The simultaneous emphasis on spiritual freedom was quite compatible with an institution destined to control nature in order to prepare the ground for the growth of morality, which was beyond the realm of politics.

But in his later works Kant expounded a closer connection between morality and civil society. He demanded not only "civil equality" and "civil liberty," that is, the protection of the rights of the individual to life and livelihood against violation by other individuals and the government but also "legislative freedom," the rights of citizens in a representative constitutional state. Kant accepted the theory of popular sovereignty. But he admitted that the ideal of a self-legislating sovereign people was "only an idea," because he could not see how to do away with a compulsory state which was needed to hold down the immoral and unfree acts of man. The ideal representative—Kant called it "republican"—constitution was a model applicable to rulers of any state. Monarchs must "rule autocratically and administer republicanly," and this meant in analogy to rational laws which a people could give itself.

In the absence of any right of the citizen to oppose an unlawful government, the practical result of Kant's philosophical construction of liberal political rights was very modest. The hope that rulers might conform to "republicanism" in their autocratic actions was proved not entirely vain in the period of Prussian Reform. But it was unrealistic that Kant, with his demand for the equality of all individuals, disregarded the class character of the existing German states altogether. Still, Kant opened a period of history in which the philosophers became the leaders in the forging of political programs.

Another attempt of Kant to relate the sensuous and the intelligible world became more immediately effective. It was his philosophy of art contained in his *Critique of Judgment.* In the *Critique of Pure Reason* and *Critique of Practical Reason* rationality went as far as the knowledge of the forms, of the general laws in theoretical reason and the universal norms in practical reason. In the former the perceived objects, and in the latter the empirical will, remained in an impenetrable shadow of irrationality. But organic nature and art did not fit into this Kantian scheme. They never are based on general rules but always related to an individual example, while at the same time claiming general approval. The judgment that a landscape or work of art is beautiful or sublime is always directed toward the specific, though it demands general validity. Kant found his solution in the teleological character of works of art and organic beings. The inherent unity of constituent parts in a whole make us look at them *as if* they had been endowed with an end by an unknown creator. Neither scientific laws nor ethical norms apply to teleological judgments, which point beyond intellect and reason. With regard to art, Kant also acknowledged a productive capacity beyond the thinking faculties of man. In the artistic "genius" appears an intelligence that acts unlike nature. In his treatment of art, Kant moved farthest away from a philosophical dualism. By way of philosophical reasoning he arrived at an intellectual position closely akin to the one that the great German writers had achieved in the same period.

The impact of Kant's critical philosophy on German thought was immense. During the next fifty years, the philosophical life in Germany did not absorb any contemporary philosophical ideas of Western Europe, which seemed strangely dated to the German philosophers. Only after 1840 did a new wave of Western influence flow into Germany. But Germany, or for that matter Protestant Germany, did not turn Kantian. The great figures that abounded at the end of the eighteenth century, both in the older and younger generations, were too strongly individualistic simply to embrace Kantianism as a new, or final, creed. Moreover, the ultimate meaning of Kant's system, over which philosophers have struggled for almost two centuries, contained a number of grave ambiguities. Kant, no doubt, was convinced that he had made reason unassailable against the skepticism that the

British empiricists had raised. It is true that in "criticizing" reason he had established limits of reason, but only to restore its authority the more safely. He believed that he had laid a foundation on which philosophers could build with assurance. Still, even those who in general accepted this objective of Kant's philosophizing remolded his thoughts according to their own needs. Friedrich Schiller, who among all nonprofessional philosophers probably did most to make Kant's ideas known among a wider public, was too much of a worshiper at the altars of Greek gods to like the Christian connotations of Kant's philosophy. He changed Kant's moralism into estheticism. Friedrich Schleiermacher (1768–1834) rejected the Kantian ethics and philosophy of religion as artificial rationalism, incapable of expressing the Christian faith. Thus, with the active response it found, the Kantian philosophy was at once exposed to important modifications. Probably the most general applause was given to Kant's gospel of the creative spontaneity of human reason.

But just to those who welcomed this encouragement of a fresh expansion in the realm of the spirit, the demarcation lines that Kant had drawn were bound to seem to be new fetters. The Kantian approach did not really produce a *Weltbild*, that is, a unified reproduction of the universe and man's place in it. It placed pure reason and practical reason far apart and yielded only a "formal" or "conceptual" knowledge. The "thing-in-itself," though logically necessary, was declared unknowable. To many, then, skepticism did not seem to be conquered. As long as reason remained a function of consciousness and did not have any grasp over objective reality, it remained a subjective quality, and a big gulf between thought and existence was yawning. Hegel once remarked that in Kantian philosophy the intellect had defeated reason.

✑ Johann Fichte

JOHANN GOTTLIEB FICHTE (1762–1814) was the first philosopher who transformed the Kantian system in an attempt to solidify its results. The son of a poor weaver's family in Lusatia, he impressed an active character and imperious mind on all the ideas he formulated. The study of Kant gave him a methodic discipline. During the 1790's in Jena, thereafter in Berlin, Fichte led the Kantian philosophy back to metaphysics, though it was not the old metaphysics that constructed an objective world. Fichte started from the subject, which also in Kant's thinking partook in universal reason. Kant, however, had set a second prerequisite of human experience beside reason, namely the variety of external objects. This objective world Fichte declared as much a part of human consciousness as the rational faculties. Fichte described self-consciousness as ego and nonego, and he discovered in the rational ego the capacity to make itself the object of thinking. This act of "intellectual intuition" to him—as subsequently to Schelling and Schleiermacher—was the true organ of philosophy. Through "intellectual intuition" man gets all knowledge of perception, intellectual concepts, and reason, as well as of moral ideas, which to Fichte represent the absolute. But all that the study of the objects brought into consciousness, that is, the nonego, can achieve is to organize them step by step, but never in their totality. This creative process, however, can find justification only in an absolute moral law. Reason is moral action. In proceeding in time, the ego limits itself by the setting of nonegos. But the experience of the finiteness of all these posited contents of thinking is the revelation of the absoluteness of morality. Thus the moral will and its freedom appears as the true sovereign of existence. The growth of freedom is the justification of the unsolved problems and the task of the world. Fichte completely subordinated theoretical reason to practical reason. But he reached the limits of his rational deductions when he had to admit the existence of unintentional free actions. In order to overcome these difficulties, he was driven in his later years closer to a philosophical irrationalism.

Still, Fichte did not give up his idealism, in which spirit or reason was only an element of ethics. The whole empirical life is in continuous labor to transform itself into a moral order. It is determined by an absolute ego, the image of the divine. Its eternal being is reproduced in the free actions of the individuals, which must contribute to the realization of reason according to the potentialities of the individual and by its free self-determination. Fichte construes the history of humanity as a single life proceeding from an original state of an unconscious or half-conscious rationality through stages of growing disregard of the moral authority and final anarchy of opinions and passions to a state in which the individual begins to discover behind its own decisions a higher and universal regularity. Arbitrariness then transforms itself into moral and intellectual freedom, and self-discipline and the artful use of reason are capable of realizing reason in life.

What distinguished Fichte from Kant was not so much the greater radicalism of his ethical idealism as his bold trust in the pliability of reality. Reason creates the world and leads humanity to its ordained goal. In this light the historical forms of state and society become transitory and questionable organizations which could be created or abolished at will to serve the cause of reason. In outlook and temper Fichte showed some kinship with the leaders of the French Revolution. But compared to the progress of humanity, practical politics always played a secondary role in Fichte's thinking. Originally he expected everything from the cultural growth of the individual and consequently demanded the utmost limitation of all government activities. Soon, however, he accepted the Kantian justification of the state as a necessary institute for the protection of the individual's freedom against violators of this freedom. Once he had adopted this principle, Fichte carried it to great length. If the state was to guarantee its citizens life and livelihood, it was to be given the means for achieving this end, which, in Fichte's opinion, included the full control over the country's economy. Thus he presented, in 1800, his *Closed Economic State (Geschlossener Handelstaat)*, the first modern program of state socialism in Germany. Still, the socialist state remained entirely subservient to the progress of reason, which united humanity. In the further development of his philosophy, Fichte began to assign the state the task of promoting the individual's education. The state, which for Kant was a *Rechtsstaat*, government built on law, was to become in addition, as Fichte expressed it, a *Kulturstaat*, a state representing the national culture. The absolutist state, which considered itself enlightened by relying on mere force and which disregarded religion and morality, was now called sinful. Under the experience of the foreign domination of Germany, Fichte became the fiery prophet of the national state. Germany, reformed in spirit by the knowledge of mankind's destiny, was the leading nation, and therefore its outward freedom was of greatest consequence. But Fichte's nationalism, even as expounded in his *Speeches to the German Nation*, which he gave in Berlin in the winter of 1807–08, was directed toward the liberation of humanity through ideas of reason.

Fichte's philosophy, as it came to light in the 1790's, formed the stepping stone for the development of the metaphysical systems of F. W. J. Schelling (1775–1854) and G. W. F. Hegel (1770–1831). Like Fichte, these two Swabian thinkers began as theologians, and even more than Fichte they were influenced by the revival of Spinoza's pantheism. The analysis of the subject-object relationship was the starting point of their early studies, and, following to some extent the

Fichtean model, both defined this relationship as one of identity. However, Schelling's world was no longer that of Kant or Fichte but of
Goethe. Goethe's contemplation of nature was translated by the young
Schelling into a metaphysical system in which the moral emphasis was
replaced by a prevalent esthetic interest. In Hegel's philosophy, which
came to maturity somewhat later and, as we shall see,[2] dominated
German intellectual life after 1815, world history became the meeting
place of the intelligible and empirical realm.

∽ Other Philosophers

THE NUMBER OF PRODUCTIVE GERMAN philosophers of this age is too
large to allow discussion of all of them, however brief. During the
nineteenth century, some of them were to find more students abroad
than in Germany, as was the case with K. C. F. Krause (1781–1832) in
Spain. Side by side with figures such as J. F. Fries (1773–1843), J. F.
Herbart (1776–1841), Franz Baader (1765–1841) stood Arthur Schopenhauer (1788–1860), who, in spite of his brilliant literary gifts,
seemed a dismal failure in the epoch of German idealism, only to become the most widely influential philosopher in Germany after 1850.
Schopenhauer, whose chief work, *The World as Will and Idea*, appeared in 1819, drew conclusions from Kant that made him an absolute
opponent of the schools of Fichte, Schelling, Fries, and Hegel. While
all of them were bent on vindicating the power of reason over life and
on harmonizing rationalism and Christian religion, Schopenhauer did
not have any faith in reason or Christianity.

The Kantian contention that the world of objects was given to us
only in the intuitions of our consciousness was turned in an irrational
direction by Schopenhauer. If the world was nothing but a phenomenon in our consciousness, and if not even such concepts as space and
time could be traced to the "thing-in-itself," we are forced to assume
that our intuitions are mere appearances or illusions of reality which
life creates as a mirage. Together with Kant, Schopenhauer looked for
an access to the absolute through practical rather than theoretical
reason, but the younger philosopher deprived also the human will of
all rationality and morality. The human will is a blind urge and desire,
forever trying to still a need or deficiency or suffering. The fulfillment
of one desire only raises many other wishes. So long as man is driven
by his will, he is ridden by the anxiety of hope and fear and will not

[2] See pp. 510–17.

find happiness or peace. Man is ruled by vital instinct rather than by reason. Schopenhauer was the founder of the modern psychology of the unconscious, which Nietzsche and Freud were to develop later. Theoretical knowledge is only the secondary manifestation of the unconscious human will and would not hold any attraction for man if the objects of knowledge were not objects of will and desire.

If we want to recognize the real truth, the interests of the will must be abandoned. In esthetic contemplation we can reach a state of vision free from desire. Art liberates from the serfdom and suffering that the will imposes, and the genius of the artist provides a better realization of the world than science can produce. Science is bound by categories that cannot lead beyond empirical reality. The imagination of the artistic genius, however, reaches to eternal ideas. It is true that the works of art are forms of illusion, but for that very reason they reflect correctly the character of this illusory world. The true essence of life is presented in tragedy, and even deeper truth is revealed in music. In contrast to literary art, music is not bound by any objects of the will. Therefore, music is the language in which the world itself philosophizes. But esthetic contemplation, which this son of the age of Goethe and Schiller placed so high, was not an aim in itself. Schopenhauer agreed with Kant and Fichte that only morality could give or restore dignity to man. But for Schopenhauer morality could only mean the abnegation of the will for life. The ascetic saint who has suppressed this will has thereby grasped the highest philosophical truth. He has recognized the illusory quality of the world and has been enabled to overcome the illusion of a difference between himself and other individuals. In fact, it is the same force that lives in myself and others. Once the fallacy of the principle of individuation has been discarded, sympathy with your fellow-men will well up, and this sympathy is the foundation of true morality. In terms of Indian philosophy, which was just becoming known in Germany, Schopenhauer described individuality as nothingness or nirvana, which was the ultimate ground to which all individuals would return.

Schopenhauer's pessimism and nihilism made no impression on his contemporaries. Although the roots of his thought were imbedded in the same soil from which the idealistic schools had sprung, he was considered a wild shoot of the philosophical tree. Among the aspects of Schopenhauer's philosophy that set him apart from a Schelling and Hegel was the central position that such fundamental Christian doctrines as original sin, predestination, and salvation through love assumed in his philosophical system. When Søren Kierkegaard (1813–55), who had been a student of Hegel and Schelling, read Schopenhauer's writings shortly before his own death, he was struck with how much ground he had in common with Schopenhauer. But although Schopenhauer understood some of the basic Christian ideas better than many an eminent theologian, Christianity fell under his general condemnation of the senselessness of life. Schopenhauer was the first German of name who displayed an outright hostile attitude toward Christian religion. Actually, as had not been possible in Germany before, he had grown up without coming into contact with church religion. However, this was still extremely rare in Germany, and philosophers such as Fichte, Schelling, and Hegel had the ear of the educated class because they had a place for religion in their systems of reason.

The trend toward religion characterized many members of the generation that formed its own personal attitude toward life during the 1790's. All of them were already beneficiaries of the achievements of Kant, Herder, Goethe, and Schiller, and they wished to continue the progress toward a higher dignity of man and an ever-growing intellectual horizon. In brief, this progress could be defined by the word *Kultur*, which soon was to be abused a great deal by the Germans. As in English, *Kultur* (culture) was originally used as a synonym for civilization. The first German writer to draw a distinction between the two terms was Kant. It was Rousseau's criticism of the pernicious elements of civilization that led Kant to his redefinition. Art and science he declared to be part of *Kultur*, while conformity to external customs was in the realm of mere civilization. Morality, too, belonged to civilization as long as it aimed at nothing but outward decency, and Kant complained that under the existing political conditions the development of a higher morality was largely stifled. This higher morality, which did not ask for gratification and honor but rested exclusively on personal conviction, was for Kant the heart of *Kultur*.

✑ *The Romantic School*

IT WAS THE DRIVE for such a *Kultur* that was carried into new fields by a group of younger men, among whom Friedrich Schlegel (1772–1829), his elder brother August Wilhelm Schlegel (1767–1845), Friedrich von Hardenberg who was known by his pen name Novalis (1772–1801), Ludwig Tieck (1773–1853), Heinrich von Kleist (1777–1811),

Friedrich Hölderlin (1770–1843), Clemens Brentano (1778–1842), Achim von Arnim (1781–1831), E. T. A. Hoffmann (1776–1822), and Jean Paul (Jean Paul Friedrich Richter, 1763–1825) were the most outstanding figures. These poets and writers represented a vast range of literary talent and achievement. In the beginning this movement had its center in Jena and subsequently in Berlin, where it fought lively feuds with the indigenous rationalism. It usually has been called the "Romantic School" (or *romantisme* in France), and there has been a general inclination in Germany to establish a strong contrast between the "classicism" of Goethe and Schiller, on the one hand, and the "romanticism" of the next generation, on the other. But both groups were actually parts of a single German movement, which began with the *Sturm und Drang*. It is true that the mature Goethe and Schiller accepted general laws and forms, for which Hellenic antiquity served as a model. Still, the Greek ideal was of their own making and a projection of their own faith rather than a binding standard, as had been the case in the French classicism of Corneille and Racine. In his later years, Goethe did not even fully adhere to the Hellenic ideals of his middle years, but also made the Orient an object of his intellectual and poetic interests. The classicism of Goethe and Schiller rested upon the subjectivism that also characterized the Kantian and post-Kantian philosophy. What distinguished the younger generation from that of Goethe and Schiller was its refusal to accept those limitations that the two older writers had imposed upon themselves and that had enabled them to achieve the unified form of their personality and work. The romanticists went back to the young Goethe and Herder and the *Sturm und Drang*, unwilling to accept any curtailment of the freedom of the individual by submission to general laws and ideals. For Goethe and Schiller in their classicist period it had been fundamental that, under the cover of the sensual world, the empirical life contained permanently valid forms of truth and beauty. It was the task of all philosophical and artistic effort to lay bare these forms and make them effective in a higher perfection of the individual. Ultimately time and eternity, ideal and reality, liberty and norm could be harmonized.

Against this "objective idealism" the romanticists placed their "subjective idealism." They denied the validity of such eternal forms of truth and beauty and the possibility of expressing the meaning of life in timeless symbols. To them life was the emanation of the absolute spirit in the world; therefore it was not "being" but "becoming," an eternal movement of unique individual acts, which could be understood and reproduced only by the active application of the individual's sensitive empathy. Since the separation of reality and spirit in the world was rejected, understanding was proclaimed to depend on the undivided sensuous and intelligible nature of man, best exemplified in his esthetic sense. Through this sense, rather than a system of general truth, an inner elevation was gained, an awareness of participation in the eternal movement that was the life of the universe. By such poetic apperception, which could be considered some sort of creative receptiveness, the individual won higher strength without, however, arriving at a permanent form. It could win a distant adumbration of the absolute, while recognizing the multitude of individual phenomena of the spiritual world. Joyful as this personal experience might be, it could not fail to intensify the feeling of the individual's finiteness and to cause an ever-renewed search for the absolute. Nostalgia was a central sentiment of romanticism, which only humor and irony, attitudes showing the relativity of all circumstances and viewpoints of human life, could temporarily overcome.

Romanticism carried subjectivism to great, often absolute length. Essentially, the poetic genius was admired as the highest personification of man's power by a generation that experienced its deepest historic impression in the observation of Goethe's personality and work. Individuality, it was concluded, ought to be left free to follow its own inner law and mode of life. Romanticism radically rejected the concept of natural law, which the *Sturm und Drang* movement had first challenged but which, to a greater or lesser degree, had still exercised an influence on Kant and the classic writers. But without a firm lodestar, the romanticists found themselves on the open sea. They surrendered themselves to the sentiments and moods of the heart, which they explored to a new depth and presented poetically. The romantic imagination succeeded in discovering a spiritual content in all reality and, in addition, found new worlds beyond the real one in myth, fairy tale, and dream. It was not only a magic spell which was spun over all appearances but also a new warming glow brightening human life. Only romanticism made love the foundation of marriage, as it reformed many other human relationships. If Frenchmen such as Victor Hugo could talk of *romantisme* as a synonym for liberalism, they actually referred to the new trust in individuality which the romanticists championed.

Yet romanticism by itself was not likely to produce model standards.

The German romantic writers did not produce any literary genius comparable to Goethe or Schiller. All of them lacked the plastic vision of the classicists, although, instead, their lyrics showed a profound affinity to music. Characteristically, the romanticists were at their best when they could wind their thoughts around an existing work. Beginning with Friedrich Schlegel, they were truly great critics of literature and art. They were also great translators, able to transpose fully the artistic form and meaning of a foreign work into German. If in the nineteenth century Shakespeare practically assumed the place of a German "classic," this was due to the translation of A. W. Schlegel and L. Tieck, and has sometimes been called the greatest poetic achievement of the romantic school. However, it was only the most significant effort in an attempt to realize what Herder had envisaged, the opening of the literature of all nations and all ages for an active intellectual enjoyment. The creation of a "world literature" accessible to all people was a lasting accomplishment of German romanticism.

At the same time this was an expression of the new attitude toward history that animated the romanticists. The Enlightenment had secularized history and, in the works of Montesquieu, Voltaire, and Gibbon, had given history a new significance. The new interpretation of history had found its representatives in Germany, although the academic historians, writing textbooks for students rather than works for the general public, lacked literary distinction. But these studies, carried on particularly by the scholars in Göttingen, were something more than mere emulation of Western European Enlightenment and application of its methods and thoughts to the problems of the history of the German Empire. Pedantic and juridical as this treatment of history was, it paved the way for a more individualized historiography. To an even greater measure, this was demonstrated by Justus Möser (1720–94), the legal councilor of the curious German bishopric of Osnabrück, in which after 1648 a Catholic bishop alternated with a Protestant administrator as ruler. In Osnabrück the most peculiar forms of the law of the Empire and of the dualistic territorial state had survived, together with an old peasant society. In his *History of Osnabrück* and *Imaginary Patriotic Discourses* (*Patriotische Phantasien*), Möser displayed a lively sense for the human values which might be hidden even in anomalous historical developments.

But only Herder had fundamentally challenged the Enlightenment's philosophy of history, which in history had found the demonstration of the unchanging nature of man and human reason, which, though modified, distorted, or enhanced by historical circumstances, remained essentially identical. With the belief in the rational character of man, the Enlightenment had risen to a comprehensive reinterpretation of universal history. Its strength lay in its conception of the unity of world history and its insistence upon clearly defined causal explanations. But the unique value of all historical phenomena was not recognized. Primitive nations, or for that matter practically all centuries of history, were judged to be nothing but imperfect stages in humanity's development, presumably even avoidable stages in the light of reason. In contrast, for Herder individuality was a manifestation of unique ideas of equal significance, and historical development to him was the organic unfolding of unique forces. Yet the classicists from Winckelmann to Schiller had established a highest norm, surpassing all others, in their Greek ideal, and this trend was so strong that even Herder in his later years adjusted himself to the classicist spirit that prevailed in Weimar.

The romanticists, however, boldly proceeded on the road which Herder had shown. This did not necessarily mean that the devotion to ancient Hellas was abandoned. With ecstatic feeling Friedrich Hölderlin longed for Greece, although it was no longer Winckelmann's serene Apollonian Hellas but the land of Dionysus and the religious mysteries. Yet on the whole the romantic interest in history tended toward the nonclassical civilizations, especially the Germanic past. The dawn of Germanic history as well as the Middle Ages came into full view. Romantic poetry led directly to the scholarly work of Jakob and Wilhelm Grimm (1785–1863; 1786–1859), with their collection of the early literary monuments, and that of Friedrich Karl von Savigny (1779–1861) and the Historical School of Law, with the study of the institutions of the early periods of Germany.

The attention given to the individual and his growth, which was to become one of the main sources of the new critical study of history, was accompanied by an insufficient grasp of the structure of universal history. In general the romantic consciousness, with its expansion into the infinite, was jeopardized by the absence of a clear position. Many romanticists, therefore, were attracted by the turn to religion which Friedrich Schleiermacher was the first to take. In his *Speeches on Religion to the Educated Among its Detractors*, of 1798, the man who was to act in later life as the chief reformer of the Protestant Church and theology in Germany admonished a philosophical audience that the unity of all spiritual life could be found only in religion. Accepting

Kant's critical analysis of human knowledge, he maintained that a synthesis of the sensuous and rational world required a prior relation of the individual to the universal ground of life. No pure or practical reason could provide this but "a sentiment of absolute dependence," that is, a feeling of complete subordination under a divine destiny. Schleiermacher's definition ultimately changed the character of Christian theology. No longer were doctrines and dogmas considered to be the true substance of religion, not even faith in God and personal immortality, but the feeling of immanence of the infinite in the finite.

Schleiermacher's desire to establish the total unity of spiritual life despite the inadequacy of rational understanding struck a sympathetic chord among his contemporaries, but it also led to the demand to have such unity represented in an integrated organization of life and society. One year after the publication of Schleiermacher's *Speeches on Religion*, Novalis issued an article entitled *The Christendom and Europe* (1799), which became one of the foremost statements of romantic social philosophy. All the romantic poets and writers were opposed to the absolute state. The French Revolution was originally welcomed by them as much as by Kant, and in later years it was still understood as an inevitable, if deplorable, consequence of despotism's sins. But whereas Kant looked toward the future, which he hoped would bring progress beyond the former and present stages of history, Novalis saw the ideal embodied in the stage preceding the age of absolutism. He glorified the Middle Ages as the period of unity and peace, in which Europe formed a spiritual empire under the leadership of a wise clergy. Religion was the breath of medieval civilization, and the Church gave the human mind ideals of supreme beauty and truth. Novalis found symptoms of decline as early as the later Middle Ages, but the full decay was caused by Protestantism and modern rationalism. The religious division gave soulless states the opportunity for usurping ecclesiastical authority. Rational scientific thought destroyed the beauty that sprang from the medieval order and finally dethroned God by making Him an idle observer of a self-propelled mechanical universe.

Novalis's interpretation of the medieval Church and culture was the expression of an enthusiastic pantheism. It obviously disregarded many historical realities and also put the essence of Catholic religion in a somewhat artificial light. But in subsequent years the romantic idealization of the Middle Ages contributed greatly to the revival of German Catholicism, particularly among the educated groups. Its prelude was the conversion to the Catholic Church of a number of individual romanticists, among them Friedrich Schlegel. In the Catholic faith many a romantic soul found the authority that the restless search for individual truth and beauty did not yield. The ground was also prepared for a more definite commitment in politics, which the romanticists had originally rather loosely approached as an arena of enjoyable intellectual contests. But when French domination spread all over Europe after the battles of Austerlitz and Jena, in 1805–06, romantic ideas, enlivened by Edmund Burke's conservatism and the traditionalism of the French emigrant writers, helped to fashion general political theories. In his *Elements of Statecraft* of 1808–09, Adam Müller (1779–1829), a native of Berlin and early convert to Catholicism, presented the first extensive application of romantic ideas to the concrete problems of politics. With utmost vigor, Müller aimed at the destruction of the mechanistic state of the absolute age as well as of the French Revolution's egalitarianism and liberalism. Feudalism and a social hierarchy were declared to be society's ideal organization and the only forms guaranteeing the state's organic and moral nature. Adam Müller, Friedrich Schlegel, and Friedrich Gentz, the German translator of Burke, went in those years to Vienna in order to win over the Austrian state to support their ideas.

✍ The New German Culture

OBJECTIONS HAVE BEEN RAISED against the conception of a unified romantic movement, and it is true that with the exception of the small groups that formed in Jena and Berlin just before the turn of the century, and a little later in Dresden and Heidelberg, personal contacts among the various representatives of the romantic school were limited. From the beginning, the contrasts among personalities were great with regard to social background and intellectual outlook as well as character. In these many different hands the romanticist ideas, in themselves rather flexible, were developed in quite different directions, which defy easy generalizations. As early as 1788, Mirabeau observed the growth of German literature and poetry in the midst of an intense pursuit of theoretical reflection, and he predicted that the German movement would produce fruits before flowers, because reason had gained the better over imagination. Whether this prediction came true is difficult to decide, and it would probably be correct to say that the fruits of thought grew simultaneously with the flowers of imagination. It was characteristic of the German intellectual movement that it advanced by alternating between esthetic vision and philosophical contemplation. Thus once more the attempt was made to find a systematic philosophical view of all the elements of thought that classicism and romanticism had created. It was undertaken by F. W. J. Schelling and G. W. F. Hegel. The latter gained the greatest following in Germany after 1815 and held it well into the 1830's. But side by side with the builders of metaphysical systems, young scholars were already at work in the period after 1815. The line of poets was thinning, and talent was attracted to academic studies. It was a group of men who fell heirs to the great conceptions of the poets and philosophers, but Goethe and the romanticists had taught them also the value of the individual phenomenon, which both generalizing abstraction and poetic intuition are apt to miss. The sciences of language and literature, of history in all its departments, and finally the natural sciences formed the subjects in which the German universities acquired a leadership which continued almost undisputed, even after the breakdown of the great philosophical systems.

The rise of the new German culture between 1770 and 1815, first described by Madame de Staël, whose book (1810) traveled fast around the world, was the work of German burghers, though a few noblemen were actively represented in the later stages. Cut off from political power as well as from full participation in political life, and denied social equality, these German burghers looked for the realization of their personality in the realm of the spirit. It is possible to discover in this attitude a silent protest against the existing political and social conditions, and occasionally this came into the open. But on the whole the leaders of German idealism were persuaded that a reform of public life was a matter of education rather than political action, and they were grateful for the freedom to philosophize granted them by the governments. They remained tied to the existing states for the additional reason that their own existence depended largely on their posts in the civil service of state and church. Even the free-lance writers wrote largely for a public of civil servants. If the burghers in the cities had shown political interest beyond the local sphere, there might have been a temptation to start a political group. But no signs of such an interest could be discovered. It was better, therefore, to seek distinction from the Philistine of the towns, not to mention the inchoate mass of the German population, the peasants. It was a strictly aristocratic ideal which the German thinkers established with their cult of genius. The social divisions were accepted as natural. Where, as in romanticism, a deeper interest in the life of the common man developed, it retained a strong air of superiority. The word *fraternité* had no place in the German political vocabulary.

The members of the new German intelligentsia formulated an ideal of man that claimed to be far above the barriers of state and nations. They wished to be citizens of all worlds and all ages. For Kant, national feeling was a beastly infatuation which had to be overcome by the acceptance of maxims of reason. Such national sentiment existed in the lower classes to a greater extent than the educated realized, and in the Wars of Liberation it proved its remarkable force. Kant was perhaps not entirely wrong when he considered it a rather primitive disposition. This dormant nativistic nationalism needed for its activation the leadership of the traditional indigenous authorities, the princes and the Church. But the German idealists aimed at a higher and more individualized feeling. For this, however, a concrete framework was lacking. The German Empire had ceased to inspire any moral loyalty. Its final collapse in 1806 met with complete apathy. After hearing the news, Goethe, who was at that moment on a journey, made the following entry in his diary: "Conflict between the servant and coachman on the coachbox, which excited us more than the dissolution of the Roman Empire." Among educational leaders, the feeling of German nationality was confined entirely to the cultural field. Such national pride as existed centered around the special contribution that German philosophy and literature were making to the advancement of humanity as a whole. While other nations, and this meant France and Britain, were spending their energies in political struggles, Germany was creating spiritual ideals that were valid for all nations. The absence of any concrete political program was thus declared to be an element of strength. The French Revolution did not change this attitude. Although the Revolution in its early stages found warm approval among the German writers, nobody of significance demanded the same rights of citizens for the Germans. The regime of the Terror, as well as the subsequent period of foreign wars, convinced most German thinkers that the Revolution was an outgrowth of the fallacious rationalism of the French Enlightenment.

The outlook of the German educated classes remained cosmopolitan even after the French had overrun the Rhineland. When the Peace of Basel neutralized North Germany in the decade from 1795 to 1805, every incentive for a practical approach to politics had vanished. Only

after the dissolution of the Empire and the defeat of Austria and
Prussia in the years 1805–07 were new voices heard. In the winter of
1807–08, Fichte delivered his *Speeches to the German Nation* in Berlin.
He preached a new conception of nationality. Nations were not
mere subdivisions of humanity but individualities in which the human
mind realized itself. A universal spirit could be only the secondary
product of the development of individual nations. Fichte called upon
his audience to resist French domination and to defend their nation-
hood. But in defining the meaning of the German national idea, he
saw it in cosmopolitan terms. To him the Germans were guardians of
the highest ideas of humanity. They deserved their national freedom
not because they were Germans, but because their culture could serve
as a model for any future culture of humanity.

It was the new philosophy of individuality that led Fichte to his
new nationalism. Romanticism, with its even greater emphasis on
individuality, produced a less abstract love of German history and
tradition. Still, the romanticists identified the nation not with a national
state but rather with culture, and German culture to them was imbedded in a common European and Christian civilization. Only in
Ernst Moritz Arndt (1769–1860), the son of unfree peasants on the
island of Swedish Rügen, and even more radically in Ludwig Jahn
(1778–1852), a strong, untrammeled nationalism broke through. Both
represented a relentless antiforeign attitude conceived as a means of
keeping the German folk-spirit (*Volksgeist*, or in Jahn, *Volkstum*)
unadulterated. Arndt was directly affected by Swedish political tradition, and Jahn showed even more pronounced democratic tendencies.
Jahn, the father of *Turnen* (gymnastics), wished to restore not only
the old-Germanic prowess, but also liberty through disciplined sport.
Arndt, master of a popular German prose, served as an official writer
to Baron Stein during the War of Liberation. This fact, however, protected him as little as Jahn from difficulties with the Prussian reaction
after 1819. The immediate influence of both writers on their contemporaries was small, but they found followers in the younger generation and through them contributed greatly to the growth of modern
German nationalism.

CHAPTER 12

Germany and the French Revolution, the End of the Empire and the Collapse of Prussia, 1789-1807

THE GERMAN THINKERS who built an empire of poetic and philosophical imagination in the last third of the eighteenth century and the first years of the nineteenth were little affected by the political events that began with the outbreak of the French Revolution. Originally, not even the German governments were particularly alarmed by the upheaval on the Seine. Joseph II, who, on a journey to France, had formed an idea of the brewing dangers to the French monarchy, was himself both threatened by the revolts in Belgium and Hungary and, after 1787, involved in the war with Turkey. Prussia, however, was pleased with France's internal weakness. In 1788, Frederick William II had intervened in the Netherlands' internal affairs, where the republicans had driven out William V of Orange, his brother-in-law. A Prussian army under Duke Ferdinand of Brunswick brought the *stadholder* back to The Hague. Surprisingly enough, the Prussian invasion proved an easy promenade, which gave Prussia's rulers an unjustified confidence in the quality of their army. A foreign conqueror was soon to make his entry into Berlin through the Brandenburg gate.

The Prussian government, in alliance with England and the Netherlands, believed it could seek aggrandizement by making Austria's life more difficult. Contacts were made with the leaders of the revolt in Hungary, Galicia, and Belgium, and relations with Turkey and Poland were strengthened. For a while it seemed that Prussia would try to win her objectives by force. However, Frederick William II was persuaded to accept a peaceful settlement on the basis of the *status quo ante*. In the Convention of Reichenbach (July 27, 1790), Leopold II promised to conclude the Turkish war without territorial acquisitions, while Prussia ceased supporting revolutionary elements in the various Habsburg lands. The Emperor made peace with Turkey in 1791. Russia fought on and, through the Peace of Jassy (1792), gained the Dnjestr line and recognition of her Crimean possessions.

If the Reichenbach Convention made sense, which Bismarck denied, it did only in its attempt to bury the Austro-Prussian antagonism, which had led to a race for Russian favor and thus made possible the Russian Empire's steady expansion. Therefore, it was logical to extend the field of co-operation. When, in the spring of 1791, the Polish diet adopted a monarchical constitution designed to give the state a workable national government, Austria and Prussia agreed to recognize Poland's integrity and constitution. But the Austro-Prussian understanding stood on shaky ground. Prussia still anticipated further Polish annexations, particularly Danzig and Thorn, and even Krakow. Further, at this time Prussia took over the government of Ansbach-Bayreuth, thereby assuming a political role in South Germany for the first time. Austria felt uneasy about the Prussian acquisition of the Franconian principalities and wished to restore the balance in Germany. Plans for absorbing Bavaria, in exchange for Belgium or an Alsace recovered from France, were contemplated by Austrian statesmen.

This divergence of views undermined from the beginning the foundation on which a common policy vis-à-vis revolutionary France might have been built. Actually both governments were unwilling to intervene in France. Leopold, much suspected in France as the ruler of the feudalistic state and as Marie Antoinette's brother, was careful not to be dragged into any action, least of all by the ultraroyalist emigrant groups, who circulated propaganda detrimental to the best interests of Louis XVI and his queen.

∽ Franco-German Friction

THE FIRST FRICTION between France and Germany developed over the abolition of feudal burdens. A number of German princes and counts owned estates in Alsace. After the French occupation of Alsace, they had managed to draw income from these estates under special arrangements with the French government. Legislation passed in the summer of 1790 nationalized the property of the French Church, dissolved monasteries, and prohibited the jurisdiction of bishops residing outside of France. The archbishops of Trier, Mainz, and Cologne and the upper Rhenish bishops officially complained to the Emperor and demanded action by the Empire. The misfortunes of some of the imperial noblemen and ecclesiastical princes along the Rhine contributed to the warm reception German nobility gave the high-born emigrants from France, who soon crowded many places in the Rhineland, particularly Coblenz and Mainz. Among them was the youngest brother of Louis XVI, the Count of Artois (later Charles X), who aimed at the full restoration of the crown's and the nobility's political and social rights. In Germany, these emigrants tried to persuade their hosts that the revolutionary order would collapse like a house of cards upon the slightest show of force.

Austro-Prussian Intervention

LEOPOLD II AND FREDERICK WILLIAM II were little affected by the emigrant French nobles. In August, 1791, the two rulers met in Pillnitz in Saxony; they rejected the uninvited Count of Artois' demands. The Austro-Prussian declaration, issued weeks after the French royal family's attempt to flee from Paris had been foiled, stated that events in France affected all sovereigns and that, if other powers would contribute forces proportionate to their power, emperor and king would intervene to restore Louis XVI's freedom of action and introduce a moderate constitution. It was a rather weak gesture, since it was well known that England opposed any intervention. When, in September, 1791, Louis XVI accepted the new French constitution, Leopold considered concerted European intervention completely unlikely. But internal forces in France drove toward conflict, and the Pillnitz declaration, given a twisted meaning by the mischievous public interpretation of the royalist emigrants, served well the purposes of the Jacobin leaders, who wanted to deflect the revolutionary regime's internal difficulties to the international field. Contacts existing between royalist circles in France and abroad could be played up for the same purpose. Leopold went far toward meeting demands that he suppress the emigrants' military demonstration in the Rhineland; but the development toward war was irresistible. In February 1792, Austria and Prussia concluded a defensive alliance. On April 20, 1792, the French legislature almost unanimously voted a declaration of war against Francis II (1792–1835), who had succeeded his father the month before. The Girondists expected a short war. Twenty-three years of only briefly interrupted wars were to follow. They devoured many children of the Revolution, and many of its original ideas were lost, while the French nation went from its greatest triumph to ultimate defeat. Still, the ideas of the French Revolution and French arms created a new Germany and Europe.

On July 14, 1792, the third anniversary of Bastille Day, the last coronation of a German emperor took place in Frankfurt. But the subsequent meeting of German princes in Mainz, the last big celebration held by the Holy Roman Empire's high nobility, showed little unity, and even less willingness to participate actively in the war against France. Prussia had mobilized large forces, but the Austrian troops were weak. The two allies argued about possible "spoils." Prussia felt that she should seek them in Poland, whereas Austria renewed the Bavarian-Belgian exchange project. No binding arrangements were made, and the open issue spoiled the two allies' mutual confidence. In spite of the Revolution in France, they were completely obsessed by the old game of power balance. Late in July the main army finally started its march to Paris from Coblenz. It was commanded by Duke Ferdinand of Brunswick, so enlightened a prince that only a few months earlier the French had tried to gain his services. Just the same, before crossing into France he signed a slightly revised draft of a manifesto, written by a French emigrant, which, in bombastic terms, made the national assembly and city council of Paris responsible for the royal family's security and, in case of violation, threatened the complete destruction of Paris and other cities.

The manifesto galvanized French popular sentiment and enabled the French revolutionaries to proclaim the war as one of national defense against tyranny. At the same time, it gave the radical elements their chance to overpower the moderates. The king became a prisoner. In early September, while the allied army took first Longwy and then Verdun and the road to Paris seemed open to it, the mob murdered helpless political prisoners in the jails of Paris and other cities. Under the shadow of these atrocities, the election of the Convention took place. It convened on September 20 and abolished the monarchy on the following day. On the same day, the denouement of the military campaign happened. The allied armies proved far superior to the poor and not even numerous troops the French were able to send into the field. It was not the mass of the *sansculottes* that was decisive in the campaign of 1792, but the good quality of the officers, most of whom were bourgeois officers rapidly promoted after the nobility had been removed from senior commands. Fighting in their own country and supported by the population, the French troops had the advantage of greater mobility than the invading forces bound by their supply lines. Allied losses through sickness were heavy that autumn. But the worst difficulties were in the mind of the allied commander. Duke Ferdinand did not really believe in the offensive strategy he had been persuaded to execute. Contrary to the emigrants' predictions, the population remained sullen and hostile; the Austrians failed to send the originally promised numbers of men; events in Paris indicated that the allies could not save the monarchy. The duke became hesitant. It was clear, too, that both the Austrian and the Prussian governments were primarily concerned with their territorial compensations, not with subduing France. On September 20, the allies met a French corps at Valmy. An artillery duel which would not have blocked the march toward Paris, took place. The duke ordered a rest and, ten days later, began to retreat to Germany. Goethe was right in telling Prussian officers at the campfire that from this day a new chapter in world history would begin. The old Europe had proved its helplessness in the face of the novel forces the French Revolution engendered. Now they had gained time to organize.

☙ The Allies Retreat

THE OCTOBER RETREAT of the allied army beyond the Rhine permitted the French armies great successes. Belgium in the north and Savoy and Nice in the south could be conquered. Limited forces opened a northward offensive from Alsace. Speyer was captured on September 30, Worms four days later. On October 21, Mainz fell into French hands, and a French detachment could even occupy Frankfurt for five weeks. The effect upon the Germans of the appearance of the French was disastrous. The government of Palatinate-Bavaria loudly assured the world of its neutrality, and the landgrave of Hesse-Darmstadt sent his soldiers as far away from the Rhine as he could. The elector of Mainz, together with his opulent court, left his capital. Small wonder that the petty princelings of this corner of the Empire quickly called their small contingents home.

Meanwhile, in unpleasant negotiations with Austria, the Prussian government insisted on compensations in Poland. Catherine of Russia, her hands free after the Peace of Jassy, had resumed her expansionist policy against Poland, using the opposition among the Polish nobility to the constitution as an entering wedge. She was a sharp and noisy critic of the French Revolution, but even more anxious to see Austria and Prussia fight in western Europe so that she might garner fruits in the east. Prussia and Austria were in the uncomfortable situation of either letting Russia advance alone or defending the integrity and constitution of Poland in a simultaneous war against Russia and France. But Prussia was only too anxious to reap profits. Frederick William II felt not the slightest moral scruple in breaking the Prusso-Polish treaty of alliance (1790) or in bypassing the Austrian government altogether.

ᔎ The Second Polish Partition

BEHIND AUSTRIA'S BACK, Prussia and Russia agreed on the second Polish partition. Russia grabbed the rest of Lithuania, Podolia, and Wolhynia; Prussia took Danzig and Thorn as well as the territories around Posen (Poznan) and Kalish, which were brought together as "South Prussia." In January, 1793, Prussian and Russian troops took possession of their spoils. The director of Austrian foreign policy, Count Philip Cobenzl, was compromised and was replaced by the anti-Prussian Baron Thugut, an austere and somewhat heavy-handed diplomat, who, however, brought fresh momentum into Austria's war effort against France. The Austro-Prussian alliance was no longer a reliable instrument in this struggle.

ᔎ England Enters the War

ON THE EVE of the Russian and Prussian onslaught on Poland, Louis XVI was guillotined in Paris; the commotion this event produced in England enabled William Pitt to convince the English people that war was necessary. He had taken pains to avoid war for a long time, since the Revolution had originally caused divided opinions, and even some unrest, in Britain. The French conquest of Belgium and disregard of the international arrangements for the Scheldt traffic had been the original cause for open Anglo-French conflict, which had finally led, in 1792, to an English demand for the evacuation of all lands occupied by the French. It was also the reply to the decree of the French Convention of November 19, 1792, which promised fraternal support to all people who wanted to regain their liberty. France declared war not only on England but also on the Netherlands. Pitt began building the first great coalition, which included Spain, Sardinia, Naples, Portugal, and officially also Russia, although no active help was expected from Catherine. The German Empire had finally declared war on

France, in March, 1793, but the imperial estates remained passive until in the fall of the year a few German states, prompted by English subsidies, could be moved into action.

The actual burden of fighting, however, was carried by Austrian and Prussian armies. One Austrian army, under the duke of Coburg-Saalfeld, successfully drove the French from the Low Countries and might have broken into France, if Austria and England had not been chiefly interested in the full occupation of Belgium. A Prusso-Austrian army under the duke of Brunswick retook Mainz after a lengthy siege and fought with good results in the Palatinate and Alsace. Further progress was expected in this theater in view of the French military weakness, but Austro-Prussian political dissensions and the lack of mutual confidence among the commanders had grown so deep as to exclude a large-scale offensive. In addition, France, now in the throes of civil war, appeared hopelessly debilitated and consequently her subjugation did not seem a matter of immediate urgency. The allied statesmen were gravely mistaken. True, the revolutionary convulsions threatened complete chaos, but out of the fratricidal domestic struggles and their heinous crimes the Jacobins erected a centralized governmental power, which neither France nor for that matter any other country had ever known.

✑ Carnot, "the Organizer of Victory"

In Lazare Carnot, the Committee of Public Safety had a member who became "the organizer of victory." Carnot brought new military talents, such as Jourdan, Hoche, and Pichegru, into command positions, and the young Major Bonaparte was tested in a desperate attempt at the recapture of Toulon. Carnot created the mass armies that defeated the foreign invaders by the *levée en masse*. The army of citizen-soldiers, which by the spring of 1794 reached an unheard of strength of 800,000 men, adopted new methods of warfare. In contrast to the mercenary armies of the *ancien régime*, held together by an iron discipline, the new army appealed to an ideal—that of an egalitarian nation. Desertion was at first a serious problem, but it was borne more easily with large numbers of men at the government's disposal. As the first victories were won, the French armies gained superiority over their enemies not only through sheer numbers but also by their novel tactics. Whereas the old armies had to be treated as compact units on the march or on the battlefield, the modern army divisions were created as fighting entities that permitted new types of maneuver before and in battle. The new citizen-soldier could also be used as an individual fighter, and skirmishing and *tirailleur* tactics could be developed. Most important, Carnot and his generals discarded belief in the superiority of the defensive and the necessity of limited strategic objectives. A new spirit, which saw in strategic offensive the best defense and looked for quick battle decisions, developed in the armies of the French Revolution. Napoleon Bonaparte was to bring the new strategy to its highest perfection.

In the late fall of 1793, the tide began to turn. In December, the lack of proper Austro-Prussian co-operation enabled Hoche to force the Austrians from their positions in the Palatinate. As a consequence, both allies had to withdraw to the eastern bank of the Rhine. The French were enabled to invade Belgium again. In June, 1794, Jourdan defeated the duke of Coburg-Saalfeld's Austrian army. During the winter of 1794–95, Holland was invaded and a Batavian Republic proclaimed. In October, 1794, French troops reached Cologne, Bonn, and Coblenz. The French successes in 1794–95 were largely the result of continued Austro-Prussian disagreement and of the impact the Polish question had on the policy of the two powers. Prussian participation in the fighting along the Rhine became perfunctory as early as 1794; Prussia was preoccupied with the trouble brewing in Poland. In March, 1794, a general revolt broke out, in which the lower nobility, the clergy, and the townspeople, under the courageous and able leadership of Thaddeus Kosciuszko, rose against the foreign oppressors of their national freedom. The Prussian army was not overly successful in fighting these eastern revolutionaries. The intervention of a strong Russian army under Suvorov, which conquered Warsaw in November, 1794, proved decisive. Catherine preferred to negotiate the third and final partition of Poland with Austria rather than Prussia. Afterwards, the state of Frederick the Great was granted Warsaw and other Polish territories, grouped together as "New East Prussia." They were entirely Polish lands, and even by contemporary Prussian observers the loyalty of their inhabitants was considered forever doubtful. Russia, moving westward, became Prussia's immediate neighbor at the Njemen and Bug rivers.

✍ *The Peace of Basel*

THE CIRCUMSTANCES of the third Polish partition brought on the full collapse of the Austro-Prussian alliance. Since Prussian finances were exhausted, the wish to make peace became irresistible. After Robespierre's fall in July, 1794, and with the progress of French arms to the coveted "natural" frontiers of France—that is, the Pyrenees, the Alps, and the Rhine—the desire for peace grew in Paris as well. Frederick William II originally thought of his role as mediator between Austria and the Empire on the one side and France on the other, but eventually he was pressed into negotiations for a separate peace. On April 15, 1795, Prussia and France signed the Peace of Basel. In this open treaty, the occupation of the Prussian territories on the left bank of the Rhine by troops of the French Republic was conceded. The ultimate disposal of these lands was left to a final peace treaty between France and the Empire. Prussia was to mediate this peace, and meanwhile the war was to be kept away from northern Germany. A secret agreement provided that Prussia would discuss specific compensations east of the Rhine if, in a future peace treaty, the Empire should cede the left bank of the Rhine to France. North Germany was to be neutralized under a Prussian guarantee. A line of demarcation was drawn in a subsequent agreement, which already contained the idea that Hanover might possibly be coerced into neutrality by Prussian occupation.

The separate treaty between Prussia and France, in which the cession of the German territories west of the Rhine and also the future dissolution of the ecclesiastical principalities was clearly indicated, aroused loud criticism in Germany. Resentment against Prussia was felt very deeply, particularly in southern Germany, henceforth fully exposed to French pressure. It was the beginning of an anti-Prussian attitude in many circles, which helped to determine the policies of the South German states during the next decades. The Prussian government under both Frederick William II and, from 1797 on, Frederick William III thought it had gained a truly great position as the protector of all of northern Germany from the Rhine to the Vistula. This was an obvious self-deception, because the small North German states were likely to look to Prussia only so long as the war between Austria and France continued. Once these two powers made peace, the small states were bound to reassert their independence by leaning toward France. There can be hardly any doubt that the ten years of Prussian neutrality which began with the Peace of Basel led to the situation in which Prussia had to fight Napoleon all by herself in 1806. But probably not even the maintenance of co-operation with Austria would have staved off the coming disaster, so long as the Prussian and

Austrian statesmen did not understand the enormous power let loose by the French Revolution and considered themselves free to carry on their old policies of maneuver and subterfuge. Leopold Ranke has said that the most important historical result of the Peace of Basel was the calm it provided for the growth of German literature in its greatest years. His suggestion contains a great deal of truth, though it must be added that the unrealistic political peace of North Germany isolated the intellectual movement from contact with the stern realities of political life.

↩ *The Peace of Campo Formio*

AFTER THE PEACE OF BASEL, Austria, the Empire, and England faced a France which, in the fall of 1795, after Robespierre's execution, organized the government of the Directory. France's internal struggles were still rather serious, and the results of the fighting in 1795 remained inconclusive. This continued to be so at the Rhenish and southern German front in the following year, but in 1796 the young General Bonaparte conquered northern and central Italy and broke into Carinthia and Styria. A preliminary peace was signed between Austria and Napoleon at Leoben, which was followed in October, 1797, by the less favorable Peace of Campo Formio. Belgium and Lombardy were formally ceded. In their place, Austria received Venice and Venetia, the independence of which Napoleon had just destroyed. In secret articles, France was promised the whole left bank of the Rhine, with the exception of the Prussian possessions. By excluding the latter, Austria wished compensation west of the Rhine withheld from Prussia. In contrast, France undertook to support compensations for Austria, among them the archbishopric of Salzburg and a parcel of Bavarian land. Austria and France agreed to guarantee that the German princes, who lost territories west of the Rhine, would be requited by gains on the right bank of the river. A congress was to be convened at Rastatt for such purposes and for the conclusion of a final peace between France and the Empire.

While France began to intensify and extend her control over the Italian peninsula, and in addition subordinated the Swiss Confederacy by the creation of the Helvetian Republic, the Congress of Rastatt started its work. Representatives of France, Austria, and Prussia met here with those of the various other estates of the Empire. The small German princes realized that they could profit most if they won

French favor. This was also true of Prussia. For Austria was not pre-pared to sacrifice all ecclesiastical dominions, on which the Emperor's influence in the Empire so largely depended. A general race for French support was the result. The Austrian government was unpleasantly surprised that France demanded the whole left bank of the Rhine and held out high hopes to Prussia and the German princes. There was a moment when Austria offered to forego all compensations, provided Prussia would do the same. Then she turned vainly to Prussia as mediator only to try in new negotiations to gain new concessions from France in Italy and, at the expense of Bavaria, in Germany. New war ensued, in which the Russia of Czar Paul I intervened. In 1799, an Anglo-Russian army landed in North Holland, but was quickly forced to evacuate. But the Russian army, which Suvorov led into Italy in the spring of 1799, completely changed the balance. By fall, the French were completely driven out of Italy, and Switzerland fell largely into the hands of Austrian and Russian forces. Friction between Archduke Carl and Suvorov made effective military co-operation impossible, and the Russian, Austrian, and English governments proved incapable of forging a common policy for this "Second Coalition" against France.

✑ The Treaty of Amiens

LATE IN SEPTEMBER, the Austrians and Russians were individually defeated and had to retreat from Switzerland. Even before Napoleon returned from Egypt, France's military position was again consolidated, and the recall of Suvorov further strengthened the chances of France's new ruler, Napoleon Bonaparte, First Consul since the Brumaire *coup d'état* (November 9, 1799). His new Italian campaign, in 1800, culmi-nating in the battle of Marengo, forced the Austrians to accept an un-favorable armistice in Italy. On December 3, 1800, the northern Aus-trian army was decisively beaten by Moreau at Hohenlinden in Bavaria. Austria was compelled to seek peace, which was signed in Lunéville on February 9, 1801. England was now totally isolated. Napoleon planned to defeat her by blocking all continental ports to English shipping and trade. The situation seemed auspicious. Through the reconquest of Italy and an alliance with Spain, the southern ports could be closed. In the north, Czar Paul was apprehensive of the rise of English sea-power in the Mediterranean, particularly after the aims of Napoleon's expedition to Egypt had been thwarted by Nelson's victory at Abukir and the English had conquered Malta. Paul persuaded Sweden and

Denmark to join with him in defense of the neutrals' maritime rights against England. Prussian policy chose a parallel course. In April, 1801, Prussia even occupied Hanover and Bremen, which otherwise might have been invaded by either France or Russia. The grave dangers these policies of the continental powers spelled for England were eased by the assassination of the Russian czar and the succession of Alexander I (1801–25) to the Russian throne, as well as by the destruction of the Danish fleet in April, 1801. Both France and England were in the mood to compromise. After lengthy negotiations, they signed the peace treaty of Amiens in March, 1802. Fourteen months later the two powers were to resume the war.

↶ Reorganization of Germany

THIS WORLD-WIDE STRUGGLE formed the background of events culminating in the final collapse of the old German Empire. In the Empire's reorganization, which took place after the Peace of Lunéville, the preponderance of France over the emperor was overwhelming. Only the czar's influence, for obvious reasons, carried some weight with Napoleon at this time. The German princes' endeavor to curry favor with the French victor knew no limits. The diet of the Empire turned over the business of compensations for losses of territories west of the Rhine to a "deputation," consisting of the electors of Mainz, Bohemia, Saxony, Brandenburg, and Palatinate-Bavaria, the duke of Württemberg, the landgrave of Hesse-Kassel, and the Franconian grandmaster of the Teutonic Order. Their recommendations, presented to the diet as a "final recess," were adopted as the so-called *Reichsdeputationshauptschluss* on March 24, 1803.

Many of the boundaries drawn by the final recess have existed well into the twentieth century. All the Empire's ecclesiastical princes were victims of the territorial redistribution, with the exception of two members of the deputation. But the Archbishop of Mainz, archchancellor of the Empire, had to give up Mainz and accept Regensburg as his see. Karl Theodor von Dalberg (1744–1817), a subtle and versatile diplomat, impressed Napoleon as a useful figure in the game of German politics. The Teutonic Order's small possessions were preserved as an asylum for the many noblemen who lost their chapter positions. All imperial cities, with the exception of Bremen, Hamburg, Lübeck, Frankfurt, Nürnberg, and Augsburg, were deprived of their autonomy, together with a group of petty secular rulers. Out of this mass, the new German "middle" states were formed, intended to be large enough to feel the pride of sovereignty, but too weak to live independently. Bavaria became the relatively strongest state, and Austro-Bavarian enmity was kept alive by the ever-renewed Austrian attempts to annex Bavarian territory. Bavaria received the adjacent bishoprics of Passau and Freising and the Swabian bishopric of Augsburg, as well as the Franconian bishoprics along the Main, Bamberg and Würzburg, and in addition many cities and abbeys in Franconia and eastern Swabia. Thereafter Bavaria was no longer a homogeneous "tribal" (*Stamm*) duchy, whereas its western neighbor, Württemberg, in spite of large annexations, remained a predominantly Swabian state. Württemberg received a large number of cities and abbeys, chiefly in Upper Swabia.

The relatively largest increments were given to Baden. It won the bishopric of Constance and all the territories on the right bank of the Rhine, which had belonged to the bishoprics of Basel, Strasbourg, and Speyer or to the Electoral Palatinate. Henceforth, Baden extended along the Rhine from the Lake of Constance to Mannheim, which lent it some geographical unity. But the strip of land called Baden lacked breadth and could not even temporarily be defended against France. Napoleon wished to have the western bank of the Upper Rhine and the major passes of the Black Forest in the hands of a state that could not resist a French invasion. In spite of the ulterior motives of French policy in the establishment of the southern German states, to which the greatly aggrandized Hesse-Darmstadt and Nassau should be added, these states were to take roots among the people.

While the new southern states could be expected to lean on France and oppose Habsburg influence in the Empire, other provisions made the anti-Austrian intentions of the settlement equally clear. Austria received only the small bishoprics of Brixen and Trent, but the Habsburg grand duke of Tuscany received the archbishopric of Salzburg and the prince of Modena, another Habsburg prince who was removed from Italy, had to be installed as the ruler of an old Austrian dominion, the *Breisgau*. In contrast, a large bounty fell to Prussia. She got the bishopric of Paderborn and parts of Münster, rounding out her Westphalian possessions. She also received many districts and places around the Harz and north of Thuringia, such as the bishopric of Hildesheim and the lands in this region which had belonged to Mainz, as for example, Erfurt and the *Eichsfeld*, and also the imperial cities of Goslar, Nordhausen, and Mühlhausen. Although Prussia did not gain a bridge between her eastern and western provinces through these central German accretions, she did improve connections between them.

The final recess wrecked the Empire, although the document was intended to seem a mere reform of the hallowed institution. Exact voting tables for the diet were worked out, and in the electoral college Cologne and Trier were replaced by Salzburg, Württemberg, Baden, and Hesse. But it was idle to hope that the Empire could survive. Among the one hundred and twelve imperial estates abolished were those that had served as the emperor's main support and the Empire's few surviving common organs. Most remaining princes were interested in their own sovereignty, not common national bonds, and in their foreign policy were taking their cue from the French dictator. The Empire had become a mere pretension. This was strongly felt in Vienna.

✍ *Proclamation of the Austrian Empire*

FROM 1795 ON, Austria had carried the burden of the war against France all by herself, without any support from the Empire, and the final recess brought the German Empire in close relations with France. The news of Napoleon's intention to make himself "Emperor of the Frenchmen" matured the plan of giving the Habsburg lands a position of their own, irrespective of the German Empire's uncertain future development. On August 11, 1804, Francis II assumed the title and dignity of a hereditary emperor of Austria for all his dynastic possessions. The proclamation stated that the new rank would not affect the rights of any of the individual territories, in particular those of Hungary, and would not loosen the ties of the German hereditary lands with the Roman Empire. Actually, the establishment of an Austrian imperial crown was incompatible with the constitution of the Holy Empire, but in view of the latter's effacement, the wish for strengthening the unity of the Habsburg realms was irresistible.

✍ *The Third Coalition*

AT THE TIME OF THE FINAL RECESS, France and England were rapidly approaching the state of open warfare. In May, 1803, the Peace of Amiens was terminated, and war began in earnest. But in the absence of a sufficiently strong French navy, fighting at first was dilatory. English naval forces had to be content with blockade operations, answered by Napoleon's excluding English trade from countries he controlled. He at once occupied Hanover with French troops and closed the Elbe and Weser ports. Meanwhile building naval vessels kept French dockyards busy, while Napoleon brought a large army together in Boulogne. An invasion of England was planned but again and again postponed, since Britain's naval superiority made crossing the Channel too hazardous. Pitt, however, succeeded in forging a new continental alliance against the French emperor, consisting of Russia, Sweden, and Austria.

Austria joined this third coalition with great reluctance. None of the powers felt any need for opposing the French Revolution; Napoleon seemed to have vanquished it. The coalition was formed not to intervene in French internal affairs, but to restore the European balance. France was to be pushed back over the Rhine and excluded from Holland, Switzerland, and Italy. But neither Austria's eminent general, Archduke Carl, nor the new director of Austrian foreign policy, Count Philip Cobenzl, believed that Austria had sufficiently recovered from her earlier wars. Only Napoleon's assuming the Italian crown, in May, 1805, made the Austrian government willing to fight France again. Prussia was sought by Napoleon as well as by Czar Alexander I as an ally. Napoleon offered Hanover, and Prussia might have gained full domination of North Germany if she had joined France, though such a policy would have made her dependent on France thereafter. Napoleon was already thinking of winning a foothold on the right bank of the Lower Rhine and demanded the cession of the Prussian Rhine fortress of Wesel. Frederick William III refused the French alliance, but also declined to join the coalition. However, when French troops on their march from Hanover to the Danube marched through the Prussian Ansbach in early October, 1805, Prussia warned Napoleon to accept a peace on the basis of Lunéville or see Prussia become a member of the coalition. It was on the eve of the battle of Austerlitz that the Prussian representative, Count Haugwitz, arrived at Napoleon's headquarters. He did not have the courage to present the Prussian demands. On the contrary, two weeks later Haugwitz signed a defensive and offensive Franco-Prussian alliance at Schönbrunn. It was the culmination of a long period of indecision, fear, and a false sense of security on the part of the Prussian government, which will have to be more fully discussed later.

The year 1805 saw the greatest triumphs of Napoleon's continental conquests. By persuasion and pressure, Napoleon secured the active co-operation of Bavaria, Baden, and Württemberg. Southern Germany became the main field of operations, contrary to the expectations of the Austrians, who had sent Archduke Carl to Italy and left the German front in the hands of the incompetent General Mack. In one of his most brilliant campaigns, Napoleon managed to cut the Austrian army's rear communications and force Mack to capitulate in Ulm on October 20, 1805. The victor marched directly on Vienna, which he occupied on November 13. The Russians and small Austrian forces under Kutusov fell back to the northern bank of the Danube in Moravia. Napoleon's situation in Austria was untenable in the long run. His army was depleted by the detachment of occupation forces, and Kutusov's superiority in numbers was bound to grow if Archduke Carl arrived with his troops from Italy. The czar's ambition led to the decision not to wait for either the archduke or possible Prussian intervention, and thus Napoleon was able to inflict the crushing defeat of Austerlitz on the two emperors on December 2, 1805. It was almost exactly fifty years after Prince Kaunitz, the statesman who was buried in the church of Austerlitz, had brought together the alliance of the three powers against Frederick II. Over his grave the battle was fought that destroyed two of the chief pillars of Habsburg power, the Austrian position in Italy and southern Germany. But French arms also broke up the alliance between Austria and Russia. Czar Alexander retired with his army into Russia, and Austria was compelled to accept the humiliating Peace of Pressburg.

✍ *The Peace of Pressburg*

AUSTRIA HAD TO RECOGNIZE all the arrangements Napoleon had made in Italy and to cede Venice, Istria, and Dalmatia. In addition, she had to surrender Tyrol, Vorarlberg, Brixen, and Trent to Bavaria, and the "anterior Austrian" lands to Württemberg and Baden. Baden received the major part of the Breisgau, the city of Constance, and some abbeys and lordships, while Württemberg received sections of the Breisgau, several cities, and other accretions. Austria annexed Salzburg, and the greatly expanded Bavaria gave up one of its recent pieces of booty, the bishopric of Würzburg, to serve as a principality for Archduke Ferdinand, the ruler of Salzburg. The three electors of Bavaria, Württemberg, and Baden were made completely sovereign. Austria recognized them as kings or, in the case of Baden, as grand duke. In these circumstances, the Empire could no longer claim to have any meaning. The last southern German free cities, the free imperial knights, and most of the imperial counts were annexed by the new sovereign territorial states. These "mediatizations" (*Mediatisierung*) of 1806 followed the "secularizations" of 1803.

For all practical purposes the new German states were tied to the French emperor's throne. As Napoleon placed his relatives on European thrones in Naples, Italy, Spain, and Holland, or created the German grand duchy of Berg on the right bank of the lower Rhine for his brother-in-law, Joachim Murat, so he also tried to establish bonds with the German dynasties through Bonaparte marriages. Eugène Beauharnais, vice-king of Italy, married a Bavarian princess; Carl of Baden, heir presumptive, married Napoleon's stepdaughter, Stephanie Beauharnais, and Napoleon's younger brother, Jérôme, married a Württemberg princess. But Napoleon realized that the German princes' connections with the Habsburgs and Romanovs could not easily be outweighed. Moreover, he wanted to exploit Germany's resources for his own political and military schemes. On July 12, 1806, negotiations with the small German states were cut short by Napoleon's imperious proposal for the establishment of a Rhenish Confederation.

∽ The Rhenish Confederation

SIXTEEN STATES ORIGINALLY JOINED the Confederation. In addition to Bavaria, Württemberg, Baden, Hesse-Darmstadt, and Berg, ten small "nonmediatized" counts or princes were included under the chairmanship of the "prince-primate" Dalberg, who received the city of Frankfurt and surrounding lands as his own principality. Napoleon proclaimed himself protector of the Confederation. The confederated states were placed under an obligation to maintain armies of 63,000 men, and they entered into a permanent military alliance with France. If one of the members of the alliance was involved in a war, all others would join. Napoleon could count the Rhenish Confederation as a part of his own federative system, or rather of the French empire. The act of the Confederation also seemed to hold forth some hope that the new federation might develop a growing community of its German member states. Apart from the presidency of the prince-primate, it mentioned the establishment of two colleges, those of the kings and princes. But the federal act stated that the forms of meeting of these organs, the subjects of their deliberations, and the execution of their decisions were to be determined by a future "fundamental statute."

However, the councils of the Rhenish Confederation never met to discuss plans for this fundamental statute. States such as Bavaria and Württemberg were jealously guarding their newly won sovereignty, which in their opinion would have been impaired by the creation of a federal power. They realized, too, that such an authority would be completely controlled by Napoleon, who, not without reason, had preserved ten small princelings as members of the organization. Napoleon could have intervened more drastically and frequently in the domestic affairs of the German states than he did between 1806 and 1812. The approaching Prussian war induced Napoleon to content himself with establishing an organization for recruiting auxiliary troops and for general support of his foreign policy. The chain of wars that began in the fall of 1806 kept Napoleon from returning to the project of strengthening the Confederation's federal authority.

On August 1, 1806, the members of the Confederation declared their secession from the Empire. On August 6, Emperor Francis laid down the crown of the German Empire and simultaneously separated all his German lands from the Empire. No doubt under the German constitution the emperor had no right to vacate the throne and thereby dissolve the Empire, but the constitution, so fragile for a good many centuries, had indeed become an unenforceable and meaningless document. How unreal the German Empire had become can be seen from Napoleon's unwillingness to assume the German crown.

∽ The Decline of Prussia

WHILE, A THOUSAND YEARS AFTER ITS INCEPTION, the German Empire fell into dust, the hour approached when the youngest great power which had developed in its lap, the monarchy of Frederick the Great, was to be shaken to its very foundations. "We went to sleep on the laurels of Frederick the Great," was the explanation Queen Louise, the wife of Frederick William III, gave for the Prussian disaster of 1806, and it contained a great deal of truth. But the twenty years after Frederick's death were full of developments that contained not only the seeds of catastrophe but also elements of future strength. Most people had received the news of old Fritz's demise with sighs of relief. His will power had dominated his state completely, and by the same token stifled individual initiative. The solitary remoteness of his life and personality could not fail to have a chilling effect on the sentiments even of his admirers. His contempt for religion bewildered the common people, and his acid criticism of German intellectual and artistic effort alienated the burghers, who began to take pride in their cultural achievements. The changes of mercantilism which Frederick introduced in his last years, hurt the people's purses, and though the French administrators of the excise tax and the tobacco and coffee monopoly were the chief targets of popular resentment, the king was not absolved of his responsibility.

∽ *Frederick William II*

THE NEW KING, FREDERICK WILLIAM II (1786–97), was welcomed by the Prussian people, and his early official actions aroused general enthusiasm. Great satisfaction was shown when the new king appeared at church or when he denounced the superiority of French culture. The royal theater in Berlin, hitherto devoted to French drama, was made a German national theater. The Berlin Academy was deprived of its French character, and although its new members represented the spirit of a shallow rationalism which had found its home in Berlin and soon was to be challenged not only by the writers of Weimar and Jena but also by the young romanticists who assembled in the Prussian capital, the institution was brought into direct contact with the indigenous intellectual movement.

The French tax administrators were dismissed, and the administration of the excise tax was restored to the General Directory. The tobacco and coffee monopolies were abolished. The Prussian government was moving in the direction of a general reform of mercantilism. The chief part of Prussian mercantilistic practices, rigid control of the grain trade, was liberalized. But on the whole, these measures were more attempts to win popularity than steps of constructive policy. These changes, it was soon discovered, would seriously diminish revenues. The plan of a general tax, however, graded in accordance with social class divisions, was quickly dropped, in fear of encountering the opposition of the propertied class. After a few years, all liberal measures were abandoned, and taxes were increased on the most essential consumer goods. If economic conditions did not become fully intolerable, this was due to the considerable expansion of commerce and trade, which increased again after 1795, when Prussia's status as a neutral permitted her to reap great profits from international trade. But the state finances suffered, largely as a result of numerous wars, but also as a consequence of political indecision and incompetence.

The war chest of fifty million which Frederick II had left his successor was rapidly exhausted, and ten years later a public debt of forty-eight million thaler had piled up. The acquisition of new provinces was of no avail, since the king liked to give away domains to his favorites in a grand style.

Frederick William II was a man of friendly disposition who craved personal recognition. He had quite a few amiable qualities and talents. For example, he played the violoncello well and devotedly, or, as the Berlin people (then as later given to sardonic jokes) expressed it, "as if he were paid for it," and to this royal interest posterity owes some of the finest of Mozart's string quartets. But although Frederick William wanted to be the autocratic ruler of the state, he had no political gifts. Those people had most influence over him who flattered his personal inclinations and catered to his personal tastes. He was a weak personality, driven by his sensuality as much as by compunction over his aberrations. The Prussian court saw the regime of both mistresses and favorite advisers who knew how to impress the king with strange mystic exercises. In the palace garden of Charlottenburg, where a century before Queen Sophie Charlotte had held pleasant and profound philosophical conversations, preposterous spiritualistic séances were staged for the king by his Rosicrucian companions, among whom Johann Rudolf von Bischoffswerder and Johann Christoph Wöllner gained the role of chief advisors, the former in foreign and military affairs, the latter in domestic administration. The heads of the Protestant state Church demonstrated their scandalous subservience by blessing two bigamistic ventures of Frederick William, using Luther's attitude toward the bigamy of Philip of Hesse as precedent.

It was illogical that his regime should undertake any attempt to reform the Evangelical Church. No doubt the state of the Church and religion in Prussia was deplorable in many respects, but further authoritarian intervention by the state could only make a bad situation worse. Wöllner's edict on religion of 1788 tried such intervention in the clumsiest fashion. It is true that the edict in its first part codified the policy of toleration toward all religious beliefs and groups, which so far had been only a practice. But the second part stipulated that in the Protestant churches the authority of the old tenets of faith should be enforced. In particular, the ministers were to be held strictly to the orthodox doctrines. The edict was executed in a petty fashion and aroused great annoyance. Inevitably, it led to nothing but hypocrisy. Since even the bureaucracy was honeycombed with rationalists, evasion was possible. The commission charged with the administration of the policy of the Church, school, and censorship had to admit in 1794 that the results hoped for had not materialized. But Frederick William urged sterner action. At that time Kant was reprimanded and forbidden to write on religion.

The immorality of Frederick William's court naturally was reflected in Berlin society, and the mild affluence which was produced by favorable economic conditions tended to promote still further libertinage. Still, it was not only the bad example set by the court which led to the society's moral slackness but often enough it was also the influence of the new ideas of literature and philosophy. Practically all of them criticized mere conformity to traditional norms of conduct and encouraged the individual to form his life in accordance with his own inner longings. The rejection of old social obligations, however, was more easily accomplished than the realization of the positive ethics of German idealism, which in these years of transition not infrequently had a more corrosive than constructive impact on the individual's moral conduct. Opposite examples could be found as well, but in the relaxed atmosphere they could not impress themselves deeply on the general character of public life.

∽ *Frederick William III*

THE ACCESSION TO THE THRONE of Frederick William III (1797–1840) brought an improvement, though not a complete change. The twenty-seven-year-old prince was an honest man of modest taste. He lived in happy marriage with the vivacious and pretty Louise of Mecklenburg (1776–1810), who was already interested in modern German literature and occasionally exercised a beneficial political influence through her enthusiastic temper. The personal favorites and mistresses of Frederick William II were at once banned from the court, and although his son maintained the customary military front of the royal household of Prussia, it was almost the style of a German burgher home that Frederick William III introduced to the court of Berlin and Potsdam. This style was continued by his two sons and successors, Frederick William IV and William I. Leopold Ranke has called Frederick William III the "simple" king and with this name has characterized not only his aversion to luxury but also his great personal modesty, which made him impervious to all flattery. As a matter of fact, he was shy and, particularly in the early period of his long reign, unsure of himself. Actually he had only a mediocre and prosaic mind, which made it impossible for him to reach great political decisions. Of tolerant religious convictions, he also wanted to become a well-meaning, enlightened ruler.

Still, Frederick William III wished to be the real ruler of the state. But as little as his father was he able to perform the work of a Frederick the Great. Frederick William II had already given up the direct management of military affairs, for which a Supreme War Council (*Oberkriegskollegium*) was founded in 1787. Otherwise he ruled with a few ministers possessing his personal confidence. His successor, however, avoided the ministers and, in need of advice, relied on his personal secretaries. Frederick the Great had employed as technical assistants so-called cabinet secretaries, who had never played a role in the formulation of policy. Under Frederick William III, they emerged, to the distress of the ministers, as the king's real political advisors, a part for which they were exceedingly ill-cast since none of them possessed statesman-like gifts. This system only accentuated the king's indecision. At the same time, the ministers, who often had to execute policies with which they disagreed, became resentful over the intrusion of subaltern figures. The pride and self-consciousness of Prussian ministers had grown since the days of Frederick II, and around 1800 a great deal of talent was found in the Prussian bureaucracy. It was in its ranks that new developments were fermenting.

✑ Reforms before 1806

FREDERICK WILLIAM III himself was convinced that the state was in need of reform. When it appeared, however, that any reform of a single department of the state led inevitably to the necessity of reorganizing its whole structure, he hesitated to take drastic action. The most important reform, which was successfully carried out in the years 1799–1805, was the liberation of the peasants on the crownlands. The peasants were first freed from the obligatory labor services they owed the managers of the royal domains. In the future they paid rent in money or kind. Their *Erbuntertänigkeit* was abolished, that is, the form of serfdom which tied the peasant to the land and made marriage as well as the appointment of an heir dependent on the lord's consent, provided the tenancy was inheritable at all. Through this reform, for which the cabinet councilor Beyme was largely responsible, the crownland peasants received a proprietary right on the lands they were holding.

It was the greatest agrarian reform ever carried out in Prussia. In the eastern provinces, not counting Silesia, 50,000 freehold farms were created, as against 45,000 created between 1816 and 1850 by legislation dealing with the nobility's lands. Frederick William III actually would have liked to proceed immediately from the liberation of the crown peasants to that of the peasants on the nobility's estates. But the *Junkers* objected to a change in their own privileges. To be sure, the privileged position of the landed nobility had certain disadvantages. The nobility's very monopoly in the ownership of landed estates depressed land prices, because it excluded the investment of urban capital in land values. Since there were many political implications connected with the nobility's exclusive right to own landed estates, the king dodged a decision on the underlying principle but adopted a very liberal practice in granting exemptions to burghers wishing to acquire noble estates. But even more complex was the problem of the "private" peasants, whom Frederick William desired to see freed like the crown peasants. The nobleman had certain obligations to his serfs. He was expected to keep the peasant's hut in repair, to provide him with food if the harvest failed, and to loan him money to pay his tax if he was in exceptional need. The lord was not permitted to evict his tenant and make his land part of the manorial lands (*Bauern legen*). However, the government had never made any systematic attempt to enforce these customary rules except for the last one, and even in this respect many violations occurred. The apparatus of the Prussian monarchy was not developed highly enough to survey the remote countryside, and the rural government was almost completely in the gentry's hands.

Still, if serfdom was to fall and thereby the guarantee of a labor supply in agriculture, the *Bauernschutz*, the protection of the peasants against eviction by their lords, had to be completely abandoned. Some East Prussian *Junker* families were relatively quick to see this connection, and since the economic conditions made an expansion of agricultural production attractive, they set their serfs free without paying special attention to the *Bauernschutz*. It also dawned on some *Junkers* that the labor of downtrodden peasant serfs would always be unsatisfactory and that in the long run free peasants and agrarian workers might be both cheaper and more effective. But Frederick William III was afraid of moving too fast in view of the strong *Junker* sentiment opposing any change in this field. Reforms in individual provinces perhaps offered a better approach, and East Prussia seemed most propitious. Here then, in 1806, Minister Friedrich Leopold von Schrötter, together with a group of younger high officials, was at work drafting plans for an agrarian reform for the province when catastrophe overtook the Prussian monarchy.

Similar reform ideas were canvassed in the financial field. A decent administration of Prussian finances had been restored after 1797. By 1806, 22 million thaler of debt were paid off and 17 million placed in the war chest, but a 53 million debt remained, a rather high sum considering that the annual budget balanced under 30 million. This budget was inadequate for the state's greater needs. Direct taxes had not been increased since the days of Frederick II, nor had army pay been raised since those of Frederick William I. The army's equipment was old, and the fortresses were in poor condition. Annexations of new provinces and the relative prosperity of these years should have made it possible to tap new sources of revenue. In 1798, Frederick William III established a royal commission on finance and directed it in particular to study the possibility of making the nobility liable to a land tax, and in general to lift a number of exemptions of special groups. But about the only practical result of these deliberations, which ranged very far, was the withdrawal of a few minor tariff exemptions of the nobility, which caused excited protests. Even though the army received a 25 per cent raise in pay, it still remained necessary to find for them opportunities for remunerative civilian employment on the side. Friction and conflicts with the guilds over the intrusion of such unlicensed and tax-exempt people into the trades of the towns resulted. In view of the clash of army organization and the order of the civilian economy, some ministers already argued, though still in vain, that the monopoly of the guilds would have to be abolished. Some of the ideas produced by the royal finance commission were used for practical legislation when Baron Stein became minister of the excise and factory department of the General Directory, in October, 1804. His energy pushed through a reform of the excise administration that moderated the separate treatment of towns and countryside. In a reorganization of the salt monopoly he took a big step toward abolishing interior customs lines, which strangled commerce between the individual provinces. In 1806, we find him busy designing a general income tax after the English model, a plan that was to be realized in Prussia only half a century later. But prior to 1806, even Stein conceived of the improvement of the government as a step-by-step process.

Frederick William III also had an eye on the correction of some weaknesses of the army, which had shone in the wars between 1793 and 1795. The full significance of the new type of army the French Revolution had brought into existence was recognized only by a few officers in Prussia. The changes in tactics, the use of *tirailleurs* at the beginning of a battle, the formation of divisions as self-sufficient units, the greater use of artillery, as well as the reliance on foraging and the resulting possibility of doing without large supply trains, made an impression on the Prussians. But no other answer was found except for the organization of two dozen battalions of fusiliers, who were to fight in extended order like the *tirailleurs*. A change in general army tactics was impossible so long as the army was composed largely of untrustworthy soldiers. For the new tactics, with their reliance on the individual soldier, called for the alertness and loyalty the French citizen soldier possessed. Half of the Prussian army consisted of mercenaries, who could not be depended on and necessitated old-fashioned tactics and a brutal discipline. The rest of the army was composed of native peasants and journeymen. They were not likely to desert and could be handled with a more civilized discipline.

Among young intelligent officers touched by the new philosophical teachings on the dignity of all humans, the old discipline aroused great uneasiness. They wished the army built exclusively on soldiers coming from the cantons and the basis of recruitment broadened to include larger sections of the town population. The wars of the French Revolution and Napoleon closed most centers of the Empire and other countries that had delivered mercenaries. On the other hand, if the *Bauernschutz* were abandoned in the course of agrarian reforms, many a rural hearth might disappear and the yield of the canton system become inadequate. Nowhere did it become clearer than in this dilemma how the whole social and political structure was aimed at the army's maintenance. Once a single stone was removed, the whole arch would topple. Any decision on the future of the Prussian army system was evaded by recruiting soldiers in the new Polish provinces. The officers who wished to see a thorough reform could not make themselves sufficiently heard. The army was top-heavy with superannuated officers and generals. The survivors of the great days of Frederick II seemed to vouchsafe the Prussian monarchy's invincibility, and the kind-hearted king hesitated to dismiss them.

Frederick William III's timidity and lack of imagination, together with his dogged determination to remain master of affairs, contributed to his inability for making full use of the talents available in Prussia. He felt ill at ease in the presence of commanding personalities. Frederick II had directed all military affairs, with the exception of mere administration of economic matters, which were in the hands of the war department of the General Directory. Frederick William III was supposed to have given the actual exercise of command functions to the Supreme War Council, but at the same time he relied on his personal military aides. However, in addition to the war department, the war council, and the adjutant-generals of the king, still other people, such as army inspectors and commanding generals, had largely independent functions. The confusion in the military high command's organization was great and was to have fatal consequences.

✌ *Foreign Policy*

THE KING'S INDECISION multiplied not only the internal government's laxity but also the international dangers. There was nothing in him of the burning desire for greater power that had been alive in Frederick II. He was more deeply impressed by the financial exhaustion which, after a series of wars, had forced Frederick William II to conclude the Peace of Basel. To keep Prussia at peace through the preservation of North Germany's neutrality, was the keystone of his whole foreign policy. Prussia did not join the second coalition (1799), and when in the end Russia and Austria fell apart, this policy appeared justified. The rapprochement between Czar Paul and Napoleon in 1800 seemed to open a chance for Prussia to act as go-between for France and Russia and collect profits by rounding out the Prussian possessions in northern Germany. This policy threatened to bring Prussia into conflict with Britain and did not enhance her political reputation with Napoleon, who wanted to deal with Russia directly. The assassination of Czar Paul and the friendlier attitude of his successor Alexander toward England threatened Prussia with complete isolation. Still, the Peace of Amiens (1802) between France and Britain eased the situation temporarily, and the Final Recess of the Imperial Deputation of 1803 brought Prussia rich spoils. But she did not gain the accession of the North German territories as a result of her own strength, but because Napoleon, with the czar's consent, wished to break up the German Empire and confine Austria to southeast Europe.

With the conclusion of peace between France and the Empire, through the Treaty of Lunéville (1801), the provision of the Peace of Basel for the neutrality of northern Germany had lapsed. When, in the spring of 1803, war broke out again between France and England,

Napoleon sent French troops into Hanover. A French army was poised in between Prussia's western and eastern provinces, but even then Frederick William III intended to maintain neutrality and persevered in this policy when the break between Russia and France occurred. It has already been told that only the violation of the Franconian possessions, through the entry of French troops, led Frederick William III —advised by Hardenberg, who on this occasion established his reputation with Alexander I—to the agreement of Potsdam of November 3, 1805, offering armed mediation and, if Napoleon refused, accession to the coalition. Even then the king hoped for peace, and this explains in part the willingness of Count Haugwitz, after the battle of Austerlitz, to sign the humiliating Treaty of Schönbrunn. The treaty recognized beforehand the territorial changes Napoleon wanted to make in southern Germany. It promised the cession of the Franconian principalities and of Cleves, for which Prussia was to receive Hanover. The occupation of Hanover was bound to bring Prussia into conflict with England, and it was Napoleon's real objective to force Prussia into subservience to France's European policy. In fact, the treaty contained an open Franco-Prussian alliance.

The Berlin government refused to ratify the Treaty of Schönbrunn without modifications. Haugwitz was sent to Paris and the Prussian army unwisely demobilized. Napoleon, who had in the meantime made peace with Austria, at once raised the price. The Treaty of Paris, to which Frederick William III gave his assent in February 1806, brought Prussia into even greater dependence on French policy. The Prussian occupation of Hanover and the ensuing rupture of relations with England meant the complete annihilation of Prussia's maritime trade, which in the preceding decade had contributed so greatly to her prosperity. The impact upon the Prussian economy was immediate and caused distress among the merchant class. Soon it was realized that Napoleon was not going to treat Prussia as an equal ally. Word was received that Napoleon had offered Hanover to England in an attempt to reach an understanding with his foremost enemy, while at the same time the disposition of French troops seemed to indicate further plans against Prussia. Among the high bureaucracy and even in the royal family, open criticism was voiced against the abject policy followed by the king under the influence of his cabinet secretaries. Frederick William III grew apprehensive. The army was mobilized and an ultimatum presented to Napoleon, chiefly demanding the withdrawal of the French troops from the Prussian frontiers. Napoleon countered with a request for the demobilization of the Prussian army. On October 9, 1806, Frederick William III issued a war manifesto.

✍ *The Battle of Jena and Its Aftermath*

THE BANKRUPTCY of Prussian foreign policy was equaled by the ineptitude of her military high command. Duke Ferdinand of Brunswick, now seventy-one years of age, who was appointed commander-in-chief, had not gained in determination and was unable to assert himself amidst the various personalities who claimed a part in the major decisions. The Prussian army was not even assembled when, with lightning speed, Napoleon fell upon it in northern Thuringia. He succeeded in placing himself between the Prussian army and their line of communications with Berlin. On October 14, he attacked the army of Prince Hohenlohe at Jena. The battle was won by Napoleon almost before it began. The emperor had secured for himself the dominant positions and had superior forces at his command. On the same day, Marshal Davoust met the Prussian main army under the duke of Brunswick farther north at Auerstädt. Confused leadership, worsened by the fatal wound the duke received as well as by the king's personal interference, enabled Davoust to win a full victory despite his outnumbered troops. Both at Jena and at Auerstädt the Prussian soldiers fought bravely. But in defeat the bonds of discipline broke down completely.

Little was saved of the vaunted Prussian army, and the generals' cowardice turned the loss of the battles into total catastrophe for the state. Two weeks later, Prince Hohenlohe capitulated with the remnants of his troops not far from Stettin. General Blücher displayed a courageous and dashing spirit even in adversity, but had finally to surrender his small corps in the neighborhood of Lübeck. In the meantime, the Prussian fortresses, which, though ill-equipped to resist long sieges, were still heavily garrisoned, capitulated ignominiously, often without making so much as the pretense of resistance. Not only Erfurt, Magdeburg, and the Elbe line, but also the fortresses of the Oder valley fell into French hands. Only Danzig and Graudenz on the Vistula put up a strong fight, and in the small fortified Baltic port of Kolberg, Major von Gneisenau rallied garrison and townspeople to a brilliant defense, which the French failed to break. Deeds of courage were equally rare among the bureaucracy. While Stein saved the coffers of the state treasury, the governor of Berlin issued a proclamation to the population: "The king has lost a battle; it is the duty of citizens to preserve calm." When Napoleon approached the Prussian capital, the governor went to Königsberg, where the court had gone, without destroying the large arms deposits in the Berlin arsenal.

On October 27, 1806, Napoleon arrived in Berlin. The ministers and officials who had remained behind in the capital took an oath to the foreign conqueror. With the administration intact, Napoleon could immediately extract large payments. Frederick William III opened peace negotiations, but to the emperor Prussia was of secondary importance. His mind was completely occupied with the great struggle against Britain. On November 21, 1806, he issued from Berlin the proclamation excluding all British trade and all Englishmen from the Continent. The Continental System was the greatest program of economic warfare conceived to that date in history, but if it was to succeed, it required Russia's accession. Prussia was to be used only as a pawn in the war, which was to compel the czar to join the anti-British front. Napoleon first offered Prussia peace, but subsequently when he saw the full measure of Prussian demoralization, only an armistice on the basis of the cession of all provinces west of the Elbe, the complete withdrawal from all federative ties with other Germanic states, and the debarment of the approaching Russian troops from Prussia. The last condition was designed to get Prussia into war with Russia. This was one of the major reasons why Frederick William III decided, on November 21, against the majority of his ministers and generals, for the continuation of the war on the side of Russia.

Stein was selected by the king as foreign minister. But he felt too inexperienced in diplomacy to accept, though he used the occasion to urge establishing a ministerial council and abolishing the king's cabinet as the highest political organ of the state. Frederick William was unwilling to see himself cut off from his intimate political advisors, the cabinet secretaries. Still, he conceded the appointment of three ministers for war, interior affairs, and foreign affairs, who should consult with the king but still remain greatly dependent on the cabinet secretaries' co-operation, and even direction. Stein refused with passion to work in such a relationship. The relentless insistence on a change in the organization of the state's supreme offices aroused the ire of the king, who, in the worst manner of an absolute ruler, dismissed Stein in the first days of 1807.

The Prussian court went from Königsberg to Memel, the easternmost town of the monarchy, and here connections were made with the Russians. Peace was made between England and Prussia, but the negotiation of a financial subsidy treaty came too late. Austria was not persuaded to join in the war against France. General revolts broke out in Prussia's Polish provinces and were supported by Napoleon, who had gone to Warsaw. But Prusso-Russian co-operation made progress, and Napoleon's situation, so far from his home bases, was not without dangers. In the battle of Eylau in Prussia (February 7–8, 1807), he failed to defeat the Russian army under Bennigsen. A Prussian corps, properly employed by its chief of staff, Scharnhorst, took a substantial part in this French setback. Hardenberg convinced Frederick William to persevere in the war, despite Napoleon's attempts to split the Russo-Prussian co-operation. Through the Treaty of Bartenstein (April 26, 1807), Alexander I and Frederick William concluded an alliance to continue the war until the French were driven over the Rhine. A program for restoring the old European system of powers was drafted. In particular, Italy, Germany, and possibly Holland were to be freed from French domination. In Germany, Prussia was to regain her status of 1805 with better frontiers. A confederation of German states, under the military leadership of Austria and Prussia, was to take the place of the former German Empire. The war aims agreed upon at Bartenstein were in harmony with the objectives William Pitt had formulated in 1805 at the time of the formation of the third coalition. But seven years were to pass before such a program served as the blueprint of a restored Europe.

✍ The Peace of Tilsit

It was in these months that Hardenberg conditioned Frederick William to working with a responsible minister of state. What the impetuous and imperious Baron Stein had failed to achieve, Count Hardenberg accomplished through suave diplomatic manners. The respect in which Czar Alexander held Hardenberg also impressed Frederick William. Important as this event was in Prussia's internal history, everything depended immediately on the course of military events. This proved disappointing. In the battle of Friedland (June 14, 1807), Napoleon roundly defeated the Russians, forcing their retreat behind the Njemen. The military reverse raised opposition to any active Russian policy in western Europe, and the czar easily succumbed to such criticism. Without consulting Prussia, Alexander hurried to make peace with Napoleon. On July 7, 1807, a treaty of peace and alliance was signed between Russia and France at Tilsit. The event could have meant the end of Prussia, and Napoleon on his part left no doubt that he agreed to the survival of a crippled Prussia only in deference to Russia's wishes. Czar Alexander promised to assist in bringing the war between France and England to a close, while Napoleon, in a less explicit manner, offered his co-operation in a settlement of the Russo-Turkish war. In these two issues lay the cause of renewed conflict between the two emperors five years later. But even at Tilsit, their mutual trust was not without strong reservations. Napoleon granted Alexander the favor of tolerating the existence of a Prussian state as a sort of cushion between the French and Russian empires. He also abstained from a full restoration of Poland. Only the territories Prussia had taken in Poland's second and third partition and the Netze district were formed into the grand duchy of Warsaw. The ruler of Saxony, after making peace with Napoleon and joining the Rhenish Confederation as "King of Saxony," became the grand duke of the revived Polish state. But Prussia not only lost all her possessions west of the Elbe, including Magdeburg and the Altmark, but also had to cede Lower Lusatia to Saxony and grant her a road that linked Saxony and Poland. The Oder was further brought under French control by the occupation of the Prussian Oder fortresses. French power was extended even to the Vistula. Danzig became a free city, though with a French garrison. All these measures served not only to subjugate Prussia but also to drive Russia out of the old Europe and allow her to expand only around the northern Baltic. Napoleon permitted the Russian conquest of Finland.

In the peace settlement of Tilsit, which marked the height of Napoleon's power over Europe, Prussia was a negligible factor. Actual negotiations did not take place between France and Prussia. Hardenberg, the architect of the Russo-Prussian alliance, was declared by Napoleon unacceptable as a representative of Prussia and had to resign as minister. The Prussians had to sign the conditions of peace handed to them within forty-eight hours. This Franco-Prussian Peace of Tilsit (July 9, 1807) was made even more oppressive by a convention of July 12, which provided for the French evacuation of Prussia east of the Elbe, for this evacuation was made dependent on the payment of a large indemnity, which, however, was left undetermined. Decimated Prussia remained at her conqueror's mercy.

CHAPTER 13

Reform and Liberation, 1807-15

A FTER THE PEACE OF TILSIT, the territories of the former German
Empire were split in a fourfold manner. Those on the left
bank of the Rhine were an integral part of the French empire. The main regions of Germany formed the Confederation of the Rhine, while Austria and Prussia were confined to the
southeastern and northeastern borderlands. In varying forms, all of
Germany experienced the influence of French ideas and institutions in
this period, but the intensity and results of this influence differed
greatly in these various regions.

✍ French Influence on Germany

FOR ALMOST TWENTY YEARS the left bank of the Rhine, organized in
seven *départements*, was ruled directly by France, and the reforms
introduced by the French took deep roots in the Rhineland. The
French administration was highly competent and effective. The chaos
of divided authorities in a land broken up among many lords gave way
to a more rational order, which, however, was firmly centralized in
Paris. But progress over the feudal government of the ecclesiastical
and petty secular princes was enormous and was welcomed by the
population. The abolition of all feudal privileges, the introduction of
Napoleon's *code civil* and of the French organization of the judiciary
as well as the organization of the local administration met with general
approval. Socially and economically, the Rhineland was closer to
French conditions than the rest of Germany. The distinction between
countryside and town was less pronounced, although the urban and
industrial elements were more fully developed. The egalitarian society
Napoleon created in France was transplanted here to kindred soil. As
part of the French empire, the Rhineland benefited from some of the
economic advantages which accrued from the Continental System. The
exclusion of all English products from the Continent permitted an

expansion of French industrial production, which also took place in the Rhineland. Particularly the district around Aachen profited from this industrial spurt. The French regime's absolute features aroused no resentment among the mass of the Rhenish people, who were used to more arbitrary forms of government. On the other hand, French school and church policies apparently were received with great distrust.

The states of the Rhenish Confederation had no unified development. In North Germany, two major groups of states existed. In the old German states, particularly Saxony and Mecklenburg, in the east, the impact of the French system was minimal. They remained what they had been, states with old dualistic constitutions and privileged classes. In Saxony, the ancient constitution did not express the actual superiority over the estates which its electors had gained long ago. Still, King Frederick August I was not unhappy that Napoleon ordered equality for Catholics, a grant the king might not have gotten from the estates. While Frederick August introduced the *code civil* in Poland, he made no changes in the laws of Saxony. A different situation prevailed in the states created by Napoleon. He gave his brother-in-law Murat the grand duchy of Berg, on the right bank of the Rhine. The largest new state, composed of Hanover, Brunswick, Electoral Hesse, and the territories of Prussia west of the Elbe, received the name of the kingdom of Westphalia. Napoleon's gay, good-hearted, but dissolute youngest brother, Jérôme Bonaparte, was installed in Kassel as king. Napoleon himself paid much attention to the governments of Berg, Westphalia, and also the grand duchy of Frankfurt, which he created in 1810 for Dalberg. Westphalia in particular was to set a model of enlightened French government in order to attract the sympathies of the people of the neighboring German states, including Prussia. Actually, the Westphalian system had a considerable influence on the thinking of German statesmen. It was an exact replica of the French empire, resting on an egalitarian society, the removal of all local immunities, and the strict centralization of all political controls. Representative bodies were not altogether abolished, but whether it was the national senate and tribunate or the councils in the departments or municipalities, though in theory they were left with consultative faculties only, in practice they were unable to maintain even that much. Through the Concordat of 1801, Napoleon also made the Church a subservient arm of the government.

Still, in northwestern Germany, the Napoleonic regime did not succeed in winning ready popular support. Although the peasants liked the free agrarian laws and everybody was pleased with the new officials' general politeness, the social and economic forces which could have taken full advantage of the French order were lacking in this predominantly agrarian region. With all the shortcomings of its aristocratic regime, Hanover took pride in its traditional forms of political life, and despite the despotism and class differentiation of their administration, the Prussian lands shared in Prussian patriotism. The people of Electoral Hesse had witnessed much immorality at the court of Kassel and suffered the indignities of their rulers' trade in soldiers, but the libertinage of a French king appeared more objectionable and conscription for the new army not much better than the former sale of soldiers. In addition, the French administration in northwestern Germany during the six years of its existence failed to translate its general political principles into practice. In 1814, consequently, it was easy to remove all the institutions it had been in the process of building and to restore the indigenous order. French ideas were not entirely forgotten, however.

Southern Germany proved receptive to both French ideas and institutions. The new "middle" states—Bavaria, Württemberg, Baden, and also Hesse-Darmstadt and Nassau—which had come into existence between 1803 and 1806 were actually new states, but each was built around the kernel of an old territorial state under a legitimate dynasty. The scope of the changes and the speed with which they were introduced were still greater than those attempted in Westphalia, but they were executed by native governments. German national sentiment was weak in southern Germany except among small intellectual circles, who complained about Prussia's betrayal of Germany through the Treaty of Basel and the discord caused by Austria's scheming against Bavaria. Although the South German governments' subservience to Napoleon could not be hidden, it could be used as an excuse for many unpopular actions. On the other hand, the indigenous governments could claim, not altogether without reason, that their existence protected the people against further intervention by the French emperor. But many old customs and laws were suddenly trampled upon and discarded. Still, to a large extent the Napoleonic system could be considered another form of Josephinism, which had found many believers in southern Germany. The Austrian Breisgau, which now became a part of Baden under Carl Frederick, had been moving, though more cautiously, in the same direction. In South Germany, the new French system could not appear as entirely alien.

ꙩ *Reform in the German States*

THE NATURE OF THE PROBLEMS all these states faced made a radical reform inevitable. In former centuries, a new territory was joined to a state by a simple personal union. Existing local laws and institutions, such as estates or law courts, were preserved, and in the central government an agency was created which dealt with the affairs of the particular territory. But not even the largest state, Bavaria, could possibly have absorbed the large number of heterogeneous new lands in this fashion. Principalities and bishoprics, large and small, abbeys, cities, and estates of imperial knights could not be annexed by the old methods. Nor could one hope to protect historic rights. Everywhere these were completely disregarded. Geographically or economically convenient local and district units were formed and treated as equal parts of the state, though, of course, they might vary in area and population. On the whole, the organization followed the example of the French *départements* and *arrondissements*, which had been created for the same reason, to blot out local and provincial diversities and special privileges. This entirely rationalistic planning also made it logical to adopt the French system in the central government. The departments concerned with special regional problems were abolished. Ministries exercising functions over the whole state replaced the confused organization of the old central offices.

These reforms set the framework of the new unified states in which absolutism, freed from considerations for time-honored laws, could hold sway. Here the sovereignty of princes was used not only as a justification for the denial of any superior authority, be it of the German Empire or the Rhenish Confederation, but also of any participation of domestic forces in government. All historic estates were dissolved. For the time being, none of the South German states took the risk of introducing popular representatives, even in the emasculated form of the Napoleonic councils, although, in 1808, Bavaria promised the establishment of such a national representation. The self-government of the towns was practically suppressed. The absolutist regimes were usually directed by bureaucratic ministers. Only in Württemberg was the monarch himself in charge of the government. King Frederick I, a brutal, base, vicious, if shrewd, man, wrote another unpleasant chapter in the records of German princely tyranny. The scandalous abuse of his despotic position for the satisfaction of his personal pleasures and whims was one of the causes of the hatred and contempt Baron Stein felt for the "sultanism" of the lesser German princes. But although the Swabian people's indignation grew, there can be no question that in this period the foundation was laid for an integrated modern Württemberg.

In Bavaria, the minister Maximilian von Montgelas, the son of a Savoyard aristocrat who had settled in Munich, held the reins of government from 1799 to 1818; in Baden, Sigismund von Reitzenstein. Both these men were radical pupils of the rationalistic Enlightenment. For a while the Baden government attempted to find a moderate transition to the new system from the relatively advanced methods which Carl Frederick (died 1811) had employed. But under Grand Duke Carl the bureaucracy moved at a dangerous rate of speed. Much confusion ensued. Every so often orders and laws had to be revised, if not countermanded, shortly after they had been issued. The officialdom of this period was ill-prepared to cope with the multitude of problems it tried to solve. Moreover, the integrity of these officials left much to be desired. Against the opposition of the nobility, which resented the loss of its freedoms, the governments of the new states introduced an egalitarian order. In Baden, the *code civil* was adopted with slight modifications, in Bavaria its acceptance was under discussion. But everywhere the peasants were declared to be personally free, although economic servitudes were not abolished. Henceforth, such obligations were considered removable (*abgelöst*) through payment, but since the states did not provide funds or any clear procedure, the economic burdens of the peasantry continued for another half-century.

The equality of the citizens, however, was expressed by a new tax system, which abolished all exemptions based on social rank and aimed at a taxation on the basis of financial capacity. The states of southern Germany shied away from a straight income tax as much as Paris. Great progress was achieved by lifting all internal customs barriers, though the duties levied at the external frontiers remained high. In southern Germany's state of economic development, a liberal foreign economic policy was probably unadvisable. But it might be questionable whether the preservation of guilds was economically justifiable. The briefness of the period in which all the reforms were initiated explains why they were not in all cases pushed to their logical conclusion. No violent popular revolt, as in France, had preceded the bureaucratic revolution from above. Even the Napoleonic legislation, which the Germans emulated, had compromised with existing social forces. Universal conscription, the *levée en masse*, had been revised by Napoleon in favor of the bourgeoisie by granting exemption in return for the payment of a tax. In this socially selective form, conscription became the rule in southern Germany. But in contrast to France, some concessions were made not only to the bourgeoisie but also to the nobility. However, it was important that they were made as free grants of the state, not through negotiations between the government and a single estate, which demanded privileges as a matter of historic right.

The state's sovereignty was also asserted against the Church. In former centuries, the power of the Bavarian dukes and electors over the Church had been very extensive. Subsequently, Joseph II's church policy had made a deep impression in Munich, but the government of Carl Theodore, which wished to control the indigenous clergy, had needed the Pope's support. But with the old Church of the Empire wrecked by secularization and with Napoleon's struggle against the papacy, the way was open for the establishment of a territorial Church. The Bavarian Church was to be confined to the Bavarian territories, and the ecclesiastical dioceses were to conform to the political boundaries. The clergy was to be selected from among the indigenous population and to be trained in Bavarian institutions. Behind this policy was not only the desire for the expansion of political power but also the conviction of the Enlightenment that people would be happier with a Church shorn of secular authority, and thereby, as it was assumed, directed toward a more rational type of religion. Therefore, the statesmen did not feel any scruples in confiscating the great properties of the monasteries. Schools were now generally declared to be state institutions and directed chiefly toward the education of citizens. This separation of education from the Church in southern Germany meant a great change, because in many places it coincided with the end of denominational uniformity.

In Munich, it is said, only three Protestants were living in 1800. They were unable to profess their faith and could worship only by taking an occasional trip to Augsburg. The new Bavaria of King Maximilian I Joseph (1799–1825), who was married to a Protestant princess, assured full protection to the churches, and Count Montgelas fostered a spirit of toleration in Bavarian education. Opposition to these measures among the people was rather strong. The attempt to found interdenominational elementary schools failed. If a new spirit was to be created, it had to be undertaken first on the higher levels, and there was no other choice but to bring men from northern Germany into Bavaria. Montgelas brought Schelling to Würzburg, drew Friedrich

Heinrich Jacobi and Friedrich Thiersch to the academy in Munich, and made Hegel the director of the "Gymnasium" in Nürnberg in 1806. Thiersch was to become the reformer of the secondary schools in the neohumanistic spirit of Weimar. For German national history it was of great significance that the long cultural isolation of old Bavaria and of the bishoprics on the Main was broken and a free interflow of ideas could take place between all regions of Germany. The reorganization of the University of Heidelberg—stymied for more than a century by the bitter religious enmities of the Palatinate—through the Baden government under von Reitzenstein, laid the foundation of Heidelberg's great role in the national history of the next century.

Yet neither Montgelas nor Reitzenstein had any national aims. On the contrary, all their policies were directed exclusively toward the integration of the heterogeneous dominions which had fallen to them. In Bavaria, there was hopeful talk about the new Bavarian "empire" and widespread reference to the creation of separate "nations," which meant the diffusion of patriotic loyalty to the new states. On the whole, the South German statesmen were successful in gaining the people's adherence to the new political units. It was not surprising that within the individual states considerable mutual distrust remained among the people of the various historic sections and was kept alive, particularly by the religious division. But not even the national sentiment during the War of Liberation could endanger the existence of the South German middle states. The internal institutions took roots amazingly quickly, and the resentment naturally felt by the nobility did not prevail after 1815 over the general assent to the achievements of the short-lived Rhenish Confederation. As a matter of fact, where some laws of this period had been abolished, their reintroduction occasionally became a demand of the popular political movement. Strong opposition was building up among the people against the unlimited absolutism of the governments. This opposition would have assumed an explosive character if the power of Napoleonic France had not thrown its shadow over Germany; therefore it was appeased by internal concessions. But not even then did the political life of southern Germany lose the deep imprint the French system had made. While the conservative forces defended the bureaucratic omnipresence, the opposition tried to develop the libertarian ideas also contained in Napoleon's political philosophy. The new middle states of southern Germany not only survived the Napoleonic period physically but also made the institu-

tions and ideas of that period a fundamental part of their future
political aspirations.

↶ *Prussia*

IN CONTRAST TO THE LANDS of the Rhenish Confederation, which in the
years after 1806 devoted themselves exclusively to strengthening their
own particular states within the limits set by their French protector,
mutilated Prussia oriented her policies toward restoring her external as
well as her internal strength. Frederick the Great had deeply imbued
this state with a sense of European power. For the last ten years, this
ambition seemed to have disappeared, but now, after the defeat, some
heat was still found in the ashes. Yet it was revealed, too, that since the
last years of the great king, new forces had been infused into the Prussian state, although they had not sufficed to remold the government's
character. Only the catastrophes of Jena and Tilsit gave them an opportunity for gaining a decisive influence on the monarchy's policies.
All the Prussian reformers were united in the belief that the Frederician
state, as they put it, had been a "machine state," in which the individual
was to function as a cog in a mechanism. The individual was treated as
a mere means to an end, and his moral energies were suppressed. But
the disregard of the moral character of man had also undermined the
foundations of the state. The apathy with which the population had
gazed at Prussia's collapse and the eagerness with which people had
adjusted themselves to foreign domination, as if the events from Jena
to Tilsit had been but the king's personal misfortunes, were the logical
outcome of a governmental system which had demanded blind obedience from its subjects instead of gaining the loyalty of free citizens.
Now, the individual's free development was proclaimed one of the
government's fundamental objectives, as was his education for participation in public life. A state which would absorb the highest ideals of
human culture and make itself the protector of the individual citizen's
moral aspirations could hope to win its people's voluntary co-operation.

The state was to be placed on a broad popular basis and its political
aims were to be identified with the ideals which the German Enlightenment, German idealism, and neohumanism had formulated. From the
outset, this gave the Prussian reformers' policies a strong German note.
It is true that they wanted most immediately to transform the Prussian
state into a "nation," but the culture they wished to instill into the

Prussian monarchy was German, and it was natural that they conceived of their Prussian reform work as a mission from Germany. The concrete political task pointed in the same direction. Prussia could free herself from French domination only if the French were thrown out of Germany. It was not exclusively among the reformers born outside of Prussia that German aims assumed certain significance.

The Prussian reform movement originated in the high bureaucracy, and this meant that it could become effective only with the king's support. The disaster which had befallen the monarchy convinced Frederick William III that reforms should be introduced speedily. But he was a cautious and unimaginative man, and though occasionally capable of making brave decisions, he was frightened by the scope of the proposed reforms. One of the major reasons for the fragmentary character of the actual reform lay in his nature. Enthusiastic and self-confident as the reformers were, they could have overcome the king's hesitations only if they had been backed by a strong popular movement. But a popular political life did not exist in Prussia. Needless to say, the peasants were without political ambitions, but this was also true of the townspeople, consisting mostly of artisans and small merchants. Insofar as they displayed any political attitude at all, it was a conservative longing for being left in their old orders. The upper circles, particularly in the few larger cities, such as Königsberg and Berlin, could not act by themselves, but waited for the signals to come from the bureaucracy.

The nobility held the greatest power. Not only did the *Junkers* rule on their estates without governmental interference, but they also provided the king's army with most of its officers and the government with the majority of its high officials. But not even the *Junkers* were capable of a fully concerted political opposition. The Prussian noblemen, except for those who were actually proponents or supporters of reform, had not challenged the monarchical absolutism for two generations. When the *Junkers* were adversely stirred up, they could react first through intrigues at the court and in the government. In addition, they had their meeting places in the county diets (*Kreistage*), the organs which elected the county councilors (*Landräte*). These local and provincial agencies served as the chief centers of vocal opposition, the more so since the conservative *Junkers* wanted to defend local and provincial institutions before all others. The *Junker* opposition, therefore, did not constitute a unified front but represented very different ideas. But the *Junkers* were able to express their dissatisfaction, and their opposition made an impression on the king.

The reform of the Prussian state was carried out by the government's high bureaucracy and a group of army officers who gained Frederick William's confidence. Some were members of the old German and Prussian nobility, others were men who had acquired their patent of nobility in the course of their own governmental career, and others were bourgeois councilors. Their education and ideals made them a distinct group, and their main support outside the government came from among the educated people. The reform movement's social basis was small and somewhat artificial. To a large extent it depended on the absolute powers of the old monarchy, which it intended to transform into a modern state. It could not arouse too much opposition among the nobility, because the services of this class were needed for liberation from the foreign yoke.

The conditions after the Peace of Tilsit were frightful. Immediately after Jena, Napoleon had begun to squeeze high indemnities from every province, and even after the Peace of Tilsit the French intendants collected every pfennig they could find. The moderate prosperity Prussia had enjoyed in the decade before Jena was destroyed overnight, and the Continental System threw the Prussian economy into complete chaos. The whole export trade with grain, the main source of economic expansion, was blocked. Since its recent growth had led to a boom in real estate values, a collapse of that market followed. The number of foreclosures was great. Meanwhile the French victor maintained an army of 150,000 men in Prussia, while he continued to collect contributions and refused to evacuate the country.

✍ Baron Stein

THE CIRCUMSTANCES called for action. It was primarily the achievement of Baron Stein (1757–1831) that the action taken was more than a temporary solution to shore up the traditional order; it was to realize a higher ideal of humanity and to restore Prussia to her place among the European powers. At the time of Tilsit, Napoleon insisted on the removal of Hardenberg as minister and even suggested Stein as his successor. Apparently he thought that Stein would not steer an anti-French course, since his Nassau estates were located in the French orbit, and that his conflict with the king would make his ministry less effective. But it was Hardenberg and the "patriots," including Queen Louise, who prevailed on Frederick William III to recall Stein, and at this moment the latter readily forgot the painful altercations which had been the cause of his dismissal early in the year. On October 4, 1807, he became the leading Prussian minister, and though he served in this capacity for only a little less than fourteen months, his ministry left an indelible mark on modern German history.

Stein came from a family of imperial knights, and his birth gave him a sense of personal independence, which left him entirely unimpressed by the exalted claims of princes and kings. His origin did not, as has often been asserted, endow him with a faith in a strong and unified German Empire. The value still attached to the Empire's constitution in these circles during Stein's youth lay in the protection it offered to the surviving special privileges of class or land. A certain diffidence on Stein's part toward the absolute and bureaucratic practices of the modern territorial states probably had its roots in the world of imperial knighthood in which he grew up.

But Stein's mind was decisively formed by the ideas he absorbed during his years of study in Göttingen and his subsequent travels in Germany and England. He was deeply impressed by Montesquieu, whose doctrine of the division of powers as the method for establishing a balanced and harmonious society accompanied Stein throughout his life. The German Justus Möser's writings gave him a belief in the existence of a free community life among the original Teutons. Montesquieu had already spoken of these old-Germanic ideas of liberty and actually traced England's free constitution back to them. The study of England's constitutional life was a logical step for Stein, particularly in the setting of Hanover, where many people pretended to be half-English. In August Wilhelm Rehberg and Ernst Brandes, his two closest friends of student days, Stein met kindred admirers of English institutions. In 1790, Brandes introduced Edward Burke's treatise against the French Revolution to Germany. In the refutation of natural law and popular sovereignty, as well as the conception of an organic historical growth of national institutions, Stein found a justification of his own thinking. He felt repelled by the French Revolution, particularly once it led to the abolition of the monarchy, and he became a determined "Anglophile," an attitude much emulated in nineteenth-century German liberalism.

But the distance from French political thought was much less than Stein realized. Stein or Rehberg saw England through the eyes of Montesquieu, and they studied the French physiocrats closely. Once Stein was called to actual leadership, he entered upon a position quite comparable to Turgot's, not only because he imposed reforms from above but also because he too attempted to reform states which had gone through an age of absolutism unknown to England. As a matter of fact, English institutions could not be transplanted to German soil, and the ideas Stein and others held with regard to English politics were significant chiefly as expressions of their desire not to proceed by rationalistic construction but by the cautious development of traditional forms. In this respect, Stein's administrative experience was his foremost teacher.

Stein had risen quickly in the Prussian bureaucracy. He wanted to be a domestic administrator. He had mastered mining, commerce, manufactures, and finance thoroughly in the course of his career, which took him to Prussia's Westphalian territories. He was the high president (*Oberpräsident*) of all the Westphalian chambers when, in 1804, he was called to Berlin. The western lands were quite different from Prussia's central and eastern provinces. Smaller, but more densely populated and more highly urbanized, they did not have the sharp division between town and country. The nobility was relatively weak and the peasants freer than in the east. Prussian absolutism had failed to impress its character completely on these rather distant western provinces. The historic estates had not so completely vanished as in the east, and there were local meetings in which even representatives of the peasants took part. The power of these assemblies to reach political decisions was minimal, but they formed a useful link between all propertied social groups and the bureaucratic state administration. To Stein they seemed the way to achieve a true public spirit. Such institutions, he believed, would keep the bureaucracy from servility to orders from above and would direct the mind of the people beyond materialistic interests or the "useless cobwebs of metaphysics" toward the practical tasks of the community. Stein's thinking was entirely dominated by his moral ideals. He, as the new German idealism, desired a full development of the individual. This tenet he had not derived from either Kant or Goethe and Schiller. The sources of his own convictions lay in the optimistic moralism of the German Enlightenment, though its rationalism and optimism were restrained by a strong Lutheran faith. Thus to him the growth of personality meant chiefly the development of man's capacity for fulfilling his duties toward his fellow men. Individual and communal responsibilities were complementary.

Stein no doubt wished to make the state strong against outward dangers, but power as such was not his aim. More than anything else he wanted a state that was healthy because of its citizens' devotion to the moral betterment of mankind. Conquest and expansion seemed abominable to him. In his personal life, too, he never struggled for power. His fierce sense of independence did not allow him to enter into factional schemes. This attitude distinguished him not only from Hardenberg, his contemporary, but also from Bismarck, who, until his death, fought for the possession of power. Moreover, in contrast to Bismarck, whose concern was so predominantly with Germany's military and diplomatic position in Europe, Stein was primarily interested in reforming the state's social foundations, much as the liberation from Napoleon inevitably occupied him between 1807 and 1814.

Stein's conflict with Frederick William III, in the winter of 1806–07, could be called a revolt of the high bureaucracy against the autocracy of the Prussian monarchs. What he demanded with the suppression of the cabinet secretaries' political role was the recognition of the heads of ministries as the government's chief executives. The king's supreme authority was not challenged, but henceforth the monarch was to reach his decisions in the council of ministers which was to be established. Stein's insistence on the independence of the ministers was an expression of his sense of personal honor and self-respect. But the younger generation of Prussian state officials and officers shared his yearning for personal responsibility. In Theodor von Schön, the East Prussian administrator, or in Hermann von Boyen, the officer from Pomerania, the Kantian teaching had contributed to freedom from servility. In general, German idealism had been a powerful influence in producing the large group of self-confident men who brought into the Prussian government a new spirit, at the same time more enterprising and less authoritarian.

What Stein had failed to achieve in 1806–07, the smooth and diplomatic Count Hardenberg had practically won in the summer of 1807. The king got used to Hardenberg's advice, and that meant to a minister's advice instead of a cabinet secretary's. When Stein assumed the office of the principal civil minister in October, 1807, the removal of the king's civil *Kabinett* no longer proved very difficult. But the formal reorganization of the state's administrative structure was only partially accomplished by Stein during the subsequent year. Reform of the state ministries followed the French model. The provincial departments of the former General Directory were abolished. Five ministries were created—for interior, foreign affairs, finance, justice, and war. In a way, this centralization was the final consummation of the work which Prussian absolutism had performed since the days of the Great Elector in unifying the Hohenzollern dynasty's heterogeneous territories.

For Stein, however, the institution of centralized ministries was connected with the introduction of more liberal forms of government. The five ministries were to form a council and act as one body. For fundamental legislation he proposed the establishment of a state council composed of the ministers, their undersecretaries, and the princes. Obviously Stein was afraid that without such a council system a new absolutism, in the form of the omnipotence of a single leading minister, might develop. Stein also expected that in the future the king would rule with and through the ministerial council. But Frederick William did not possess the personal gifts for such a rule "in council." He wanted to lean on a single man, and therefore, in 1810, Hardenberg was appointed as prime minister with the title of State Chancellor. Stein's successors also disliked the idea of having their power limited by a state council, and the project was shelved.

The abolition of the General Directory necessitated reorganizing the war and domain chambers in the subordinated districts. A great change did not take place on this level, and some of Stein's reforms did not last. The old war and domain chambers, renamed "governments," were responsible for the whole administration, including school and church matters in the districts, which in size could be broadly compared to the *départements* in France. They were now largely deprived of judicial functions, an application of the theory of the division of powers, but conflicts between the individual citizen and the state were not altogether turned over to the ordinary courts. Only financial cases could be taken to the courts, all other complaints about administrative malpractices could be launched only with the government. In the formation of the district governments, Stein followed his preference for council decisions. The presidents were not, like the French *préfets*, the superiors of the district officials, but chairmen of a board of councilors.

Such a collegiate system seemed to contain a greater guarantee against arbitrary dictatorial decisions. While this may have been true, it also made for a more pedantic administration and was likely to tie the hands of a progressive official. The usefulness of the board principle, in any event, depended upon the actual composition of these bodies. Stein aimed at giving the governments a more liberal character by adding estate representatives as members. But if he hoped to drive the dust from the offices by the addition of laymen, his method was ill-chosen. What still existed of the old estates was under the control of the privileged class, and its representatives were defenders of the *status quo*. Moreover, the co-operation of honorary members with professional bureaucrats responsible to ministers and king proved entirely impractical and was quickly dropped.

Another idea of Stein's, aiming at the decentralization and liberalization of the government, proved more fruitful. Once the monarchy's highest agencies were made fully representative of the state's unity, as had been done by the suppression of provincial ministers, it seemed both desirable and possible to strengthen the life of the provinces. Stein himself, prior to becoming a minister, had been high president in Westphalia, in which capacity he had been the chief of a number of war and domain chambers. Now he wished to send a representative of the central government into each province in order to maintain close mutual contact between the province and the center. The new officials existed for only two years. They were unnecessary in the small rump-Prussia of 1807–15, but became a general institution after 1815. During the nineteenth century, this uniquely Prussian office preserved a great many of the historical traditions of the various regions of which the Prussian state was composed. The annexation of territories unrelated to the old Prussia, in 1815 and 1866, was greatly facilitated by these special officers. It is true that the creation of this additional level of state administration increased the governmental paperwork when the high presidents conceived of their position in a narrowly bureaucratic fashion. But there were highly successful personalities among them, most conspicuously so Theodor von Schön (1773–1856) in East Prussia and Baron Ludwig von Vincke (1778–1844) in Westphalia, both of whom became beloved fathers of their provinces and wove them into the unity of the monarchy. The office gained real significance when the high presidents were made the government's representatives with the reorganized provincial estates. This brought them into close relation with the population's public life. They became more popular figures than the members of the closeted district governments.

Beneath the level of the provinces and governmental districts, no bureaucratic administration was to be maintained, but all public functions were turned over to elected officials, or what was later called "self-administration." In a way, such institutions existed in the rural counties (*Landkreise*). The county councilor (*Landrat*) was a representative of the county estates, though a state official by royal appointment. But the county diet consisted only of noble landowners, and the *Junker Landrat* naturally respected the political privileges of his cousins, among which the police power and patrimonial jurisdiction on their estates were the most important. It was self-administration by and for a single class. Stein planned a radical reform of the county organization. By incorporating the small county towns into the counties, he wanted to create local diets composed of the landed gentry, townsmen, and peasants. He also wished to abolish the patrimonial jurisdiction. All these ideas at once aroused the strongest protestations of the *Junkers*, which Stein's iron will might have overcome if he had been in office longer. There was no point in forcing a showdown of these issues so long as the legislation with regard to the peasant's social status, begun in 1807, was still incomplete. Hardenberg took up these problems again in his *Gendarmerie-Edikt* of July 30, 1812. He simply abolished the *Landrat* altogether and replaced him by a "director" (*Kreisdirektor*) appointed by the government. County deputies, who were placed alongside him, had only the shadow of authority. This bureaucratic solution aroused the furor of the *Junkers*, and the government decided not to execute the edict. Actually the political predominance of the *Junkers* over the counties was in the end strengthened during the Prussian reform period, insofar as the small county towns, which had been under tax councilors, were added to the rural counties. Only sixty years later, in 1872, were the counties reorganized and they only then received a modern type of self-administration.

ᗡ Städteordnung

STEIN'S CENTRAL ACHIEVEMENT, through which he made the idea of self-administration an essential part of the German political heritage, was the new order for the urban communities (*Städteordnung*) promulgated on November 19, 1808. Without Stein's initiative and enthusiasm, this city order would not have come into existence. Its detailed formulation, however, Stein had to leave largely in the hands of younger and more liberal assistants, among whom J. G. Frey, police director of Königsberg, was most influential in shaping the new order. Actually through the Königsberg pupils of Kant and Adam Smith it became more liberal than in retrospect Stein would have liked it to be. It is true, however, that the general notions Stein entertained with regard to the reorganization of the cities, the idea that it should be a step

toward the renewal of their proud medieval life or toward the adaptation of English urban constitutions to the German city, were not
particularly practical for what Stein wanted to produce. The corrupt
state of English cities excluded them as models. Almost all the old
free German cities, with their medieval constitutions, had been absorbed by the neighboring territorial states just a few years earlier,
and the three Hanseatic cities, Hamburg, Bremen, and Lübeck, were
deprived of their freedom by Napoleon in 1810. Only these three cities
and Frankfurt were restored in 1814 and could pride themselves on an
unbroken internal development from the days of the medieval German
city republics.

These constitutions did not provide the pattern for the Prussian
reformers, however. For what they had in mind, they were inevitably
driven closer to the precedents set by the French Revolution. They
did not intend to establish self-governing republics but only to endow
urban communities with certain rights of self-administration. The new
local rights were not supposed to endanger the state's unity. Therefore
those rights that had constituted the core of the medieval German
cities' republican freedom—and are an integral element of Anglo-
American self-government—namely the administration of law and law
enforcement, were withheld from the Prussian towns and cities. The
city courts became royal law courts, and the police departments in the
large cities were placed under royal directors. In the small cities, the
mayor administered the police, not by municipal right but under the
district government's orders and supervision, a legal distinction taken
from France. In the construction of the city government, the French
model shone through even more clearly. The traditional view, which
saw in the crafts the constituent members of the government, was
abandoned, as was the exclusive exercise of governmental functions
through a mayor and a group of city councilors.

A constitutional system was introduced in which legislative and
executive power were divided. The chief organ was really a city assembly of elected deputies (*Stadtverordneten-Versammlung*), for all
practical purposes a city parliament. It elected the mayor and town
councilors, who together formed the *Magistrat*, the city government.
The city assembly approved the budget and supervised all executive
actions of the city government. The assembly was elected by all citizens balloting in boroughs. The Prussian city did not identify inhabitants and citizens, as the French Revolution had more or less done.
The property qualifications on which full citizenship depended were,

however, very low and admitted even the small craftsman and merchant. On the other hand, the "residents" (*Schutzverwandte*) were composed not only of the poor but also the formerly "exempted" people, among them the civil servants and ministers. As a result, town hall politics, once it got under way, was probably too much under the influence of petty local interests.

Originally, Stein wanted to compose the *Magistrat* entirely of elected honorary members serving without remuneration for a period of time. But his collaborators persuaded him to accept a salaried mayor, elected for six years, and a number of city councilors for the legal and technical departments, elected for twelve years and receiving pension rights. The idea of voluntary service survived only in the formation of so-called deputations for the administration of some technical branches, such as building construction, schools, and health. These deputations had a member of the *Magistrat* for chairman, but they consisted of city assemblymen and co-opted citizens willing to devote themselves to these special tasks. Still, the character of the Prussian city administration was molded primarily by the full-time executives. The mayors and city councilors were actually trained professional managers and formed a service not essentially different from the state's civil service. They had the same education, usually in law, as those who went into the state administration, and in the course of their career they often went from one city to another. The municipal civil servants were more responsive to the public than their counterparts in the state services, but they were not likely to stray off the official line too far, since they needed the government's placet for appointment. It was through the approval of the members of the *Magistrat* that the government imposed a further limit on the scope of self-administration. The larger cities even had to nominate three candidates for mayor, from among whom the government would elect one. On the other hand, the state government's direct supervision of city affairs was largely lifted, and the tax councilor disappeared from the urban scene.

The reorganization of city government, which could not fail to have great consequences for the social life of the cities, was for Stein only one measure in his general conception of a state freed of stifling bureaucratic absolutism and pulsating with popular energies. Rural county reform, the creation of representative organs in the provinces, and finally in the nation, were to follow and to complete the new structure. As it came to pass, the reform of city government remained the only action in which the idea of self-administration was realized.

If Stein hoped that through municipal self-administration the burghers would develop a civic spirit, this hope was fulfilled only later. At the end of the century, every German city by its mere external appearance bore witness to the civic pride alive in it. Within the limits set by the state, the administration was competent and free of corruption. The combination of professional managers with popular bodies was the chief source of the technical efficiency of German municipal government. But in the absence of truly democratic functions, the civic spirit it developed was of a narrow type. All the great issues of the century —national unification, liberalization of state and national government, the problems of an industrial society, or the great decisions on church and school policies—though somehow reflected in the life of the urban communities, could not be brought much closer to solution on this basis. They had to be fought on a stage more general than the locality, and the people attracted by them never devoted much energy to municipal politics. The character of city government was largely determined by that section of the socially conservative propertied classes whose interests were centered around local affairs. The deplorable districts built for housing the working class testify to this aspect of German city government, which, it should not be forgotten, has had parallels in other nations. Still, local self-administration in Germany was in a limited way a school for public activity. To provide an education in constructive political thought the cities would have needed broad political responsibility and direct links with self-government on the supralocal level. In England, local government and a national parliament strengthened each other mutually.

How German self-administration would have developed if Stein could have carried his reform plans to their full conclusion, nobody can say exactly. But there is no question that the new City Order of 1808 went far beyond the existing conditions toward a time which had not yet arrived. Frey warned Stein not to present the law to the town councilors, and actually, this law, designed to restore some autonomy to the cities, was introduced without any prior consultation with them, by mere fiat of a bureaucratic government. Popular response to the new municipal order was not encouraging. The old guilds and ruling families resented the attack on their social position. J. G. Frey was defeated when he offered himself as candidate for the mayor's post in Königsberg. Berlin elected as its first mayor a chamber president who had just resigned in protest against the reforms which ruined the Prussian state. This mayor was the father of the two Gerlach brothers, who were the leaders of Prussian reaction under Frederick William IV. Possibly even worse was the attitude of those towns which simply re-elected their old heads because they found it too expensive to pay them a pension.

Stein's reforms envisaged a society which had not yet come into being. The absolutist state had treated the burghers as mere servants. It was not surprising that they found it difficult to act as upright men when their masters suddenly told them to do so. It was even harder to breathe some public spirit into the peasant class, which still formed the majority of the population. Nothing could be expected from them in the way of ready patriotic service, let alone free public responsibility, so long as a minimum of human dignity had not been restored to them. A good beginning in this direction had been made in the years before Jena, with the liberation of the peasants on the royal domains. But the liberation of the "private" peasants, that is, those on the *Junker* estates, had proved thornier, since the interests of the Prussian gentry could not be disregarded lightly. The revolutionary methods which in France had created a free, landowning peasant class could not be ap-plied in Prussia, where the state was grounded on the co-operation of the nobility. In certain respects, this co-operation was even more needed at a time when foreign conquerors were in the country. In New East Prussia, one of the provinces formed out of the Polish lands which had come to Prussia through the third Polish partition, the Prussian administration had abolished serfdom and created larger farms without paying attention to the Polish nobility, but this could not serve as a model for reform in Prussia itself. Yet, together with the eman-cipation of the peasants on the royal domains, the Polish policy set a precedent for the liberation of the Prussian private peasants, and the breakdown of the state after Jena made the king bolder than before.

∽ Liberation of the Peasants

WE HAVE ALREADY SEEN that agrarian reform plans were under dis-cussion in East Prussia. When Stein assumed his office in Königsberg, in October, 1807, he found drafts of a reform legislation prepared by the provincial minister for East Prussia, Baron von Schroetter, and the young councilor, Theodor von Schön. In this province's high bureauc-racy Kant's liberal ideas had found enthusiastic followers, and from the University of Königsberg, through C. J. Krauss, the new gospel of Adam Smith had been spread. Schön was this idealistic group's most intelligent and most doctrinaire member. Stein's first political decision, made in the first week of his ministry, was to accept Schön's proposed plan of agrarian reform, and he prevailed on the king to make it applicable to all the provinces, not only to East Prussia. The Royal Edict of October 9, 1807 proclaimed: "After St. Martin's day of 1810 there shall be only free people, as is already the case on the domains in all our provinces." The first clarion call of the reform legislation did not, however, tear down all the walls with which the feudal past had surrounded the peasantry.

The Edict's immediate significance was of a general political nature. It proclaimed the abolition of the three estates on which the state had rested. The law declared not only that a nobleman could acquire peasant as well as burgher land, and the peasant and burgher that of the nobleman, but also that a nobleman as well as peasant could take up any trade, while a burgher could become a peasant. The traditional division of society into separate estates was superseded by classes which the individual could join according to his economic capacity. In their practical application, these liberal principles could not by themselves transform a stubborn reality. Economic liberalism was bound to favor the economically strongest class, which in Prussia was the landed gentry. The Prussian *Junkers* had no wish to enter into bourgeois occupations. Naturally, they were willing to take advantage of the opportunities which a free economy offered them for improving their economic fortunes, and on the whole they learned quickly to run their estates as capitalistic enterprises. But they were by no means inclined to give up the political and legal privileges they had enjoyed in the past and felt to be useful for the future. The admission of burghers to the ownership of land did not bring the nobility closer to the towns and to bourgeois consciousness. On the contrary, the burghers who became owners of estates adopted the *Junker* style of life and usually, within two or three generations, merged with the nobility.

What the peasant gained through the Edict of October 9, 1807 was not very clear. The term *Erbuntertänigkeit* was never well defined. Obviously the peasant was freed of a good many personal duties, such as getting his lord's permission for marriage, but it was most doubtful what was meant when the Edict stated that the peasant owed his lord only those obligations "derived from the tenure of land or special contracts." For the time being, the squires' economic power was hardly touched and remained secure through their possession of local police authority and patrimonial justice.

It was in the nature of feudal law that no clear distinction existed between servitudes attached to the personal status of peasants and those incumbent upon the tenure of land. Beyond this, feudalism had tended to build the exercise of political authority on the ownership of land. A real liberation of the peasants required reforms on three levels —a reform of personal status, which the edict actually inaugurated, of land tenure, and of public administration. Stein attacked the last of these. He wished to dissolve the local units ruled by the squires, the *Gutsbezirke*, and create rural communities in which small and big landowners would have equal rights. Patrimonial jurisdiction was to be taken away from the squires, and they also were to lose their exemption from the land tax. But the first steps which Stein took in this direction involved him in serious conflicts with the *Junker* opposition. Perhaps Stein would have broken this resistance had he stayed longer in office, but none of his successors took these matters up again. Only after the revolution of 1848–49 was patrimonial jurisdiction wrested from the nobility, while the exemption from the land tax was only lifted in 1861, and self-government of the rural communities according to Stein's principles was first introduced in 1891. Another significant prerogative of the country squire, his rights as patron of the parish, was abolished only after the revolution of 1918.

The reform of the political conditions of the countryside came to a standstill before Stein could force a showdown. The reform of the proprietary relationships was undertaken with great hesitation. Theodor von Schön originally assumed that personal freedom would enable the capable peasant to gain a satisfactory economic position through bargaining, and Stein at least was never anxious to intervene in favor of the small peasants. But he tried to put some brakes on the process by which the *Junker* might greatly enlarge his own land by removing tenants or buying up peasant land. How far he might have gone in the long run is again impossible to say. The decision came under Hardenberg, first through the Edict of September 14, 1811, which was then drastically changed by the Declaration of May 29, 1816. Two major burdens had to be removed from the peasants, those connected with the uncertainties of landholding and with the obligations in services. In both respects, the peasants' actual situation was vastly variegated. But three groups stood out: (1) peasants who were hereditary leaseholders (*Erbpächter*); (2) those who had the usufruct of the land either in hereditary or nonhereditary tenure (*Lassiten*); (3) peasants holding leases of temporary duration (*Zeitpächter*).

The Edict of 1811 did not deal with the hereditary leaseholders, since their tenure was considered secure. It ruled that the hereditary *Lassit* who wanted to become a freeholder should cede one third of the land which he occupied, while the nonhereditary *Lassit* and the temporary leaseholder were to turn over one half to the landlord. This regulation did not include such compensation as the peasant might owe in addition for compulsory services. Although the Edict aroused strong complaints among the nobility, it was actually very favorable to their interests. To be sure, few *Junkers* complained because the agrarian reforms destroyed the time-honored patriarchal relationship between lord and peasant and turned land into a mere commodity. Adam Müller's glorification of medieval feudalism was not taken very literally, even by the most stalwart conservative opponent of all reforms, the Brandenburg *Junker* Ludwig von der Marwitz. The majority of the landed gentry, most clearly so in East Prussia, was not opposed to the introduction of free capitalistic forms into agriculture. The boom in the grain trade before 1806 had given them a taste of the opportunities which they could exploit if they increased their production by the expansion of acreage and the modernization of husbandry. Most of the *Junkers*, therefore, did not object to the removal of feudal landholding laws and servitudes, but only to the assertedly inadequate compensation.

‿ *Declaration of 1816*

PARTLY ON ACCOUNT OF sheer indifference toward agrarian problems, partly because of sympathy with the nobility, Hardenberg gave in to the *Junkers'* remonstrances and issued the Declaration of 1816, which was supposed to be an explanation of the Edict of 1811, but was actually a new law. Under this law, all those peasants were excluded from the adjustment of their tenure who were not *spannfähig*, that is, did not own a team of draft animals, as well as those whose farms were not registered in the official tax records or whose tenure was not of relatively long standing. Since, after 1816, the Prussian government discontinued all activities directed toward the preservation of a numerous peasant class, all peasants not covered by the Declaration found it difficult to make a living on their reduced acreage. The transition from the ancient three-field system to an improved crop rotation added to the arable land, and the dissolution of the commons operated in the same direction. But since, in contrast to the landed gentry, the peasants had no sources of financial credit, they were often unable to change to more intensive forms of land cultivation. In the great agrarian crisis of the early 1820's, which, incidentally, forced many *Junkers* to sell their family estates to burghers, a large number of the new peasant holdings, sometimes whole villages, disappeared.

After 1816, the owners of the large estates were at liberty to extend their land and could be sure of an adequate labor supply. Within the next thirty years, they made full use of these opportunities. It has been estimated that up to one million hectares (1 hectare = 2.4710 acres) were added to their properties and that 46,000 to 54,000 peasant farms, together with 70,000 small family places, came into the hands of the nobility. The population formed the new class of laborers on the estates. The highest group among them were the *Instleute*, workers hired by the year, mostly one year after the other, and housed by the owner. The workers' wages were paid in money and kind or the use of scraps of land. As a rule, their labor contracts included the labor of wives and children. To all of them the stiff Ordinance of 1810 applied, an ordinance the nobility had extracted from the government as a first protection of their control of labor. This *Gesindeordnung* regulated relations between lord and servant in any household and was not abolished until 1918. Under it no laborer or maid could resign prematurely, striking was punishable by imprisonment, "paternal discipline" could be applied, and obedience enjoined, in an absolute manner. In these conditions, the farm laborers were not better off than the former unfree peasants and were often hardly distinguishable from peons. Although feudalism had been replaced by economic liberalism, paternalism lived on in this world. Small wonder that in this atmosphere no easier forms of social intercourse developed and full subordination to the ruling class was considered natural.

The existence of small groups of freeholders, particularly in East and West Prussia, to whom were added now those peasants who emerged from the rigors of liberation and economic crisis, did not change the social climate of East Elbian Prussia. On the whole, they were rather substantial peasant landholders, and though their social outlook was not identical with that of the *Junkers*, their economic interests were largely the same, and using laborers like the big landowners, they were dependent on cheap labor. They tended to act and feel like little *Junkers* and, with few temporary exceptions, constituted a thoroughly conservative element well into the most modern period of German history. After 1816, the agrarian reforms, so hopefully begun by Stein in 1807, with the intent of creating a freely intermingling society of small and larger proprietors, served the growth of a rigid social structure of authoritarian character. The exigencies of the economic situation in the years after the Peace of Tilsit contributed greatly to this evolution. The destructions of the war were too great to allow rebuilding all farms. The strengthening of the threatened credit of the nobility was almost the only way to save some of the Prussian state's ruined financial credit. Thus, all elements conspired to petrify the social and political order of East Germany.

✍ *Plans for National Representation*

HAD THE REORGANIZATION of the political government made progress, this development might have been considerably modified. It was not necessary to proceed step by step from local through provincial to national government, as Stein ideally felt. As a matter of fact, he himself disregarded this sequence. As early as December, 1807, the pressing need for funds to pay the contributions the French had imposed on the Prussian provinces led to the convention of provincial estates in East Prussia. But Stein made plans for the creation of a national representation, which reached a definite stage in the fall of 1808. This projected assembly could not be called a real parliament. It was merely to be given the right to debate legislation, which, however, included the right to initiate laws. Nor was it to be elected by the people, but by estates and occupational groups, though in such forms that the nobility could not dominate. It was to have regular and fully publicized meetings. Stein again stressed the value of such an institution for the education of the people in political consciousness and ability: "Participation of the nation in legislation and administration creates love of the constitution, a correct public opinion on national affairs, and in many individual citizens capacity for administering public business. History teaches how far greater the number of great commanders and statesmen has been under free constitutions than in despotic states."

Stein's plan for national representation was, however, closely linked up with his foreign policy. While he had directed all his policies toward the ultimate liberation of Prussia, the situation with which he had to deal as minister made it doubtful whether rump-Prussia could survive at all. The state could continue only because the Franco-Russian alliance had induced Napoleon to respect Alexander's wishes. The czar held his hand over Prussia, which made Frederick William look up to his Russian friend. But the demand for a huge contribution and occupation by French troops enabled Napoleon to weaken Prussia still further and keep her in a state of miserable subjection. There were moments during the winter of 1807–08 when Stein and Scharnhorst saw no way of getting relief from French oppression except by offering an auxiliary corps to fight in Napoleon's service. Instead, new negotiations were resumed in the spring of 1808. At the same time, another train of thought matured in the minds of Stein, Scharnhorst, and Gneisenau. Napoleon's treacherous deposition of the legitimate dynasty had led to a national rising of the Spanish people against the foreign invader and to grave losses in the French army. In these circumstances, the Prussian reformers discovered new and unexpected possibilities for driving the French from Germany.

The insurrection in Spain was indeed an event of great historic significance. It was the first eruption of a nativist nationalism, soon to be repeated in Tyrol. An old and homogeneous nation, still living in rather primitive conditions and, in its vast majority, accepting the traditional monarchical and ecclesiastical institutions as the divine law, rose against alien and heretical intruders. Favored by the nature of the country, the brave popular defenders inflicted terrible punishment on the French. Yet their heroic battle would not have brought them final success had England not intervened with an expeditionary force and war supplies. The peculiar circumstances of the Peninsular War were only dimly recognized in Königsberg or, for that matter, in Vienna.

For in Vienna Napoleon's removal of the Spanish dynasty and the reaction of the Spanish people had caused both alarm and fresh hopes. The Austrian government was directed by Count Philip Stadion who, like Baron Stein and Count Metternich (then Austrian ambassador in Paris), was a German imperial knight. Archduke Carl, who had proved his great military abilities in the wars of 1796 and 1799, was minister of war and generalissimo of the Austrian armies. Stadion prepared for the war chiefly through a reform of the army, since in the multi-national Habsburg empire the grant of self-administration appeared dangerous. Archduke Carl modernized the Austrian army in many respects, which set a number of precedents for what was subsequently done in Prussia. Among his reforms was the creation of a national guard in the various Habsburg lands. Popular forces and sentiments began to permeate the dynastic army of older days, and patriotic feeling could be sensed in most provinces. But it was strongest in the German provinces, and here the national sentiment of the leading groups had a twofold orientation. It was attachment to the homeland

and the dynasty as well as a feeling for Germany, which in these circles was still considered to include the old imperial power.

The Spanish War and the Austrian armament raised fervent hopes among the Prussian reformers for an early liberation. Stein, together with Scharnhorst and Gneisenau, made bold plans. They envisaged arming the whole population, not only in Prussia but also in the whole of northern Germany, which they thought could be aroused to revolt against its French rulers. The promise of national representation was to highlight the popular freedom Germany would gain after the liberation from Napoleonic despotism. Frederick William III resisted these counsels. If Russia had been willing to fight, he might have been persuaded to undertake the heavy risks, but at Erfurt in the summer of 1808, Czar Alexander renewed his alliance with Napoleon, thereby enabling him to lead his forces to Madrid. But while the Prussian government continued to negotiate in Paris, Stein went on to prepare a national revolution. A poor diplomat and even worse conspirator, Stein wrote a most uncautious letter, which was intercepted by the French police. Napoleon used the incident to present the Prussian negotiators in September with a convention which imposed not only an exorbitant indemnity but also, going beyond the Treaty of Tilsit, a limitation of the Prussian army to 42,000 men. Stein urged the rejection of the convention, but his position had become untenable. Even among some friends of reform, the stormy pace Stein set in foreign and domestic politics caused opposition. Frederick William was discomforted by his minister's way of proposing to use Prussia as a mere means for liberating Germany. He was prepared to suffer humiliation for the preservation of his throne, and Stein's policy seemed foolhardy. On November 24, 1808, Stein had to give up his office. Shortly thereafter, Napoleon issued a ban against him and had his estates seized. Warned by the French minister in Berlin, Stein went to Austria, whence he was called by Czar Alexander, in 1812, to serve as his advisor.

Austria's war in 1809 failed to incite popular national revolution in Germany. Austrian arms did not succeed in creating the basis for such movements. The Austrian army was maneuvered out of Bavaria, and Austria became the battleground of the war. Archduke Carl imposed on Napoleon a serious reverse at Aspern, but failed to exploit his success, and soon the war was decided at Wagram. Only in Tyrol did the peasants rise in a heroic struggle, not for the German fatherland but against the Bavarian regime, which was destroying the old constitution of the land and its ties with the Habsburg dynasty. Everywhere in

Germany, the people's political loyalties were predominantly anchored in the dynastic states' particularism. Since the German dynasties refused to lead a popular movement in 1809, the few attempts at revolt which occurred in northern Germany quickly fizzled out. In Prussia, the debate over participation in the fight against France was renewed once Austria had gone to war, but the king remained firmly set against any involvement. With the acceptance of subservience to Napoleon, the internal reforms of the state became less pressing.

✍ Baron Hardenberg

NOTHING OF CONSEQUENCE WAS ACHIEVED by the ministry of Count Alexander Dohna and Baron Karl Altenstein, who followed Stein. Neither of them was a reactionary, but both lacked the qualities of leadership needed in Prussia's desperate situation, which grew even worse, since the Franco-Russian alliance began to strain and crack after 1810, when Baron Karl von Hardenberg (1750–1822) took the helm again. The king made him the actual prime minister with the title of State Chancellor. The Hanoverian nobleman, since 1790 in the service of the Prussian state, was a dexterous administrator and diplomat. To him, an amiable and debonair eighteenth-century cavalier, politics was the art of the possible, but within these limits he liked to help not only himself but also others to the pleasures of life. A versatile and cosmopolitan mind enabled him to absorb the practical political wisdom of enlightened despotism as well as of the French Revolution and Napoleonic administration and to apply it to the Prussian state as far as circumstances permitted. "Democratic principles in a monarchical government," was the motto of his own administration, but much as he liked to dispense freedom, he saw to it that the government did not lose control of its decisive prerogatives. A national representation seemed to him quite desirable, provided it did not acquire real power.

While Hardenberg gave the reform of the state a more radical direction than Stein, owing to his belief in economic liberalism, and a more authoritarian note, due to his faith in bureaucracy, he was at the same time more sensitive to the wishes both of the nobility and the king. We have already seen where this policy led in the questions of agrarian reform and rural self-government. Hardenberg's immediate endeavor centered around consolidating the public debt and a tax program which was to produce the means for paying the French indemnity. One measure of the finance reform was the secularization of

Church properties, which in the future made the Churches financially
fully dependent on the state. It is true that for a long time the Protestant Church's property had been treated as a mere part of the state
budget, but the Catholic Church in Silesia still owned large holdings.
The new financial policy launched by Hardenberg required social and
economic reforms as well. Complete freedom of trade was proclaimed.
Thereby, not only the monopoly of the guilds was abolished but also
the economic separation of town and country was torn down. The
attack on the guilds was much resented at that time, and the grant of
civil equality to the Jews, too, was unpopular.

The equal treatment of town and country was achieved through a
general tax system which attempted to do away with the distinctive
methods of excise and contribution. Hardenberg's finance reform was
only partly successful, however. In particular the land tax, which he
wanted to be levied universally, met with the stern opposition of the
nobility, which again secured its exemption from such a tax. Hardenberg attempted to win public support for his policy by calling a
National Assembly of Notables in 1811. Apparently he hoped to persuade the group by rational argument and personal charm to give him
its support in the country. But the Assembly, heavily loaded in favor
of the nobility, only served as the focus for the growth of an oppositional movement among the nobility. Its chief outlet, however, it found
in the provincial estates, the *Junkers'* exclusive domain. The outbursts
of the Brandenburg estates under the leadership of Marwitz and Count
Finckenstein, whom Hardenberg had locked up in Spandau for a few
weeks, looked almost like an impending recrudescence of the struggles
in the days of the Great Elector. Hardenberg dodged the opposition
by concessions and the speedy adjournment of the Assembly. Still,
among some of its members as well as in the government, the Assembly
aroused the wish for a true national representation with more clearly
stated authority and of broader social composition. A Provincial National Assembly, composed of eighteen noblemen, twelve townsmen,
and nine peasants, elected by the county and city councils, held sessions
from 1812 to 1815, but Hardenberg was temperamentally unfit to
breathe political life into this convention.

In Berlin, the imminent Franco-Russian war caused a repetition of
the passionate debates of 1808 and 1809 over foreign policy. The
patriots Scharnhorst, Gneisenau, and Boyen wanted to fight with
Russia and renewed Stein's plans for a national revolt in Germany.
Frederick William III persisted in his conviction that the monarchy

could not undertake a war of liberation except in alliance with Russia and Austria. The Austria of Metternich refused to turn against Napoleon, and England denied subsidies. Finally, in February of 1812, Prussia agreed to place a corps of twenty thousand men at Napoleon's disposal for the Russian war. The country, as the base of the French operations, was burdened again with the quartering of troops and all the forced deliveries for their maintenance. In despair over the king's policy, a number of officers, among them Carl von Clausewitz, went to Russia. "The world divides," said Gneisenau, "into those who fight voluntarily or involuntarily for or against Napoleon's ambition. In this situation geographical boundaries seem to matter less than principles." Gneisenau and Scharnhorst, too, laid down their offices, though they remained active in minor state functions. In a way the king's policy was proved right by the actual course of events, but nobody expected the catastrophe of the *grande armée*, and the king could by no means count on the Prussian state's survival in the case of a French victory. France's debacle in Russia made the liberation of Prussia possible. Prussia's contribution to the ultimate defeat of Napoleon would not have been so great if she had not regained the services of those men who in 1812 lost hope in Prussia's character.

Military reforms were begun immediately after Tilsit. In July, 1807, the king made General Gerhard von Scharnhorst head of a Commission for Military Reorganization, to which Neithard von Gneisenau and Carl W. von Grolman were also appointed, together with other more conservative officers. The reformers gained the majority when Hermann von Boyen and Count W. von Goetzen joined the Commission. Scharnhorst was the dominating spirit of this group. A Hanoverian by birth, this son of a Low-Saxon peasant had entered an officer's career through the military school of one of the small German princes. He had fought with distinction in the revolutionary wars in the Hanoverian army but gained his public reputation as a military writer and as the director of the war college in Hanover. In 1801 he accepted an offer to come to Prussia in the same capacity. Quickly his genius as a teacher began to make itself felt among a large group of younger officers. However, his teachings did not change the high command's thinking. He himself had little influence on the duke of Brunswick, on whose staff he served in the fateful battle of Auerstädt. The catastrophe of 1806–07 at last gave him the chance for the realization of his ideas. He remained self-composed in the face of many a slight he suffered in his career on account of his common birth, nor did his tenacity weaken when his proposals met with temporary defeat. Fortunately, the king liked the even temper and the simple manners of this seemingly shy and reticent man. Scharnhorst gave the appearance of an unassuming scholar, but he was a fearless soldier in battle. Few people ever became aware of the profundity of his mind and the glowing passion of his will.

Gneisenau, too, was a non-Prussian. He came from a Saxon burgher family only recently ennobled. His was an extraordinary nobility of mind and feeling. He always considered Scharnhorst greater than himself. Although this was probably true with regard to power of intellectual analysis, the range of Gneisenau's feelings, which reached from the most tender human sentiments to the strongest emotions of war, was certainly not smaller and found expression in a dramatic and lordly personality. Some of his friends judged hyperbolically that in France Gneisenau might have vied with Napoleon politically as well as militarily. As it was, he proved himself an equal to the Corsican only in the art of war when, after Scharnhorst's death on the threshold of liberation, he became the leading strategist of the Prussian army in the campaigns of 1813–15. Whereas Gneisenau thus consummated Scharnhorst's work on the battlefields, it fell to Boyen to complete it in the councils of state. Boyen, who became minister of war in 1814, had sat in Kant's lecture room as a young officer and absorbed the Kantian ethics. Born an East Prussian, he had deep roots in the state of Frederick the Great, in contrast to Scharnhorst and Gneisenau, who were often inclined to use Prussia as a mere vehicle of their German plans.

If it was Stein's supreme objective to arouse a new patriotic spirit among the people by founding the state on the nation's moral energies, it was Scharnhorst's highest intention "to bring army and nation into a close union." Military and civilian reforms were running side by side and were supporting each other. Without the personal liberty of the peasants, without the abolition of the political separation of the social classes, and also without the new organization of the governmental structure, the building of a new army would have been impossible. It is true that Stein and Hardenberg could not have gained the king's approval for many of their reform measures if the need for new military forces had not been so urgent. But as Stein looked beyond national liberation to a German state prospering through the cultivation of domestic freedom, Scharnhorst, together with his friends and disciples, saw in such freedom not only the generator of strong military power but also the guarantor of human dignity.

Prussia's catastrophic defeat in 1806–07 brought the new military leaders to the fore. They had been reform-minded before 1806, but they, too, had gained their radical determination to insist on fundamental changes only through the bitter experiences of the past year. On the other hand, the conditions of a beaten state depending on the will of the victor made full reforms extremely difficult, if not impossible. This was true, in the first place, of the most cherished ideal of the reformers, mobilizing the state's full manpower, regardless of class, for defense. The old methods of recruitment were impractical. Hiring mercenaries outside of Prussia was impossible; Napoleon controlled all of Germany and Prussia was without funds. It was doubtful whether the "canton system"[1] could produce the necessary number of soldiers after Tilsit had reduced Prussia to few provinces. The canton system, as will be remembered, was a method of conscription which applied chiefly to the peasants. To turn it into universal conscription all that was needed was the abolition of local and social exemptions. But upon those the Prussian state's caste character rested. The idea of a general liability to military service was resented not only by the nobility but also by the bourgeoisie. In fact, the latter was even more vociferous in opposing the loss of its only important privilege. It could be pointed out that Carnot's universal conscription had been kept by Napoleon only in theory, since he had allowed substitutions, which meant that the rich could buy off military service. But Scharnhorst wanted to avoid exactly this violation of principle. Only universal service would instill a general sense of obligation to the state, and this, together with the citizen's new rights, could realize a new ideal of manhood.

In 1808, the Military Reorganization Commission recommended introducing universal service and creating a reserve militia. But Frederick William III, though inclined toward universal conscription, did not approve of it then. The idea of a militia, moreover, frightened the king as a revolutionary move. Apparently what was decisive with him was not so much his abhorrence of arming the people, and even less the internal opposition to universal service, but the fear that Prussia's adopting an ambitious military program would give Napoleon an excuse for intervention. This was the time when Stein wanted to launch a national war of liberation and finally was forced out of the Prussian service. Simultaneously Napoleon had imposed strict armament limitations on Prussia. For an army of 42,000 men, the canton system delivered a sufficient number of recruits, and it was left unchanged with

[1] See p. 199.

all its exemptions till 1813. The only way of evading the terms of the
Paris Convention of 1808 was the call-up of additional canton men for
brief training. In order to make this possible, a small percentage of
each regiment's old soldiers were sent on home leave. The people called
these special trainees *Krümper,* probably because they looked sloppy,
krumm, beside the spick-and-span soldiers. It has been one of the
legends of German history that the *Krümper* system enabled Prussia
to build up large trained forces, and the framers of the disarmament
provisions of the Versailles Treaty of 1919 were affected by it. Actually,
the numbers involved were relatively small. In the spring of 1813, the
Prussian army and its trained reserves numbered less than 66,000 men.

While only the cornerstones of the national military establishment
could be laid, the military reformers could carry their other plans beyond the blueprint stage. With the disappearance of foreign mercenaries, the brutal discipline could no longer be defended. Brutality
might turn human beings into machines, but it would not produce
courageous soldiers who could be depended upon in good and adverse
circumstances. Discipline rested on a live sense of honor and not on
the use of the cane. The new articles of war, introduced in August,
1808, practically abolished corporal punishment and established orderly
processes of military justice. The reform was introduced also with a
view to making army life less repulsive to the burghers, who were
expected to enter the army under a system of universal conscription.
The burgher's son was not to be forced down to the level of a peasant-
serf. In addition, the reorganization enabled him to compete to some
extent with the nobleman.

In 1806–07 the aristocratic officer corps had displayed not only a
great lack of qualities of military leadership but also, in many instances,
lack of an ordinary sense of duty and honor. Apart from investigating
guilty commanders, reducing the size of the army made it possible to
get rid of fossilized generals and superannuated officers. All the reformers agreed that personal honor, bravery, and knowledge were not
the natural monopoly of noblemen. The French officers exhibited all
these qualities in high measure. Thus, to the disgust of most Prussian
Junkers, it was now declared that a claim to an officer's commission
could in the future be established in peacetime only "by knowledge
and education" and in war "by extraordinary bravery and perspica-
cious judgment," and that individuals from all classes were eligible to
positions of military command. The old order, whereby *Junkers* in
their early teens could serve as privileged corporals (*Gefreite-*

Korporal) till they automatically received an officer's commission, was abolished. After three months in the army, everybody who was beyond seventeen years of age could compete for one of the available cornet positions. Another examination was required before a cornet could receive an officer's commission. Obviously, book learning could not be made the only criterion of a good officer; general intelligence, exactness in the fulfillment of duties, and suitable deportment were other standards to be met. But they were less objective tests and open to social and political biases, especially since the senior regimental officers were given a part in selecting and promoting officers. This was probably useful for producing an *esprit de corps* among the officers, but it was not necessarily the best spirit which might have been produced. The system tended to bring about the absorption of only those bourgeois candidates who seemed most adaptable to the style of the nobility. Against Scharnhorst's wish, Frederick William III also saved the military cadet schools, the foundations of Frederick William I, in which the young *Junker* boys had been taught. They were opened to sons of officers, but continued to the end of the Prussian monarchy in 1918 to send into the army boys who from the time when they left the nursery had been surrounded by military tutors and had been inculcated with a blind faith in monarchy and Prussian military virtues. Albrecht von Roon and Paul von Hindenburg, among many other generals and military statesmen, were typical products of these cadet schools.

A very considerable opening had been torn into the wall of social privilege which had surrounded the old Prussian army, and fresh talent could enter the service. Equally important was the fact that study and intellectual effort found a home among the officers, noble or bourgeois. Scharnhorst succeeded in a complete reorganization of the army schools. A general war school for officers, later called *Kriegsakademie*, was created in Berlin for training in specialized branches, such as artillery and engineering. The school also contained a select class of officers preparing for higher staff work. Here Carl von Clausewitz (1780–1831) taught in 1810. He became the administrative director of the school in 1818. In the following decade, the most philosophical disciple of Scharnhorst and Gneisenau wrote his book *On War*, the great theoretical testament of the strategic thinking of this generation of Prussian officers. Their great teacher was Napoleon, and they endeavored to decipher the causes of his success in order to become his equals in future battles. These theoretical studies laid the ground for what became the Prussian General Staff, which represented an effort to substitute a brain trust of officers in the absence of a genius of Frederick the Great's stature.

The transition from autocratic absolutism to a bureaucratic government had its parallel in the military field. It was not, however, confined to the command in war and strategic planning. For the time being, the general staff remained a subordinate organ of the general army administration, which in the course of Stein's reorganization of the central government was unified in a single war ministry. The war ministry consisted of two departments, the general war and the military economy departments. In the former, all matters of administration and command were centered. Three sections were created, one for personnel, a second for training, war plans, and mobilization, and a third for the supervision of special arms and ordnance. The military economy department was in charge of finance and supply. At no time was the Prussian military establishment as strictly organized as under this plan of December, 1808, but the concentration of so much power was disliked by many factions. At the time of the promulgation of the plan, the king was afraid that a war minister might cut the direct royal contact with the army. Frederick William III refused to appoint a minister of war till 1814. In 1809, Scharnhorst was made chief of the general department only. But since he had direct access to the king, who also gave him the title of chief of general staff, and since he found co-operation in the economy department, army reform was not jeopardized. In all these years, the least spectacular but technically most important part of the reform took place in the training and maneuver grounds. The formation of smaller army units composed of all branches of arms was perfected, though the army's small size made only brigades instead of divisions possible. The co-operation of infantry, cavalry, and artillery in such units adapted the army to fighting in broken-up terrain and to attacking in deep columns. The abandonment of a rigid single battle line placed greater responsibility than before on the subordinate officers, and the new tactics called for more personal self-reliance in the lower ranks. The field service regulations of 1812 did away with the old drill techniques and emphasized the contributions to be made by the individual soldiers.

Prussia's participation as a satellite of France in the war against Russia in 1812 seemed to pervert everything for which the Prussian reformers, civilian and military, had striven. They had aimed at an intimate marriage of the national culture and the state, and in order to achieve it had made room for the individual's autonomy. But the international situation pressed the Prussian state into the servitude of France and forced the individual to ignore his moral ideals. In these circumstances many a reformer felt it to be his right and duty to continue the fight against Napoleon wherever he could. Prussia was not identical with Germany, and to the reformers the idea of Prussian or German nationality was subordinated to universal ethical ideals. As Stein could say: "The fatherland is where honor and independence is found."

ᴄ᷇ Stein in Russia

BARON STEIN WAS THEN IN ST. PETERSBURG on the invitation of Czar Alexander I. He refused to enter Russian service but acted as the czar's adviser, particularly on German problems. His presence in Russia was of great importance. His courage and confidence in the ultimate victory over Napoleon helped to carry the czar and the Russian aristocracy over the bitter disappointments of early defeats. His activities to organize a national revolution in Germany were less successful. His and Gneisenau's attempts to persuade the British government to launch military landings in northwestern Germany were entertained in a dilatory fashion. It was doubtful whether they could have set the spark to large popular risings. The propaganda Stein and his German Committee directed toward the German soldiers in Napoleon's army and to the people in Germany had little visible results, though in Ernst Moritz Arndt, Stein had on his side one of the great masters of popular German prose. But the vast mass of the German people were incapable of political action. Even the loose network of conspirational cells which existed in places among the higher middle classes was clumsy and futile. The republican ring assumed by Stein's and Arndt's propaganda at this moment when all the German princes obeyed French orders found no echo in a staunchly monarchist population. The German Legion organized in Russia out of German prisoners and volunteers did not become a large unit.

The greatest contribution made by Stein, however, was the part he played in persuading Alexander to carry the war westward beyond the frontiers of Russia after disaster had overtaken the *grande armée* on its march back from burning Moscow. With the invaders driven from the holy soil of Russia, no further Russian war aims existed. So argued the commander of the army, Kutusov, the foreign minister, and many nationally minded Russians. To move forward would mean to conduct Britain's war and involve Russia in European enmities. The

Russian army had shrunk and could not fight alone in the heart of the Continent. The key lay in Austria's policy, which was not encouraging, while Prussia could not offer an equivalent substitute. Stein was instrumental in convincing the czar that Germany could be mobilized against Napoleon and kept him determined to risk the great struggle for the liberation of Europe in the spring of 1813, even in the event that only Prussia joined forces with Russia in the beginning. Alexander I decided in favor of such a policy, since he wanted to make himself master of Poland. This he could only hope to become if the French empire were dissolved, and the role of the liberator of Europe appealed to him.

The Prussian corps under General Ludwig von Yorck (1759–1830) had operated in the Baltic provinces and was not drawn into the catastrophe which befell the main army of Napoleon. In its retreat, it approached the East-Prussian frontier in the last days of 1812. With no authorization from the Prussian government, which was undecided on its policy, General von Yorck, on December 30, 1812, boldly signed a convention with the Russians pledging the neutrality of his troops. Yorck was a fierce reactionary in politics and as such had been an absolute opponent of the Stein-Scharnhorst reforms. It was proud Prussian patriotism which, in disregard of the ingrained Prussian virtue of discipline, drove him to the Convention of Tauroggen, which was welcomed by the patriots in the whole country as the first sign of an impending historic change.

No less important was the impact of the event on the czar. In continuing the war against Napoleon he had considered mobilizing the Polish nation and endearing himself to the Poles by restoring the kingdom of Poland under Russian sovereignty, which would have moved the western frontiers of the Russian empire to the mouth of the Vistula. But the Poles remained sullen in response to all blandishments, whereas the East Prussians showed great enthusiasm for the common war against France. The energy of Stein, who appeared in Königsberg, was needed to stir up the notables of the province to organize for war without the approval of the government in Berlin. The province assumed the burden of maintaining Yorck's corps and, in addition, of raising twenty thousand men as a national guard. It was a manifestation of the people's willingness for sacrifice which impressed both the czar and also the hesitant Frederick William III, who always underrated the strength of popular convictions. He was, indeed, in danger of being disregarded by his people, since in the other provinces the people as well as the army grew restless.

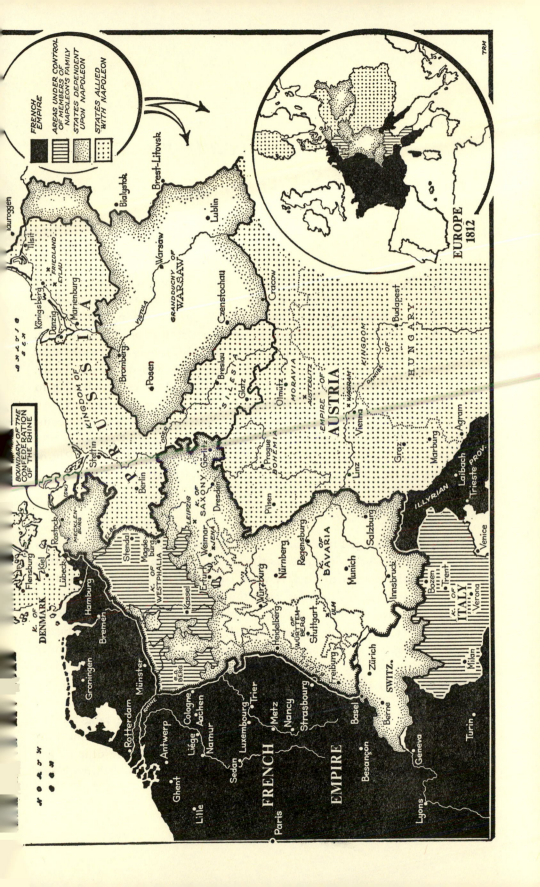

EUROPE 1812

FRENCH EMPIRE

AREAS UNDER CONTROL OF MEMBERS OF NAPOLEON'S FAMILY

STATES DEPENDENT UPON NAPOLEON

STATES ALLIED WITH NAPOLEON

BOUNDARY OF THE CONFEDERATION OF THE RHINE

FRENCH EMPIRE

Paris
Lille
Ghent
Sedan
Namur
Liége
Antwerp
Rotterdam
Groningen
Bremen
Hamburg
Münster
Luxembourg
Metz
Nancy
Strasbourg
Trier
Cologne
Aachen
Besançon
Lyons
Geneva
Berne
Basel
Turin
Milan

RHINE

DENMARK
Flensburg
Kiel
Lübeck
Rostock
MECKLEN-BURG

K. OF WESTPHALIA
Kassel
Magdeburg
Stendal
Erfurt
Weimar
JENA

SAXONY
Leipzig
Dresden
Görlitz

BERG
Heidelberg
Würzburg
Nürnberg
Regensburg
Freiburg
Stuttgart
K. OF WÜRTEMBERG
ULM
K. OF BAVARIA
Munich
Salzburg
Innsbruck
Bozen
Trent
Verona
Venice
ITALY
K. OF

SWITZ.
Zürich

PRUSSIA
KINGDOM OF PRUSSIA
Königsberg
Danzig
Marienburg
FRIEDLAND
EYLAU
Tilsit
Tauroggen
Stettin
Berlin
Bromberg
Posen
VISTULA
ODER

GRAND DUCHY OF WARSAW
Białystok
Lublin
Warsaw
Brest-Litovsk
Czenstochau
Cracow

SILESIA
Breslau
Glatz

BOHEMIA
Prague
Pilsen
Olmütz
MORAVIA
AUSTERLITZ

EMPIRE OF AUSTRIA
Vienna
Linz
Graz
WAGRAM
DANUBE

KINGDOM OF HUNGARY
Budapest

ILLYRIAN
Laibach
Trieste PROV.
Marburg
Agram

TRM

CHAPTER 14

The Wars of Liberation and the Peace Settlement of Vienna

FROM DECEMBER, 1812 ON, while the sad and wretched remnants of the *grande armée* staggered through the land, Hardenberg had contemplated the possibilities of liberation. But without Austria it seemed unrealistic to wage war against Napoleon, and Austria was unmovable. Understandably, the czar's Polish plans aroused concern. Yet negotiations were finally opened with Russia. Again Stein had to intervene. Actually, Alexander was now willing to leave West Prussia and a strip of Polish territory, creating an easy connection between West Prussia and Silesia, with Prussia. As compensation for the other parts of Poland that Prussia had owned before 1806, she was to receive German territories. On this basis the Russo-Prussian treaty of alliance was concluded on February 27, 1813.

✂ *Prussia Mobilizes*

ON FEBRUARY 3, Frederick William III had agreed to the formation of ranger (*Jäger*) detachments through the call-up of volunteers from among the propertied class. A week later all exemptions from military service were invalidated. But even though he was arming, the king had not made up his mind whether to fight. When he moved from Berlin to Breslau, the attitude of the people showed him that he had practically no choice. He signed the Russian alliance, and on March 15 Alexander I entered Breslau. Two days later the creation of a national guard (*Landwehr*) comprising all men from the age of seventeen to forty who were not in the regular army or the ranger corps was announced. Universal service through conscription, except for the rangers, was achieved as Scharnhorst and the military reformers had wished. In 1813, Prussia managed to mobilize 280,000 men or 6 per cent of her population. Thanks to the new military organization, and through this impressive striking force, she enhanced her influence among the powers far beyond her slender size. In the spring of 1813, however, the Prussian army was hardly a good army. The national guard was untrained and arms were scarce. But morale was high and the local self-government, entrusted with organizing and equipping the national guard units, proved the value of popular institutions. Yet if the war, after an initial phase, had not been followed by an armistice during the summer, the shortcomings of the army might have proved very serious. It became particularly important that the ranger detachments produced good officers for the national guard. This was one reason why Boyen could stave off attempts to use the national guard as a mere reservoir for the replenishment of the regular army. He wanted to keep it as a distinct citizens' army. And in battle the national guard regiments fought side by side with those of the regular army.

The general patriotism shown by the Prussian population was in stark contrast to the apathy of 1806, and there can be no question that the reformers had worked hard to bring about this change. They had rightly judged that great moral forces were slumbering in the people which could be activated for the state. Whether they had diagnosed the nature of these forces quite correctly can be doubted. Their own philosophy of life was too idealistic and individualistic, their nationalism too lofty and moralistic to serve as the belief of the masses. Even their political action had looked too far ahead to be immediately cherished by the people. Apart from the reactionary opposition of certain *Junker* circles, the townspeople disliked freedom of trade and had little appreciation of self-government. By 1815, the agrarian reform had hardly gone beyond promises. Though the reformers had a following among the officer corps and upper bureaucracy as well as among the educated groups, they did not dominate these groups completely. It will be seen later[1] how Wilhelm von Humboldt, as chief of education in the years 1809–10, had aimed at making the humanism of Weimar the foundation of Prussia's educational system. Great as the results of Humboldt's reforms finally proved to be, they had not as yet produced a general effect, nor had the active interest of the Prussian government in the modern German culture moved the intellectual leaders to support the Prussian reformers' national policies. Goethe, Hegel, and Schelling remained aloof from all efforts of national liberation.

The patriotism of 1813 rested on more elementary forces than the

[1] See pp. 475–7.

lofty ideas of Stein and Scharnhorst. The reformers recognized this and on their part attempted to arouse popular passions to the full. In April, 1813, Scharnhorst created provincial militias (*Landsturm*) consisting of all men not in the army or national guard. Their function was to act as home defense by all means of popular resistance, for which the Spanish War served as the model. Yet in Prussia the call-up and the arming of the common men met with strong criticism. This appeal to sansculottism aroused fears among the nobility and bourgeoisie, and care was taken to keep the mobilization of a *Landsturm* on a small scale and control it by placing it under the police authorities. Everywhere the established state authorities directed the popular movement. As a matter of fact, where such agencies did not give the signal and take charge, people failed to act. It was one of the reformers' bitter disappointments that no uprisings occurred in the states of the Rhenish Confederation and that only the people of "Old Prussia," that is, of the four eastern provinces which formed Prussia between 1807 and 1815, made far more than ordinary sacrifices. Among the Prussian reforms the greater equality among the classes and the improved conditions of army life were most generally important for engendering the common spirit shown by the Prussian people during the war. Hatred of the foreign oppressor and desire for the restoration of normal economic life were the predominant motives of the popular war spirit. Although the hope for further liberalization of the Prussian government and the national liberation of Germany may have played a role in the thinking of a good many educated people, the patriotism of the masses, most of them peasants, did not need these special incentives. They were animated by Prussian loyalties. The dynasty was still considered the supreme authority ordained by God, and it was not modern philosophy but the old religious teachings which served as the justification of political beliefs and actions. The war revealed in general that the traditional forms of religion were much more alive among the people than the literature of the age would indicate. The motto "With God for King and Fatherland" expressed rather well the prevailing sentiment of these years. Monarchism, antiforeign feeling, and a vague nationalism, partly Prussian, partly German, were fused into a quasi-religious obligation.

Napoleon was able to mobilize fresh troops at short notice. They were not as well trained and officered as in former years but still better and larger forces than the allies were able to put in the field in the spring of 1813. In the battle of Gross-Görschen, on May 2, Napoleon forced the allies to retreat from Saxony and three weeks later at Bautzen compelled them to withdraw to Silesia. As a matter of fact, the Russians were at the point of going back to Poland. But none of the battles had been more than a tactical victory for Napoleon, in spite of his great superiority in numbers. French losses were much heavier, and each time the allied armies had made an orderly retreat. The Prussian army displayed excellent morale and fine leadership. The reformers had to forego the honor of direct command. Field Marshal Blücher (1742–1819) was chosen as a commander. He was a rather illiterate old warrior who had been more devoted to hunting, gambling, and women than to study. But his dashing and colorful personality made him the hero of soldiers and people. Moreover, he was sufficiently honest and shrewd to respect the talents of Scharnhorst and Gneisenau. He relied entirely on their advice, and thus during this war the Prussian general staff system took root. Scharnhorst served as Blücher's chief of staff. He was wounded in the battle of Gross-Görschen. Hurrying to Prague during the summer in order to win Austria over to the allied side and neglecting his wound, he died. His place as Blücher's chief of staff was taken by Gneisenau, while Grolmann, Boyen, Clausewitz and others served as chiefs of staff with the individual corps commanders. In this way the new strategic school, the Prussian general staff, implanted itself as a sort of nerve system into the body of the Prussian army.

✑ Austrian Policy: Count Metternich

DISSATISFACTION WITH THE RESULTS of the spring campaign induced Napoleon to offer a two-month armistice. As in 1807, he thought it still possible to reach a separate peace with Russia by concessions in Poland or to gain Austria's support. In both respects he was mistaken, and the pause in the fighting gave the Russians and Prussians the chance for perfecting their armaments. But the policy of Austria, whose government since 1809 had been in the hands of Count Clemens Lothar Metternich (1773–1859), was decisive. This descendant of an old Rhenish noble family had been Austrian ambassador in Paris in 1806–09 and was a strong champion of war against the France of Napoleon. Austria's defeat had cured him forever of an emotional approach to politics. When he became Austrian foreign minister in 1809, he viewed the realities of power relationships with cold skepticism. Behind his methods of *raison d'état* was still a strong belief in the value of the old European state system and the balance of power among independent states. In internal politics, too, Metternich found the health of governments in a balance of the forces of progress and of continuity. In an age in which the French Revolution had aroused people to reckless change, governments had to insist on preserving stability and authority. Metternich believed in absolutism as a universal principle and in the balance of power as Europe's natural order. A rationalist, and in his private life an epicurean, he conducted for almost forty years an Austrian policy intended to serve the interests not only of the Habsburg empire but also of Europe as a whole.

Nobody among the leading European statesmen was intellectually so deeply opposed to the ideas of the Napoleonic empire as was Metternich. He did not forget that Napoleon had subdued the revolutionary chaos in France. Nevertheless, Napoleon remained to Metternich a child of the Revolution who by his conquest of the Continent had ruined the old state system. Its restoration became the true aim of Metternich's diplomacy. But in the first years his concern had to be Austria's very survival, and little could be done to ease the grip Napoleon held over the country. The marriage of Marie-Louise, daughter of Francis I, to the French emperor did not create a Franco-Austrian alliance comparable to the one of Kaunitz's days. Although Austria, in contrast to Prussia, received some political promises, she had to place an auxiliary army at Napoleon's disposal in 1812.

The Russian debacle in 1812 opened a new chapter. Many Austrian patriots felt that Austria should annihilate the remnants of Napoleon's retreating army and place herself, as was intended in 1809, at the head of a national rising in Germany. Metternich did not share this feeling. Austria was poorly armed and financially depleted and would have become dependent on Russia. The Austrian statesman saw no gain in the full defeat of Napoleon if this was to lead only to the overweening power of the other of "the two biggest colossi of ancient or modern history." French predominance even seemed preferable to that of the czar, since the death of Napoleon would presumably shake the foundations of the French empire. Metternich wanted to see the "colossi" in balance in order to be able to bring back under Austrian guidance the general balance of power in Europe, which to him rested "on eternal and unalterable laws." Therefore he encouraged the alliance between Prussia and Russia and while rearming kept Austria in a state of neutrality in order to intervene at the right moment through diplomatic mediation or force of arms.

Cold and wily, but in its objectives inflexible, Metternich's diplomacy had accomplished the general recognition of Austria's decisive role by August, 1813. Both Napoleon and the allies had to accept Austria's armed mediation. The barren results of the spring campaign made it impossible for Metternich to present his program of reducing France to her "natural" frontiers. But he trusted that the conqueror was not likely to make even the small concessions to alleviate Prussia's and Austria's positions and that Francis I would then be persuaded to enter the war on the side of the allies. Actually, after fruitless negotiations, Austria declared war on August 11, 1813. The allied cause was thereby greatly strengthened, but at the same time considerably changed in itself. The reformers in Prussia, and Stein at the side of the czar, lost influence. They wanted the freedom of nations and were ready to use even revolutionary means and daring military strategies to achieve it. Metternich, on the other hand, wanted to restore the old states through the time-honored methods of legitimate governments and carefully calculated military operations. While Kutusov's Kalisch proclamation of March 25, written under Stein's aegis, threatened German princes collaborating with Napoleon with extinction if they did not join the national liberation, Metternich soon began to build golden bridges for them. On his part the czar was not inclined to dispense completely with legitimacy.

This divergence of views also affected the conduct of the campaign. The Austrian Prince Karl von Schwarzenberg, a brave but somewhat conventional general, became the supreme commander of the large army which assembled in Bohemia and was composed of Austrians, Russians, and Prussians. Bernadotte, crown prince of Sweden, joined the allies north of the Elbe with a small corps, which, augmented by Russian and Prussian troops, became the northern army. Bernadotte wanted to conquer Norway on the Continent. Napoleon's former marshal was a good officer, but he had to move cautiously on account of his still precarious political position in Sweden. The third and smallest army was formed out of two Russian and one Prussian corps in Silesia and placed under Blücher. Here the new military thinking of the Prussian school quickly proved that only a determined offensive spirit and bold strategic moves could match Napoleon's great military leadership. The Prussian army and national guard showed the capacity for sustaining the unusual efforts which their leaders demanded from them. Napoleon was still in a powerful position. Quite apart from the fortresses in eastern Germany held by French garrisons, he was in command of the whole Elbe line from Dresden to Hamburg, and with his main army centered around Dresden he enjoyed the advantage of interior lines. He could throw himself with superior forces upon any of the three armies.

✍ *The Allied War Plan: Leipzig*

THE ALLIED WAR PLAN provided that each time the attacked army would retreat the two others would advance toward Napoleon's base, thus forcing him to turn around. At this moment the attacked army was to attempt to overwhelm the French rear guard. The plan, most difficult to execute in practice, was on the whole rather successful. In a number of fierce battles the Silesian and northern armies inflicted heavy punishment on Napoleon. But he pushed the Bohemian army back over the mountains when it approached Dresden, only to be forced to a tactical draw by the defeat of one of his army corps that had followed Schwarzenberg's army into Bohemia. Yet all the heavy fighting of the weeks in late August and early September did not bring a strategic decision. It was achieved by Gneisenau's plan to lead the Silesian army northward and persuade Bernadotte to force the crossing of the Elbe in combined strength. Largely owing to the heroic fighting of the Prussians, the two armies won the southern bank of the Elbe. They side-stepped a northward push by Napoleon by moving west and thereby threatened his communications with the Rhine in possible co-operation with the Bohemian army. Napoleon was forced to accept battle against the allies around Leipzig beginning on October 14, with the heaviest and bloodiest fighting taking place on October 16 and 18. Napoleon lost about one third of his army, but the allies failed to block the chief line of retreat and even failed to arrange an effective pursuit of their foe. But when they entered Leipzig on October 19, they knew that all of Germany east of the Rhine had been freed.

It was the high watermark of allied co-operation, in which the contribution made by the Prussian reform group was much greater than Prussia's actual strength. Beyond the battlefield, however, Prussia's influence was much more limited, and politics ruled the hour after the arms had done their work. Already before victory at Leipzig, Metternich had achieved a success in his diplomacy which had the most far-reaching consequence for the future of Germany. Through the Austro-Bavarian Treaty of Ried (October 8), Bavaria declared her withdrawal from the Rhenish Confederation and joined the coalition.

Austria guaranteed Bavaria's full sovereignty. For certain territorial concessions to Austria she was to receive equal compensation. The military gain of this co-operation was considerable, although an attempt of a Bavarian-Austrian army under Prince Wrede to stem Napoleon's retreating army at Hanau on the Main failed on October 30. The political results were manifold. The treaty laid to rest a century of Austro-Bavarian enmity and inaugurated a half-century of close co-operation between Vienna and the South German governments. Since the treaty implied the retention of the Franconian principalities of Ansbach and Bayreuth by Bavaria, Prussia, which had owned them from 1791–1806, was kept from trespassing into South Germany again.

∽ Revival of Small States

BAVARIA'S DEFECTION led to the dissolution of the whole Rhenish Confederation. Reluctantly King Frederick of Württemberg and Grand Duke Carl of Baden, Napoleon's son-in-law, joined the coalition and were accepted as allies. In northern Germany, events moved in a similar direction despite Stein's efforts. In his opinion the struggle of liberation was to culminate in the abolition of the territorial German princes, who had become tyrants through their absolutism and traitors by their alliance with Napoleon. He proposed to place all these territories under allied administration, which, with the participation of the populations, was to organize national guards and militias and mobilize the resources of these countries for the war. Stein hoped that such a common endeavor would set free the national spirit which would produce a better unified Germany. An agreement between Russia and Prussia of March 19 provided for a Central Administrative Council, of which Stein became the head. But neither Frederick William III nor Alexander I were the men to ride roughshod over their most serene cousins. An exception was made in the case of the King of Saxony, who had been held as a prisoner-of-war since the battle of Leipzig. The wish to annex Saxony outweighed Frederick William's feeling of royal solidarity. Otherwise Stein was directed to work through the governments. After the battle of Leipzig, Metternich saw to it that the Council was changed into a Central Administrative Department which received its political directions from a diplomatic council of the major allied powers. The functions of the Department were those of a general war commissariat or, in modern terms, an office of war mobilization. As an agency through which the future constitu-

tional order of Germany could be prepared, it lost almost all significance. The allied powers abolished only the kingdom of Westphalia
and the grand duchy of Berg, with their Bonapartistic rulers, and the
grand duchy of Frankfurt, since Dalberg was not of princely birth. The
princes north of the Main who had been deposed by Napoleon in
1806 were allowed to return in this whole region. Otherwise the
German princes who happened to be in possession of a throne were
accepted as rulers and no restoration of the princes and counts who had
been absorbed by other states before the war of 1806 took place. Stein
was dismayed by the survival of what he called "the thirty-six chief-
tains," but he helped to restore four aristocratic city-republics, Hamburg, Bremen, and Lübeck in the north and Frankfurt in the southwest.

The stamp of approval was given to the continued existence of all
these particular sovereignties. But much as Metternich had in mind the
establishment of a conservative Germany over which Austria could
exercise a strong influence, he could rightly argue that his policy was
in harmony with the prevailing sentiment of the German people.
Stein's expectation that people in the Rhenish Confederation waited
only for the signal to band together for guerilla war and were eager
to take substantial governmental functions into their hands was an
illusion. Everywhere they displayed the desire to receive orders from
what they considered their legal princes, and even the worst of them
they took to their bosom. Where a slightly more critical spirit came to
the surface, it was not caused by the wish for greater national unification but for the return to former dynasties, as for example in the case
of the people of the Breisgau, who wanted to have the Habsburgs
back, or those of Ansbach-Bayreuth, who preferred Prussia to Bavaria.
But under their state governments the Germans showed perfect willingness to fight the French. The Bavarians gave a very good account
of themselves in the winter campaign and so did the northwestern
Germans, mobilized by Stein's department, when they joined the
allied troops in the spring.

But the most controversial question among the allies in the weeks
and months after the battle of Leipzig was the continuation of the war
against Napoleon itself. Military and political considerations of conflicting character were hard to reconcile even within individual governments and led to even greater antagonism within the coalition. The
liberation of Germany to the Rhine had been accomplished. An invasion of France with her strong fortresses and patriotic people might
get an allied army into the same difficulties as in 1792–93. This thought

originally made all the leading statesmen reject Gneisenau's correct appraisal and accept new negotiations with Napoleon. Gneisenau argued that Napoleon's forces had grown too weak to offer strong resistance and were no longer sufficient to man all the fortresses. But from Frankfurt, where the allied headquarters had been moved, Napoleon was offered the "natural" frontiers of France. The French nation was assured a greater extension than it had ever enjoyed under its kings. For Napoleon, however, such conditions were unacceptable. English diplomacy, too, was not satisfied with subscribing to the Rhine frontier. Particularly after Holland revolted against the French regime, it wanted to see the liberation of the mouths of the Rhine and Scheldt. Once it became clear that Napoleon would not resign himself to the role of a national leader the conflict over war aims among the allies became heated. The fickle czar considered the moment propitious for presenting an ambitious program of Russian hegemony in Europe. Alexander demanded the complete defeat of Napoleon and his replacement by Bernadotte. With France removed as a potential counterbalancing power to Russia, the czar would be able to make himself master of all of Poland. Prussia could be compensated for her Polish provinces by Saxony, and Austria for Galicia by Alsace. Thus strengthened Russia could devote herself thereafter to the conquest of the Near East without Austrian interference.

Metternich fought this threat against the balance of power with all the means at his disposal. When the allied armies invaded France, spearheaded by the Prussian troops which crossed the central Rhine on New Year's Day of 1814, the main army under Schwarzenberg was still guided by the aim of gaining peace with Napoleon rather than destroying him. The lack of a common policy was reflected in the lame and disunited conduct of the campaign in France and was further enhanced by Napoleon's diplomatic moves. On February 3, a diplomatic congress was opened at Châtillon which, with interruptions, negotiated with Napoleon till March 19, offering him the frontiers of 1792. The negotiations mirrored the hopes and disappointments the partners entertained with regard to their military chances. The congress opened under the impression of Blücher's victory at La Rothière on February 1, but two weeks later Blücher's troops were badly mauled on the Marne, largely owing to the inactivity of Schwarzenberg's army. While Napoleon finally refused to accept the proffered peace conditions, the allies succeeded in establishing agreement among themselves. On March 1 they concluded the Quadruple Alliance of Chaumont in which they pledged themselves not only to the common pursuit of the war and the avoidance of separate peace negotiations but also to the common enforcement of the peace against French violations for a period of twenty years. Napoleon's stubborn refusal to come to terms compelled even Metternich to give up all attempts to maintain him on the throne of France, and the return of the Bourbons was envisaged.

In order to gain freedom of strategic initiative, Blücher had marched north and joined with a Prussian corps which arrived from Belgium after liberating Holland. The Prussian troops, lacking many substantial supplies, were in a poor state, and the French population suffered many outrages at their hands. But at Laon, on March 9–10, Napoleon failed to gain a victory, though the Prussians missed out on taking advantage of his defeat. Napoleon's last gamble to march east in order to induce the allies to retreat to Lorraine miscarried. Both Schwarzenberg and Blücher marched against Paris, which was surrendered by Napoleon's marshals. On March 31, Alexander I and Frederick William III made their entry into the French capital with their guard troops. Louis XVIII became king of France, and the czar, Castlereagh, Metternich, and Hardenberg negotiated with Talleyrand's provisional government the articles of peace, known as the first Peace of Paris. A quarter century of revolution and war drew to a close.

The first Peace of Paris (May 30, 1814) was negotiated with France by the four major allied powers. Three other powers—Spain, Portugal, and Sweden—were subsequently allowed to add their signatures. As soon as Napoleon was defeated, Czar Alexander had assumed the role of a benevolent protector of Louis XVIII's new regime and had even promised that royalist France would receive better terms than those offered the French emperor. Britain, too, aimed at gaining an understanding with the Bourbon monarchy, while it was Metternich's settled policy to preserve France as a great European power. France actually received more territories and stronger boundaries than the "frontiers of 1792" would have implied. Compared to 1792, France won lands with half a million inhabitants and her only territorial losses were the colonies which she lost to Britain. Of German territories, in addition to the bulk of Alsace, she retained all the enclaves on the left bank of the Upper Rhine that had still belonged to the German Empire at the time of the French Revolution. But she also gained new territories. To Saarlouis she added the whole southern bank of the Saar river.

∽ The Congress of Vienna

WHILE THE PEACE OF PARIS settled the French problems, all the issues concerning the "intermediary Europe" were left to a general congress which convened in Vienna late in September. The czar and Frederick William III, as well as many German princes and former lords were present together with diplomatic representatives of two hundred states, princes, and cities. In addition, Vienna attracted a large number of social pleasure seekers and people bent on profit. The imperial court staged numerous lavish social events, and the high Austrian aristocracy as well as the smaller families did their utmost to entertain the visitors. The gaiety and luxury of these festivities was a revival of the happy days the ruling classes had enjoyed before the Revolution. But class lines were not quite as tightly drawn any longer and the czar set the example in relaxing the etiquette, while the diplomats did not revive the pomp and circumstance of eighteenth-century protocol. It is true that they did not know how to run this Congress as a working conference. In a strict sense the Congress met only once, namely for the signing of the final treaty. Its work was done by deliberations of the four victor powers or, particularly when their interests began to clash more seriously, of the four powers and France or, in more formal procedure, of the eight signatories of the Peace of Paris. In addition, other committees worked on special problems. Among them, the German committee, consisting of Austria, Prussia, Hanover, Bavaria, and Württemberg, worked on the question of a Germanic constitution. As Metternich once expressed it, the gathering in Vienna was *"Europe sans distance,"* which meant that it brought the leading statesmen of Europe together before an audience composed of all states.

The balance of power in Europe was the strongest single idea in the thinking of the diplomatic protagonists in Vienna. It was Metternich's lodestar, but no less that of Lord Castlereagh. After gaining from the Peace of Paris England's war aims vis-à-vis France, world maritime hegemony, the British Tory statesman was able to devote himself with calm detachment to building a concert of Europe in which no single power could dominate the rest. This included the creation of barriers against the renewal of any French attempt at the conquest of the Continent and also the limitation of Russian progress toward Central Europe. Prussia was to receive sufficient recognition to keep her from committing herself entirely to Russia without, however, making her strong enough to antagonize Austria or France. Britain's relative aloofness from most of the specific Continental conflicts and the powerful position she held as the financier of the alliance enabled Castlereagh to play a decisive part in Vienna as the mediator of clashes among the states and as an architect of reasonable compromises. This Tory statesman knew little about the sentiments of people, and even if he had, he would not have paid any attention to them. Castlereagh intended to found a restored balance upon states rather than nations.

Anglo-Austrian co-operation was easily achieved. As in the days of Marlborough and Prince Eugene, the two powers had fought together in the revolutionary wars against France as the champions of a universal monarchy. During the War of Liberation this political tradition had revived and, in the common diplomacy of Metternich and Castlereagh during the Congress, had reached new intensity. Both statesmen were sensitive to the Russian threat not only with a view to Central Europe but also to the Balkans and the Mediterranean. In his fundamental political outlook the Prussian representative, Hardenberg, was not too far removed from the thinking of the Austrian chancellor and British secretary. He shared with them the view that Europe should be restored as a plurality of states held together not only by their own interests but also by the well-being of the European community as a whole. The *convenance* of the individual state was limited by the *convenance* of Europe or the existence of what was called "the public law" of Europe. This belief in a European system into which the individual nations' ambitions ultimately had to be fitted was held by Hardenberg as much as by Metternich, Castlereagh, and Talleyrand. It was the major cause of the final success of the Congress. Despite its highly rationalistic and absolutist nature, the Vienna settlement lasted longer than any comparable peace. Many boundaries drawn in Vienna are still in existence. Even more important was the fact that for a full century no general war took place and that even the great upheaval caused by the wars attending the national unification of Italy and Germany after the middle of the century could be absorbed by the European system created in 1815.

But Hardenberg was distinguished from Metternich, Castlereagh, and Talleyrand not only by his more liberal political ideas, which were to some extent means to gain more influence over people and also made him inclined to listen to the Prussian reformers' national hopes, but also by his position as the chancellor of the youngest and weakest of the great powers. Unlike the other great powers, Prussia was not satisfied with mere restoration, but wanted to overcome the shortcomings of her power basis caused by the wide spread of her separate possessions. Moreover, Prussia wanted to win a role in Germany comparable to the contribution she had made to the nation's liberation. Supported by Wilhelm von Humboldt, whose fine critical mind produced one memorandum after another, Hardenberg pressed the Prussian case. The Hanoverian aristocrat was a great diplomat, though in the art of diplomatic finesse and legerdemain slightly inferior to the *"comte de la balance,"* Metternich. Both had to make substantial concessions to their monarchs. This was more serious in Hardenberg's case, since there were fewer arrows in his quiver. Originally, Hardenberg leaned to close co-operation with Austria and England, who in turn were willing to pay a high price for Prussian collaboration against Russia, but this policy was from the beginning gravely handicapped by Frederick William III's determination not to endanger his relationship with Czar Alexander, in whom he now saw the Prussian monarchy's savior.

Czar Alexander I, introduced by his tutor, the Swiss, La Harpe, to the ideas of the French Enlightenment, saw in the liberation of suppressed nations and the granting of constitutions means of internal and external peace. A federation of nations was one of Alexander's chief ideals. His intervention in European affairs had a missionary intention which, however, did not prove incompatible with an expansionism in the tradition of Catherine II. He failed to shed autocracy and expansionism even when, in 1813–14, his philosophical notions were replaced by religious motives derived from his contact with pietistic circles in Baden and Württemberg and the writings of German romanticism. He dreamed of erecting a theocratic order on earth through God-chosen rulers and a fraternal community of nations. This mixture of ideas made a disturbing impression on the statesmen of the Congress, and no steadying influence of a single minister was discernible. Closest to the thinking of the Western ministers was Count Nesselrode, a Westphalian by birth and Russian chancellor in later years, and Count Razumovski, Russian ambassador in Vienna, whose name has reached posterity through Beethoven's dedications. But the czar seemed to prefer the advice of the old La Harpe, the Polish Prince Czartoryski, the Greek Capodistria, the Corsican Pozzo di Borgo, and of Baron Stein, who was invited by Alexander to serve him as advisor in German affairs and who naturally presented his ideas to the Prussian and some German statesmen as well.

The opening months of the Congress were already under the cloud of Alexander's demands to be left free to restore the kingdom of Poland and make himself king of this constitutional national state. Austria and Britain opposed this plan vigorously and tried to gain Prussia's adherence to a common Western policy. But Frederick William III refused to hinder Alexander's Polish program. In exchange for Russian concessions in West Prussia and the promise of Russian support of Prussia's chief peace aim, the acquisition of Saxony, the Prussian government abstained from placing obstacles in the way of the czar's plans for Poland. This step led to a drastic change of Metternich's policy not only in European relations but also in the German question. Both he and Hardenberg were convinced that Germany's future depended upon Austria's and Prussia's "peaceful dualism." Metternich had gone far to meet Prussian wishes, even where they seemed rather steep, as in the case of the desired annexation of Saxony. But Metternich was determined to keep a Prussia that separated herself from the solidarity of the Western states from bold German aspirations.

Prussian annexation of Saxony had the strongest overtones of an active national policy. Frederick the Great had already coveted this richest and most industrious country in East Central Germany, which was contiguous to Brandenburg, Silesia, and the Prussian possessions between the Elbe and Harz. The annexation of Saxony would have rounded out and solidified the center of the Hohenzollern monarchy. In the north and east, Prussia would have clung around Bohemia and at its southernmost point touched Bavaria. In this respect Saxony was the most desirable compensation Prussia could acquire, but the new strength was demanded by the Prussian patriots as the best means for giving Prussia a leading position in the German nation. The claim was most passionately defended by the historian Barthold Georg Niebuhr. He wrote: "Prussia is proud of the mission to defend herself and Germany; it must, however, be strengthened for this mission in order not to exhaust herself and bleed white." To him this Prussia was not a self-contained state but the heart and brain of the German nation; "it is the common fatherland of every German who excels in scholarship, arms, administration." Strangely enough, at this moment the national patriots cared as little as the princes about the feeling of the people. The demonstrations of loyalty to their old dynasty by the Saxons counted for nothing. Even Boyen thought that a well-devised constitution would turn the heterogeneous members into a "magnificent nation."

Frederick William III ordered Hardenberg to stop opposing the czar's Polish plans, and this led to the split of the Quadruple Alliance. The annexation of Saxony by Prussia was most unpopular in Austria and equally detested by the German "middle states." Metternich placed himself at the head of this German opposition. But in promoting these states' interests and helping them realize their territorial claims, he prejudiced the future of a German federation still further. If Austria and Prussia had reached agreement on a constitution prior to the Polish-Saxon conflict, the federation would have become better integrated, and the two great German powers could have broken the resistance of the small states by withholding fulfillment of their territorial aspirations.

✂ *Prussia Brought to the Rhine*

THE DIVISION IN THE QUADRUPLE ALLIANCE made Metternich and Castlereagh anxious to secure French assistance. Talleyrand had his opportunity for displaying the prestige of the restored monarchy in European and German affairs. In a way, the events were a first rehearsal of the revived balance-of-power principle. The diplomatic struggle assumed a bitter character, and cold, harsh words were exchanged. On January 3, 1815, Britain, Austria, and France concluded a secret alliance by which the three promised to fight together if they were attacked because of their common stand. In Berlin there was talk about war against Austria. But there was much bluff and bluster on both sides, and the solution of the crisis was found a few days later. Czar Alexander conceded to Austria both the Polish possessions in Galicia she had gained in the first Polish partition and agreed to letting Krakow, city of Polish kings, become a free republic. Prussia gave all of her acquisitions from the third partition to Russia; however, she retained not only Danzig and West Prussia, finally augmented by Thorn, but also a substantial land bridge, subsequently forming the province of Posen (Poznania). This fourth partition brought a population of an additional three and a half million Poles under the scepter of the czar. Russian Poland cut deeply into Prussia's eastern provinces, but from a Prussian military point of view the frontier was greatly improved beyond what Alexander had originally intended to grant. Metternich, rightly or wrongly, comforted himself with the thought that with the concessions of the czar a full-blown Polish national revival had been averted.

Prussia had to forego complete annexation of Saxony and to content herself with the northern half, containing two fifths of Saxony's population. Upper and Lower Lusatia, the land around Wittenberg, on which in days now past the electoral dignity had rested, and northern Thuringia, with Erfurt, became Prussian. Even these limited additions contributed very considerably to tying together the center of Prussia, but the diplomats counted heads, or as they said "souls," and found that Prussia had a just claim to receive many more of them. It was Castlereagh who wished to find the compensation on the Rhine. He had already done his best to make the restored Netherlands as strong as possible. Under the prince of Orange they were to include the Belgian provinces, which Austria did not wish to have returned to her, the bishopric of Liége, and Luxembourg. The United Netherlands appeared sufficiently strong to deter a new French sally into the strategic region of river estuaries and at the same time serve as a useful gate to the Continent for England. But behind these Netherlands, Castlereagh wanted to place a big military power, and Prussia seemed the ideal state to assume sentry duties along the Rhine. The idea, which in its origins went back to the younger Pitt, implied giving Prussia the whole left bank of the Rhine from, broadly speaking, Bingen to Emmerich on the Rhine to a line from Cleves to Aachen and Trier in the west. Together with the restored Westphalian possessions of Prussia on the right bank of the river, this created a territorial bloc which made Prussia the complete master of the Lower Rhine, but on the other hand was separated from its eastern provinces by Hanover and Hesse-Kassel.

In this British proposal, which found Metternich's support, Prussian statesmen saw an attempt to weaken Prussia. They wished to resume the Prussian position at the northern Rhine and in general to contribute, largely through a federation of Germanic states, to the defense of the western borderlands of Germany, but actual rule over the major part of the Rhineland, which placed Prussia in direct contact with France, was resisted. The Prussians preferred to transfer the king of Saxony from Dresden to Bonn and endow him with a Rhenish kingdom. But eventually Prussia had to give in. She had to make still another concession by turning over East Friesland to Hanover, thereby losing her only access to the North Sea, the port of Emden. Castlereagh wanted to keep the district adjacent to the Netherlands under Anglo-Hanoverian control. In exchange, Prussia received the last Swedish foothold on the Baltic mainland, the district around Stralsund and the island of Rügen.

It was one of the most fateful decisions to transplant Prussia against her will to the Rhineland. Strategic considerations and, to some extent, regard for the future relations of the German princes were the paramount motives. No attention was paid to popular wishes. None of the diplomats foresaw the future. Prussia, giving up simultaneously most of her Polish provinces, became a German state to a much greater extent than would have been the case if she had annexed all of Saxony. Henceforth Prussia was insolubly involved in all vital German political problems. The state straddled the whole North German plain from the Niemen to the Rhine. It had a strong position on the Vistula, owned the Oder valley in its entirety, controlled the central Elbe valley, and became the strongest power on the Rhine, the river that linked North and South Germany in peace and war. The new Prussia's widespread nature and the division into two separated parts made both defense and a unified economic policy a serious problem. Inevitably Prussia had to make arrangements with her neighbors and to conduct an active German policy. The rich natural resources of the Rhineland were not entirely overlooked by the statesmen in 1815. Nobody, of course, could have foreseen that through the Rhineland Prussia could gain supremacy in industry and commerce.

The Smaller States

IN THE REARRANGEMENT of Germany's territorial order the smaller states depended largely on the protection of the great powers. Baden and Württemberg maintained their boundaries because they could rely on their dynastic ties with the czar. These relations proved profitable also in the enlargement of Oldenburg, Saxony-Weimar, and Saxony-Coburg. Count Münster, the representative of Hanover, with Castlereagh's support, was able to reap important additions to the former electorate, now raised to a kingdom. Apart from East Friesland, Hanover got important territories in northern Westphalia, including Osnabrück. In the east she received Goslar and the bishopric of Hildesheim. Yet the most difficult territorial question arose between Austria and Bavaria. Under Napoleon, Bavaria had won Tyrol, Salzburg, and Berchtesgaden and the Treaty of Ried, which brought Bavaria to the allied side, had guaranteed Bavaria the size she gained through Napoleon's favor. In exchange for Tyrol, Bavaria readily accepted Würzburg and Aschaffenburg on the Main, but she was not willing to give all of Salzburg to Austria unless she received compensations which would have cut off Baden and Württemberg from direct contact with the north and made Bavaria the actual leader of South Germany. The negotiations proved unusually difficult and led in the final days of the Congress to an Austro-Prussian front against these Bavarian ambitions. The two major German powers reached an agreement which placed the region on the left bank between the Prussian Rhineland and the French Alsace at Austria's disposal, but the future of this region was not settled before the time of the second Peace of Paris or even the final Austro-Bavarian treaty of April 14, 1816.

Metternich realized in 1815 that a full Austrian retreat from the Rhine might jeopardize Austria's leading position in Germany. He had not renewed Austrian claims for Belgium and recommended leaving Alsace with France. He forewent, as will be seen, the prestige Austria might have derived from a revival of the German imperial title. But he felt that Austria could not refuse a direct part in the western defense of Germany, which for centuries had been her main contribution to the life of the nation. Therefore, he wanted to make the strategic Mainz and the Palatinate Austrian, and he also thought of regaining the Breisgau for the Habsburgs. His Rhenish origin made him think highly of the German tradition of Austrian policy. Yet his plans were defeated not by the European powers, not even by France or Prussia, but exclusively by internal opposition in Vienna. Here the view prevailed that Austria should be organized as a compact empire around the eastern Alps, Danube, and Adriatic, and Metternich had to bow to Emperor Francis. Austria finally received all of Salzburg, though without Berchtesgaden, and also the *Inn-Viertel* with Braunau. Mainz, which became a federal fortress, went to Hesse-Darmstadt, while the mass of territories on the left bank of the Upper Rhine was given to Bavaria. Then and later Bavarian wishes to gain a direct land bridge to the distant Palatinate remained unfulfilled.

The territorial rearrangement delayed, and in many respects prejudiced, the reconstruction of a German constitution. Only after Napoleon's return to France were official discussions resumed. Already at Bartenstein, in 1807, Prussia and Russia had spoken of creating a Germanic federation, and the alliance treaty of Kalisch had made it a declared war aim. Kutusov's manifesto of March, 1813 even promised the restoration of "a dignified empire." The hope for reviving the German Empire was in a good many hearts at a time when the romantic writers awakened interest in the glories of the medieval Empire. The sentiment was strongest in the regions where the territorial division had gone furthest. When Francis I journeyed to Frankfurt after the battle of Leipzig, he was widely welcomed as German emperor. All through the period of the Congress, the small states expressed themselves in favor of the renewal of the imperial dignity. It was doubtful, however, to what extent they desired an emperor merely as a protector of their own freedom against the middle states.

Baron Stein was similarly hostile to the middle states, which appeared to him as traitors to Germany and internally as representative of "sultanism." He struggled in a series of projects to find a constitution for Germany which would make the country secure against new aggression from the west and give the individual constitutional and civil freedom. Therefore he wanted to weaken the middle states, possibly even to revive the independence of the small counts and knights. The small states, however, were not to have sovereignty, but only limited administrative authority. Foreign policy, defense, and common economic affairs would come under a strong central authority which would also exercise a certain jurisdiction over the guarantee of constitutional and individual rights. It was clear to Stein that such a system could not be imposed on Austria and Prussia. Consequently, in his opinion, it was either possible to have two Germanys, a North Germany under Prussian leadership and a South Germany under that of Austria, or to give the central power to one of two great German powers, in which case the other would have to stand on the side. Stein argued paradoxically that the imperial rank should be given to Austria because she was less German and therefore should be tied to Germany through the German imperial crown.

Stein's plans for a German constitution are memorable, since for the first time they brought out the complexity of the political problems which a movement toward the establishment of a German national state would have to solve. The strength of the middle states in the defense of their sovereignty and the tradition of *Libertät* among the small states—what came to be called German "particularism"—was an imposing force. Yet to a large extent it fed on the tensions created by the existence of two major German powers, neither of which wanted to subordinate itself to the other. The founding of a federal state was impossible in these circumstances, as even Stein had to see, though at the end he returned to his dream of a revived Empire. Metternich and the Prussian statesmen, Hardenberg and Humboldt, agreed from the outset that only a federation could be created. The Treaty of Ried and the other treaties Metternich concluded with the southern German states in the fall of 1813 created a situation in which a strict subjection of these states to a central authority became unthinkable. Metternich had already decided not to restore the imperial dignity to the Austrian ruler and even less the old constitution of the Holy Empire. Its political weakness had been shown by the events of the last twenty-five years, and the imperial title had proved hollow. In Metternich's view the reassumption of the imperial title could only induce the small states to resume their collusion with foreign powers. The Treaty of Chaumont and the first Peace of Paris provided only bonds of federation for the German states.

But a federation could assume very different forms. As long as Prussia and Austria co-operated in a so-called system of "peaceful dualism" the degree of integration could go quite far, and the early negotiations between Austria and Prussia had been begun in this spirit. Hardenberg and Humboldt wished to place Austria and Prussia in charge of the confederation and make its executive responsible for foreign and military affairs as well as the guarantor of the political and legal rights of citizens. Besides, they were aiming at the extension of Prussian superiority in the north, expecting Austria to act similarly in southern Germany. The Saxon-Polish controversy, however, stymied "peaceful dualism." Metternich strengthened Austrian relations with the middle states not only in the south but also, as a result of the successful intervention on behalf of Saxony, in the north, where Hanover was already apprehensive of Prussian pressure. Metternich could even threaten with a separate federation of German states under Austrian presidency.

The impact of the smaller states was clearly shown in the final document which emerged from the German Committee of Five (Austria, Prussia, Bavaria, Württemberg, and Hanover). The resistance of Bavaria and Württemberg to any common institutions produced results not always to the liking of even the Austrian chancellor, but Metternich was convinced that only a federation of equal states was possible, that this federation should be based exclusively on governments and not lend support to a German liberal or national movement. By the spring of 1815, Nassau, Bavaria, Württemberg, and Baden had already promised their people constitutions in order to stave off Prussian insistence on a federal guarantee of constitutional principles and had, thereby, compelled the Prussian government to issue, on May 22, 1815, a new proclamation assuring the Prussians of provincial as well as general representative organs. The constitutional movement was thereby deflected from the national field and could now serve the builders of particular states as well. But Metternich was also anxious to stop the liberal trend. The result was the ambiguous article 13 of the Federal Act. "*Landständische* constitutions will exist in all German states." The article did not impose an obligation on the members under the law of the federation to introduce constitutions, and it avoided any definition of the type of constitution contemplated. *Landstände* could mean the old feudal bodies, which had continued in Austria, Saxony and other states, or it could be interpreted as constitutions like the French *Charte* of 1814.

✂ The Germanic Confederation

THE GERMANIC CONFEDERATION was a loose federation of thirty-five monarchical states and four city republics. The Federal Act adopted by the German governments at the last moment (June 8, 1815) declared as its objective "the preservation of the external and internal security of Germany and of the independence and inviolability of the individual German states." Its fundamental provisions were incorporated into the Vienna Treaty of June 9, 1815, and through Article 11, Austria, Prussia, and all the other member states pledged mutual aid against attacks on their lands that had belonged to the Holy Empire or now to the Germanic Confederation. This left out the Prussian provinces of East and West Prussia and Posen, as well as Austria's Polish, Hungarian, and Italian possessions. The foreign powers which were princes of territories belonging to the Confederation, the King of England as King of Hanover, the ruler of the Netherlands as Duke of Luxembourg, and the Danish King as Duke of Holstein and Lauenburg, were not committed to such help.

The chief organ of this security association was a permanent diplomatic conference, the Federal Diet at Frankfurt. When it met as a plenary council, each of the members had at least one vote, Austria and the five kingdoms as many as four. The Plenary Council was to convene only for decisions regarding fundamental laws or organic institutions. It could reach these decisions by a two-thirds majority, though for constitutional changes and religious matters unanimity was required. The Plenary Council met very rarely between 1822 and 1847 and never thereafter. The regular business was carried out by the Select Council (*Engerer Rat*), on which eleven larger states had one vote each, as had each of the seven "curias," in which twenty-eight small states were bundled together. Here a simple majority decided, while a tie could be broken by the vote of the Austrian president.

The Confederation was not a state but rather an association under international law. Yet the sovereignty of its members was limited in certain respects. They could not leave the Confederation, conspire against its security with other powers, or take the law into their own hands against another member. Once the Confederation had declared war, they could not negotiate a separate armistice or peace. All these provisions were an improvement over the Holy Roman Empire, as was the clearer definition of the German boundaries. In spite of the dynastic bonds between some of its members and foreign countries, the Confederation was a more closely knit union than the old Empire. In 1821–22, a military organization was created which laid down the size of the contingents to be contributed to a Confederate army of 300,000 men. Austria and Prussia each had to present three corps, and the remaining four corps were to be formed by the small and middle states. Unfortunately, the problem of the command of this German army was not solved, but the organization was still superior to that of the Empire. In other fields, the Confederation never implemented the possibilities it possessed. The Federal Act promised deliberations on the promotion of trade and commerce. But nothing came of it unless one wants to mention the agreement on a German copyright, which pleased a nation of prolific writers and avid readers.

Weakest were the rights granted individuals. "The law of citizens" consisted of equal rights for the Christian churches, the right of a German to acquire real estate in any member state, of migration, of entrance into the civil service or army of other states, as well as of the suppression of double taxation. The question was whether the Confederation would enforce individual rights, especially since no Confederate courts were established. Member states were bound to execute laws enacted by a two-thirds majority, and, if it so chose, the Confederation could take strong action to force compliance. Individuals had only the comfort of the vague promise that the Confederation would protect "wronged subjects" (*bedrängte Untertanen*). One group of the latter already experienced the benevolence of the leading statesmen at the Congress. Legal equality had been granted to the Jews not only in the Rhenish territories incorporated into France but also, with some reservations, in the states of the Rhenish Confederation. Hardenberg had emancipated the Jews in Prussia in 1812. Whereas Hardenberg's motive was his belief in a free competitive economy, Metter-nich's interest in the Jewish problem stemmed from the position the Jewish bankers had acquired in the management of Austrian state finances and debts. Wilhelm von Humboldt, through his contacts with the Jewish literary circles of Berlin, had gained a great human liking for Jews early in his life. Together with Metternich and Hardenberg, he struggled successfully at the Congress to defeat attempts by some of the states such as Bavaria, Württemberg, and Saxony, and also the Hanseatic cities and Frankfurt, the home of the Rothschilds, to deny full equality to the Jews. The Federal Act forbade the cancellation of positive rights the Jews had won in indi-vidual states and envisaged a discussion by the Federal Diet of improve-ments of their civil status. Still, it needed Austro-Prussian diplomatic intervention, joined by Russia and England as guarantors of the Vienna settlement, to make the four cities accept the equality of Jews.

When we look at the Germanic Confederation as a whole, it is ob-vious that it contributed greatly to the growth of a national cohesion the patriots quite wrongly asserted already existed. It did not exist even in the cultural field, much less in the relations of the social classes, and least of all in political affairs. The Confederation was not at all an ideal structure, but it ought not to be judged with the eyes of the liberals of 1848 or the generation of Bismark. The nature of the Con-federation, its predominantly diplomatic character and its aloofness from the broad stream of popular concerns, again made the individual states the chief scene of German political life, as they had been in the past. Yet the world of German states was better protected against foreign invasion or pressures and more pacified within itself than had been the case for many centuries. If Germans were far from reaching political unification under the Confederation, they could at least feel a sense of unity.

∽ Waterloo and the Peace of 1815

WHILE THE CONGRESS OF VIENNA was entering upon its last phase, Napoleon returned from Elba, in March, 1815, and won back the allegiance of the French army. News of the rift among the big powers over the Polish-Saxon issue had reached him, but he did not know that the conflict had been settled. His reappearance helped bolster unity among the allies. Napoleon's forces were limited when he decided to cripple the British and Prussian armies before the Austrian and Russian armies would approach. Wellington and Blücher, having made contact without having effected a union, operated south of Brussels. On June 16, 1815 Blücher and his chief of staff, Gneisenau, accepted Napoleon's attack at Ligny in the expectation that Wellington would join them. But this hope failed, and the Prussian army suffered a severe setback. While Napoleon turned against Wellington at Waterloo, believing the Prussians disorganized and in full retreat, Gneisenau boldly directed the withdrawal of the Prussian troops to a point not too far away from Wellington's army. He also achieved the reorganization of the badly shaken corps and led them in an exhausting march toward the battle-field of Waterloo, where, in the afternoon of June 18, Napoleon had flung his slightly superior army against the defensive battleline of Wellington's army composed of seventy thousand men, of whom 25,000 were English, the rest Hanoverian and Dutch. The English troops showed what an eighteenth-century army could do if possessed by magnificent bravery and ably commanded. Still, the appearance of the Prussians threatening the flank and rear of the French was de-cisive. Gneisenau managed to stir up the tired Prussian troops to con-duct a relentless pursuit of the enemy through the night. Napoleon's army was completely destroyed. By-passing the French fortresses, the Prussians advanced quickly to the French capital, followed by the army of the Duke of Wellington, who brought Louis XVIII back to France.

Napoleon's reappearance had stirred up in Germany a new and powerful wave of national sentiment. In the *Rheinische Merkur*, edited by Joseph Görres in Coblenz, this passionate feeling had its chief mouthpiece. This time, particularly in southwest Germany, it came to the formation of popular patriotic associations. Hopes, dis-appointed by the course of the diplomatic negotiations in Vienna, rose to new heights of expectation. In Blücher's headquarters the will to use the victory for imposing a humiliating peace on France seemed for a while to push aside all other considerations, even those of subordina-tion to the policy of the state. Blücher assumed the role of the cham-pion of the live national conscience determined not to have "the quill-drivers" again spoil what the sword had won. Vengeance was to be taken not only on Napoleon but also on the French people. The soldiers were allowed great freedom in oppressing the population. Large war contributions were demanded, and restoration of the Bourbon king's authority was opposed. Various schemes were pre-sented by which France could be forever kept down. National feeling turned into a vindictive hatred, which was blind to the rights of other nations and to the needs of a stable order in Europe. It was ominous that the Prussian army, in days past a silent tool in the hands of the king but now a force with a will of its own, identified itself with radical nationalism.

As a prelude to subsequent events in German history the outbreak of this "military-republican" Prussian spirit—as Castlereagh called it—had some significance, but it did not represent the whole officer corps. Clausewitz, conscious that war was to have a constructive political end, was alarmed by the undisciplined conduct of the headquarters, and Gneisenau, under Hardenberg's influence, calmed down. Of all the ideas to weaken France through substantial territorial annexations, only the acquisition of Alsace had a certain chance, since it had supporters in Austria as well. But the time had passed when the return of Alsace could have been justified in terms of nationality. Alsace was still German in its folklore, but the French Revolution and Napoleon had turned the Alsatians into devoted French citizens. The bourgeoisie and peasants had sullenly watched the allied armies enter the country in 1814, full of fear that feudalism and dismemberment of the province might follow in their wake. It would be wrong to argue that if Alsace had gone back to Germany in 1815, the allegiance of its people might have shifted. For the Germany of the small states in the age of the Restoration could not have made national converts.

In any event national arguments were not used in the discussion of the Alsatian problem in 1815. Military and strategic reasons dominated, but did not prevail. Britain and Russia insisted from the beginning that the principles of the first Peace of Paris should not be abandoned. Temporary occupation of some French fortresses would suffice as a safety measure till the royalist regime would take roots. Depriving the French of their self-respect as a great power would drive them into revolutionary adventures again. But even Metternich favored a strengthening of the frontiers of France's eastern neighbors. As a result, France had to make concessions to Piedmont, Switzerland, and the Netherlands, while Prussia received Saarbrücken and Saarlouis, a small but strategically important district with a population which desired to belong to Germany. On the Upper Rhine, Landau came to the Bavarian Palatinate. The "frontiers of 1790" superseded the "frontiers of 1792" in the second Peace of Paris of November 20, 1815. France also had to pay a moderate contribution to the allied powers.

CHAPTER 15

The Restoration After 1815

ETWEEN 1812 AND 1815, Metternich had succeeded in leading
Austria to the pinnacle of her power. For a while, the dominant position of an empire which, more than any other
power, represented the universalist traditions of Europe and
which at the same time was void of all aggressive tendencies, was beneficial for a Europe anxious to recover from twenty-five years of
division and war. But the question may be raised whether European
diplomacy had not brought Austria much more than she could hope
to maintain by the governmental methods of the past. The Habsburg
Empire contained at least ten different nationalities and claimed leadership not only in Germany but also in Italy. Not even the old "hereditary lands" formed a strongly integrated dominion, while the Habsburg
Empire as a whole was only loosely knit together. The resources of
Hungary were in the hands of the Magyar magnates and practically
out of reach of the Vienna government. The apparatus of the monarchy of Maria Theresa and Joseph II was inadequate for dealing with
the complex problems of a multinational empire. Although Metternich
felt the need for a better organized central government, he did not
prevail against the suspicious and unimaginative Emperor Francis.
Actually, much more than administrative reorganization was called for.
The new national and social movements were still in their early infancy. A far-seeing statesman would have tried to mold them, and
social reforms might have served him as a lever. Nobody can assert
that such policies would have forestalled the ultimate crisis of the
Habsburg empire, but it can be said that Metternich's reliance on
repressive methods for the preservation of the existing political and
social order never faced up to the historical situation. Metternich had
no sense of organic growth but saw social organization only in mechanistic terms.

ᔥ *Metternichian Absolutism*

METTERNICH WAS THE TRUE SCION of eighteenth-century despotism, untouched by the new ideas of nationality and popular government. Nor did contemporary religious and political philosophies impress him. The theories of Adam Müller, Friedrich Schlegel, and other Viennese romanticists did not express the doctrines of his rule. Metternichian absolutism continued the Josephinian system of state control over the teaching of universities and schools and enforced conformity with governmental thinking by police methods. Since the German states, including Prussia, were never reduced to political apathy to this extent, Austria erected strong barriers to free intercourse between her people and the rest of Germany. Despite these obstacles, the German literary and humanistic culture of the classic and romantic age took a firm hold on the educated classes. In Franz Grillparzer (1791–1872), Austria possessed the greatest German dramatic talent of the period.

But political particularism was even greater in Austria than in Germany, and where such patriotism did not content itself with local or provincial life, it was directed toward the tasks of the Habsburg rather than the former German Empire. The German element was the chief support of the Austrian imperial government. Until 1870, large numbers of non-Austrian Germans entered the officer corps, upper bureaucracy, and higher education. But these contacts did not contribute to close connections between Austria and Germany. To most Germans, Austria appeared as the immovable guarantor of the old public order. When the quickening pulse of economic life tended to bring Germans of the various states into closer contact, Austria stood apart. The growth of the Austrian economy between 1815 and 1848, once the internal customs barriers between the Austrian provinces of the empire had been removed, was not inconsiderable. But on the whole it started on a lower level, and the old forms of economic organization were preserved. Internally, the government favored guilds, while externally it imposed a strict protectionism.

While the ties between the Austrian and German people grew weaker over the following decades, the policy of the Austrian government in Germany lost much of its moral appeal. Since she did not participate in the solution of Germany's economic problems or very prominently in the Confederation's military defense, Austria's presiding function rested more on European than German grounds. It is true that Austria continued to enjoy the sympathies of the particularist

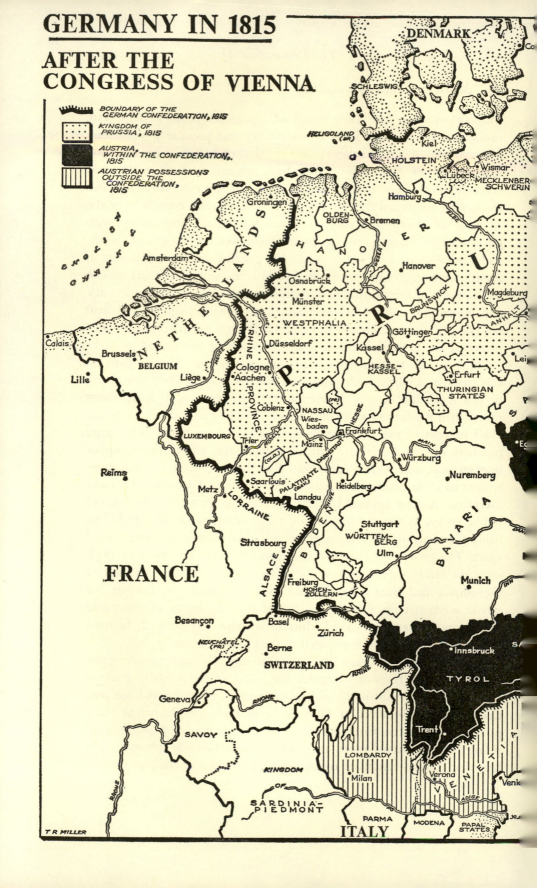

GERMANY IN 1815

AFTER THE CONGRESS OF VIENNA

BOUNDARY OF THE GERMAN CONFEDERATION, 1815	
KINGDOM OF PRUSSIA, 1815	
AUSTRIA, WITHIN THE CONFEDERATION, 1815	
AUSTRIAN POSSESSIONS OUTSIDE THE CONFEDERATION, 1815	

DENMARK

SCHLESWIG

HELIGOLAND (BR.)

HOLSTEIN

Kiel

Wismar

MECKLENBER-SCHWERIN

Lübeck

Hamburg

Bremen

OLDEN-BURG

Groningen

NETHERLANDS

HANOVER

Hanover

Amsterdam

Osnabrück

Münster

WESTPHALIA

P R U

BRUNSWICK

Magdeburg

ANHALT

Göttingen

ENGLISH CHANNEL

Calais

Brussels

BELGIUM

Liège

Düsseldorf

RHINE

Cologne

Aachen

P PROVINCE

Kassel

HESSE-KASSEL

Lei

Erfurt

THURINGIAN STATES

Lille

Coblenz

NASSAU

Wiesbaden

(PR.)

HESSE

Frankfurt

MAIN

Würzburg

Nuremberg

LUXEMBOURG

Trier

MOSEL

(OLD.)

Mainz

DARMSTADT

Reims

Metz

LORRAINE

Saarlouis

PALATINATE (BAV.)

Landau

Heidelberg

BADEN

Stuttgart

WÜRTTEM-BERG

Ulm

BAVARIA

Munich

Strasbourg

ALSACE

RHINE

FRANCE

Besançon

Freiburg

HOHEN-ZOLLERN

Basel

Zürich

RHINE

Innsbruck

SA

NEUCHÂTEL (PR.)

Berne

SWITZERLAND

TYROL

Geneva

SAVOY

RHONE

Trent

VENETIA

LOMBARDY

Milan

Verona

Veni

KINGDOM OF SARDINIA-PIEDMONT

ADIGE

PARMA

MODENA

PAPAL STATES

ITALY

T R MILLER

forces and of the main body of German Catholicism, but she did so for political rather than intellectual reasons. Austrian Catholicism did not radiate ideas which could have given it a strong influence in Germany. Instead, Munich became the intellectual center of German Catholicism. Slowly but steadily, Germany and Austria became more distant.

We have been looking far beyond the years following the Congress of Vienna. In the decade after 1815, Austrian influence in Germany asserted itself with great vigor to ensure the realization of the Vienna program.

∽ *Prussian Reforms after 1815*

IT WAS OF THE GREATEST IMPORTANCE that Prussia, not without Metternich's prodding, revised her policy after the war. As early as 1814, the Prussian reformers had met with an opposition of increasing strength, not only among the allies but also in Prussia.

In the military field, the reform legislation was brought a decisive step closer to completion. In June 1814, Frederick William III had finally agreed to the full unification of the war ministry and appointed Boyen as minister. Together with Grolman, Boyen drafted the law for universal military service which embodied Scharnhorst's ideas. It made all Prussians from the age of twenty to thirty-nine liable to military service. For three years they would serve in the active army and remain for two years in the army reserve. Thereafter, they would be assigned for seven years to the first levy of the national guard (*Landwehr*), which in time of war would serve with the field army, and for another seven years to the second levy of the national guard, which when mobilized would assume garrison and fortress duties. Beyond the age of thirty-nine, they could still be called in a national emergency for service in a militia (*Landsturm*). The institution of "one-year volunteers" (*Einjährige*) for high-school graduates was incorporated in the law. In the opinion of its authors, this law would give Prussia an army of 500,000 men in war, while the state had to provide for only 130,000 men in peace. The financial advantages were obvious and helped convince the king, who himself was no friend of the national guard and was already being urged by the reactionaries to abandon Scharnhorst's conception of a popular army. The wish to see Prussia possess a large military establishment as a means of strengthening the hands of her diplomatic representatives at the Congress of Vienna induced Frederick William to sign the law on September 3, 1814. For almost half a century it regulated the organization of the Prussian army, with some modifications for a full century. With greater or lesser changes, it was adopted in many other countries.

But the passionate struggle Blücher and Gneisenau conducted for their nationalistic war aims after Waterloo chilled the king's lukewarm feelings toward the reformers and their ideas. The old marshal retired, and Gneisenau resigned from active service a year later. Frederick William III had followed the advice of the reformers reluctantly in perilous times. Now, when the danger had passed, he fell back into his natural indecisiveness. He felt more at ease in the company of the conservative *Junkers* and became distrustful of any further change that might weaken his monarchical authority. In the selection of ministers, Hardenberg made great concessions to the reactionary groups, trusting that as chancellor he would be able to control them, as he hoped that his talents would not fail him in managing the king. But he did not move as surely as in his younger years, nor did the liberties he took in his private life strengthen his personal leadership. In the practical execution of the agrarian reform, as we have already seen, Hardenberg compromised with the *Junkers* in an unfortunate manner, though he still was determined to introduce a constitution as his ultimate aim in reorganizing the Prussian government. In Hardenberg's opinion, however, the plan for a constitution was subordinate to reestablishing the administrative structure of the Prussian monarchy, which had just been enlarged in the west by new provinces adding five and a half million citizens to the five million in the old east. The royal announcement of May 22, 1815 had defined the future estates' function as "the discussion of all matters that concern the personal and property rights of citizens, including taxation." Only a consultative body was contemplated, whose scope was to be restricted to financial matters. Considering the Prussian chancellor's liberal economic views, it might seem that he intended that the estates should represent property owners rather than feudal corporations. This became the central political problem. The conservative nobility did not oppose the creation of assemblies, provided it dominated them. Therefore it objected to the disregard of corporate rights. These feudal forces were antiabsolutist in a reactionary way, since they actually aimed at restoring the dualistic state. In contrast to them, a bureaucratic government imbued with ideas of general welfare and the rule of law could think of itself as the bearer of progress. However, as a bureaucratic absolutist, Hardenberg was unprepared to grant any real power to a modern representative organ. The army, foreign affairs, and police were always held to be within the area of the royal prerogative, as was the right to convene and dissolve the future estates. In Hardenberg's view, the national estates were to serve as a meeting place of the government and the productive forces of society, where a benevolent government could secure the support of the leading classes by concessions and adjustments.

∽ *The* Staatsrat

IN ORDER TO GIVE THE GOVERNMENT itself greater coherence, Hardenberg, in 1817, created a Council of State (*Staatsrat*) composed of the princes of the royal family, ministers of state, heads of government departments and provinces, commanding generals, and thirty-four men in public administration appointed by the king, who would preside over the meetings. It was a typical organ of enlightened absolutism which had turned from autocracy to bureaucracy. Under the leadership of Hardenberg, the Council became an important organ for the initiation of legislation. Later, its political significance declined, though it continued to serve as a check on arbitrary policies of individual departments and to insure exactness in the formulation of laws.

In these early years of its existence, the Council of State debated not only administrative reorganization but also financial reforms. The financial situation of the Prussian state was grave. The payments exacted by the French, the cost of the war, and the public debts of some of the new territories had created a state debt of around 250 million thaler. The budgetary needs of around 50 million were not fully covered by revenue, and the state credit had fallen very low. The urgency of economic rehabilitation led first to the customs law of 1818, which abolished all internal customs and only collected duties at the external frontiers. The tax law of 1820 found a substitute for the former excise revenues in the so-called class tax, a head-tax differentiated for four classes. Although it was a crude levy, it was at least a step in the direction of an income tax. Together with the land tax, which continued to be collected on quite different levels in the various provinces, the class tax made direct taxation the source of half the public revenues. In spite of a good many social and technical shortcomings, the Prussian tax system restored order. The state debt was consolidated and partly repaid in subsequent years, while the properties of the state, which were relatively greater than those of any other state, were ably developed and brought increased returns. Beginning in the 1830's, Prussian public finance had outgrown all signs of weakness. For the first time, the expenditure for the Prussian army decreased to somewhat less than half the state revenues, at least if the 20 per cent needed for debt service is counted in. Austria in this period spent one sixth of her budget for military ends, Bavaria one fourth.

✑ Constitutional Plans

THE FINANCIAL REFORM was the work of an independent bureaucracy, and no public debates took place. Yet Hardenberg inserted into the law of 1820 a clause that in the case of future loans the king would request the supporting guarantee of the estates. This promise did not hold out hope for the grant of budgetary powers to the estates. It seemed practical in the interest of the state credit to make some sort of a popular organ a cosignatory of loans. Actually, the king considered this an innocuous concession to Hardenberg, since he expected to manage state finances without loans, which in fact was possible for more than twenty-five years. Hardenberg's plans for a Prussian constitution were already beyond hope of realization. Disturbed by the violence resulting from agitation carried on by a large segment of German students, the king had been won over by Metternich to a repressive policy against the liberal movement in universities, press, and associations. He increasingly leaned toward the reactionary groups at the court and in the government. Hardenberg accepted the policy expressed in the Karlsbad Decrees of September 20, 1819, about which more will have to be said later. But he still believed it possible to introduce a constitution providing for general representation, built on communal organs on the local, county, and provincial levels, and defining some rights of the individual citizen. Wilhelm von Humboldt was made a special minister of "constitutional and communal affairs." The draft of a constitution which he presented was actually not very different from Hardenberg's, but he conceived of the government in a different spirit. Ten years' active work as a statesman and the experience of the national liberation had not turned the intellectual individualist of the Weimar period into a bureaucrat of Hardenberg's type. He had become convinced that the individual would grow through participation in public affairs, as the state would gain strength through such participation. But this view, which still reflected the great motives of Stein's ministry, clearly envisaged representative organs which were not fully subordinated to the government but possessed some measure of independence.

Unfortunately, the issue was not joined. Humboldt considered Hardenberg unbearable as leader of the reform, and he judged that the chancellor's political position had grown weak. Sensitive and proud as Humboldt was, he resented the dictatorial manner of the chancellor. But when he attacked the acceptance of the Karlsbad Decrees as an action giving up an autonomous Prussian policy and placing the state in the tutelage of Austria, he did not realize how much he criticized the king, and his demand for the virtual abolition of the superiority of the chancellor over the ministers aroused Hardenberg to angry counteraction. On the last day of 1819, Humboldt had to leave the government. Shortly before, his closest political supporter in the cabinet, Boyen, had resigned, because he was unwilling to accede to the king's wish to place the training of the national guard under regular army supervision. Boyen wanted to keep the national guard a distinct people's force and did not wish to see its close connection with the civilian agencies of self-administration weakened by the intrusion of the army.

✎ *The End of the Era of Reform*

THESE EVENTS MARKED THE END of the era of Prussian reforms. Hardenberg remained chancellor, but found himself politically isolated. The constitutional work fell entirely into the hands of the reactionaries, who also enjoyed the support of the crown prince. In 1821, Frederick William III, against the chancellor's advice, accepted the proposal to desist from creating national estates and to introduce only provincial estates. After Hardenberg's death, in 1822, laws on provincial estates were promulgated in 1823–24. Owners of large estates received the strongest representation. In old Prussia, they got half of all seats, while the peasants were most discriminated against. Roads, poorhouses, asylums, and fire insurance were some of the more important matters in which the estates were competent. Considering these estates' reactionary complexion, it was to the good that they had only such small functions. They could not endanger the monarchy's unity nor hamper the state bureaucracy, in which liberalism still retained a foothold. The *Junkers'* position was even stronger in the county administration. The new laws for the individual provinces (1825 and 1827–28) gave each owner of a large estate a single vote, the peasants altogether three, and the towns one. A county where 65 landowner votes, three peasant votes, and three town votes represented 29,000 urban and 27,000 rural inhabitants was nothing unusual. As in the past, the county councilors (*Landräte*) were nominated either by the *Junkers*, as in old Prussia, or by the county council, as in the west.

Friedrich Meinecke has rightly called the year 1819, together with 1848 and 1866, the three tragic turning points of modern German history. Neither Hardenberg nor even Humboldt intended to introduce a full-fledged liberal constitution, but the creation of national estates would have served as an antidote to bureaucratic absolutism and arrogant "junkerdom." It might have paved the road toward the progressive acceptance of the rising middle and lower classes into an integrated political community. Prussia's return to a little-tempered authoritarianism separated the government from the new popular forces coming to the fore in the tremendous social transformation of the nineteenth century. They could find an opening only through revolution, and revolution was crushed. Although under Bismarck the state's social basis was greatly broadened and modernized, Prussia's authoritarian character was deeply implanted in the new German Empire of 1866–71.

In proportion as new elements were added to the Prussian absolutism of the age of restoration, the nobility's influence on the government had become clearly marked. Its role as a pillar of the monarchy was more openly recognized by the king, and the *Junkers* very frankly defended their privileges as unchangeable rights. The army remained, or again became, the center of co-operation between the king and the Prussian aristocracy. The influx of officers from the bourgeoisie did not change the aristocratic style of the officer corps. Quite apart from the fact that this influx over the next decades was nowhere very great, and negligible in the guard troops, the untitled officers came largely from families who had acquired former *Junker* estates, had rented state domains, or belonged to the civil service. Their mode of life was not very different from that of the *Junkers*, whom they were inclined to emulate. Although the small general staff and the war academy continued on the high level demanded by Scharnhorst, the average education of the officers remained low compared with corresponding civilian groups. The great emphasis placed on the army as the defender of the throne and the existing order tended to give the inculcation of blind obedience and parade drill an undue place in military training. The Service Regulations of 1847 were a step back from Scharnhorst's Regulation of 1812. Politically more important was the alienation of the army from the people. By 1848, the gulf which separated the army from civil society was as great as in the days of Frederick the Great. Resentment against the military's arrogant and scornful attitude was one of the major reasons for the revolution of 1848.

On the other hand, Prussian absolutism after 1819 retained strong liberal elements. By and large the feudal elements occupied the ministerial posts, but the civil service was studded with men, *Junkers* and burghers, who tried to carry forward the reform era's tradition in the administration. If the people did not lose all their trust in the government in the period after 1819, it was largely the merit of the great number of educated and competent high officials who placed the general welfare above any class interest, though they were not free of bureaucratic propensities either. But they believed they were guided by the highest ideals as transmitted by the German universities, and that in their endeavor to translate them into reality they represented the nation's best interests as well as the progressive course of history. This sentiment was shared by the majority of the educated classes, who saw in the higher bureaucracy a sort of national representation, "a selection of the ablest of the whole nation," as Leopold Ranke expressed it. While not every member of the higher middle classes would have shared Ranke's conservative estimate that the monarchy would see to it that "the right man would get into the right position," most of them would have accepted the creed which in 1815 G. B. Niebuhr stated thus: "Liberty rests far more on administration than on constitution."

This attitude of the university graduate reflected a feeling that the expert administrator should not be hampered by unenlightened popular criticism. The authoritarian character of bureaucracy was, therefore, not fundamentally distrusted. The extraordinary power of the nobility and army were judged to be imperfections which could be overcome in due course, and the violations of personal freedom and freedom of expression which followed the Karlsbad Decrees were considered to be temporary aberrations. The German bourgeoisie had been too thoroughly steeped in a spirit of obedience and social hierarchy in centuries past not to fit itself into an authoritarian system. No doubt, its liberal political ambitions had grown in the last generation, but the experiences of the Napoleonic period and of the national liberation had also spread an awareness of the significance of power which tended to serve as an excuse for the survival of the militaristic nature of the Prussian state.

↶ Economic Policy: The Zollverein

THE COLLAPSE OF CONSTITUTIONAL PLANS did not eliminate liberal ideas from Prussian economic policy, though even in this field the strength of existing social forces could not be disregarded. The Prussian customs law of 1818, the work of the director-general of customs, Karl Georg Maassen, boldly abolished all internal imposts and levied duties only at the external frontiers. A very low tariff was introduced, which admitted raw materials free and imposed on foreign industrial products a duty of 10 per cent, while luxury goods, such as coffee, tea, or wine, paid 20 or even 30 per cent. No other action did as much as this law to undermine the separate life of the provinces, in which the conservatives found the bulwark of their privileges. But the creation of a large market was in the interest of the grain producers of the east, and so were cheap industrial imports. For the urban industrialists, greater protection against the advanced British industries would have been preferable. From the beginning, the Prussian government looked toward the expansion of the economic area of Prussia. In the first place, it wanted to link the separate halves of the state. The collection of duties on goods passing through Prussia served as the foremost weapon in this struggle. For the other states were unwilling to surrender easily, although Prussia offered them attractive terms. She suggested a simple division of the revenue on the basis of population. In 1828, the Prussian minister of finance, Friedrich von Motz, concluded the first treaty with one of the middle states, Hesse-Darmstadt, but in the same year Bavaria and Württemberg formed a South German Customs Union, whereas Saxony, the Thuringian states, and Hesse-Kassel united in a Central German Trade Association. Motz succeeded in effecting a rapprochement of the north and south which weakened the Central German group. Hesse-Kassel joined the Prussian customs union in 1831, and in the following two years Maassen achieved a merger of the Prussian and South German systems. On January 1, 1834, the Prusso-German *Zollverein* began to operate. By 1836, Baden and Nassau had joined. Only the northwestern states, Hanover, Oldenburg, Brunswick, Holstein, and the Hanseatic cities remained outside the area, which had a population of twenty-five million and whose external frontiers were slightly shorter than those of the Prussia of 1818. At the very threshold of the railroad age, the foundations for a German economy were laid, and Maassen was right when he expected this economic union to form the greatest step toward political unification under Prussian auspices.

∽ *Popular Movements*

ALTHOUGH STRONG LIBERAL and even German national elements survived in the Prussian bureaucracy and found expression in both economic policy and, to a lesser degree, as will be seen later, in the administration of education, no integration of popular forces into the state organization took place. The appearance of the first entirely independent popular movements in modern German history contributed to this result. Free associations had sprung into existence in Germany from the seventeenth century on, but their aims had been only religious and educational. Freemasonry in eighteenth-century Germany did not have real political significance. During the Napoleonic occupation, however, lodges or similar associations, such as the Virtue League (*Tugendbund*), had served as centers for the cultivation of patriotic sentiment and action. In 1815, a lawyer, Karl Hoffmann, had formed a German Society in Nassau, which after Waterloo advocated national unification. Gneisenau and Hardenberg saw in this League a useful tool for building up public support for Prussian war aims. On the other hand, governmental voices were heard protesting the "senseless and illegal idea that private associations want to compete with the state in order to intervene in national affairs." The League dissolved after the second Peace of Paris.

But the idea of such patriotic associations was used by the students. It was an unusual generation of German students, since many of them had served as volunteers during the wars of liberation and from these experiences had brought back an exalted idealism and patriotism they wanted to preserve in their academic life. The life of students in the German universities called for thorough reform. The idealistic philosophers, from the 1790's on, had attempted to awaken a sense of moral responsibility among the untamed and coarse German students, though with little result. After 1815, these efforts found a strong echo. Under the influence of Ludwig Jahn and the historian Heinrich Luden, a novel student organization was founded in Jena on June 12, 1815. Whereas formerly student fraternities had been formed largely on the

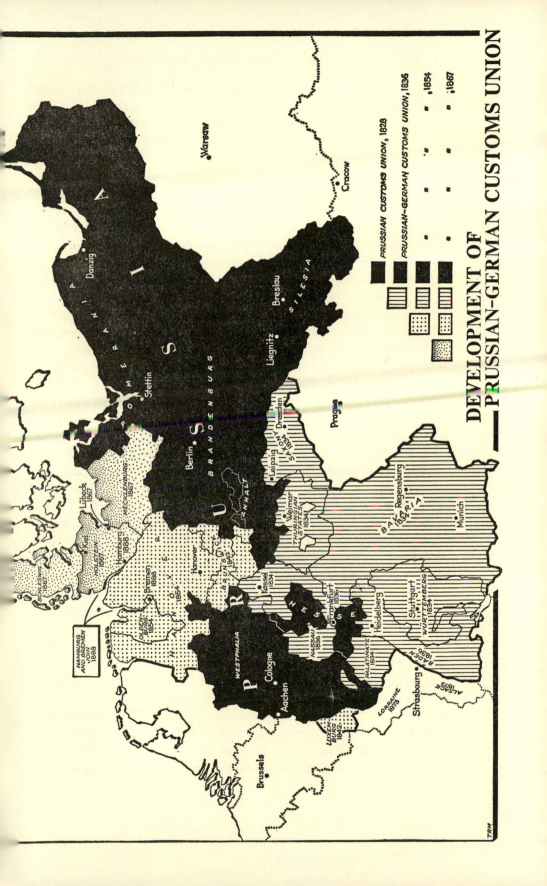

DEVELOPMENT OF
PRUSSIAN–GERMAN CUSTOMS UNION

PRUSSIAN CUSTOMS UNION, 1828

PRUSSIAN–GERMAN CUSTOMS UNION, 1836

1854

1867

basis of the regions of origin, the new union (*Burschenschaft*) wanted to express the unity of Germany and was open to all students. The former student corporations (*Corps*) had carried on the old style of life which had characterized and marred the German student. The new union established a new ideal of personality, in which morality and earnest devotion to intellectual and religious matters found a place beside dedication to the nation. Personal and political reform were joined together. As a demonstration of their new convictions, the students adopted a novel simple dress, which they incorrectly declared to be the old-Germanic costume. Without good reason, they identified their tricolor with the colors of the Holy Roman Empire. But the black-red-gold banner of the Jena *Burschenschaft* was to become the flag of the democratic movement in Germany.

Soon the Jena events were emulated in other universities, such as Heidelberg, Giessen, Erlangen, and Halle. Berlin, Göttingen, and Leipzig were little affected. Among the Catholic universities, only Würzburg and Freiburg participated. To strengthen the bonds of unity, a national convention was held at the Wartburg castle on October 18, 1817, the anniversary of the battle of Leipzig, and at the same time a suitable date for the commemoration of the tercentenary of Luther's Reformation. Almost five hundred students came together and marched to the castle, where Luther, in 1521–22, had translated the New Testament into German. The commemoration had the character almost of worship. Luther, as the "internal liberator," was linked with the external liberation under Blücher. In this period it became fashionable to see in the Reformation a step toward the national freedom of contemporary Germany, as Metternich and the Catholic conservative ideologists in Germany and France saw in Protestantism the pacemaker of the revolution. The Wartburg celebration did not produce any specific political demands, and the only gesture of defiance was committed by a small group in the evening, when a victory fire was lit and a torch parade staged. As a re-enactment of Luther's burning of the papal bull, old printed paper inscribed with the names of despised reactionary authors was thrown into the fire.

This childish prank evoked serious anger in the chancelleries. To be sure, for the first time in German history young people from all parts of Germany had freely assembled, and the universities, as the most closely connected national institutions of German life, constituted an effective sounding board for political ideas. But the opinions vented by the vast majority of these students were exceedingly vague sentiments and not always of a political nature. Jeers and threats from those in power, however, could not win their allegiance either, nor could the pent-up energies of this youth easily have found a constructive function in the authoritarian order which Metternich and his colleagues were building.

In the personal and social reform of German students' life the effect of the new students' union was immediate. Once students stopped acting like urchins playing noblemen, the gulf which had separated them from society for so long closed. As a matter of fact, the German bourgeoisie preferred to look with friendly eyes on the academic youth, so much so as to be ready to tolerate some glaring shortcomings. Exaggerated conviviality remained a disciplinary problem, and like the old corps before, the students' unions knew no way of satisfying their vaunted social honor except duelling. In this respect, they were the blind children of a society ridden with unfulfilled dreams of rank and social prestige. In finally refusing to accept Jewish students into their unions, they also reflected their families' social attitude. The believers in a Kantian concept of universal man lost out. Only "Germans and Christians" were admitted. This did not mean the adoption of racist principles, for converted Jews were not rejected, and in this age many German Jews joined Christian churches. But it was a bad sign that German education could not overcome these barriers of religion.

The students' unions, after 1818 united throughout Germany in a General German Students' Union, produced groups which placed the emphasis of their thinking decidedly, or even entirely, on political action. Among them, the so-called Blacks (*die Schwarzen*) or Unconditionals (*Unbedingte*), who gathered in Giessen around the young university lecturer Karl Follen, became the center of the greatest agitation. The young prophet was endowed with a cold and irresistible logical brain and a glowing mystical mind, which fascinated many students. He preached the necessity of a unified republic, which only self-effacing individual ethical action could achieve. For such ends, conventional morality should be disregarded, and the murder of tyrants was justified. This German Robespierre came from the people of Thomas Müntzer, and the Christian idea of sacrifice gave his rationalism its revolutionary determinism. A young and feeble student, Karl Ludwig Sand, found in Follen's philosophy the doctrines which steeled his courage to carry out an assassination. As his victim he selected the playwright August von Kotzebue (1761–1819), who was known to write reports on German conditions for the czar and to have made fun of the activities of the German students. On March 23, 1819, Sand stabbed the writer to death in Mannheim.

This insane deed gave Metternich the chance to stamp out all open signs of political opposition. He was helped by the fact that many liberals, among them even professors of theology, publicly lauded Sand's motives. The government in Berlin, particularly the king, was frightened. Ludwig Jahn was arrested. E. M. Arndt, who had just been appointed professor at the new University of Bonn, was placed under police investigation, while Schleiermacher's sermons were officially spied upon. In late summer, Metternich met Frederick William III in the spas of North Bohemia and persuaded him to accept a program of suppression of "demagoguery" in the universities, the press, and the diets of the states throughout the Germanic Confederation. Ministers of Austria, the five kingdoms, and the three grand duchies were called to Karlsbad in order to draw up a list of decrees. Article 18 of the Federal Act, which envisaged "equal regulations on the freedom of the press," was cynically construed as legal permission for the introduction of general censorship. The states agreed to remove every teacher who disseminated ideas inimical to existing political institutions. A state commissioner was to be appointed at each university to direct the lectures of professors into wholesome channels. The students' unions were banned. In Mainz, a Central Investigating Commission was established by the Confederation but no confederate court was created, because this seemed too great an infraction of the member states' sovereignty. No agreement was reached on a final interpretation of article 13, concerning the character of representative organs.

ༀ The Final Act of Vienna

WITH THE MAJOR STATES UNITED, the Karlsbad Decrees of September 20, 1819 were railroaded through the Frankfurt Diet. Being constitutional law, they would have required the consent of the Plenary Council, but they were only perfunctorily discussed by the Select Council, without time being given to its members to write for instructions. Due to this stealth and pressure, the decrees became law before October 1. Ministerial conferences of the seventeen states represented on the Select Council were held in Vienna during the winter of 1819–20. The interpretation and augmentation of the Federal Act of 1815 were debated. The results were embodied in what became the second fundamental law of the Germanic Confederation, the Final Act of Vienna (*Wiener Schlussacte*) of May 15, 1820. Although the Final Act once more stressed the sovereignty of the member states, it laid down more specific general principles binding for all. The most important issue, the definition of *landständisch* in article 13 of the Federal Act, was regulated in article 57 of the Final Act. However, it was not a clear-cut victory for the reactionary aims of Metternich's councilor Friedrich Gentz, who had urged the Karlsbad Conference to declare only corporate estates, and no representation of the whole people, as compatible with the monarchical principle. It was asserted that the state could have only one representative, the king or prince, and that the corporations (*Stände*) had to be of a nonpolitical character. Parliaments were called products of French revolutionary thought and for that reason "un-German," a slogan heard in Germany again and again in the twentieth century. No historical justification exists for such an assertion. For almost five hundred years German political tradition had seen the state represented in two organs, emperor and Empire, prince and territorial estates. Largely under the influence of the French monarchy, German absolutism had adopted Bodin's principle of undivided sovereignty resting in the king. What Gentz and other conservative romanticists defended as German was essentially monarchical absolutism, which they felt was less threatened by old-fashioned corporate estates than by bodies representing modern social forces.

With a view to the political developments in South Germany, Metternich was satisfied with a less explicit statement of monarchical principle. Article 57 declared that the full power of the state must be concentrated in the head of state and that only in the exercise of some of his rights could a monarch choose to be bound to the consent of estates. The nature of these estates was still left somewhat in the dark, though it was clear that governments could and should keep them on a short leash.

The Karlsbad Decrees were enforced with great zeal everywhere in Germany. It shows the difference between Austria and the rest of Germany that even the greatest efforts of the Austrian police could not find the shadow of any "subversive" or, as it was then called, "demagogic," activities. But even in the other parts of Germany the results of the persecutions were rather limited. Only two or three professors fell victim to immediate police actions. A number of younger intellectuals were driven abroad. Among them was Joseph Görres, who had acted as the most active German national voice in the Rhineland in 1815 and who took refuge in French Strasbourg. Another exile of this period was Niebuhr's young disciple, Franz Lieber, who was to make important contributions to American political thought. One of them, the creation of a humane code of military government at the time of the Civil War, was to benefit Germany after 1945. Many careers of students were broken or warped by the prosecution of the students' unions, and the harassment by police and spies drove the professors back into the aloofness from personal political convictions and action which had characterized the German academic profession in former centuries. The growth of a productive interaction between the idealism of the age of Kant and Goethe and the practical interests of the nation, which during the War of Liberation had made substantial progress, was suddenly interrupted.

It did not take much effort on the part of the government to quell independent thinking in Germany. In France, where regard for German philosophy and scholarship was very high in the half-century after 1815, there was great surprise at how meekly German intellectuals accepted even the violation of their freedom of expression. The *Burschenschaft* dissolved, and the professors retired to the privacy of their studies. The secret student organizations which developed slowly remained weak. Naturally, they were more political in their aims than the movement between 1815 and 1819 had been, but radicalism comparable to Follen's ideas was conspicuously absent, and the open associations in the universities became less and less distinguished from the older students' clubs. The conditions of Germany were entirely unpropitious for an active political opposition. The burghers at large were occupied with parochial concerns. As in the past, they looked to the government for the solution of the grave economic problems which beset them in these years. The spirit of obedience was easily restored in Germany. During the decade after 1819–20, a longing for freedom could be expressed only vicariously as in the demonstrations of sympathy for the Greek national revival.

✑ South German Constitutions

YET THE KARLSBAD DECREES could not undo all the popular institutions introduced after 1815. In the South German states, which had acquired so many new and heterogeneous territories and subjects after 1803, the fall of their protector Napoleon, and the ensuing rise of both restorative and national tendencies, induced the governments to look for means of solidifying their separate existence. They found them in the creation of constitutions. The duchy of Nassau, composed of many patches in the Rhine and Lahn valleys, received a constitution as early as September 1814. The constitutional development of Bavaria, Württemberg, and Baden after 1815 was of lasting historical significance. In a general way, all these constitutions followed the example of the French *Charte* of 1814, though with deviations of some consequence. The German constitutions adopted the principle of the *Charte* which denied the people's sovereignty and considered all rights as free grants by the king. They also accepted the bicameral system of the *Charte*. But whereas in France the second chamber was elected by the citizens of regional districts and therefore, despite the high property qualifications of the suffrage, represented a modern egalitarian society, the second chambers in Germany were elected through corporate bodies. This showed the more conservative character of German politics, which stemmed not only from the monarch's absolutist wishes but also from the nature of the antiabsolutist forces. In addition, it was one of the chief objects of the South German constitutions to give the former imperial counts and knights a place in the new order, and the creation of first chambers offered such an opportunity.

Of the three South German constitutions, the Bavarian one of 1818 was the most conservative. Here Crown Prince Ludwig, together with a group of noblemen, finally succeeded in toppling the regime of Count Maximilian Montgelas. But the administrative system of this founder of the modern Bavarian state was essentially preserved. Three months later, Baden followed. The Baden constitution, the work of the liberal councilor Karl Nebenius, was the only one that, like the French *Charte*, had the second chamber composed of representatives of districts and not of corporations. Thus the Baden parliament became the first modern representative organ in Germany, as Baden became the model land of German liberalism. Its southern region, the formerly Austrian Breisgau, had been deeply affected by the ideas of the Enlightenment, which Joseph II's government had planted, and under Carl Frederick the margraviate had absorbed similar influences. Naturally, Baden closely followed events on the other side of the Rhine.

In Württemberg, a stormy struggle accompanied the introduction of a constitution, which in the final result stood somewhere halfway between those of Bavaria and Baden. Württemberg had retained her medieval dualistic structure through the last century. The peculiarity of her estates had been the virtual absence of the nobility, which in old

Swabia had been an imperial nobility. The Württemberg estates were dominated by Lutheran ministers and burghers. In spite of all the tyranny the country had suffered from its rulers, the estates in some fashion had existed until Frederick could make himself king, in 1805, and abolish them. This autocratic ruler realized, however, that the new situation demanded concessions to the constitutional principle. In 1815, he attempted to impose a constitution which was to be valid in the old and new parts of the state. But indignation at Frederick's despotic regime was too great in the whole kingdom. The diet, composed of the burghers of the old duchy, representatives of the recently acquired imperial cities, imperial nobility, and ecclesiastical principalities, challenged the king's right to impose a constitution. They demanded the restoration of the "good old law," under which a constitution could only be the result of bargaining and contract between prince and estates. It was curious how here in Württemberg the labels of old and new were strangely mixed up. Originally, the aristocrats had joined the burghers in their opposition to a prince who offered not only an authoritarian regime but also a unity of the state beyond the old corporations. The conflict was bitterly fought over even after the death of Frederick I in 1816. His able and ambitious son, William I (1816–64), made further offers, which were scornfully rejected. In 1819, a compromise was finally achieved. The Karlsbad Conference, with its threat against the sovereignty of the confederate states as well as against liberal rights brought king and estates together. The constitution took the form of a compact between king and estates, and a number of special institutions and usages of old days were revived. But for all practical purposes, the Württemberg constitution of September 25, 1819 was a constitution similar to the Baden and Bavarian constitutions, and it produced the same results.

In southern Germany, the constitutions created agencies through which a popular movement could, or at least could hope to, operate. This fact alone made it possible to achieve the unification of the new states in surprisingly short time. For the realization of liberal objectives these constitutions remained, however, more a framework for the future than a tool for immediate application.

Metternich's intervention through the Karlsbad Decrees frustrated the South German parliaments. Friedrich Gentz pressed for the complete abolition of the constitutions, and Metternich undoubtedly was in essential sympathy with him as to their revolutionary nature. In terms of the Karlsbad Decrees and the Final Act of Vienna, the Baden constitution was particularly objectionable. But Metternich preferred stability to doctrinal uniformity. To him it seemed unwise to coerce the middle states into full and open submission. This would have compromised the sovereignty of the members of the Germanic Confederation and placed monarchical government in a bad light. The Austrian chancellor was satisfied with crippling the growth of liberal institutions, which the constitutions might have permitted. In this endeavor, he found the ready support of the South German governments themselves.

Everywhere the first meetings of the state diets had been lively or even stormy. The demands of the representatives ranged far and were pressed with vigor and often enough with doctrinaire stubbornness. In general, they aimed at a speedy realization in the actual administration of the states of rights the constitutions promised and at the fulfillment of tasks the Confederation was pledged to undertake. The governments resented the parliaments' initiative. They did not want to be pestered by motions but intended to confine the diets to the acceptance of the budget and government-sponsored legislation. The governments wanted to retain a maximum of absolute power. The new weapons the Karlsbad Decrees placed at their disposal were used with alacrity to stifle the political influence of the diets and their members. The complete control of press and associations made it possible to deny the parliaments all publicity, thwart all party organization, and manipulate elections. Thus, as a consequence of the Karlsbad Decrees, independent political life ceased to pulsate in the constitutional organs of southern Germany. But at least the constitutions were not destroyed, and after 1830 they could serve as protection for reviving political agitation.

CHAPTER 16

Schools and Churches in the Early Nineteenth Century

THE INTELLECTUAL AND SPIRITUAL MOVEMENT which, between 1789 and 1815, had seemed to move closer to politics, appeared once more to retire into the private homes, the schools, and churches during the 1820's. Actually, however, under a calm surface, great transformations were taking place, reorienting the individual and creating a new balance of forces in public life. One of the most important changes was the establishment of a universal school system by the German states. Others were the partial revival of the German Protestant churches and the rebuilding of the Roman Catholic Church. These events have had a determining influence on German life ever since.

➷ Education

ENLIGHTENED DESPOTISM had been greatly concerned with educational reforms. It needed capable state officials and people useful in the mercantilistic enterprises of the governments. In accordance with the class character of society, the scions of the nobility were kept separate from the burgher sons in *Ritterakademien* (Knights' Academies) and military cadet schools. When the young noblemen attended the university, usually accompanied by private tutors, they would sit on separate benches and be excused from regular examinations. In addition to the traditional Latin schools, frequented by the sons of burghers preparing for the university, there had come into existence in the age of absolutism special schools for those intending to enter practical occupations. These schools emphasized knowledge of the *realia* of life. They were commonly known as burgher or "realistic" schools (*Realschulen*), in contrast to the humanistic schools or *Gymnasia*. Conditions in Germany were extraordinarily variegated, but under the influence of the Enlightenment the trend of education was running toward a closer adaptation of schools to practical life and in the direction of education by secular authorities. In France, a similar development after the French Revolution led to the national government's educational monopoly and a school system which made allowance for practical occupational needs. The German state governments, too, assumed the direction of all educational activities after 1815, but the further development of "realistic" schools was blocked for a long time by the rise of neohumanism.

Even before the enlightened humanitarians, the Pietists had given growing attention to popular education. In 1717, Frederick William of Prussia had issued an edict ordering parents to send their children to school. But schools did not exist everywhere, least of all in the countryside, and the teachers, often simple artisans or handicapped veterans, were a sad lot. Only during the last years of the century was progress made. Rousseau's teachings prepared the ground for new methods of education, but even more influential was the model set by J. H. Pestalozzi (1746–1827) in Ifferten, Switzerland. Christian-humanitarian impulses had led the Swiss reformer to devote his life and fortune to the education of poor children. He wanted to show that education was not the authoritative imposition of knowledge but the cultivation of the innate capacity of each individual. The educator could only cautiously assist in the growth of the child by removing obnoxious social influences and strengthening the natural qualities of "head, hand, and heart." Pestalozzi did not forget the educational role of the family or the peculiar gifts of the individual pupil, but he believed that men had a common nature, which a wise educator could hope to make strong through the development of the totality of inborn faculties. Education then was essentially a training, or "gymnastics" of budding personalities, not a mechanical distribution of information or a one-sided stimulation of special skills. General education was to precede any specialized instruction.

The belief in the individual's power to rise from a state of nature through a social stage to true morality had great appeal to German idealism and neohumanism, which were in full revolt against the pedagogics handed down from the Middle Ages. In the last years of the eighteenth century, Goethe, Schiller, Herder, and Jean Paul were presenting ideas on education which paved the way for Pestalozzi in Germany. Fichte was the first German philosopher to place Pestalozzi on a pedestal in his *Speeches to the German Nation* of 1807–08. The revival of the fatherland, so Fichte argued, could only be the result of a wealth of moral personalities such as the pedagogics of Pestalozzi would produce. But whereas Pestalozzi's work had been the outflow of an altruistic sentiment for the poor and oppressed, Fichte wanted to create a nation representing the highest ideals of mankind. In a truly authoritarian fashion, he did not hesitate to make the state the sole authority of national education. If the state could enforce war service, Fichte said, it could enforce school attendance as well. He proposed boarding schools, run as self-supporting socialist communities, which were to be breeding places of the new national philosophy. They were to be under the state's exclusive direction, though Fichte conceded that as soon as one generation had passed through the contemplated schools, the family might again be given a greater role in education. He was not altogether unaware of the danger that governments might act for low political rather than high philosophical ends, but he comforted himself with the consideration that the existence of many German states would produce the needed corrective.

Fichte's program of national education was not adopted by the German governments, but the idea that the state must gain not only prestige but also moral force by allying itself with the nation's cultural life found general approval. Surprisingly, it was the Prussian state, till recently not conspicuous for cultural endeavor, in which these ideas were first formulated in a systematic manner and translated into reality. One of Stein's last actions before leaving Prussia, in 1808, was his recommendation to appoint Wilhelm von Humboldt chief of the department of education. Humboldt, a Brandenburg *Junker*, had lived as an intimate friend of Schiller and Goethe in Jena and thereafter in Rome, where he occupied the sinecure of a Prussian minister. The untrammeled development of his own personality had been the dominating aim and pleasure of his life. Like Stein, he had resented absolutism's crippling effects on the free personality. Now circumstances made him a leader in the movement which extended the state's activities into new regions of life. From March 1809 to June 1810, he directed Prussia's educational policies and in this short period created the institutional forms of Prussian and German education which were to last until 1933.

Humboldt made the state the sole authority for education, which at the same time was extended to all classes of the population. But in deliberate opposition to the trend of the thinking of Enlightenment, which was running toward the practical and specialized schools, Humboldt threw his support behind schools of general education on every level. A tripartite organization of educational institutes was adopted, a universal "people's school" (*Volksschule*), a "higher" school, preparing for the pursuit of scholarship, and the universities. He wished to exclude schools serving special classes and allow only as supplementary institutions schools training for special occupations. This aim was not fully achieved. Although Scharnhorst agreed with Humboldt's intentions, neither of them succeeded in getting the military cadet schools abolished. Otherwise the principle was generally adopted that every child was to receive a "general" education and that the acquisition of any special vocational or professional skill was to be left to additional schools, if not to practical life itself. For the *Volksschule* this meant the adoption of the Pestalozzi method, and "normal schools" were created as models for training teachers. The three R's, singing, and gymnastics formed the chief subjects, together with religion, which was supposed to provide the foundation for the development of character. It took many years before the elementary school was generally established, particularly in the rural districts, but during the early and middle nineteenth century, Germany was far ahead of other countries in the actual organization of such a public school system.

❧ *The* Gymnasium

BEYOND THE ELEMENTARY SCHOOLS, the "realistic" schools continued to exist, but they were not substantially augmented for the next fifty years. The true love of the reformers was the *Gymnasium*. Its educational methods, too, were founded on the philosophy of Rousseau and Pestalozzi, but at the same time the *Gymnasium* was filled with the spirit of German neohumanism represented so well by Humboldt and his closest collaborator, J. W. Süvern (1775–1829), a disciple of F. A. Wolf. They remodeled the old "Latin schools," still essentially Melanchthon's institutes, into schools designed to develop the full capacity of their pupils in a ten-year course of study centered around Latin, Greek, mathematics, and German. These were the subjects judged to be best suited for the development of the fundamental faculties of mind, though the program was rounded out by a number of minor subjects to insure a universal outlook. A special class of teachers for the *Gymnasium* emerged from the universities. As a rule, the teachers at the old Latin schools had been theologians, and for that matter usually second-rate theologians. The teachers of the new *Gymnasia* were graduates of the philosophical faculties, who had to pass a state examination. The *Gymnasia*, on their part, were made the guardians of admission to the universities through their final examinations.

Primary and secondary schools were thus strictly separated. Since the course of study of the *Gymnasium* was planned as a unified ten-year course, the transfer from the elementary to the higher school had to take place after three to four years of elementary school, and whoever did not enter the *Gymnasium* at the age of nine or ten, found himself forever cut off from all opportunities of higher education. He was also automatically excluded from access to the university, for the only way leading there was the *Gymnasium*. Predictions with regard to future intellectual capacity are inevitably difficult to make at such an early age. Moreover, the social circumstances of a family might make it impossible to contemplate a higher education even for the patently most gifted child. As a rule, the decision was not even one arrived at by consideration of a child's ability but by the parents' social ambitions. Another shortcoming of the *Gymnasium* was its virtual monopoly on any higher education. As a consequence, its first six grades were crowded with boys intending to enter upon commercial and practical occupations or eager to acquire the privilege of serving one instead of three years in the army. The full benefit of the humanistic curriculum was denied them, for it lay in the study of the great classical authors, which occupied the last years, whereas the earlier ones had to be devoted largely to languages. Many youths left the *Gymnasium* after six years without having been exposed to the true aims of a humanistic education and without, on the other hand, having received the personal or technical preparation best suited for their future careers. A substantial segment of society, and one that, with the growth of an industrial society, became increasingly more important, remained ill-educated and constituted a group easily susceptible to philosophies of mere success or materialism and naturalism. In the latter part of the century, and even more so after 1890, the "realistic" schools multiplied, but they never quite established themselves as an equal partner in the German high-school system.

Aside from these incidental social, and ultimately also cultural, results of the establishment of the *Gymnasium* as the normal type of high school, there is no question that the *Gymnasium* made the new German culture, as it had come into being during the half century prior to 1815, the common property of a large class of Germans. Naturally, much of its depth was lost once it was diffused on a general basis, and it would be unrealistic to assume that the teachers could have risen above the general intellectual trends of the age. Soon they reflected the changed approach to the classics inaugurated by the generation following F. A. Wolf and Wilhelm von Humboldt. From the days of Winckelmann on, German neohumanism had found in the Greeks the absolute model of *humanitas*. It assumed that in grasping Greek art, thought, and character we enter a spiritual world which will mold our personality according to the highest ideals. In Humboldt's opinion, the *Gymnasium* was to provide the experience of this "classic" character of antiquity. For this purpose, the study of the greatest expressions of Greece was demanded, not an encyclopedic knowledge of antiquity.

With August Boeckh (1785–1867), the first professor of classics at the University of Berlin, the study of the classics assumed a historical rather than esthetic and ethical intent. The Greeks lived "on bread and wine," and not "on poetry and philosophy," Boeckh said, and he set out to reconstruct the full reality of Greek life. The "science of antiquity" (*Altertumswissenschaft*) soon led to a vast accumulation of historical information and to a specialization among classical scholars which introduced to the *Gymnasium* a type of learning likely to detract attention from this school's original educational aim. Like the old Latin school, the *Gymnasium* became again more of a preparatory school for future scholars. The formation of personality was further hampered by the conflict of ideals the curriculum contained. For German neohumanism, Christian religion was subordinated to Greek ideals. In Goethe and Humboldt this attitude had a strongly pagan note. Religion held a definitely minor place in the German *Gymnasia*, particularly in the Protestant schools, but it inevitably competed with humanistic values. In addition, there was the German past, upon which the romanticists opened a wide vista. Whether this past was interpreted as the beautiful synthesis of Christian and Germanic elements or was one-sidedly seen either as the realization of the Christian spirit or the expression of the Teutonic element in world history, it was more directly and concretely linked with the German realities than the ethereal vision of Hellas.

No school program could have settled the conflict of Christian, classical, and national ideals which characterized German cultural life, but Humboldt's philosophical and esthetic humanism neglected forces and problems bound to assert themselves. Soon attacks were directed against the humanistic *Gymnasium*. Humanists complained about its degeneration into a preparatory school for professional scholars, parents accused it of overburdening its pupils, social reformers objected to its divisive influence on society, Christian leaders castigated its aloofness from religion, while nationalists deplored its neglect of the German national tradition. In the course of the century, no single cultural movement gained a position from which it could have unified the ideal trends. Thus, while the general organization of German schools was never changed, many concessions were made in the curriculum which tended to blur the ultimate educational aims even more.

When Humboldt made the state the only authority over schools, he did not intend to turn them into agencies for political indoctrination. On the contrary, schools were to serve as gateways to the free realm of absolute ideas. Humboldt believed that the state had the duty of opening the doors to universal culture and that this supreme obligation was not properly discharged if the state interfered in the free formation and traffic of ideas. His liberalism was both radical and genuine in this respect. It rested on the faith, which he shared with Goethe, that the greatest human happiness was found in the development of personality ("*Höchstes Glück der Erdenkinder ist nur die Persönlichkeit*"). But he also assumed that the fully educated individual would quite naturally be an ideal citizen as well. This did not mean that he would be a blind supporter of the existing political order. Humboldt himself subsequently became the foremost champion of constitutional reform in Prussia. But education was directed toward the acquisition of philosophical wisdom, individual moral distinction, and artistic taste rather than toward the development of political ideas. In contrast to modern English humanism, the potentialities inherent in the classics for the promotion of political convictions remained unused in German schools. Rather than making some special contribution to the formation of political opinion, the *Gymnasia* merely reflected society's dominant political sentiments, particularly of the social groups whose sons populated these schools. Esthetic Hellenic humanism did not provide its disciples with much capacity for public activities, as for example the Latin humanism of France, which preserved much more of the rhetorical tradition of the older European humanism.

∽ Reorganization of the Universities

HUMBOLDT'S EDUCATIONAL REFORMS culminated in the reorganization of the universities. The stagnation of the universities in the seventeenth and eighteenth centuries had not been confined to Germany. The leading minds absented themselves from the universities and tried to create in the academies new centers for the advancement of science and scholarship. Leibniz had led this movement in Germany. But simultaneously attempts were made to improve the state of German universities. The founding of Halle, in 1694, had been the first step away from the medieval type of academic teaching. But this Prussian university was arrested in its development under the regime of Frederick William I, and his successor, Frederick II, cared little about Halle and was chiefly interested in the Berlin Academy. Beginning in 1734, Göttingen became the first academic institution to break not only with the teaching in the Latin language but also with the supervision of the university by theologians. Here, in Hanover, the professors received freedom from censorship for their publications and lectures. Preferably they were chosen from among the people who had acquired a name in practical professions and they were encouraged to maintain their public activities. The free and refined intellectual atmosphere of Göttingen benefited particularly the study of law and politics, and even young noblemen were attracted by the university. Stein, Hardenberg, and Humboldt, among many others, studied at Göttingen.

The new "academic freedom" practiced in Göttingen was carried into the field of speculative thought in Jena at the turn of the century, when Schiller, Fichte, Schelling, and Hegel taught at the university of Saxony-Weimar. The new ideal of a university was presented in a philosophical form by Schelling in 1803. Science (*Wissenschaft*) was conceived as a *universitas*, an organic totality of knowledge. Special studies had to be pursued in the light of a single all-embracing truth. They were meaningful only to the extent to which they mirrored the highest truth in a special application. The value of any knowledge could be determined not in terms of its practical usefulness but of its participation in the totality of science which can and must be approached from every side by critical methods. The demonstration of the search for the ultimate truth was the proper subject of all academic instruction. The dispensation of all factual knowledge could be left to books. It is the professor's task to introduce his students to the creative process of searching out the truth and to arouse in them the intellectual sense and moral enthusiasm for scientific inquiry. Only the productive scholar can be an ideal academic teacher; research and teaching belong together.

This theory of the university was an attempt to re-establish the unity of knowledge the medieval schoolmen had assumed. But the autonomy of human reason was fully retained as in the Enlightenment, only that, in contrast to the Enlightenment's uniform rationalism and pragmatism, German idealism asserted the spontaneity of the human mind. In the reform of the German universities after 1803 the new philosophy found an organizational expression. The secularization of the prince bishoprics meant the abolition of almost all their universities, and the subsequent political turmoil brought other universities to an end. Heidelberg and Würzburg were successfully reconstituted, but the new philosophical idealism found its fullest realization in the founding of the University of Berlin, the chief personal achievement of Wilhelm von Humboldt, who was supported by Schleiermacher.

The loss of Halle by the Treaty of Tilsit left Prussia with only the small provincial universities of Frankfurt-on-the-Oder and Königsberg. After some hesitation, Humboldt decided to situate a university in the Prussian capital as a manifestation of Prussia's intent to support German arts and letters. At the same time, he did not merely reassemble Halle University but created a new university in accordance with new principles. The University of Berlin was opened in the fall of 1810. It took over the institutes of the Berlin Academy of Sciences and some of the medical facilities of the Prussian capital. The hope that it would attract many students from all over Germany was not fulfilled. Only after the peace of 1815 did the university begin to live up to the expectations of its founders. At that time, the reorganization of the Prussian universities was completed by the reopening of Halle, to which Wittenberg was joined, by the moving of the University of Frankfurt to Breslau, and by the founding of Bonn University in the Prussian Rhineland. The other German universities before long adopted the new academic style of Heidelberg, Würzburg, and the Prussian universities. Particularly important was the transfer of the old Bavarian University of Ingolstadt and Landshut to Munich, in 1826.

The German universities were institutes for the development of the intellect exclusively. Humboldt believed that the experience of creative scholarly research communicated by eminent professors would not only make the student informed but also provide the force for his personal self-education. The professor was free to select his subject in a way he deemed best, as the students were free to select universities, professors, and courses. Since science was assumed to be a single realm, it seemed of little import where the individual started his study, though philosophy was still thought to provide the master key to all departments. Each department, it was believed, supplied a liberal education. It was unnecessary to make a distinction between undergraduate and graduate studies, the more so since the *Gymnasium* was supposed to furnish the training preparatory to advanced study. The baccalaureate was abolished, and the liberal arts, augmented by the disciplines of natural science, history, politics, economics, and linguistics, as the philosophical faculty, reached equal status with the faculties of theology, medicine, and law.

Many of the assumptions on which the new German university rested were questionable and became patently untenable as the century proceeded. Even in the beginning, the spark of idealistic scholarship did not set every student aflame, while many, abusing academic freedom, did not even expose themselves to this idealistic experience. Otto von Bismarck was only one among the innumerable students who avoided every contact with the ideal life of the university. He lived in and for the student corporation to which he belonged and finally prepared himself for his law examination by cramming. These corporations, however, did not cultivate the spirit of scholarship but only successfully attempted to impose on their members the social forms and manners of junkerdom, which were incompatible with the intentions of Humboldt's university. With the grant of unlimited "academic freedom," the professors denied themselves all institutional means of exerting a decisive influence on the personal education of the academic youth. Formerly, German universities had had their halls (*Bursen*) where students lived together under the supervision of the university authorities. But with the exception of a number of Catholic universities and theological institutes, no collegiate arrangements had survived the Thirty Years' War. What such institutions could have achieved, was amply demonstrated by the Tübingen *Stift* (foundation) for theological students, which was also provided with a group of tutors (*Repetenten*) supervising the studies of its junior fellows. The graduates of the *Stift*, such as Hegel and Schelling, made a deep mark on German academic and intellectual life during the century.

The expectation that philosophy would act as the integrating element of science became illusory after 1830, when the idealistic systems broke down, and with the growth of knowledge even the greatest minds were incapable of presenting the whole field of science. No doubt, the contribution philosophy made to a critical awareness of the methodological problems of all research was greater in Germany than anywhere else. The number of towering figures to appear in the academic history of Germany was astonishing, and almost without exception their achievements rested in good measure on the universality of their interests and their philosophical minds. But at the same time, emphasis on research led to the proliferation of overspecialized departments, which in the hands of unphilosophical scholars became educationally sterile fields. After 1870, the German universities turned out chiefly specialized experts, whose general education was poor.

A great deal of the "academic freedom" remained perfunctory, because the universities did not serve merely as an arena for the development of the moral and intellectual capacities but also as professional schools. Even the most idealistic student could not help being to some extent a "bread-student," as Schiller called him, that is, a student preparing for a remunerative career. The three old faculties essentially had always had professional aims, and the new philosophical faculty, too, became a school training for professional services, among which the career of teacher at the *Gymnasium* attracted the largest number. However, academic degrees did not gain their bearer admission to the church ministry, higher government service, law practice, medical practice, and the teaching profession. Here admission depended on state examinations, and inevitably their character and organization determined the courses that students would take and professors offer. With these stipulations, the governments exercised a great influence on the study programs of the universities. But the authority of the state reached far beyond such measures by the very fact that the universities remained state institutions. They received practically all their funds from the annual state budget, and the appointment of professors remained the right of the government. Humboldt was aware of the tensions which might develop between the interests of the state and the free pursuit of scholarship. He, as well as Schleiermacher, sighed that without the state "everything would go infinitely much better." But the endowment of universities and their establishments as corporate bodies was not in accordance with the spirit of a bureaucratic state.

Humboldt gave the universities many rights of self-government and the professors important privileges. He hoped that state interference would wane further in the future. He placed his trust in the future government officials who as graduates of the new universities would respect principles of academic freedom. His expectation was not entirely in vain. Baron Karl von Altenstein, who was Prussian minister of education from 1817–40 and as such the chief organizer of Prussian schools and universities in the nineteenth century, was a tolerant man, desirous of giving competing schools of thought a representation in the educational system of the state and protecting scholars from political persecution. But he was unable to shield education against the Karlsbad Decrees and the ensuing witch hunt, and in general was only able to mitigate some of the excesses of governmental policies. In the latter part of the century, political conflicts between government and universities hardly occurred, since the liberal professors had made their peace with the state of Bismarck. The German universities did not represent the full breadth of German intellectual life. Roman Catholics were under a certain handicap; democrats, and even more so Social Democrats, were not admitted. Particularly after 1848–49, the universities showed a far more conservative outlook than German arts and literature.

The creation of educational systems by the states in the nineteenth century supplemented the growth of the political power of these modern states. For the molding of the character of modern nations, state education has been an elemental force. This does not mean that the original plans of the reforming statesmen came true. A general school organization is inevitably an integral part of the social and political order of a people, and the ideas of the educational founders are bound to be modified by the social and political realities. Moreover, the impact of new intellectual movements may fill the organization with a very different content. All this happened in Germany, and it would be quite a mistake to lay all the causes of certain dangers and shortcomings of the German schools which we have tried to indicate at the doorstep of Humboldt. Together with the French reform, Humboldt's plan was the most comprehensive system of state education ever conceived, and its realization was pushed with utmost vigor after 1815. The French philosopher Victor Cousin, visiting Berlin in 1831, called Prussia "the classic country of schools and barracks." By 1840, Altenstein's regime had reorganized or established about 30,000 elementary schools and 38 normal schools. Eighty per cent of the children attended school in the Rhine province on the eve of the Revolution of 1848 and as many as 93 per cent in the province of Saxony, though only 61 per cent in the Polish province of Poznania. In half a century illiteracy was wiped out. This was a great achievement, which also had a great impact on the transfer of people from rural to urban communities during the industrial revolution. The most immediate consequence was a breakdown of the barriers which had existed between people in the various local and regional communities. This did not only apply to the Prussian state but also to Germany as a whole, since all states followed at once or a little later the Prussian example of school reform. The German universities, entering upon a century of productive scholarship and research unequaled in any country, exercised an influence far beyond Germany.

✑ Literary and Artistic Culture

THE GREAT AGE OF THE GERMAN UNIVERSITIES was the half century after 1815, when they were carrying the conceptions of classic German philosophy and literature over into pure research. The wealth of talent in the universities was most impressive. Obviously science gained by the attraction which the universities exercised upon imaginative people who one or two generations earlier would have known no other outlet than poetry. The impulses of German art, literature, and philosophy were still omnipresent. Goethe was still alive, and his own literary production turned from poetry toward the philosophical interpretation of his own visions and experiences. Also romantic literature was still flowering, although a certain decline of original literary production became noticeable. Germany did not produce anything quite comparable to the great French and English novel of the nineteenth century. Only in music was the continuity of creation never ended. In the decade before his death, in 1827, Beethoven reached the highest stage of his artistic expression in such works as his *Ninth Symphony*, *Missa Solemnis,* or the last four string quartets. His sufferings were transposed into a heroic struggle of man against the tragic adversities and illusions of life and resolved by an idealistic faith.

As Beethoven's music was the musical realization of classic German idealism, Franz Schubert's (1797–1828) compositions were deeply permeated by the spirit and form of classic German literature. His *Lieder* in particular were the direct translation of lyric poetry into a language which knows no frontiers. Carl Maria von Weber (1786–1826), through his own operas as well as his direction of the Dresden opera, gave German operatic art a definite place on the German stage. Dresden itself remained the center of the romantic opera in Germany to the time of Richard Wagner's musical directorship in 1843–49. By his many-sided creative art and as the leader of the *Gewandhaus* and Thomas choir in Leipzig, Felix Mendelssohn Bartholdy (1809–47) had perhaps the greatest influence of any single person on the formation of nineteenth-century musical taste. He brought about the acceptance of Bach and Händel as the equals of the great classic Viennese school. His attempt to make religious music one of the major means for the revival of church life largely failed, however. Even his own oratorios made their greatest appeal in concert halls rather than in churches. The subjectivist character of this music interfered with its easy acceptance in general Christian worship. As with Robert Schumann (1810–56), modern German music had its centers essentially in the concert hall and opera, and its public was the educated classes. They did not constitute an entirely passive audience, for the cultivation of piano and chamber music was widespread in the homes of the German bourgeoisie of the century. Here musical culture, together with participation in dramatic art, assumed something of the role which church and religion had played in earlier centuries. While all over Germany, in cities large and small, citizens built temples dedicated to drama, opera, and music, it was not amiss to speak of the devotees of these arts as members of an "esthetic Church," or *Kulturkirche*.

✺ *Religion*

THIS DEVELOPMENT WAS THE ULTIMATE OUTCOME of the emancipation of secular from ecclesiastical culture. The German Enlightenment of the eighteenth century had never displayed an antireligious attitude but had tended to subordinate religion to rationalism by a rather facile synthesis of reason and revelation. From the second half of the eighteenth century on, religion ceased to be a major regulatory force in human affairs for the German bourgeoisie, and this trend was made incontrovertible in the mass of the middle classes through the growth of modern natural science. In this respect one may say that the Enlightenment continued in a more or less vulgarized form right into our century. Even among the theological schools, the Enlightenment retained important strongholds up to the middle of the nineteenth century. With Gesenius and Wegscheider, the University of Halle remained a citadel of the Enlightenment well into the 1830's, while in Heidelberg H. E. G. Paulus, until his death in 1851, presented an arid rationalistic theology to large academic audiences. In the state bureaucracies, the creations of enlightened absolutism, rationalism retained many believers, but in the educated classes in general German idealism modified, or even greatly changed, this fundamental outlook.

Beginning with Lessing, German idealism objected to the monopoly of reason which the Enlightenment established in the realm of the spirit. We have seen that Pietism was a contributing element to this opposition to rationalism as it was in the religious revival which occurred after the Wars of Liberation. Yet almost all the representatives of German idealism shared with the Enlightenment the firm conviction that man could rely on his own powers, among which reason was, if not the only, still the foremost human faculty. In Goethe, Schiller, or Humboldt the emphasis on the subjective personality led to ideals derived from classic antiquity rather than Christianity. Kant, with his doctrine of the radical evil in man, recovered some of the deepest Christian notions, but he confined religion entirely to morals and saw in religion a lower form of philosophy, useful as a crutch for the unenlightened and needed by the state for building a public spirit. Philosophical idealism as well as humanism stressed the distinction between educated and uneducated people, a separation which was to have serious consequences in a nation already strongly divided by many class barriers.

Large groups of the people, however, were not affected by German idealism and neohumanism. They continued to live as orthodox members of the Protestant churches. Their response to the French Revolution and the wars which followed in its wake had been of an entirely negative nature. The French Revolution and its belief that man's reason could build an ideal world were held a proof of human hubris, and the ensuing terrors of war and destruction were explained as God's judgment on a sinful world. It was a piety of inwardness and aloofness from secular history. As far as it considered action in the world, it was directed toward Christian mission or, as it was called, the "awakening" of fellow men to Christian truth. In Württemberg, the refusal to adjust to the political events produced a genuine chiliastic movement. Thousands identified Napoleon with the Apollyon of the *Revelation* and migrated to Poland and southern Russia, in order to await there the advent of the kingdom of God. In general, however, the new piety, which cared little for philosophy and took the Bible as its authority, was cultivated in a quietistic spirit by many small and remote circles.

Pietism and Lutheran orthodoxy had been drawing together when the Enlightenment had risen to power in state and church. In the first decade of the new century, Pietism and orthodoxy were only weakly represented among the clergy but undoubtedly were much stronger among those lay groups that were little touched by the intellectual currents of the age. Among them were not only the peasants and small artisans but also many of the rural squires. During and after the War of Liberation, Luther's doctrine of justification became for them the central tenet of the revived faith, and the old historic creeds, especially the Augsburg Confession, gained fresh life. Over this bridge, orthodoxy and Pietism came together. These "positive" Christian groups, as they were soon called, strengthened their fraternal bonds by their common views of the state. Man must accept the eternal order of God, which was simply equated with the time-honored historic order of German society. Thus it was said now "throne and altar" belonged together, or that a positive Christian faith called for a conservative belief in the divine right of princes. Only in Württemberg was this conclusion avoided. Here the time-honored order was identified with the "good old law" of the estates, for which in these very years after the war the Swabian people made a strong stand against the king.

Outside of Württemberg, neo-orthodoxy and neo-Pietism helped to fill the sails of the new conservatism. But the monarchical governments lacked an understanding of these religious forces. The absolute state of the eighteenth century and of the days of the Rhenish Confederation had tended to make the Church administration a mere department of state government. Still, the absolute state had left religious life within the churches relatively free. The political reforms of the period of 1806–15 abolished the remaining ecclesiastical boards, which had existed alongside the bureaucratic organs of the state. The Vienna settlement finally created states which in many cases contained both Catholic and Protestant territories or brought Lutherans and Reformed Protestants together. Thereby it destroyed the situation in which the Protestant prince could serve as head of the Church because both in theory and in practice he was the "foremost member" of a religiously homogeneous community. Henceforth, his authority in Church affairs was construed as an attribute of his sovereignty and thereby became even less questionable than his prerogatives as a political ruler, which could be challenged by the estates.

Monarchistic sentiment was ingrained in German Protestantism, and new Catholic rulers were readily accepted as heads of the Church.

Thus, for example, the Franconian and Palatinate Churches recognized the Bavarian king. By itself, however, this would not have necessitated state control over the religious activities of the Churches, including the common creed and the forms of worship. If the religious renascence was to spread its roots far, it had to grow on a popular basis.

✑ Reorganization of the Protestant Churches

YET IN POPULAR PARTICIPATION in the direction of church affairs kings and princes, quite mistakenly, saw only a move toward political liberalism. Actually, the presbyteries and synods which existed in the Reformed Churches of the Rhineland and had been adopted even by the Westphalian Lutherans did not aspire at the exercise of church government. Hardly any room was left for the independence of the individual congregation when in 1815 consistories were reintroduced in Prussia or, as in Rhineland-Westphalia, newly introduced, and the whole church administration turned over to bureaucratic bodies, at the side of which in each province a "superintendent general" acted as the highest theological authority. At the same time when Hardenberg's plans for a political constitution were abandoned, original projects for a complementary ecclesiastical organization were discarded by Frederick William III.

The struggle for the reorganization of the Protestant churches became closely linked up with the conflicts which arose over a Protestant union and a new order of worship. Under the influence of the Enlightenment and early Pietism, the old division between the Lutheran Church and the Reformed Churches, for which German Protestantism had paid so dearly in its history, had waned during the eighteenth century. Particularly in the regions along the Rhine, where Protestants lived in immediate proximity to Roman Catholics, relations grew very close. In Prussia, Frederick William III, who personally was greatly affected by the Lutheran faith, intended to close the gap which had existed between the dynasty and the people since 1613, when Elector John Sigismund had adopted the Calvinist creed. At the time of the tercentenary of Luther's *Ninety-five Theses*, the king called for a union of the two denominations. On October 31, 1817, twenty Berlin ministers attended a communion service, in which rites and formulas were used which left it to the communicant to interpret the Lord's Supper in either the Lutheran or Calvinist manner. King and court held a similar service in Potsdam.

✎ *The Prussian* Agende

BUT WHEREAS IN BADEN, Nassau, and the Bavarian Palatinate formal union was brought about in 1817–21 through synods or congregational approval, Frederick William III imposed the merger by a new order of worship which he himself drafted. This *Agende* of 1822 aroused the opposition not only of those who found the new forms of church services ill chosen but also those who resented the introduction by royal command. Few were in full agreement with the king. A long and noisy struggle ensued, which, however, produced more verbal arguments than determined deeds. On the whole, the ministers and laymen active in the Church were too closely tied to the existing social and political order to be ready to carry their opposition to clear disobedience to the government. Frederick William stubbornly pressed his *Agende,* and although he denied that the congregations would be forced to adopt it, the government used every means to make ministers conform and deliver the assent of their congregations.

The king's preoccupation with the liturgical side of religion obviously was a sign of his uncertainty in doctrinal matters. Still, he was attracted by the assurance which the old creed breathed. His simple mind longed for uniformity of faith, and he wished to make the Augsburg Confession the official creed. Actually, this would have ruined all the chances for the unification of German Protestantism. Therefore, he eventually contented himself with demanding the adherence of all ministers to the "symbolic books" of the historic Protestant churches, and in 1830 he ordered that preference should be given to orthodox ministers. What this meant in practice, remained doubtful. Negatively, these actions amounted to a declaration of royal opposition to the ideas of the Enlightenment and modern German philosophy. But the selection of an official creed could have made sense only if this creed had been grounded in the living faith of the Church members. Furthermore, it was never settled what the official creed was to be from now onward. Was the minister under an obligation to the substance only of the various creeds or might he consider one creed of his choice the expression of his own faith? It was a curious way of promoting orthodoxy.

Just the same, the mass of the orthodox and Pietistic groups in the eastern provinces of Prussia were gratified by the favorable attitude shown by the government toward "positive" Christianity, and the Reformed congregations of the Rhineland and the Westphalian Lutherans were appeased in 1835 by the grant of a presbyterial and synodal constitution. This constitution made only small concessions to lay influence. In Silesia, where Lutherans still preserved memories of the long fight for survival under the Catholic rulers of Austria, opposition to the *Agende*, to Union and absolutist ecclesiastical intervention was bravely upheld by many congregations. The Prussian government was not ashamed to defame them as dangerous sectarians, and even military coercion was used. Thousands of these Silesian Lutherans emigrated to America. The remaining "old Lutherans" finally received from Frederick William IV the precarious status of a separate church.

In other German states, church constitution and creed were somewhat more liberally defined. This was particularly true of Baden. But the system of absolute state churches, which excluded lay elements from all participation in the direction of religious activities, prevailed everywhere. A new type of division within German Protestantism resulted from the diversity of constitutions and creeds in the various states. The Lutheran Churches of Saxony or Hanover looked disdainfully upon the "Evangelical," that is United Lutheran-Reformed Church of Prussia. The German state churches became staunch defenders of the sovereignty of the individual German states. With the demise of the *Corpus Evangelicorum* of the diet of the old Empire, in 1806, not even the shadow of an institutional bond survived among the German Protestant churches. They excluded themselves from the national movement of the century. The churches were still more lacking in consciousness of ecumenical duties. The conception of the church as a community of faith and work founded on principles holier than the authority of the state seemed to have disappeared in Germany. No doubt, Luther had never paid much attention to the external church. Yet in Sweden, the most Lutheran country, the state Church developed into a true "people's church" and, through its archbishop and Church assembly, wielded great influence on national life. It was the power of political absolutism which warped the character of modern German Protestantism.

The identification of the Church with an ill-defined supranaturalistic creed interfered with the flow of ideas which had originated with German idealism and which continued to dominate the universities. Two major attempts were made to bridge the conflict between German idealism and Christian religion. The first was undertaken by Hegel. In his philosophical system there was no place for a church independent from the state. Although the absolute ideas of religion, art, and science still belonged to a higher realm than that of the state, the latter was the actual realization of the absolute spirit in historic time and embodied not only the law but also the total morality of a nation. Hegel assigned the greatest significance to religion. According to his interpretation, all the great turning points or new ages in world history were initiated by a new stage of religious history. But the churches, in Hegel's eyes, were chiefly schools which through their doctrines laid the ground for new human attitudes. Still, the full realization of a new morality could only be achieved in the state, which, therefore, would absorb the Church. Hegel seemed to offer a philosophical justification for the church policies of the government. He also seemed to support orthodoxy by his positive reinterpretation of such key dogmas as the Trinity, or God's incarnation and sacrificial death, which had been discarded by the rationalists for a long time.

Yet Hegelian philosophy contained elements which placed Christianity in great jeopardy. According to Hegel world history was the unfolding of the absolute spirit in the world through the development of human consciousness. The Christian religion thus became a mere moment in this process of reason, and not even its supreme hour. For religion was not the highest form of consciousness. It was only a stage on the way to rational philosophical concepts. Moreover, religious ideas represented forms of the *human* consciousness. Hegel's philosophy of history and religion placed the historical study of Christian religion on a new basis. Ferdinand Christian Baur (1792–1860) of Tübingen became the leader of a school devoted to a new historical study of early Christianity. But before this earnest Swabian scholar, who combined the philosophical impulses of Hegel with the critical methods of Niebuhr, started to publish the results of his research in 1844, one of his young students had already drawn the radical conclusions which one might discover in Hegelian thought. David Friedrich Strauss (1808–74), with his *Life of Jesus*, caused a storm of excitement by describing the original Christian religion as a product of the national Jewish spirit, and Jesus as the representative rather than creator of the Christian ideas.

∾ Schleiermacher

FRIEDRICH SCHLEIERMACHER DEVOTED HIS LIFE to healing the breach between religion and philosophy. As preacher and professor in Berlin and as collaborator of Stein and Humboldt during the Prussian reform period, his influence on the renascence of religion and the Church was very great. When he began his literary career in 1799 with his famous *Speeches on Religion to the Educated Among Its Detractors* he fought against the general indifference toward religion. Re-editing his treatise in 1821, he pondered whether any educated detractors were left and discovered instead a multitude of "superstitious and superpious." He expressed fear that in the future Christianity might come to be identified with barbarism and scholarship with atheism. For him, critical knowledge gained certainty and the self true freedom only through religion, which he found in the human consciousness of "absolute dependence on God." Philosophy and religion are as inseparably linked as ethics and piety. But Schleiermacher dissolved both rationalistic and supranaturalistic metaphysics, which so far had formed the chief contents of Christian theology. Critical thinking leads to the mere assumption of a creator and prime mover, while human consciousness possesses God only in subjective feeling. Theology is not capable of making valid statements on supranatural subjects. Therefore, not dogmatics but the study of religion as it has come to life in history becomes the central task of theology. The Christian dogmas are only derivatives of religious experience and finite symbols of the various forms of piety, which for Schleiermacher are by no means of equal value and altogether are no more than inadequate attempts.

The heart of religion is the dynamic power of religion itself. It is a necessary element of human life, because it perfects all the higher capacities of man. Consequently, religion enters, and should enter, into all human relations. Religion originates in the depth of individual consciousness, but in Schleiermacher's view tends to expand into a social consciousness or, in other words, to form churches. Still, the individual Christian should not be immured in his church. In all his activities he may consider himself as an organ of the divine reason which determines the world. This belief conditioned Schleiermacher's own ideas of church and state as well as his own public actions. His original ideal of the church had been the small and self-contained congregation. During the years of foreign occupation and national liberation, when he rallied his friends and congregation to patriotic sacrifice, he gained a higher appreciation of people and state and wished to see arise a "people's church" which could permeate all public life with its spirit. But in harmony with his whole religious thinking, this could only be a free church unregimented by the state and, least of all, bound by narrow creeds. Thus Schleiermacher became the chief opponent of the official Prussian Church policy.

Hegel and Schleiermacher felt a world apart, and the intellectual and academic Berlin of the 1820's was divided largely by the position which everyone had to choose in the controversy between the two thinkers. Their philosophical conflict comprised more than the issues of religion and seemed to both of them irreconcilable. But certain common trends appeared in their thought, as for example in the significance which both attached to history, because both started from an analysis of human consciousness. For this reason their influence could often mix in the later part of the century. The strongly intellectual character of the religious thought of Hegel as well as Schleiermacher denied both a wide popular appeal, although particularly the latter found many followers among the members of the theological faculties, the natural place for working out a synthesis of religion and modern philosophy. The "mediating theology" (*Vermittlungstheologie*) found its place side by side with the "positive" schools. The "mediating" theologians made great contributions to the critical understanding of religion, but their impact on the religious life of the nation remained small. Even the response of the educated classes was weak. When in the 1840's German idealism ceased to hold sway and German scholarship turned empiricist and positivist, while the German bourgeoisie displayed increasingly materialistic attitudes, the "mediating theology" found itself isolated.

Liberal and Positive Christianity

IN THEIR ENDEAVOR NOT TO LOSE contact with the spirit of the age, liberal theologians were easily tempted to construe Protestant religion merely as the spiritualizing element of a progressing world history. Luther then was judged to have been the liberator from the bondage of the medieval Church and the spearhead of modern secular civilization. The Reformation which Luther had begun was to be carried forward by each generation in alliance with the progressive forces of the epoch not only against Catholicism but also against Protestant obscurantism. In general, these theologians tended to find the realization of spiritual and moral ideas in the history of the state rather than the church. The vast majority of the educated people lapsed into a state of indifference, although they retained their outward church membership. They looked to science and the arts to gain a higher content for their lives. Often enough, these *Kulturprotestanten* did not retain anything of the historic faith of the Reformation except an anti-Catholic attitude.

While liberal theology failed to win the adherence of large groups, neo-orthodoxy and neo-Pietism, after temporary gains until about 1840, proved incapable of stopping the movement away from the Church among the urban population. Pietism never quite overcame its aversion to philosophy and systematic learning, whereas the renewed orthodoxy, with its simple supranaturalism and biblicism, refused to come to grips with modern science. In addition, its absolute reliance on monarchy and authoritarian government, as evinced by its foremost spokesman, E. W. Hengstenberg (1802–69), alienated the growing political liberalism. "Positive" Christianity became the religion of the old ruling classes, the rural population, and the lower middle classes in the towns, although substantial sections of the latter forsook religion after the middle of the century.

✍ *Neo-Pietism*

FROM THE OUTSET, and this meant from the time of the War of Liberation, the reviving religious movement had found its most active representatives in the upper social groups. Already during the time of the French occupation a Silesian nobleman in Berlin, Baron H. E. von Kottwitz (1757–1843), through his Pietistic faith and philanthropic activities, attracted an important circle of gifted young men, among them the heir to the Prussian throne, the future Frederick William IV, and his friends, the brothers Leopold (1790–1861) and Ludwig von Gerlach (1795–1877). The movement spread quickly from Berlin to the eastern provinces. Among the Pomeranian *Junkers* particularly the new piety found many believers. In the 1830's and 1840's Adolf von Thadden of Trieglaff (1792–1882) was the central figure of this circle. It was here that the young Otto von Bismarck found his faith. But at the same time, the "awakening" was carried to the common people through revivalist preachers.

The reaction of the people was originally quite considerable, but although the movement was religiously as well as politically conservative, the Protestant churches did not have at their disposal the means for making these forces fruitful for the ecclesiastical life. The Prussian police was even suspicious of the religious excitement on the Pomeranian *Junker* estates. It is true that in Württemberg the awakening led to some doctrinal differences and even separation. Contacts with English nonconformists, probably established by Swabian emigrants to the New World, brought into existence Baptist congregations which upheld their belief against the state Church and government and defended it as the true meaning of Scripture. But beyond this religious protest, the dissident groups did not develop a diversionary political or social program. In their religious group life they looked for shelter from the harsh realities of the world.

In this respect the orthodox Pietists were not different from these dissenters, although their humanitarian effort had wider aims. Still, in order to launch such an ambitious scheme as foreign missions in Germany, the Württemberg Pietists needed the co-operation of Swiss citizens, with whom they founded the Basel Missionary Association. Societies for the distribution of Bibles and Christian tracts sprang up in many places in Germany. In the northern Rhineland and the Wupper valley around Elberfeld with its Reformed traditions all these missionary and social activities were still grounded in the congregations themselves. Theodor Riedner (1800–64), Protestant minister in Kaiserswerth, was the first German to organize the collaboration of women in social work. And from this predominantly Catholic little Rhenish town the drive was begun for the construction of hospitals, which were also training centers of Protestant nurses or "deaconesses," as they were called.

◈ *Johann Wichern*

IN ALL THESE CHARITABLE ENTERPRISES Protestantism almost unintentionally moved closer to the field of social action. In Hamburg, pastor Johann Hinrich Wichern (1808–81) became the greatest preacher and public figure whom German Protestantism had produced since Luther. With the help of some of Hamburg's patricians he founded in 1833 the *Rauhe Haus*, an institution devoted to the rehabilitation and education of delinquent youths, for which task Wichern developed unusually understanding and successful methods. But whereas all the former institutions of this type had attended only to local needs, Wichern conceived of it as a model for all the German churches. For he felt that the social problems could be solved only if they were attacked on a broad front. He realized that the problems of poverty and moral dissolution which he found in the proletarian elements of the port city of Hamburg were only examples or harbingers of what modern civilization might produce. It was the measure of his stature as a religious personality that in such a degeneration he saw very clearly a failing of the Christian church. The Christian message was one to be presented not only by words but also by deeds.

Yet Wichern thought of sin as the cause of this grave deterioration of social conditions. His traditionalistic, conservative views did not allow him to recognize in society a conflicting process of social claims nor in pauperism the unhappy result of the fluctuations of modern economy. The inequalities of property as well as of social and political status were never questioned by Wichern, nor did he believe that social conditions could be improved through the legislation of the state. Only the spread of the Christian faith could restore organic health to society. While, therefore, the conversion of the individual remained the center of all Christian efforts, Wichern attached to it a Christian significance as well as a social one. Although the divinely ordained order of this world was a punishment of human sin, the kingdom of God could not only be experienced in the anticipation of a transcendental realm but was already foreshadowed in the triumphs of good over evil in the conscience of the faithful. The spiritual and moral strength which faith created had its effects upon the social order, on family, church and state.

Wichern acknowledged that social circumstances could threaten the very existence of religious life. Against these conditions, such as sickness, crime, or broken homes, he wished to mobilize Christian love through free associations of laymen. Luther's ideal of the priesthood of all believers was turned into an imperative for such action. Wichern took care not to minimize the function of the ministers and their service to the Word, but faith to him was not doctrine alone but also action, and he saw in it the means for making the Church a "people's church" and for creating a common consciousness among the German churches beyond all doctrinal differences.

Wichern's deep piety, together with his great gift of organization and oratory, made him an eminent ecclesiastical leader. Institutions similar to his *Rauhe Haus* in Hamburg were created elsewhere, and he spun a network of relations between all the welfare agencies which the pietistic awakening had brought into being. He was watched with great suspicion by official churchmen, who feared that the movement was undermining the dominant position of ministers and the supremacy of doctrine. Wichern incurred the greatest hostility among the orthodox Lutheran Churches of Hanover, Mecklenburg, and Saxony. But he gained sufficient support among the North German nobility, and eventually even from King Frederick William IV, to carry his cause forward. When, in 1846, the Prussian king appointed a general synod to advise him on the development of the church constitution, a resolution was adopted recommending the introduction of deacons in all congregations. Yet the ruler disliked most of the recommendations of the synod and refused to execute any of them. Thus also the resolution which would have given welfare and social activities a firm institutional function in the church was shelved. In the midst of the revolutionary upheaval of 1848, however, a general German church convention, the Wittenberg *Kirchentag*, accepted the establishment of a national committee of all charitable associations of German Protestantism, about 1,500 in number. The actual conduct and administration of Protestant charities remained in the hands of local associations, which were represented on land or provincial committees. But in the so-called Central Committee of the Inner Mission a national council of these voluntary activities was achieved.

But Wichern's fervent hope that the "organized work of believing congregations in free associations" would lead to the Christian and social revival of a sinful people in state and church, was not to be fulfilled. It was the historic achievement of Pietism, and in particular of Wichern, to grasp a connection between the social conditions of his age and the future spiritual history of the people, but his traditionalistic views of society, together with his unflexible theological outlook, did not allow him to become a modern social reformer. Through the awakening of faith he wanted to restore the old social order. The paternalistic forms of an agrarian society seemed to him quite adequate for ordering the new relationship, as the corporate molds of ancient towns seemed suitable for the modern city. Moreover, Wichern's Lutheran inheritance let him deny any capacity for changing the fundamentals of the social order. Although laws were needed to prohibit abuses and make adjustments to fluctuating circumstances, these were the business of the state.

In spite of his sensitive understanding of many psychological needs of the proletarians, Wichern failed to recognize the novelty of their human situation as children of modern individualism facing a wretched mass existence. The proletarians were not just another case in the eternal fall from grace, nor was the social reality which had thrown them into the utmost poverty the old "God-given" order. Wichern was already quite wrong in his idealization of agrarian society. The recent gains of the landlords and the misery of the agrarian workers spoke loudly. And although the leader of the "Inner Mission" occasionally seemed almost ready to enter upon the path of social reform, he was unable ever to discover the rise of a new class and its right to develop its own social and moral attitudes. The Inner Mission was also far from addressing itself to all the workers. On the whole, it catered to the sickly and dejected rather than the healthy and strong.

If Wichern and the Inner Mission failed to produce a Christian regeneration of the nation and in particular to win substantial sections of the working class, the reason lay largely in their political ties with the ruling classes. In order to overcome the opposition in the Church, Wichern had always leaned on the powers that be. When, in the turbulent circumstances of the revolution, the conservatives helped decisively in making the general organization of the Inner Mission possible, Wichern was only too ready to entrust its practical direction to them. In the years after the collapse of the Revolution of 1848–49, the Prussian *Junkers* made the Inner Mission one of the chief vehicles of their restoration policies. It never became, as Wichern had dreamed, a movement of the people, nor was the German proletariat attracted to the Protestant state churches. For a solution to its ills it looked exclusively to politics, thereby following the example of German liberalism. Liberalism, however, considered social problems negligible, because they would solve themselves in a free economy of a national state. Thus the nascent German working class was practically isolated. While the Protestant churches remained appendages of the state, the workers' movement formulated its longings in a radical program which renounced both the truth of religion and the state.

✎ Roman Catholicism

ROMAN CATHOLICISM, still the prevailing religion in the population of the German Confederation, reacted differently to the development of the new century. The policies of the French Revolution and of Napoleon had played havoc with all the ancient institutions and ideas of the Roman Church. All the old "Church states" had disappeared, and their property had been taken over by the secular state governments. Chaos had followed in the whole Church administration. Only five of the German bishops' sees were occupied by a bishop in 1815,

numerous monasteries had been dissolved and educational and charitable activities brought to a sudden halt. The majority of the universities in the Catholic territories had been closed. The spiritual principalities on the average had been governed neither better nor worse
than the majority of the secular ones, but the religious function of
the Church had been weakened by its endowment with worldly
authority and wealth. Bishops' sees and positions in the chapters had
been the domain of the high nobility, and its members had used the
income of their benefices to defray the expenses of a mundane life. All
this was now over. The modern leaders of the Church came from
among the low clergy, and even the noblemen, a good many of whom
to the present day have risen to high Church offices, were henceforth
theologically trained and proven in Church work. The annihilation of
the political power of the German Church was ultimately shown to
have been a blessing in disguise.

Yet in 1815 Church conditions were really desperate. The Congress
of Vienna had refused to make arrangements for the German Church
and had handed the problems over to the Diet of the Germanic Confederation. But it soon became clear that the Diet was not willing to
order the Church on a national scale. The wish of the individual states
to deal with ecclesiastical matters on a strictly territorial basis was
responsible for this failure. Strangely enough, the reorganization of
the political map of Germany had left (apart from the little Hohenzollern) only two predominantly Catholic states, Austria and Bavaria.
Very large groups of Catholics had become citizens of Prussia, Hanover, Württemberg, Baden, Hesse, and some smaller Protestant states.
Still, the Catholic states were not less determined to maintain the rule
of the state over the Church. Austria continued the practices of
Josephinism and declined to negotiate with the Vatican on anything but
the practical application of governmental orders.

Bavaria concluded a concordat with Rome which cut the old bonds
of the Bavarian bishoprics with Salzburg. The boundaries of the new
dioceses conformed to the boundaries of the state. Two archbishoprics
were created, Munich-Freising and Bamberg. Each of them had three
suffragans (Augsburg, Regensburg, and Passau; Würzburg, Eichstätt,
and Speyer). The state assumed the obligation of granting these new
ecclesiastical dignitaries a proper endowment. Although the concordat
gave the king the right to nominate all the bishops as well as other
far-reaching privileges of appointment, the Bavarian government, to-

gether with the constitution, published a religious edict which extended the state supervision over every aspect of Church life. The state also failed to provide a permanent endowment for the Church.

The other South German governments, which had decided to conduct common negotiations with the Curia, demanded the same privileges for the state as the Bavarian concordat had conceded. The Church refused to make these concessions to Protestant princes. The Pope restored the old right of the cathedral chapters to elect the bishop, which actually went back to the Worms Concordat of 1122, but the individual princes were given the right to eliminate candidates "less agreeable" to them from the lists of candidates. The Vatican circumscribed the dioceses in accordance with the territorial boundaries, Freiburg for Baden, Rottenburg for Württemberg, Mainz for Hesse-Darmstadt, Fulda for Hesse-Kassel, Limburg for Nassau and Frankfurt. The five bishoprics formed the ecclesiastical province of the Upper Rhine, and Freiburg was finally raised to the archepiscopal see. But the states recognizing the papal bull which established the new ecclesiastical organization asserted by a mere ordinance (*Landesherrliche Verordnung*) the full control over the Church by the state.

The Roman Church did not reach any better results with Hanover and Prussia. From 1816–21, the historian Niebuhr, as Prussian minister in Rome, conducted negotiations with the Curia. The bull *De salute animarum*, which subsequently was also printed in the series of official publications of Prussian state laws, contained the circumscription of the Prussian bishoprics and the measures which the Prussian government was to adopt for their financial sustenance. Beyond these agreements Frederick William III was unwilling to go. In the western provinces the archbishopric of Cologne was re-established with suffragan bishops in Trier, Münster, and Paderborn. In the east the archbishopric Posen-Gnesen with the bishopric Kulm was created, also the exempted bishopric of Ermland and the bishopric of Breslau. Hanover agreed in 1824 to the restoration of the bishoprics of Hildesheim and Osnabrück.

The re-establishment of a regular Church organization was bought at the price of the acceptance of dominant state control over the Church. This was an ill foreboding for the religious life in Catholic Germany. But whatever the shortcomings of the Church settlement were, it created at least a working order, and as much as the governments wished to safeguard the principle of state superiority, within their territories they were interested in peace between state and Church. No doubt, however, the insecure position of the Church made the clergy, and before long also the Church members, look toward Rome as the source of strength in their struggles with inimical or callous political authorities.

In its causes and impact the revival of traditional Catholic piety during the years of war and French domination was not essentially different from the Protestant revival. As far as can be judged, the rationalism of the Enlightenment never penetrated far beyond the upper classes. Not only the rural population but also many groups of the lower clergy were little affected by modern ideas. Particularly the monasteries proved largely impervious to the movements of the time. German philosophical idealism and the modern literature so closely connected with its growth were almost entirely a product of German Protestantism. They reached the Catholic society with some delay and, more important still, were absorbed in a more critical spirit. Then the romantic movement had brought a new respect for religion in its old forms and expressions. It taught that religion could not exist in the abstract but only in concrete historical realization. At the same time, the romantic thinkers had demonstrated a deep meaning in the universalism of the Roman Church as the sustaining force of European life in its greatest period, the Middle Ages, which the romantic poets revived in a golden light. The conversion of a good many of the romantic writers gave the Church a group of brilliant defenders.

Outstanding among them was Friedrich Schlegel, who arrived in Vienna in 1808, almost simultaneously with Clemens Maria Hofbauer, in whom the popular piety found its most appealing representative. A simple monk from a Moravian village, Hofbauer radiated a new devotion to the Church in the imperial city through the saintly model set by his ascetic life and his warm and open faith. Hofbauer's activity as popular preacher, confessor, and teacher gave the criticial genius of Schlegel its practical application. While Schlegel dedicated himself to a Christian reinterpretation of art, literature, and history, Hofbauer's presence was the living witness of the continual creativity of Christian life. Others, such as Adam Müller, the political thinker of German romanticism, Anton Günther, the philosopher of religion, who attempted to utilize German idealism, or Zacharias Werner, the somewhat dissolute poet, were active in this revival. For a number of years Vienna seemed to assume the leadership in the regeneration of German

Catholicism, but the heavy hand of absolute state control throttled the progress of the movement. From the 1830's on, too late and with little success, Metternich tried to moderate the excesses of Josephinism.

In the regeneration of German Catholicism Munich became an increasingly important center. Johann Michael Sailer (1751–1832), the son of poor parents, was a teacher who trained a new generation of Catholic youth. He grew up in the Enlightenment while giving its humanitarian and moralistic pedagogy a positive religious foundation, which was the inheritance of his upbringing among the people. He also eagerly absorbed the classic German literature, but to him it was a means for developing a style and language of noble simplicity which could be easily understood by both the learned and the uneducated. One of Sailer's early students, Christoph Schmid (1768–1854), became the actual founder of children's literature in Germany. Sailer's religion was built on the essential teachings of biblical Christianity. Much as he wished to see the individual fully dedicated to Christian wisdom, he disliked exaggeration and superfluous adornment. His was a serene piety of classic proportions. As a professor in Landshut he educated many priests who were able to become true fathers of their parishes. But Sailer also had great influence on laymen, among them his colleagues in all the faculties. When, in 1826, Landshut University was moved to Munich, Sailer's friends extended his model to a larger field.

The young King Ludwig I (1825–48) had listened to Sailer's academic sermons as a student. For him as crown prince, Sailer, a Bavarian Fénelon, wrote a "mirror of princes." Ludwig I was a man of great talents and marked complexity in his intellectual interests. Romantic and classicist inclinations were both alive in him. When he made Munich into a center of German culture and attempted to give it also the outward appearance of a modern capital, he followed his artistic taste in adorning the city with classical buildings. Friedrich Thiersch had the king's support in his endeavor to fill the Bavarian schools and universities with the ideas of German neohumanism. The Greek revolution evoked strong philhellenic feelings in Ludwig, and he had the eventual satisfaction of seeing his brother Otto become the first king of the Greeks.

Ludwig's dynastic consciousness entered into almost all his preferences and decisions. Thus he was unwilling to give up any of the controls over the Church which the government had acquired during the Napoleonic period. But it was the reviving Catholic piety, and not the spirit of the Enlightenment, which he tried to implant in Church and state. In 1827, he brought Joseph Görres (1776–1848) as professor of history to Munich. Eight years before, the passionate Rhenish publicist had had to flee from the wrath of the Prussian king to Strasbourg, and had found his way to the Church among the leaders of Alsatian Catholicism. Now he became the chief figure in the group of men at the university, men such as the philosopher Franz von Baader, the jurist Georg Phillips, the philologist Ernst Lasaulx, and the church historian Ignaz Döllinger (1799–1890), who worked for the regeneration of the Church. As they pressed their ideas, these men began to feel the cold hand of the state-church system.

The Bavarian Catholic revival did not originally produce a scholarly foundation for a modern Catholic theology. The new Catholic theological faculty in Tübingen was the first school that presented works of theological scholarship which revitalized both the faith of the Church and faith in the Church. Johann Adam Möhler (1796–1838) was the head of this group which eventually was to drive rationalism from theological teaching. Möhler was the first to use modern historical methods for understanding the development of the Church, and through the reinterpretation of scholasticism he prepared the way for the revival of Thomism.

While the Swabian university planted the seeds of new scholarship, Mainz proved to be the source of most of the efforts directed toward a popular pastorate. The "golden Mainz," the hallowed Christian metropolis of Germany, was shorn of its glories by the collapse of the Holy Empire and the French annexation. But after the re-establishment of the French Church, a new diocese of Mainz was created, and an Alsatian, Johann Ludwig Colmar, was appointed bishop by Napoleon. Thus the work of ecclesiastical reconstruction was already well underway when Mainz was joined to Hesse-Darmstadt in 1815. The training of a new clergy was given first attention. The seminar of Mainz, first under Franz Leopold Liebermann, then under another Alsatian, Andreas Räss, became the model institute for the education of the new clergy and also restored scholastic theology as a major element of instruction. These Alsatians, all born in simple circumstances, had seen the furor of anti-ecclesiastic fanaticism unleashed by the Jacobins and had fulfilled their pastoral duties in danger of their lives. But they had also gained the conviction that the Church possessed a reservoir of loyalty among the people which could be activated if the clergy would observe the high demands of their calling.

A democratic air could be sensed about these Catholics who set out to meet the challenge of revolutionary democracy. They recognized early the decisive role which the common people were likely to play in the great decisions on the future of state and Church. The Mainz circle attempted at once to break the virtual monopoly on all publications which Protestantism held in Germany. A flood of apologetic and polemic pamphlet literature, together with classic Christian texts, issued from the presses of the city of Gutenberg. A monthly journal, *The Catholic*, was founded in 1821 and quickly gained wide distribution, though also immediate difficulties with state censorship. From 1822–27, the journal had to be published in Strasbourg. The Mainz school was extremely critical of the state-Church system and also curialist, since it saw in a centralized Church the best guarantee against the encroachments by the state. A new type of ecclesiastical leadership originated in Mainz. In 1830, Räss went back to Strasbourg, where, in 1841, he became bishop, which he remained until Alsace was annexed by Germany. The two foremost pupils of Räss, Johannes Geissel and Nicolaus Weiss, succeeded each other on the bishop's see in Speyer. Geissel, son of a vineyard farmer in the Palatinate, was made archbishop of Cologne after 1840. In Mainz itself Baron Wilhelm Emanuel von Ketteler (1811–77) was enthroned. Though the scion of an old Westphalian noble family and not a direct student of the Mainz circle, Ketteler did more than anybody else to bring its ideas to full maturity and public acceptance by the whole of German Catholicism.

The Cologne Troubles

IN 1837 THE SO-CALLED COLOGNE TROUBLES (*Kölner Wirren*) forced the German Catholics into a passionate political conflict. Since after 1815 many German states contained members of more than one denomination, mixed marriages had occurred more frequently. In the Rhineland, where the Prussian government employed many Protestant officials from the eastern provinces, mixed marriages had become rather frequent. The Prussian law of Frederick the Great had ruled that in such cases the male children should follow the religion of their fathers and the female children that of their mothers. In the spirit of the Enlightenment, the Roman Catholic clergy of eastern Prussia had been accommodating to the wishes of the state, although the canon law did not allow the assistance of priests at mixed marriages, unless the education of all the children in the Roman Catholic faith was pledged by the parents. But it was difficult to enforce the Prussian law in the predominantly Catholic Rhineland as the Prussian government intended. The Vatican went far in 1830 by accepting civil marriages as valid and only withholding the blessing of the priest if the conditions of the canon law had not been met. Yet the government was not satisfied and secretly prevailed on the archbishop, Count Spiegel, to advise the clergy to assume a decidedly more conciliatory attitude than the papal brief permitted.

Count Spiegel, a grand seigneur who had grown up in the age of state-dominated churches, was followed by the austere Clemens August von Droste-Vischering, who declined to tolerate any deviation from the papal brief. When the archbishop refused to resign, the Prussian government had him arrested and incarcerated in the fortress of Minden on November 20, 1837. This arbitrary action, which lacked any legal justification, caused an enormous sensation. Much dissatisfaction had already collected among the Rhenish people over the unfriendly attitude which the Prussian government from the king down to the county councilors displayed toward Catholicism. The imprisonment of the archbishop, whose actions were publicly recommended by the Pope, provoked popular demonstrations of a threatening character. Joseph Görres in Munich lifted the Rhenish conflict into a national light by the publication of his *Athanasius,* a masterpiece of popular polemics which found the widest distribution. Görres described the policy of the Prussian government as the result of modern individualism and rationalism, and bound to lead to revolution and the complete disintegration of society. Passionately, he demanded lawful freedom for the Roman Catholic Church and parity of the denominations.

The impact of the Cologne troubles was tremendous. The revival of religious life after 1815 had strengthened denominational feeling as well as mutual polemics. But it had also brought the leaders together into common opposition to rationalism and an exclusively secular culture. In politics, as a rule this had created a common conservative front against liberalism and democracy. Until 1837 the chief political organ of German conservatism, the *Berliner Politische Wochenblatt,* was edited by Protestant and Catholic writers. This co-operation between the leading spirits of the Churches ceased when Prussian Protestants defended the policy of Frederick William III. In 1838, Görres and others founded the *Historisch-Politische Blätter für das katholische Deutschland* in Munich. The name indicated that the Munich circle felt itself responsible for the Catholic cause in all of Germany. Prussia was branded as the state impersonating the worst consequences of the Reformation, rationalism, and Erastianism. To these Catholics it seemed logical that the Prussian policy vis-à vis the Catholic Church was loudest applauded by liberals and radicals. Deep as the disappointment at the tyrannical action of the Prussian monarch was, German Catholics remained profoundly suspicious of the democratic movement. For the time being, they looked for a revival of corporate institutions under a legitimate monarchy as a cure for the ills of the absolutist state.

∽ The Beginnings of Catholic Social Action

FOR AN ALLIANCE OF CATHOLICS and liberals, which had made the Belgian revolution of 1830 possible and successful, the prerequisites were lacking. Still, the use of liberal and democratic methods by the Irish under O'Connell in these decades or of constitutional rights by the Poles made an impression. The great freedom enjoyed by the Church under the Belgian constitution served as an example that a modern constitution could not only promote rights of the individual but could also protect the independence of corporations, particularly the Church. But the German Catholic leaders were slow in approving political liberalism, because they were afraid that it might open the gates of the Church to philosophical liberalism as well. The popular Catholic movement, especially of the younger generation, adjusted itself more readily to such ideas. In Württemberg and Baden the diets proved a most important school for the parliamentary representatives of Church interests.

For the first time, the Cologne conflict unveiled the existence of a nationwide Catholic grouping in which all the old classes, from the nobility to the bourgeoisie and the peasantry, shared. The awareness of social problems within the Church kept the Catholic movement in touch with the slowly emerging class of the industrial workers. As the active Catholics eyed with distrust the political ideas of the French Revolution, so also they were critical of the new social and economic conditions which they saw develop in Western Europe as a consequence of the rise of industries. The Munich philosopher Franz von Baader (1765–1841), who had lived in England for four years and was influenced by Lamennais's thought on the subject, analyzed in 1834–35 the dangers threatening society from a split into a propertied and proletarian class. Baader described the depersonalizing power of the machine on the worker and the law of falling wages in a system of growing production in terms which almost anticipated Karl Marx. He demanded limitations on free competition and opportunity for the workers to voice their grievances. To the clergy he assigned the function of "Christian deaconry," to act as solicitors of the proletariat. Thus, on the basis of critical sociological diagnosis, a social policy to be undertaken jointly by state and Church was postulated by a Catholic thinker.

Yet Baader was neglected by his contemporaries. The time was not yet ripe for approaching the social problems in such a fundamental way. Still, social demands were raised. A Freiburg professor, Franz Josef Buss (1803–78), was the first to discuss social legislation from the rostrum of a South German parliament in 1837. But his social activities were devoted more to individual charitable work than to the reform of society. This was largely true of the work of Adolf Kolping (1813–65), who had been a shoemaker's apprentice before he entered the priesthood. He knew the distressing needs of the migratory journeymen and formed journeymen's associations, which under the direction of a local priest were to provide the journeymen with the protection and the physical and spiritual bread which the Christian family normally supplied. From 1845 on, this early social priest tested his ideas in Elberfeld, and after 1851 the movement was carried from Cologne all over Germany and even into foreign countries. In the same year of 1845 the first St. Vincent conferences, which followed the model set by Antoine Ozanam and his students in Paris, were held in Germany. Laymen of all classes came together in an endeavor to bring practical and religious assistance to the needy.

All these social and political actions kept the Catholic movement in closest contact with the popular social trends of the age, as the movement itself was representative of many strata of society. The formal and often hostile relations of the states and the Catholic Church, strengthened by the desire of the official Church leaders not to be absorbed even by a friendly state, enabled the Church to build a much broader popular foundation than the Protestant churchmen, with their reliance and dependence on the state and the ruling classes, could ever hope to do. Therefore, the German Catholics could act even when the Revolution of 1848 put the monarchical governments temporarily out of business. The year 1848 brought developments of the last thirty years to a close and set the stage for a new century in the history of German Catholicism. It saw the first conference of German bishops convene in Fulda, saw Catholic priests and laymen in the German parliaments successfully defend and advance the rights of the Church, and witnessed the first national assembly of representatives of the Catholic associations. In Mainz, Baron von Ketteler, who was to become bishop in this see in 1850, declared the social question to be the foremost problem to be solved by the Church. All the elements and aims which characterized German Catholicism during the century after 1850 and were to make it a major force in German politics manifested themselves for the first time in the years of the German revolution.

The Prussian policy in the Church question was no doubt consciously or unconsciously motivated by the feeling of strength which animated Protestantism at that time. After all, it seemed to that generation of German Protestants that the Roman Catholic Church had gained its restitution only by the benevolence of the princes in 1815. Not only were they entirely blind to the new vitality which the Church had acquired from popular sources, but they also forgot the hopeless division within Protestantism itself. The Prussian government appealed to the other German governments for a statement of solidarity in the question of mixed marriages. But all of them protected themselves by insisting on their sovereignty. Matters grew worse by an almost identical incident concerning the archbishop of Prussia's Polish territories. The only applause that Frederick William III received came from the liberals and the democrats, and this sounded hollow in the ears of the senescent authoritarian monarch.

ᴈ Efforts at Church-State Reconciliation

His son, Frederick William IV, who ascended the throne in 1840, was deeply affected by romanticism and its veneration of the Christian-German Middle Ages. He disapproved of the control of the state over the Church and hoped to gain the co-operation of the Church in counteracting all revolutionary movements. The conflict over mixed marriages was settled in favor of Church doctrine, and many practices of state supervision were quietly abandoned. Direct and free communications between the bishops and Rome were allowed, and state intervention in the elections of bishops was liberalized. The new policy of Frederick William IV, which was accompanied by earnest efforts to calm the interconfessional controversies, was highlighted when, in 1842, Frederick William IV attended the celebrations in Cologne. The great cathedral had remained incomplete as a consequence of the religious division of the Reformation. The resumption of construction was made the occasion for a demonstration of peace between state and Church as well as of the solidarity of all Christian forces in the preservation of the historic German culture.

Frederick William IV's endeavors at reconciliation were not without some political results. In a time when the beginnings of industrialization made the population of the Rhineland aware of the palpable advantages of belonging to a large state, the absence of serious friction in ecclesiastical matters assisted in making the Rhenish provinces acquiesce in the Berlin administration. But the experiences which the German Catholics had had in the period after 1815 were not forgotten. The rude interference in inner Church affairs and the toleration of such actions by orthodox Protestants and secular liberalism had forced German Catholicism back upon its own resources. And these had grown immensely, since it had sunk its roots deep into the life of the people and had become responsive to the developments of a new age. In the new generations of its priests and bishops Catholicism had leaders who represented the Church with prudence, dignity, and courage. They did not lose sight of the tasks posed by its popular support, as indeed the Catholic revival was even more the work of laymen than of the hierarchy. If future statesmen, such as Bismarck, believed that the Catholic Church in Germany could be brought into submission by the coercion of the clergy, they showed ignorance of the strong social foundation which German Catholicism had acquired by the middle of the century.

CHAPTER 17

The Transition from Idealism to Realism

THE DISCUSSION OF SCHOOLS AND CHURCHES in the preceding chapter has led us far into the nineteenth century. For an understanding of the general history of Germany, however, it will be necessary to return to the period which started with the 1830's. A new generation began to appear on the scene. In 1831 death removed Stein, Gneisenau, Niebuhr, and Clausewitz. In addition to these political figures of the liberation era, the leaders of classic idealism died in quick succession; Hegel in 1831; Goethe in 1832; Schleiermacher in 1834; Wilhelm von Humboldt in 1835. New voices became dominant, and criticism of both religious supernaturalism and philosophical idealism became widespread, while the preoccupation with social problems was growing.

∾ Hegel

THE SPLITTING OF THE GERMAN idealistic movement into a good many differing schools, the survival of eighteenth-century rationalism, and the regeneration of suprarationalist religion among Roman Catholics and Protestants created a greater variety of intellectual camps than had existed in earlier days. It was only the prelude to the rise of an even greater multitude of competing systems which occurred in the second half of the century. The last German philosopher who had come close to a monarchical position in the German intellectual world during the 1820's was G. F. W. Hegel. In 1817 he came from Heidelberg to the Prussian capital, where he exercised an extraordinary influence on students and the general world of education. The patronage of Baron Altenstein, the Prussian minister of education, afforded Hegel the opportunity for having his disciples chosen for appointment in other faculties and universities. While simple and natural in his personal manners, Hegel was not insensitive to power. But the mastery of the universe through speculative reason was the foremost concern of his imperious mind. In dramatic intellectual struggles he grew beyond the heritage of his youth. Religion, theology, and classical humanism provided the original inspirations, but the French Revolution as well as the subsequent destruction of the old German Empire, which had meant so much to his Swabian homeland, aroused his passionate interest in politics and history. What nature was to Goethe, history was to Hegel: the manifestation of the reality of the spirit.

In Berlin Hegel's work received its final form through the publication of his *Encyclopedia of the Philosophical Sciences* (1817, 1827, 1830), the *Philosophy of Right* (1821), and his academic lecture courses on religion, esthetics, philosophy of history, and the history of philosophy. Hegel was convinced that Kant had left philosophy in an untenable dilemma. Kant had confined all knowledge to human experience and had taught that only the forms with which the human mind organized the data of experience were *a priori* to each sense impression and, therefore, constituted true universals. But Kant maintained that we had only a knowledge of things as they appeared to our consciousness, and that consequently a knowledge of the "things in themselves" was denied to us. Hegel judged that in such a "philosophy of reflection" knowledge actually remained subjective and was incapable of mastering reality. Reason, he argued, in such a system would have no power over reality, because it separated the world of subjectivity and objectivity and was dealing with the ideas of things rather than with the things themselves. Hegel judged that Kant's attempt to confine knowledge within close frontiers had failed, because Kant's transcendental postulates were proof that something beyond the frontiers could be known. Demanding the "courage of truth" Hegel proceeded to replace transcendentalism by a new metaphysics.

In contrast to the "subjective" idealism of the Königsberg sage, Hegel erected a system of "objective" idealism, which explained the world as the necessary development of the "absolute" or divine spirit. If the ultimate synthesis of all forms of being thus has a spiritual character, man can understand it only as far as he experiences it in his consciousness. Moreover, these experiences must be more than mere empirical experiences if they are to contain universally necessary truth. Hegel discovered the root of this necessity in the very nature of the spirit itself. In a process of continuous self-assertion, self-opposition, and restored unity, the absolute spirit unfolds in the world in order to realize its potentialities, making them in the course of this process the conscious and free possession of man.

ᴔ Hegel's Philosophy of History

FOREMOST AMONG HEGEL'S CONTRIBUTIONS, and the greatest one in its impact on his contemporaries and on posterity, was his philosophy of history. His philosophy of nature, which largely followed Schelling, was not very original nor were his relations with modern science very intensive. Nature Hegel called the "idea in its otherness," dormant reason. The true dynamic character of the absolute spirit manifests itself only in history, the explication of the absolute spirit in time. With regard to history he made his often-quoted and much misunderstood statement: "What is rational is real, and what is real is rational." This did not mean that reason could be ascribed to everything that subsisted. Hegel made a sharp distinction between mere appearance and actual reality. Real and rational is only what is part of the spiritual process of universal history, which in its progress from one stage to the next rests on conscious acts of man. Still, the mind of the individual remains subjective and gains rational consciousness only to the extent to which it realizes the ordered movement of the absolute spirit as the supreme law of the universe. Thus the individual is led beyond itself to the participation in the collective forms in life, in which a higher reality, namely that of the "objective spirit" reveals itself.

National cultures are the expression of the communal historical consciousness. Law is the abstract formulation of the principles of community, while the main source and guarantor of law is the state. In the idea of the state the divine spirit appears on earth. No single state realizes this idea. According to the stage which the absolute spirit has reached, one or the other state becomes the vehicle of the absolute spirit and thereby the protagonist of progress. Hegel traces the migration of the spirit that underlies history from the Orient through Greco-Roman civilization to the medieval and modern European worlds. It is a dialectical movement proceeding from thesis through antithesis to synthesis or, concretely, from the Oriental, who only knew that one man was free, to the Greeks, who knew that some men were free, to the Christian-German nations which knew that man, as man, is free.

By making the state the exclusive organ of all the great historical decisions Hegel left the individual in a subordinate place. Happiness is not the goal of history; on the contrary the times of happiness are "blank pages" in the book of history. Moreover, the ideals of individual morality cannot be made the criteria of the actions of states. Rather, these embody the movement of the absolute spirit and follow ethical norms quite different from the moral precepts of individual life. In order to execute the moves of the absolute spirit in actual history, the state is to have power and to follow the laws of power. Hegel accepted Machiavelli's teachings with regard to the overriding nature of state interests. Politics is a struggle for power, in which passions drive men forward, though in the background the universal spirit perfects its course. It is the "cunning of reason," which uses the labors, hopes, and sufferings of finite forces to realize its supreme aims. The state is the vessel of the absolute, but at the same time it remains a historical entity bound by the particular circumstances of time and space. States must assert their peculiar nature, and wars, therefore, are inevitable. Any attempt to construe an ideal state or an ultimate eternal peace is declared to be illogical. Hegel's philosophy rejects the whole tradition of natural law, which had constituted one of the strongest liberalizing forces in Western civilization. The theory of the "inalienable rights" of the individual, which in the eighteenth century had found such strong philosophical support even in Germany, was treated with particular scorn.

Hegel's apotheosis of the state offered a justification for an absolutist and authoritarian government against which the individual was essentially unprotected. Still, for Hegel the state is the embodiment of the national spirit (*Kulturstaat*), with its internal government based on lawful procedures (*Rechtsstaat*) and consequently not to be simply identified with power (*Machtstaat*). The philosopher of spirit saw in the statesman the executor of the idea and not, as modern fascist theory does, the creator and manipulator of the idea. For Hegel the state still belongs to the finite world, and although there is no judge on earth to pass sentence on the actions of the state, the state is under the judgment of universal history, in which the full totality of the absolute spirit is revealed. In this sense Hegel could say: "World history is the world court of justice." Moreover, the state is obliged to respect the independence of art, religion, and philosophy as the great manifestations of the absolute spirit. Here the internal experiences of the individual were protected, at least in theory.

The state as agent of reason and spirit was seen by Hegel as an enlightened and generous power. His political theory was by no means blind reaction. The doctrine of Haller, who conceived of the state as an institution of nature, in which God had intended to have the strong rule over the weak, was the prevalent political philosophy among the conservatives. Hegel called such doctrines products of fanaticism, imbecility, and hypocrisy. To him reason was the principle of the state, and he resented any theory that made the state the battlefield of blind forces of chance. Throughout his life he expressed his deep admiration of that "glorious mental dawn," the French Revolution, which was "a result of philosophy" and had drafted a constitution "in harmony with the concept of right." Hegel also rejected the teachings of another influential conservative school as being essentially naturalistic. The romantic conservatism of the so-called Historical School of Law, of which Friedrich Karl von Savigny (1779–1861; professor in Berlin, 1810–42) was the most eminent representative, stressed the nonconscious working of the *Volksgeist* as the source of all the legal institutions of a nation and opposed any rational creation of law as a presumptuous interference in historical custom.

But Hegel's philosophy was grounded on a conservative faith of its own. Hegel believed that it was not the task of philosophy to set new aims to history, rather that it was the function of philosophy to understand past developments and to bring into consciousness the present stage of history. He was convinced that history had entered a late stage, and he saw this proved by the capacity of the modern philosophers to interpret history in terms of reason as well as by the rise of the Prussian monarchy. The glorification of Prussia as the "state of intelligence" drew him into strange reasoning. In stark contrast to his general insistence on the historical and rational character of the state, his defense of monarchy rested on the argument that birth, a fact of nature rather than history, gave monarchs an objective role far above the particular interests of individuals and social classes. Another expression of Hegel's conservative mood could be found in his apparent satisfaction with the existence of the German Confederation. In view of the close connection that Hegel established between state and national spirit, one might have expected him to plead for a unified German state.

Such subjective judgments betrayed some of the basic dilemmas of the Hegelian philosophy. But its consequences were even more far-reaching. In spite of all the efforts made by the idealistic philosopher to soften such a conclusion, it is true that in his system the actual criterion of historical progress lay in the outcome of the conflicts of power. With the idea realizing itself only in concrete states, no absolute ideals for regulating and evaluating the course of history remained. What was true in international relations was equally true in the internal life of states. In the face of the sovereignty of the state, individual rights had only a relative value, and individual morality and political ethics were separated. The idea of absolute justice disappeared in the clouds, and the positive law of the existing state could demand unquestioning obedience from any citizen.

∽ *The Extinction of Natural Law*

THE RISE OF HEGEL'S PHILOSOPHY completed the intellectual development that German romanticism had begun. The religious and philosophical foundation on which the political and social thought had relied for almost two millennia, the belief in natural law, was abandoned. It was an infinitely more radical philosophical revolution than the change of thought that the French Revolution had accomplished. For the French Revolution had only replaced the absolutist version of natural law by a democratic interpretation without questioning its underlying philosophical assumptions. Germany, which only a generation ago had produced in Kant a great thinker who had presented his political and social theories in terms of the common European tradition of natural law, resolutely turned away from this heritage in the age of Hegel. Thereby, a deep cleavage was opened between Germany and Western Europe such as had never existed in any earlier century of European history.

German Catholicism retained a natural law tradition as embodied in the teachings of the Church, but within the educated groups of Protestant Germany, which dominated the civil service and the universities, this tradition became extinct and was not revived, even after Hegel's system itself had lost its appeal. Those historical forces which actively pursued democratic reform in Germany after 1830 were compelled to look for theoretical support in the arsenal of Western European thought. But the failure of the German Revolution of 1848–49 and Bismarck's victories, two decades later, reduced these forces to relative impotence among the German bourgeoisie, and it was only in the democratic socialism which the German working classes embraced in the last third of the nineteenth century that a closer affinity to Western ideas prevailed again.

The simple appearance of a new philosophy of individuality that the romantic writers cultivated and that Hegel combined with his grandiose "panlogism" does not really explain the separation of German political thought from the mainstream of European ideas. If educated men in Protestant Germany were so eager to give up Kant for Hegel, the philosophy of the latter must have appeared to them as offering solutions to their own vital problems and aspirations. In the preceding generation some of the outstanding personalities, such as Stein, Scharnhorst, or Gneisenau, had been able to assert their individual genius. They had put their stamp on the policies of the Prussian state, and where they did not succeed, as in the crisis of 1812, had even fought this state. In this period the cultivation of individuality and political reform had still to be compatible. But the reaction after 1815 gave the individual no such scope, and to advocate revolution was not in the blood of an intelligentsia which depended for its existence on the traditional German state. They resigned themselves rather easily to a new absolutism, especially since it could be rightly argued that unlike the state of Frederick the Great this new absolutism was not a personal despotism but gave the bureaucracy an important share in all political decisions. Moreover, compared to the mercantilistic practices of the eighteenth century, the German states of the Restoration gave great freedom to the free economic enterprise of civil society. Progress was undeniable. In addition, had not this Prussia in the Wars of Liberation played an outstanding role in restoring the liberty of European nations, and particularly had it not revived national life in Germany? In view of these events, even the objectionable militaristic aspects of Prussia might be excused, especially as they were also counterbalanced by the flowering of arts and sciences.

Hegel's philosophy fitted exactly the situation of people who were deeply convinced of the power of reason over reality, but wanted to be persuaded that progress toward freedom was possible within an authoritarian political order. The hard realities of history had to be spiritualized, especially the cruel injustices of sheer might, and the experience of freedom turned largely into an internal experience of the individual. Councilors of state could pride themselves on being workers in the realm of the objective spirit, and professors could feel themselves as friends of the world spirit. The peculiar historical circumstances of the educated class in the Germany of the age of Restoration make the wide acceptance of the Hegelian philosophy understandable. Similarly, the changing political and social climate of the 1830's as much as new scientific ideas caused the waning faith in Hegel's system. Still, many of the social and political conditions which had favored the growth and acceptance of Hegel's system continued to exist in Germany, and some of his ideas were used to rationalize these conditions. In the age in which the German people struggled for unification, only to receive it in the end as a result of the power politics of an authoritarian government, and even more in the subsequent age of imperialism, Hegelian ideas were widely current in Germany. But these later generations conceived of the state as the final absolute in positive reality, or often enough as a force of biological nature and not as a passing moment in the dialectic movement of the spirit. Although these later champions of power politics and denigrators of international law employed a partly Hegelian language, they were no longer inspired by Hegel.

Opposition to Hegel

The immediate influence of Hegel had by no means only benefited conservatism. Many conservatives, among them the circle of the Prussian crown prince, who later became King Frederick William IV, felt a deep suspicion, which was proved well-founded by the development of Hegel's school after the master's death. The conservative critics called his philosophy a "negative" philosophy, because it employed reason to question the given reality and order. Every form of life changes into its opposite and achieves its complete actualization only through this process. The "negation" of all given reality by the Hegelian dialectic seemed to F. J. Stahl (1802–61), who in the 1840's became the leading German theorist of conservatism, to contain the "principle of revolution." Since social theory was an essential part of Hegel's philosophy, this assertion was not entirely groundless. But even more important in the eyes of Hegel's contemporaries was his transformation of religion into mere logic. While orthodox theology opposed him on this issue, some of his students drew radical consequences from his teachings. The *Life of Jesus* (1835) by D. F. Strauss has already been mentioned. This interpretation of the New Testament as a myth created by the absolute spirit opened the gates to the most radical criticism of Christian religion.

Ludwig Feuerbach (1804–72), who began as an enthusiastic apostle of Hegelian pantheism, proceeded to criticize Hegel for his neglect of nature as the conditioning element of man and human thought and developed a sensual materialism as the negation of Hegelian philosophy. According to Feuerbach, Hegel still remained caught in theological prejudices. Actually the individual and matter is the true reality, and Hegel's universal is a mere abstraction. What man wishes to be, he conceives of as another world, as a transcendental ideal, and worships as his God. Feuerbach's *Essence of Christianity*, published in 1841, proclaimed Christian religion to be the illusionary creation of man's wishful thinking. For the first time in German history an antireligious and naturalistic materialism made its appearance and began to spread fast among the urban middle classes, particularly among the lower strata. The mechanistic interpretation of both the psychic and physical world, which had originated with the French materialism of the eighteenth century, was soon appropriated by the German materialists. The simultaneous progress of natural science led to a complete rejection of all speculative philosophy of nature, and the new materialism could pose as the philosophy of life most appropriate to the modern scientific age. Its optimistic ethics promised happiness to the individual, and its politics leaned toward democracy.

✑ *Marx and Engels*

WHILE THE NATURALISTIC MATERIALISM of Feuerbach had an immediate effect on popular thinking, the historical materialism of Karl Marx (1818–83) was not to gain any influence for decades to come. It was in the "Young Hegelian" circles of the Prussian capital that this young student from the old bishops' town of Trier steeped himself in Hegel's philosophy and began to question its validity. But up to the year 1843, Karl Marx had not visibly grown beyond a democratic radicalism. In that year, however, the Prussian government expelled him from the country because, as an editor of the Cologne newspaper *Rheinische Zeitung* in 1842–43, he had directed the heaviest attacks against official policies. The years between 1844 and early 1848, spent in Paris and Brussels, enabled him to study the impact of the industrial revolution and also of Western European socialism. At this time he met Friedrich Engels (1820–95), who had just made a name for himself by the publication of his book *The Condition of the Working Class in England*, and an intimate friendship and close intellectual and political co-operation, which was to last until the end of their lives, developed between the two prophets of social revolution.

Karl Marx, who came from a family that had cut its ties with the Jewish community completely, nonetheless by his intense rationalism showed traces of the long rabbinical tradition of his family. The strongest human motive that one can discover in his original rebellion against the bourgeois society, his live sense of equal justice, in his later years almost took on the character of a cerebral principle rather than that of a deeply felt conviction. In contrast to the abstractness of Marx, Friedrich Engels showed a free and open attitude to world and life. The son of a well-to-do cotton manufacturer in Barmen, he had wished early to escape from the narrowness of his home town and from what seemed to him the unbearable hypocrisy of its Pietistic merchants and industrialists. He went to Manchester in order to assist in the management of the English branch of his family's firm. The income from his business activities allowed him to provide the means for the Marx family in their London exile after 1850. Although busy with his practical job, Engels was an industrious student of history. His amazing linguistic faculties permitted him to roam far and wide in universal history. Since serving as an officer in the revolutionary army during the Baden campaign of 1849, he had also acquired a great knowledge of military affairs. Engels always maintained that his contribution to the development of Marxian theory had been largely confined to special aspects, and that in particular the strong foundation of the whole structure had been the work of Marx. This is quite correct, for Engels did not possess the piercing theoretical ability of Marx. Still, the services that Engels rendered Marx were great. His understanding criticism helped the birth of many an idea, and the information that Engels was able to give to Marx added much concrete matter to Marx's writing. Next to his happy family life, the continuous exchange that went on between the two men was, no doubt, the chief source of strength that supported Marx in his heroic efforts to produce his work, in spite of the most irksome and discouraging circumstances that plagued his life.

The decisive stage in the growth of historical materialism was the collaboration of Marx and Engels that culminated in the publication of the *Communist Manifesto* in London in January 1848, on the eve of the European revolutions of 1848–49. This masterpiece of political demagogy did not evoke a response from the masses in those years. It was only thirty or, maybe, even fifty years after its publication that its full force in making world history began to be revealed. But the *Manifesto* contained in a nutshell the new socialism, which Marx called "scientific," in contradistinction to the "utopian" socialism of all his predecessors, such as Fourier, Proudhon, or Owen. The demonstration of necessary laws of history, which made the ultimate realization of socialism inevitable, constituted the scientific nature of the new social-ism. The failure of the revolutions of 1848–49 induced Marx and Engels to modify their ideas in some respects, but on the whole they rather elaborated on them and in the *Capital*, of which the first volume ap-peared in 1867, while the second and third were edited posthumously by Engels in 1885 and 1893, Marx transposed his socioeconomic theories into a strict system of economics.

Marx found fault with Hegel's assertion that in the monarchical state the stage had been reached at which reason was realized. The proletariat was clear evidence that the existing society denied to a whole class the fulfillment of its human potentialities. The proletarian does not own property, a prerequisite of personal freedom, nor does he participate in religion, philosophy, and art, the avenues of human access to the world of the absolute. Bourgeois society condemns the proletarian to "universal suffering" by subjecting man to the blind rule of an alien force. Commodities, the products of human labor, which for that very reason enhance human freedom, have become the brutal masters of man in capitalistic society. Marx was convinced of the creative power of capitalism and often talked about it in a language of high admiration. Capitalism had not only multiplied the productive capacity of man immensely, but had also achieved the organization of mankind into a universal society and thereby created the conditions for a unified movement of world history.

Capitalism was a necessary stage of history, but by no means the fulfillment of reason or human freedom. This called for the abolition of class society and of private property as the cause of class division. But there was hope for the early arrival of an age of a classless society in which all would share in the fruits of production and in which the individual would be able to realize his full potentialities. Within the growth of capitalism itself Marx found the seeds of its own destruction. By depriving the worker of the ownership of the means of production, bourgeois society forces him to sell his labor at a price that is far less than the value he gave to commodities through his labor. The capitalist appropriates the surplus value. The exploitation of the worker, in-tensified by the replacement of human labor through machines, drives the proletariat into a state of extreme pauperization (*Verelendung*). At the same time the free competitive system devours its own masters. In the competitive struggle capital tends to concentrate in fewer and fewer hands, and a growing number of capitalists are pushed into the proletariat. This process of concentration will wreck the whole structure of bourgeois society. While its dire economic circumstances would turn the proletariat into a homogeneous class, the class of capitalists would dwindle. Thus the day when the last expropriators would be expropriated by the proletariat would approach.

Karl Marx never departed from the Hegelian tradition to the extent that Ludwig Feuerbach and other Young Hegelians did. Marxist theory retained the goal of history that Hegel had established, the realization of reason and human freedom, and the model of Hegelian dialectics was equally essential. But whereas for Hegel the actual course of history was only part of a great metaphysical drama, Marx employed the critical tools of Hegelian philosophy exclusively for the understanding of actual history. The absolute denial of metaphysics and religion, much strengthened by Feuerbach, induced Marx and Engels to speak of their "materialistic" interpretation of history. But this label is misleading, and "economic" interpretation is more fully descriptive. History was declared by Marx to be the history of class struggles and ideas were "ideologies" or "superstructures" of social reality. But this was true only of history prior to the destruction of capitalism and of bourgeois society, which Marx liked to call the "prehistory" of man. Moreover, Marx was far from judging ideas, whether religious, moral, political, or artistic, as unimportant. They were active agents in history, and although their forms as well as their movements were conditioned by economic realities, they were no simple reflections of economic motives.

Marx's statement that he had placed philosophy on its feet again after Hegel had made it stand on its head, expressed his opposition to the philosophy of spirit but not to reason. It was not in the metaphysical progress of mind, however, but in the concrete struggle of man with the material conditions of life that the decision on the future freedom of man and man's reason had to be sought. Mere philosophical interpretation of history was not enough to achieve this end. The actual change of society and of the forms of economic production on which society rested was imperative. Guided by a scientific theory, the philosopher turned into the leader of the proletarian revolution. Marx and Engels always claimed that the modern working-class movement was not only the child of Western European socialism, but also of classic German philosophy, and this is correct with regard to the original Marxist theory, although the socialist movement of a subsequent age was little conscious of this link.

∾ A Science of Reality

THE DEVELOPMENT OF MARXISM in the 1840's was a further sign of the growing disbelief in speculative idealism and of the turn toward a science of reality. Representatives of Young Hegelianism remained excluded from academic faculties, but the shift away from philosophy to the empirical sciences steadily proceeded in the period after 1830. Even romanticism, as far as it had taught respect for the specific value of individual forms, had helped to prepare a new sense for reality. The studies of the Grimm brothers (Jacob, 1785–1863; Wilhelm, 1786–1859) were motivated originally by the romantic wish to recapture the moment in which the youthful Germanic spirit awoke and created language and poetry. The *Children's and Domestic Tales* (1812–22) and the *German Legends* (1816–18) were the ripe fruits of their early years. Together with the recovery of Germanic folk-poetry they accomplished the mastery of the problems of the history of the German language, to which the two brothers devoted the major part of their lives. Jacob Grimm's *German Grammar* (1819–37) founded comparative Germanic philology, and after 1852, together with his brother, he created the *German Dictionary*, that big storehouse of historical Germanic linguistics. Franz Bopp (1791–1867) carried his research into all the Indo-Germanic languages and became the father of comparative linguistics. The work of the Grimms, of Bopp, and a good many other scholars of their generation laid a secure scientific basis for scholarship in the humanities. Historiography, too, benefited from their achievement.

∾ Barthold Georg Niebuhr

BARTHOLD GEORG NIEBUHR (1776–1831), in his *History of Rome* (1811–12, rev. ed. 1827–32), had for the first time in the history of European historiography radically broken with the practice of using the classic historians as sources for their treatment of the past. He was not the first scholar to question the value of the great Roman historians for the understanding of the early period of Roman history, but he was the first one to show methods with which to reconstruct the past that the classic literary sources misrepresented or misunderstood. From a critical appreciation of the outlook of the secondary writers as well as of their position in the midst of the institutions and events of their own age the modern scholar had to make his way to authentic documentation and information, which then had to be woven into a new unified conception of the historical subject under study. This so-called "critical method," essentially the application of an expanded philological text-criticism, which became the prerequisite of all modern historical research, was for the first time successfully demonstrated by Niebuhr.

Not only his critical sense, sharpened by an enormous learning, but also his intense participation in the intellectual and political movements of his time made Niebuhr's scholarly achievements possible. His child-hood in the free peasants' community of northern Friesland provided him with a vision of a free agrarian society, as which he was later on to diagnose the early Rome. He took over the direction of the Prus-sian State Bank on the eve of the battle of Jena in 1806, and he was greatly involved in the politics of the period of reform and liberation. From 1816–23 he served as Prussian minister in Rome and negotiated the treaty that regulated the state-Church relations in Prussia for the next century. Niebuhr was always close to the realities of political and economic life, but he approached history chiefly with the intention of finding the right social and political order, and the Roman state of the early period served him as the ideal testing ground. In this respect he was still a representative of the pragmatism of the historiography of the Enlightenment, and he also shared its moralizing attitude. The influence of early romanticism, particularly of Herder's concept of organic growth, tended to strengthen his concentration on the indi-vidual at the expense of the interest in universal history. Moreover, the romantic theories of the national spirit, by their dogmatic application, impaired the full power of his extraordinary historical divination. Niebuhr did not possess the literary gift that might have enabled him to turn his critical studies into a great narrative that would have ap-pealed to a wide audience. It was only after the middle of the century that Theodor Mommsen (1817–1903), with his *Roman History* (1854–56), succeeded in arousing such a general interest.

✑ Leopold Ranke

THE CALM DAYS AFTER 1815 favored the maturing of a genius who could blend the experiences of the preceding political storms with those of the Restoration, and the philosophical and literary atmosphere of Germany helped to create a history that found its strength in objective contemplation. Leopold Ranke (1795–1886), descendant of a family that had been dedicated to the Lutheran ministry in Saxony for cen-turies, came to history by way of theology and the classics. In 1824, he published his first book, *Histories of the Latin and Germanic Nations from 1494–1514*, which secured for the young high-school teacher a professorship at the University of Berlin. The *History of the Popes in the Sixteenth and Seventeenth Centuries* (1834–36) carried his fame far beyond the frontiers of Germany. In steady succession his other great masterpieces appeared thereafter, the *German History in the Time of the Reformation* (1839–43), the *Prussian History* (1847–48), the *French History in the Sixteenth and Seventeenth Centuries* (1852–61), and the *English History Chiefly of the Seventeenth Century* (1859–68). As an octogenarian he undertook the writing of a *Universal History* (1881–88), which at the time of his death had reached the fifteenth century. Together with many monographic studies, Ranke's works, which filled about sixty volumes, covered practically the whole of European history, and in his seminars many historians were trained who gave the study of history a secure place in all the German universities.

In the introduction to his first book, Ranke stated that the historian should not draw lessons for the future nor pass moral judgments, and he added the often misunderstood and even ridiculed remark: "I only wanted to show what actually happened." He intended to express his opposition to a moralizing and pragmatic history, as he also rejected the novelistic treatment of historical subjects with which at that time Walter Scott and other romantic writers entertained a large public. The "actual past" could only be known from the documents and monuments of the past, and the literary art that the historian might employ in the presentation of historical subjects was absolutely bound by the available evidence. In Ranke's hands the "critical method" proved the key to unlock the wealth of historical life in many fields. A catholic taste for the variety of historical forms enabled him to penetrate deeply into the unique character of historical events. But all individual persons, incidents, or historical ages appeared to Ranke as integral parts of wider developments. Beyond the subjective forces, Ranke, like Hegel, recognized dominant objective powers, and states and nations formed the most important entities in the course of universal history for both men.

Yet Ranke did not identify human history with the movement of the absolute spirit, nor did he accept a law of inevitable progress. His firm, if undogmatic faith in a personal God made him distinguish between a spiritual and historical world, although they were not fully separated. All of history showed the operation of spiritual elements, and Ranke felt that at times divine action could be adumbrated. The great political struggles were not mere conflicts of interests and passions but represented the contests of ideal principles as well. The real and the ideal were united in history, and Ranke liked to speak of the *real-geistig* essence of all historical life. In these ideas, that seemed to him the living principles of states, nations, or ages, the universal character of history revealed itself. Ranke, though hardly matched as a master of the critical historical method and as an artist in the rendering of historical individuality, from the beginning aimed at understanding the totality of history. His life work found its logical crown in his *Universal History*. For Ranke, however, world history could not be reduced in the Hegelian manner to rational ideas and laws of progress. To him, history was the demonstration of the potentialities of man, which could be understood only if history was contemplated in its fullness. Ranke admitted that there might be progress in the material and technological conditions of civilizations, but he denied general progress. He found it illogical that past periods of history should be considered mere stepping stones toward an enlightened present or future age. In contrast, he argued: "Each epoch is equally close to God."

In his first work, *Histories of the Latin and Germanic Nations*, Ranke stated his conviction that European history received its fundamental character from both the diversity and the unity of the European nations. While each of these kindred nations in the course of history had developed its own individuality ever more distinctly, they had at the same time formed a community on the basis of their common historical experiences. In modern times this unity was expressed chiefly in the system of great powers that had asserted itself victoriously against attempts at imposing the rule of a single nation all over Europe, as Charles V, Philip II of Spain, Louis XIV, and again Napoleon had tried. For Ranke, the survival of this system was the best assurance of the continuity of European history, as on the other hand the tensions within the system seemed to guarantee the vitality of its member nations by spurring them on to their highest effort. Power and state interest played a decisive role in Ranke's view of history. But power to him was never only physical or military power, but moral power as well. Universal and national ideas were woven into the great political decisions.

In his own age Ranke found the dominant conflict in the contrast between the ideas of the French Revolution and those of the old Europe. In this struggle between the sovereignty of the people and legitimate monarchy Ranke's heart was with the conservative forces, although he realized that Prussia would have to adjust herself to the conditions of modern politics. This process had already begun with the reforms of the years 1807–19 and with the liberal political and economic policies for which the Prussian bureaucracy was chiefly responsible. Also, Ranke was not an opponent of representative institutions provided the supremacy of the monarch was not imperiled. Basically, Ranke believed that a prudent monarch supported by a capable civil service would be able to cope with the problems of the modern age. His faith in monarchy made him grateful for the unbroken tradition of dynastic rule in Germany, and in the sovereignty of the individual German princes and their loose federation in the Germanic Confederation he saw the natural form of German political life. Ranke was not a champion of the political unification of Germany but was content with the cultural unity of the nation. In later years he followed Bismarck's policy with considerable apprehension and welcomed the new German Empire in the end, because he could construe its founding as a victory of conservative principles rather than the result of nationalism.

Undoubtedly Ranke's political views impaired somewhat the objectivity of his writings on the nineteenth century, though he was always far from presenting his own political ideas in a militant manner. When, after the July Revolution of 1830 the Prussian government enlisted his help to propagate sound conservative ideas, he remained so detached from a narrow controversy over the political issues of the day that the *Historisch-Politische Zeitschrift*, the magazine which he edited from 1832–36 and largely filled with articles from his own pen, left all the warring political factions cold. This journalistic venture remained Ranke's only interlude in practical politics. Thereafter he devoted himself exclusively to his historical work, and in it he achieved a breadth of universal understanding such as had never been reached before nor has been equalled since.

Ranke exercised some influence on practically every historian of the later nineteenth century in Germany and abroad. But the religious and philosophical motives that had led Ranke to history were hardly understood by midcentury scholars. To them the critical method by itself seemed the key to all historical knowledge, and philosophical interest in the problems of universal history had faded. In Germany Ranke's historiography was taken as proof of the supreme role of the state in world history. Actually, Ranke's historical conceptions were much

broader. Religion, churches, literature, and art were within his purview, and he had his eyes also on social history, although it is true that
in his works statesmen and political events occupied the better part
of the stage.

The first generation of Ranke's students not only confined history
dogmatically to past politics but also demanded that the historian
should not avoid judging the past in terms of a firm political ideal and
should preach to his contemporaries definite lessons from the past.
Johann Gustav Droysen (1808–84), Heinrich von Sybel (1817–95),
Ludwig Häusser (1818–67), and Heinrich von Treitschke (1834–96)
were the chief representatives of this "political"—or "Prussian"—
school of German historiography. It was a group of many-sided talents,
quite different in their personal temper and convictions, but united in
their determination to link their studies to the great national questions.
As advocates of constitutional government and even more of German
national unity under the leadership of Prussia, they wielded considerable power over the political sentiments of the liberal bourgeoisie,
particularly between 1848–71. In this period historical thought spread
far, but it was bought at the price of an accommodation to the political
movements of the age.

✌ Natural Sciences

IN THE DISCOVERY OF HISTORY, which has added a new dimension to
Western thought, the Germany of the first half of the nineteenth
century made its most original intellectual contribution to the modern
world. From Herder and the romantic writers to Hegel and Ranke,
German thinkers and scholars had formulated their new ideas about
history and their methods for reconstructing the past rather independently. But in the natural sciences Germany had remained far behind and had to rely on Western Europe for instruction. From the
seventeenth century on, England and France as well as the Netherlands
held the undisputed leadership in the scientific mastery of nature.
Whereas Italy even then retained a prominent place in the cultivation
of science, Germany's creative participation in the growth of science
was sporadic.

Even the reception of the results of modern science had to overcome
some reluctance in Germany. In Western Europe, and particularly in
France, with which German scholars were in closer touch than with
England, the rise of the natural sciences had led to mechanistic and

even materialistic interpretations of life. Therefore, inductive and experimental science was viewed with suspicion by German idealistic and romantic philosophers. In the early decades of the nineteenth century strong movements arose in Germany aiming at the creation of a speculative philosophy of nature that was to be superior to science. Schelling and his disciples, who were the foremost representatives of this school, were not altogether wrong in stressing the limitations of scientific knowledge, and this was particularly true with regard to the still modest results of the scientific research of that period. But their philosophical speculation failed to produce a sure basis of scientific method. It even tended to encourage dilettantism and quackery. For example, biomagnetism, which the Austrian Franz Mesmer (1733–1815) invented and presented as the best therapeutic method to high Paris society on the eve of the French Revolution, had its greatest vogue in Germany after 1815.

ᔆ *Alexander von Humboldt*

IF GERMAN SCIENTIFIC METHODS did not get lost in romantic speculation, this was due to an extraordinary extent to the personality and work of Alexander von Humboldt (1769–1859). Alexander grew up under the same influences as his elder brother Wilhelm, and he, too, enjoyed the friendship of Goethe and Schiller. But while Wilhelm's interests always centered on the study of man, Alexander's more practical mind was directed toward nature. The inductive research of the Enlightenment, which reached a new productive stage in the France of Napoleon, was blended by Alexander von Humboldt with the esthetic neo-humanism of Germany. For many years Humboldt lived in Paris and returned there again to write the extensive scientific report on his expedition to Central America undertaken in 1799–1804. This epoch-making event in the history of modern science was crowned with rich results not only in general geography but also in many special sciences, such as geology, biology, botany, and anthropology. From the exact observation of individual phenomena, however, Humboldt proceeded to a higher synthesis. In his old age he aimed at a "world physics," which meant a systematic treatment of the totality of nature. His *Kosmos* (1845–62), which was read all over the world, absorbed an encyclopedic knowledge of science into a panoramic view of the universe. Goethe's all-embracing curiosity as well as his sense of clear literary form were reflected in Humboldt's work.

Even after 1815, Alexander von Humboldt, a titular chamberlain at the royal Prussian court, remained a believer in the ideals of the French Revolution. But his prestige and authority as scientist were unchallenged, and he used them to promote scientific talent wherever he found it. One of his early protégés was the young Hessian Justus Liebig (1803–73), whom he met in Paris and helped to obtain a professorship at the University of Giessen. Here Liebig created the first chemical laboratory dedicated both to academic instruction and research. Practically every field of chemistry was advanced in a fundamental way by Liebig's experiments as well as by his theoretical vision. One hesitates to single out his contributions to organic chemistry, but his studies on the chemical aspects of physiology and finally his application of chemistry to agriculture that led to a revolution of agronomy, were particularly notable. At the same time Friedrich Wöhler (1800–82) enlarged the field and methods in chemical science in many new directions. His synthetic creation of urea in 1828 in particular broke down the absolute division between organic and inorganic chemistry and established a new theoretical framework for chemical research.

Liebig and Wöhler were the founders of chemical science in Germany. Wöhler was a professor in Göttingen, which in the nineteenth century became one of the great world centers of natural science. It was Carl Friedrich Gauss (1777–1855) who more than any other gave the small university town in South Hanover this distinction. In him the first modern German mathematical genius of Newtonian stature appeared. He was little affected by the post-Kantian German philosophy but was rather a child of the German Enlightenment which, as will be remembered, combined trust in reason with a simple faith in the transcendental world. The mathematical theories of Gauss laid the foundations for the modern natural sciences from astronomy to all the other departments of experimental and measuring physics. For Gauss mathematics was a worshipful contemplation of the universe. The technological implications of modern science appeared to him as irrelevant, though he knew about them. Thus, together with the physicist Wilhelm Weber, he constructed the first electro-magnetic telegraph in 1833. But Gauss and Weber were interested only in the scientific principles of their experiment, and although Liebig's science found a practical application in agriculture, other branches of the German economy were not as yet sufficiently developed to exploit inventions in physics.

But the growth of scientific research itself depended on a measure of technological development. As the musical culture of the eighteenth century had stimulated technical inventions, such as the *Hammerclavier* and other musical instruments, so the new science called for its instruments. The Bavarian Joseph Fraunhofer (1787–1826) was an artisan who perfected telescopes for astronomic observation. He acquired all the absolute mathematical knowledge and more than this, laid the foundations of modern optics. Through his workshop Munich acquired a leading position in the production of scientific instruments. While telescopes and to a lesser degree microscopes formed the chief products, the development of methods of precision mechanics as such was the event of most far-reaching historical significance. The skill and knowledge acquired in servicing science constituted an important resource for the future growth of German industrial manufacture.

∽ *Medicine*

LIKE SCIENCE IN GENERAL, German medicine depended for its revival originally on the importation of ideas from Western Europe. The German Enlightenment had begun to intensify these contacts, and it was notable that Catholics assumed the early lead in improving medical care and medical science. Gerhard van Swieten, the personal physician of Empress Maria Theresa, had studied at the clinics of Leyden University and became the head of the first medical school of Vienna. Joseph II built the Josephinum and the general Vienna hospital, medical institutions that for a long time were not equaled anywhere.

The example of Vienna was emulated in South Germany, and in the days of the Rhenish Confederation Paris became easily accessible. In the early years of the century, Bamberg, Würzburg, and Landshut became the centers for a medicine strictly based on anatomy and relying on practical diagnostics together with the use of all the departments of science. Johann Lukas Schönlein (1793–1864) of Bamberg was the first German professor of medicine who made the clinical demonstration and the scientific experiment the chief content of his research and teaching. As professor in Würzburg from 1817–33 he made his clinics the training place of a new generation of doctors. Though a sincere member of the Catholic Church, he fell victim to the intrigues of the romantic prejudices against his inductive scientific methods, which to the medical advisers of the Bavarian king, Ludwig I, seemed to run closely parallel to Schönlein's liberal political views.

Schönlein found a new position at the newly founded University of Zurich, which, like its older sister Basel, gave many a German scholar refuge from political oppression in this period. In 1840, Schönlein was brought to Berlin.

✍ *Realism Reigns Supreme*

BY THIS TIME VIENNA HAD BROUGHT FORTH its new medical school, and the medicine taught here compared favorably with the best of French medical science. If the great Viennese doctors were still handicapped in therapeutics, this was due to the lagging development of physiology. It was the co-operation of Schönlein and Johannes Müller in Berlin that made physiology fruitful and gave the new Berlin school its scientific significance. Johannes Müller (1801–58) came from the Rhineland and, like Schönlein, was the son of a simple Catholic craftsman, and he retained his Catholic faith. The scope of Müller's scholarship was universal. He enriched all fields of biological science and taught astronomy, pathology, and physiology. The speculative philosophy of nature was by him fully replaced by the inductive and experimental science of nature. His disciples, among them Hermann Helmholtz (1821–94), Rudolf Virchow (1821–1902), Emil Du Bois-Reymond (1818–96), and Ernst Haeckel (1834–1919) built on the ground that he had laid. But as inductive research was carried further and further into new fields the unity of science gave way to greater specialization. The religion of a Gauss, Schönlein, and Johannes Müller or the universal idealism of an Alexander von Humboldt was replaced by positivism or, as in Haeckel, by an outright naturalism.

The transformation of German thought after Goethe's and Hegel's deaths was motivated to a great extent by the growing urgency of the social problems after 1830. The existing economic institutions were incapable of sustaining the general standard of living that was modest enough, while the first spurts of modern economic activity originally produced more dislocation than improvement. From philosophical, literary, and purely scholarly preoccupations the new generation turned to politics. Its dreams of a national empire and justice for all were still steeped in the idealistic tradition. But the failure of these aspirations in the Revolution of 1848–49 caused the widespread loss of idealistic faith. In the following half-century realism ruled supreme in Germany. It was in this period that German life and German political and economic institutions were thoroughly recast.

Index

BY ANNEMARIE HOLBORN

(Dates given after the names of persons indicate the years of the reigns of emperors, kings, princes, and ecclesiastical dignitaries, and the years of birth and death for all others.)

The text of this book was set on the Linotype in JANSON, a recutting made direct from type cast from matrices long thought to have been made by the Dutchman Anton Janson, who was a practicing type founder in Leipzig during the years 1668–87. However, it has been conclusively demonstrated that these types are actually the work of Nicholas Kis (1650–1702), a Hungarian, who most probably learned his trade from the master Dutch type founder Dirk Voskens. The type is an excellent example of the influential and sturdy Dutch types that prevailed in England up to the time William Caslon developed his own incomparable designs from these Dutch faces.

This book was composed, printed, and bound by
The Riverside Press, Cambridge, Mass.
Typography and binding designs based on originals by
GUY FLEMING